MW01224758

Ancient Israel's
HISTORY

An Introduction to Issues and Sources

EDITED BY
BILL T. ARNOLD
RICHARD S. HESS

Baker Academic

a division of Baker Publishing Group
Grand Rapids, Michigan

Published by Baker Academic
a division of Baker Publishing Group
P.O. Box 6287, Grand Rapids, MI 49516-6287
www.bakeracademic.com

Printed in the United States of America

Library of Congress Cataloging-in-Publication Data
Ancient Israel's history : an introduction to issues and sources / edited by Bill T. Arnold and Richard S. Hess.
        pages cm
    Includes bibliographical references and index.
    Summary: "Leading experts offer a substantive history of Israel textbook that values the Bible's historical contribution without overlooking critical issues and challenges"— Provided by publisher.
    ISBN 978-0-8010-3930-0 (cloth)
    1. Bible. Old Testament—History of Biblical events. 2. Bible. Old Testament—Criticism, interpretation, etc. 3. Jews—History—To 70 A.D. I. Arnold, Bill T. II. Hess, Richard S.
    BS1197.A6195 2014
    221.95—dc23   2014026186

14   15   16   17   18   19   20   7   6   5   4   3   2   1

Contents

Preface

BILL T. ARNOLD AND RICHARD S. HESS

The impetus for this work came through the Institute for Biblical Research (IBR). Professor Lee Martin McDonald was president of IBR at the time and suggested that volumes focusing on each Testament be produced. One of us (Richard Hess) served on the board as editor of the *BBR* and volunteered to proceed with the project. We planned the work in collaboration with Jim Kinney of Baker Academic, to whom we express our appreciation for his help on a number of issues.

Our objective in this volume is to provide a current state of research on issues relative to the history of ancient Israel. Consequently, we chose separate individuals to write the chapters, with each contributor chosen because of demonstrated expertise on the subject matter of that chapter. They represent a variety of backgrounds. The contributors would not all necessarily agree on a number of topics regarding the history of Israel, a fact that we believe strengthens the volume. We allowed our contributors to express their own points of view on controverted issues, while insisting that all points of view be represented fairly. The contributors have written chapters that we believe are within the spirit of the IBR, and each has produced an outstanding contribution.

The volume's structure reflects our methodological commitments. First, we chose to assume neither a negative stance toward the biblical literature nor a naive fideism on difficult issues. Second, we designed chapters that move chronologically through the periods of Israel's history with a focus on the primary sources and the major scholarly issues regarding the interpretation of history in the period under consideration. While this book is intended as an introductory volume, the research represented here also provides new insights and reconstructions for further study of the subject. We hope that this work will be of benefit to students and researchers alike, as all of us strive to understand more about this fascinating and important subject.

Abbreviations

General

//	parallel text(s)	idem	by the same author(s)
AD	*anno Domini* (in the year of our Lord)	IA1	Iron Age I (1200–1000 BCE)
		IA2	Iron Age II (1000–586 BCE)
Akk.	Akkadian	i.e.	*id est*, that is
art.	article	LBA	Late Bronze Age (ca. 1550–1200 BCE)
BC	before Christ		
BCE	before the Common Era	lit.	literal, literally
ca.	circa	LXX	Septuagint (Greek version of the Jewish Scriptures)
CE	Common Era		
cf.	compare	masc.	masculine
chap(s).	chapter(s)	MBA	Middle Bronze Age (ca. 2100–1550 BCE)
col(s).	columns		
Dyn.	Dynasty, Dynasties	no(s).	number(s)
ed.	edition, edited by, editor	pl.	plural
e.g.	for example	repr.	reprint
esp.	especially	rev.	revised
ET	English translation	sg.	singular
et al.	and others/another	s.v.	under the word
etc.	and the rest	trans.	translated by, translation, translator
fem.	feminine		
fig(s).	figure(s)	v.l.	*varia lectio*, variant reading
Heb.	Hebrew	v(v).	verse(s)
ibid.	in the same source		

Modern Versions

ESV	English Standard Version		*according to the Traditional Hebrew Text*
NJPS	*Tanakh: The Holy Scriptures: The New JPS Translation*		
		NRSV	New Revised Standard Version

Old Testament

Gen.	Genesis	Song	Song of Songs
Exod.	Exodus	Isa.	Isaiah
Lev.	Leviticus	Jer.	Jeremiah
Num.	Numbers	Lam.	Lamentations
Deut.	Deuteronomy	Ezek.	Ezekiel
Josh.	Joshua	Dan.	Daniel
Judg.	Judges	Hosea	Hosea
Ruth	Ruth	Joel	Joel
1–2 Sam.	1–2 Samuel	Amos	Amos
1–2 Kings	1–2 Kings	Obad.	Obadiah
1–2 Chron.	1–2 Chronicles	Jon.	Jonah
Ezra	Ezra	Mic.	Micah
Neh.	Nehemiah	Nah.	Nahum
Esther	Esther	Hab.	Habakkuk
Job	Job	Zeph.	Zephaniah
Ps./Pss.	Psalm/Psalms	Hag.	Haggai
Prov.	Proverbs	Zech.	Zechariah
Eccles.	Ecclesiastes	Mal.	Malachi

New Testament

Matt.	Matthew	1–2 Thess.	1–2 Thessalonians
Mark	Mark	1–2 Tim.	1–2 Timothy
Luke	Luke	Titus	Titus
John	John	Philem.	Philemon
Acts	Acts	Heb.	Hebrews
Rom.	Romans	James	James
1–2 Cor.	1–2 Corinthians	1–2 Pet.	1–2 Peter
Gal.	Galatians	1–3 John	1–3 John
Eph.	Ephesians	Jude	Jude
Phil.	Philippians	Rev.	Revelation
Col.	Colossians		

Old Testament Apocrypha and Pseudepigrapha

1 En.	*1 Enoch (Ethiopic Apocalypse)*	1–2 Macc.	1–2 Maccabees
1 Esd.	*1 Esdras*	Sir.	Sirach
Let. Arist.	*Letter of Aristeas*	*T. Iss.*	*Testament of Issachar*

Dead Sea Scrolls and Related Texts

CD-A	Damascus Document[a]
CD-B	Damascus Document[b]
1QpHab	1QPesher to Habakkuk
1QS	1QRule of the Community
4Q169 (4QpNah)	4QNahum Pesher
4Q171 (4QpPs[a])	4QPsalms Pesher[a]

4Q175 (4QTest)   4QTestimonia
4Q379 (4QapocrJoshua^b) 4QApocryphon of Joshua^b
4Q394 (4QMMT^a)   4QHalakhic Letter^a
4Q396 (4QMMT^c)   4QHalakhic Letter^c

Philo

Good Person	*That Every Good Person Is Free (Quod omnis probus liber sit)*	*Hypoth.*	*Hypothetica (Hypothetica)*

Josephus

Ag. Ap.	*Against Apion*	*J.W.*	*Jewish War*
Ant.	*Jewish Antiquities*		

Mishnah, Talmud, and Related Literature

b.	Babylonian Talmud	*Sanh.*	*Sanhedrin*
m.	Mishnah	*Ṭahŏr.*	*Ṭahorot*
y.	Jerusalem Talmud	*Yad.*	*Yadayim*
		Yebam.	*Yebamot*
Šabb.	*Šabbat*	*Yoma*	*Yoma (= Kippurim)*

Greek and Latin Works

Appian

Hist. rom.	*Historia romana (Roman History)*

Diodorus Siculus

Bib. hist.	*Bibliotheca historica (Library of History)*

Herodotus

Hist.	*Historiae (Histories)*

Livy

Hist.	*Ab urbe condita libri (History of Rome)*

Pliny the Elder

Nat.	*Naturalis historia*

Polybius

Hist.	*Historiae (Histories)*

Tacitus

Hist.	*Historiae (Histories)*

Secondary Sources

AAA	Approaches to Anthropological Archaeology	*ABD*	*The Anchor Bible Dictionary.* Edited by D. N. Freedman. 6 vols. New York, 1992
AASOR	Annual of the American Schools of Oriental Research	*ABR*	*Australian Biblical Review*
ÄAT	Ägypten und Altes Testament	ABRL	Anchor Bible Reference Library
AAWG	Abhandlungen der Akademie der Wissenschaften in Göttingen	*ACF*	*Annuaire du Collège de France*
AB	Anchor Bible	*AcSum*	*Acta sumerologica*

ADAJ	*Annual of the Department of Antiquities of Jordan*	ATDan	Acta theologica danica
AfO	*Archiv für Orientforschung*	*ATJ*	*Ashland Theological Journal*
AfOB	Archiv für Orientforschung: Beiheft	BA	*Biblical Archaeologist*
ÄgAbh	Ägyptische Abhandlungen	BabAr	Babylonische Archive
AH	Achaemenid History	BAMA	British Academy Monographs in Archaeology
AJA	*American Journal of Archaeology*	*BAR*	*Biblical Archaeology Review*
AJN	*American Journal of Numismatics*	BARIS	British Archaeological Reports International Series
ÄL	*Ägypten und Levante*	*BASOR*	*Bulletin of the American Schools of Oriental Research*
AnBib	Analecta biblica	*BBR*	*Bulletin for Biblical Research*
ANESSup	Ancient Near Eastern Studies Supplement Series	BBRSup	Bulletin for Biblical Research Supplements
ANET	*Ancient Near Eastern Texts Relating to the Old Testament.* Edited by J. B. Pritchard. 3rd ed. Princeton, 1969	BEAM	Beiträge zur Erforschung der antiken Moabitis (Ard el-Kerak)
AntOr	*Antiguo Oriente*	BEATAJ	Beiträge zur Erforschung des Alten Testaments und des Antiken Judentums
AOAT	Alter Orient und Altes Testament	BEHE	Bibliothèque de l'École des hautes études
AOS	American Oriental Series	BES	Brown Egyptological Studies
ARAB	*Ancient Records of Assyria and Babylonia.* Daniel David Luckenbill. 2 vols. Chicago, 1926–1927	BETL	Bibliotheca ephemeridum theologicarum lovaniensium
		Bib	*Biblica*
		BibA	Bibliotheca aegyptiaca
ARCER	American Research Center in Egypt Reports	BibJudSt	Biblical and Judaic Studies
ARM	Archives royales de Mari	BibOr	Biblica et orientalia
ARMT	Archives royales de Mari: Transliterated and Translated Texts	BibSem	Biblical Seminar
		BIFAO	*Bulletin de l'Institut français d'archéologie orientale*
ARWAW	Abhandlungen der Rheinisch-Westfälischen Akademie der Wissenschaften	BIW	The Bible in Its World
		BJS	Brown Judaic Studies
AS	Assyriological Studies	*BN*	*Biblische Notizen*
ASAE	*Annales du Service des antiquités de l'Égypte*	*BO*	*Bibbia e Oriente*
		BPC	Biblical Performance Criticism
ASORAR	American Schools of Oriental Research Archaeological Reports	*BRev*	*Bible Review*
		BSac	*Bibliotheca sacra*
		BT	*The Bible Translator*
ASORB	American Schools of Oriental Research Books	*BurH*	*Buried History*
		BW	Bible World
ASORDS	American Schools of Oriental Research Dissertation Series	BWANT	Beiträge zur Wissenschaft vom Alten und Neuen Testament

BZAW	Beihefte zur Zeitschrift für die alttestamentliche Wissenschaft	DOTHB	*Dictionary of the Old Testament: Historical Books.* Edited by B. T. Arnold and H. G. M. Williamson. Downers Grove, IL, 2005
CAD	*The Assyrian Dictionary of the Oriental Institute of the University of Chicago.* Chicago, 1956–		
		DOTP	*Dictionary of the Old Testament: Pentateuch.* Edited by T. D. Alexander and D. W. Baker. Downers Grove, IL, 2003
CAJ	*Cambridge Archaeological Journal*		
CANE	*Civilizations of the Ancient Near East.* Edited by J. Sasson. 4 vols. New York, 1995	EA	*Egyptian Archaeology*
		EA	El-Amarna Tablets. According to the edition of J. A. Knudtzon. *Die el-Amarna-Tafeln.* Leipzig, 1908–1915. Reprint, Aalen, 1964. Continued in A. F. Rainey, *El-Amarna Tablets, 375–379.* 2nd rev. ed. Kevelaer, 1978
CBQ	*Catholic Biblical Quarterly*		
CHANE	Culture and History of the Ancient Near East		
ChrEg	*Chronique d'Egypte*		
CIS	Copenhagen International Series		
CMD	Classica et mediaevalia: Dissertationes		
ConBOT	Coniectanea biblica: Old Testament Series	ÉABJ	Études annexes de la Bible de Jérusalem
CorBC	Cornerstone Biblical Commentary	EAEHL	*Encyclopedia of Archaeological Excavations in the Holy Land.* Edited by M. Avi-Yonah. 4 vols. Jerusalem, 1975–1978
COS	*The Context of Scripture.* Edited by W. W. Hallo and K. L. Younger Jr. 3 vols. Leiden, 2003		
		EAH	Entretiens d'archéologie et d'histoire
CRIPEL	*Cahiers de recherches de l'Institut de Papyrologie et d'Égyptologie de Lille*	ÉAHA	Études d'archélogie et d'histoire ancienne
		ÉBib	Études bibliques
CRSAIBL	*Comptes rendus des séances de l'Academie des inscriptions et belles-lettres*	EEFM	Egypt Exploration Fund Memoir
		EH	Essential Histories
CUSAS	Cornell University Studies in Assyriology and Sumerology	ÉPRO	Études préliminaires aux religions orientales dans l'Empire romain
CWA	Cambridge World Archaeology		
DCH	*Dictionary of Classical Hebrew.* Edited by D. J. A. Clines. Sheffield, 1993–	ÉRCM	Éditions Recherche sur les civilisations: Mémoire
		ErIsr	*Eretz-Israel*
DHA	*Dialogues d'histoire ancienne*	ETL	*Ephemerides theologicae lovanienses*
DJ	*Denver Journal*		
DJD	Discoveries in the Judaean Desert	FAT	Forschungen zum Alten Testament
DMOA	Documenta et monumenta Orientis antiqui	FCI	Foundations of Contemporary Interpretation

FOTL	Forms of Old Testament Literature	*JAAR*	*Journal of the American Academy of Religion*
FRLANT	Forschungen zur Religion und Literatur des Alten und Neuen Testaments	*JANESCU*	*Journal of the Ancient Near Eastern Society of Columbia University*
FSBP	Fontes et subsidia ad Bibliam pertinentes	*JAOS*	*Journal of the American Oriental Society*
GAP	Guides to Apocrypha and Pseudepigrapha	*JARCE*	*Journal of the American Research Center in Egypt*
GAT	Grundrisse zum Alten Testament	*JAS*	*Journal of Archaeological Science*
GM	*Göttinger Miszellen*	*JBL*	*Journal of Biblical Literature*
HACL	History, Archaeology, and Culture of the Levant	*JBQ*	*Jewish Bible Quarterly*
		JBS	*Jerusalem Biblical Studies*
HALOT	L. Koehler, W. Baumgartner, and J. J. Stamm, *The Hebrew and Aramaic Lexicon of the Old Testament.* Translated and edited under the supervision of M. E. J. Richardson. 5 vols. Leiden, 1994–2000	*JCS*	*Journal of Cuneiform Studies*
		JCSMS	*Journal of the Canadian Society for Mesopotamian Studies*
		JDS	Judean Desert Studies
		JEA	*Journal of Egyptian Archaeology*
HAR	*Hebrew Annual Review*	*JERD*	*Journal of Epigraphy and Rock Drawings*
HBM	Hebrew Bible Monographs		
HCOT	Historical Commentary on the Old Testament	*JESHO*	*Journal of the Economic and Social History of the Orient*
HO	Handbuch der Orientalistik	*JHS*	*Journal of Hebrew Scriptures*
HR	*History of Religions*	*JJS*	*Journal of Jewish Studies*
HS	*Hebrew Studies*	JLSP	Janua Linguarum: Series Practica
HSM	Harvard Semitic Monographs		
HSS	Harvard Semitic Studies	*JMA*	*Journal of Mediterranean Archaeology*
HTIBS	Historic Texts and Interpreters in Biblical Scholarship	*JNES*	*Journal of Near Eastern Studies*
HTR	*Harvard Theological Review*	*JNSL*	*Journal of Northwest Semitic Languages*
HUCA	*Hebrew Union College Annual*	JPSTC	Jewish Publication Society Torah Commentary
HUCM	Monographs of the Hebrew Union College	*JSJ*	*Journal for the Study of Judaism in the Persian, Hellenistic, and Roman Periods*
IAAR	Israel Antiquities Authority Reports		
IBC	Interpretation: A Bible Commentary for Teaching and Preaching	*JSOT*	*Journal for the Study of the Old Testament*
		JSOTSup	Journal for the Study of the Old Testament: Supplement Series
ICC	International Critical Commentary		
IEJ	*Israel Exploration Journal*	JSPub	Judea and Samaria Publications
Int	*Interpretation*		

JSS	*Journal of Semitic Studies*
JSSEA	*Journal of the Society for the Study of Egyptian Antiquities*
KUSATU	*Kleine Untersuchungen zur Sprache des Alten Testaments und seiner Umwelt*
LAI	Library of Ancient Israel
LAPO	Littératures anciennes du Proche-Orient
LBI	Library of Biblical Interpretation
LBNEA	Library of Biblical and Near Eastern Archaeology
LCL	Loeb Classical Library
LD	Lectio divina
LHBOTS	Library of Hebrew Bible/Old Testament Studies
LSS	Levant Supplementary Series
LSTS	Library of Second Temple Studies
MARI	*Mari: Annales de recherches interdisciplinaires*
MC	Mesopotamian Civilizations
MDAIK	*Mitteilengen des deutschen archäologischen Instituts, Abteilung Kairo*
MPAIBL	Mémoires présentés à l'Academie des inscriptions et belles-lettres
NABU	Nouvelles assyriologiques brèves et utilitaires
NAC	New American Commentary
NCamBC	New Cambridge Bible Commentary
NCB	New Century Bible
NDA	New Directions in Archaeology
NEA	*Near Eastern Archaeology*
NEAEHL	*The New Encyclopedia of Archaeological Excavations in the Holy Land*. Edited by E. Stern. 5 vols. Jerusalem, 1993
NEASB	*Near East Archaeology Society Bulletin*
NICOT	New International Commentary on the Old Testament
NIDB	*The New Interpreter's Dictionary of the Bible*. Edited by K. D. Sakenfeld. 5 vols. Nashville, 2009
NIDOTTE	*New International Dictionary of Old Testament Theology and Exegesis*. Edited by W. A. VanGemeren. 5 vols. Grand Rapids, 1997
NSA	New Studies in Archaeology
NSR	Numismatic Studies and Researches
OA	*Opuscula Atheniensia*
OBO	Orbis biblicus et orientalis
OEAE	*The Oxford Encyclopedia of Ancient Egypt*. Edited by D. B. Redford. 3 vols. Oxford, 2001
OEANE	*The Oxford Encyclopedia of Archaeology in the Near East*. Edited by E. M. Meyers. 5 vols. Oxford, 1997
OHAE	*The Oxford History of Ancient Egypt*. Edited by I. Shaw. Oxford, 2000
OHBW	*The Oxford History of the Biblical World*. Edited by M. Coogan. Oxford, 2001
OIC	Oriental Institute Communications
OIE	Oriental Institute Essays
OIP	Oriental Institute Publications
OIS	Oriental Institute Seminars
OLA	Orientalia lovaniensia analecta
OMROL	*Oudheidkundige mededelingen uit het Rijksmuseum van Oudheden te Leiden*
OPBF	Occasional Publications of the Babylonian Fund
OPBIAA	Occasional Publications of the British Institute of Archaeology in Ankara
OPSNKF	Occasional Publications of the Samuel Noah Kramer Fund

Or	*Orientalia*		SBLAIL	Society of Biblical Literature Ancient Israel and Its Literature
OTL	Old Testament Library			
OtSt	Oudtestamentische Studiën			
PÄ	Probleme der Ägyptologie		SBLBES	Society of Biblical Literature Biblical Encyclopedia Series
PBA	Proceedings of the British Academy			
PDRI	Publications of the Diaspora Research Institute		SBLDS	Society of Biblical Literature Dissertation Series
PEFM	Palestinian Exploration Fund Monographs		SBLMS	Society of Biblical Literature Monograph Series
PEQ	*Palestine Exploration Quarterly*		SBLRBS	Society of Biblical Literature Resources for Biblical Study
PSBA	*Proceedings of the Society of Biblical Archaeology*		SBLSBS	Society of Biblical Literature Sources for Biblical Study
QM	Qumranica Mogilanensia		SBLSCSS	Society of Biblical Literature Septuagint and Cognate Studies Series
RA	*Revue d'assyriologie et d'archéologie orientale*			
RB	*Revue biblique*		SBLSS	Society of Biblical Literature Semeia Studies
REg	*Revue d'égyptologie*			
RH	*Revue historique*		SBLSymS	Society of Biblical Literature Symposium Series
RHDFE	*Revue historique de droit français et étranger*		SBLWAW	Society of Biblical Literature Writings from the Ancient World
RIMA	Royal Inscriptions of Mesopotamia, Assyrian Periods			
RINP	Royal Inscriptions of the Neo-Assyrian Period		SBLWAWSup	Society of Biblical Literature Writings from the Ancient World: Supplement
RlA	*Reallexicon der Assyrologie.* Edited by E. Ebeling et al. Berlin, 1928–		SBT	Studies in Biblical Theology
			SBTS	Sources for Biblical and Theological Study
RSO	Ras Shamra-Ougarit			
SAA	State Archives of Assyria		SCCNH	Studies on the Civilization and Culture of Nuzi and the Hurrians
SAAS	State Archives of Assyria Studies			
SAHL	Studies in the Archaeology and History of the Levant		ScrHier	Scripta hierosolymitana
			ScrM	*Scripta Mediterranea*
SAOC	Studies in Ancient Oriental Civilization		*Sem*	*Semitica*
			SFSMD	Studia Francisci Scholten memoriae dicata
SAr	Serie archeologica			
SARI	Sumerian and Akkadian Royal Inscriptions		SHANE	Studies in the History of the Ancient Near East
SBLAB	Society of Biblical Literature Academia Biblica		SHCANE	Studies in the History and Culture of the Ancient Near East
SBLABS	Society of Biblical Literature Archaeology and Biblical Studies		SHJPLIMS	Studies in the History of the Jewish People and the Land of Israel Monograph Series

SJLA	Studies in Judaism in Late Antiquity	*UF*	*Ugarit-Forschungen*
SJOT	*Scandinavian Journal of the Old Testament*	UISK	Untersuchungen zur indo-germanischen Sprach- und Kulturwissenschaft
SO	Symbolae Osloenses	ULIAOP	University of London Insti-tute of Archaeology Occa-sional Publications
STO	Studi e testi orientali		
SWBA	Social World of Biblical Antiquity	UNHAII	Uitgaven van het Nederlands Historisch-Archaeologisch Instituut te Istanbul
TA	*Tel Aviv*		
TANE	Themes from the Ancient Near East, BANEA Publica-tion Series	UNINOL	Uitgaven van het Nederlands Instituut voor het Nabije Oosten te Leiden
TAUIAM	Tel Aviv University Institute of Archaeology Monographs	UZKÖAI	Untersuchungen der Zweigstelle Kairo des Öster-reichischen Archäologischen Institutes
TAUIAP	Tel Aviv University Institute of Archaeology Publications		
TCRPOGA	Travaux du Centre de recher-che sur le Proche-Orient et la Grèce antiques	VAB	Vorderasiatische Bibliothek
		VOK	Veröffentlichungen der Orien-talischen Kommission
TCS	Texts from Cuneiform Sources	*VT*	*Vetus Testamentum*
TDOT	*Theological Dictionary of the Old Testament.* Edited by G. J. Botterweck, H. Ringgren, and H.-J. Fabry. Translated by J. T. Willis, D. E. Green, and D. W. Stott. 15 vols. Grand Rapids, 2006	VTSup	Supplements to Vetus Testamentum
		VWGT	Veröffentlichungen der Wis-senschaftlichen Gesellschaft für Theologie
		WBC	Word Biblical Commentary
Them	*Themelios*	WMANT	Wissenschaftliche Monogra-phien zum Alten und Neuen Testament
THOTC	Two Horizons Old Testament Commentary		
ThSt	Theologische Studien	*WUB*	*Welt und Umwelt der Bibel*
TLZ	*Theologische Literaturzeitung*	*WZKM*	*Wiener Zeitschrift für die Kunde des Morgenlandes*
TOTC	Tyndale Old Testament Commentaries	YNER	Yale Near Eastern Researches
Transeu	*Transeuphratène*	*ZAW*	*Zeitschrift für die alttesta-mentliche Wissenschaft*
TranseuSup	Supplements to Transeuphratène	ZDMGSup	Zeitschrift des deutschen morgenländischen Gesell-schaft: Supplementbände
TSS	Texts and Studies for Students		
TynBul	*Tyndale Bulletin*	*ZDPV*	*Zeitschrift des deutschen Palästina-Vereins*
TZ	*Theologische Zeitschrift*		
UÄA	Urkunden des ägyptischen Altertums		

Introduction

Foundations for a History of Israel

RICHARD S. HESS

Why is history important? The well-known words of George Santayana, "Those who cannot remember the past are condemned to repeat it," are more than a century old and yet continue to provide a pragmatic rationale for the study of the past.[1] It is a sufficient argument in itself for study of the human past. Perhaps never in the history of the world has there been a generation of so many people who have been devoted to severing their ties with the past and embracing a present and future without an identity or self-reflection on who they are. In part, this is a factor created by the explosion of a generation of youth who outnumber those who are older. The United States Census Bureau estimates that about 44 percent of the world's population is under the age of twenty-five. The speed of electronic media and the interest placed on what is new mitigate value and concern for the past and the study of history.

This was not the case in the ancient world in which the Hebrew Bible[2] first appeared. Indeed, the sense of the past provided identity for people and

1. George Santayana, *Introduction and Reason in Common Sense* (vol. 1 of *The Life of Reason; or, The Phases of Human Progress*; London: Archibald Constable, 1906), 284. The quotation is considered a paraphrase of a similar statement made earlier by Edmund Burke.

2. The terms "Hebrew Bible" and "Old Testament" may be used interchangeably in this book. Both refer to those thirty-nine books comprising the Protestant canon of the Old Testament and the Jewish canon of the Hebrew Bible.

oriented them to a narrative yielding aspects that endured far beyond their own time and place. Thus the prophet Jeremiah could charge his listeners, "This is what Yahweh says, 'Stand at the roads! Look and ask for the ancient paths where the good road is. Walk in it and you will find a place of rest for your souls'" (Jer. 6:16).[3]

The prophet promised guidance and rest in the good way of history, of the past. That the people rejected this was attributed not to a new level of enlightenment but to a failure to connect with the heritage that gave them all the good things that they possessed. The past was a source of hope, strength, and encouragement. To reject it was to reject one's relationship with God, one's community, and one's family.

The study of history was in no way disconnected from the practices of faith and worship or from the daily activities of life. The former was true because God's presence and identity were recognized in the nation's past and in its hope for the future. Thus the Decalogue—the first series of statutes given in the Torah—began with a statement of self-identification that connected Yahweh, the lawgiver, with claims to the formation of the nation: "I am Yahweh your God, who brought you out of the land of Egypt, out of the house of slaves" (Exod. 20:2). How was God known? Yahweh was recognized by his historic acts of goodness in the context of Israel's history.

In the daily activities of life, there was also a connection with history. The people of Israel were just that: a people who recognized their origin from a common ancestor and were joined in kinship with one another through families and tribes whose lines traced back to a common origin. The land that produced the wealth for Israel to live as it did was recognized as a gift from God. God gave this land at a historical point in time through the disenfranchisement of the Canaanite peoples. The land was then allotted to families, and these inherited estates were passed down through history.

If perceptions of history in the twenty-first century differ significantly from those of biblical times, the role of history nevertheless is an important discipline. Whether in Israel or elsewhere, the ancients saw history in the context of the will of the divine. Modern study of history has shifted its overarching presuppositions away from the religious and into the realm of the ideological. Informed by the philosophies of this present age, history becomes an important means of identifying where we have been and thereby of understanding where we are going. That much of the Western world has lost that sense does not make the study of such history any less urgent.

One may ask, why study the history of ancient Israel? After all, if we have

---

3. Scripture translations in this introduction are by the author.

limited time in our fast-paced society, and if there is so much to learn of technology and related areas merely to survive, would it not be better to limit our study of history to that of our own country and perhaps of those other nations that are so powerful and exercise an influence on who we are to become in the future?

There are two fundamental fallacies to this. The first lies in the nature of humanity and its relationship to the purpose of the study of history. Contrary to the views of some social engineers, humanity has not fundamentally changed throughout the past centuries of recorded history. It may have refined its understanding of aspects of science and the manipulation of the world in which we live; however, the fundamental nature of the human condition, in terms of the basic virtues and vices of individuals, families, and cities and nations, has not changed. One need only read the personal correspondence between kings, queens, and officials at and near Mari, a city in Syria from nearly four thousand years ago. The texts there reveal all the same emotions and personal concerns at root that modern exchanges on email, Facebook, Twitter, or the variety of other communication sources may contain.[4] People have not changed fundamentally, and so the study of the ancients is just as important as that of moderns.

It is even more important because, as the study of classics did for many centuries in the West, the study of ancient Israel provides an examination of a society different from the present, so much so that it becomes possible to stand outside of our own world and look at ourselves more critically and objectively than the perspective available to any philosopher of politics and sociology of the present age who ignores the past. Thus the ancient world is at once similar and different. Its history enables us to identify the enduring values, both virtues and vices, that remain common to all humanity. It also gives us a place to stand that is truly outside our own present age and the means to view this age from a profoundly different perspective.

Second, the study of ancient Israel's history is not merely the examination of a random and otherwise unrelated ancient civilization. Instead, it forms a foundation to the development of Western history and thought. On the level of arts and letters, no book has provided more of a model in terms of literary forms and expressions than the Hebrew Bible. In terms of law and society, no set of texts has more frequently provided the basis for legal bodies and jurisprudence in the history of Western civilization than the laws of the Old Testament. And, of course, the entire direction of Western civilization and of world history cannot be understood without the faiths most closely attached

4. See Wolfgang Heimpel, *Letters to the King of Mari: A New Translation, with Historical Introduction, Notes, and Commentary* (MC 12; Winona Lake, IN: Eisenbrauns, 2003).

to and evolved from ancient Israel: Judaism and Christianity. While the West no doubt built upon the ancient Greco-Roman culture for its understanding of philosophical categories and in those terms taught people for centuries how to think, it derived almost exclusively from ancient Israel and its heirs the morality and ethics that informed countless generations concerning the principles of how to live.[5]

Thus the study of the history of ancient Israel is not merely a footnote in the great collection of all human knowledge. Rather, it is the essential starting point for discerning more than two thousand years of human culture and history, for perceiving what remains today that is most important, and for preserving what we dare not forget as we prepare ourselves, our children, and our grandchildren for the future.

Purpose

In light of the importance of the topic, the purpose of this volume is to inquire into and to synthesize the major sources relevant to ancient Israel's history and to evaluate key issues of interpretation required of a critical study of that history. This work is designed to serve as an introductory text in the subject. It does not presuppose any knowledge of the region. However, it assumes that the interest for this particular subject lies especially with those who have a familiarity with the basic concepts and terms of the world of the Hebrew Bible or at least a willingness to become acquainted with them.

The book is designed to serve as a portal into the study of ancient Israel's history. The authors envision a text that brings the reader familiarity with major critical issues of interpretation. Because this history represents a wide variety of contributors, our concern is not to espouse any one confessional or ideological position. The authors of this volume hold in common a respect for the biblical text as a legitimate source in the study of Israel's history, but they also represent a variety of views within that general perspective. As such, this volume seeks to appreciate the value of various critical positions, even where authors may disagree with them. At the same time, we also wish to provide readers with an understanding of the major issues, an awareness of the sources, and a means to judge for themselves in reconstructing the history of Israel.

This introductory section briefly considers the major approaches to understanding what biblical history and Israelite history are and the methods used to

---

5. For recent treatment of the influence of the Old Testament on the foundations of modern democracies, see Eric Nelson, *The Hebrew Republic: Jewish Sources and the Transformation of European Political Thought* (Cambridge, MA: Harvard University Press, 2010).

interpret the sources in order to arrive at their historical understanding. It also considers a major element of any study of history: chronology. By describing the means by which historians have attempted to set events onto a time line in the context of known events contemporary with Israel in the ancient Near East, it becomes possible both to identify the sequence of those events and to place the biblical narrative within the larger flow of history. This introduction concludes with an outline of the book and its organization.

Definition and Methods

Early Study (ca. 1850 to 1970)

The modern study of history begins with the German historian Leopold von Ranke (1795–1886). In his research and writing, he rejected views of evolution and the development of humanity. In place of generalizations, he examined particulars and especially based his research and writing on the sources to which he would refer. In this he rejected the universal history approach of Hegel that sought similarities and themes across civilizations. Although not interested in broad evaluations of historical directions, von Ranke did emphasize the role of God in understanding how history worked. Von Ranke is best remembered for defining his approach to history as "wie es eigentlich gewesen"—that is, "as it really happened." This interpretation of the phrase has led to a general rejection of von Ranke as overly simplistic and hopelessly idealistic, given the selectivity and bias inherent in all history writing. Yet in the view of many, the sense of the German "eigentlich" is misunderstood when translated as "really." Instead, in this context it is better translated as "essentially." This understanding comports well with von Ranke's emphasis on examining and remaining close to the sources in his approach to history.

When one turns to consider the role of the history of Israel, this complex subject has been and remains closely tied to the study of the biblical text. Most famous in this study from the late nineteenth century is the work of Julius Wellhausen (1844–1918), whose *Prolegomena to the History of Israel* identified the development of the Pentateuch by describing four discrete literary sources. He consummated generations of research by placing them in a generally accepted historical sequence. While contributing to the history of Israel, this work proved far more influential as a study of the history of the literature of the Pentateuch.[6]

6. It also represents the most influential of many important works in the study of ancient Israelite religion and the history of Israelite religion. Although that is important as a field of research in itself, our focus in this volume is on history rather than on the history of religion(s).

Hermann Gunkel (1862–1932) served more directly to address the question of Israel's history through the study of traditions. He identified those materials that lay behind the written texts of the Bible. Although they had passed through generations of oral and perhaps written forms that may have molded and shaped them before being written in the form found in our present Bible, the original core of the history and its themes could be identified. In this latter process of identification of history, Gunkel was aided by the discovery of common literary forms and themes occurring in (what was then) the newly discovered and translated texts of Babylon, Assyria, and Egypt, along with the myths and other narratives found in them.

No historian of the twentieth century has had as much of an enduring impact on the study of ancient Israel as has Albrecht Alt (1883–1956). His theories on Israelite law, the ancestral "gods of the fathers," the formation of the state of Israel, tribal backgrounds, and a host of other matters either remain the starting point for discussion today or provide a major model that continues to be accepted. Alt used the understanding of societies and the social sciences contemporary to his time. This became influential in his models that synthesized the ancient Near Eastern, classical, and biblical evidence.

A final figure in the chain of early influential German scholars is Martin Noth (1902–1968). Along with Gunkel and Alt, Noth developed his theories of the historical growth of traditions now preserved in the Bible and of the use of the ancient Near Eastern and classical worlds as key sources for interpreting the biblical text. Noth's emphasis on the covenant "league" of twelve tribes as the key to early Israel's formation made a lasting contribution to the field even though some aspects of the hypothesis were rejected. To this should be added his contribution of the Deuteronomistic History—the theory that a single editor prepared and completed the history of Israel that we now have in the books of Joshua, Judges, 1–2 Samuel, and 1–2 Kings. As is the case with Alt's work, Noth's analysis of the Deuteronomistic History remains an anchor in the discussion of Israel's history.

William F. Albright (1891–1971) was the dominant American scholar in biblical studies and related archaeological fields for some fifty years of the twentieth century. He pioneered biblical archaeology as it came to be understood methodologically, and he remains the chief American proponent of this area, which has brought untold numbers of students, volunteers, and readers into the study of the subject.

For a survey of studies and approaches to the latter, see Richard S. Hess, *Israelite Religions: An Archaeological and Biblical Survey* (Grand Rapids: Baker Academic, 2007). For more on Wellhausen and other scholars discussed here, see Bill T. Arnold, "Pentateuchal Criticism, History of," *DOTP* 622–31.

Albright's primary interest was to provide an understanding of the historical claims of the Hebrew Bible and to use his mastery of the material culture of the ancient Near East and of the written texts from all relevant languages to assist in that effort. He contributed to the study of ancient Israelite history in too many areas to mention, but it should be noted that his major analysis of pottery stratigraphy from excavations at Tell Beit Mirsim provided the foundation for the correlation of all strata at all archaeological sites in the ancient Near East to absolute chronology. In this way it is possible to determine, for example, which level of ancient Lachish (Tell ed-Duweir) was attacked and destroyed by the Assyrian king Sennacherib in 701 BCE. As a means for understanding the customs and culture of the Bible, Albright promoted the use of the texts from Ugarit, those from Nuzi, and others from Mari, all of which were discovered and many published during his career.

Albright was the first to announce the dating of the Dead Sea Scrolls to their now-accepted production between the second century BCE and the first century CE and thereby (along with his earlier dating of the Nash papyrus) to recognize the earliest Hebrew Bible manuscripts in existence. His rigorous typological methodology in pottery analysis and stratigraphy, historical geography, comparative Semitics, and cross-cultural customs contributed to a profound synthesis of biblical history that remains significant to the present. With the passing of many of his students, who themselves influenced so much of the field in the latter twentieth century, there emerged a variety of criticisms of his legacy. However, the very existence of these disagreements forty years after his death attests to the profound influence that he continues to exercise.

Of course, this is all too limited a list of influential scholars of the history of Israel who flourished between 1850 and 1970. One might also include the British archaeologist Kathleen Kenyon, whose excavations in Jerusalem and Jericho, along with her publications, overturned assumptions and paved the way for the present study of the history of this region. There is also the French scholar Roland de Vaux, whose work in so many areas provided the magnificent synthesis of his own history of Israel—one that has stood the test of time. One might also mention the Ukrainian-born Israeli philosopher and scholar Yehezkel Kaufmann, whose writing on the history of Israel provided one of the first major studies from that land. His multivolume work remains perhaps the best example of the analysis of ancient Israelite history in opposition to the cultures and peoples contemporary with it.

Another important figure was Benjamin Mazar, president and chancellor of Hebrew University, whose essays pioneered many aspects of historical geography and can still be read with profit. He taught many of the major biblical historians and historical geographers who have profoundly influenced these fields of Israeli scholarship, and his legacy includes a veritable family of archaeologists who have made an equally significant contribution to archaeology and its impact on biblical studies. Finally, Cyrus Gordon might be added because of his independent thinking that attempted to make connections across the Mediterranean and beyond, his influence on a generation of students, his mastery of the ancient Near Eastern languages and texts that few scholars could match when working with biblical Hebrew, and his advocacy of a method that held the Masoretic Hebrew text as being virtually without need of text-critical emendation.

1970s and 1980s

All these people and influences, as well as many others, have left an imprint on the field of ancient Israelite history that remains to this day. Where does one proceed from here? The past forty years of the discipline have seen an explosion both of knowledge and of competing methods not unlike that found in many other disciplines. The field remains extremely active, if less coherent.

In the 1970s and the 1980s one could identify important (English language) historical studies in the works of J. Maxwell Miller and John Hayes, John Bright, John Van Seters, J. Alberto Soggin, and Yohanan Aharoni. The work of Miller and Hayes represented an approach that accepted higher critical assumptions about the biblical text and made use of connections with the extrabiblical evidence.[7] Their volume presented the most detailed discussion of the sources and a careful recounting of the narrative. This work enjoyed sufficient popularity that a second edition was published in 2006.

John Bright's work had already appeared in 1959.[8] The second edition (1972) and then the third (1981) would come out in the period under consideration. His work represents the closest example of the ongoing influence of Albright, who was Bright's teacher. Many of the traditional arguments for Albright's particular interpretation of the Bible are retained. The study contains a great deal of information, but little in the way of new syntheses was added in the later editions.

Close to the Albright school, but cutting a path of his own, is Eugene Merrill and his *Kingdom of Priests*.[9] This work carefully follows the biblical texts and integrates archaeology and other extrabiblical sources as appropriate.

---

7. J. Maxwell Miller and John H. Hayes, *A History of Ancient Israel and Judah* (2nd ed.; Louisville: Westminster John Knox, 1986).

8. John Bright, *A History of Israel* (Philadelphia: Westminster, 1959).

9. Eugene H. Merrill, *Kingdom of Priests: A History of Old Testament Israel* (Grand Rapids: Baker Books, 1987; 2nd ed., Grand Rapids: Baker Academic, 2008).

Although John Van Seters had published an earlier critical analysis of the Abraham narratives of Genesis, his historical method as applied to the whole of the Hebrew Bible relied heavily upon genre analysis and the nature of the historical material that one might expect in a particular genre.[10] A heavy emphasis was placed upon the classical Greek sources as legitimate forms that most closely resembled anything like history writing in the Hebrew Bible. Thus Van Seters understood that the Israelites borrowed from the Greeks and therefore wrote in a time subsequent to them. Operating on these assumptions, he dated the production of historical literature in Israel into the Persian period and later.

The Italian scholar J. Alberto Soggin continued the traditional view that stressed the importance of sources.[11] The sources most useful in the reconstruction of history were those that used administrative and other documents that might be considered neutral in terms of bias. Therefore the earliest evidence for legitimate historical inquiry lay in the period of the monarchy and the preservation of records, lists, and other documents in the Bible. These should be essential elements in the reconstruction of any history.

The Israeli archaeologist Yohanan Aharoni produced a historical geography of the Hebrew Bible that resulted in two English editions, in 1967 and 1979.[12] As with Bright's work, the first edition appeared before 1970, but it gained influence during the 1970s and 1980s. This relied on the combined disciplines of the study of the geography and toponymy of the land of Israel as well as the analysis of all available historical sources. The effect of this study was to provide a summary of the available sources for the history of Israel and a close connection between these sources and the places where the events occurred.

1990 to the Present

The 1990s ushered in a new era of historiography of ancient Israel. It drew on the roots of the previous period but divided into three separate methodological approaches to how a history should be written. *The first approach* has been to read the biblical sources suspiciously and to build a history derived from social science models and reconstructions that either ignore the Bible or treat it as fundamentally flawed in comparison to other ancient Near Eastern sources. Although many using this perspective disagree with aspects of his

10. John Van Seters, *In Search of History: Historiography in the Ancient World and the Origins of Biblical History* (New Haven: Yale University Press, 1983).

11. J. Alberto Soggin, *A History of Israel: From the Beginnings to the Bar Kochba Revolt, AD 135* (trans. John Bowden; London: SCM, 1984).

12. Yohanan Aharoni, *The Land of the Bible: A Historical Geography* (trans. Anson F. Rainey; Philadelphia: Westminster, 1967; 2nd ed., Philadelphia: Westminster, 1979).

methodology, Van Seters remains the figure most representative of this view from the previous period who continues to be productive up to the present. *The second approach* has been to draw on the "critical orthodoxy" of the interpretation of biblical sources and use their testimony primarily within that context. This continues the basic approach of Miller and Hayes and that of Soggin. Behind them lay the work of Alt and Noth. *The third general avenue of approaches* has tended to treat the biblical text as a source similar to that of other sources. This category includes those who share the traditional critical approach with the second group, as well as those who do not rely heavily on this method. Rather, they see in the Hebrew Bible an ancient source that should be weighed and critically evaluated along with other ancient sources. This approach inherits the assumptions of Albright and Bright, who used the text as a foundation for comparisons with other sources. It also includes that of Aharoni, who saw how repeatedly the text provided a reliable source for the study of geography in the various periods in which it appeared.

Key to the development of these decades is the recognition that the literary nature of a text and the degree of its historical value have no relationship necessarily. There are several aspects to this point. V. Philips Long exemplified this concern with his appreciation of genres in terms of larger literary units that may be studied for their intent and purpose, and yet at the same time they should not be used to predetermine what a biblical text may and may not contain regarding history.[13] It is preferable not to classify biblical literature as fictional, ahistorical, or antihistorical only on the basis of its literary form or artistry. The nature of the literature as referential to historical and other truth claims should not be understood as compromised by the form or literary quality in which the text is presented. Long understood the biblical literature in terms of theological, literary, and historical dimensions. Indeed, most (perhaps all) of the ancient Near Eastern historical sources may be examined with these perspectives. Each one complements, rather than negates, the other. As Long noted, the historical dimension requires careful attention to what the text communicates and an evaluation of both internal consistency within the biblical literature and external consistency with other historically relevant sources.

Of similar importance is K. Lawson Younger Jr., whose 1990 study examines historical questions of the Bible within the context of ancient Near Eastern literature, specifically considering problems of genre identifications

---

13. V. Philips Long, *The Art of Biblical History* (FCI 5; Grand Rapids: Zondervan, 1994). For important reading in the broad field, see idem, ed., *Israel's Past in Present Research: Essays on Ancient Israelite Historiography* (SBTS 7; Winona Lake, IN: Eisenbrauns, 1999).

in previous scholarship.[14] On the one hand, history writing (or historiography) is not the opposite of fiction. That is to say, bad historiography does not necessarily make good fiction. On the other hand, history writing does not produce a record of fact. Instead, it provides a discourse that claims to provide a record of fact. Rather than fiction, Younger found figurative language in the historiography. Like Long, Younger identified internal elements and external elements. The latter comprised themes, motifs, and rhetorical devices that could be identified across the biblical and the ancient Near Eastern literary horizon. The former, the internal elements, comprised what Younger referred to as transmission codes. These comprised specific ideological components unique to the biblical historiography, as would be true of other ancient Near Eastern historiography with reference to its own particular culture and time. For Younger, ideology is not propaganda. Instead, he follows Clifford Geertz, the late and influential sociologist of religion, in arguing that it should be understood less prejudicially as a schematic image of social order. In this sense, ideology is a means of imposing order on the past that incorporates both literal and figurative language. The desire here is to avoid oversimplified conclusions of bias without appreciating the full impact of the cultural background that leads the author to communicate history in the manner that he or she chooses.

Having examined significant advances in literary and comparative/ideological studies with reference to historical investigations, we must consider the archaeological dimension. Two archaeological "discoveries" would have lasting impact on all future studies of ancient Israel's history. The first summarized some of the regional surveys that had been done by archaeologists in the previous two decades. In 1988 Israel Finkelstein published *The Archaeology of the Israelite Settlement*. Although more survey results would be published in the following decades (and although Finkelstein would reconsider his own conclusions), this work firmly established the fact that a previously unattested sedentary population appeared in the central hill country of the land of Israel around 1200 BCE,[15] as attested by almost three hundred new villages. This was stunning, as the previous period of time attested to hardly two dozen population centers in the same region. Since this coincided with the understanding of most biblical historians as to exactly when and where Israel first appeared in the southern Levant, it created a unique and key element for further study in this earliest period of Israel's history as a people.

14. K. Lawson Younger Jr., *Ancient Conquest Accounts: A Study in Ancient Near Eastern and Biblical History Writing* (JSOTSup 98; Sheffield: JSOT Press, 1990).

15. Scholars work with both BC ("before Christ") and BCE ("before the Common Era") as designations for the same time period. We have tended to use BCE without any disrespect for the alternative but have also allowed the use of BC where authors have preferred it.

A second archaeological element was more in line with what could be called a discovery. This was the result of the work of archaeologist Avraham Biran, who had excavated for nearly three decades at the north Israelite site of Tel Dan.[16] On July 21, 1993, expedition surveyor Gila Cook was cleaning around the large gate area after a day of digging. As the evening light bathed the stones, she noticed that an inscribed fragment had been reused in an ancient wall. This discovery and that of an additional fragment a year later from the same Aramean monumental stela constituted the remains of a victory inscription set up by an Aramean king from Damascus in the late ninth century BCE.[17] In it the Aramean king mentions the Judean "house of David," a reference that has parallels only in the Hebrew Bible and only with reference to King David's family and dynasty. This attestation of the biblical David and his dynasty within about a century and a half of the monarch's life (by traditional dating) has, in the minds of most historians, established the reality of a David from this early period.

"SUSPICIOUS" HISTORIES

These methodological evaluations became significant because the decade of the 1990s was also the period that witnessed the rise of what some have referred to as the minimalists. They have been called this on the basis of their general skepticism toward any historical value to the contents of the Hebrew Bible. Centered at the University of Copenhagen (Niels Peter Lemche and Thomas Thompson) and at Sheffield University (Philip Davies), this group has exercised significant impact upon the study of biblical history, even though their method cannot be described as the dominant one.

Thompson's 1992 *Early History of the Israelite People: From the Written and Archaeological Sources* provides the most important illustration of this approach and will be reviewed here more completely.[18] The book's basic premise is that the biblical text is unusable as a source for ancient Israelite history.

Thompson begins his construction of Palestinian (not Israelite) history by using as his guide the ecological transformations brought about through cycles of wet and dry periods in the eastern Mediterranean world. He finds no evidence of any group called "Israel" before the first millennium BCE and so

16. Avraham Biran and Joseph Naveh, "An Aramaic Stele from Tel Dan," *IEJ* 43 (1993): 81–98.

17. Avraham Biran and Joseph Naveh, "The Tel Dan Inscription: A New Fragment," *IEJ* 45 (1995): 1–18.

18. Thomas L. Thompson, *Early History of the Israelite People: From the Written and Archaeological Sources* (SHANE 4; Leiden: Brill, 1992). The following discussion is adapted from Richard S. Hess, "Recent Studies in Old Testament History: A Review Article," *Them* 19, no. 2 (1994): 9–15.

denies any validity to the generally accepted mention of Israel on the Egyptian Merneptah Stela of 1209 BCE.

Thompson maintains that no political union could have existed in the time and place in which the Bible remembers the united monarchy of David and Solomon. This is apparently because the settlement of much of the Judean hill country had not yet taken place, and so there was no population to support a kingdom. However, the lack of population is sometimes itself a motivation for wars of conquest, such as those undertaken by the Hittites to replenish their own population.[19] Further, we do know that the Benjaminite region was settled at this time. This is also true for Jerusalem and Hebron along with other major sites in the Judean low hill country to the west. These are the same regions from which the early leaders of a unified Israel emerged and where they had their centers of rule. What does it mean to argue that the population was insufficient? Was the population of Macedonia sufficient for Alexander to create an empire, albeit short lived, of the known world from Greece to India? The already-mentioned Tel Dan Stela, with its inscription of the "house of David," calls into question all disputes concerning the existence of a David. This expression is used elsewhere (e.g., "house of Omri") to describe a dynasty and the historical founder of that dynasty. Hence this provides evidence for a David.

When Thompson considers the biblical text itself, he concludes that Genesis through 2 Kings has no coherent plot development, theme, ideology, or historiography; it is the product of antiquarian and traditionalist interests, a collection of a variety of tales and traditions within an editorial framework. In a major break with Van Seters, Thompson does not see the Hebrew Bible as containing historiography in the Greek sense of a critical intent to identify history. Thompson seems to be guided by the absence of a Hebrew word equivalent to the Greek word *historia*. Unfortunately, he does not provide the necessary and detailed comparative analysis from texts, especially those Hittite and Assyrian sources that he does understand as historiographic.

This same approach was followed by Mario Liverani, as expressed in the English title of his work *Israel's History and the History of Israel*.[20] "Israel's History" serves as creation of history with no necessary relationship to the time, place, and people that it purports to represent. In part two of the book, Liverani titles his discussion of this sort of history as "An Invented History."

19. Bustenay Oded, *Mass Deportations and Deportees in the Neo-Assyrian Empire* (Wiesbaden: Reichert, 1979).

20. Mario Liverani, *Israel's History and the History of Israel* (trans. Chiara Peri and Philip R. Davies; BW; London: Equinox, 2005); original ed., *Oltre la Bibbia: Storia antica di Israele* (Rome: Laterza, 2003).

However, the "real" history of Israel that Liverani purports to describe is titled "A Normal History." As with Thompson and the others, Liverani adopts a suspicious reading of the biblical text. However, unlike these others, he uses the text of the Old Testament as a significant source.

Also written from a suspicious perspective is the approach of the late Gösta Ahlström in his posthumously published *History of Ancient Palestine from the Palaeolithic Period to Alexander's Conquest.*[21] This text, however, moves us toward the second category, that of traditional critical orthodoxy. While Ahlström remains closer to the skeptical approach regarding the period before the united monarchy, he interacts with traditional higher criticism in the period from the united monarchy onward. Along with a fundamental trust in and detailed catalog of archaeological evidence, this approach anticipates much of the critical analysis of ancient Israel up to the present.

CRITICAL ORTHODOXY IN HISTORIES

In addition to the already-mentioned second edition of Miller and Hayes, the second and third editions of the multiauthored volume edited by Hershel Shanks also appeared at this time. While the first edition of this work (with the exception of the first chapter) closely integrates the evidence of archaeology, extrabiblical texts, and Hebrew Bible sources read in a traditional manner, many of the chapters of the later editions closely follow the critical approaches of this second category.[22]

Other histories were written in part as a response to the skepticism of the first category. A critical response was made to those who considered the Hebrew Bible of little or no historical value. The Oxford Old Testament seminar brought together the papers of some seventeen scholars under the editorship of John Day.[23] They argued that there was indeed evidence for history in the Hebrew Bible, and that elements of this history extended much earlier than had been maintained by those in the first category.

One of the contributors, the Syro-Palestinian archaeologist William G. Dever, wrote two volumes of his own that demonstrated where and how the preexilic texts of the Hebrew Bible correlated with known and current

21. Gösta W. Ahlström, *The History of Ancient Palestine from the Palaeolithic Period to Alexander's Conquest* (ed. Diana Vikander Edelman; JSOTSup 146; Sheffield: JSOT Press, 1993).

22. Hershel Shanks, ed., *Ancient Israel: A Short History from Abraham to the Roman Destruction of the Temple* (Englewood Cliffs, NJ: Prentice-Hall; Washington, DC: Biblical Archaeology Society, 1988); idem, *Ancient Israel: From Abraham to the Roman Destruction of the Temple* (2nd ed.; Washington, DC: Biblical Archaeology Society, 1999); idem, *Ancient Israel: From Abraham to the Roman Destruction of the Temple* (3rd ed.; Englewood Cliffs, NJ: Prentice-Hall, 2010).

23. John Day, ed., *In Search of Pre-Exilic Israel: Proceedings of the Oxford Old Testament Seminar* (JSOTSup 406; London: T&T Clark International, 2004).

archaeological evidence and its interpretation.[24] Together these works demonstrated an important value to these data for questioning the assumptions of various postmodern social science models and for reexamining the value of the textual record from the periods of earliest Israel and the united monarchy.

A second arena of concern that Dever addressed was to critique the assumptions of the work of Israeli archaeologist Israel Finkelstein, popularized with the assistance of Neil Asher Silberman, in his volume *The Bible Unearthed*.[25] Their stated purpose is to present how new discoveries of the discipline of archaeology have overturned long-held assumptions about the essential reliability of the Hebrew Bible as a historical record. For each chapter the authors present a summary of the biblical account and then discuss ways in which archaeology has controverted this traditional understanding. The authors always present their interpretation of the archaeological data but do not mention or interact with contemporary alternative approaches.

An alternative approach to reading the biblical text through social science methods has been to apply the benefits of social science models to the data gained from archaeology. The detailed analysis and emphasis on archaeological method distinguished this approach from some in the first category. Thomas E. Levy edited the best example of this approach, covering the Holy Land from prehistoric to modern times, with each chapter written by an archaeologist who is a specialist in the period under consideration.[26] With the emphasis on the social archaeology and not on the biblical text, the work provides essential perspectives on the historical periods not available elsewhere.

Daniel E. Fleming has provided a recent synthesis of biblical, extrabiblical textual, and critical discussion.[27] His work isolates strata of historical text based on the understanding that the history represented by the northern kingdom of Israel predates that of Judah. He seeks to isolate the former and note where Judean editing occurs.

Among the many other scholars who work with these methods, we must mention finally the important work of Nadav Na'aman. Although his research

24. William G. Dever, *What Did the Biblical Writers Know, and When Did They Know It? What Archaeology Can Tell Us about the Reality of Ancient Israel* (Grand Rapids: Eerdmans, 2001); idem, *Who Were the Early Israelites, and Where Did They Come From?* (Grand Rapids: Eerdmans, 2003).

25. Israel Finkelstein and Neil Asher Silberman, *The Bible Unearthed: Archaeology's New Vision of Ancient Israel and the Origin of Its Sacred Texts* (New York: Free Press, 2001).

26. Thomas E. Levy, ed., *The Archaeology of Society in the Holy Land* (New York: Facts on File, 1995).

27. Daniel E. Fleming, *The Legacy of Israel in Judah's Bible: History, Politics, and the Reinscribing of Tradition* (Cambridge: Cambridge University Press, 2012).

has appeared primarily in the form of articles, a three-volume collection of his scholarly papers reveals how he has integrated the archaeological and extrabiblical textual evidence into an appreciation of critical views as applied to all periods of ancient Israel.[28]

HISTORIES BALANCING BIBLICAL AND EXTRABIBLICAL SOURCES

As we move into the third area of research, that which emphasizes the biblical text and the extrabiblical evidence but does not accept without question either the results of higher criticism or the skepticism of the first group, we can consider a variety of studies, both those that primarily react to the other areas and those that present new syntheses. Even here there is overlap as many of the studies seek to do both. Thus, while Kenneth Kitchen's *On the Reliability of the Old Testament* presents much in the way of critique against critical positions by applying comparative ancient Near Eastern evidence, we have in this tome a survey of the history of ancient Israel that provides a unique integration of the comparative data and biblical literature.[29] Again, conferences were convened and papers published in six volumes that ostensibly addressed concerns initially raised by Van Seters and later by the so-called minimalists, as well as other scholars who follow postmodern approaches.[30] These collected essays also advance the historical interpretation and understanding of every area of ancient Israelite history. The same may be said of the analysis that searches the philosophical foundations and critiques the assumptions of historians, as set forth by the Danish scholar Jens Bruun

28. Nadav Na'aman, *Ancient Israel and Its Neighbors: Interaction and Counteraction* (vol. 1 of *Collected Essays*; Winona Lake, IN: Eisenbrauns, 2005); idem, *Canaan in the Second Millennium B.C.E.* (vol. 2 of *Collected Essays*; Winona Lake, IN: Eisenbrauns, 2005); idem, *Ancient Israel's History and Historiography: The First Temple Period* (vol. 3 of *Collected Essays*; Winona Lake, IN: Eisenbrauns, 2005).

29. Kenneth A. Kitchen, *On the Reliability of the Old Testament* (Grand Rapids: Eerdmans, 2003).

30. Alan R. Millard, James K. Hoffmeier, and David W. Baker, eds., *Faith, Tradition, and History: Old Testament Historiography in Its Near Eastern Context* (Winona Lake, IN: Eisenbrauns, 1994); V. Philips Long, David W. Baker, and Gordon J. Wenham, eds., *Windows into Old Testament History: Evidence, Argument, and the Crisis of "Biblical Israel"* (Grand Rapids: Eerdmans, 2002); James K. Hoffmeier and Alan R. Millard, eds., *The Future of Biblical Archaeology: Reassessing Methodologies and Assumptions; The Proceedings of a Symposium, August 12–14, 2001 at Trinity International University* (Grand Rapids: Eerdmans, 2004); Daniel I. Block, ed., *Israel: Ancient Kingdom or Late Invention?* (Nashville: B&H Academic, 2008); Richard S. Hess, Gerald A. Klingbeil, and Paul J. Ray Jr., eds., *Critical Issues in Early Israelite History* (BBRSup 3; Winona Lake, IN: Eisenbrauns, 2008). A sixth volume, though not the product of a congress, continues this tradition: James K. Hoffmeier and Dennis R. Magary, eds., *Do Historical Matters Matter to Faith? A Critical Appraisal of Modern and Postmodern Approaches to Scripture* (Wheaton: Crossway, 2012).

Kofed.[31] Perhaps the best example of a critical evaluation of the approach of traditional higher criticism, integrated with a historical survey of ancient Israel, is the 2003 history by Iain Provan, V. Philips Long, and Tremper Longman III.[32] Of the approximately three hundred pages of text, one hundred are devoted to the questions of method and a critique of other approaches. The authors' strong background of literary analysis (see the summary of Long's earlier work above) and awareness of the critical approaches provide a unique contribution to the field of Israelite history.

The third method will always rely heavily on the comparative evidence and especially the written texts. In addition to what has already been noted, important contributions of the past two decades have included significant editions of Neo-Assyrian texts and other new texts from this ancient empire, as well as new readings of cuneiform and alphabetic texts from the southern Levant of the second and first millennia.[33] To this may be added the archive from thirteenth-century BCE Emar as well as the new readings and many new texts published from contemporary Ugarit, eighteenth-century BCE Mari, and the Luwian texts of the late second and early first millennia BCE.[34] For

31. Jens Bruun Kofoed, *Text and History: Historiography and the Study of the Biblical Text* (Winona Lake, IN: Eisenbrauns, 2005).

32. Iain Provan, V. Philips Long, and Tremper Longman III, *A Biblical History of Israel* (Louisville: Westminster John Knox, 2003).

33. See, e.g., Hayim Tadmor, *The Inscriptions of Tiglath-Pileser III, King of Assyria: Critical Edition, with Introductions, Translations, and Commentary* (Jerusalem: Israel Academy of Sciences and Humanities, 1994); Eckart Frahm, *Einleitung in die Sanherib-Inschriften* (AfOB 26; Vienna: Institut für Orientalistik der Universität Wien, 1997); Shigeo Yamada, *The Construction of the Assyrian Empire: A Historical Study of the Inscriptions of Shalmaneser III (859–824 BC) Relating to His Campaigns to the West* (CHANE 3; Leiden: Brill, 2003); Hayim Tadmor and Shigeo Yamada, *The Royal Inscriptions of Tiglath-pileser III (744–727 BC) and Shalmaneser V (726–722 BC), Kings of Assyria* (RINP 1; Winona Lake, IN: Eisenbrauns, 2011); Earle Leichty, *The Royal Inscriptions of Esarhaddon, King of Assyria (680–669 BC)* (RINP 4; Winona Lake, IN: Eisenbrauns, 2011); Kirk Grayson and Jamie Novotny, *The Royal Inscriptions of Sennacherib, King of Assyria (704–681 BC), Part 1* (RINP 3/1; Winona Lake, IN: Eisenbrauns, 2012); Wayne Horowitz and Takayoshi Oshima, *Cuneiform in Canaan: Cuneiform Sources from the Land of Israel in Ancient Times* (Jerusalem: Israel Exploration and Hebrew University of Jerusalem, 2006); Shmuel Ahituv, *Echoes from the Past: Hebrew and Cognate Inscriptions from the Biblical Period* (trans. and ed. Anson F. Rainey; Jerusalem: Carta, 2008).

34. See, e.g., (on Emar) Daniel E. Fleming, *The Installation of Baal's High Priestess at Emar: A Window on Ancient Syrian Religion* (HSS 42; Atlanta: Scholars Press, 1992); idem, *Time at Emar: The Cultic Calendar and the Rituals from the Diviner's Archive* (MC 11; Winona Lake, IN: Eisenbrauns, 2000); Richard S. Hess, "Multi-Month Ritual Calendars in the West Semitic World: Emar 446 and Leviticus 23," in Hoffmeier and Millard, *Future of Biblical Archaeology*, 233–53; (on Ugarit) Marguerite Yon and Daniel Arnaud, *Études Ougaritiques I: Travaux 1985–1995* (RSO 14; Paris: Éditions recherche sur les civilisations, 2001); Brian C. Babcock, *Sacred Ritual: A Study of West Semitic Ritual Calendars in Leviticus 23 and the Akkadian Text Emar 446* (BBRSup 9; Winona Lake, IN: Eisenbrauns, 2014);Wilfred G. E. Watson and Nicolas

the large quantity of written evidence recently published from the fifth and fourth centuries BCE, see chapter 13 below, authored by André Lemaire. His mastery of relevant epigraphy is well known, and his publications of many primary sources from this period (and other periods) are too numerous to chronicle here.

For an awareness of the strengths and weaknesses of this method, as well as the full use of newly published comparative data, see, in addition to the works of Kitchen and the six volumes of collected essays already mentioned, many of the entries in *Dictionary of the Old Testament: Historical Books* and the collection of essays in *Archival Documents from the Biblical World*, whose titles describe their contents: James K. Hoffmeier, "Understanding Hebrew and Egyptian Military Texts: A Contextual Approach" (xxi–xxvii); Harry A. Hoffner Jr., "Hittite-Israelite Cultural Parallels" (xxix–xxxiv); K. Lawson Younger Jr., "The 'Contextual Method': Some West Semitic Reflections" (xxxv–xliii); David B. Weisberg, "The Impact of Assyriology on Biblical Studies" (xliv–xlviii); and William W. Hallo, "Sumer and the Bible: A Matter of Proportion" (xlix–liv).[35] Finally, there is the useful discussion and enormous bibliography of Kenton L. Sparks's *Ancient Texts for the Study of the Hebrew Bible*.[36] Although not concerned only with historiographical matters, this could be a starting point for a comparative survey of the relevant texts of any given period in Israel.

The philosophical underpinnings of all three methods continue to enjoy study and reflection. A good example is the recent study by Koert van Bekkum that critiques the philosophical assumptions behind the first two methods and seeks to use the comparative approach by first allowing the biblical text and the archaeological witness to speak for themselves, with their distinctive tools for analysis and interpretation.[37] Only then are the two compared and contrasted.

Wyatt, eds., *Handbook of Ugaritic Studies* (HO 1/39; Leiden: Brill, 1999); K. Lawson Younger Jr., ed., *Ugarit at Seventy-Five: Proceedings of the Symposium "Ugarit at Seventy-Five," Held at Trinity International University, Deerfield, Illinois, February 18–20, 2005, under the Auspices of the Middle Western Branch of the American Oriental Society and the Mid-West Region of the Society of the Biblical Literature* (Winona Lake, IN: Eisenbrauns, 2007); (on Mari) Heimpel, *Letters to the King of Mari*; (on Luwian) John David Hawkins, *Inscriptions of the Iron Age* (vol. 1 of *Corpus of Hieroglyphic Luwian Inscriptions*; UISK 8; Berlin: de Gruyter, 2000).

35. Bill T. Arnold and H. G. M. Williamson, eds., *Dictionary of the Old Testament: Historical Books* (Downers Grove, IL: InterVarsity, 2005); William W. Hallo and K. Lawson Younger Jr., eds., *Archival Documents from the Biblical World* (vol. 3 of *The Context of Scripture*; Leiden: Brill, 2003).

36. Kenton L. Sparks, *Ancient Texts for the Study of the Hebrew Bible: A Guide to the Background Literature* (Peabody, MA: Hendrickson, 2005).

37. Koert van Bekkum, *From Conquest to Coexistence: Ideology and Antiquarian Intent in the Historiography of Israel's Settlement in Canaan* (CHANE 45; Leiden: Brill, 2011).

Today, if one were to look for an exemplary integration of the comparative method with a close attention to all relevant ancient Near Eastern, classical, and biblical texts and manuscripts, there is none better than the contribution of the late Israeli scholar Anson Rainey in *The Sacred Bridge*.[38] In a massive undertaking, he provides these original textual sources (as well as rabbinic sources) in transliteration and translation and integrates a comprehensive understanding of geography and archaeology to present a unique synthesis that portrays as closely as possible the history of ancient Israel.

With such a varied and enormous background in sources and interpretive approaches, there is not available any volume that can evaluate all that has gone before and provide a new and more complete synthesis in light of the most recent available evidence bearing upon the interpretation of ancient Israel. No work can serve as the final word on the subject. However, here we seek to introduce the interested reader to the study of ancient Israel by examining the story as traditionally told, the most important sources for interpretation, the major critical issues and problems with our understanding of the sources, and how they might best be synthesized.[39]

Chronology

There are two types of chronology: relative and absolute. Relative chronology seeks to place events and people in sequence. Examples of this are the sequence of Abraham, the exodus, and the monarchy. The biblical witness is unanimous in confirming this chronological sequence. Relative chronology can be much more specific. Thus 1–2 Samuel and 1–2 Kings provide the length of each king's reign in Judah and Israel. So one can calculate the number of years from the beginning of the first king (Saul) and his reign through that of David and Solomon to the end of the united monarchy. And one can calculate the number of years from that event to the destruction of Jerusalem and the deportation of Judeans to Babylon. It is also possible to relate the reigns of other kings in sources outside the Bible. Thus, for example, Abram is contemporary with Tidal of the Goiim, Rehoboam with Shishak of Egypt, Hezekiah with Sennacherib of Assyria, Josiah with Neco of Egypt, and Jehoiachin with Nebuchadnezzar of Babylon. Except for Tidal, all of these leaders are attested outside the Bible and can be placed within a sequence of kings and

---

38. Anson F. Rainey and R. Steven Notley, *The Sacred Bridge: Carta's Atlas of the Biblical World* (Jerusalem: Carta, 2006).

39. For further analysis, see Megan Bishop Moore and Brad E. Kelle, *Biblical History and Israel's Past: The Changing Study of the Bible and History* (Grand Rapids: Eerdmans, 2011).

rulers from their native lands. The Roman-period figure Ptolemy recorded lists of Assyrian and Babylonian kings, as Manetho did of Egyptian dynasties and their rulers. These can be correlated with the ancient Near Eastern records and—since the decipherment of the Egyptian, Babylonian, Assyrian, and other languages and scripts—with the thousands of texts that attest to rulers and sequences of kings.

The second type of chronology is absolute. This allows one to calculate exactly how many years ago an event took place. Historically, this system has used the birth of Jesus Christ as a dividing point in the eras, so that events before the birth are designated "BC" (before Christ) and those after the birth "AD" (anno Domini, "in the year of the Lord"). In biblical studies, as here, these designations are sometimes replaced with "BCE" (before the Common Era) and "CE" (Common Era).

In order to provide an absolute chronology for the events of ancient Israel, one would need some means of counting back from the present to an event mentioned in the sources of that time. This would be difficult since we do not have reliable lists of years between the present and so long ago in the past. However, in 1867 one of the first great Assyriologists, Henry Rawlinson, published an eponym list from the period of the Neo-Assyrian kings that changed the picture completely. The Assyrians named each year according to a king or important official, and they kept a list of these year-names in sequence according to the rulers. One of the names had attached to it a note that an eclipse occurred on a particular month. It was possible to calculate that date astronomically as June 15 or 16 in 763 BCE.[40] As a result of this piece of data, it was possible to fix the dates for the reigns of the kings of the Neo-Assyrian Empire, the Neo-Babylonian Empire, and the Persian Empire. Corresponding connections with Egyptian chronology allowed for absolute dates there as well.

However, the resultant, detailed chronology in these empires did not solve the apparent contradictions in the biblical chronologies. Indeed, even within biblical books such as 1–2 Kings (setting aside the issues with 1–2 Chronicles) there seemed to be contradictions between the northern and southern reigns and their lengths and sequences. It was Edwin R. Thiele who solved the main elements of the problem and produced a reliable chronology for the rulers of Israel and Judah.[41] He found two systems of dating each king's length of

---

40. See Alan R. Millard, *The Eponyms of the Assyrian Empire 910–612 BC* (SAAS 2; Helsinki: Neo-Assyrian Text Corpus Project, University of Helsinki, 1994), 2.

41. Edwin R. Thiele, *The Mysterious Numbers of the Hebrew Kings: A Reconstruction of the Chronology of the Kingdoms of Israel and Judah* (Chicago: University of Chicago Press, 1951; 2nd ed., Grand Rapids: Eerdmans, 1965; 3rd ed., Grand Rapids: Eerdmans, 1983). See also Kenneth A. Kitchen, "Chronology," *DOTHB* 181–88.

reign. The king's predecessor died during year X. In one case year X was not counted by the new monarch (it was called the "accession year" system), and in the other case year X was counted as one year. The former system was used in Babylon and Assyria, and the latter system was used in Egypt. The northern kingdom of Israel, perhaps influenced by the first king Jeroboam's stay in Egypt, began with the Egyptian system. The southern kingdom mostly followed the Assyrian system, as did both kingdoms in the eighth century BCE and later, when Assyria controlled the region.

Thus the major dates in the first millennium BCE include the following: David, in about 1000; death of Solomon and beginning of the divided monarchy, 931; end of Hoshea and the northern kingdom of Israel, 722; reform of Josiah, 622; Babylonian destruction of Jerusalem and Judah, 587/586; beginning of Cyrus and the Persian Empire, 539.

As for the second millennium BCE, there are no certain connections to obtain an absolute chronology. Further, the dates in the biblical text are not intended to express precision, as seen by one of the first, that found in Genesis 15:13, 16, where the "four hundred years" from Abraham to the exodus are made equivalent to four generations. There is debate about when the Bible perceives the exodus, Israel's key event of deliverance from Egyptian slavery, to have taken place. Some say early, at 1447 BCE, on the basis of 1 Kings 6:1. Others contend that this date is similar to that in Genesis 15 and not intended to be exactly 480 years (a symbol for 12 generations of 40 years each). Instead, they propose that the traditions preserved in Exodus and the known archaeological realities of Egypt suggest a date sometime in the middle of the thirteenth century BCE.

Layout

We have divided the volume into chapters that move forward in time roughly according to the biblical story of Israel. Chapters 1, 2, and 3 consider important pentateuchal material that has special historiographical interest: the Genesis narratives, the exodus and wilderness records, and the covenants. In some cases the biblical texts were not written as history. In every case the literature was selective in its treatment of the events. Often the nature of the literature governed much of what was chosen and why it was chosen for inclusion in the written texts. Even where the literature comes closest to what looks to the modern reader as history, choices were made contingent on the purpose of what was being written. The same happens today, although we may have different purposes in mind when we write history or read and evaluate sources for history. This section therefore is concerned with examining the type of literature involved and the manner in which it may and may not be used for historical purposes. Foundational to all history is the manner in which an understanding of the past is derived from ancient written texts. Historiography is more than the casual writing about past events; it also involves the evaluation of sources for their use in the re-creation of places or times.

The following chapters consider questions of Israelite history. Here the chapters appear in chronological order, from the beginning of the Iron Age (ca. 1200 BCE) until the end of the Hellenistic period (63 BCE). The former constitutes the earliest generally recognized appearance of an entity or people known as Israel in the southern Levant. The latter date marks the conquest of that same area by the Roman general Pompey and the beginning of Roman imperial rule. An exception to this is chapter 8, where we consider the historiographical value of the prophetic traditions. The acts and words of prophets dominate much of the Hebrew Bible and thus provide an important area for consideration.

As each chapter develops its theme, there is a concern to present four major areas for consideration. First, the chapter provides a summary of the biblical texts traditionally associated with the period or type of literature under consideration. This allows readers, regardless of their familiarity with the topic, to review the oldest and best-known source that has been used more than any other in the reconstruction of ancient Israelite history. It also prepares for a description and examination of other historical sources of importance. These are evaluated as to their worth. Second, the author considers major issues in the analysis of these sources and especially in their application to the study of the historical period or type of literature under consideration. Third, the dominant positions in the scholarly literature are outlined and discussed. Fourth, these are then evaluated in the light of existing evidence. The authors of the chapters organize these areas according to the manner they feel best addresses their topic. They present their own understanding of the issues and provide a summary of where the evidence and the major discussions lead. Authors have flexibility to address the issues under consideration in each chapter because of the distinctive features of each historical period.

1

The Genesis Narratives

Bill T. Arnold

The first book of the Bible presents several challenges when approached from the perspective of history and historiography. First and foremost among those problems is that the opening chapters describe characters and events in a world dramatically different from our own: a world with talking serpents, with life before cities, before agriculture, before music or metallurgy; a world in which humans were unified with one language; and more. We cannot begin to locate these characters and events in a particular time or place, which is, of course, one of the tasks of any study of history. These chapters are, in fact, presented from a perspective *before* history, if we assume that history is properly understood as a time when humans began to write accounts of the past (a definition that itself is difficult to refine). And so we will need to start by asking how these materials in the early chapters of Genesis may be examined, or even if they may be examined at all, from the perspective of history and historiography.

Second, and closely related to this first challenge, is the realization that the genre or type of literature that we find in the book of Genesis is unlike others, with its own subset of characteristics raising numerous questions when examined, again, from the perspective of history and historiography. We will need to explore the specific characteristics and qualities of these literary types and how exactly they speak to issues of history, or whether they in fact speak to issues of history at all. And as we will see, these distinctive literary features relate to the ancestral accounts of Genesis 12–50 as much as they do to the so-called Primeval History of Genesis 1–11.

Third, in the case of Genesis we are left with even less evidence from the ancient Near East than usual when studying the Old Testament and its parallels with the surrounding environment. We famously have literary parallels in creation accounts (especially from Mesopotamia), comparative materials in creation concepts (including from Egypt), and cultural features from the ancient world that are suggestive as parallels to certain elements in the ancestral narratives. But in terms of archaeological context, or extra-biblical confirmation of the characters and events of Genesis, we are left completely without trace. As a result, this chapter on the materials in the book of Genesis is especially challenging for a volume devoted to, as stated in the introduction, exploring "the major sources relevant to ancient Israel's history" and evaluating "key issues of interpretation required of a critical study of that history."

Methodology and the Refinement of Our Task

We have set as our purpose in this volume the exploration of the sources, those within the Bible and all other sources beyond it, in order to see what may be said about the historical realities treated in the Bible itself. Before getting far in this endeavor, however, we must admit certain obvious limitations on how much we can say, due to a lack of details in those sources. The challenges already introduced here make the task especially difficult in a chapter devoted to the book of Genesis. In such a setting our task is necessarily attenuated; we are left with searching for what one scholar has called "a critically assured minimum."[1] On the one hand, it is naive to think that we are capable of reconstructing what actually happened in the history of early Israel, especially in the period of Israel's ancestors, or even more especially the beginnings of world history. On the other hand, historians of all periods operate with degrees of probability and are tasked with discerning the likelihood of this or that event regardless of the time period or even the amount of relevant material available for investigation.[2]

---

1. Tryggve N. D. Mettinger, *In Search of God: The Meaning and Message of the Everlasting Names* (trans. Frederick H. Cryer; Philadelphia: Fortress, 1988), 56. We should note, however, that Mettinger is using the phrase in a somewhat broader way in his discussion. See his discussion for more on what follows here about "possibilities," "probable conclusions," and "facts."

2. On the dangers of extreme skepticism and nihilism in the historical task, and with specific examples related to Israel's history, see Wilfred G. Lambert, "Mesopotamian Sources and

Because of these challenges and limitations, we are like scholars of all traditions and "schools" of investigation, using the best of our critical acumen and methods to draw conclusions about the historical realities of the biblical world.[3] In this process we must be willing to discern between (1) those conclusions that we consider essentially established, or "proven" and sometimes regarded as "factual"; (2) conclusions that seem most likely, although the evidence is less than sufficient to settle the matter once and for all; (3) conclusions that have sufficient evidence to establish their reasonable credibility, and for which we may use the term "plausible"; and (4) conclusions that are only possible, but for which we have no real evidence and about which we cannot make definitive statements. The latter are only possibilities in the sense that we can imagine them in the realm of human intellectual investigation; it is possible for rational, thinking humans to believe them. But to go beyond these conclusions is to assert mere fantasy or, in some cases, to explore the nature of faith itself, which is, of course, beyond the boundaries and capabilities of historical research.[4]

Our task of exploring the possible historical realia in Genesis is complicated still further by developments in the study of Israel's Scriptures in recent decades. Among many scholars it has become a common methodological datum to assume that the biblical text cannot be trusted when it comes to historical specifics (see the three methodological approaches discussed under "1990 to the Present" in the introduction). The basis for such an assertion, it is alleged, is that the textual evidence contained in the Bible has been "transmitted" or preserved through centuries by scribes, which, in the minds of some researchers, essentially disqualifies the biblical text as a primary historical source. In such an approach, archaeology and contemporary epigraphic data become "primary," and the biblical witness to ancient events is relegated to a "secondary" status.[5] An extreme version of this approach contends that

---

Pre-Exilic Israel," in *In Search of Pre-Exilic Israel: Proceedings of the Oxford Old Testament Seminar* (ed. John Day; JSOTSup 406; London: T&T Clark International, 2004), 352–65, esp. 362–64.

3. The use of "critical" here in no way implies a negative approach to our sources but rather refers to rigorous and intensive investigation of those sources, culling our greatest intellectual traditions in order to discern the most likely conclusions, whether we draw conclusions that we consider proven, probable, or only possible.

4. Absolute certainty of historical knowledge is impossible, but adequate certainty and reasonable certainty are entirely different matters. For theoretical introduction to this topic and recent bibliography, see Michael R. Licona, *The Resurrection of Jesus: A New Historiographical Approach* (Downers Grove, IL: IVP Academic; Nottingham, UK: Apollos, 2010), 31–107, and esp. 67–70 on absolute, adequate, and reasonable certainty.

5. For this approach, although in a more nuanced way than usually stated, see Lester L. Grabbe, *Ancient Israel: What Do We Know and How Do We Know It?* (London: T&T Clark, 2007), 6–10, 35.

we must attempt to reconstruct Iron Age history in the Levant as though the Bible does not exist at all.[6]

The problem, of course, is that archaeology and epigraphy themselves need interpretation, and sometimes scholars are as inclined to privilege or overinterpret these data as severely as they accuse others of overreading the biblical text. Whatever status one attributes to the biblical text, primary or secondary, it is methodologically problematic to exclude the possibility of *any* historical realia being preserved in the written testimony simply because it is transmitted over long periods of time.[7] The possibility must always be left open that late sources, which typically are assumed to be secondary or tertiary, may contain more accurate historical information than sources taken as primary only because those sources are older or perceived as more tangibly related to the events such as archaeology or epigraphy.[8] More care is needed with all sources on a case-by-case basis when exploring these earliest periods of Israel's history. In the case of the book of Genesis, we are left with no specific evidence from archaeology or extrabiblical sources, as we have already noted. This leaves us only with the text of Genesis, and the methodology employed in this chapter does not assume an essentially skeptical stance relative to that textual witness. But I will also endeavor to avoid overreading or overinterpreting the text of Genesis as if it were a historical document, since this biblical book, perhaps above all others, requires particular attention to its genre or literary type. Our task requires that we ask in what sense the terms "history" and "historiography" may be applied to a book such as Genesis.

Finally, our task is complicated further by research in the past two hundred years on the origins and early sources behind the current text of Genesis. The book itself has been the primary starting point for investigations of alleged original sources of the Pentateuch, famously resulting in the isolation of

6. Gary Rendsburg has argued that this approach has a particular agenda, unsupported by facts and driven by ideology alone. He shows that one can, in fact, write a modest history of ancient Israel as though the Bible does not exist, based solely on archaeology and epigraphy, and that such a history would not be much different from the portrait found in the Bible. See Gary A. Rendsburg, "Israel without the Bible," in *The Hebrew Bible: New Insights and Scholarship* (ed. Frederick E. Greenspahn; New York: New York University Press, 2008), 3–23.

7. A point that Grabbe (*Ancient Israel*, 220) helpfully notes and at times models. See also the comments of Baruch Halpern in Baruch Halpern and William G. Dever, "Two Views of a History of Ancient Israel," review of Lester L. Grabbe, *Ancient Israel: What Do We Know and How Do We Know It?*, BASOR 357 (2010): 77–83, esp. 77.

8. On the need for "finer discrimination" of sources in the historical endeavor, see Jens Bruun Kofoed, *Text and History: Historiography and the Study of the Biblical Text* (Winona Lake, IN: Eisenbrauns, 2005), 41–43; Iain W. Provan, V. Philips Long, and Tremper Longman III, *A Biblical History of Israel* (Louisville: Westminster John Knox, 2003), 56–62.

Ancient Alalakh

As we have noted, we have no specific evidence from archaeology or epigraphy confirming events described in the book of Genesis or mentioning any of the characters of the book. However, we have a body of literature from the ancient Near East suggesting cultural parallels to Israel's ancestors. For example, more than five hundred texts were discovered from two distinct periods in the history of the ancient city of Alalakh (modern Tell Atchana): the eighteenth–seventeenth and fifteenth centuries BCE. Alalakh was located on the southeast corner of the Hatay plain, on the Orontes River, in what is now southern Turkey (see fig. 1.1). Most of these inscriptions were written in Akkadian cuneiform on clay tablets, but reflect features of the local dialect. The Alalakh archive contains administrative records, a few treaty texts, and literary texts such as hymns and omens, as well as a statue inscription of King Idrimi from around 1500 BCE (although discovered in a later stratum). The Idrimi Inscription is an autobiographical account of the king's exploits after fleeing the kingdom when his father was murdered, living in exile for years, returning to Alalakh to reclaim the throne, and extending his rule into Hittite territory.[a]

Collectively, the texts of Alalakh illuminate the society and economic life at an important city-state of Syria-Palestine during the Middle and Late Bronze Ages. Numerous social customs attested at Alalakh and known also from other sites, such as Ugarit and Nuzi, have been compared to the customs in the ancestral narratives. But such customs have been criticized as not necessarily distinctive to the Bronze Age and not helpful as direct comparisons to the ancestral practices. The method of drawing such comparisons has been refined, and we understand the limitations of making such connections. Nevertheless, the concentration of such a large number of these cultural parallels in a Bronze Age society on the Mediterranean coast remains suggestive as background to the ancestral narratives. These include (1) a betrothal gift for the wife's father, allowing the bridegroom to marry (Gen. 34:12); (2) provisions for the use of a surrogate mother in cases of barrenness after seven years (Gen. 16:1–4); and (3) seven years of barrenness before a second wife compared to Jacob's seven years of service before he was allowed to marry Rachel (Gen. 29:15–35).[b]

a. Tremper Longman III, "The Autobiography of Idrimi," *COS* 1.148:479–80.

b. Richard S. Hess, "The Bible and Alalakh," in *Mesopotamia and the Bible: Comparative Explorations* (ed. Mark W Chavalas and K. Lawson Younger; JSOTSup 341; Grand Rapids: Baker Academic, 2002), 209–21, esp. 210–12; see also idem, "Seven Years of Barrenness before a Second Wife," *COS* 3.101C:252–53.

four primary sources (known as JEDP) and several secondary and redactional sources in the nineteenth century. The twentieth century saw significant revisions of this documentary hypothesis, as well as more than one challenge to

Figure 1.1.

World of Genesis

such a source approach altogether. In the first decade of the twenty-first century, investigation continued unabated into the original sources of the Pentateuch, including again Genesis as a primary focus, with special attention given to the literary parameters of each source and their relative dating. Today, little

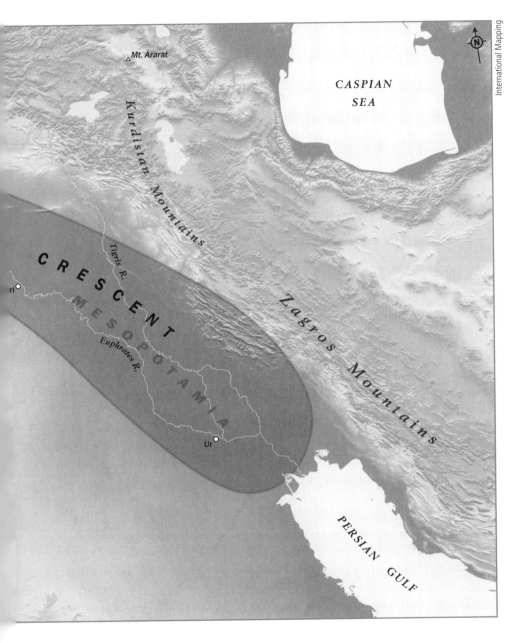

consensus has been reached on these issues, and a thorough review of the
research is beyond the scope of the present task.

For our purposes it is sufficient to explain that the book of Genesis has
largely been perceived as composed from two primary threads of materials,

priestly and nonpriestly traditions (sometimes referred to as P and non-P materials), although no general consensus has been achieved as to their extent or relative dates. The nonpriestly materials were compiled at some unreconstructed point in early Israel as an epic history (sometimes referred to as J, JE, or some similar siglum), and they formed one of the three expansive narrative complexes from ancient Israel.[9] It has been combined with the priestly materials to comprise the book of Genesis as an introduction for the Pentateuch as a whole. As such, this older epic history introduces the reader to the beginnings and development of the cosmos and humanity generally (parts of Gen. 1–11) and to the ancestors of Israel as explanation of Israel's origins (portions of Gen. 12–50). Regardless of one's conclusions about the specifics of how these materials were compiled in the present text of Genesis, I think it is helpful to acknowledge the two types of materials found in the book, priestly and nonpriestly.[10] In my view, either type of literary tradition is capable of preserving reliable historical information, and so I eschew skepticism as a legitimate position vis-à-vis the textual evidence. However, I also believe that literary features of these materials occasionally alert us to genres and literary types that are not intended to be taken as historiography in any modern sense of that term. Such complexity requires a nuanced methodology that takes each episode of the narratives individually in the process of assessing them for historical value.

Mytho-Historical/Pre-Ancestral Accounts (Gen. 1–11)

The people, places, and events described in the opening chapters of Genesis have no corresponding association with what we might call verifiable history. Events of these chapters (especially Gen. 1–4) cannot be confirmed or denied by the study of history, because history begins with the invention of writing. We know what we know about ancient people, society, and events primarily by the written records left behind, although archaeology and other social sciences contribute to our understanding of ancient history. The Primeval History (Gen. 1–11) addresses the origins of the universe, the creation of humanity, and the first institutions of human civilization.[11] We retain the term "history" in the title of this first unit of the Bible—the Primeval History—because, on the one hand, it arranges themes along a time continuum using cause and effect

9. See Bill T. Arnold, "History and Historiography, OT," *NIDB* 2:833–37, esp. 834–35.

10. See Richard S. Hess, *Israelite Religions: An Archaeological and Biblical Survey* (Grand Rapids: Baker Academic, 2007), 46–59.

11. For details on the structure and content of Genesis, see Bill T. Arnold, *Genesis* (NCamBC; Cambridge: Cambridge University Press, 2009), 1–12.

and generally uses historical narrative as the literary medium for communication. On the other hand, those themes themselves are the same ones explored elsewhere in the ancient Near East in mythological literature (creation of the universe, creation of humanity, the great flood, etc.). The Primeval History narrates those themes in a way that transforms their meaning and import, and for these reasons we may think of these chapters as a unique literary category, which some have termed "mytho-historical."[12] This designation in no way identifies these chapters as myths or mythical, but rather draws attention to the way certain themes that are explained through mythmaking elsewhere in the ancient Near East have been transformed in the Genesis narrative account.[13]

This unique blending or merging of literary categories—myth and history—in Genesis 1–11 is readily apparent in the way the chapters have been composed. These chapters are no simple history or example of ancient historiography. At most, we may say that mythical themes have been arranged in a forward-moving, linear progression, in what may be considered a historicizing literary form, using genealogies especially, to make history out of myth.[14] The famous personal names Adam (humanity) and Eve (life) provide both literary wordplay in the first biblical narratives and possess elements and roots that occur in the earliest West Semitic names attested outside the Bible.[15] The place name Eden (well-watered) also attests to an ideal garden with a description that contains clues connected to ancient realities.[16] Along with these, the land of Assyria and the rivers Tigris and Euphrates (Gen. 2:14) illustrate the merging of literary forms. This is Israel's version of ancient Near Eastern mythic history, in which a founding account is given of the universe, and events are traced back to a time in which the gods are the principal actors and reality is given essential features. In Israel's distinctive founding, mythic history events

---

12. Thorkild Jacobsen, "The Eridu Genesis," *JBL* 100 (1981): 513–29, esp. 528; Patrick D. Miller Jr., "Eridu, Dunnu, and Babel: A Study in Comparative Mythology," *HAR* 9 (1985): 227–51, esp. 231 (both reprinted in *I Studied Inscriptions from before the Flood: Ancient Near Eastern, Literary, and Linguistic Approaches to Genesis 1–11* [ed. Richard S. Hess and David Toshio Tsumura; SBTS 4; Winona Lake, IN: Eisenbrauns, 1994]). Although Jacobsen and Miller are drawing comparisons esp. between ancient Near Eastern mythology and the priestly materials of Gen. 1–11, the literary category itself is helpful for all of the Primeval History.

13. On the near impossibility of defining "myth" and "mythology," see John N. Oswalt, *The Bible among the Myths: Unique Revelation or Just Ancient Literature?* (Grand Rapids: Zondervan, 2009), 32–46.

14. Richard H. Moye, "In the Beginning: Myth and History in Genesis and Exodus," *JBL* 109 (1990): 577–98, esp. 598.

15. Richard S. Hess, *Studies in the Personal Names of Genesis 1–11* (Winona Lake, IN: Eisenbrauns, 2009), 14–24, 111–12, 131.

16. Richard S. Hess, "Eden—a Well-Watered Place," *BRev* 7, no. 6 (1991): 28–33; James A. Sauer, "The River Runs Dry: Creation Story Preserves Historical Memory," *BAR* 22, no. 4 (1996): 52–57, 64.

are traced back to a single creator, God, and the historicizing features are more prominent because of the prevalence of genealogies, as we will see.[17]

The prevalence of genealogical lists in the Primeval History is one of the most important literary features of this portion of Genesis (4:17–24, 25–26; 5:1–32; 10:1–32; 11:10–26). We have related materials from other cultures of the ancient Near East, and yet none of the extrabiblical examples have precise parallels with the use of genealogies in Genesis 1–11, either in form or function. Most ancient Near Eastern genealogies are intended to establish a certain status for a political leader or official, whereas in the Primeval History genealogies are blended with narrative portions to move the reader forward in history.[18] The characters involved are not political leaders rooted in the past; rather, they are key figures in religious history highlighted for their failures as much as for their successes.

Anthropological explorations of the genealogies of Genesis have demonstrated the highly sophisticated way in which they function in the book.[19] In general, Genesis has two types of genealogies: the "linear" or vertical genealogy, tracing a single line of descent, and the "segmented" or horizontal genealogy, which traces various descendants. Which of these two forms is used depends on its function in the text. In addition to these two forms, the genealogies of Genesis have three functions. First, by means of a process known as "divergence," each patriarch of ancient Israel is the father of other children who are not part of the Israelite ancestry and who become the ancestors of other people groups in the ancient world. Through such a process of differentiation, Genesis explains how Israel related to other populations of the ancient world. Second, Israel's lineage itself is traced through a straight line from Adam to Jacob in a process known as "invergence," in which only one son continues the Israelite ancestry. This lineal descent gives way to twelve subunits in a single generation with the children of Jacob (Gen. 29:31–30:24, counting Dinah; the birth of Benjamin is recorded in 35:16–21), and from that point forward a third process, known as "segmentation," becomes primary. With the children of Jacob, the genealogies of Genesis focus on the branches of the ancestral family, all considered within the covenant blessing

17. For comparison of Gen. 1–11 with Sumerian historiography (and ancient Near Eastern materials more generally) using the categories "contemporary history," "previous history," "legendary history," and "mythic history," see Richard E. Averbeck, "The Sumerian Historiographic Tradition and Its Implications for Genesis 1–11," in *Faith, Tradition, and History: Old Testament Historiography in Its Near Eastern Context* (ed. Alan R. Millard, James K. Hoffmeier, and David W. Baker; Winona Lake, IN: Eisenbrauns, 1994), 79–102, esp. 97–100.

18. Richard S. Hess, "The Genealogies of Genesis 1–11 and Comparative Literature," *Bib* 70 (1989): 241–54 (reprinted in Hess and Tsumura, *I Studied Inscriptions*).

19. For some of what follows, and more bibliography on this topic, see Arnold, *Genesis*, 9–10.

of Israel's ancestry. Thus the book traces through this system of genealogies a line of descent for all humanity through twenty-five generations from Adam to the children of Jacob, creating a literary framework or skeleton for the entire book.

Most anthropologists and historians working with genealogies emphasize their origins in the oral culture of tribal societies and their fluid nature in telescoping and reorganizing details of a given genealogy. They function to provide social identification for a person or people group, or to establish the legitimacy of individuals within certain groups, rather than to trace the history of those individuals or groups. They are fluid because they can be adapted to reflect changing realities of the social groups. Some argue that such fluidity makes genealogies fictitious and of no historical value. A more fitting approach is to recognize that genealogies are not intended as historiographical documents in the first place, although at times they can contain elements that have historical value.[20] Their use in Genesis is more natural in the ancestral narratives (Gen. 12–36), and so it is possible that genealogies have been extended into the Primeval History in Genesis 1–11 as a means of overlaying formal literary continuity with those ancestral narratives and to provide unity for the book as a whole. In any case, the presence of genealogies in Genesis cannot simply preclude the possibility of historical value in these materials, any more than their presence can be taken as documented historical events.

The account of Noah and the great flood (Gen. 6:9–9:29) resembles similar accounts in the ancient world, especially in Babylonia, where we have remarkably close literary parallels in the famous Gilgamesh Epic.[21] The similarities between the Genesis account of the flood and Gilgamesh are so exact, especially in the episode of the birds—the raven and the dove (Gen. 8:6–12)—that we must admit some literary dependence in either direction, although there is little agreement about which direction. It is therefore possible to argue that the story arose from a specific historical flood that took place in parts of southern Mesopotamia, perhaps as early as 2900 BCE.[22] Yet the nature of the literary presentation is quite beyond anything like a verifiable historical account, so the characterization of these chapters as "proto-historical" seems most appropriate.[23]

20. For more discussion, and esp. for the helpful analogy of a corporation's "organization chart," see John H. Walton, "Genealogies," *DOTHB* 309–16, esp. 314.
21. For survey, see David Toshio Tsumura, "Genesis and Ancient Near Eastern Stories of Creation and Flood: An Introduction," in Hess and Tsumura, *I Studied Inscriptions*, 27–57, esp. 44–57; Arnold, *Genesis*, 106–7.
22. William W. Hallo, "Antediluvian Cities," *JCS* 23 (1970–1971): 57–67, esp. 61.
23. Gordon J. Wenham, *Genesis 1–15* (WBC 1; Waco: Word, 1987), 166.

Sumerians

Sumer is the name of the alluvial plain at the mouth of the Persian Gulf in what is modern Kuwait and southern Iraq. The origins of the inhabitants of ancient Sumer (the Sumerians) remain completely shrouded in mystery, although we know much about their society and culture in the third millennium BCE. The earliest written texts in human history appear to have been in the Sumerian language, which is currently thought to be independent from known language families. The Sumerians appear to have been the inventors of writing itself, developed in their distinctive cuneiform impressions on clay, stone, and occasionally other materials.

Among other important cultural innovations, the Sumerians invented the sexagesimal system of counting, which gave us the 24-hour clock and the 360-degree circle. Scholars have also investigated the likelihood that Sumerian towns and neighborhood councils were the earliest experiments with democracy in human history. Together with their successors in southern Mesopotamia, the Babylonians, the Sumerians may be credited with establishing the philosophical, religious, and social infrastructure for ancient Mesopotamian culture for the next two millennia.[a]

The Akkadian versions of the Gilgamesh Epic, perhaps the greatest literary composition to come from ancient Mesopotamia, had Sumerian precursors. The Old Babylonian version of the epic from the early second millennium BCE probably was compiled by scribes using older disparate Sumerian stories about the great third-millennium king Gilgamesh from Uruk. They were then arranged in a single composition.[b]

a. Harriet E. W. Crawford, *Sumer and the Sumerians* (2nd ed.; Cambridge: Cambridge University Press, 2004).

b. See William L. Moran, "The Gilgamesh Epic: A Masterpiece from Ancient Mesopotamia," *CANE* 4:2327–36, esp. 2328–30. For translation of the Gilgamesh Epic, see Andrew R. George, *The Epic of Gilgamesh: The Babylonian Epic Poem and Other Texts in Akkadian and Sumerian; Translated and with an Introduction* (New York: Barnes & Noble, 1999), which includes translation of the Sumerian poems of Gilgamesh (141–208).

In sum, many readers of the opening chapters of Genesis will leave open the question of the historicity of these events, taking them as possible, no matter how remote the possibility may seem to us now. Others will admit the implausibility of those events as real or historically factual, largely because of specific literary features of the Genesis account. In truth, the situation perhaps is more complex because there may be vestiges of historical features embedded in the text, especially in Genesis 6–9; 10. But each such text needs to be examined on a case-by-case basis, and opinions will, of course, vary widely. Here it may be helpful to retain a distinction between "historical" and "literal." In other words, a text may be essentially metaphorical or symbolic and still retain historical features or elements that reflect real events in time and space. Some of the events of the Primeval History may be historical but not literal.

Ancestral Narratives (Gen. 12–36)

The next extended unit of the book of Genesis traces events in the lives of ancient Israel's first ancestors, especially Abraham, Isaac, and Jacob, and their families.[24] The task we have set for ourselves in this volume is to explore as much as can be known about the historical realities behind these narratives. As with the mytho-historical/pre-ancestral materials of Genesis 1–11, we have precious little to go on here—no extrabiblical references to these characters, no definitive archaeological traces of their lives or the events described in these chapters.

However, we are not completely left in the dark about Israel's ancestors. As we will see, we have a few Bronze Age cultural parallels that seem to relate to this early period, and the texts themselves preserve vestiges of what we may take as signs of the great age of the narratives, even if much of it may have been preserved orally and therefore beyond our ability to research.[25] In particular, the question of when the ancestors lived and how (or, some would say, whether) they actually relate historically to the later Israelites is tied to another question that we must address briefly: the "emergence" of ancient Israel in Syria-Palestine. I have put "emergence" in quotation marks because to speak of Israel's "conquest" of the land is already to prejudge the issues that scholars attempt to evaluate when assessing when and how Israel first appeared in the land.[26] The issues are exceedingly complex, but simply stated, scholars attempt to explain the evidence of archaeological surveys revealing a sudden population increase in a region previously sparsely populated in the central highlands of Syria-Palestine toward the end of the

---

24. We should not deny the essentially patriarchal nature of these accounts, although the term "patriarchal" in contemporary English imposes an inaccurate and pejorative connotation on Israelite culture. In point of fact, the wives of Abraham, Isaac, and Jacob, and other women in the narratives, often play roles that are surprisingly egalitarian in their perspectives. We must be careful not to impose our own egalitarian sensitives upon such an ancient culture in a way that reflects our arrogance more than it does the realities of that society and its treatment of women. See Phyllis Trible, "Depatriarchalizing in Biblical Interpretation," *JAAR* 41 (1973): 30–48, esp. 31; Carol L. Meyers, "Was Ancient Israel a Patriarchal Society?," *JBL* 133 (2014): 8–27.

25. We must think of ancient Israel as an "oral-and-written" culture and abandon the concept of orally preserved traditions developing first and then followed by their textualization. See Robert D. Miller, *Oral Tradition in Ancient Israel* (BPC 4; Eugene, OR: Cascade Books, 2011).

26. For details, see the discussion in chaps. 4 and 5 below.

Late Bronze Age.[27] These archaeological data are not in themselves in dispute or controversial; they are considered to be proven, or irrefutable, facts. Yet scholars are not agreed on their significance. And this illustrates the problems involved in reconstructing a history of early Israel and explains why the conclusions in this chapter especially are so tentative. One particular conclusion—entirely reasonable to consider, based on these archaeological realities—is that Israel's arrival in the land from outside Syria-Palestine is attested by the sudden population increase in the central highlands. But this is not the only possible explanation of the evidence. Scholars have explored the possibility that harsh weather conditions around 1200 BCE destabilized the major cities of Syria-Palestine and elsewhere, making it impossible for large urban sites to support their populations, which opted for living in villages in the highlands. Others have investigated the influence of a weakened Egyptian control of the coastal cities of the Levant, leading to migration of their inhabitants to the highlands. And, of course, the arrival of the so-called Sea Peoples along the coastal regions of the eastern Mediterranean was likely a contributing factor.

Regardless of these other contributing factors, it seems most likely that the new inhabitants in the central highlands of Syria-Palestine were population elements of what may be safely identified as "Israel" (see discussion in chap. 4, pp. 152–53), and that at least a portion of them escaped from slavery in Egypt and arrived in the central highlands after many years in the desert. Our task, then, is to consider the claims of the Pentateuch that this new group in Canaan had ancestry extending back to "wandering Arameans" (Deut. 26:5), presumably seminomads relying predominantly on small-cattle pastoralism for subsistence and having possession of no land of their own. The ancestral narratives of Genesis claim to fill in the details of this ancestral heritage. The text contains hints at the historical context, although, as we have noted, no extrabiblical evidence has confirmed the details. So, for example, Abram is promised that his descendants would return to Canaan and settle there "in the fourth generation" from his lifetime (Gen. 15:16). The ancestral family is consistently perceived in Israelite tradition as living "long ago" (mēʿ ôlām, "from of old, since ancient time" [Josh. 24:2–4]) and "from the days of old" (mîmê qedem, "from days of antiquity" [Mic. 7:20]). These biblical references and others suggest a setting for the ancestral age many centuries before the period of Moses and the exodus (Exod. 12:40; 1 Kings 6:1), which itself is impossible to date precisely. Thus the

---

27. An increase from 25 to nearly 300 excavated sites in the hill country, with an estimated population growth from 12,000 to approximately 60,000. See Israel Finkelstein and Neil Asher Silberman, *The Bible Unearthed: Archaeology's New Vision of Ancient Israel and the Origin of Its Sacred Texts* (New York: Free Press, 2001), 114–15.

authors of the Bible assumed an ancestral period in the Bronze Age, perhaps in the early second millennium BCE.[28] The question for the historian, then, is precisely when their ancestors lived, or, in the mind of some, if they existed at all.

Parallels with ancient Near Eastern cultural features have been investigated as a means of understanding the historical background of Israel's ancestors, with mixed results. It was argued nearly forty years ago that the Genesis account contains closer parallels to the customs reflected in first-millennium-BCE Babylonian legal texts than in the second-millennium texts, and that the ancestral narratives in particular contain historical anachronisms reflecting their late date of composition and lack of historical value.[29] Many cultural parallels from the second millennium BCE had been proposed for ancestral customs, especially from the ancient city of Nuzi in Mesopotamia.[30] However, closer scrutiny of those parallels reflected a flawed comparative methodology, so that the results have been largely abandoned. Arguments for the antiquity and authenticity of the ancestral accounts in Genesis based on those comparisons have been dropped as invalid. Some scholars have concluded that the Genesis accounts of the ancestors were ideological fictions from a much later period, as late as the postexilic period. Taken in this way, the ancestral traditions of Genesis reflect only the Israel of the Iron Age, not that of any Bronze Age ancestors. In fact, the period of the ancestors disappears altogether.[31] Others of a more moderate approach have concluded that the ancestral narratives contain bits of data reflecting great antiquity, and they prefer to speak of the ancestral narratives as a composite "of historical memory, traditional folklore, cultural self-definition, and narrative brilliance."[32]

28. For a dated but still helpful summary of the possible dates for the ancestral period, see J. J. Bimson, "Archaeological Data and the Dating of the Patriarchs," in *Essays on the Patriarchal Narratives* (ed. A. R. Millard and D. J. Wiseman; Leicester, UK: Inter-Varsity, 1980), 53–89, as well as other essays in that volume.

29. Thomas L. Thompson, *The Historicity of the Patriarchal Narratives: The Quest for the Historical Abraham* (BZAW 133; Berlin: de Gruyter, 1974); John Van Seters, *Abraham in History and Tradition* (New Haven: Yale University Press, 1975). For a helpful survey, see Gordon J. Wenham, "Pondering the Pentateuch: The Search for a New Paradigm," in *The Face of Old Testament Studies: A Survey of Contemporary Approaches* (ed. David W. Baker and Bill T. Arnold; Grand Rapids: Baker Books, 1999), 116–44.

30. Barry L. Eichler, "Nuzi and the Bible: A Retrospective," in *Dumu-E₂-Dub-Ba-a: Studies in Honor of Åke W. Sjöberg* (ed. Hermann Behrens, Darlene Loding, and Martha T. Roth; OPSNKF 11; Philadelphia: Samuel Noah Kramer Fund, University Museum, 1989), 107–19; Maynard Paul Maidman, *Nuzi Texts and Their Uses as Historical Evidence* (ed. Ann K. Guinan; SBLWAW 18; Atlanta: Society of Biblical Literature, 2010).

31. Maynard Paul Maidman, "Historiographic Reflections on Israel's Origins: The Rise and Fall of the Patriarchal Age," *ErIsr* 27 (2003): 120*–28*.

32. Ronald S. Hendel, *Remembering Abraham: Culture, Memory, and History in the Hebrew Bible* (New York: Oxford University Press, 2005), 46.

When it comes to archaeology and epigraphy, which some would call the "primary" sources of evidence, we must admit that the ancestral narratives are no better attested than the Primeval History. Investigation of individual sites mentioned in the ancestral narratives has been inconclusive, although we have a great deal of information about many of the locations mentioned in Genesis 12–36.[33] Recent investigation has turned attention to a consideration of what we can know about the original homeland of Israel's ancestors in and around Haran or, more generally, in northern Iraq and inland Syria. We have evidence of a long tradition of urbanization in the region, with large autonomous city-states and tribal polities. While this type of investigation is suggestive, it leaves us with nothing in the archaeology specifically attesting to the Israelite ancestors or confirming the text of Genesis. This leads one scholar to argue that the archaeological details are able only to "provide a plausible context for early Israel, if not provide subtle hints about its origins."[34]

Potentially more fruitful have been attempts in recent years to study the tribal confederacies revealed in thousands of texts from the ancient city of Mari as the cultural background for the Israelite heritage extending back to the Middle Bronze Age.[35] This comparative research has been reinvigorated by a surge of publications and information from the French team working on the Mari archives, led by Jean-Marie Durand since 1981.[36] One tribal confederation in particular, the Yaminite (or Binu Yamina), occupied locations such as Haran in North Mesopotamia and presents a tantalizing possible connection with the biblical "Benjaminites." It is possible to argue that Israel included the tribe named "Benjamin," because of its background in the Syrian tribal division. The shared names present a clue "that there were ancient Binu Yamina somewhere in Israel's ancestry, probably not limited to the tribe of Benjamin."[37] Since Israel's

33. Bimson, "Archaeological Data," 65–82. For a defense of the idea that the so-called anachronisms of the ancestral narratives are instead adaptations, or literary updates, see Edwin M. Yamauchi, "Abraham and Archaeology: Anachronisms or Adaptations?," in *Perspectives on Our Father Abraham: Essays in Honor of Marvin R. Wilson* (ed. Steven A. Hunt; Grand Rapids: Eerdmans, 2010).

34. Mark W. Chavalas, "The Context of Early Israel Viewed through the Archaeology of Northern Mesopotamia and Syria," in *Critical Issues in Early Israelite History* (ed. Richard S. Hess, Gerald A. Klingbeil, and Paul J. Ray Jr.; BBRSup 3; Winona Lake, IN: Eisenbrauns, 2008), 151.

35. Daniel E. Fleming, "Genesis in History and Tradition: The Syrian Background of Israel's Ancestors, Reprise," in *The Future of Biblical Archaeology: Reassessing Methodologies and Assumptions; The Proceedings of a Symposium, August 12–14, 2001 at Trinity International University* (ed. James K. Hoffmeier and Alan R. Millard; Grand Rapids: Eerdmans, 2004), 193–232.

36. For introduction and overview, see Jack M. Sasson, "The King and I: A Mari King in Changing Perceptions," *JAOS* 118 (1998): 453–70, esp. 457–59.

37. Fleming, "Genesis in History," 219; idem, "Mari and the Possibilities of Biblical Memory," *RA* 92 (1998): 41–78.

ancestral origins are identified in Genesis as associated with pastoralists near Haran in northern Mesopotamia, it seems more than plausible that those origins can be illuminated by the Mari texts as a specific tribal heritage descended from the Syrian Binu Yamina of the Bronze Age. In light of this connection, a further link could be the Amorite tribal term *ḥibrum*, used at Mari to refer to the component of the Binu Yamina population based in the backcountry and traveling with the flocks. This could be related to the biblical Hebrew term *ʿibrî*, "Hebrew."[38] All of this information from Mari is suggestive as background for Israel's ancestors, but at least one prominent scholar has warned against an overly eager "historicizing effort" that will distort the study of the Bible by chasing "that most elusive of Grails, the quest for the historical Abraham."[39] While his cautionary note and scholarship are laudable, the possibility of a historical Abraham seems far more likely than that of someone finding *the* Holy Grail. The quest for the historical Abraham will no doubt continue, and it seems that the Mari evidence is a rich resource for future investigation.

Sociologically, the ancestral family would have been much the same as other people groups living in the Levant. The "father's house" (*bêt ʾāb* [e.g., Gen. 12:1]) was the most important feature of the society. It consisted of an extended family of up to three generations and served as the center of religious, social, and economic life. These households were structured further into "families" or "clans" (*mišpěḥôt*), social spheres between the smaller "father's house" and the larger tribe.[40] These distinctions occur more than once in the ancestral narratives (Gen. 20:13; 24:7). For example, this includes the initial call of Abram to leave his father's house, which was essentially a call to launch out as a new *paterfamilias*. He did this even though he was childless and had no assurance that he himself would in fact become a father and therefore be able to establish a new "house" (Gen. 12:1).

Whereas later Israelites lived in permanent structures made of sun-dried bricks placed on stone foundations and roofed over with wood crossbeams, their ancestors are consistently portrayed as living in tents (e.g., Gen. 12:8; 13:3, 12; 18:1).[41] This claim of a tent-dwelling heritage for Israel's ancestors is corroborated by (1) an extensive vocabulary in biblical Hebrew for things tent-related, (2) a generally favorable perception of tents and nomadism in

38. Fleming, "Genesis in History," 220–21.

39. Jack M. Sasson, "Mari and the Holy Grail," in *Orientalism, Assyriology and the Bible* (ed. Steven W. Holloway; HBM 10; Sheffield: Sheffield Phoenix Press, 2007), 198.

40. Lawrence E. Stager, "The Archaeology of the Family in Ancient Israel," *BASOR* 260 (1985): 1–35, esp. 20–22.

41. Oded Borowski, *Daily Life in Biblical Times* (SBLABS 5; Atlanta: Society of Biblical Literature, 2003), 16–21; Philip J. King and Lawrence E. Stager, *Life in Biblical Israel* (LAI; Louisville: Westminster John Knox, 2001), 21–35.

Mari

The ancient city of Mari (modern Tell Hariri, located near the present-day border between Syria and Iraq) was an important exchange city on the west bank of the upper Euphrates River (see fig.1.1). The city existed from the early third millennium BCE until its destruction by Hammurapi around 1760 BCE. We have extensive archives from the kingdom period of Mari's history, from the end of the nineteenth and the first half of the eighteenth centuries BCE. The nearly twenty-five thousand documents discovered at Mari cast remarkable light on the Amorite culture and society of the region, even while we have a wealth of other documentation and resources for the Old Babylonian period of Mesopotamian history (ca. 2003–1595 BCE).[a]

In particular, the Mari texts have revealed how Zimri-Lim, a powerful king of Mari during the early eighteenth century BCE, ruled over an Amorite tribal state (specifically, a "Sim'alite" tribal state), balancing his roles as Amorite tribesman and king of an urban-based empire.[b] The tribal culture of Amorite Mari shares proximity in space, language, and chronology with ancient Israel, as the two share a physical region and a family of languages. In most chronological reconstructions, the end of Old Babylonian Mari culture was separated from the beginning of Israel's culture by a few centuries. Therefore, cultural features may easily have been transmitted, borrowed, or otherwise shared between Amorite Mari and early Israel.

In addition to the comparisons between the Mari evidence and Israel's ancestors, we have reason to explore comparisons between Mari and David's united monarchy. The Mari archive has challenged our traditional assumptions that tribal groups necessarily abandoned their patrimonial structures when establishing new urban-based state polities and therefore our assumptions about conflict between "town and tribe." Such comparisons may eventually illuminate even further our understanding of Saul and David as both tribal chieftains and the first royal figures in early Israel.[c]

a. Jean-Claude Margueron, "Mari," *OEANE* 3:413–17.

b. Fleming, "Mari and the Possibilities," 54. The details of this Amorite tribal culture raise fascinating possibilities for homologous comparisons with Israel's ancestors (as opposed to analogous comparisons, which are less direct parallels). On the distinction between "analogy" and "homology," see Jack M. Sasson, "About 'Mari and the Bible,'" *RA* 92 (1998): 97–123, esp. 98–99.

c. Daniel Bodi, *The Demise of the Warlord: A New Look at the David Story* (HBM 26; Sheffield: Sheffield Phoenix Press, 2010).

biblical literature, (3) an ability to move between permanent and impermanent buildings (e.g., Gen. 33:17–18), and (4) the possibility that the later Israelite architecture of permanent houses evolved from tent structures.[42] Separately,

42. Michael M. Homan, *To Your Tents, O Israel! The Terminology, Function, Form, and Symbolism of Tents in the Hebrew Bible and the Ancient Near East* (CHANE 12; Leiden: Brill, 2002), 29–59. Although generally favorable toward nomadism, later Israel did not embrace a

each piece of evidence is inconclusive, but together they converge to lead us to this general conclusion: "It is unlikely that someone would invent a tent-dwelling heritage were it not true."[43] This conclusion about the improbability of later Israelite authors inventing such a feature of their ancestral heritage is one that can be repeated, as we will see, when we consider a number of religious features of the ancestral narratives.

However, such a nomadic or seminomadic and pastoralist heritage for Israel's ancestors is not completely disconnected from the land. Each of the patriarchs—Abraham, Isaac, and Jacob—is closely associated with specific geographic regions of the promised land, and even with specific villages and cities within those regions. So the children of Jacob settled in the central hills of what would become northern Israel, especially in the area north and northeast of Shechem (Gen. 33:18; 35:4).[44] His grandfather Abraham is associated with the southern highlands, around Hebron and its open-air sanctuary at Mamre (e.g., Gen. 13:18; 18:1). Isaac appears to have lived in the Negev around Beersheba (Gen. 26:23). The Genesis narratives do not portray Israel's ancestors as vagabonds or nomadic drifters, moving from place to place, with no association or connection to the settled areas. On the contrary, they appear as tribal chieftains, connected to the settled areas and interacting with the local inhabitants. In this way, Israel's ancestors appear in the Genesis narratives with both tribal and pastoralist features, again perhaps related to the older Amorite tribal culture illustrated in the Mari archives, showing how tribal structures related to the older settled society.[45]

The religious expressions and practices of Israel's ancestors, as portrayed in the Genesis account, are quite different from later Israelite religion. Perhaps the most obvious is the name of the God they worshiped, which is almost always an "El"-type name (e.g., "El-Shaddai" [Gen. 17:1]; "El-Elyon" [Gen. 14:18]), rather than "Yahweh" as defined and worshiped by later Israelites. The concept of "holiness" so central to later Mosaic conceptions of relating to God (from Exod. 3:5 onward) is missing in the ancestral accounts of Genesis. Not only that, but also ancestral worship was unmediated; it was not regulated by a priest or prophet. Israel's ancestors worshiped in open-air sanctuaries near trees

---

romantic notion of nomadic life, making it unlikely that they invented such a tradition about their origins from thin air. See Kenton L. Sparks, "Israel and the Nomads of Ancient Palestine," in *Community Identity in Judean Historiography: Biblical and Comparative Perspectives* (ed. Gary N. Knoppers and Kenneth A. Ristau; Winona Lake, IN: Eisenbrauns, 2009), 9–26.

43. Homan, *To Your Tents*, 45.

44. For conjecture about the historical circumstances that led to their departure from northern Mesopotamia in the second millennium BCE, see André Lemaire, "La haute Mésopotamie et l'origine des Benê Jacob," *VT* 34 (1984): 95–101.

45. See Fleming, "Mari and the Possibilities"; idem, "Genesis in History."

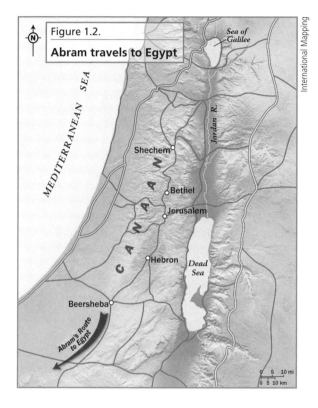

Figure 1.2.

Abram travels to Egypt

(e.g., Gen. 12:6–7; 13:18) or pillars (e.g., Gen. 28:18; 31:13), apparently unaware of any prohibitions against the worship of Baal or injunctions against Canaanite religious expression. Later religious festivals and holy days receive hardly any attention in the ancestral narratives. Israel's ancestors related to the religions of the surrounding peoples without hostility and, in at least one case, with open acceptance (Gen. 14:17–21).[46] These features and others mark the religion of Israel's ancestors as distinct from the Mosaic Yahwism of the rest of the Pentateuch and from later Israel as reflected in the Historical Books and the Prophets. The data suggest that the Genesis traditions about the religion of Israel's ancestors are genuinely ancient and pre-Yahwistic: "The depiction of religion in Genesis 12–50 may indeed have a claim to origins in part from the period prior to the emergence of Israel as a national Yahweh-worshiping community."[47]

All of this points to the conclusion that Israel's ancestors known to us in the Genesis accounts were real individuals, living during a period of time only imprecisely understood but likely in the Bronze Age, and at some distance from the authors of the biblical texts. The extrabiblical evidence does not

46. For a more complete list of features of ancestral religion, see the convenient summary in Hess, *Israelite Religions*, 149–51. In a more theological, even homiletical vein, John Oswalt has argued the Bible's claims that it derived its understanding of reality, an understanding radically distinct from all others in the ancient world, directly from the "human-historical experiences" of Abraham, which Oswalt contends is a strong argument for the historicity of Abraham ("Abraham's Experience of Yahweh: An Argument for the Historicity of the Patriarchal Narrative," in *Perspectives on Our Father Abraham: Essays in Honor of Marvin R. Wilson* [ed. Steven A. Hunt and Marvin R. Wilson; Grand Rapids: Eerdmans, 2010], 33–43, esp. 42).

47. Hess, *Israelite Religions*, 151.

demand the historicity of Abraham, Isaac, and Jacob, but "it certainly allows it, in accord with the biblical data."[48] Israel understood these accounts to be fundamentally factual, and without that factuality "the patriarchal narratives have sense but not reference."[49]

The Joseph Narrative

As we have seen, the Primeval History is justifiably identified as "mytho-historical" literature. Given what we have seen in the ancestral narratives of Genesis 12–36, those narratives might best be understood as Israel's protohistorical "traditional epic."[50] When we come to the final portion of Genesis, the Joseph narrative (Gen. 37–50), we find a different type of literature altogether, one that is most often identified as a "novel" because of its continuous story line with multiple scenes, carefully plotted suspense, and artfully crafted denouement.[51] For some, this genre identification means that these chapters are complete works of fiction, or that they must be an artistic invention of the author. But such an assumption is not necessary. We might just as easily think of the Joseph novel in terms of a "historical" novel, written with a high degree of literary sophistication, which does not, however, preclude authentic historical features of the account.[52] We have seen that genuine historical memories can be preserved in "secondary" and later sources, and similarly they can easily be preserved in artful and polished literary compositions. We should not presume a skeptical approach to the text simply because it is well written.

48. Alan R. Millard, "Abraham," *ABD* 1:40.

49. John Goldingay, "The Patriarchs in Scripture and History," in Millard and Wiseman, *Patriarchal Narratives*, 29. For the philosophical foundations for a "qualified correspondent" theory of truth emerging among nonminimalists working in the field, see Megan Bishop Moore, *Philosophy and Practice in Writing a History of Ancient Israel* (LHBOTS 435; London: T&T Clark, 2006), 29–31, 108–35, 183.

50. Frank Moore Cross, "Traditional Narrative and the Reconstruction of Early Israelite Institutions," in *From Epic to Canon: History and Literature in Ancient Israel* (ed. Frank Moore Cross; Baltimore: Johns Hopkins University Press, 1998), 22–52; David Damrosch, *The Narrative Covenant: Transformations of Genre in the Growth of Biblical Literature* (San Francisco: Harper & Row, 1987); Abraham Malamat, "The Proto-History of Israel: A Study in Method," in *The Word of the Lord Shall Go Forth: Essays in Honor of David Noel Freedman in Celebration of His Sixtieth Birthday* (ed. Carol L. Meyers and Michael Patrick O'Connor; Winona Lake, IN: Eisenbrauns, 1983), 303–13.

51. Arnold, *Genesis*, 17, 313–17. The Joseph novel itself in the narrower sense is Gen. 37; 39–45; and bits of Gen. 46–50. Provan, Long, and Longman (*Biblical History*, 108, 122) refer to the "novella-like Joseph story" and to its "novella-like quality."

52. Roland de Vaux, *The Early History of Israel* (trans. David Smith; Philadelphia: Westminster, 1978), 295–96.

The task before us, then, is to explore what we can and cannot know about the historical details of the Joseph narrative. As with the Primeval History and ancestral narratives, we have no direct confirmation in extrabiblical evidence for any of the events narrated here. We have no ancient Near Eastern sources naming Jacob or his children. We do not know the name of the pharaoh who knew Joseph, nor do we possess archaeological data confirming Israel's presence in Egypt. In the twentieth century, this absence of evidence led to the conclusion among some that we have no historical traces in the Joseph narrative, and that (together with the ancestral narratives of Genesis) the Joseph narrative is "hardly possible and totally improbable."[53]

Yet no one would deny that there "is no narrative in the Old Testament that reflects so immediately and vividly acquaintance with and wonder at a foreign land" as much as the Joseph narrative reflects ancient Egypt.[54] Since the development of Egyptology as a technical discipline, numerous scholars have investigated the Egyptian background to the Joseph narrative as a means to discern historical realia in the text of Genesis.[55] Of the Egyptian elements that have been investigated, a few of the most pertinent examples are slavery in Egypt, Egyptian personal names, the presence of Semites from Canaan living in the Egyptian Delta, perceptions and practices of dreams and magic in ancient Egypt, and the potential significance of Joseph's investiture and status.[56] Although some of these many Egyptian elements in the Joseph narrative may be denied or contested in their individual particulars, the cumulative weight of the evidence affirms that the picture portrayed in the Joseph narrative is "compatible with what is known from Egyptian history," and that the body of evidence suggests that the main points of the Joseph narrative are "plausible."[57] As with the ancestral narratives of Genesis 12–36, plausibility is the most that we can expect when searching for confirming details of these events.[58]

53. Thompson, *Historicity of the Patriarchal Narratives*, 328. This conclusion often is accompanied by the assertion that biblical narratives do not need to contain any historical value in order to be true (ibid., 326–30).

54. Claus Westermann, *Genesis 37–50: A Commentary* (trans. John J. Scullion; Minneapolis: Augsburg, 1986), 29.

55. For convenient introduction to this body of research, see James K. Hoffmeier, *Israel in Egypt: The Evidence for the Authenticity of the Exodus Tradition* (New York: Oxford University Press, 1997), 78–79.

56. Ibid., 83–95; Kenneth A. Kitchen, *On the Reliability of the Old Testament* (Grand Rapids: Eerdmans, 2003), 343–52; de Vaux, *Early History of Israel*, 297–310.

57. Hoffmeier, *Israel in Egypt*, 223, 226.

58. The Mari texts discussed above are also pertinent to the pastoralist mode of subsistence illustrated in Joseph and his family (Gen. 37:12–17), leaving us with a picture in the Joseph novel that is, as Daniel Fleming says, "remarkably plausible." See Daniel E. Fleming, "From Joseph to

I close with one particularly striking textual connection between an Egyptian source and the Joseph narrative. The so-called Report of Bedouin is a model letter or scribal exercise from the time of Pharaoh Merneptah (ca. 1213–1203 BCE), referring to certain Shasu tribes that apparently were Semitic pastoralists allowed to enter the eastern Nile Delta peacefully from the region of Edom.

> We have just let the Shasu tribes of Edom pass the Fortress of Merneptah-hetephermaat—Life, Prosperity, Health!—to the pool of Pithom of Merneptah-hetephermaat, of Tjeku, in order to revive themselves and revive their flocks from the great life force of Pharaoh—Life, Prosperity, Health!—the perfect Sun of every land.[59]

The phrase "in order to revive themselves and revive their flocks" is reminiscent of Joseph's assertion that God sent him ahead of his brothers in order to preserve life and "to keep alive" survivors from among them (Gen. 45:5, 7; cf. 47:25). This Egyptian text and others referring to the Shasu confirm the presence of Semitic tribal groups from Syria-Palestine moving to Egypt and rising to positions of power and influence. It would be premature to assume that these pastoralist Shasu tribes were related to the early Israelites. However, their journey and experiences are at least reminiscent of those described in the Joseph narrative for Jacob's family. And the parallel is attractive because of the Bible's witness that Israel and Edom were close relatives (Gen. 25:23–24), and that Yahweh is a deity who emerged from Seir and Edom (Deut. 33:2; Judg. 5:4; Hab. 3:3). In my view, it is plausible, perhaps probable, that the Report of Bedouin reflects the same general social movement represented by the settlement of Jacob's family in the Nile Delta—that is, the movement of Semitic pastoralists (small-cattle shepherds, tending sheep and goats) into the eastern Nile Delta in order to sustain themselves and their livestock, presumably in a time of famine.

David: Mari and Israelite Pastoral Traditions," in *Israel: Ancient Kingdom or Late Invention?* (ed. Daniel I. Block; Nashville: B&H Academic, 2008), 78–96, esp. 84–86.

59. Adapted from the translations by James P. Allen, "A Report of Bedouin," *COS* 3.5:16–17; John A. Wilson, "The Report of a Frontier Official," in *The Ancient Near East: An Anthology of Texts and Pictures* (ed. James B. Pritchard; Princeton: Princeton University Press, 2011), 235–36. Compare also pp. 51–52 below.

2

The Exodus and Wilderness Narratives

James K. Hoffmeier

Passover, also called the Feast of Unleavened Bread, is the religious festival celebrating Israel's "exodus" from Egypt. It was so important to the ancient Israelites that it was one of the three times a year that every Israelite household was required to appear at the Lord's sanctuary (Exod. 23:14–15). Within the Hebrew Bible there is mention of the observance of the Passover in the book of Joshua and in the days of Samuel the prophet (ca. 1000 BC).[1] Furthermore, one of ancient Israel's creeds emphasizes the sojourn in and the exodus from Egypt as foundational to Israel's origins as a people:

> A wandering Aramean was my father. And he went down into Egypt and sojourned there, few in number, and there he became a nation, great, mighty, and populous. And the Egyptians treated us harshly and humiliated us and laid on us hard labor. Then we cried to the Lord, the God of our fathers, and the Lord heard our voice and saw our affliction, our toil, and our oppression. And the Lord brought us out of Egypt with a mighty hand and an outstretched arm, with great deeds of terror, with signs and wonders. (Deut. 26:5–8)[2]

1. See Josh. 5:10–11. In King Josiah's day, when Passover was observed in Jerusalem, the Chronicler reports, "No Passover like it had been kept in Israel since the days of Samuel the prophet" (2 Chron. 35:18).
2. The ESV is the translation used throughout this chapter unless otherwise specified.

After departing from Egypt, the Hebrews did not go directly to settle in Canaan, the land promised to Abraham (Gen. 15), Isaac (Gen. 26), and Jacob (Gen. 46), and the book of Exodus (15:22–19:1) records their pilgrimage under the leadership of Moses to Mount Sinai. There their encounter with their God, YHWH (Exod. 20), included the "giving of the law," or Torah. This law stands at the heart of the Hebrew Scriptures as those texts are to this day. For forty years Israel lived in the Sinai, mostly in the area of Kadesh Barnea (Num. 13–19), possibly 'Ain Kudereit in the Wilderness of Paran (Num. 13:3), on the border of the Negev (south of Canaan), and near the territory of Edom (Num. 20:16).

From the perspective of the Old Testament, then, the sojourn-exodus and wilderness traditions are the foundation on which ancient Israel's self-understanding as a people and their religious origins were based. Even Israel's neighbors, the Bible reports, recognized their origins as a people in Egypt. King Balak of Ammon described them as "a people . . . come out of Egypt" (Num. 22:5). Despite this, many Old Testament scholars and biblical archaeologists today question the authenticity of the Bible's reports or reject them altogether.

J. Maxwell Miller and John H. Hayes, in their influential *A History of Ancient Israel and Judah*, declare, "We hold that the main story line of . . . [the] entrance into Egypt, twelve tribes descended from the twelve brothers, escape from Egypt, complete collections of laws and religious instructions handed down at Mt. Sinai, forty years of wandering in the wilderness, miraculous conquests of Canaan, . . .—is an artificial and theologically influenced literary construct."[3] Along similar lines, Niels Peter Lemche opines, "The traditions about Israel's sojourn in Egypt and the exodus of the Israelites are legendary and epic in nature. The very notion that a single family could in the course of a few centuries develop into a whole people, a nation, consisting of hundreds of thousands of individuals, is so fantastic that it deserves no credence from a *historical* point of view."[4]

More recently, in a popular book coauthored by a leading Israeli archaeologist, Israel Finkelstein, we are told that "the historical saga contained in the Bible—from Abraham's encounter with God and his journey to Canaan, to Moses' deliverance of the children of Israel from bondage"—is "a brilliant product of the human imagination."[5] These statements well reflect the current

3. J. Maxwell Miller and John H. Hayes, *A History of Ancient Israel and Judah* (Philadelphia: Westminster, 1986), 78.
4. Niels Peter Lemche, *Ancient Israel: A New History of Israelite Society* (BibSem 5; Sheffield: JSOT Press, 1988), 109.
5. Israel Finkelstein and Neil Asher Silberman, *The Bible Unearthed: Archaeology's New Vision of Ancient Israel and the Origin of Its Sacred Texts* (New York: Free Press, 2001), 1.

attitude toward the historicity of the narratives in the books of Genesis and Exodus. The question is, why?

The reason is straightforward: there is a general skepticism toward the Bible as a reliable source for history. If it were not still Scripture to Jews and Christians, the Bible probably would not be treated in such a condescending and dismissive manner. Because of this hermeneutic of suspicion, the Bible is not treated as a historical source unless there is external corroborating archaeological or historical (textual) evidence. In the case of the Israelite sojourn and exodus, no direct, clearly identifiable support has come to light in Egypt.

The demand that the Bible's historical claims (especially those relating to the book of Exodus) be substantiated by an external historical source raises a serious methodological flaw. The Bible should not be regarded as a *single* source. For those who still accept the traditional synthesis constructed by Julius Wellhausen, there are three primary sources present in the book of Exodus (Jahwist, Elohist, and Priestly), as well as whatever the redactor (whoever that may be) brings to the final form.[6] Then too we have the testimony of the book of Deuteronomy that represents a fourth tradition. All four of these sources in the Pentateuch, plus redactors, agree that there was a sojourn in Egypt and an exodus from Egypt, followed by a Sinai wilderness experience. Consequently, those who adopt the classical formulation of the Pentateuch as a mosaic of sources and traditions cannot then view the Bible as a lone historical witness. Rather, according to such an approach, multiple voices give testimony to the exodus and wilderness narratives despite some variations between them on certain details. They concur on the main points.

In addition to the testimony of the Pentateuch (all five books place the Hebrews in Egypt or refer back to the sojourn retrospectively), aspects and details of the exodus and wilderness stories are used in a multiplicity of ways in the books of Joshua, Judges, 1–2 Samuel, 1–2 Kings, Psalms, and in the Prophets.[7] Exodus and Sinai references or motifs are found in what are believed to be some of Israel's earliest poetic texts, such as Exodus 15 and Judges 5.[8] The earliest literary prophets—eighth-century-BC Hosea (11:1; 12:9, 13; 13:5–6), Amos (2:10; 3:1; 4:10; 9:7), and Micah (6:4)—are familiar

6. See, e.g., J. Philip Hyatt, *Commentary on Exodus* (NCB; London: Marshall, Morgan & Scott, 1971), 14–28; William C. Propp, *Exodus 1–18: A New Translation with Introduction and Commentary* (AB 2; New York: Doubleday, 1999), 125–27.

7. See James K. Hoffmeier, "These Things Happened—Why a Historical Exodus Is Necessary for Theology," in *Do Historical Matters Matter to Faith? A Critical Appraisal of Modern and Postmodern Approaches to Scripture* (ed. James K. Hoffmeier and Dennis R. Magary; Wheaton: Crossway, 2012), 99–134.

8. Frank M. Cross and David Noel Freedman, "The Song of Miriam," *JNES* 14 (1955): 237–50; idem, *Studies in Ancient Yahwistic Poetry* (SBLDS 21; Missoula, MT: Scholars Press, 1975).

with aspects of the exodus and wilderness traditions. Often simple, passing allusions are given, indicating that the audience needed no further elaboration. With this overwhelming evidence within the Bible regarding the Egyptian sojourn, exodus, and wilderness episodes, evidence coming from a variety of types of literature and used in a host of different ways, it is methodologically inadvisable, at best, to treat the Bible as a single witness to history, requiring corroboration before the Egypt-Sinai reports can be taken as authentic. To be sure, external support for the biblical tradition would be welcome, but I maintain that it is not a prerequisite for regarding the exodus narratives as authentic memories.

This does not mean, however, that we should ignore the indirect information that provides background material to the biblical narratives. Egyptian literature, various texts, artistic illustrations, various archaeological data, and topographic considerations shed light on events and details treated in the exodus-wilderness narratives. In fact these data (some of which will be reviewed below), in my judgment, beyond merely providing local Egyptian color and general contextual material for the biblical narratives, go a long way toward demonstrating the authenticity of the biblical tradition. I have already undertaken detailed studies of these matters in earlier publications.[9] What follows here are only some of the background data relevant to the sojourn-exodus and Sinai wilderness narratives, largely in the book of Exodus.

Israel in Egypt

Above, I quoted from the creed in Deuteronomy 26:5–9. Gerhard von Rad understood this pericope to be a credo, one of "the oldest pictures of the saving history" for Israel.[10] The immigration to Egypt, the harsh treatment, and the miraculous delivery are rehearsed when the firstfruits are presented to the priest and offered to God (Deut. 26:3–4). Can the historian take such a religious confession seriously? So deeply was this memory seared into the minds of the ancient Israelites and ubiquitous throughout the Old Testament that it is hard to believe that it was "a brilliant product of the human imagination."

The historian often has to work by analogy or with contextual data in the absence of direct evidence about the past and so can speak only in terms of

9. James K. Hoffmeier, *Israel in Egypt: The Evidence for the Authenticity of the Exodus Tradition* (New York: Oxford University Press, 1997); idem, *Ancient Israel in Sinai: The Evidence for the Authenticity of the Wilderness Tradition* (New York: Oxford University Press, 2005).

10. Gerhard von Rad, *Old Testament Theology* (trans. D. M. G. Stalker; 2 vols.; New York: Harper & Row, 1962–1965), 1:121.

what is plausible or probable.[11] The same is true with regard to the biblical tradition that the Hebrews were pastoralists who emigrated to Egypt due to famine in Canaan. No serious archaeologist thinks that direct archaeological evidence will be found that can verify the historicity of Abraham, Isaac, and Jacob, or that the latter and his clan moved to Egypt. The question, rather, is, Does evidence exist from Egyptian sources to demonstrate that Egypt was a place where pastoralists came for refuge from droughts to preserve their flocks and livelihood? Could it be that the portrayal of the Hebrews emigrating to Egypt is reflective of a broader pattern? Here the data from Egypt make it very clear that pastoralists from the southern Levant, Transjordan, and Sinai regularly came to Egypt under such circumstances. The evidence falls into two categories, textual and archaeological, which are mutually supportive.

Throughout pharaonic history, Egypt had to deal with pastoralists from the more arid areas of the southern Levant and Sinai who were eager to enter the fertile Nile Valley, which was a verdant magnet for pastoralists and normally was unaffected by the weather patterns of the eastern Mediterranean region.[12] Egypt's fertility was based on the Nile and the rains in central Africa, not the precipitation that rolls in from the sea. Margaret Drower describes Egypt's situation: "On the borders of the Delta, from time immemorial small groups of these bedawin [Bedouin] came to pasture their flocks, tempted by the proximity of better grazing-grounds and possible loot."[13] Normally Egypt was able to control the main entry points to Egypt in north Sinai along the "Ways of Horus,"[14] the route that runs parallel to the Mediterranean coastline,[15] and the more southerly entrance at the Wadi Tumilat, the narrow green valley that extends east from the Nile Delta toward the modern city of Ismailiya.[16] During

11. See the section "Methodology and the Refinement of Our Task" in chap. 1 above. Historians must operate with degrees of probability and must conscientiously distinguish between conclusions that are proven, probable, plausible, or only possible.

12. See recent Landsat or Google Earth images of Egypt and Sinai; e.g., Adrian Curtis, ed., *Oxford Bible Atlas* (Oxford: Oxford University Press, 2007), 18–19. On recent archaeological and geological developments in northwestern Sinai that have revealed the more precise path of this approach to Egypt, see James K. Hoffmeier and Mohamed Abd el-Maksoud, "A New Military Site on 'the Ways of Horus'—Tell el-Borg 1999–2001: A Preliminary Report," *JEA* 89 (2003): 169–97.

13. Margaret S. Drower and J. Bottéro, "Syria before 2200 B.C.," in *Early History of the Middle East* (vol. 1.2 of *The Cambridge Ancient History*; Cambridge: Cambridge University Press, 1971), 351.

14. Known in the Bible as "the way of the land of the Philistines" (Exod. 13:17).

15. Anson F. Rainey and R. Steven Notley, *The Sacred Bridge: Carta's Atlas of the Biblical World* (Jerusalem: Carta, 2006), 92; Curtis, *Oxford Bible Atlas*, 78–79.

16. Curtis, *Oxford Bible Atlas*, 18.

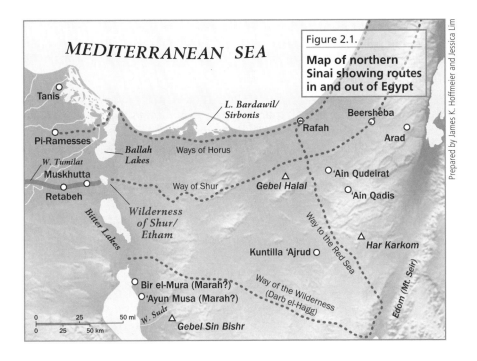

Figure 2.1.

Map of northern Sinai showing routes in and out of Egypt

Prepared by James K. Hoffmeier and Jessica Lim

the New Kingdom (ca. 1550–1200 BC) these entry points were well guarded by forts that monitored movements of pastoralists or invading armies (fig. 2.1).[17]

A late thirteenth-century-BC letter from a scribe to his superior (presumably back in the royal residence at Pi-Ramesses) reports that a group of pastoralists were granted permission to pass his fort in the Wadi Tumilat to water their flocks. This letter is found in Papyrus Anastasi VI: "Another information for my lord that we have just let the Shasu tribes of Edom pass the Fortress Merneptah-hetephermaat, LPH,[18] of Tjeku, to the pool of Pithom of Merneptah-hetephermaat, of Tjeku in order to revive themselves and revive their flocks."[19]

17. For review of the border forts, see James K. Hoffmeier and Stephen Moshier, "A Highway Out of Egypt: The Main Road from Egypt to Canaan," in *Desert Road Archaeology in Ancient Egypt and Beyond* (ed. Heiko Riemer and Frank Förster; Africa Praehistorica 26; Köln: Heinrich Barth Institut, 2013), 485–510; Ellen Fowles Morris, *The Architecture of Imperialism: Military Bases and the Evolution of Foreign Policy in Egypt's New Kingdom* (PÄ 22; Leiden: Brill, 2005). I discovered the two forts of the Eighteenth Dynasty and Ramesside periods at Tell el-Borg. See Hoffmeier and Abd el-Maksoud, "New Military Site"; James K. Hoffmeier, "Tell el-Borg on Egypt's Eastern Frontier: A Preliminary Report on the 2002 and 2004 Seasons," *JARCE* 41 (2004): 85–111; idem, "Recent Excavations on the 'Ways of Horus': The 2005 and 2006 Seasons at Tell el-Borg," *ASAE* 80 (2006): 257–79.

18. Abbreviation for the epithet "Life, Prosperity, and Health."

19. James P. Allen, "A Report of Bedouin," *COS* 3.5:16–17.

"Tjeku" is the Egyptian name for the area of the present-day Wadi Tumilat, and linguistically it corresponds to the Hebrew term "Succoth," found in Exodus 12:37; 13:20.[20] The fortress is named for the reigning pharaoh, Merneptah (1213–1205 BC). It permitted a group of Shasu, or Bedouin,[21] to water their flocks in the pools of Pithom (more on this below). These were Shasu of Edom, apparently from the area of Edom in the southern Transjordan. In the biblical tradition the Edomites are descendants of Esau, also called "Edom" (Gen. 25:30; 36:8). Since the Edomite Bedouin are mentioned in this late thirteenth-century letter, Papyrus Anastasi VI indicates that these pastoralists likely had traversed from southern Transjordan, across Sinai, to come to Egypt to water and feed their flocks.[22]

As this text further reveals, during the Middle Kingdom (2106–1786 BC) and New Kingdom (ca. 1550–1200 BC) Egypt was able to control the borders and limit infiltration, but in the First (2190–2106 BC) and Second (1786–1550 BC) Intermediate periods, when central authority had broken down and the border forts had been abandoned by the military, the door was wide open for unfettered access to the Nile Delta by pastoralists from the east. Echoes of this problem for Egypt are heard in a number of literary works that reflect on the calamities for Egypt when large numbers of pastoralists occupied the Nile Delta.

In the Wisdom for Merikare, from the First Intermediate period, King Meryibre Khety laments the presence of troublesome "Asiatics" (i.e., ʿamu = Semitic-speaking people from western Asia):

> Now speaking about these foreigners,
> As for the miserable Asiatic, wretched is the place where he is;
> Lacking in water, . . . Food causes his feet to roam about.[23]

The king advises his son to build defenses in the Bitter Lakes region (i.e., the Isthmus of Suez) and to defend the region.[24]

---

20. William F. Albright, *The Vocalization of the Egyptian Syllabic Orthography* (AOS 5; New Haven: American Oriental Society, 1934), §20B; Wolfgang Helck, "*Ṯkw* und die Ramses-Stadt," *VT* 15 (1965): 35; *HALOT* 2:753.

21. Raphael Giveon, *Les Bédouins Shosou des documents égyptiens* (DMOA 18; Leiden: Brill, 1971).

22. On pastoralists in the New Kingdom, see Manfred Bietak, "Nomads or *mnmn.t*-Shepherds in the Eastern Nile Delta in the Late New Kingdom," in *"I Speak the Riddles of Ancient Times": Archaeological and Historical Studies in Honor of Amihai Mazar on the Occasion of His Sixtieth Birthday* (ed. Aren M. Maeir and Pierre de Miroschedji; 2 vols.; Winona Lake, IN: Eisenbrauns, 2006), 1:124–36.

23. Translation in Hoffmeier, *Israel in Egypt*, 55.

24. For commentary on this passage, see ibid., 56–58.

An early twentieth-century-BC text, the Prophecy of Neferti, seemingly reflects on the period before the Middle Kingdom when people from western Asia penetrated the Nile Delta and were upsetting the status quo:

> All happiness has gone away, the land is cast down in trouble
> because of those feeders, Asiatics [*sttyw*] who are throughout the land.
> Enemies have arisen in the east, Asiatics [*ʿamu*] have come down to
>   Egypt.
> A fortress is deprived of another beside it, the guards pay no attention
>   to it.[25]

To remedy this crisis, Neferti prophesies that a messianic-like king named Ameny (short for Amenemhet) will come to stabilize Egypt: "One [i.e., the king] will build the 'Walls of the Ruler' . . . to prevent Asiatics [*ʿamu*] from going down into Egypt. They will beg for water in the customary manner in order to let their flocks drink."[26] What is so informative about this statement is the assumption that when the forts are fully functional, the pastoralists will once again need to seek permission to enter Egypt to water their flocks. The reference to this defensive network, the "Walls of the Ruler," is also mentioned in the Story of Sinuhe. Sinuhe was a court official who, upon learning of the assassination of King Amenemhet I, fled Egypt for Canaan because he feared being implicated.[27] As he approached Sinai, he reports, "I reached the 'Walls of the Ruler' which were made to repulse the Asiatics [*Sttyw*], to trample the Bedouin [*nmiw šʿw* = lit., "sand-farers"]. It was in fear that I took to crouching in a bush lest the sentry on the wall on duty see (me)."[28]

There are, then, two references to the defense system called the "Walls of the Ruler" in the twentieth century BC, but so far no corresponding feature has been discovered from the Twelfth Dynasty in the Bitter Lakes region or north Sinai. Nevertheless, Egyptologists tend to view these literary references as reflecting reality.[29] Certainly the purpose of such a defensive network is clearly understood.

The foregoing texts demonstrate that Egypt had an ongoing problem with pastoralists trying to enter it to graze and water sheep and, if possible, to stay

---

25. Translation in ibid., 58.
26. Translation in ibid., 59.
27. For full translation of the Story of Sinuhe, see Miriam Lichtheim, *The Old and Middle Kingdoms* (vol. 1 of *Ancient Egyptian Literature: A Book of Readings*; Berkeley: University of California Press, 1973), 222–36; idem, "Sinuhe," COS 1.38:77–82.
28. Translation in Hoffmeier, *Israel in Egypt*, 60.
29. For a review of the literature on the "Walls of the Ruler" and archaeological data, see James K. Hoffmeier, "'The Walls of the Ruler' in Egyptian Literature and the Archaeology Record: Investigating Egypt's Eastern Frontier in the Bronze Age," *BASOR* 343 (2006): 1–20.

there. Border forts, some of which have been discovered only in the past two decades, were erected to control such activities. The literature is unanimous in its testimony about the problem of infiltrating pastoralists, but a logical question follows: is there any direct archaeological data to support the textual testimony?

Surprisingly, the answer is affirmative. It is a surprise because one normally does not expect pastoralists to leave much evidence of their presence, other than burials, given the short duration of their visits and movements. And presently, archaeologists and anthropologists are unable to distinguish the various ethnicities of pastoral groups from the Semitic world when they leave their traces in Egypt. This means that Hebrews, Shasu, or ʿAmu cannot be differentiated archaeologically. The evidence at most Nile Delta sites reflects the sedentarizing of pastoralists.

Once in Egypt, especially in the Second Intermediate period, many pastoralists became sedentary, and their Syro-Canaanite cultural remains are discernable. In the Wadi Tumilat, the sites of Tell el-Maskhuta and Tel el-Retabeh have yielded signs of Middle Bronze Age Syro-Canaanite presence, including burials with pottery and weapons from the Levant.[30] In the east Nile Delta, Tell el-Yehudiyeh was the first site to yield the presence of settling Asiatics. Nineteenth-century excavations conducted by Édouard Naville and then Flinders Petrie produced what appears to have been a Middle Bronze Era defense system.[31] Syro-Canaanite remains from the Second Intermediate period have been discovered at other Nile Delta sites such as Inshas, Tell Farasha, and Tell el-Kebir,[32] but the most important site is Tell el-Dabʿa. This latter site has been investigated by Manfred Bietak of the University of Vienna regularly since 1966, and it is the long-sought capital of the Hyksos, Avaris, mentioned in Josephus's quotation of Manetho (*Ag. Ap.* 1.78). Avaris was a major urban center, with Levantine-type tombs, pottery, and architecture.[33]

---

30. For a convenient review, see Hoffmeier, *Israel in Egypt*, 65–67. See also John S. Holladay, *Cities of the Delta: Preliminary Report on the Wadi Tumilat Project; Part 3, Tell el-Maskhuta* (ARCER 6; Malibu, CA: Undena, 1982); Carol Redmount, "On an Egyptian/Asiatic Frontier: An Archaeological History of the Wadi Tumilat" (PhD diss., University of Chicago, 1989).

31. For a review of work there, see Hoffmeier, *Israel in Egypt*, 67. For a more recent treatment of this type of site, see Aaron Burke, *"Walled Up to Heaven": The Evolution of Middle Bronze Age Fortification Strategies in the Levant* (SAHL 4; Winona Lake, IN: Eisenbrauns, 2008), chap. 1.

32. For a review of this site, see Hoffmeier, *Israel in Egypt*, 67–68.

33. See Manfred Bietak, *Avaris, the Capital of the Hyksos: Recent Excavations at Tell El-Dabʿa* (London: British Museum Press, 1996); idem, *Avaris and Piramesse: Archaeological Exploration in the Eastern Nile Delta* (Oxford: Oxford University Press, 1979). More than 20 volumes of final reports are now available in the Tell el-Dabʿa series from the Austrian Academy of Sciences publications in Vienna, and scores of studies and preliminary reports appear in the journal *Ägypten und Levante/Egypt and the Levant.*

Currently a major Hyksos period (Second Intermediate period) palace is being excavated in Area F II, which shares architectural features with Middle Bronze Age Syro-Canaanite palaces.[34]

Egyptian textual sources and archaeological evidence conclusively demonstrate, especially in the Second Intermediate period, a substantial foreign presence in the Nile Delta, including the Hyksos rulers. When the Hyksos ruling and military elite retreated to Canaan after being attacked by the Theban king Ahmose around 1525 BC, it is generally believed, the majority of the Semitic-speaking population remained in Egypt. The Hebrews probably were included among these "Asiatics" in the Nile Delta who prompted the paranoid pharaoh in the book of Exodus (1:8–10) to begin the subjugation of the Israelites.

The Oppression of the Hebrews

The image of the Hebrews pressed into hard labor for the pharaoh is fixed into the mind of the reader of the early chapters of Exodus: "Therefore they set taskmasters over them to afflict them with heavy burdens. . . . So they ruthlessly made the people of Israel work as slaves and made their lives bitter with hard service, in mortar and brick, and in all kinds of work in the field. In all their work they ruthlessly made them work as slaves" (Exod. 1:11, 13–14).

Two areas of forced labor are mentioned: brickmaking and building, and agricultural work. While the perspective of the book of Exodus is focused on the suffering and forced labor of the Hebrews, when the exodus occurs, "a mixed multitude also went up with them [the people of Israel]" (Exod. 12:38). This "mixed multitude" (*'ereb rab*) is what Umberto Cassuto understood to mean "a motley mob who were not of Israelite origin."[35] Nahum Sarna more specifically ties "mixed multitude" to "varied groups of forced laborers" who took advantage of the opportunity to leave Egypt with the Hebrews.[36] It seems, then, that this mention of the "mixed multitude" shows that other non-Egyptian people experienced the same fate as the Israelites.

As suggested above, we have reason to believe that there was a significant number of the foreign elements in the Nile Delta, especially those of the lower

---

34. Manfred Bietak and Irene Forster-Müller, "Eine palatiale Anlage der frühen Hyksoszeit (Areal F/II): Vorläufige Ergebnisse der Grabungskampagne 2006 in Tell el-Dabʿa," *ÄL* 16 (2006): 61–76.

35. Umberto Cassuto, *A Commentary on the Book of Exodus* (trans. Israel Abrahams; Jerusalem: Magnes, 1967), 147.

36. Nahum M. Sarna, *Exodus: The Traditional Hebrew Text with the New JPS Translation* (JPSTC; Philadelphia: Jewish Publication Society, 1991), 62.

classes who remained in Egypt after the expulsion of the Hyksos, as well as the subsequent military campaigns of the Eighteenth Dynasty pharaohs in which thousands of prisoners of war were taken to Egypt.[37] Thutmose III conducted numerous military campaigns to Canaan and Syria between 1458 and 1425 BC. His yearly reports record that, after he defeated the city of Megiddo, 340 were taken. In year 30 over 200 were removed, in year 31 492 prisoners were relocated, in year 33 over 500, in year 34 over 600 were taken to Egypt, and in year 38 more than 500 were transferred to Egypt.[38] These numbers tally to several thousand, but to this figure we must add large numbers taken from Nubia to Egypt. During the reign of Thutmose III's son and successor, Amenhotep II (1427–1400 BC), the numbers of prisoners brought to Egypt escalate precipitously. He claims to have captured and deported 89,600. Scholars remain divided on whether to take this figure literally or as an artificially exaggerated number.[39] In favor of taking this figure at face value is that 89,600 is a total of smaller units of prisoners[40] from different ethnic groups and different areas, and such a figure does not look symbolic or hyperbolic.[41] Regardless of which position one takes, the claims of this stela minimally indicate that large (perhaps even larger) numbers of prisoners were relocated from western Asia to Egypt at the end of the fifteenth century BC, a practice that continued over the next 150 years. Consequently, from the seventeenth century BC and on through the New Kingdom, significant numbers of foreign people from the Semitic-speaking world were living in Egypt and especially in the Nile Delta.

Well known is the work scene from the tomb of Rekhmire, a vizier of Thutmose III, in which foreign prisoners from western Asia and Nubia are shown making bricks for building a construction ramp of the Akh-Menu temple, in the Karnak complex in Thebes.[42] Taskmasters with sticks are depicted

---

37. For a review of the data, see Hoffmeier, *Israel in Egypt*, 112–16.

38. Kurt Heinrich Sethe, *Urkunden der 18. Dynastie* (3 vols.; UÄA 4; Berlin: Akademie-Verlag, 1961), 3:690.7, 691.2, 698.7, 699.5, 706.4, 717.10.

39. For example, this total is viewed as exaggerated by Anthony Spalinger, "The Historical Implications of the Year 9 Campaign of Amenophis II," *JSSEA* 13, no. 2 (1983): 89–101. In support of the high figures, based on the comparison of these numbers with prisoner-of-war numbers of the Hittites and Assyrians, see Amin Amer, "Asiatic Prisoners Taken in the Reign of Amenophis II," *ScrM* 5 (1984): 27–28.

40. Actually, this figure is not an accurate total of the smaller units. The actual total is even higher, 101,128 (for discussion of this text, see Hoffmeier, *Israel in Egypt*, 113).

41. Compare this figure with grandiose statements in Thutmose III's Poetic Stela, where the king claims to have captured "ten thousand thousands" (*ḏbꜥ ḥꜣw*) and "hundred thousands" (*ḥfnw*). See Adriaan de Buck, ed., *Egyptian Readingbook: Exercises and Middle Egyptian Texts* (3rd ed.; Leiden: Nederlands Instituut voor het Nabije Oosten, 1970), 54.1–2.

42. Norman de Garis Davies, *The Tomb of Rekh-mi-Rē at Thebes* (New York: Plantin, 1943), plates 56–57.

Figure 2.2. Brickmaking scene from the tomb of Rekhmire

as supervising the workers. Exodus reports that the Hebrews had to meet production quotas (Exod. 5:4–14). Kenneth Kitchen has demonstrated that as early as the Old and Middle Kingdoms, brickmakers had to meet quotas, and the evidence from the Louvre Leather Roll is that missing the targeted quantity was normal practice.[43] In the thirteenth century BC, during a construction project at Pi-Ramesses, the Nile Delta royal residence, Papyrus Leiden 348 mentions "the ʿApiru who are dragging stone to the great pylon of [text broken] Raʾmesse-miamun, Beloved of Maʾet."[44] The reference to Apiru in this Nile Delta setting is intriguing, as the term is possibly cognate with the word "Hebrew."[45] However, it is generally recognized that the term ʿApiru is not an ethnic designation but rather a sociological one that refers

43. Kenneth Kitchen, "From the Brickfields of Egypt," *TynBul* 27 (1976): 143–44.

44. Ricardo Caminos, *Late-Egyptian Miscellanies* (BES 1; London: Oxford University Press, 1954), 491.

45. See Niels Peter Lemche, "Ḫabiru, Ḫapiru," *ABD* 3:6–10. On linguistic challenges for equating "Hebrew" with "Ḫabiru, Ḫapiru," see Rainey and Notley, *Sacred Bridge*, 88–89; Richard S. Hess,

to displaced people.[46] Thus it is possible that the biblical Hebrews would have been understood to be Apiru, but the term has broader application throughout the Levant. Regardless of the specific identity of the Apiru, they are foreigners from western Asia who are engaged in forced labor for Ramesses II (1279–1213 BC).

Then too, foreigners are found engaged in agricultural work in New Kingdom times. In a recent study Ellen Morris has drawn attention to the numerous scenes in Eighteenth Dynasty tombs that show various foreigners working in diverse types of farmwork, including tending vineyards and winemaking.[47]

It can be concluded, then, that the very two areas where the Bible claims that the Hebrews were compelled to work, brickmaking/construction and agriculture, are precisely where the Egyptian data show that deportees from the Levant were forced to work. Consequently, the biblical portrayal cannot be regarded as "a brilliant product of human imagination." It seems probable that the Hebrews, already in the land, were treated like prisoners of war being brought into Egypt during the New Kingdom.

Excavations at Tell el-Dab'a since the 1990s have uncovered a number of major mud-brick architectural structures. After clearing Avaris of the hated Hyksos rulers, Ahmose had a substantial citadel constructed that measured 229 x 153 feet.[48] Then in the fifteenth century, likely during the reign of Hatshepsut and Thutmose III, a complex of three palaces was constructed, the largest of the mud-brick palaces (Palace G) measuring 1,791 x 843 feet, and then a mud-brick enclosure surrounded the thirteen-acre area.[49] This palace complex appears to have been abandoned in the fourteenth century BC. In the final decades of the fourteenth century Horemheb engaged in a building program at Avaris, and then in the Nineteenth Dynasty, to the northeast, Ramesses II built his megalopolis, Pi-Ramesses.[50]

"The Bible and Alalakh," in *Mesopotamia and the Bible: Comparative Explorations* (ed. Mark W. Chavalas and K. Lawson Younger; JSOTSup 341; Grand Rapids: Baker Academic, 2002), 211.

46. Moshe Greenberg, *The Ḫab/piru* (New Haven: American Oriental Society, 1955); Giorgio Buccellati, "ʿApirū and Munnabtūtu—The Stateless of the First Cosmopolitan Age," *JNES* 36 (1977): 145–57; Jean Bottéro, "Entre nomads et sédentaires: Les Habiru," *DHA* 6 (1980): 201–13. Lemche (*Ancient Israel*, 430–31) is one scholar who believes that Israel's origin evolved from ʿapiru/ḫabiru.

47. Ellen Morris, "Mitanni Enslaved: Prisoners of War, Pride, and Productivity in a New Imperial Regime," in *Creativity and Innovation in the Reign of Hatshepsut* (ed. J. Galan, P. F. Dorman, and B. M. Bryan; Chicago: University of Chicago Press, forthcoming).

48. Bietak, *Avaris, the Capital of the Hyksos*, 68–72.

49. Manfred Bietak, "The Thutmoside Stronghold of Perunefer," *EA* 26 (2005): 13–17; idem, "Perunefer: The Principal New Kingdom Naval Base," *EA* 34 (2009): 15–17.

50. Labib Habachi, *Tell el-Dabʿa I: Tell el-Dabʿa and Qantir, the Site and Its Connections with Avaris and Piramesse* (ed. Ernst Czerny; UZKÖAI 2; Vienna: Verlag der Österreichischen Akademie der Wissenschaften, 2001).

These recent discoveries in the northeastern Nile Delta, what the Bible calls "the land of Goshen" (Gen. 45:10; 46:28–29; 47:4–5; Exod. 8:22; 9:26) and "the land of Rameses" (Gen. 47:11), indicate that huge building projects were periodically undertaken throughout the New Kingdom. It stands to reason that the Bible preserves a memory of the servitude imposed on the sojourning Hebrews in Egypt. A careful reading of Exodus 1–5 indicates that the forced-labor events imposed on the Hebrews occurred over a protracted period of time and are telescoped. The climax of the hard labor came with the construction of Rameses, when the exodus possibly occurred.

Geography and the Exodus

In the early days of Egyptology in the nineteenth century, archaeologists were interested in identifying and excavating sites mentioned in the exodus narratives. One might naturally think that if the geography in the book of Exodus could be shown to be authentic, narratives associated with those places would reflect accurate memories from the period of the exodus. Here the pioneering investigations of Édouard Naville and Flinders Petrie are exemplars.[51] Alan Gardiner, the renowned Oxford Egyptologist, was harshly critical of Naville and others who, he thought, were treating the Old Testament uncritically in their attempts to correlate biblical and Egyptian geographical terms.[52] Despite his negativity toward the Bible at times, he produced an authoritative study on the location of the Nile Delta residence built by Ramesses II and named for the pharaoh himself: "House of Ramesses Beloved of Amun, Great of Victories" which in abbreviated form occurs most commonly as "Pi-Ramesses" or even simply "Rameses."[53] Concerning the name of the Ramesside residence and Rameses in Exodus 1:11, Gardiner concluded, "Whether or no[t] the Bible

51. For a recent review of this material, see James K. Hoffmeier, "Major Geographical Issues in the Accounts of the Exodus: The Pitfalls and Promises of Site Identification in Egypt," in *Israel: Ancient Kingdom or Late Invention?* (ed. Daniel I. Block; Nashville: B&H Academic, 2008), 99–104.

52. Alan H. Gardiner, "The Geography of the Exodus," in *Recueil d'études égyptologiques dédiées à la mémoire de Jean-François Champollion à l'occasion du centenaire de la lettre à M. Dacier relative à l'alphabet des hieroglyphes phonétiques, lue à la l'Académie des inscriptions et belles-lettres le 27 septembre 1822* (BEHE 4/234; Paris: E. Champion, 1922), 203–15; idem, "The Geography of the Exodus: An Answer to Professor Naville and Others," *JEA* 10 (1924): 87–96.

53. Alan H. Gardiner, "The Delta Residence of the Ramessides," *JEA* 5 (1918): 127–271. Donald Redford has argued that the Hebrew writing of "Rameses" without the element "Pi" is indicative of a late period writing, reflective of the period of authorship ("Exodus I 11," *VT* 13 [1963]: 401–18). Wolfgang Helck ("*Tkw* und die Ramses-Stadt," *VT* 15 [1965]: 35–48) demurred, providing examples of Ramesside period writings without "Pi." Therefore, the absence of "Pi" cannot be used as an indication of lateness of the Hebrew text.

narrative be strict history, there is not the least reason for assuming that any other city of Ramesses existed in the Delta besides those elicited from the Egyptian monuments. In other words, the Biblical Raamses-Rameses is identical with the Residence-city of Pi-Ramesse."[54]

In recent decades the geography of the book of Exodus has once again been the subject of scholarly discussion. For most of the past seventy-five years, the book has been considered to reflect historical and geographical reality,[55] but in recent years challenges to this understanding have arisen. Gösta Ahlström, for example, promoted the notion that the geography and especially the sea-crossing story are attempts to "historicize" a mythological tale, and hence he sees the entire narrative as "mythological historiography."[56] Similarly, Bernard Batto proposed that the postexilic priestly writer attempted to historicize the myth of the sea crossing of Exodus 14 by surrounding it with what appears to be genuine geography.[57] Donald Redford summarily dismissed this approach to interpreting the geography of the exodus: "This is a curious resort, for the text does not look like mythology (at least on the definition of the latter as a timeless event set in the world of the gods). The biblical writer certainly thinks he is writing datable history."[58] That datable history, Redford suggests, points to the sixth century, based on his study of geographical names of the Saite period and later.[59] Many biblical scholars have followed Redford's position because he is an eminent Egyptologist. It will be shown in the following section that Hebrew toponyms that find linguistic correlations with Egyptian

54. Gardiner, "Delta Residence," 266.

55. For examples, see some Bible atlases: J. Simons, *The Geographical and Topographical Texts of the Old Testament: A Concise Commentary in XXXII Chapters* (SFSMD 2; Leiden: Brill, 1959); Herbert G. May, ed., *Oxford Bible Atlas* (2nd ed.; London: Oxford University Press, 1974), 58–59; and some commentaries: Hyatt, *Exodus*, 139–61; Nahum Sarna, *Exploring Exodus: The Origins of Biblical Israel* (New York: Schocken Books, 1987), 103–29.

56. Gösta W. Ahlström, *Who Were the Israelites?* (Winona Lake, IN: Eisenbrauns, 1986), 45–55.

57. Bernard Batto, "The Reed Sea: *Requiescat in Pace*," *JBL* 102 (1983): 27–35; see also idem, *Slaying the Dragon: Mythmaking in the Biblical Tradition* (Louisville: Westminster John Knox, 1992), 115–17.

58. Donald B. Redford, *Egypt, Canaan, and Israel in Ancient Times* (Princeton: Princeton University Press, 1992), 409.

59. Donald B. Redford, "An Egyptological Perspective on the Exodus Narrative," in *Egypt, Israel, Sinai: Archaeological and Historical Relationships in the Biblical Period* (ed. Anson F. Rainey; Tel Aviv: Tel Aviv University, 1987), 137–61; idem, *Egypt, Canaan, and Israel*, 409–15. He continues to hold his earlier position in a recent article without considering criticisms of his position by scholars such as Helck ("*Tkw* und die Ramses-Stadt"), Kenneth Kitchen (e.g., "Egyptians and Hebrews, from Ra'amses to Jericho," in *The Origin of Early Israel—Current Debate: Biblical, Historical and Archaeological Perspectives; Irene Levi-Sala Seminar, 1997* [ed. Shmuel Ahituv and Eliezer D. Oren; Beer-Sheva: Ben-Gurion University of the Negev Press, 1998], 65–131), and Hoffmeier (*Israel in Egypt*, 116–20, 169–72, 176–91; *Ancient Israel in Sinai*, 50–109; "Major Geographical Issues," 99–129).

terms and place names are at home in the thirteenth century BC, while some of the names do, however, linger on into the later period.

Raamses/Rameses

Due to the importance of this city to thirteenth-century Egypt and to the book of Exodus, the discovery of Pi-Ramesses was a priority of early Egyptologists. The earliest proposals located Pi-Ramesses at Tell Farama (Pelusium), on the farthermost northeast corner of the Nile Delta.[60] But with Petrie's excavations at Tell el-Retabeh in the first decade of the twentieth century, focus shifted to this site as a possible location for Pi-Ramesses,[61] with nearby Tell el-Makshutta thought to be Pithom.[62] Pierre Montet's excavations at San el-Hagar (i.e., Tanis) from the late 1920s onward led several generations of Egyptologists to believe that it was ancient Pi-Ramesses.[63] The Egyptian scholar Labib Habachi began investigating the area around the northeast Nile Delta town Qantir and believed that he had found the site of the elusive Ramesside city. Unfortunately, the full publication of his investigations did not appear until 2001, more than fifteen years after his death.[64] Subsequent work at Qantir by Edgar Pusch has fully confirmed Habachi's proposals.[65] There is no doubt among Egyptologists that Qantir was the location of the Ramesside royal residence, Pi-Ramesses, and that it was built adjacent to the old Hyksos capital and earlier Eighteenth Dynasty stronghold of Avaris.[66] Among the most interesting discoveries made by Pusch was the main stable for the chariot horses.[67] Hitching stones and other

60. Max Müller, "A Contribution to the Exodus Geography," *PSBA* 10 (1888): 467–77.

61. W. M. Flinders Petrie, *Hyksos and Israelite Cities* (London: School of Archaeology, University College, 1906), 28–34.

62. Édouard Naville, *The Shrine of the Saft El-Henneh and the Land of Goshen* (EEFM 4; London: Trübner, 1887); idem, *The Store-City of Pithom and the Route of the Exodus* (3rd ed.; EEFM 1; London: Trübner, 1888; 4th ed., 1903); idem, "The Geography of the Exodus," *JEA* 10 (1924): 18–39.

63. Pierre Montet, "Tanis, Avaris, et Pi-Ramses," *RB* 39 (1930): 5–28.

64. Early writings on his survey appeared in Labib Habachi, "Khatana-Qantir: Importance," *ASAE* 52 (1954): 443–559. For the full publication, see Habachi, *Tell el-Dab'a I*.

65. Edgar Pusch, "Piramesse," *OEAE* 3:48–53; idem, "Towards a Map of Piramesse," *EA* 14 (1999): 13–15. For a recent review of the history of the building phases of Avaris to Pi-Ramesses, see Manfred Bietak and Irene Forstner-Müller, "The Topography of Avaris and Per-Ramesses," in *Ramesside Studies in Honour of K. A. Kitchen* (ed. Mark Collier and Steven Snape; Bolton: Rutherford, 2011), 23–50.

66. Kitchen, "Egyptians and Hebrews," 69–71; Nicholas Grimal, *A History of Ancient Egypt* (trans. Ian Shaw; Oxford: Blackwell, 1992), 246; Jacobus van Dijk, "The Amarna Period and the Later New Kingdom," *OHAE* 292.

67. Edgar Pusch, "'Pi-Ramesses-Beloved-of-Amun, Headquarters of Thy Chariotry': Egyptians and Hittites in the Delta Residence of the Ramessides," in *Pelizaeus-Museum Hildesheim: The Egyptian Collection* (ed. Arne Eggbrecht; Mainz: von Zabern, 1996), 131–34.

finds related to horses and chariotry were uncovered. Pusch estimates that this stable could accommodate five hundred horses (fig. 2.2).

From the Eighteenth Dynasty (late sixteenth century) and through the building of Pi-Ramesses (early thirteenth century), continuous large-scale mud-brick building projects were underway at Avaris-PiRamesses, which may represent the climax of the enslavement of the Hebrews as reported in the book of Exodus.[68] Biblical mention of Rameses as the place associated with the Hebrew building efforts (Exod. 1:11) and the place of departure for the exodus (Exod. 12:37; Num. 33:3, 5) is significant because this huge city functioned only from around 1275 BC and into the Twentieth Dynasty, thus the late twelfth century to early eleventh centuries BC. By 1070 BC, Smendes, the founder of the Twenty-First Dynasty, had constructed a new capital out of the abandoned remains of Pi-Ramesses at Tanis, about twelve miles north of Qantir. Tanis remained the principal city of the northeast Nile Delta down to Roman times.[69] During the first millennium BC the biblical writers knew of the political and economic importance of Tanis, or "Zoan," as it is written in Hebrew (cf. Isa. 19:11, 13; 30:4; Ezek. 30:14). When the writer of Psalm 78 muses about the exodus, he identifies the area Zoan/Tanis (Ps. 78:12, 43), not Rameses, as the place where God worked his miracles to free Israel. The omission of Rameses in this text may be explained as the writer using the name of the current dominant city of the northeast Delta, and not the previous one now gone for centuries.[70] The fact that Rameses occurs only in the pentateuchal books indicates that these references, traditionally understood to harken back to the era of Moses, do accurately recall the name of the earlier city.

Pithom

The meaning of this name is not disputed. Hebrew "Pithom" is the accurate writing for Egyptian *pr-itm*, meaning "house of Atum." During the second millennium BC final *r*'s in words were not vocalized, hence the writing *pi*.[71] This name occurs but once in the Old Testament, in connection with

68. Habachi (*Tell el-Dab'a I*, 107–9) reports on Seti I's building activity that preceded Ramesses II's massive expansion of the site when it was named Pi-Ramesses.

69. Geoffrey Graham, "Tanis," *OEAE* 3:348–50.

70. Some scholars have tried to explain the use of Rameses in the exodus narratives as reflecting not the thirteenth-century Ramesside city but rather the memory of the names of cults and chapels set up at Tanis from ancient Pi-Ramesses. For discussion and critique of this position, see Hoffmeier, "Major Geographical Issues," 112.

71. Friedrich Junge, *Late Egyptian Grammar: An Introduction* (trans. David Warburton; Oxford: Griffith Institute, 2001), 35.

the building efforts of the Hebrews (Exod. 1:11). The fact Pithom occurs alongside Rameses in Exodus 1:11 does not mean that the two were close to each other. In 1885 Naville was the first excavator to work at Retabeh.[72] He discovered what he thought, wrongly, was a Roman-period camp, which is likely why he moved east to Maskhuta, since he was interested in the period of the exodus. As mentioned in the previous section, when Petrie began work at Tell el-Retabeh, he thought that it was Pi-Ramesses, while Tell el-Maskhuta, eight miles to the east, was believed to be Pithom by Naville, based on discovery of the so-called Pithom Stela. The stela dates to the reign of Ptolemy II Philadelphos (282–246 BC) and twice mentions *pr-itm* (Pithom), while there are twelve occurrences of Tjeku (i.e., Succoth). It is imprudent to use this late-dated text as the main datum to identify the site at an earlier period, since the name may have changed.

Excavations at Tell el-Maskhuta in the late 1970s and early 1980s by John Holladay, using far more controlled and precise modern excavation techniques than those of Naville's day, suggested to him that the site was occupied during the Second Intermediate period (seventeenth century BC), followed by a long hiatus until 610 BC, when Necho II established a townsite in connection with the Red Sea Canal project, as reported by Herodotus.[73] As a consequence of the absence of pottery and stratigraphy during the New Kingdom (1525–1100 BC), Holladay and others think that the Pithom of the Bible must reflect the period after 600 BC, when this site was reestablished.[74] Hence its appearance in Exodus 1:11 is anachronistic, Holladay maintains, for the purported thirteenth-century setting.

This position, however, ignores textual evidence demonstrating that there was a site known as Pithom in the Wadi Tumilat during the New Kingdom (fig. 2.1). Papyrus Anastasi VI, introduced above, reports that pastoralists from Edom were permitted to enter Egypt to water and feed their flocks.[75] Petrie's excavations demonstrated that Tell el-Retabeh had some sort of occupation from the Old Kingdom down through the New Kingdom and even to Roman

---

72. Naville, *Shrine of the Saft El-Henneh*, 24–25, plate xi.

73. A. D. Godley, trans., *Herodotus* (4 vols.; LCL; London: Heinemann, 1931), 2:158; Alan Lloyd, *Herodotus, Book II, Commentary 99–182* (ÉPRO 43; Leiden: Brill, 1977); idem, "Necho and the Red Sea: Some Considerations," *JEA* 63 (1977): 242–71.

74. Holladay, *Tell El-Maskhuta*; idem, "Tell El-Maskhuta," in *Encyclopedia of the Archaeology of Ancient Egypt* (ed. Kathryn A. Bard; London: Routledge, 1999), 786–89; John Van Seters, "The Geography of the Exodus," in *The Land That I Will Show You: Essays on the History and Archaeology of the Ancient Near East in Honor of J. Maxwell Miller* (ed. J. Andrew Dearman and M. Patrick Graham; JSOTSup 343; Sheffield: Sheffield Academic Press, 2001), 255–76.

75. Alan H. Gardiner, *Late-Egyptian Miscellanies* (BibA 7; Brussels: Édition de la Fondation égyptologique reine Elizabeth, 1937), 76–77; translation in Allen, "Report of Bedouin," 16–17.

times.[76] He also discovered remains of a New Kingdom period stronghold,[77] which was reexposed in excavations in the 1990s by Egyptian archaeologists. Brief investigations of Retabeh in the 1970s under the auspices of Johns Hopkins University, still unpublished,[78] resulted in uncovering a good stratigraphical sequence from the Second Intermediate period through the New Kingdom and onward to the late seventh century, with the New Kingdom being the period of greatest occupation.[79] A number of Egyptian-led smaller excavations were made periodically since the 1970s but have not been published.[80] In 2007 a Polish-Slovak mission returned to Retabeh and began a systematic study of the site by conducting surface and magnetometer surveys, along with excavations.[81] This work is ongoing, but initial reports of the areas investigated during the initial two seasons have uncovered levels, objects, and pottery from the twelfth and eleventh centuries. These researchers are also reexamining the fortification features partially uncovered by Petrie to clarify the plan and dating of these features.

The text of Papyrus Anastasi VI mentions the "pools of Pithom," suggesting some sort of water source near the site that the pastoralists were permitted to access. In his investigations of the geography of the Wadi Tumilat, Bietak discovered evidence for a small lake system to the west of Retabeh, which led him to conclude that this site was Pithom of Papyrus Anastasi VI.[82] Kitchen also has concluded that Retabeh is Pithom of Egyptian texts and of Exodus 1:11.[83]

When we combine the data from Petrie, the Johns Hopkins team, and the current work, it is likely that Tell el-Retabeh is Pithom of New Kingdom times, and that it served as the principal defense installation of that period in the Wadi Tumilat (Tjeku region). The new and more precise excavation and analysis methods, along with the geophysical survey, should be able to provide a clearer picture of the history and purpose of this strategic site.

76. Petrie, *Hyksos and Israelite Cities*, 28–29.

77. Ibid., plate xxxv.

78. Slawomir Rzepka reports that his team has been given access to study this material by Professor Hans Goedicke (Slawomir Rzepka et al., "Tell el-Retabeh 2007–2008," *ÄL* 19 [2009]: 243n6).

79. Michael J. Fuller, "Tell el-Retaba: The Architectural and Depositional Sequence" (unpublished paper, Washington University, 1980). I am grateful to the author for sharing this information with me. In 2004–2005, Professor Fuller posted a report on his stratigraphical data (http://users.stlcc.edu/mfuller/retaba.html).

80. For a brief summary of these excavations based on a review of some of the unpublished notes by the Supreme Council of Antiquities projects, see Rzepka et al., "Tell el-Retabeh," 241–45.

81. Ibid., 241–80.

82. Manfred Bietak, *Tell el-Dabʿa II: Der Fundort im Rahmen einer archälogisch-geographischen Untersuchung über das Ägyptische Ostdelta* (UZKÖAI 1; Vienna: Verlag der Österreichischen Akademie der Wissenschaften, 1975), 88–90, figs. 28–37, 45.

83. Kitchen, "Egyptians and Hebrews," 72–78.

That Retabeh's occupation comes to a sudden end around 600 BC corresponds to the building up of Tell el-Maskhuta at the same time.[84] The presence at Maskhuta of a number of Ramesside-period blocks and statues with the name "Pithom" inscribed on them suggests that they likely were moved from Retabeh for the building of the late seventh-century city at Maskhuta.[85] It might be suggested that the name of the city moved to the new Pithom, meaning that Pithom was the name of Retabeh in the second millennium BC and into the first millennium, when the name Pithom was transferred to Maskhuta as the blocks and statues from old Pithom were relocated to establish the new Pithom.[86] We have already observed such a transfer of blocks and statues from Pi-Ramesses to Tanis.

"The Way of the Land of the Philistines"

When the Hebrews departed Egypt, according to Exodus 13:17a, they did not use the northern road to Canaan, which the Bible calls "the way of the land of the Philistines, although that was near" (see fig. 2.1). If one were traveling out of the northeast Nile Delta from the area of Pi-Ramesses and Avaris, that would be the route to take to get to Canaan. The road actually began at this point in the Nile Delta.[87] Known as the "Way/s of Horus" in Egyptian texts, this route has long been called the "military highway" that stretched across north Sinai to Gaza, the entryway to Canaan (fig. 2.3).[88] Until the past twenty-five years, the military nature of this route was known primarily from the remarkable and informative panoramic reliefs of Seti I (1294–1279 BC).[89] The scenic reliefs show and name the series of forts that defended this strategic military and economic corridor.[90] Particularly significant is the frontier

---

84. There now is evidence that some reoccupation of the site occurred during the Greco-Roman period (Rzepka et al., "Tell el-Retabeh," 247–49).

85. For a review of this material, see Hoffmeier, "Major Geographical Issues," 117–21.

86. I proposed this suggestion in Hoffmeier, *Ancient Israel in Sinai*, 58–65.

87. Bietak, *Avaris, the Capital of the Hyksos*, 19. For further discussion, see Hoffmeier and Moshier, "Highway Out of Egypt."

88. Alan H. Gardiner, "The Ancient Military Road between Egypt and Palestine," *JEA* 6 (1920): 99–116.

89. University of Chicago Oriental Institute Epigraphic Survey, *The Battle Reliefs of King Sety I* (vol. 4 of *Reliefs and Inscriptions at Karnak*; OIP 107; Chicago: University of Chicago Press, 1986), plates 1–6.

90. Eliezer Oren, "The Overland Route between Egypt and Canaan in the Early Bronze Age," *IEJ* 23 (1973): 198–205; idem, "The 'Ways of Horus' in North Sinai," in Rainey, *Egypt, Israel, Sinai*, 69–119; idem, "The Establishment of Egyptian Imperial Administration on the 'Ways of Horus': An Archaeological Perspective from North Sinai," in *Timelines: Studies in Honour of Manfred Bietak* (ed. Ernst Czerny et al.; 3 vols.; OLA 149; Leuven: Peeters, 2006), 2:279–92; Hoffmeier and Moshier, "Highway Out of Egypt."

Figure 2.3. Karnak relief of Seti I, right panel showing the procession arriving at Tjaru (from A. H. Gardiner, "The Ancient Military Road between Egypt and Palestine," *JEA* 6 [1920])

complex of Tjaru depicted on the rightmost of the three tableau scenes. Tjaru was known as Egypt's frontier town, and the capital of the eastern province, or nome, of Egypt called "Foremost of the East."[91] Tjaru was written as *silu* in Semitic texts such as the Amarna letters and is known as Sile in later times.[92] Various New Kingdom texts mention the fortress (*ḥtm*) Tjaru, as does the label on the Seti I scene.[93] Recent research by Morris has shown that a *ḥtm*-fort is a particular type of stronghold normally found at entry points to Egypt.[94] In other words, such border forts were official checkpoints for entry into Egypt. One was stationed on the northern or coastal entry point (i.e., Tjaru), and the other guarded the southern corridor through the Wadi Tumilat and the Way of Shur, likely at Tell el-Retabeh.[95]

During the New Kingdom (fifteenth through thirteenth centuries BC), Tjaru/Sile was the launching point for Egyptian campaigns. It served as a

91. John Baines and Jarmoír Málek, *Atlas of Ancient Egypt* (New York: Facts on File, 1982), 15.

92. William F. Albright, "The Town of Selle (Zaru) in the Amarnah Tablets," *JEA* 10 (1923): 6–8; William Moran, ed. and trans., *The Amarna Letters* (Baltimore: Johns Hopkins University Press, 1992), 331 (Amarna letters 42, 46).

93. University of Chicago Oriental Institute Epigraphic Survey, *Battle Reliefs of King Sety I*, plate 6.

94. Morris, *Architecture of Imperialism*, 5, 382–84, 404–9.

95. Ibid., 419–23.

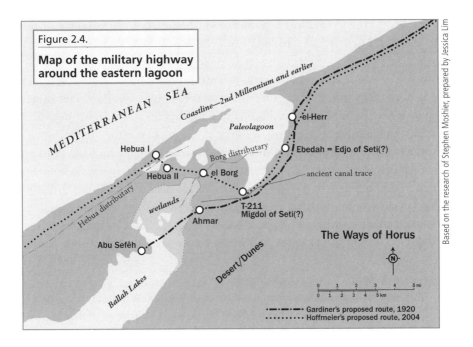

Figure 2.4.

Map of the military highway around the eastern lagoon

MEDITERRANEAN SEA

Coastline—2nd Millennium and earlier

Paleolagoon

el-Herr

Hebua I

Borg distributary

Ebedah = Edjo of Seti(?)

Hebua II   el Borg

ancient canal trace

Hebua distributary

wetlands

Ahmar

T-211
Migdol of Seti(?)

Abu Sefêh

Desert/Dunes

Ballah Lakes

The Ways of Horus

N

0   1   2   3   4   5 mi
0 1 2 3 4 5 km

●—●—●— Gardiner's proposed route, 1920
●●●●●●● Hoffmeier's proposed route, 2004

Based on the research of Stephen Moshier, prepared by Jessica Lim

strategic defensive site and as a military depot for supplying military operations across north Sinai and Canaan.[96] For most of the twentieth century, Egyptologists followed the lead of Carl Küthmann and Alan Gardiner in believing that Tjaru was located at Tell Abu Sefêh, just two miles east of the Suez Canal at Qantarah East.[97] Excavations at this important site in the 1990s and early 2000s yielded archaeological evidence of fortifications only for the Persian period through the Roman period, and nothing from the New Kingdom (fig. 2.4).[98]

Meanwhile, archaeological surveys in north Sinai in 1981 identified Tell Hebua, made up of four areas numbered I–IV, as an important site due to size and surface finds from the New Kingdom, and excavations began in the mid-1980s. Hebua is located approximately six miles north-northeast of Tell Abu Sefêh (fig. 2.4). Mohamed Abd el-Maksoud uncovered a fort that he initially

96. Oren, "Egyptian Imperial Administration"; Mohamed Abd el-Maksoud, "Tjarou, porte de l'Orient," in *Le Sinaï durant l'antiquité et le Moyen-Age: 4000 ans d'histoire pour un désert; Actes du colloque "Sinaï" qui s'est tenu à l'UNESCO du 19 au 21 septembre 1997* (ed. Dominique Valbelle and Charles Bonnet; Paris: Errance, 1998), 61–65.

97. Carl Küthmann, *Die Ostgrenze Ägyptens* (Leipzig: Hinrichs, 1911); Gardiner, "Ancient Military Road"; idem, *Ancient Egyptian Onomastica* (2 vols.; London: Oxford University Press, 1947), 2:202*–3*.

98. Mohamed Abd el-Maksoud et al., "The Roman Castrum of Tell Abu Sayfi at Qantara," *MDAIK* 53 (1997): 221–26.

thought was the second fort depicted on the Seti I relief, the Dwelling of the Lion, after the Fortress Tjaru.[99] As work continued there, and Tell Abu Sefêh produced no second-millennium levels, Abd el-Maksoud and others began to think that Hebua was indeed Tjaru.[100] The mud-brick fort, with an enclosure wall of the thirteenth century, measures 800 x 400 yards. Geological investigations in the region show that this fort was located on a long, narrow barrier island that guarded the road out of Egypt. To its north was the Mediterranean Sea, and to its south were marshlands and lakes through which the Pelusiac branch of Nile flowed.[101] In 1999 a statue of the Ramesside era was discovered that contained an epithet to the deity "Horus Lord of Tjaru"; then in 2005 a cache of statues and stelae was discovered within the New Kingdom temple precinct, one of which also mentioned Tjaru.[102] This statue is dated by Abd el-Maksoud and Dominique Valbelle to the Second Intermediate period (ca. seventeenth century BC). The discovery of these two texts removes any doubt that Hebua I is part of ancient Tjaru.

In 1999 brief excavations at Hebua II, less than a mile southeast of Hebua I, uncovered some remains from the New Kingdom.[103] However, full-scale excavations by Abd el-Maksoud in 2006 began to reveal another huge fortress complex, and work is ongoing. The Hebua II mud-brick fortification walls are 45 feet thick and cover an area of 14 hectares (about 34.6 acres).[104] A number of impressive carved reliefs and inscriptions have been discovered at Hebua II and demonstrate that this fort functioned during the Eighteenth and Nineteenth

99. Mohamed Abd el-Maksoud, "Une nouvelle forteresse sur la Route D'horus: Tell Heboua 1986 (Nord Sinaï)," *CRIPEL* 9 (1987): 13–16.

100. Mohamed Abd el-Maksoud, *Tell Heboua (1981–1991): Enquête archéologique sur la Deuxième Période Intermédiaire et le Nouvel Empire à l'extrémité orientale du Delta* (Paris: Ministère des Affaires Étrangères; Éditions Recherche sur les civilisations, 1998); idem, "Tjarou." When I visited Hebua I in 1994, I began to think that it could be Tjaru (see Hoffmeier, *Israel in Egypt*, 185–86).

101. James K. Hoffmeier and Stephen O. Moshier, "New Paleo-Environmental Evidence from North Sinai to Complement Manfred Bietak's Map of the Eastern Delta and Some Historical Implications," in Czerny et al., *Timelines*, 2:167–76; Stephen O. Moshier and Ali el-Kalani, "Paleogeography along the Ancient Ways of Horus (Late Bronze Age) in Northwest Sinai, Egypt," *Geoarchaeology* 23, no. 4 (2008): 450–73.

102. Mohamed Abd el-Maksoud and Dominque Valbelle, "Tell Héboua-Tjarou l'apport de l'épigraphie," *REg* 56 (2005): 19–20.

103. Abd el-Rahman el-Ayedi, "The Dwelling of the Lion: A New Fortress on the Ways of Horus," *ASAE* 80 (2006): 35–44. It now appears that the walls that el-Ayedi discovered were possibly the enclosure walls around the temple complex rather than the fort's enclosure walls.

104. I was able to visit the work in progress at the invitation of Dr. Abd el-Maksoud in 2008 and 2009. See now Mohamed Abd el-Maksoud and Dominique Valbelle, "Tell Héboua II: Sur le décor et l'épigraphie des elements architectoniques découverts au cours des campagnes 2008–2009 dans la zone centrale du *Khétem* de Tjarou," *REg* 62 (2011): 1–17, and plates 1–6.

Dynasties.[105] This fort clearly is the one represented on the Seti I relief on the left side of the waterway that separates it from the building complex on the other side of the water, which most certainly is Hebua I. It is now apparent that the Hebua II fort is the *ḥtm*-fort of Tjaru (fig. 2.3).

These recent discoveries are significant to the study of the geography of the exodus on a number of levels. Locating Egypt's east frontier capital and defensive stronghold permits the remainder of the military road to be traced. Thanks to my excavations at nearby Tell el-Borg, we have demonstrated that this fort is likely the Dwelling of the Lion, the second fort on the Seti I sequence.[106] Additionally, the direction of the route for the Ways of Horus can be determined by combining geological study of this area and the location of New Kingdom military sites. The road heads southeast from Hebua II, passes Tell el-Borg on its way south toward the southern tip of the eastern lagoon (fig. 2.4). Migdol is the next site after the Dwelling of the Lion (it will be treated below). The route continues north on the east side of the lagoon and then turns east toward Canaan.[107] Most significant for exodus geography, these discoveries provide the military realities behind Exodus 13:17 and explain why the Israelites avoided the way of the land of the Philistines and headed toward the southeast rather than moving northeast from Rameses.

Succoth

Concerned that the Hebrews would "see war and return to Egypt" if they took the expected but well-defended route out of Egypt, God directed them to leave "by the way of the wilderness toward the Red Sea" (Exod. 13:17–18). This datum indicates that the route taken was toward the other road out of Egypt, the Wadi Tumilat (figs. 2.1).

This understanding is confirmed by the itinerary sequence detailed in Exodus 12:37, "The people of Israel journeyed from Rameses to Succoth," and repeated in the Numbers 33 itinerary (Num. 33:3, 5). Linguistically, Hebrew "Succoth" corresponds to Egyptian "Tjeku."[108] The word Succoth is the plural of *sukkâ*, which is a Semitic (and Hebrew) word for "hut," or "booth."[109] This name was likely applied to the Wadi Tumilat in New Kingdom Egypt because

105. Ibid.
106. Hoffmeier and Abd el-Maksoud, "New Military Site"; Hoffmeier, "Tell el-Borg"; idem, "Recent Excavations on the 'Ways of Horus.'"
107. Hoffmeier and Moshier, "Highway Out of Egypt."
108. Yoshiyuki Muchiki, *Egyptian Proper Names and Loanwords in North-West Semitic* (SBLDS 173; Atlanta: Society of Biblical Literature, 1999), 232–33.
109. *HALOT* 2:753; *DCH* 6:153.

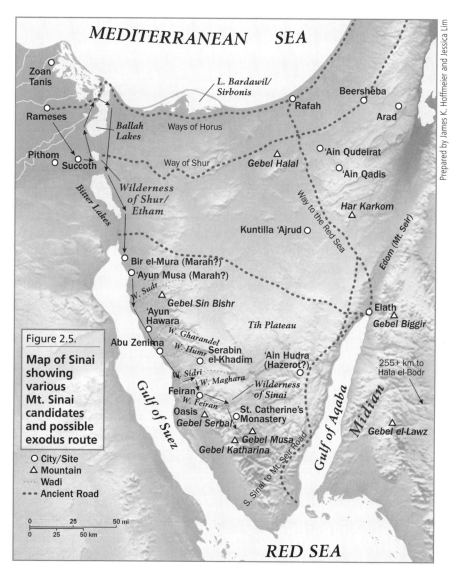

Figure 2.5.

Map of Sinai showing various Mt. Sinai candidates and possible exodus route

O City/Site
△ Mountain
···· Wadi
•-•- Ancient Road

Prepared by James K. Hoffmeier and Jessica Lim

of the Semitic-speaking pastoralists who set up their camps with booths and tents for their temporary stay in the area.

The Egyptian name Tjeku is found on various inscriptions at Tell el-Retabeh and Tell el-Maskhuta. A block found by Petrie at Retebeh depicts Ramesses II smiting the head of a desert dweller before the standing figure of the god Atum, who bears the epithet "lord of Tjeku" (fig. 2.6).[110] This and other references

110. Petrie, *Hyksos and Israelite Cities*, plate 30.

indicate that Tjeku was a regional name for the Wadi Tumilat as well as the site of a specific "keep" (sgr) of Tjeku, according to Papyrus Anastasi V.[111] Then too, the aforementioned reference to Pithom in Papyrus Anastasi VI places it "in Tjeku." These references suggest that the term "Tjeku" applied to the region as a whole and to a specific fortress with that name. It was noted above that even on the Pithom Stela (282–246 BC) Tjeku is written twelve times. This name survives in the Arabic name "Maskhuta," suggesting that it may have been the site where the sgr, or "keep," of Tjeku was located in the thirteenth century BC. True, Holladay's excavations did not uncover any remains from this period. It could be that the present-day village of Maskhuta is built over the area where the New Kingdom fort and settlement were located. Just two years ago the Supreme Council for Antiquities, conducting a salvage clearance of an area at Tell el-Maskhuta, discovered more than thirty tombs from the Roman era; to everyone's surprise, the tomb of a Ramesside-period official named Ken-Amun was also discovered.[112] The tomb was made of mud brick, but the inside walls were covered with a veneer of limestone decorated with various funerary scenes and included his title as "overseer of royal records." Such an official at this remote location on Egypt's frontier would likely have been attached to the fort that must have been located in the area.

Mention of Succoth in the exodus geography is significant because the name is attested both in the New Kingdom and later, and it also demonstrates that when the Hebrews departed Pi-Ramesses, they were heading toward the Wadi Tumilat or Tjeku region, the other means of egress from Egypt.

Etham

Etham is found only once in the exodus itinerary. After camping somewhere in the Succoth area, the Hebrews proceeded east and were "on the edge of the wilderness," where they camped at Etham (Exod. 13:20). The specific reference to "the edge of the wilderness" implies that Sinai had not yet been reached. The etymology of the name remains uncertain, though the most promising suggestion is that it is a toponym that includes the name of the god Atum, the patron of that area.[113] Kitchen suggests i(w) itm, "the isle of Atum."[114] The Isthmus of Suez contained numerous lakes of various sizes in ancient time, some of which (i.e., the Small and Great Bitter Lakes and Lake Timsah) are

---

111. Gardiner, *Late-Egyptian Miscellanies*, 67.
112. Reported at http://www.drhawass.com/blog/press-release-new-tomb-discovered-ismailia.
113. Muchiki, *Egyptian Proper Names*, 230.
114. Kenneth A. Kitchen, *On the Reliability of the Old Testament* (Grand Rapids: Eerdmans, 2003), 259.

Figure 2.6. Ramesses II smiting an easterner before Atum, Lord of Tjeku, Succoth (from W. M. F. Petrie, *Hyksos and Israelite Cities* [London: British School of Archaeology, 1906], plate 30)

still active. In addition, there is the larger Ballah Lake system, desiccated since the nineteenth century AD.[115] It seems appropriate to use the word "island" in this border area, with its lakes and marshlands, punctuated with tracts of land. In fact, in the Egyptian Story of Sinuhe, the Egyptian official passes through this very region when he tries to flee Egypt. In the Bitter Lakes area (i.e., *km wr*) he rests at a spot called *iw km wr*, "the Isle-of-Kem-Wer."[116] So there is a toponym in this same watery border area that uses the initial element *iw*. *I(w)-itm* works linguistically, fits the geographical realities of the region, and mentions Atum as the deity associated with the site. The name *Iw-itm* is not presently known in Egyptian sources, but it is reasonable to conclude that it was somewhere at the end of the Wadi Tumilat, at the edge of the Sinai wilderness, and perhaps in the vicinity of the present-day Lake Timsah.

Turn Back!

At Etham on the edge of the wilderness, the trek to Sinai takes an unexpected turn. Exodus 14:2 reports that God instructed Moses "to turn back

---

115. See various maps in Bietak, *Tell el-Dab'a II*; idem, *Avaris, the Capital of the Hyksos*, fig. 1; Hoffmeier and Moshier, "New Paleo-Environmental Evidence."
116. Lichtheim, *Old and Middle Kingdoms*, 224.

and encamp in front of Pi-hahiroth, between Migdol and the sea, in front of Baal-zephon; you shall encamp facing it, by the sea." This same rerouting is recorded in the Numbers 33 itinerary (33:7). The cluster of names indicates that a degree of precision is offered in the text to locate "the sea," also called *yam suf* (Reed Sea), through which the Israelites reportedly passed (cf. Exod. 15:4, 22; Deut. 11:2–4; Josh. 2:9–10; 4:23–24).

Since the route followed moves from Rameses southeast to Succoth or the Wadi Tumilat, and Etham probably is located farther east, the straightforward meaning of "turn back" (Heb. *šûb*) indicates a turn in the opposite direction of where they had been heading—that is, in a more northerly direction. Commentators on the Torah generally agree on the meaning of this change of course. Cassuto explains it as "let them turn round and not continue to travel in a south-easterly direction."[117] More recently, William Propp understands it to mean "change direction, most likely back to Egypt."[118] According to biblical geographer J. Simons, in this passage "the verb used means not only a change in direction but more particularly a change involving a set back, in this sense namely that by this maneuver the Israelites moved somewhat away from their immediate goal—the crossing of the border of Egypt."[119]

Lately, Angela Roskop has proposed that Exodus 13:20; 15:22 represents a dual departure from Egypt and does not offer a coherent linear itinerary that reflects reality but rather is a literary construct of the priestly writer's design.[120] This is not a compelling explanation, since Exodus 13:20 does not describe a departure from Egypt into the wilderness. The text is plain enough that the Israelites camped at Etham "on the edge of the wilderness" (*bě'ētām biqṣê hammidbār*). There is no dual departure from Egypt. A better explanation for the peculiar call to "turn back" is offered by John Durham, who argued, regarding the toponyms of Exodus 14:2, "The purpose of so precise a location, one that provides no less than four points of reference, not only suggests a historical base for the exodus route described in this narrative, but also implies that the directions specified are important for understanding the narrative."[121] Benjamin Scolnic also sees that the collocation with the geographical terms "is attempting to provide a precise set of referents. . . . It may be an attempt to ensure identification."[122] So while the reason for turning back remains a

---

117. Cassuto, *Exodus*, 159.

118. Propp, *Exodus 1–18*, 490.

119. Simons, *Geographical and Topographical Texts*, 242.

120. Angela R. Roskop, *The Wilderness Itineraries: Genre, Geography, and the Growth of Torah* (Winona Lake, IN: Eisenbrauns, 2011), 215–16, 246–47.

121. John I. Durham, *Exodus* (WBC 3; Waco: Word, 1987), 186.

122. Benjamin E. Scolnic, "A New Working Hypothesis for the Identification of Migdol," in *The Future of Biblical Archaeology: Reassessing Methodologies and Assumptions; The*

mystery, there is good reason to believe that the detour is fundamental to the narrative, while the location of the destination is very precise.

What is the purpose of the narrative? We have already noted that the northern route out of Egypt was dangerous for military reasons and treacherous because of lakes, marshy wetlands, and Nile River distributaries (fig. 2.4). So the Hebrews avoided the area in favor of a southeast route to the Wadi Tumilat, the very area where the narrative reports that God directed the Israelites in Exodus 14:1–2. This rerouting seems illogical because the Israelites were trying to leave Egypt and enslavement to the pharaoh. Consequently, turning back into the teeth of the lion makes no sense, unless the divine purpose, according to the Torah, overrides logical considerations. In Exodus 14:1, 3–4 it becomes clear that a trap is being set for the pharaoh and his armies:

> "For Pharaoh will say of the people of Israel, 'They are wandering in the land; the wilderness has shut them in.' And I will harden Pharaoh's heart, and he will pursue them, and I will get glory over Pharaoh and all his host, and the Egyptians shall know that I am the LORD."

The area between the end of the Wadi Tumilat (i.e., Etham) and north to the area of the Ways of Horus (i.e., the way of the land of the Philistines) was made up largely of the Ballah Lakes. To its north there is a narrow stretch of land before reaching the Nile River distributaries and surrounding wetlands (see fig. 2.4). With the discovery of the two fortresses at Hebua and Tell el-Borg and likely more at the southern end of the eastern lagoon,[123] the pharaoh's statement in Exodus 14:3—"They are wandering in the land; the wilderness has shut them in"—suggests his assessment that when the Israelites "turned back," it was because they were "hopelessly confused" and were "hemmed in on all sides—by Egyptian border fortresses, by wilderness, and the sea," Sarna proposes.[124] Cornelis Houtman translates this verse as "they have walked into a trap. The Wilderness blocks their way."[125] While the pharaoh thinks that the Israelites are trapped, in reality it is his armies that were marching into a trap of divine making.

Let us now consider the toponyms of Exodus 14:2.

Proceedings of a Symposium, August 12–14, 2001, at Trinity International University (ed. James K. Hoffmeier and Alan R. Millard; Grand Rapids: Eerdmans, 2004), 98.

123. See James K. Hoffmeier, "The Search for Migdol of the New Kingdom and Exodus 14:2: An Update," *BurH* 44 (2008): 3–12; idem, "Migdol auf der Spur," *WUB* 14 (2009): 68.

124. Sarna, *Exodus*, 71.

125. Cornelis Houtman, *Exodus* (trans. Johan Rebel and Sierd Woustra; 4 vols.; HCOT; Leuven: Peeters; Kampen: Kok, 1993–2002), 2:257.

Pi-Hahiroth

Scholars have long tried to make sense of the name Pi-Hahiroth, whether it was an Egyptian or Semitic term.[126] No satisfactory corresponding Egyptian place name or theoretically reconstructed name has achieved a consensus. Taken as a Semitic term, it means "the mouth of the canal." This translation was offered by William F. Albright in 1948,[127] and thirty-five years earlier by Grey Hubert Skipwith.[128] More recent linguistic study of this term supports this early proposal.[129] This proposed meaning gained more credibility with the discovery of traces of an ancient canal in north Sinai, east of the northern limits of the now desiccated Ballah Lake, by Israeli geologists in the early 1970s.[130] To learn more about this canal and investigate any archaeological evidence that would help in dating the canal, geologist Stephen Moshier and I went to north Sinai in 1998. Armed with recently declassified CORONA satellite images from the 1960s (fig. 2.7), we were able to demonstrate that the canal continued east, where it ended at an oasis, rather than turning north past the southern end of the eastern lagoon.[131] Due to deep Aeolian sands, we were unable to identify any archaeological evidence that might assist in dating the canal feature, but the trough of the canal was still visible (fig. 2.8). In our investigations at nearby Tell el-Borg, we discovered a distributary of the Pelusiac Nile that flowed by the fort there and then continued east into the lagoon (see fig. 2.4). It may be that this canal was excavated from this distributary.[132] (For a possible Egyptian textual reference to the canal, see the section "Baal-Zephon and Yam Suf" below.)

One possible interpretation of the toponym "Pi-Hahiroth" is that the "mouth" of the canal gets its name from the point where the canal begins either from the distributary or at the northmost section of the Ballah Lake through which the distributary flows.[133]

126. For a detailed discussion of this term and the history of interpretation, see Hoffmeier, *Israel in Egypt*, 169–71; idem, *Ancient Israel in Sinai*, 105–7.

127. William F. Albright, "Exploring in Sinai with the University of California African Expedition," *BASOR* 109 (1948): 16.

128. Grey Hubert Skipwith, "Pi-Hahiroth, 'the Mouth of the Canals,'" *PEQ* 45 (1913): 94–95.

129. Kitchen, *Reliability of the Old Testament*, 260. Hoffmeier, *Israel in Sinai*, 170–71.

130. Amihai Sneh, Tuvia Weissbrod, and Itamar Perath, "Evidence for an Ancient Egyptian Frontier Canal," *American Scientist* 63 (1975): 542–48. See also William Shea, "A Date for the Recently Discovered Eastern Canal of Egypt," *BASOR* 226 (1977): 31–38.

131. Hoffmeier and Abd el-Maksoud, "New Military Site," 172–73.

132. Hoffmeier and Moshier, "New Paleo-Environmental Evidence," 167–74; Moshier and Ali el-Kalani, "Paleogeography along the Ancient Ways of Horus."

133. The water levels of the lake would likely fluctuate during the annual flood season in the months of August, September, and October.

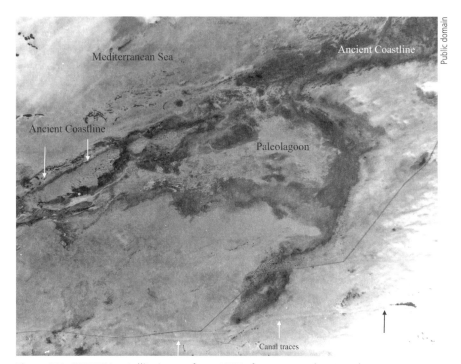

Figure 2.7. CORONA satellite image from 1967 of area around eastern lagoon

Migdol

"Migdol" is a Semitic term for a watchtower or fort[134] that is attached to the names of forts on the eastern frontier in the thirteenth and twelfth centuries BC. Mention has already been made of the fort sequence on Egypt's eastern frontier as displayed on the Seti I relief from Karnak Temple (see fig. 2.3). In Seti I's time it is called "Migdol of Men-maat-re," which includes the king's nomen or throne name. This fort retained its name but appended the name of the reigning monarch. During the reign of his successor, Ramesses II, the fort is called "The Dwelling of Sese,"[135] "Sese" being an abbreviation for "Ramesses." Finally, the same fort is depicted and named as the "Migdol of Rameses (III),"[136] the fort's name during his reign (1184–1153 BC). Among

134. *HALOT* 2:543–44; *DCH* 5:131–32. See James Hoch, *Semitic Words in Egyptian Texts of the New Kingdom and Third Intermediate Period* (Princeton: Princeton University Press, 1994), §224.

135. Hans Werner Fischer-Elfert, *Die satirische Streitschrift des Papyrus Anastasi I* (2 vols.; ÄgAbh 44; Wiesbaden: Harrassowitz, 1986), 2:150–51.

136. University of Chicago Oriental Institute Epigraphic Survey, *The Earlier Historical Records of Ramses III* (vol. 1 of *Medinet Habu*; OIP 8; Chicago: University of Chicago Press, 1930), plate 42.

James K. Hoffmeier, 1998

Figure 2.8. Picture of section of the east end of the frontier canal showing trough with oasis in background

those who have studied the identification of Migdol in Ramesside times, there is agreement that all three of these forts are one and the same, and that its location should be found somewhere east (or southeast) of Tjaru.[137] The textual evidence, especially the Seti I Karnak relief and the Medinet Habu scene of Ramesses III in connection with the Sea Peoples invasion, suggests that a location just outside of Egypt in north Sinai probably is correct. Indeed, Morris, after her exhaustive study, concluded that forts with the element "Migdol" attached to the name "had a very limited distribution in the New Kingdom. Outside Egypt itself they are found only in north Sinai."[138]

The east frontier site named Migdol occurs in the Hebrew prophets in the late seventh and sixth centuries (cf. Jer. 44:1; 46:14; Ezek. 29:10; 30:6). This fort is likely the one located at Tell Qedua in north Sinai, on the northeast

137. Gardiner, "Ancient Military Road," 107–10; Kenneth A. Kitchen, *Ramesses I, Sethos I and Contemporaries* (vol. 1 of *Ramesside Inscriptions: Translated and Annotated, Notes and Comments*; Oxford: Blackwell, 1993), 14; Donald B. Redford, "Egypt and Western Asia in the Late New Kingdom: An Overview," in *The Sea Peoples and Their World: A Reassessment* (ed. Eliezer D. Oren; Philadelphia: The University Museum, University of Pennsylvania, 2000), 13; Morris, *Architecture of Imperialism*, 718–19, 817–18; Hoffmeier, "Search for Migdol," 7–8.

138. Morris, *Architecture of Imperialism*, 818.

shore of the eastern lagoon.[139] The name "Migdol" survives into the Greco-Roman period as Magdala and was long thought to be identified with Tell el-Herr. Excavations by Dominique Valbelle during the past twenty-five years have revealed no remains prior to the fourth century BC,[140] leading to the conclusion that it is Magdala of the late period, but not Migdol of the Hebrew prophets, or the New Kingdom.[141]

Since there are two different sites equated with Migdol/Magdala of the seventh/sixth century BC (Tell Qedua) and fourth century BC to Roman AD times (Tell el-Herr), Migdol of Ramesside times (and Exod. 14:2) is likely elsewhere. It probably is between Tell el-Herr and the southern point of the eastern lagoon. Elsewhere I have proposed that it could be the New Kingdom site identified in Oren's survey, called T-211.[142] The site appears as a rectangular walled site in CORONA satellite images of the 1960s. In 2008 my team tried to locate T-211, but due to agricultural development in the area over the past decade,[143] the site is completely lost to archaeological investigation. If Migdol of New Kingdom times was located at T-211, then it was located just north of the so-called East Frontier Canal, whose name could be connected to Pi-Hahiroth.

Baal-Zephon and Yam Suf

Of the three toponyms of Exodus 14:2, Baal-Zephon (*baʻal ṣĕpōn*) remains the most elusive. The name means "Baal of the North," an epithet associated with the Canaanite storm-god Hadad or Baal (i.e., Baal Zaphon). Some scholars have followed Noël Aimé-Giron's association of Baal-Zephon with Tell Defeneh, located just east of the Suez Canal.[144] Given the new possibilities that Migdol and Pi-Hahiroth are to be found around six miles east

---

139. Eliezer D. Oren, "Migdol: A New Fortress on the Edge of the Eastern Nile Delta," *BASOR* 256 (1984): 7–44.

140. Dominique Valbelle and Etienne Louis, "Les trois dernières forteresses de Tell el-Herr," *CRIPEL* 10 (1988): 23–55; Dominique Valbelle and Giorgio Nogara, "La forteresse du IVe siècle avant J.-C. à Tell El-Herr (Nord-Sinaï)," *CRIPEL* 21 (2000): 53–64; Dominique Valbelle, "The First Persian Period Fortress at Tell El-Herr," *EA* 18 (2001): 12–14; idem, *Tell el-Herr: Les niveaux hellénistiques et du Haut-Empire* (Paris: Errance, 2007).

141. Joffrey Seguin, *Le Migdol: Du Proche-Orient à l'Égypte* (Paris: Presses de l'Université Paris-Sorbonne, 2007).

142. Hoffmeier, "Search for Migdol," 9–10.

143. A drainage canal, with paved roads running parallel to it, and a fruit farm now overlie the area where T-211 should be found. The area of the farm was covered by more than three feet of sand to raise the area above the previously low-lying land that was close to the brackish subsurface waters.

144. Noël Aime-Giron, "Baal Saphon et les dieux de Tahpanhes dans en nouveau papyrus Phénicien," *ASAE* 40 (1941): 433–60.

of the Suez Canal, a location in this general area for Baal-Zephon should be sought. The Bible does not disclose what kind of site Baal-Zephon is, complicating its identification. Aramaic Targumim understood the name to refer to a shrine.[145] The Canaanite deity's name is known in Egypt in Ramesside times and associated with a shrine in or near Memphis.[146] A cylinder seal was discovered at Tell el-Dab'a in 1979 that depicts Baal Zaphon striding over two mountain peaks with weapons in his hands. Edith Porada dates this seal to the eighteenth century BC, showing the influence of this Levantine deity in Egypt at an earlier date.[147]

Over fifty years ago Henri Cazelles noticed that Papyrus Anastasi III might contain a clue concerning the identity of the Hebrew *yam suf* (Reed Sea) and Baal-Zephon.[148] In this document the scribe Pabes writes a glowing report of the well-watered and lush area around Pi-Ramesses and the marshy areas to its east full of fishes and reeds.[149] He mentions that "the waters of Baal" and "the Waters of Horus [Egyptian *š-ḥr* = Heb. Shihor] have salt, and the *p3-ḥr*-waters natron [deposits]. Its ships sail forth and moor."[150] Bietak has long held that *š-ḥr* (Shihor) was the name for the eastern lagoon and has suggested that the parallel usage of *p3 ṯwfy* (the reed marshes) with Shihor in Papyrus Anastasi III (line 2,12) indicates that they were in close proximity.[151] If Shihor is the eastern lagoon, then the comparably large lake or marshy area near it is the Ballah Lake, which, he maintains, is *p3 ṯwfy* (the reed marshes), the same as the Hebrew *yam suf* (reed sea), the name of the sea through which Israel escaped Egypt in the Hebrew tradition (Exod. 13:18; 15:4, 22; Deut. 11:4; Josh 2:10; Judg. 11:16; Ps. 106:9, 22). The linguistic connection between the Hebrew *suf* and Egyptian *ṯwfy* has long been recognized, but it may be that the word is originally Semitic.[152]

In this text, then, we have the collocation of *p3 ṯwfy* (*yam suf*), a body of some sort that includes the name "Baal" (but not with "Zaphon"), and

145. J. W. Ethridge, trans., *The Targums of Onkelos and Jonathan ben Uzziel of the Pentateuch, with Fragments of the Jerusalem Targum from the Chaldee* (New York: Ktav, 1968), 485.

146. Gardiner, *Late-Egyptian Miscellanies*, 89.7.

147. Edith Porada, "The Cylinder Seal from Tell el-Dab'a," *AJA* 88 (1984): 485–88.

148. Henri Cazelles, "Les localizations de l'exode et la critique litteraire," *RB* 62 (1955): 346–58.

149. The text is in Gardiner, *Late-Egyptian Miscellanies*, 21–22; translation and commentaries are offered in Caminos, *Late-Egyptian Miscellanies*, 73–81.

150. Caminos, *Late-Egyptian Miscellanies*, 74.

151. Bietak, *Tell el-Dab'a II*, 137; idem, "Comments on the Exodus," in Rainey, *Egypt, Israel, Sinai*, 167. He still maintains this view, as can be seen in his map of the eastern Nile Delta and north Sinai in *Avaris, the Capital of the Hyksos*, fig. 1.

152. For a thorough review, see Hoffmeier, *Israel in Egypt*, 199–215; idem, *Ancient Israel in Sinai*, 85–89.

a feature called "the *p3-ḥr*-waters," which Caminos did not know how to translate. James Hoch, however, has proposed that it is related to the Semitic word *ḥarru*, meaning "canal."[153] Consequently, James Allen's recent translation renders this critical line as "the Lake of Horus has salt, the Canal has natron," and in a note explains that *p3-ḥr* is "the name of a navigable, brackish body of water in the eastern Egyptian Delta, perhaps joining an arm of the Nile to the Lake of Horus."[154] It is precisely between the northern end of the Ballah Lake (*yam suf*) and the eastern lagoon (Shihor) where the trace of the canal was discovered that was discussed above (see fig. 2.4).

One final datum that helps locate Egyptian *p3 ṯwfy* is found in the Ono-mastica of Amenemope, from the twelfth century BC. Included in its various lists of words by different categories is a geographical list arranged from south to north. The northernmost toponym is "Tjaru," now firmly located at the site of Hebua. The place name immediately south of Tjaru is *p3 ṯwfy*.[155] Since Bietak conducted his excellent mapping of the Nile Delta, the geological work of the North Sinai Archaeological Project, supervised by Stephen Moshier, has produced evidence that the northern reaches of the ancient Ballah Lake extend farther north than earlier realized, and the surveying at the northern end of the lake's dried-out depression shows that it reached a depth of 15 to18 feet.[156]

The point of the foregoing is to demonstrate that the terms "Migdol," "Pi-Hahiroth," *p3 ṯwfy* (*yam suf*), and "Baal" (less "Zaphon") converge in the area south of Tjaru (Hebua), north of the Ballah Lake (*p3 ṯwfy* = *yam suf*) and west of the eastern lagoon (Shihor). This appears to be the area where the Israelites would have been quite vulnerable to the marshy lakes and the nearby Egyptian forts. And yet, according to the narrative of Exodus 14 and the Song of the Sea (Exod. 15), it was the Egyptian army that was defeated while Israel was liberated.

Wilderness Narratives

The largest block in the Pentateuch is given to the activities of the Israelites in the wilderness, from Exodus 16 through Numbers 19. And from Numbers

153. Hoch, *Semitic Words in Egyptian Texts*, 232.
154. James Allen, "Praise of Pi-Ramessu," COS 3.3:15.
155. Gardiner, *Ancient Egyptian Onomastica*, 2:201*–3*. P3 *ṯwfy* and Tjaru are numbers 418 and 419, respectively, on the sequence.
156. I am the director of the North Sinai Archaeological Project. Stephen Moshier supervises the geological work. The data regarding the depth of the lake is written in reports that are not yet published.

19 through the book of Deuteronomy, the Israelites are moving into parts of the Transjordan, conquering areas and preparing to enter the land of Canaan. In this section we focus on some of the highlights of the wilderness experience.

The ultimate destination of the Israelites when leaving Egypt was Canaan, the land promised to Abraham and his descendants after a period of oppression (Gen. 15:13–16). The Torah, however, records that Moses was instructed to return to the very mountain where God had appeared: "When you have brought the people out of Egypt, you shall serve God on this mountain" (Exod. 3:12). This detail indicates that once out of Egypt, Moses was leading the people on a religious pilgrimage to the mountain of God. Three major points emerge from the wilderness narratives that will be investigated here: (1) the geography of the narratives, including the location of Mount Sinai; (2) the law or Sinaitic covenant; and (3) Israel's desert sanctuary.

Geography of the Wilderness Narratives

Because of the lack of any clear archaeological evidence to confirm that this indeed was Mount Sinai/Horeb, more than a dozen mountains have been proposed in the intervening centuries (fig. 2.5). Since the land of Midian is generally located in the northwestern area of present-day Saudi Arabia, east of the Gulf of Aqaba, different sites in Arabia have been proposed, as well as locations north in the Transjordan (Edom). Most candidates for Mount Sinai are within the Sinai Peninsula (fig. 2.5).

In the initial theophany of the burning bush, the location is rather vaguely given: "Now Moses was keeping the flock of his father-in-law, Jethro, the priest of Midian, and he led his flock to the west side of the wilderness and came to Horeb, the mountain of God" (Exod. 3:1). Known both as Mount Sinai and Mount Horeb in the Bible,[157] the location of "the mountain of God" has been the subject of intense interest since the early Christian era (fourth century), when the emperor Constantine's mother, Helena (ca. AD 330), ordered the building of a chapel at the site of the burning bush and a fortified enclosure to provide security for hermits who had been residing at the foot of Gebel Musa (Mount Moses).[158] Other monks had established themselves at Gebel Serbal, about twenty miles to the west of Gebel Musa. According to Dionysius of Alexandria, Christians fleeing persecution in Egypt came to south Sinai,

157. For a discussion of the possible reasons for this dual usage, see Hoffmeier, *Ancient Israel in Sinai*, 114–15.
158. Athanasios Paliouras, *The Monastery of St. Catherine on Mount Sinai* (Sinai: St. Catherine's Monastery, 1985), 8–9.

perhaps thinking that they would find refuge in this area as the prophet Elijah did from Queen Jezebel's persecution.[159]

One reason so many mountains have been suggested is that once the Israelites left Egypt, even though geographical information is provided and toponyms are offered, none of these can be identified with certainty. Then too, there is nothing in later biblical narratives that offers much help with location. In the entire Old Testament only Elijah is recorded as returning to visit "Horeb, the mount of God" (1 Kings 19:8). From this episode we learn that he traveled "a day's journey into the wilderness" from Beersheba (19:3–4). From there we are told only that "the way is great for you" (19:7, lit. trans.). No further geographical information or distance is provided.

The lack of specificity in the Elijah story prevents us from drawing any specific conclusions about the location of the mountain of God, except that it appears to be well south of Beersheba. Thus we must return to the data provided by the Pentateuch to assist in finding an approximate area where Mount Sinai was located. In the end, the biblical information does not allow us to locate a specific peak, but it does allow many candidates to be ruled out.

Three principal data can be cited. First is the narrative that traces Israel's journey from the departure to Egypt to the arrival at Mount Sinai in Exodus 15–19, along with the itinerary in Numbers 33. While these two sources provide some differences by naming toponyms in Numbers 33 not included in Exodus, there is general agreement between them. The third datum is found in Deuteronomy 1:2, and I begin the discussion with it.

"It is eleven days' journey from Horeb by the way of Mount Seir to Kadesh-barnea." Kadesh-Barnea is located in northeastern Sinai, on its border with Edom in the southern Transjordan. Moses observes this in his communiqué with the leader of Edom when he requests permission to pass through Edom en route to Moab and Ammon: "Here we are in Kadesh, a city on the edge of your territory" (Num. 20:16). Given this information, there are two candidates to be Kadesh-Barnea, 'Ain Qadis and 'Ain Qudeirat (fig. 2.5). Both sites are situated by springs ('Ain in Hebrew and Arabic means "spring"), the latter lying six miles north of the former. "Qadis" has attracted some attention because this Arabic name seemingly preserves the old Hebrew word for "holy" (qdš).[160] Its spring is not as robust as the one at 'Ain Qudeirat.

---

159. It was Edward Robinson who thought that this reference could point to the origination of these mountains being considered candidates for biblical Mount Sinai. See *Biblical Researches in Palestine, Mount Sinai and Arabia Petræa: A Journal of Travels in the Year 1838* (Boston: Crocker & Brewster, 1841), 180.

160. C. Leonard Woolley and T. E. Lawrence, however, argued that the Arabic word "Qadeis" refers to a "scoop or bailer" for drawing water from a well or spring by the Arabs for purification

Consequently, ʿAin Qudeirat has been labeled "Kadesh-Barnea" by recent investigators.[161]

Regardless of which site was the biblical Kadesh-Barnea, the proximity of the two means that the general area has been established, and this becomes an important anchor point for locating the mountain of God some eleven days' journey away. Throughout the Bible travel distances are measured by "day's journey" (e.g., Gen. 30:36; Exod. 3:18; 5:3; 8:27; Num. 10:33; 11:31; 33:8; 1 Kings 19:4; Jon. 3:3–4). A days' journey is generally understood as the distance a caravan can travel during daylight hours. It ranges from 17 to 23 miles, depending on terrain and conditions.[162] In the early second millennium BC, caravans from Mari could cover about twenty-two miles in a day.[163]

The mention of an eleven-day journey in Deuteronomy 1:2 is regarded by most scholars as such a specific and nonsymbolic number that it is an accurate figure.[164] This distance could range between 200 and 240 miles and eliminates any potential Mount Sinai in northern Sinai and the southern Transjordan. The other relevant datum in this verse is that between Horeb and Kadesh-Barnea the Israelites passed through Mount Seir. "Mount Seir" is another name for Edom (i.e., the territory of Esau) in southern Transjordan (e.g., Gen. 32:3; 36:8, 9, 21; Num. 24:18; Deut. 2:5; Ezek. 35:15). This point means that somehow the journey between Mount Sinai/Horeb took the Israelites through Mount Seir/Edom before reaching Kadesh Barnea (ʿAin Qudeirat/ʿAin Qadis). This means that a location in northwest Arabia or south Sinai could accommodate both the distance and passing through southern Seir. In the case of a south Sinai location, the Israelites would have traveled eastward from south central Sinai to the coast, then north along the peninsula's eastern coast to the area of Ezion-geber/Elath in southern Edom, before turning north-northwest to Kadesh Barnea (fig. 2.5).

In recent years there has been renewed interest in locating Mount Sinai in northwest Arabia, coupled with the theory of a sea crossing through the Gulf of Aqaba.[165] It is true that the Bible does call this body of water *yam suf* in

---

rituals and is not related to the Semitic word "Kadesh" (*The Wilderness of Zin* [London: Palestine Exploration Fund, 1914; repr., Winona Lake, IN: Eisenbrauns, 2003], 70n1). Consequently, this name could not be connected to Kadesh-Barnea.

161. Rudolph Cohen, *Kadesh-Barnea: A Fortress from the Time of the Judaean Kingdom* (Jerusalem: The Israel Museum, 1983); idem, "Kadesh-Barnea: The Israelite Fortress," *NEAEHL* 3:843–47.

162. Barry Beitzel, "Travel and Communication (OT World)," *ABD* 6:646.

163. Graham Davies, "The Significance of Deuteronomy 1:2 for the Location of Mount Horeb," *PEQ* 111 (1979): 93.

164. For a review of different views, see Hoffmeier, *Ancient Israel in Sinai*, 119–20.

165. Colin J. Humphreys, *The Miracles of Exodus: A Scientist's Discovery of the Extraordinary Natural Causes of the Biblical Stories* (San Francisco: HarperSanFrancisco, 2003); Robert Cornuke and David Halbrook, *In Search of the Mountain of God: The Discovery of the Real*

The Sinaitic Covenant and Its Role in Israel

More important than the location of Mount Sinai is what Scripture reports to have occurred there: the revelation of the Sinaitic covenant or law. Exodus 19:5 uses the word *běrît*, commonly translated as "covenant" in many English versions. This word has the legal nuance of a "treaty" or "alliance"[a] and is attested in various ancient Near Eastern treaty texts well back in the second millennium BC.[b] The fact that the same term is used across the Near East in this period and in the Bible creates a serious problem for the old contention of Julius Wellhausen that the idea of covenant was a late development in ancient Israel, an idea that he associated with the fifth-century-BC priestly writer (P).[c] Further militating against the late appearance of the covenant material in Exodus 20–23 has been the discovery and comparative study of actual ancient treaty texts.[d]

The later prophets view the covenant ceremony in the wilderness of Sinai as God's ultimate revelation, where he made himself "known" to the Israelites. Hosea puts it this way:

> But I am the LORD your God
>   from the land of Egypt;
> you know no God but me,
>   and besides me there is no savior.
> It was I who knew you in the wilderness,
>   in the land of drought. (Hosea 13:4–5)

This covenant is also viewed as the marriage between the Lord and Israel. In Jeremiah, God recalls, "I remember the devotion of your youth, your love as a bride, how you followed me in the wilderness, in a land not sown" (Jer. 2:2). Israel's

Solomon's day (1 Kings 9:26). It is very clear that the body of water through which the Israelites passed was close to Egypt's border, as implied by situating Etham as "on the edge of the wilderness" (Exod. 13:20), before they departed Egypt, where the journey took a turn to the north (see above) where they came to the sea (*yam suf*) through which they crossed. This means that there were only three stops between departing Rameses and the sea (a distance of 60–66 miles), three stops before departing Egypt. Once past the sea, they entered the "wilderness of Shur" (Exod. 15:22). "Shur" is the name of the route from southern Canaan to Egypt (Gen. 16:7), and it is explicitly located beside Egypt (Gen. 25:18; 1 Sam. 15:7; 27:8). After departing the sea, the Israelites traveled either eight or eleven days until reaching Mount Sinai (see Exod. 15:22–19:1;

Mt. Sinai (Nashville: Broadman & Holman, 2000); see also Cornuke's website: http://baseinsti tute.org/index.php?option=com_content&view=article&id=52&Itemid=66; Howard Blum, *The Gold of Exodus: The Discovery of the True Mount Sinai* (New York: Simon & Schuster, 1998).

infidelity to God's commandments, then, is considered to be adultery. "You have played the whore with many lovers; and would you return to me? declares the Lord" (3:1c). Ezekiel 16 frames God's relationship with Israel in an allegory telling how he rescued the baby girl, saw her develop, and claimed her for marriage by entering into a covenant with her (16:1–14). However, his beautiful bride is told, "You trusted in your beauty and played the whore because of your renown and lavished your whorings on any passerby; your beauty became his" (16:15).

The Sinai Covenant, then, was not just an event in Israel's past; it also served as the very foundation for Israel's religious and social life. The Deuteronomic covenant made it clear that Israel's status in the land promised to Abraham, Isaac, and Jacob was contingent on obedience to the laws of Sinai.

> If you act corruptly by making a carved image in the form of anything, and by doing what is evil in the sight of the Lord your God, so as to provoke him to anger, . . . you will not live long in [the land], but will be utterly destroyed. And the Lord will scatter you among the peoples, and you will be left few in number among the nations where the Lord will drive you. (Deut. 4:25–27)

Furthermore, the Sinai covenant is the grid through which Israel's history is understood. By this covenant, Israel's kings would be evaluated (especially 1–2 Kings). The covenant serves as the foundation for the indictments of the prophets against Israel and Judah.

a. Gordon McConville, "בְּרִית," NIDOTTE 1:747.
b. Kenneth A. Kitchen, "Egypt, Ugarit, Qatna and Covenant," UF 11 (1979): 453–64.
c. Julius Wellhausen, Prolegomena to the History of Ancient Israel (Gloucester, MA: Peter Smith, 1983 [1878]), 417–18.
d. See further chap. 3, "Covenant and Treaty in the Hebrew Bible and in the Ancient Near East."

Num. 33:8–15).[166] This means that it is impossible for Shur to be in the area east of the Gulf of Aqaba in present-day Saudi Arabia.[167] One must combine the information about the eight to eleven stops after crossing the sea until reaching Mount Sinai and the distance of an eleven-day journey to Kadesh-Barnea. When we take all of this into consideration, the mountains of southern Sinai, including Gebel Musa and Gebel Serbal, fit the general parameters.

The Tabernacle, Israel's Desert Sanctuary

When Moses received the law or covenant from God, in keeping with ancient legal practices, a copy of the treaty was to be deposited before the deity, in

166. For a discussion of the uncertainty here, see Hoffmeier, Ancient Israel in Sinai, 117–18.
167. For further arguments against a Saudi Arabian location for Mount Horeb/Sinai, see ibid., 130–40.

the sanctuaries of the suzerain and vassal. One ancient treaty text records, "A duplicate of this tablet is deposited before the Sun-goddess of Arinna, since the Sun-goddess of Arinna governs kingship and queenship. And in the land of Mittanni a duplicate is deposited before the Storm-god, Lord of the *kurinnu* of Kahat."[168] In the deserts of Sinai, Israel had no temple because they would be traveling from that point to the land of Canaan. Consequently, a portable sanctuary or tent shrine logically becomes the first place of worship. Instructions for its construction (Exod. 25–40), along with its various accoutrements, immediately follow the conclusion of the covenant ceremony (Exod. 24). The ark of the covenant, the gold-covered portable box with winged cherubim over it, was where the tablets containing the "book of the covenant" (Exod. 24:7) were to be placed (Exod. 25:16; Deut. 31:24–26).

A number of recent studies of the tabernacle have demonstrated that many aspects of this tent shrine find parallels from Egypt and point to the Sinai for its origins. While this might seem like an obvious conclusion, Wellhausen and his adherents believe that the tabernacle was not the prototype for Solomon's temple but rather a retrojection by the exilic priestly writer who could not envision a time when Israel did not have a place of worship.[169] Kitchen has shown that tent shrines and canopies made of various materials and fabrics are known in Egypt as early as the Old Kingdom (2700–2300 BC). These included gold-plated frames over which a covering would be placed.[170] The antiquity of the tent shrine of Exodus is further supported by comparisons with Ramesses II's tent shown on several temple façades that depict his military campaign at Kadesh in Syria (fig. 2.9).[171] His royal encampment is laid out like the tabernacle, rectangular in shape, and surrounded by an enclosure wall map of panels. This is not an insignificant detail, as the royal camps of campaigning Assyrian kings of the first millennium BC are of a different shape, circular or elliptical.

A more fitting analogy to Israel's desert sanctuary is the shrine discovered at Timna. It had been a small 7 x 9 m structure dedicated to the Egyptian

---

168. This is from the treaty between Suppiluliuma I the Hittite and Shattiwaza of Mittanni (Gary Beckman, *Hittite Diplomatic Texts* [ed. Harry A. Hoffner; 2nd ed.; SBLWAW 7; Atlanta: Scholars Press, 1999], 46).

169. Julius Wellhausen, *Prolegomena to the History of Ancient Israel* (Gloucester, MA: Peter Smith, 1983 [1878]), 36–37.

170. Kenneth Kitchen, "The Tabernacle—a Bronze Age Artifact," *ErIsr* 24 (1993): 119–29; idem, "The Desert Tabernacle: Pure Fiction or Plausible Account?," *BRev* 16 (2000): 14–21.

171. Michael Homan, "The Divine Warrior in His Tent: A Military Model for Yahweh's Tabernacle," *BRev* 16 (2000): 22–33, 55; idem, *To Your Tents, O Israel! The Terminology, Function, Form, and Symbolism of Tents in the Hebrew Bible and the Ancient Near East* (CHANE 12; Leiden: Brill, 2002), chap. 7.

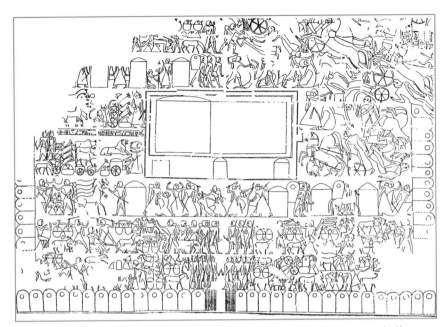

Figure 2.9. Ramesses II camp set up at Kadesh from the pylon of Luxor temple (from Hoffmeier, "Tents in Egypt and the Ancient Near East," *Journal for the Study of Egyptian Antiquities* VII, no 3 [1977], plate 3)

goddess Hathor by Egyptian miners but was later enlarged to 9 x 10 m.[172] When the shrine was abandoned by Egyptians it was altered into a Midianite tent-shrine, which became clear with the discovery by Benno Rothenberg of a "large amount of heard red and yellow cloth" that covered the low-lying stone wall of the sanctuary.[173] The Midianite tent-shrine originated in the second half of the twelfth century BC, which puts it close in time to the Israelite tabernacle.

From ancient Mari (ca. eighteenth century BC) we learn that large ceremonial tents were erected with the use of tent frames, designated by the term *qé-er-su*. This is cognate with the Hebrew word *qĕrašîm*,[174] the very word used fourteen times in Exodus 26:15–29 for the frames of the sanctuary. Additionally, we find that a number of words of Egyptian origin are used in connection with the construction of the tent. The wood frames, the ark, and other furniture of the tabernacle were to be made of acacia wood (e.g.,

172. Benno Rothenberg, *The Egyptian Mining Temple at Timna* (London: University College London, 1988), 28.

173. Benno Rothenberg, "Timna," *NEAEHL* 2:483.

174. Daniel Fleming, "Mari's Large Public Tent and the Priestly Tent Sanctuary," *VT* 50 (2000): 484–98.

Exod. 25:10, 13, 23; 26:15, 26, 32, 37; 27:1; 30:1), which probably is the only tree of the limited varieties in Sinai that could have been used to make furniture. The nineteenth-century explorer Henry Spencer Palmer, who wrote extensively about the geography and flora and fauna of Sinai, observed, "Of the native trees there are very few varieties. The most valuable for economic purposes are the date-palm, the acacia and the tamarisk."[175] The Hebrew word for "acacia," *šiṭṭâ* or *šiṭṭîm* (pl.), appears to be a loanword from Egyptian *šnd.t*.[176] Many of the wooden objects associated with the tabernacle are overlaid with gold. The Hebrew word for the process of gilding is *paḥ* (Exod. 39:3; Num. 16:38), which derives from the Egyptian word *pḥ3*.[177] Egyptian artisans were experts in gilding wooden objects with gold foil, as scores of items from Tutankhamun's tomb make clear. So it is not surprising that the Hebrews utilized the means and terminology of gilding that the Egyptians mastered.

Linen is one of the materials used in the covering of the tent of meeting (Exod. 26:1, 31, 36; 27:9, 16, 18) and to make priestly garments (39:27–29). In these texts the word for "linen," *šēš*, is the Egyptian word for "linen." The use of this word is significant because there is a Hebrew word (*bûṣ*) for "linen" used regularly outside of Exodus, and Genesis 41:42 also uses *šēš* (in the Joseph story, set in Egypt!).[178]

There is no good explanation for these Egyptian linguistic and technological elements in the book of Exodus if the narrative is "a brilliant product of the human imagination."[179] Rather, they suggest that the narratives preserve these Egyptian features because the Israelites had spent several centuries in Egypt and brought with them terminology and practices learned in Egypt that they appropriated in Sinai while they were establishing their first religious sanctuary.

The "tabernacle," the Hebrew word that literally means "dwelling place" and "abode" (*miškān*),[180] continued to be Israel's sanctuary after entering the land of Canaan. The tabernacle, or "tent of meeting," stood at Shiloh for around two centuries (Josh. 18:1; 19:51; 1 Sam. 2:22; 3:1; 4:4). After the Philistine victories against Israel, Shiloh was abandoned, and the sanctuary was

175. Henry Spencer Palmer, *Sinai: From the Fourth Egyptian Dynasty to the Present Day* (London: Society for Promoting Christian Knowledge, 1892), 46.

176. Thomas O. Lambdin, "Egyptian Loan Words in the Old Testament," *JAOS* 73 (1953): 145–55; Muchiki, *Egyptian Proper Names*, 256.

177. Lambdin, "Egyptian Loan Words," 153; Muchiki, *Egyptian Proper Names*, 253.

178. Avi Hurvitz, "The Usage of שש and בוץ in the Bible and Its Implication for the Date of P," *HTR* 60 (1967): 117–21; James K. Hoffmeier, "Flax, Linen," *NIDOTTE* 1:711–12.

179. Finkelstein and Silberman, *Bible Unearthed*, 1.

180. *HALOT* 1:646–47; *DCH* 5:527–31.

moved to Nob (1 Sam. 21:1–6) and then to Gibeon (2 Chron. 1:3, 13). Then, when Solomon dedicated the temple in Jerusalem, the old tent sanctuary was taken to Jerusalem and somehow incorporated into the new edifice (1 Kings 8:4; 2 Chron. 5:5). Richard Friedman has argued that the old tent was actually erected within the holy of holies.[181] This interesting theory lacks compelling evidence. But it is clear that including the tabernacle, perhaps even with the cloths rolled up, was intended to transfer the sanctity of the Sinai shrine into the new temple. The connection between tent and temple is echoed in a number of liturgical texts, including Psalm 27:4–6:

> One thing have I asked of the LORD,
>   that will I seek after:
> that I may dwell in the house of the LORD
>   all the days of my life,
> to gaze upon the beauty of the LORD
>   and to inquire in his temple.
> For he will hide me in his shelter
>   in the day of trouble;
> he will conceal me under the cover of his tent;
>   he will lift me high upon a rock.
> And now my head shall be lifted up
>   above my enemies all around me,
> and I will offer in his tent
>   sacrifices with shouts of joy;
> I will sing and make melody to the LORD.

Conclusion

The exodus from Egypt and the sojourn in the Sinai wilderness were the defining events for the Israelites that formed them and their understanding of their God. On the latter point, God could reveal himself as "I am the LORD your God, who brought you out of the land of Egypt" (e.g., Exod. 20:2; Lev. 19:36; 25:38; 26:13; Num. 15:41; Deut. 5:6; Ps. 81:10; cf. Hosea 12:9; 13:4). In Exodus 6:7 God declares, "I will take you to be my people, and I will be your God, and you shall know that I am the LORD your God, who has brought you out from under the burdens of the Egyptians." Rolf Rendtorff calls this the "covenant formula," which expresses God's relationship with and commitment to Israel

---

181. Richard E. Friedman, "The Tabernacle in the Temple," *BA* 43 (1980): 241–48; idem, *Who Wrote the Bible?* (San Francisco: HarperSanFrancisco, 1987), 174–87.

vis-à-vis his covenant.[182] This means that whenever the Old Testament uses the expression "my people" (and it occurs more than two hundred times), "it is a reminder to Israel that they are God's people, liberated by him from slavery in Egypt, and now bound to him by the Sinaitic covenant."[183]

182. Rolf Rendtorff, "The Concept of Revelation in Ancient Israel," in *Revelation as History* (ed. Wolfhart Pannenberg; New York: Macmillan, 1968), 23–53.

183. Hoffmeier, "These Things Happened," 113.

3

Covenant and Treaty in the Hebrew Bible and in the Ancient Near East

SAMUEL GREENGUS

Covenants and treaties play an essential role in the historiography of ancient Israel and its neighbors. The recent set of volumes by Kitchen and Lawrence identifies, translates, and studies approximately one hundred such documents, reaching from about 2500 to 46 BCE.[1] The purpose of this chapter is to discuss the types of covenants and treaties that are most important for the study of ancient Israel and to conclude with some observations regarding their value as historical sources.

The term "covenant" is the usual translation of Hebrew *běrît*, the word most often used to describe the divine covenant between God and Israel. However, *běrît* is also used in secular contexts to describe relationships between human parties, acting as individuals, as well as between larger groups and even between entire nations. In secular contexts it is therefore often customary to translate the term *běrît*, depending on the situation, as "contract, pact, treaty." While English translations will differ, the same Hebrew word *běrît* underlies all these contexts, both divine and secular. The etymology of the term *běrît* is most

---

1. Kenneth A. Kitchen and Paul J. N. Lawrence, eds., *Treaty, Law and Covenant in the Ancient Near East* (3 vols.; Wiesbaden: Harrassowitz, 2012).

plausibly explained by looking at related Semitic languages outside of the Bible. The likeliest explanation relates it to Akkadian *birītu*, which denotes an area held in common by neighbors, something "in-between," as well as a clasp holding together two ends of a chain or fetter.[2] This etymology makes sense; it conveys both the ideas of mutuality and of how two parties are tied together by agreement and obligations. In Akkadian one finds other words with similar meanings used to describe "contract, pact, treaty"; many of these likewise convey the idea of "binding" or "tying together."[3]

In the Hebrew Bible "covenant" describes the relationship between God and the people of Israel. But it is not the only way in which this important and theologically complex relationship is described. While other divine-relationship metaphors, such as shepherd and flock[4] or parent and child,[5] highlight aspects of generous nurture and caring, the term "covenant" focuses on obligations and responsibilities existing between the parties. These metaphors or poetic images are helpful in explaining theological ideas and beliefs on the kinds of relationships that were possible between a mortal humanity and a transcendent God.

In divine covenants, God is a partner to the agreement and not just a witness or observer to the agreement, as is the case in secular covenants. It is best first to look more closely at such secular or worldly uses before we examine the concept of divine covenant because exploration of exclusively human or secular covenants will help to bring important underlying ideas into sharper focus and will give us a starting point from which we may better understand how the overall concept of covenant was understood in ancient Israel. In a very real sense, the divine covenant draws upon many ideas and practices found in the ordinary, everyday life of the people.

Secular Covenants: Personal

The simplest covenant unites two persons. One such covenant is that of marriage, which is mentioned in Proverbs 2:16–17, where a young man is

---

2. See *HALOT* 1:157 (s.v. *bĕrît*); *CAD* B 252–55. For *brt*, *bryt* in Egyptian documents, see Kenneth A. Kitchen, "The Fall and Rise of Covenant, Law, and Treaty," *TynBul* 40 (1989): 122–23. See also idem, "Egypt, Ugarit, Qatna, and Covenant," *UF* 11 (1979): 453–64.

3. Note, e.g., *riksum, rikiltu, riksātum, ṣimdatum*. See Samuel Greengus, "Legal and Social Institutions of Ancient Mesopotamia," *CANE* 1:482. See also references in *CAD* R 346, 353–54; *CAD* Ṣ 194–96. The term *adē*, which is used in both divine and secular covenants, is discussed further below.

4. See Ps. 23:1; Isa. 40:11; Jer. 31:10; 50:19; Ezek. 34:12–16; Mic. 7:14.

5. See Deut. 32:6, 18; Ps. 2:7; Isa. 63:16; 64:7 (8 ET); Jer. 31:9; Mal. 1:6, 2:10.

admonished to "steer clear" of an adulterous woman who seeks to entrap him. She is described as one "who abandons the companion of her youth and forgets the covenant [with its oath sworn by the name] of her God."[6] We again see marriage and a clearer reference to oath in Malachi 2:14, where the prophet declares, "And you say: 'For what [reason does the LORD not accept our sacrificial offerings]?' (It is) because the LORD was a witness between you and the wife of your youth, whom you betrayed; and she was your friend and your wife by covenant."

In marriage, the Deity becomes a witness to covenants made by human parties. The Lord is angry because promises or oaths of marriage, invoking his name, were sworn and later broken. In Malachi the husband's failure to keep his oath of fidelity will lead to the breaking up of his marriage, as we see further in Malachi 2:15–16, where the prophet continues, "Do not act treacherously with the wife of your youth. For I hate divorce, says the LORD."[7] Earlier in this passage the prophet is using human infidelity as a poetic image to "explain" the broken relationship of faith and fidelity between God and the people of Judah, who "have profaned the covenant of our forefathers" and "husbanded the daughter of a foreign god" (Mal. 2:10–11).

The poetic image of a marriage covenant is found again in Ezekiel 16:8, where God is visualized as a man rescuing a foundling girl left in a field. The foundling grows to maturity, and then God, in the role of the man, recounts, "I passed by you again and looked on you; you were at the age for love. I spread the edge of my cloak over you, and covered your nakedness: I pledged myself to you and entered into a covenant with you, says the Lord GOD, and you became mine" (NRSV).

Later in this "story" or allegory, the wife proves to be faithless and is punished for her adultery. Here, again, while the poetic image is one of marriage, the entire purpose of Ezekiel 16 is to stress the apostasy and punishment of the people of Israel for worshiping idols and the gods of the pagans.[8]

We seem to have another simple covenant in the bond of loyalty and friendship between David and Jonathan. In 1 Samuel 18:3 we read, "And Jonathan

---

6. Scripture translations in this chapter are by the author unless otherwise indicated.

7. Here with the ancient versions we read *tbgd* in place of *ybgd*. Divorce often was the consequence of infidelity in biblical times, but forgiveness was also possible. See Samuel Greengus, *Laws in the Bible and in Early Rabbinic Collections: The Legal Legacy of the Ancient Near East* (Eugene, OR: Cascade Books, 2011), 35–40, 48–52. The themes of infidelity and covenant seem to be linked also in Job 31:1: "I have made a covenant with my eyes; how then could I look upon a virgin?" (NRSV).

8. Greengus (*Laws in the Bible*, 48–49) discusses the conflation of penalties normally given for adultery with the pain and sufferings of military conquest and exile. These are set side by side in Ezek. 16:38–41 and similarly in the tale of the two faithless sisters in 23:25–26.

and David made a covenant because he [Jonathan] loved him as his own soul."
In this passage the covenant seems to describe an action establishing a kind of
"blood-brotherhood" between close friends. But in 1 Samuel 23:16–18 their
bond, apparently renewed for a second time, takes on a quasi-political tone:

> And Saul's son Jonathan arose and went to David at Horesh and strengthened
> his hand by [invoking the name of] God. He said to him, "Do not be afraid:
> the hand of my father Saul will never find you; and you are going to be king
> over Israel and I shall be the second to you; and also my father Saul knows [this
> is] true." And the two of them made a covenant before the LORD. And David
> remained in Horesh, and Jonathan went back to his house.

One might look for further political overtones in the Hebrew phrase "made
a covenant." We can translate it literally as "cut a covenant." This phrase finds
its origin in the making of political covenants between rulers and nations
where a sacrificial animal was cut into pieces and solemn oaths were sworn.
The sacrifice served to "invite" one or more deities to be present and witness
the covenant and hear the oaths taken. The cut-up animal was also an omi-
nous sign, attached to a solemn oath, called 'ālâ in Hebrew, which included
a curse falling upon the swearer of the oath who did not keep his word.[9] Deities, by whom oaths were sworn, were expected to punish an oath taker who
violated his promised word. The phrase "cut a covenant," however, may have
anciently become an idiom that could be used in simpler contexts, even where
the taking of oaths was not accompanied by a sacrifice. This seems to have
been the situation in the hasty meeting and covenant renewal between David
and Jonathan described above in 1 Samuel 23:16–18.

We can see the actual ritual of sacrifice described very clearly in Jeremiah
34:8–22. During the war being fought by Zedekiah to repel the armies of
Nebuchadnezzar that had come against Judah, Zedekiah had "made a covenant with all the people in Jerusalem to proclaim a decree of release [for free
persons enslaved by their creditors because of unpaid debts]." (Unfortunately,
after making this covenant and releasing their debt slaves, the creditors then
recaptured them and returned them to servitude, thus breaking their oaths.)
In Jeremiah 34:18–20 the prophet describes the full ritual of covenant making,
the cutting apart of the sacrificial animal, and the oath:[10]

---

9. A cognate form of this term, 'lt, also occurs in Ugaritic; see Theodore Lewis, "The Identity
and Function of El/Baal Berith," *JBL* 115 (1996): 409–10. One should also mention the Akkadian term *māmītu*, "solemn oath," which is also used to denote "treaty." See *CAD* M/1 190–95.

10. The oath is referred to earlier, in Jeremiah 34:16: "And you went back and profaned my
name and you made go back—each person his male or female slave—(those) whom you had
(previously) set free on their own, and you captured them again to be your male and female slaves."

And those who transgressed my covenant and did not keep the terms of the covenant that they made before me, I will make like the calf when they cut it in two and passed between its parts: the officials of Judah, the officials of Jerusalem, the eunuchs, the priests, and all the people of the land who passed between the parts of the calf shall be handed over to their enemies and to those who seek their lives. Their corpses shall become food for the birds of the air and the wild animals of the earth. (NRSV)

The image of parties to a covenant walking between the divided carcass of the sacrificial victim gave rise to several other expressions used to describe the making of a covenant, such as "enter into the covenant," "enter into the oath," "pass into the covenant," and "stand in the covenant."[11] Jeremiah 34 will be revisited later when we come to discuss the subject of "divine covenant renewal."

In ancient Near Eastern contexts we also find that covenant terminology was used to describe binding agreements and relationships between individuals. This is well attested for marriage; however, there is no evidence for a bond created between individuals similar to that of David and Jonathan, except in larger, political situations—for example, between individual kings on behalf of themselves and their people.[12]

Secular Covenants: Political and Group

The making of the secular, royal covenants were of huge significance in ancient times; they were dramatic events, witnessed, widely disseminated, and shared with the people at large. While the promises made and the oaths taken

---

11. For "enter into the covenant," see 1 Sam. 20:8; Jer. 34:10; for "enter into the oath," see Ezek. 17:13; for "pass into the covenant," see Deut. 29:12; for "stand in the covenant," see 2 Kings 23:3; 2 Chron. 34:32. See further the "passing between the halves" in the discussion on Gen. 15 below.

12. See Samuel Greengus, "The Old Babylonian Marriage Contract," *JAOS* 89 (1969): 505–32. The formation of marriage agreements primarily involved oral agreements, but records were written to record important transactions, which could affect the status and rights of husbands or wives. The formation of marriage agreements (*riksu, riksātum* are the terms most often used) involved rituals other than sacrifice and, at times, sworn promises. See further Samuel Greengus, "Redefining 'Inchoate Marriage' in Old Babylonian Contexts," in *Riches Hidden in Secret Places: Ancient Near Eastern Studies in Memory of Thorkild Jacobsen* (ed. Tzvi Abusch; Winona Lake, IN: Eisenbrauns, 2002), 123–39. For Neo-Assyrian marriage agreements, see Karen Radner, *Die Neuassyrischen Privatrechtsurkunden als Quelle für Mensch und Umwelt* (SAAS 6; Helsinki: Neo-Assyrian Text Corpus Project, University of Helsinki, 1997), 157–58. We are not certain whether the "pledge" and "entering into the covenant" in Ezek. 16:8 derive from the "allegorical level" of the divine covenant with the people of Israel or reflect rituals used in ordinary marriage (see Daniel I. Block, *The Book of Ezekiel* [2 vols.; NICOT; Grand Rapids: Eerdmans, 1997–98], 1:483n120).

remained the central feature, the taking of these royal oaths occurred within elaborate formal settings and structures. The terms or provisions of these agreements were carefully negotiated and often recorded in written form to be preserved for posterity. It is the recovery of such documents through archaeology that enables us now to know more about the making of covenants in ancient times.

We possess a large number of secular, royal covenants or treaties, going back to the end of the third millennium BCE. Our most important records for comparative purposes come from the ancient Near East and are written in Sumerian, Akkadian (Babylonian and Assyrian), and Hittite.[13] One large group of documents comes from the Old Babylonian period (2000–1600 BCE) and largely involves a cluster of kings and kingdoms located in what is now Iraq and Syria.[14] A second major group dates to about 1400–1000 BCE and

---

13. Here we are dealing with fragments of treaties as well as with more completely preserved treaty texts. There are also documents that discuss rites and ceremonies as well as negotiations over the content of treaties. Thus it is difficult to arrive at a set number, but there are at least some sixty treaty transactions recorded. See further Amnon Altman, "How Many Treaty Traditions Existed in the Ancient Near East?," in *Pax Hethetica: Studies on the Hittites in Honour of Itamar Singer* (ed. Yoram Cohen, Amir Gilan, and Jared L. Miller; Wiesbaden: Harrassowitz, 2010), 17–36. A new publication that offers a serious attempt at collecting and presenting the texts of all known ancient Near Eastern treaties is Kitchen and Lawrence, *Treaty, Law and Covenant*.

14. For the earliest records, see Jerrold S. Cooper, *Presargonic Inscriptions* (vol. 1 of *Sumerian and Akkadian Royal Inscriptions*; SARI 1; New Haven: American Oriental Society, 1986), 33–53; Hans Neumann, "Der Vertrag zwischen Ebla und Abarsal," in *Staatsverträge, Herrscherinschriften und andere Documente zur politischen Geschichte* (vol. 2 of *Texte aus der Umwelt des Alten Testaments*; ed. Michael Lichtenstein; Gütersloh: Mohn, 2005), 2–8; Heidemarie Koch, "Elams Vertrag mit dem akkadischen Köning Narām-Sîn (2260–2223 v. Chr.)," in Lichtenstein, *Staatsverträge*, 283–86. For treaty documents of the Old Babylonian period, see Dennis J. McCarthy, *Treaty and Covenant: A Study in Form in the Ancient Oriental Documents and in the Old Testament* (2nd ed.; AnBib 21A; Rome: Biblical Institute Press, 1978), 86–96, 307–8; Karl Hecker, "Staatsverträge," in Lichtenstein, *Staatsverträge*, 88–91; Jean-Marie Durand, *Les documents épistolaires du palais de Mari* (3 vols.; LAPO 16–18; Paris: Cerf, 1997–2000), 1:290–93; Jesper Eidem, "An Old Assyrian Treaty from Tell Leilan," in *Marchands, diplomates et empereurs: Études sur la civilisation mésopotamienne offertes à Paul Garelli* (ed. Dominique Charpin and Francis Joannès; Paris: Éditions Recherche sur les civilisations, 1991), 185–206; additional documents in Jesper Eidem, *The Royal Archives from Tell Leilan: Old Babylonian Letters and Treaties from the Lower Town Palace East* (UNINOL 107; Leiden: Nederlands Instituut voor het Nabije Oosten, 2011); Samuel Greengus, *Old Babylonian Tablets from Ishchali and Vicinity* (UNHAII 44; Istanbul: Nederlands Historisch-Archaeologisch Instituut, 1979), no. 326, 74–77; S. Çeçen and K. Hecker. "*Ina Mātika Eblum*: Zu einem neuen Text zum Wegerecht in der Kültepe-Zeit," in *Vom Alten Orient zum Alten Testament: Festschrift für Wolfram Freiherrn von Soden zum 85. Geburtstag am 19. Juni 1993* (ed. Manfred Dietrich and Oswald Loretz; AOAT 240; Neukirchen-Vluyn: Neukirchener Verlag; Kevalaer: Butzon & Becker, 1995), 31–41; Cahit Günbatti, "Two Treaty Texts Found at Kültepe," in *Assyria and Beyond: Studies Presented to Mogens Trolle Larsen* (ed. J. G. Dercksen; UNINOL 100; Leiden: Nederlands Insituut voor et Nabije Oosten, 2004), 249–68; Michaël Guichard, "Un traité alliance entre Larsa, Uruk et Ešnunna contra Sabium de Babylone" *Sem* 56 (2014): 9–24.

focuses mainly on the diplomatic relations between the Hittite kings and their neighbors in Anatolia and Syria. These documents are mostly written in Akkadian, which functioned as the language of diplomacy; these were duplicates of the primary Hittite versions.[15] A third major group comes from around 900–625 BCE and deals with the relations between Assyria and kings of smaller kingdoms in Syria. These were also written in Akkadian and, on some occasions, with Aramaic duplicates.[16]

In the Bible political covenants or treaties were made between leaders of Israel on behalf of themselves and their people. The patriarchs Abraham, Isaac, and Jacob, as chieftains of their small bands, made pacts with their neighbors or rivals. Abraham made pacts with the Amorites, and both he and Isaac did so later with Abimelech king of Gerar (Gen. 14:13; 21:27–32; 26:28). Jacob and Laban made a covenant or pact on behalf of themselves and their large households, and they erected monuments—a pile of stones and a stone pillar—as a memorial "witness" to their agreement (Gen. 31:44–54). They both also swore oaths, and there is mention of a sacrifice and a shared meal (31:53–54).

Joshua made a treaty with the Gibeonites, who came to make peace. This created a challenging situation because the Israelites had been commanded not to make any covenants with nearby peoples. The Gibeonites misrepresented themselves as a faraway people while making the covenant. But this agreement had to stand, once it was made and oaths had been sworn (Josh. 9:6–27).[17] We read of a treaty between Solomon and Hiram of Tyre in 1 Kings 5:26 (12 ET); that passage also mentions the existence of "peace" [šālôm] between

15. For treaty documents of this period, see Gary M. Beckman, *Hittite Diplomatic Texts* (ed. Harry A. Hoffner; 2nd ed.; SBLWAW 7; Atlanta: Scholars Press, 1999); Gernot Wilhelm et al., "Texte der Hethiter," in Lichtenstein, *Staatsverträge*, 95–159; Herbert Niehr and Daniel Schwemer, "Altsyrische Texte," in Lichtenstein, *Staatsverträge*, 161–85; Emmanuel Laroche, *Catalogue of Hittite Texts*, nos. 27, 78, 132, 133, 137, 138 (http://www.hethport.uni-wuerzburg .de/CTH/). A few of these treaties are also presented in Erica Reiner, "Akkadian Treaties from Syria and Assyria," *ANET* 531–32; Itamar Singer, "The Treaties between Hatti and Amurru," *COS* 2:93–100; Richard S. Hess, "Alalakh: 1. Treaties," *COS* 2:329–32. The list in John H. Walton, *Ancient Israelite Literature in Its Cultural Context: A Survey of Parallels between Biblical and Ancient Near Eastern Texts* (LBI; Grand Rapids: Zondervan, 1989), 95–107 (with updates given here), is a useful resource, covering this period plus many of the documents from the earlier and later periods.

16. For this later period, see Simo Parpola and Kazuko Watanabe, *Neo-Assyrian Treaties and Loyalty Oaths* (SAA 2; Helsinki: Neo-Assyrian Text Corpus Project, University of Helsinki, 1988); Joseph A. Fitzmyer, *The Aramaic Inscriptions of Sefire* (rev. ed.; BibOr 19A; Rome: Pontifical Biblical Institute, 1967). It may be convenient to consult an earlier and more widely available translation by Franz Rosenthal, "The Treaty Between KTK and Arpad," *ANET* 659–61.

17. For statements against making peace with nearby peoples, see Exod. 23:32; 34:12, 15; Deut. 7:2; Judg. 2:2.

Jehu

From archaeology we learn about another Israelite ruler, Jehu, king of Israel, who became a vassal of the Assyrian king Shalmaneser III in 841 BCE. Carved into the stone of one of Shalmaneser's monuments, the Black Obelisk, is a scene that appears to show Jehu prostrating himself before Shalmaneser and his courtiers. The inscription accompanying the scene states, "I received the tribute of Jehu, son of Omri: silver, gold, a golden bowl, a golden basin, golden tumblers, golden pitchers, tin, a staff (fit) for the hand of a king (and) batons."

(A. Kirk Grayson, *Assyrian Rulers of the Early First Millennium BC* [2 vols.; RIMA 2, 3; Toronto: University of Toronto Press, 1996], 2:149)

them. Elsewhere in the Bible treaty partners are called "men who are at peace with you" (cf. Obad. 7; Ps. 55:20).

David and Abner, acting for their respective tribal groups,[18] made a treaty (2 Sam. 3:20–21), yielding the throne of Israel to David in the agreement. There is also mention of a shared feast, which, as we will see further, was a feature in non-Israelite political treaty rites.[19]

In the ancient Near East there was a difference between "parity treaties," where the participants were "brothers," and "vassal treaties," where the participants are described as "father and son" or "master and slave."[20] We see a parity treaty at the conclusion of a war between Ahab and Ben-hadad of Aram. Ahab was victorious, but at the end of the war Ahab was willing to make peace with Ben-hadad, who offered to hand over territory to Samaria, along with commercial concessions to the merchants of Israel to do business in Damascus. Ahab called Ben-hadad his "brother" in 1 Kings 20:32–33. This was more than politeness; it implied recognition of strategic realities on the part of Ahab, who, while accepting the concessions made by Ben-hadad, still professed to treat his defeated but potentially troublesome neighbor as an equal.

18. In 2 Sam. 3:6 the warring parties are called "the house of David and the house of Saul." David subsequently assumed kingship over all Israel in a covenant ceremony with a representative body of elders who came together at Hebron, as described in 2 Sam. 5:3 (retold in events leading up to 1 Chron. 12:38).

19. There may also have been a shared meal in the covenant of Joshua with the Gibeonites (see Josh. 9:14).

20. In Amos 1:9–10 Tyre is castigated for violating its "treaty of brothers" with its neighbors to the south, probably a reference to a treaty with Samaria or Judah. In the treaties with Egypt and Assyria mentioned in Hosea 12:1, Samaria, called "Ephraim" by the prophet, was likely a vassal of the great powers. For the terminology of "brotherhood" and "fatherhood" in Mesopotamian treaties, see Bertrand Lafont, "International Relations in the Ancient Near East: The Birth of a Complete Diplomatic System," *Diplomacy and Statecraft* 12, no. 1 (2001): 40–43. For "master" and "slave," see also *CAD* A/1 248; for "father," *CAD* A/1 71; for "brother," *CAD* A/1 188 (*aḫḫūtu*).

Figure 3.1. Jehu in the Black Obelisk

In 2 Kings 16:7–9 is an account of a vassal treaty between Ahaz and Tiglath-pileser of Assyria; it happened after the invasion of Judah by Rezin king of Aram and his then-ally Pekah king of Israel:

> Ahaz sent emissaries to King Tiglath-pileser of Assyria, saying, "I am (hence-forth) your 'servant and your son.' Come up, and save me from the hand of the king of Aram and from the hand of the king of Israel, who are attacking me." Ahaz also took the silver and the gold found in the house of the LORD and in the treasure houses of the king, and sent a tribute to the king of Assyria. The king of Assyria hearkened unto him; the king of Assyria went up against Damascus, and took it, and deported (its people as captives) to Kir; and he killed Rezin.[21]

We find the place of divine punishment for broken oaths uttered in the formation of secular covenants in Ezekiel 17:18–20, where God says that he will punish Zedekiah, ruler of Judah, who had made a treaty with Nebuchadnezzar to be a faithful vassal to Babylon:

21. Second Chron. 28:16–21 gives a different version of this event. Another tale of deliverance in exchange for tribute, this time of Asa king of Judah by Ben-hadad king of Aram, is recounted in 1 Kings 15:16–21 (//2 Chron. 16:1–6).

Because he despised the oath [*'ālâ*] and broke the covenant, for behold: he gave his hand and (yet) did all these things, he shall not escape. Therefore thus says the Lord GOD: As I live, I will surely return upon his head (punishment for) my oath that he despised, and my covenant that he broke. I will spread my net over him, and he shall be caught in my snare; I will bring him to Babylon and enter into judgment with him there for the treason he has committed against me.

Here the Lord states that he will punish Zedekiah for violating the solemn oath that he pronounced as part of his covenant or treaty agreement with Nebuchadnezzar.[22] The use of a sacrificial animal is not mentioned here but may have been present in a political treaty of such importance.[23] Nevertheless, in certain political treaties from Babylonia we find that sacrificial rites might be omitted when the parties were not able to take the oath at the same time and place.[24]

There was an inherent cultural ideal that all agreements and promises sworn by the name of God were not ephemeral but rather should continue to be kept in perpetuity or at least as far into the future as one could imagine. We see this idea of continuity expressed in the personal political covenant made by Abraham with Abimelech, where the king asks of Abraham, "Now therefore swear unto me here by God that you will not deal falsely with me, my posterity, and with my future descendent: (rather) corresponding to the kindness that I have done unto you, you shall do unto me, and to the land wherein you have sojourned" (Gen. 21:23).

The personal covenant between David and Jonathan likewise lived on, as can be seen in 2 Samuel 21:7, where David dooms Saul's children to death at the hand of the Gibeonites but spares Jonathan's son, Mephibosheth, "because of the oath of the LORD that was between them, between David and Jonathan son of Saul."

The expectation that a covenant will live on beyond the lifetimes of the participants is likewise seen in ancient Near Eastern secular political treaties. In one Hittite treaty, for example, the Hittite king commands his vassal, "Protect My Majesty as overlord. And later protect the sons, grandsons, and progeny of My Majesty as overlords. You shall not desire some other overlord for yourself."[25]

---

22. This oath is again mentioned in 2 Chron. 36:13: "And he [Zedekiah] also rebelled against Nebuchadnezzar the king, who had made him swear (an oath) by God."

23. Cf. Ezek. 17:13, which uses the phrase "had him enter into the oath," discussed above. An expected association of sacrifice with covenant is expressed in Ps. 50:5.

24. See Dominique Charpin, *Writing, Law, and Kingship in Old Babylonian Mesopotamia* (trans. Jane Marie Todd; Chicago: University of Chicago Press, 2010), 107–8.

25. Treaty between Tudhaliya IV of Hatti and Shaushga-muwa of Amurru (Beckman, *Hittite Diplomatic Texts*, no. 17.103–7). For further examples, see ibid., no. 11.74–82; no. 13.87–93.

In similar fashion, the Sefire Treaty between two Aramean kings presents itself as being made not only between the current participants, but also between their sons, grandsons, and other offspring. Near the end of the stela it states this hope in a different way: "Thus have we spoken [and thus have we writ]ten. What I, [Mati'el], have written (is to serve) as a reminder for my son [and] my [grand]son who will come after me."[26] However, as we saw earlier in the treaty between Zedekiah and Nebuchadnezzar, human treaties were at times broken.[27]

Divine Covenants with Individuals

We turn now to divine covenants, which show God in a close relationship with the leaders and people of Israel. Here God is not just a witness to covenants made by others, but also personally acts as one of the covenant partners. When we study the details of the divine covenants, we find valuable additional information by looking at nonbiblical political covenants or treaties. We perhaps should not be surprised to find that the divine covenants made by the "king of kings" contain many meaningful features that are also found in the political covenants or treaties made by earthly kings.

In the Bible we have divine covenants being made between God and individuals, similar in character to the "personal covenants" of political character that we have seen made between human participants—for example, between Jacob and Laban, or Jonathan and David. In these divine covenants with individuals, there is the clear expectation that the covenants would continue to be valid in the future, even beyond the lifetimes of the present partners to the covenant. This may in part be due to the eternity of God, who, as one of the covenant participants, would always be present, and God, moreover, would not break his promise once given.

This assumption of perpetuity clearly appears in God's covenant with Noah, the first divine covenant with an individual mentioned in the Bible. This covenant, earlier promised in Genesis 6:18, is made after the flood, as told in Genesis 8:20–9:17. First, Noah offers a sacrifice of animals. God, smelling the "sweet savor," vows to himself that he will never again bring a flood like this upon the earth. He blesses Noah and his sons and gives them and their posterity sway over the earth and all its creatures. Henceforth humanity—that is, the descendants of Noah—may eat the flesh of living creatures on the

---

26. Fitzmyer, *Sefire*, 42–43, 52–53 (I Face A, Face C).
27. In 1 Kings 15:19 and 2 Chron. 16:3, Asa king of Judah asked Ben-hadad to break off his treaty with Baasha king of Israel.

condition that they not partake of the blood but instead pour it out upon the ground. For the homicidal shedding of human blood, God will demand blood in return, since humankind is made in the image of God. These are the provisions of the covenant that apply to the human participants. The Bible goes on to relate the single provision that comprises God's promise (Gen. 9:8–11):

> Then God said to Noah and to his sons with him, "As for me, I am establishing my covenant with you and your descendants after you, and with every living creature that is with you, the birds, the domestic animals, and every animal of the earth with you, as many as came out of the ark. I establish my covenant with you, that never again shall all flesh be cut off by the waters of a flood, and never again shall there be a flood to destroy the earth." (NRSV)

God then also identifies a sign, as remembrance of the covenant:

> God said, "This is the sign of the covenant that I make between me and you and every living creature that is with you, for all future generations: I have set my bow in the clouds, and it shall be a sign of the covenant between me and the earth. When I bring clouds over the earth and the bow is seen in the clouds, I will remember my covenant that is between me and you and every living creature of all flesh; and the waters shall never again become a flood to destroy all flesh. When the bow is in the clouds, I will see it and remember the everlasting covenant between God and every living creature of all flesh that is on the earth." (Gen. 9:12–16 NRSV)

The rainbow in the divine covenant functions like the monuments of stone in the covenant between Jacob and Laban. A difference, of course, is that God's covenant is capable of being everlasting, for all future generations. So while a secular, personal covenant between mortals likewise aspires for longevity, its mortal scope and material limitations cannot promise eternity. This difference, as we will see, may be behind the need for covenant renewal, at least on the part of human participants in a divine covenant.

The divine covenant between God and Abraham is described in two separate accounts (Gen. 15; 17). In Genesis 15 God promises Abram (not yet called Abraham), who is still childless, that his descendants will be as numerous as the stars in heaven. God also promises the future inheritance of the land now occupied by the Amorites, Canaanites, and others. Abram is said (15:6) to have trusted in God's promise, but still he asked for further assurance. Genesis 15 describes God commanding Abram to sacrifice three animals and two fowl; Abram cut the animals into two, laying the animal halves opposite each other. While waiting, God tells Abram about the future period of slavery in Egypt and the exodus. Then, "When the sun set and it was very dark, there appeared a smoking oven, and a flaming torch which passed between those pieces" (Gen. 15:17 NJPS). This vision of fire and smoke passing between the two halves of the sacrificed animals would be anciently understood as depicting God "entering into" or "passing into" the covenant, in a manner similar to what we have earlier seen described about the covenant participants in Jeremiah 34.

The account in Genesis 17 does not describe the rite of covenant making but affirms the promises made in Genesis 15: a multitude of progeny and

> ## An Enduring Covenant
>
> The biblical concept of an enduring covenant between Abraham and God plays an important role in early Christianity as in Judaism. This is expressed in many passages in the New Testament. For example, in Romans 4:16–17 we read, "For this reason it depends on faith, in order that the promise may rest on grace and be guaranteed to all his descendants, not only to the adherents of the law but also to those who share the faith of Abraham (for he is the father of all of us, as it is written, 'I have made you the father of many nations')" (NRSV).

promise of the land. The divine covenant between God and Abraham will be everlasting, to be continued for Isaac and his progeny. Abram's and Sarai's names are divinely changed to "Abraham" and "Sarah"; Abraham is promised an heir by Sarah, to be called "Isaac."[28] Then follows the obligation for Abraham and his descendants to circumcise all male children of their households at eight days of age.[29]

The divine covenants with Abraham and his children are foundational to biblical theology.[30] Likewise, but in a different way, are the divine covenants that God makes with David and with Phinehas. The covenant with David is described as extending to his future offspring, and its continuity is mentioned specifically in connection with his descendants Solomon, Rehoboam, and Jehoram.[31] This covenant also plays a significant role in "messianic" passages,

---

28. In Gen. 26:2–5 God gives assurance to Isaac that he is indeed the inheritor of the divine covenant that God had made with Abraham prior to Isaac's birth; similarly with Jacob in 28:4, 13–15 and again in 35:9–15.

29. Note Gen. 17:10: "This is the covenant which you shall keep. . . ." But the removal of the foreskin then also becomes "the sign of the covenant between me and between you" (17:11). For circumcision as an obligation, see Gen. 21:4; Josh. 5:2–8. The existence of additional (unmentioned) obligations on the part of Abraham is suggested in Gen. 26:5.

30. God's covenant with the patriarchs is frequently recalled (e.g., Exod. 2:24; 6:3–4, 8; 32:13; Lev. 26:42; 2 Kings 13:23; 1 Chron. 16:15–18; Ps. 105:9–12 (8–11 ET).

31. The perpetuity of the Davidic covenant is mentioned in Ps. 89:1–4 and is declared by Solomon in 1 Kings 8:23–26. For Rehoboam (not mentioned by name), see 1 Kings 11:11–13; 2 Chron. 13:5; for Jehoram, see 2 Chron. 21:7. David himself declares the everlasting nature of

where the prophets of Israel look for the restoration of the Davidic rule in more distant times, even after the loss of political sovereignty and exile. One such passage is Jeremiah 33:14–18:[32]

> The days are surely coming, says the LORD, when I will fulfill the promise I made to the house of Israel and the house of Judah. In those days and at that time I will cause a righteous Branch to spring up for David; and he shall execute justice and righteousness in the land. In those days Judah will be saved and Jerusalem will live in safety. And this is the name by which it will be called: "The LORD is our righteousness." For thus says the LORD: David shall never lack a man to sit on the throne of the house of Israel, and the levitical priests shall never lack a man in my presence to offer burnt offerings, to make grain offerings, and to make sacrifices for all time. (NRSV)

The continuity of priesthood in the temple is further supported by a personal divine covenant with Phinehas son of Aaron, which is expressly mentioned in Numbers 25:12–13: "Behold, I [the LORD] am giving him my covenant of peace; and it shall be for him and for his seed after him an everlasting covenant of priesthood."[33] So in this way the two most important institutions in ancient Israelite society—the monarchy and the temple cult—were seen as being supported by God's will.

Scholars have looked for evidence of individual divine covenants in the ancient Near East, and there is at least one clear instance where this appears to be the case. It is in a prophetic vision in a Neo-Assyrian document (ca. 680 BCE) recording a series of prophecies for Esarhaddon made by the seer La-dagil-ili, a prophet of Arbela:

> This covenant tablet of Aššur enters the king's presence on a *cushion*. Fragrant oil is sprinkled, sacrifices are made, incense is burnt, and they read it out in the king's presence: The word of Ištar of Arbela to Esarhaddon, king of Assyria: Come, gods, my fathers and brothers, [enter] the cove[nant. . . .'] [Break] [She *placed*] a slice . . . on the [ter]race and gave them water from a cooler to drink; she filled a flagon of one seah with water from a cooler and gave it to them with the words: "In your hearts you say, 'Ištar is slight,' and you will go to your

---

this covenant in 2 Sam. 23:5. The continuity of the Davidic covenant is linked with the patriarchs in Jer. 33:25–26.

32. Other passages clearly mentioning the restoration of monarchy are Isa. 9:6; 11:1–15; Jer. 23:5–6.

33. In Mal. 2:1–9 a "covenant with Levi" is the subject of an admonition "to the priests," who need to be reminded that this covenant is supported by God's will. The context seems to imply that the body of priests sinned by turning against one of their number, who is described as "a messenger of the LORD of Hosts." In Neh. 13:29 both priests and Levites are in this covenant.

cities and districts, eat (your) bread and forget this covenant. (But when) you drink from this water, you will remember me and keep this covenant which I have made on behalf of Esarhaddon."[34]

The vision describes how the goddess Ištar seeks to muster additional, divine support for Esarhaddon, then in exile, fighting a rebellion led by his brothers, who sought to deny him his throne. There is brought before the king a tablet that records promises of military victory made by the chief god, Aššur. Sacrifices are made and incense is burned. Ištar, either in her temple or in heaven, invites the other gods to now signify their support by "entering the covenant," and she further binds them by having them partake of the sacrificial meal. Henceforth they will not be able to forget these actions, which signify their assent. The term used to describe the covenant written upon a tablet is *adē*, which is the familiar term used in Neo-Assyrian times.[35] In the narrative of the vision, the tablet of the covenant is also described as "the well-being [*šulmu*] placed before the image (of the god)."[36] This evokes the "covenant of peace [*šālôm*]" that God made with Phinehas.[37]

From a much earlier time comes a less clear example of a divine covenant between Uru'inimgina king of Lagash (ca. 2300) and his god Ningirsu. The king instituted a series of temple reforms, limiting the economic powers of the priestly administrators of the temples at Lagash. He also instituted measures of relief for debt slaves. The king claimed to be following the command of Ningirsu.[38] His inscription concludes, "Uru'inimgina made a covenant with

34. Simo Parpola, *Assyrian Prophecies* (SAA 9; Helsinki: Neo-Assyrian Text Corpus Project, University of Helsinki, 1997), lxx, 23–25 cols. ii 27–iii 15.

35. See Parpola and Watanabe, *Neo-Assyrian Treaties*, 180–83; Fitzmyer, *Sefire*, 57–59. These scholars agree that *adē* is a loanword from Aramaic, but, according to Jean-Marie Durand, the term *adē* may go back to Amorite ("Réalités amorrites et traditions biblique," *RA* 92 [1998]: 3–39). Fitzmyer, despite some grammatical difficulties, wants to link this term to Hebrew *ʿēd*, *ʿēdût*, which have the idea of witness, to testimony and sworn oaths. One can point to the ark, which is called both *ʾărôn habbĕrît* and *ʾărôn hāʿēdût* (e.g., Exod. 30:26; 39:35; Num. 4:5; Josh. 3:6), and to the two stone tablets of the *bĕrît* and *ʿēdût* (e.g., Exod. 31:18; 34:28). Note also 2 Kings 17:15: "They despised his statutes, and his covenant that he made with their ancestors, and the sworn oaths [*ʿēdût*] that he witnessed against them." Note further the 1QIsaiah[a] text of Isa. 33:8, which reads, "has broken the covenant, has despised witnesses [*ʿdym* in place of the Masoretic Text *ʿrym*]." See Martin Abegg Jr., Peter Flint, and Eugene Ulrich, *The Dead Sea Scrolls Bible: The Oldest Known Bible; Translated for the First Time into English* (San Francisco: HarperSanFrancisco, 1999), 320.

36. Parpola, *Assyrian Prophecies*, 26 col. ii 26.

37. The term "covenant of peace/well-being" also occurs in Isa. 54:10; Ezek. 34:25; 37:26. Compare the use of the Akkdadian cognate term *šalmu* and its dialectal variant *salīmu* to denote a "treaty of peace" (see *CAD* S 100–103). On the use of terms for "well-being, goodness" in contexts of treaty relationships and political amity, note Deut. 23:6; see discussion in Dennis J. McCarthy, "Ebla, ὅρκια τέμνειν, *ṭb*, *šlm*: Addenda to *Treaty and Covenant*," *Bib* 60 (1979): 247–53.

38. Cylinder B, C viii, 10–13.

Ningirsu that he would not permit the strong man to subjugate the widow (and) the orphan."[39] This is a unique reference, and we have no knowledge about the specific rites performed in making this covenant.

All of the foregoing divine covenants were made with individuals who received the message of negotiation from their deity either directly through personal visions or, as with Phinehas and Esarhaddon, through a prophet's vision intended for them.[40] The relationship between the human partners and the deity was close and direct; so in this sense—clearly so in the Hebrew Bible—they "knew God." In the cases of Noah, Abraham, and Phinehas, the Bible also tells us that they earned divine favor through meritorious actions on their part; similar merits are proclaimed for David as well.[41] But the covenants with Isaac, Jacob, and Solomon seem to flow from the merit of their fathers.[42] Esarhaddon's "merit," if any, seems to flow from his being the chosen one of the gods Aššur and Ištar.[43]

Divine Covenants with a People or Group

The individual divine covenants were meant to be everlasting and continue on for the human partners' offspring. This was achievable in the family lines of kings and priests. In the case of the patriarchal ancestors of ancient Israel, however, the numbers of their "inheritors" or descendants, over time, vastly increased, and the "legacy" relationship with God was felt to be less intimate and less secure. This happened despite the guidance received from the prophets and leaders. Thus, according to the Bible's "master narrative," the masses of Israelites, especially in preexilic times, were no longer mindful of the earlier covenants and strayed to worship multiple gods. Their errant behavior put the ancient covenants in jeopardy and came to affect the divine promise of the land. This lack of fidelity to God is described as a major reason for foreign invasion, conquest, slaughter, and exile, although, after punishment, as we

39. Cylinder B, C xii, 23–28. See Cooper, *Presargonic Inscriptions*, 70–74. In place of the more literal "made a covenant," he translates "solemnly promised." See further the discussion in Lewis, "Identity and Function," 405–9.

40. God appears directly to Solomon in a dream in 1 Kings 3:5–15 (//2 Chron. 1:7–12), but this vision, which concerns the building of the temple, mentions neither the divine covenant nor the perpetuity of the royal line.

41. Gen. 6:9 (Noah); Gen. 15:6; 22:16–18; 26:5 (Abraham); Num. 25:11 (Phinehas); 1 Kings 11:38; Isa. 55:3 (David).

42. Gen. 26:3–5 (Isaac); Gen. 35:12 (Jacob); 2 Chron. 1:9; 6:17 (Solomon).

43. Ištar is also referred to as "Mulissu." For this royal ideology of being the chosen of the gods, which applied to many of the Neo-Assyrian kings, see Parpola, *Assyrian Prophecies*, xxvi–xliv and passages cited there. For a biblical "response" to this ideology, see Isa. 10:5–6; 45:1–7.

will see below, there was also opportunity for repentance, forgiveness, and restoration.[44]

According to the Bible, the people of Israel, the descendants of the patriarchs, were not left to rely solely on historical memories of the covenants with their ancestors. Therefore, after the exodus from Egypt, while they were in the wilderness under the leadership of Moses, God made two fresh "group" covenants with the people: first at Sinai and then, as described in Deuteronomy, before entering the promised land. These are unique events in that God acted as a covenant partner with the people of Israel in the same way God was a partner to the covenants with the patriarchs and the others who have been mentioned.[45] In the book of Deuteronomy, Moses also laid out a program for renewal of this covenant, to be performed shortly after entering the land. In renewal ceremonies, as in ordinary covenants, God is assumed to act as a covenant partner, but he is "represented" by a leader or priest. In these settings God acts in the "conventional way" as "guarantor" and witness to the sworn oaths. Renewals (further discussed below) were subsequently led by Joshua, Asa, Jehoiada, Hezekiah, Josiah, Zedekiah, Ezra, and Nehemiah.[46] Covenant renewals were initiated to remind later generations about the existence and continuity of earlier covenant agreements and the obligations that the people were expected to fulfill.

Sinai

In Exodus 19:3–9 there is a preliminary "negotiation" to establish that the people are willing to enter into a covenant. The same kind of negotiations preceded the making of secular treaties. In the Old Babylonian texts we have examples of protracted negotiations; in advance the parties worked out the provisions of the final treaty and how the oaths were to be sworn. These negotiations normally are not recapitulated in the treaty documents themselves, but we know about them from royal and diplomatic correspondence leading up to the making of the political treaties.[47] In situations where there was a vast difference in status between the parties, it appears that negotiations were

---

44. For a treaty in which the Hittite king Mursili II forgives his vassal for earlier supporting the king's adversary, see Beckman, *Hittite Diplomatic Texts*, 83.

45. The participation of God as covenant partner is clearly stated in a number of places: Exod. 24:8; 34:10, 27; Deut. 4:23; 5:2–3; 29:1, 12, 14, 25; 31:16, 20.

46. We note but can add little to the account of the "northern" covenant renewal in 2 Kings 17:33–41. One may also explore the relationship of this tradition, if any, to the ancient covenants at Shechem, implied by references to El-*berith* and Baal-*berith* recounted in Judg. 8:33; 9:4, 46. See Lawrence E. Toombs, "Shechem (Place)," *ABD* 5:1185. For additional literature and views, see Lewis, "Identity and Function."

47. Charpin, *Writing, Law, and Kingship*, 107–14.

brief, and that the overlord dictated terms to his vassal. Thus, for example, in the text of the treaty between the Hittite king Suppiluliuma and Huqqana of Hayasa, the treaty begins abruptly with a scant introduction of the speaker, followed by a short "historical prologue": "Thus says My Majesty, Suppiluliuma, King of Hatti: I have now elevated you, Huqqana, a lowly dog, and have treated you well. In Hattusa I have distinguished you among the men of Hayasa and have given you . . ."[48]

In Exodus 19:4–6 and again at the beginning of the Decalogue in Exodus 20:1–2, there is similarly a brief introduction of the speaker along with a bit of "historical prologue": "Then God spoke all these words: I am the LORD your God, who brought you out of the land of Egypt, out of the house of slavery. You shall have no other gods before me" (Exod. 20:1–3 NRSV). The remainder of the body of the Decalogue (20:3–17) continues with a series of commandments that correspond structurally to stipulations or provisions found in political treaties. In secular political treaties, stipulations are varied in character and deal typically with matters of defense, commerce, borders, and return of fugitives. The stipulations in the biblical divine covenants, on the other hand, deal with rules of worship, moral conduct, and law. This combination of secular and religious rules is unique and is seen only in the Bible; one does not expect to find cultic and ritual rules and procedures within ancient Near Eastern treaties or law collections.[49] However, in the Bible, all these were components of the divine covenant linking Israel with God, the divine sovereign. Thus, not surprisingly, some features found in political treaties appear in commandments relating to cult and ritual. For example, in certain Hittite treaties a vassal is commanded to come before the overlord as well as to send yearly tribute.[50] In a similar fashion, the Bible commands all males to appear before the Lord three time a year, and not to come empty-handed (Exod. 23:14–17; 34:23–26; Neh. 10:34–37!). Some Hittite treaties include provisions governing the setting of boundaries by the sovereign. In the Bible, in Numbers 34, God, the divine sovereign, sets boundaries for Israel's land. This action belongs to the covenant even though the passage occurs outside the main Sinai and Deuteronomy pericopes.[51] The inclusion of laws within

---

48. Beckman, *Hittite Diplomatic Texts*, no. 3.26–34. Historical prologues can, of course, be much longer and more detailed, as in no. 2 (18–19); no. 6A (43–44). Number 2 (19) includes the statement "I, My Majesty have now given the population of the land of Kizzuwatna its freedom." For the Bible, cf. Josh. 24:2–13.

49. See Greengus, *Laws in the Bible*, 284–87.

50. "Sunashura must come before his Majesty and look upon the face of his Majesty" (Beckman, *Hittite Diplomatic Texts*, no. 2.19). For a yearly tribute, see ibid., no. 5.37; no. 8.60.

51. For some examples in treaties, cf. Beckman, *Hittite Diplomatic Texts*, no. 18B.109–11; no. 18C.114–17; no. 224, under "frontiers."

the biblical covenants is, however, without parallel: the stipulations in political treaties are not concerned with the interactions between citizens residing within the vassal nations since this was the private domain of each ruler.

There seems to be more than one set of stipulations associated with the Sinai covenant; their scope and total size are larger than anything found in the secular political treaties. After the Decalogue is an additional section beginning in Exodus 21:1 with God telling Moses, "And these are the judgments that you should set before the people." This verse introduces the lengthy Book of the Covenant, which appears to end at 23:19 and is then followed by a speech of exhortation ending at 23:33. Exodus 25–31 adds entire chapters with commandments dealing with the construction of the tabernacle and the preparation of the priestly vestments, followed by additional Sabbath laws (31:12–17). After the incident of the golden calf and the breaking of the first set of tablets, there is yet another set of stipulations, the so-called Cultic Decalogue described in Exodus 34:10–27. For these reasons, many scholars believe that the body of covenant stipulations presently before us in Exodus must be the end result of an ancient literary process that added associated material to an originally smaller, more sharply defined Sinai covenant tradition, centering on the two tablets of the Decalogue.[52]

In Exodus 24:3–11 we find a number of rites similar to those seen in the formation of secular political treaties. In Exodus 24:3, 7–8 the people, after hearing the provisions of the covenant document, affirm their acceptance of everything that God had spoken.[53] Their affirmation may be compared with the sworn oaths taken by participants in political treaties. This is followed, in Exodus 24:9–11, by sacrifices, the erection of twelve stone pillars (one for each tribe), and the sprinkling of the "blood of the covenant" upon the people. Then Moses, accompanied by Aaron, his two eldest sons, and seventy elders, ascended the mountain and saw a vision of the God of Israel standing upon a celestial pavement. They did not die after seeing God and were able to eat and drink, dining on the sacrifices that were offered. This vision of the Deity testifies to God's presence at the sacrifices as a covenant partner and his recognition of its mutually binding character. The leaders of the people, representing the community, are "invited" to join in the shared sacrificial meal, yet there was also an effort to include the masses of the people as Moses sprinkled the blood of the sacrificial animals upon them.

Covenant sacrifices are frequently mentioned as a central part of the making of political treaties in the Old Babylonian period. Thus, for example,

---

52. For discussion and literature, see Cornelius Houtman, *Exodus* (trans. Johan Rebel and Sierd Woustra; 4 vols.; HCOT; Leuven: Peeters; Kampen: Kok, 1993–2002), 3:7–16, 80–98, 310, 326–35.

53. This is in addition to the affirmation given by the people before the Decalogue in Exod. 19:8.

Zimri-Lim of Mari writes to a fellow monarch, "Let us kill donkey foals and establish an oath of the gods between us," or "I made (them) slaughter a foal of a donkey mare and arranged (thus) for a peace [salīmum] between the Haneans and the land of Idamaraṣ."[54] There are also references to the blood of the victim as symbol of the treaty—for example, "Between (the two kings) is established blood and a firm agreement." There is also mention of touching the blood and swearing the oath.[55] As for eating and drinking as part of enacting a treaty, note, for example: "After they came to agreement and made a treaty and the ass was slain, one 'brother' let the oath be sworn by other, and they sat down to the cup; after they *engaged* and drank the cup, one 'brother' with the other exchanged gifts."[56] The cup may also have had significance; in an Old Assyrian treaty ceremony each party declared, "If we cast aside our oath, let my blood be poured out like (this) cup."[57]

The Sinai covenant does not specifically mention the cutting apart of the sacrificial victims, like what is described in Genesis 15 and Jeremiah 34, but that custom was also known outside the Bible. From the Neo-Assyrian period we have two treaties from about 750 BCE involving Mati'ilu of Arpad, which was in Syria. One treaty, written in Akkadian, was with the king of Assyria; the other, written in Aramaic, was with a regional ally.[58] In both treaties the sacrificial animals were cut apart. In these treaties is a ceremonial declaration connecting the death of the sacrificial victim with the punishments that would fall on the party who broke the oath. The Aramaic treaty states, "[Just as] this calf is cut in two, so may Mati'el be cut in two, and may his nobles be cut in two."[59] The Assyrian treaty likewise states,

---

54. For these and other passages, see *CAD* Q 162 (s.v. *qatālu*); and *CAD* Ḫ 118 (s.v. *ḫāru*, *ḫa'aru*). For additional references and discussion, see Kenneth C. Way, *Donkeys in the Biblical World: Ceremony and Symbol* (ed. Jeffrey A. Blakely and K. Lawson Younger; HACL; Winona Lake, IN: Eisenbrauns, 2011), 75–82. Way adds references to treaty sacrifices involving other animals, including goats and puppies.

55. For references, see Bertrand Lafont, "Relations internationales, alliances et diplomatie au temps des rois de Mari," in *Mari, Ébla et les Hourrites: Dix ans de travaux; Actes du colloque international (Paris, Mai 1993)* (ed. Jean-Marie Durand and Dominque Charpin; Amurru 2; Paris: Éditions recherche sur les civilisations, 2001), 260–61. Eidem (*Royal Archives*, 315–17) discusses a letter (no. 89.257–58, 571) in which the royal treaty partners, negotiating from a distance, touch their own (dried?) blood that is sent from one to the other.

56. See Lafont, "Relations internationales," 266–67, citing ARM 26/2 404:60–64 (A.487 +A.3459).

57. The document is Kt n/k 794.39–42, published in Çeçen and Hecker, "*Ina Mātika Eblum*," and discussed by Lafont ("Relations internationales," 288–89), who raises the question of whether this was the cup drunk at the meal or another ceremony involving the blood of the sacrificial victim.

58. For the Akkadian treaty with Aššur-nerari V, see Parpola and Watanabe, *Neo-Assyrian Treaties*, no. 2.8–13; for the local treaty in Aramaic, see Fitzmyer, *Sefire*.

59. Fitzmyer, *Sefire*, 39–40 (I Face A).

This spring lamb has been not brought out of its fold for (ordinary) sacrifice; . . . it has been brought out for the treaty of Aššur-nerari, king of Assyria with Mati'ilu. . . . This head is not the head of a spring lamb, it is the head of Mati'ilu, it is the head of his sons, his magnates, and the people of his land. If Mati'ilu [should sin] against this treaty, just as the head of this spring lamb is c[ut off], and its knuckle placed in its mouth, . . . so may the head of Mati'ilu be cut off, and his sons [and magnates]."[60]

In the Assyrian treaty the animal appears to have been dismembered and "rearranged" rather than just cut apart. Perhaps this was an adaptation of a custom more at home in the west than in Assyria and Babylonia. The role of the sacrifices in the Old Babylonian treaties has been taken by some to be an imported, Amorite custom.[61]

We also find the setting up of a stone monument, pillar, or stela as part of the treaty ritual in a Mari text that describes an alliance relationship with a Bedouin group: "There is a stela (erected) between us; . . . the elders of Suhum have established the (terms) of the agreement and I erected a stela and also slaughtered a young male sheep."[62] When we seek to explain the significance of the stela, we can look to the Bible. In the covenant between Jacob and Laban, there was both a pile of stones and a stela or pillar, as noted in Genesis 31:51–52. There, Laban declares, "This heap is a witness, and the pillar is a witness, that I will not pass beyond this heap to you, and you will not pass beyond this heap and this pillar to me, for harm"[63] (NRSV).

In the covenant renewal ceremony in Joshua 24:27, Joshua likewise sets up a stone monument, saying, "See, this stone shall be a witness against us; for it has heard all the words of the LORD that he spoke to us; therefore it shall be a witness against you, if you deal falsely with your God" (NRSV).

60. Parpola and Watanabe, *Neo-Assyrian Treaties*, 8–9. A similar passage appears in the Succession Treaty of Esarhaddon, lines 547–50, 552.

61. Way, *Donkeys in the Biblical World*, 77–80; Jean-Georges Heintz, "'Dans la plénitude du coeur': A propos d'une formule d'alliance à Mari en Assyrie et dans la Bible," in *Ce Dieu qui vient: Études sur L'Ancien et le Nouveau Testament offertes au professeur Bernard Renaud à l'occasion de son soixante-cinquième anniversaire* (ed. Raymond Kuntzmann; LD 159; Paris: Cerf, 1995), 31–34; idem, "Nouveaux traités d'époque babylonienne ancienne et formules d'alliance dans la Bible hébraïque: Remarques préliminaires," in *Les relations internationales: Actes du colloque de Strasbourg, 15–17 juin 1993* (ed. Edmond Frézouls and Alex Jacquemin; TCRPOGA 13; Strasbourg: Université des sciences humaines de Strasbourg, 1995), 75–78.

62. Durand, "Réalités amorrites." The text is A.3572.39–46: *narûm ina birišunu . . . ši-bu-tum ša LÚ su-hi-im a-di ú-bi-ru-nim-ma d ha-mu-sà-am ah-mi-is ù* UDU A.LUM.HÁ *aṭ-bu-uh*. The term *a-di* appears to be a cognate to Neo-Assyrian *adê*; if so, it predates the Neo-Assyrian usage by many centuries.

63. Similarly in Gen. 31:48. Jacob set up a pillar next to the altar when God appeared to him in 35:9–15, although the term "covenant" is not present.

Behind the durable presence and "witnessing" of the stone is the Deity, who will punish the party breaking his oath, as stated in Genesis 31:53: "'May the God of Abraham and the God of Nahor'—the God of their fathers—'administer justice between us.' And so Jacob swore by the God whom his father Isaac feared." Similarly, in Genesis 31:49–50 Laban also says, "The LORD watch between you and me, when we are absent one from the other. . . . Remember that God is witness between you and me" (NRSV).

The twelve stones of the Sinai covenant, as the Bible says, represented the twelve tribes of Israel, which, along with their elders, were parties to the covenant. In a somewhat similar fashion, after the passage of the ark of the covenant across the Jordan (Josh. 4:3–9, 20), Joshua commands that twelve stones be erected in Gilgal as a perpetual memorial.[64]

We also find places where measures were taken to preserve memory of the terms of the covenant as well as the fact of the covenant being made. The two motives are clearly joined together in the Sefire Stela, upon which the text of the treaty is then also inscribed. Mati'iel writes, "Thus we have spoken [and thus have we wr]itten. What I, [Mati']el, have written is (to serve) as a reminder for my son [and] my [grand]son who will come after me."[65]

The two stone tablets of the covenant were regarded in a similar fashion. In Exodus 31:18; 32:15; 34:29 the stone tablets containing the Decalogue are described as "tablets of witness" or "testimony." In Exodus 25:21 God commands Moses, "And you shall place in the ark the witness that I will give you." In other words, the stone tablets were kept in a special container and placed in the heart of the sanctuary, allowing it to be called "the tabernacle of witness"; this was the religious center of the community.[66] We will return to the subject of preserving the content of written covenants again after we look at covenant in Deuteronomy and subsequent covenant renewals.

Deuteronomy

Deuteronomy 29:1 declares, "These are the words of the covenant that the LORD commanded Moses to make with the Israelites in the land of Moab, in addition to the covenant that he had made with them at Horeb" (NRSV).[67] From this verse we clearly see that Moses led the people into a second covenant prior to their entering the promised land. There has been discussion

---

64. In view of the numerical correspondence, one may wonder whether the two monuments set up in Gen. 31 were intended to represent Jacob and Laban, the two parties to the agreement.

65. Fitzmyer, *Sefire*, 52–53 (I Face C 1–4).

66. See Exod. 40:21. For the tabernacle as a center of holiness, see Num. 1:50–53; 9:15–23.

67. Horeb is also called "the mountain of God" in Exod. 3:1; 1 Kings 19:8; in Deuteronomy, "Horeb" replaces "Sinai."

on how this second covenant relates to the earlier one at Sinai. To what extent does it renew, supplement, or even replace the Sinai covenant? Deuteronomy repeats the Decalogue, which goes back to Horeb (Deut. 1:6–5:33), and also recapitulates the account of writing the second set of tablets (Deut. 9:8–10:5). However, Moses also repeatedly exhorts the people to observe the commandments, statutes, judgments, and duty[68] that God, through Moses, is commanding them "today"—that is, in the context of his final wilderness addresses.[69] So in this fashion Deuteronomy draws us to the "present tense" of the second covenant.

Deuteronomy further draws the first and second covenants together through a new way of using the term "commandment" by itself alone, either in the singular or in the plural, to describe the totality of the covenant obligations that God wishes Israel to observe.[70] In a similar fashion Deuteronomy introduces a new way to use the term "torah" (Heb. *tôrâ*). Here it is no longer used to describe one particular teaching or instruction among many other "torahs" (or *tôrôt*);[71] rather, "torah," in the singular, becomes a way to describe the totality of covenant obligations commanded by God. The impression of totality is further suggested by the repeated use of the expression "this torah."[72] Deuteronomy 1:5 helps to set this process of "consolidation" in motion, when it introduces the entire book by declaring, "On the other side of the Jordan in the land of Moab, Moses began to expound this torah as follows." There is evidence of this "unification" of diverse covenantal materials already in Exodus 24:12: "And the LORD said to Moses, 'Come up to me on the mountain, and stay there; and I will give you the tablets of stone, and the torah and the commandment, which I have written in order to instruct them.'"

What, then, are the provisions of the second covenant in Deuteronomy? In addition to the Decalogue and various pronouncements scattered in the

68. The term "duty" (Heb. *mišmeret*) is used in the singular, while the terms for "statute" (Heb. *ḥōq*) and "judgment" (Heb. *mišpāṭ*) are in the plural. The term "commandment" (Heb. *miṣwâ*) is used both in the singular and plural. There seems to be a "running together" of these terms that blurs their originally individual character to a point where they are functionally indistinguishable.

69. See Deut. 4:40; 5:1; 8:11; 10:13; 11:1–2, 32; 26:16–17; 27:10; 28:15; 30:16. In all these texts the terms "commandment, statute, judgment" appear in the plural.

70. This begins in Deut. 5:1, after concluding the events at Horeb. For singular use of "commandment" plus "today," see Deut. 7:11; 8:1; 11:8; 15:5; 19:9; 27:1; 30:11; for plural use plus "today," see Deut. 11:27–28; 13:18; 28:1, 13; 30:8.

71. For singular *tôrâ* describing particular rules, see Lev. 6:9, 14, 25; 12:7; 13:59; 15:32; Num. 5:29–30; 6:21; 19:14; for plural *tôrôt*, see Exod. 16:28; 18:16; Lev. 26:46; Isa. 24:5.

72. See Deut. 4:8, 44; 17:18–19; 27:3, 8; 28:58; 29:29; 31:9, 11–12, 24, 26; 32:46 (with "today"). In Deut. 4:8; 17:19 the terms "statutes and judgments" are set alongside "torah" in a way that suggests inclusion or parity.

first part of the book, Deuteronomy 12–26 presents what is clearly a discrete body of stipulations, provisions, and laws. Some of these measures recapitulate materials found in the Book of the Covenant in Exodus, but there is also "new" material, given in Deuteronomy for the first time.[73] So in one sense Deuteronomy represents a renewal of Sinai, but unlike later renewals, it does more than merely confirm older, established stipulations and provisions.

The second covenant in Deuteronomy is taken to be a new divine covenant in which God himself is a covenant partner even though God does not make a "personal appearance" to the people as he did at Sinai. At the same time, Moses acts as an interlocutor, in the fashion of renewal, bringing God and the people together. Both ideas are stated in Deuteronomy 29:10–16 (note added italics), where Moses says:

> You are standing (here) this day, all of you, before the LORD your God—your tribal heads, your elders and your officials, all the men of Israel, your children, your wives, even the stranger within your camp, from your hewer of wood to drawer of water—to enter into the covenant of the LORD your God and into its oath, *which the LORD your God is making with you this day*, so that He may establish you this day as His people and be your God, as He promised you and as He swore to your fathers, Abraham, Isaac, and Jacob. *Not just with you alone do I* [Moses] *make this covenant and this oath*, but both with those who are standing here with us this day before the LORD our God and with those who are not with us here this day.

It is interesting to note that there is no reference to Sinai here. Deuteronomy links itself directly to the patriarchs. This presentation helps to give the second covenant a separate identity, with its own direct link to the foundational patriarchal covenants.

Another important feature related to covenant making appears in Deuteronomy 28:1–68; this is the recitation of blessings and curses that help secure the observance of the covenant by the participants. Their inclusion is not a biblical innovation; they are in fact a well-known part of secular political treaties in the ancient Near East. Blessings are frequently mentioned, but we have not encountered the juxtaposition of blessings and curses in the other biblical covenants that we have reviewed thus far.[74] The blessing section in

---

73. For an interesting reconstruction of this relationship, see Bernard M. Levinson, *Deuteronomy and the Hermeneutics of Legal Innovation* (Oxford: Oxford University Press, 1997).

74. Blessings are mentioned in covenants with Noah (Gen. 9:1), Abraham (12:2; 22:17–18), Isaac (26:3–4), Jacob (35:9), and at Sinai (Exod. 23:25–31). Genesis 12:3 promises blessings and curses upon Abraham's enemies.

Deuteronomy is shorter than the curse section; this is in keeping with what is typical in most of the ancient Near Eastern treaties. Blessings and curses can also be found on royal monuments, protecting them from removal, reuse, or destruction. The blessings (Deut. 28:3–14) deal with well-being at home and in the field, progeny of humans and animals, rainfall and food sufficiency. There is a promise of military victory and security. The curses (28:15–44) deal with the reversal of the blessings, plus physical affliction, suffering crime and abuse at home, military defeat, and exile.

In all covenants divine participation, presence, and retribution are implicit in oath taking.[75] We encounter our earliest examples of the full articulation of both blessings and curses together in the Hittite treaties of the second millennium BCE. These seem to be part of every treaty. Note, for example, the treaty between Muwatalli II of Hatti and Alaksandu of Wilusa:

> If you, Alaksandu, transgress these words of the tablet which stand on this tablet, then these (aforementioned) Thousand Gods shall eradicate you, together with your person, your wife, your sons, your lands, your cities, your vineyard, your threshing floor, your field, your cattle, your sheep, and together with your possessions. They shall eradicate your progeny from the Dark Earth. But if you do observe these words, then these Thousand Gods whom I, My Majesty, Labarna,[76] Muwatalli, Great King, have summoned to assembly—the deities of Hatti, the deities of Wilusa, and the personal Storm-god of Lightning of My Majesty—shall benevolently protect you, together with your wife, your sons, your grandsons, your cities, your threshing floor, your vineyard, your field, your cattle, your sheep, and together with your possessions. You shall thrive in the hand of My Majesty, and you shall live to an old age in the hand of My Majesty.[77]

The blessing themes of person, life, and livelihood are similar to what we see present in Deuteronomy 28:3–6:

> Blessed shall you be in the city, and blessed shall you be in the field. Blessed shall be the fruit of your womb, the fruit of your ground, and the fruit of your livestock, both the increase of your cattle and the issue of your flock. Blessed shall be your basket and your kneading bowl. Blessed shall you be when you come in, and blessed shall you be when you go out. (NRSV)

75. Thus 2 Chron. 6:22–23 describes how God, on hearing an oath, will punish one who swears falsely and reward the one telling the truth.

76. "Labarna" is a royal title, conferring divine approval and legitimacy (see F. Starke, "Labarna," *RlA* 6:404–8).

77. Beckman, *Hittite Diplomatic Texts*, no. 13.92–93. For other examples, see 29, 33, 40–41, 48, 52–53, 58, 64, 68–69, 86, 92–93, 112, 121–22. These are not preserved on all of the treaties but must have been part of the original texts.

The curse section in Deuteronomy is expansive and adds graphic images to the many enumerated misfortunes. These images, as observed by many scholars, find many close parallels in the Neo-Assyrian Succession Treaty of Esarhaddon.[78] Among the striking similarities in images shared by Deuteronomy 28 and the Succession Treaty, note the following examples:[79]

> Deuteronomy 28:23–24: "The sky over your head shall be bronze, and the earth under you iron. The LORD will change the rain of your land into powder, and only dust shall come down upon you from the sky until you are destroyed" (NRSV).
>
> Esarhaddon, lines 528–33: "May they [the gods] make your ground like iron; let nothing sprout from it. Just as rain does not fall from a brazen heaven, so may rain and dew not come upon your fields and your meadows; instead of dew may burning coals rain on your land."
>
> Deuteronomy 28:26: "Your corpses shall be food for every bird of the air and animal of the earth, and there shall be no one to frighten them away" (NRSV).
>
> Esarhaddon, line 425: "May Ninurta, the foremost among the gods, bring you down with his fierce arrow; may he fill the plain with your blood and feed your flesh to the eagle and the vulture."
>
> Deuteronomy 28:27: "The LORD will afflict you with the boils of Egypt, with ulcers, scurvy, and itch, of which you cannot be healed" (NRSV).
>
> Esarhaddon, line 461: "May Gula, the great physician, put sickness and weariness [inside of you], set an unhealing wound in your body. Bathe in [blood and pus] as if in water!"
>
> Deuteronomy 28:29: "You shall grope about at noon as blind people grope in darkness, but you shall be unable to find your way; and you shall be continually abused and robbed, without anyone to help" (NRSV).
>
> Esarhaddon, line 422: "May Šamaš, the light of heaven and earth, not judge you justly. May he remove sight (from) your eyes and (so) walk about in darkness!"

78. Parpola and Watanabe, *Neo-Assyrian Treaties*, 28–58.

79. For more discussion and literature, see Delbert R. Hillers, *Treaty-Curses and the Old Testament Prophets* (BibOr 16; Rome: Pontifical Biblical Institute, 1964), 43–79; McCarthy, *Treaty and Covenant*, 172–82; Jeffrey H. Tigay, *Deuteronomy* (JPSTC; Philadelphia: Jewish Publication Society, 1996), 489–97. There is also a blessing-and-curse section in Lev. 26 with many of the same motifs as in Deut. 28. It seems that these were added in order to set the legal material within the book of Leviticus into a covenantal framework. Leviticus 26:46 concludes, "These are the statutes, judgments, and teachings [*tôrōt*] that the LORD gave out between himself and the Israelite people on Mount Sinai, through the hand of Moses."

Deuteronomy 28:30: "You shall become engaged to a woman, but another man shall lie with her. You shall build a house, but not live in it. You shall plant a vineyard, but not enjoy its fruit" (NRSV).

Esarhaddon, line 428: "May Venus, the brightest of the stars, before your eyes make your wives lie in the lap of your enemy; may your sons not take possession of your house; may a stranger divide your possessions."

Deuteronomy 28:38: "You shall carry much seed into the field but shall gather little in, for the locust shall consume it" (NRSV).

Esarhaddon, lines 442–44: "May the locust who diminishes the land devour your harvest; may the sound of mill or oven be lacking from your houses."

Esarhaddon Succession Treaty

In the Esarhaddon Succession Treaty the list of gods, by whom the oaths were sworn, are presented in their "ranking" according to the theology of the Assyrian king. Thus the list begins with Aššur and his consort Mulissu; these are the national gods of Assyria. They are followed by Anu, Sin, and Šamaš, who represent "sky, moon, and sun." Ninurta, a god of war, follows next in the hierarchy. Gula, whose curse we noted in the main text (see Esarhaddon, line 461), actually comes much later in this list (no. 17); she is a goddess of healing. There are still five more listed after her, and finally unnamed others, "all the great gods of heaven and earth." There is a separate curse associated with every one of the gods in the list; these gods were invoked to witness the swearing of the oath by the vassals and to punish any violations.

However, despite the similarities, it must also be pointed out that these are traditional curse themes and were used in other formulations in treaties and royal monuments from earlier periods as well as appearing in Neo-Assyrian treaties.[80]

The Succession Treaty of Esarhaddon was different from the usual political treaties that we find between heads of state because it explicitly involves the "masses."[81] Esarhaddon here created an elaborate vehicle in order to ensure an

---

80. See the detailed discussions in Markus Zehnder, "Building on Stone? Deuteronomy and Esarhaddon's Loyalty Oaths (Part 1); Some Preliminary Observations," *BBR* 19 (2009): 341–74; idem, "Building on Stone? Deuteronomy and Esarhaddon's Loyalty Oaths (Part 2); Some Additional Observations," *BBR* 19 (2009): 511–36. Zehnder concludes, "On the other hand, this does not exclude in principle the possibility that [the Succession Treaty of Esarhaddon] could have had more limited influence on the text of Deuteronomy at certain points. . . . This is especially true with respect to the curse sections" (534). He nevertheless argues that "the safest conclusion would be that the similarities . . . are the results of dependence on shared literary traditions" (535).

81. We know of treaties made between the overlord involving groups of vassals who took the oath together. From the time of Assurbanipal, we have the Zakutu Treaty and his Treaty with

orderly royal succession after his death and to preserve the large empire that he had achieved. It involved every citizen of the empire. To this end the king "convened the people of Assyria, great and small, from coast to coast, made them swear a treaty oath by the gods and established a binding agreement to protect my crown-princeship and future kingship over Assyria."[82] The large number of coparticipants said to be involved in the Succession Treaty is unusual and, to our knowledge, is matched only by the masses of participants in the biblical covenants of the wilderness and their renewals. But here too, given the limitations of our present historical-archaeological evidence, some scholars question how Esarhaddon could effectively have brought together masses of people rather than selected officials and military officers. Moreover, while the Succession Treaty exists in many copies, the ancient copies found so far come mainly from the eastern periphery of the empire, and the swearing of Esarhaddon's oath of allegiance by the Judean monarchy is as yet undemonstrated.[83]

Renewal of Divine Covenant

Renewal covenants are found only in the Bible. They were organized by a leader of the people who acted as a representative of God, inviting the people to reaffirm obligations deriving from earlier divine covenants. Although we usually assume that these earlier covenants are one or both of the divine covenants made in the wilderness, this linkage is not always clearly stated. In the

---

Babylonian Allies (see Parpola and Watanabe, *Neo-Assyrian Treaties*, 62–68). From an earlier time, see the treaty between Arnuwanda I of Hatti and the Men of Ismerika, in Beckman, *Hittite Diplomatic Texts*, 13–17 (this last treaty is extensively discussed in Joshua Berman, "CTH 133 and the Hittite Provenance of Deuteronomy 13," *JBL* 130 [2011]: 25–44). Beckman (*Hittite Diplomatic Texts*, 7) cites additional examples (mentioned but not treated in his book) listed in Laroche, *Catalogue of Hittite Texts*, CTH 27, 137, 138. From a still earlier time, see the Old Assyrian treaties (Kt. n/k 10 and 794), considered in Günbatti, "Two Treaty Texts." Such "group documents" clearly involved leaders but not the participation of the masses of subjects "great and small," as claimed by Deuteronomy and Assurbanipal. For biblical examples of "group treaties," see my discussion above in the section "Secular Covenants: Political and Group."

82. This is an excerpt from an inscription of Assurbanipal, recounting how Esarhaddon, his father, had arranged for his succession. See Parpola and Watanabe, *Neo-Assyrian Treaties*, xxix. This passage is from vol. 2 of Maximilian Streck, *Assurbanipal und die letzten assyrischen Könige bis zum Untergange Niniveh's* (VAB 7; Leipzig: Hinrichs, 1916), 4, i 11–22, partly cited in *CAD* Š/1 123.

83. This argument is made by Wilfred G. Lambert, review of Hans Ulrich Steymans, *Deuteronomium 28 und die adê zur Thronfolgeregelung Asarhaddons: Segen und Fluch im Alten Orient und in Israel*, *AfO* 44–45 (1997–98): 396–99. It is taken up again in Zehnder, "Building on Stone? Some Additional Observations," 533–35. However, in addition to the known copy from Iraq, a new copy of Esarhaddon's treaty has now been found in Turkey at Tell Tayinat (it is discussed below).

renewals the covenant is made between the people and God, but there is no expectation in the ceremony that God will appear or respond. In this sense, the covenant renewals are somewhat like present-day "religious revivals" or renewals of marriage vows.

The renewal ceremony in Joshua 8:30–35 follows the prescription given in Deuteronomy 27:1–8 for a ceremony, which was to take place after crossing the Jordan River into the promised land. The people were to set up an altar, offer sacrifices, and also cover the stones of the altar with plaster and to write "upon the stones all the words of this torah, explaining them well" (Deut. 27:2, 8). At that time and place, described further as located between the opposing hilltops of Ebal and Gerizim, which overlook Shechem,[84] the people (27:11–13) were to divide themselves into two groups, in recognition of the blessing and the curse, which were to be recited to them by the Levites in a loud voice (27:14). This very ceremony of recitation is also prescribed in Deuter-

Samaritans

Mount Gerizim at Shechem was later the site of a temple built by the Samaritans, who claimed that it was indeed the place chosen by God "to place his name there." That language is repeated many times in Deuteronomy, especially in chapters 12–14, but the name of the site is not given. For the Judeans, it came to mean the temple built by Solomon in Jerusalem and rebuilt again later, after the Babylonian exile. Although the Samaritans shared the Pentateuch with the Judeans, they did not consider any of the other books of the Hebrew Bible as Scripture. The schism between the Samaritans and the Judeans seems to have developed after the exile and even led to actual warfare in the time of the Hasmonean high priest John Hyrcanus. He conquered the northern territory of the Samaritans in 129 BCE and destroyed the temple at Shechem shortly thereafter; the Samaritan temple was never rebuilt. The number of Samaritans has dwindled over the centuries; at present there are small communities of Samaritans still residing at Shechem as well as in the city of Holon, near Tel Aviv, in modern Israel.

onomy 11:26–30. The "blessing and the curse" to be recited would seem to be what follows in Deuteronomy 28. However, the context is interrupted in Deuteronomy 27:15–26 by a series of twelve curses with no corresponding blessings.[85] What is interesting here is the absence of the term "covenant,"

---

84. This is described in Judg. 9:7.

85. The relationship between the curses in Deut. 27:15–26 and the blessings and curses in Deut. 28 is difficult to resolve. There is likewise uncertainty, going back to ancient times, about what was or could have been written upon the plastered stones. See S. R. Driver, *A Critical and Exegetical Commentary on Deuteronomy* (3rd ed.; ICC; 1901; repr., Edinburgh: T&T Clark, 1986), 296–300; Tigay, *Deuteronomy*, 252, 486–88; McCarthy, *Treaties and Covenants*, 194–99.

yet so many covenantal elements are present: sacrifice, recitation of blessings and curses, and the people's response, signifying acceptance. There is also the writing down (Josh. 8:32) of the words of God, as was done after the Sinai covenant in Exodus 24:4.

Retention and public reading of the covenant text often appear as important requirements for the future maintenance of the agreement. In Deuteronomy 31:9–13 Moses writes down "this torah" and commands the priests, sons of Levi, to gather the people and to read it out to them every seven years. In Deuteronomy 31:25–26 Moses also commands the Levites to keep "this inscribed text of the torah and set it beside the ark of the covenant of the LORD your God, and let it be there for you as a witness." Similar measures can be found in some of the ancient Near Eastern treaties. For example, in the treaty between Muwatalli II and Alaksandu, mentioned above, it states, "Furthermore, this tablet which I have made for you, Alaksandu, shall be read out before you three times yearly, and you, Alaksandu, shall know it."[86] Retention in a sacred place is stipulated in a treaty between Suppiluliuma I of Hatti and Shattiwaza of Mittanni: "A duplicate of this tablet is deposited before the Sun-goddess of Arinna, since the Sun-goddess of Arinna governs kingship and queenship. And in the land of Mittanni a duplicate is deposited before the Storm-god, Lord of the *kurinnu* of Kahat. It shall be read repeatedly, for ever and ever, before the king of the land of Mitanni and before the Hurrians."[87]

The text goes on to warn against altering the text of the treaty tablet, hiding it away, or destroying it.[88] The enumerated gods will be witnesses and guarantors of the treaty and will punish the participant who fails to keep the agreement. Similar warnings are found in Neo-Assyrian treaties—for example, "[And one who will] give orders to efface these inscriptions from the temples of the gods wherein they are written." The text goes on to include that if anyone orders someone else "who does not understand" to efface it, "may [he] and his son die in oppressive torment, etc."[89]

---

86. Beckman, *Hittite Diplomatic Texts*, 91. See also in the treaty between Mursili II of Hatti and Kupanta-Kurunta (ibid., 81).

87. Ibid., nos. 6A–B, 46–48, 51. This provision may be compared with the commandment given for a future Israelite king in Deut. 17:18–20.

88. Compare Deut. 13:1 (12:32 ET): "Every word that I command you, you shall be mindful to do it; you shall not add to it or take away from it."

89. Fitzmyer, *Sefire*, 124–25 (II Face C 1–11). Note also Esarhaddon's Succession Treaty, lines 397–409: "whoever changes, disregards, erases . . . You shall guard [this treaty tablet which] is sealed with the seal of Aššur, king of the gods, and set it up in your presence like your own god" (see Parpola and Watanabe, *Neo-Assyrian Treaties*, 44–45). A new copy of the Succession Treaty was found in Turkey in 2009 in a temple at Tell Tayinat. The treaty tablet (TT 1801) was prominently displayed in antiquity within the holy place. For photos and preliminary information, see Timothy P. Harrison, "Tayinat Archaeological Project Annual Reports" for 2009–2010

Another covenant renewal is described in Joshua 24:1–27. With the people "assembled before God," Joshua narrates a lengthy historical prologue (vv. 1–13); we have already noted this as a feature in covenants. Joshua has the people swear fidelity to God, eschewing all other gods (vv. 14–15); the people reply in the affirmative (vv. 16–18). Joshua alludes to punishments awaiting failure to do so (vv. 19–20) and calls on the people to bear witness against future backsliding and to put away any tokens of these gods (vv. 21–23). The people then again affirm their acceptance of these terms, and so "Joshua made a covenant for the people on that day, and he fixed it as 'statute and judgment' in Shechem. And Joshua wrote all these words in a torah of God, and he took a large stone and set it up under the oak tree, which was in the sanctuary of the Lord. And Joshua said to all the people, 'Behold, this stone will be a witness for us because it has heard all the words of the Lord which he spoke with us'" (vv. 24–27). The words spoken by the Lord must, of course, be the words spoken by Joshua in the name of God.

We see in the covenant renewal accounts in Joshua, as mentioned previously in Deuteronomy, how the term "torah" is again being used in a general but indeterminate fashion, leaving open for us, as readers, the question of whether it is being used to describe a subset of the covenant obligations or their totality. Fidelity to the Lord and rejection of other gods is the only obligation or "commandment" that is specified in Joshua 24. In Joshua 8:32, 34 the text content of the torah being spoken and written by Joshua is likewise not specified; the focus there was, of course, on the curses and blessings that supported the covenant. In the perspective of the Hebrew Bible, any and all of God's covenant stipulations, provisions, and so on must be observed. It thus is possible here in Joshua, as well as in later covenant renewals, to use the term "torah" in the broadest fashion.

Covenant renewals were instituted by the Judean kings Asa, Hezekiah, and Josiah. Asa's covenant renewal is presented in 2 Chronicles 15:10–17 and adds little to what we have already seen.[90] Hezekiah's intention for a covenant renewal is mentioned briefly only in 2 Chronicles 29:10; his subsequent actions

---

(http://www.utoronto.ca/tap/). See further Jacob Lauringer, "Some Preliminary Thoughts on the Tablet Collection in Building XVI," *JCSMS* 6 (2011): 5–14. On the temple itself, see Timothy P. Harrison, "Temples, Tablets and the Neo-Assyrian Provincial Capital of Kinalia," *JCSMS* 6 (2011): 29–37; Timothy P. Harrison and James F. Osborne, "Building XVI and the Neo-Assyrian Sacred Precinct at Tell Tayinat," *JCS* 64 (2012): 125–43. The treaty document is fully published in Jacob Lauringer, "Esarhaddon's Succession Treaty at Tell Tayinat: Text and Commentary," *JCS* 64 (2012): 87–123.

90. There is only the barest reference, if any, to a covenant document, but there may be an indirect reference to a curse in 2 Chron. 15:13: "And anyone who will not seek the Lord, the God of Israel, will be made to die, including minor or adult, man or woman."

relate to temple and cult, but there is no further reference to covenant. We have a fuller picture of Josiah's covenant in 2 Kings 23:1–24 (repeated in 2 Chron. 34:1–35:19). Josiah's covenant revolves around the discovery of a text stored in the temple, according to 2 Kings 22:13, describing the great wrath of the Lord that would come upon the people "because our forefathers did not hearken to the words of this book, to act according to all that is written concerning us."[91] These seem to correspond, certainly in content, with the blessings and curses in Deuteronomy 28. After receiving divine verification of the book's authenticity, we are told in 2 Kings 23:2–3:

> The king went up to the house of the Lord, and all the people of Judah, all the inhabitants of Jerusalem with him—priests, prophets, and all the people, from minor to adult; he read in their hearing all the words of the book of the covenant that had been found in the house of the Lord. The king stood upon a pillar[92] and made the covenant before the Lord, to follow after the Lord, to observe his commandments, "sworn testimonies" and his statutes, with total heart and total soul, to fulfill the words of this covenant that were written in this book. And all the people "stood" in the covenant.[93]

Later in the narrative, the book that was found in the temple is referred to as "torah of Moses" or "book of Moses" (2 Kings 23:25; 2 Chron. 35:12). But here too, despite the sweeping language, the resulting focus of the covenant renewal seems to be narrower in scope. In the accounts of Josiah as well as of Hezekiah, the covenant renewal is followed by three actions: the extensive destruction of idols and shrines, the removal of religious practitioners outside the temple, and the revival of the long-neglected observance of the Passover (2 Kings 23:3–24; 2 Chron. 29:11–31:21).[94]

The covenant-renewal ceremony in Jeremiah 34, as we have already noted, is focused on one issue only: release of debt slaves. Likewise of narrow scope is the covenant in Ezra 9–10, which covers only the "sin" of intermarriage. In Ezra 10:2–5 we are told how Ezra was asked to lead the people in making "a covenant with our God to remove all wives and offspring from them, according to the counsel of my lord [v.l. Lord] and of those who tremble at the

---

91. Thus 2 Chron. 34 reports Josiah declaring, "The wrath of the Lord that is poured out on us is great, because our forefathers did not keep the word of the Lord, to act according to all that is written in this book" (v. 21), and the prophetess Huldah replying for God, "I will indeed bring evil upon this place and upon its inhabitants, all the curses that are written in the book that they read before the king of Judah" (v. 24).

92. According to 2 Kings 11:14 this was a ceremonial venue for public appearances.

93. Compare 2 Chron. 34:30–32 for some small but interesting variants.

94. So 2 Chron. 31:1 mentions the destruction of outside shrines; the rest of the content describes activities taking place in the temple at Jerusalem.

commandment of our God; and let it be done according to the torah" (10:3). Intermarriage plus other obligations relating to the observance of the Sabbath and of temple support are the focus of Nehemiah 10. Thus Nehemiah 9:38 tells how the people commissioned a written agreement ('ămānâ) that recorded the names of leading priests, elders, plus

> the rest of the people, the (other) priests, the Levites, the gatekeepers, the singers, the temple servants, and all who separated themselves from the peoples of the lands in (observing) the torah of God—their wives, sons, and daughters, all who know and understand, stand fast with their brethren, their noble leaders, and enter the sworn oath and promise to follow the torah of God, which was given through Moses the servant of God, and to observe and do all the commandments of the LORD our master, and his statutes and judgments. (Neh. 10:28–29)

Nehemiah 10:29 talks about "entering the solemn oath and promise," but no sacrifice is mentioned here; perhaps this expression had also become just a figure of speech.[95]

A "blend" of covenants is described in the narrative about the accession of Jehoash told in 2 Kings 11:1–20 (retold in 2 Chron. 23:1–17). Jehoash was hidden away to protect him from his grandmother Athaliah, who ruled Judah after the death of Ahaziah, father of Jehoash. The priest Jehoiada arranged a coup to unseat Athaliah. He summoned the palace guard, "and he brought them to him in the temple of the LORD, and he made for them a covenant; and he had them swear an oath and (then) showed them the son of the king" (2 Kings 11:4). This covenant was "limited," binding the guards in loyalty to the young king. Shortly thereafter, after increasing the ranks of supporters, Jehoiada arranged a coronation ceremony; he "brought out the king's son, and set the crown on him, and (gave him) the testimony; they made him king and anointed him; they clapped hands and shouted, 'May the king live (long)!'" (2 Kings 11:12).[96] Thus far we appear to have a political covenant, similar to what we have earlier noted in 2 Samuel 5:3: "And the elders of Israel came to the king at Hebron, and King David made a covenant with them in Hebron before the LORD. And they anointed David to be king over Israel."[97]

---

95. In Neh. 5:7–13 Nehemiah gathers the community and leads them in an oath ceremony, pledging relief to debtors in their community, but there is no mention of "covenant" or "torah." For discussion, see Greengus, *Laws in the Bible*, 94–98.

96. Retold in 2 Chron. 23:11. For discussion of this ceremony, see Moshe Weinfeld, *Deuteronomy and the Deuteronomic School* (Oxford: Clarendon, 1972), 85–91.

97. A formal coronation of Solomon is also described in 1 Chron. 29:1–25, but it is not identified as a covenant.

Later, however, after executing Athaliah, Jehoiada convened what appears to be a religious covenant renewal, described in 2 Kings 11:17: "And Jehoiada made a covenant between the LORD and between the king and between the people, to be the LORD's people; [in addition to the covenant] between the king and the people."[98] Following this ceremony, as described both in 2 Kings 11:18 and 2 Chronicles 23:17, the people tore down the temple of Baal, just as they did later in the times of Hezekiah and Josiah.

There are places where the Hebrew Bible speaks of God initiating a renewal of his covenant with the people of Israel. Such action, however, is always described as taking place in a future time. It is possible, as many scholars have done, to read such passages as applying to the resettlement of Judea after the exile under the benign rule of Persia. But in places the poetic images of restoration are so sublime and beyond normal experience that readers of the Bible, from ancient to modern times, have looked beyond the chronological framework of the biblical narratives for their literary intent and purpose. Thus, for example, Micah 4:3–4: "He shall judge between many peoples, and shall arbitrate between strong nations far away; they shall beat their swords into plowshares, and their spears into pruning hooks; nation shall not lift up sword against nation, neither shall they learn war any more; but they shall all sit under their own vines and under their own fig trees, and no one shall make them afraid" (NRSV).[99]

These prophetic passages often speak of God as establishing "a new covenant, an everlasting covenant," and "a covenant of peace."[100] Sometimes they employ motifs of the relationship between husband and wife, which we have already seen in the discussion of personal covenants above, and also that of a close, responsible family member.[101] In Deuteronomy 30:1–10 we see a promise of divine forgiveness and restoration, although the term "covenant" is not specifically mentioned. Yet covenant is implicit in the references to "blessings and curses" that are described as having already befallen the errant people (Deut. 30:1, 7). Deuteronomy 30:6 also expects the people "to love the LORD your God with all your heart and all your soul." To help the errant

---

98. The account in 2 Chron. 23:16 has only the religious covenant renewal: "And Jehoiada made a covenant between himself and the people and the king (affirming them all) to be the people of the LORD." Chronicles elevates the status of the priest, who here is not just a facilitator but also a major covenant participant alongside of the king.

99. See also Isa. 2:2–4; 65:17–25; Dan. 12:1–4.

100. See Jer. 31:31 (new covenant); Isa. 54:10; Ezek. 34:25; 37:26 (covenant of peace); Isa. 61:8; Jer. 32:40; Ezek. 16:60; 37:26 (everlasting covenant).

101. For husband and wife, see Jer. 31:32; 31:34 (perhaps) (cf. Hosea 2:20–22 [21–23 ET]); Isa. 54:6–8; Ezek. 16:59–63. For close relative (i.e., "redeemer"), see Isa. 54:8 (cf. "redeemer" in, e.g., Lev. 25:25; Num. 5:8; Ruth 3:9, 12).

people achieve this, God will "circumcise your hearts and the hearts of your offspring." The use of this figure of speech makes a link back to God's first covenant with Abraham, bringing Israel full circle back to its beginnings.[102] This motif of "love," repeated many times in Deuteronomy, is also found in the ancient Near Eastern treaty traditions as an expression for the expectation of loyalty and friendship between allies.[103] In theological terms, this translates into rejection of other gods, fidelity to the one God of Israel, and keeping the precepts of his covenant.

Implications for Historiography

1. It is clear that covenant is an ancient practice, with deep roots in ancient Near Eastern history. Covenants are attested in sources going back to before the second millennium BCE.

2. We have seen that covenants in the Bible have many features that are analogous to those found in the ancient Near Eastern treaties; these similarities occur both in accompanying rituals and in the texts of the treaties. Features include prior negotiation, introduction of speaker, historical prologue, stipulations, various sacrificial rites (including dismemberment and blood), a shared meal, erecting a stone monument or stela as a memorial, writing stipulations on the stones, preservation of covenant document and its contents, periodic reading of covenant document, blessings and curses.

3. Not all features appear in every treaty, nor do these features appear in any fixed order. Comparisons are complicated by the fact that the Bible also maintains a larger narrative, which describes the events surrounding the making of the covenant as well as reproducing the covenant content itself. We therefore should be hesitant to rely upon the presence or absence of features as an indicator of origin or dating.

4. While the custom of erecting stone monuments as a memorial of a covenant or treaty is ancient and attested outside of the Bible, the writing down of the treaty or covenant stipulations on the stone monument is known only from Neo-Assyrian times. At the same time, the practice of writing down laws upon stone monuments is attested earlier, and the

---

102. In Deut. 10:16 and Jer. 4:4, God urges the people to accomplish this on their own; God's action in Deut. 30:6 acknowledges their human frailty. Note also that God replaces their "heart of stone" (Ezek. 11:19; 36:26), urges "a new heart and new spirit" (Ezek. 18:31), and bestows a "pure heart and upright spirit" (Ps. 51:10).

103. See Heintz, "'Dans la plénitude du coeur'"; Weinfeld, *Deuteronomy*, 81–85, 334–35. See also *CAD* G 38 (s.v. *libbu gamru*); Eidem, *Royal Archives*, 331–32, where, in treaties, one finds the expression "negotiating with whole heart."

divine covenant stipulations in the Bible include a substantial body of legal formulations.[104]

5. Divine covenants between gods and individuals are rare in the ancient Near East; they clearly exist in the Neo-Assyrian period, yet one cannot rule out their existence in earlier times, especially in view of the elevated role of kings in the ancient Near East and the well-attested role ascribed to deities in watching over their birth, nurture, and career.[105]

6. Divine covenants with a people or a group are known in the ancient Near East. However, covenants involving the masses of people as partners are seen only in the Bible (Sinai, Deuteronomy, and later renewals); mass participation was also anciently claimed for the Succession Treaty of Esarhaddon.

7. There are strong similarities between the formulation of the curses listed in Deuteronomy and Leviticus and the curses in the Succession Treaty of Esarhaddon. These are, nevertheless, variations out of a larger and older tradition.

8. Rituals are definitely part of covenant and treaty making, but they are not at its center; primary focus is on the obligations agreed on between the parties and the oaths that were sworn. In ancient Near Eastern treaties these oaths were sworn by many gods, but in biblical covenants only by the one God of Israel.

9. Covenants with Noah and patriarchs have fewer stated obligations than the covenants of Sinai and Deuteronomy. A narrow focus seems also to be the case in many of the covenant renewals.

104. For laws inscribed on stone monuments in Old Babylonian and Old Assyrian contexts, see *CAD* N/1 364–65; G. R. Driver and John C. Miles, *The Babylonian Laws* (corrected ed. with additions; 2 vols.; Aalen: Scientia Verlag, 1975), 1:28–29. For Lipit-Ištar, in the Ur III period, see the statement in the epilogue to his laws, xxi, 49–60 (Martha T. Roth, *Law Collections from Mesopotamia and Asia Minor* [ed. Piotr Machalowski; SBLWAW 6; Atlanta: Scholars Press, 1997], 34). See further Kitchen, "Fall and Rise of Covenant," 124–33; idem, *On the Reliability of the Old Testament*, 283–89. Kitchen argues for a "confluence of law and treaty" and points in addition to the presence of blessings and curses on these monuments. But these are added to protect the monument itself, not the laws written upon it, which are upheld by royal authority and divine oversight of justice.

105. See Gösta W. Ahlström, "Administration of the State in Canaan and Ancient Israel," *CANE* 1:590–91; Greengus, "Legal and Social Institutions," 470–71; Henri Frankfort, *Kingship and the Gods: A Study of Ancient Near Eastern Religion as the Integration of Society and Nature* (OIE; Chicago: University of Chicago Press, 1978), 237–43.

4

Early Israel and Its Appearance in Canaan

Lawson G. Stone

Disagreement swirls around how we describe the process by which a community calling itself "Israel" came to live in the region of the southern Levant loosely designated as "Canaan." Early on, scholars such as William F. Albright unhesitatingly called it the "conquest."[1] Doubts about the accuracy of that description led others to refer to the peaceful infiltration of Israelite seminomads from Transjordan, or a "settlement."[2] Then, doubting that the Israelites ever lived outside of Canaan, scholars began envisioning preexisting elements in the land congealing into a new group, "Israel." Some characterized the process as a social revolution.[3] Others appealed to models of social evolution, part of the rhythm of settlement shift in the Levant, or the cyclic movement

---

1. William F. Albright, "The Israelite Conquest in the Light of Archaeology," *BASOR* 74 (1939): 11–23.
2. Albrecht Alt, "The Settlement of the Israelite Tribes in Palestine," in *Essays on Old Testament History and Religion* (trans. R. A. Wilson; New York: Doubleday, 1967 [German original, 1925]), 173–221.
3. George Mendenhall, "The Hebrew Conquest of Palestine," *BA* 25 (1962): 66–87; idem, *The Tenth Generation: The Origins of the Biblical Tradition* (Baltimore: Johns Hopkins University Press, 1985); Norman K. Gottwald, *The Tribes of Yahweh: A Sociology of the Religion of Liberated Israel, 1250–1050 B.C.E.* (Maryknoll, NY: Orbis Books, 1979).

Canaanites
The terms "Canaan" and "Canaanite" appear 160 times in the Old Testament, the preponderance of them in Genesis through Judges. In general, the geographical term denotes the traditional boundaries of the promised land, from a line between the southern tip of the Dead Sea to the "Brook of Egypt" (i.e., the Wadi al ʿArish) to as far north as the city of Dan (cf. Josh. 15:2–5; 19:24–31). One would expect the term "Canaanite" to denote anyone living in this region, but such is not the case. As named in the Bible, the occupants of "Cannaan" are diverse, including Amorites, Perizzites, Hivites, Jebusites, and, of course, Canaanites. "Canaanite" in the Old Testament denotes someone in Canaan who represents the polytheistic culture that the Hebrews sought to replace with a culture oriented around devotion to the one God, Yahweh, and obedience to his covenant. Thus a "Canaanite" such as Rahab can be assimilated into Israel and not be treated to the fate decreed for Canaanites during the conquest.
The terms "Canaan, Canaanite" appear in extrabiblical texts spanning upper Mesopotamia, Syria, Ugarit, and Egypt from the 1700s BCE through the Iron Age I. The New Kingdom pharaohs of Egypt used "Canaan" to denote their province in the southern Levant. The ruler of Mitanni addressed a letter to the "kings of the

between pastoralism and agriculture.[4] As scholars became doubtful about describing with certainty how elements of the indigenous Canaanite population formed a community defined by ethnic ties that repudiated important elements of the religion and culture of Late Bronze Age (LBA) Canaan, the term "emergence" became popular, as if Israel arose by spontaneous generation out of the primordial ethnic soup of LBA Canaan.[5] This chapter's title uses "appearance" as the operative word, which might imply a kind of ex nihilo generation of Israel in the early Iron Age I (IA1), or could simply express a neutral stance about the process.

The shifting of terms itself betrays the shifting currents in Old Testament scholarship. Here I sketch an understanding of how Israel became constituted in the land of Canaan, with its own coherent identity and self-differentiation

4. For the hypothesis of a settlement shift, see Philip R. Davies, *In Search of "Ancient Israel"* (JSOTSup 148; Sheffield: Sheffield Academic Press, 1992). For the alternation between pastoralism and agriculture, see Israel Finkelstein, *The Archaeology of the Israelite Settlement* (trans. D. Saltz; Jerusalem: Israel Exploration Society, 1988).

5. See Robert B. Coote and Keith W. Whitelam, *The Emergence of Early Israel in Historical Perspective* (2nd ed.; SWBA 5; Sheffield: Almond, 1987); Israel Finkelstein, "The Emergence of Israel in Canaan: Consensus, Mainstream and Dispute," *SJOT* 5, no. 2 (1991): 47–59; Volkmar Fritz, *The Emergence of Israel in the 12th and 11th Centuries BCE* (trans. James W. Barker; SBLBES 2; Leiden: Brill, 2011) (the original German title [1996] employed *Entstehung*).

land of Canaan," though the Egyptians refrained from calling the city rulers of its province "kings." This may explain the book of Joshua's preference for "king" in denoting the rulers of Canaanite cities as a specimen of anti-Egyptian polemic. Whatever the complexities of interpreting the evidence, the biblical material and the ancient Near Eastern textual data overlap significantly, with the main bulk of occurrences appearing in biblical materials that take their ostensible, temporal horizon in the Late Bronze Age/Iron Age I, however much later they might have been redacted.

Archaeologically, a reasonably consistent material culture unites the regions designated "Canaan" in extrabiblical (especially Egyptian) texts. However, it does not appear to point to a single ethnic group, but rather a population consisting of many ethnic identities subsumed under a city-state system dominated by New Kingdom Egypt. Thus the biblical recognition that many different "nations" lived in "Canaan" touches on a vital fact. This diversity naturally would arise from Canaan as a crossroads and bottleneck for the major trade routes. As such, Late Bronze Age Canaan became the object of imperial exploitation, opportunistic occupation, and overt colonization. As the regional empires of the Late Bronze Age splintered and collapsed in the thirteenth century, Canaan experienced increasing instability and violence. This led to the emergence of the Israelite state in the Iron Age.

from neighboring or competing groups, possessing its own social structure and advancing its own territorial claims. In doing so, the appeal of William Dever for a dialogue between the two discourses of biblical studies and archaeology, broadly understood, figures strongly.[6] This chapter begins with the biblical narrative because many scholars argue that the very nature of the biblical materials forces the question of how, or whether, they should play any role in a historical reconstruction. A review and summary of extrabiblical data, both documentary and material, provides a context for defining parameters to shape a proposal regarding Israel's appearance in Canaan. A comprehensive proposal would need to explain not only how an ethnic group calling itself "Israel" came to claim possession of Canaan and evolve into a monarchic state that would last for centuries but also how it ultimately produced the Hebrew Scriptures and birthed three world religions. Such a proposal would also tax even extended monographic treatment.[7] Here the issues can only be

6. William G. Dever, *What Did the Biblical Writers Know, and When Did They Know It? What Archaeology Can Tell Us about the Reality of Ancient Israel* (Grand Rapids: Eerdmans, 2001), 53–95.

7. An even-handed review of the options in an article-length presentation appears in Richard S. Hess, "Early Israel in Canaan: A Survey of Recent Evidence and Interpretations," *Palestine Exploration Quarterly* 126 (1993): 125–42; repr. in *Israel's Past in Present Research: Essays on*

introduced and set in context, citing the most prominent or pertinent scholarly literature. The assessment of the various models used in trying to integrate the data ultimately poses the question of whether only an analysis of factors and forces is possible, or whether a linear narrative, however modest, can be constructed—that is, whether Israel's appearance, from a scholarly perspective, has a story.

The Biblical Material

Traditionally, scholars have observed that the biblical material itself offers diverse perspectives on the process by which Israel gained possession of portions of Canaan.[8] Joshua 1–12 is typically cited as presenting a blitzkrieg-like "conquest" in which Israel invades Canaan, rapidly destroys many cities and towns, and slaughters their populations, thus wresting the land from its native inhabitants in order to possess and settle it. Following on the heels of that story, Joshua 13–24 frankly and without censure admits that much territory did not fall into Israel's hands and constituted an ongoing challenge (see fig. 4.1). Judges 1:1–2:11 recapitulates the partial settlement, repeating, with minor alterations, passages from Joshua 13–24 verbatim. However, it locates the time frame as "after the death of Joshua." Further, Judges 1:1–2:11 evaluates this partial conquest as faithlessness and thus draws rebuke from the angel of Yahweh (2:1–5). The possession of Canaan in Judges is seen as gradual, as largely unsuccessful, and ultimately as incomplete. The portrayal in Judges also recognizes the shifting of some tribes from their original settlement areas, recounting the migration of the tribe of Dan from its original location in the Shephelah up to the city of Laish in the far north (Judg. 18). Judges 2:20–3:6 offers several interpretations of this partial settlement, ranging from seeing it as a failure in and of itself, to analyzing the failure as a judgment on Israel for other sins, such as idolatry. This same pericope also attributes the Canaanite remnant to Yahweh's desire to test Israel's faithfulness or, alternatively, as a needed education for each generation to learn war. The biblical authors had no problem with diverse interpretations of the same state of affairs. In addition, Numbers 13–14 implies an unsuccessful attempted entry into Canaan

---

Ancient Israelite Historiography (ed. V. Philips Long; SBTS 7; Winona Lake, IN: Eisenbrauns, 1999), 492–518. Monographic treatments are represented by Fritz, *Emergence of Israel*; William G. Dever, *Who Were the Early Israelites, and Where Did They Come From?* (Grand Rapids: Eerdmans, 2003); Ralph K. Hawkins, *How Israel Became a People* (Nashville: Abingdon, 2013). Of the three monographs, Hawkins's is the most systematic and accessible.

8. For the standard critical analysis of the relevant biblical materials, see Fritz, *Emergence of Israel*, 1–66.

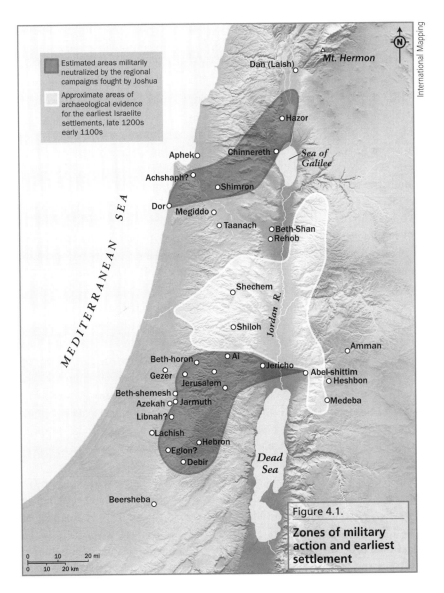

Figure 4.1.

Zones of military action and earliest settlement

from the south, one that conceivably could have resulted in a few Israelite communities in the wadi systems around Beersheba or Arad.

The diversity manifest in the biblical materials raises a caution about sweeping generalizations regarding its historical character. Even recognizing that the materials have been edited from a Deuteronomistic perspective, the presence of so many sharp differences in presentation and perspective precludes ascribing to the Bible a monolithic view of Israel's appearance in Canaan.

Likewise, such diversity, and the difficulties of harmonization that it creates, resists characterizing the biblical account as propagandistic fabrication. This is because the dominant note of the propaganda becomes hard to discern amid the competing voices in the text. However, the diversity of viewpoints has led scholars to hypothesize a complex process of composition behind the text, reaching back centuries before the material's canonical form. The dominant view sees in Joshua-Judges the activity of compilers and editors of the Deuteronomistic school(s), who sought to present the early history of Israel as an extended case study of its religious and political outlook. The presence of multiple editorial layers, the lateness of the final form of the text, and the presence of an explicit point of view—all these have led scholars to question the biblical material's historiographic pertinence. Such a "rewritten Bible" might incidentally preserve historical information, but like a stopped clock that is nevertheless right twice a day, it cannot be relied upon consistently. Skepticism is inspired by the axiom of Julius Wellhausen and nineteenth-century critics that a text is evidence not for the era it narrates but rather for the era of its composition. In addition, some scholars have argued that the biblical materials employed literary genres that did not aspire to be historical reports in the modern sense but instead served purposes of symbolic social, religious, and political advocacy. Therefore, their very nature cancels out their trustworthiness as consistent guides to ancient realities. Consequently, when a historian asserts that a particular archaeological find seems to support the historical claims of the biblical text, the increasingly common reply is that the text makes no such historical claims. Thus there is nothing to be supported or confirmed in the first place, rendering the confluence between archaeology and the text merely coincidental.

But are matters so clear? As H. G. M. Williamson has asked, "Can we safely ignore the Bible?"[9] To be sure, questions must be asked when the matter of "rewritten" texts arises. On the surface, the text produced by the proposed redactional processes evinces great ideological diversity, which is how those redactional processes were discerned in the first place. Additionally, hypotheses of scribes and editors redacting the biblical text remain projections based on models that are partly grounded in empirical evidence, but that also remain strongly speculative in nature. Again, the glory of contemporary biblical criticism is its diversity. Theories explaining the emergence of the Deuteronomistic History (Deuteronomy + Joshua + Judges + Samuel + Kings) range widely

---

9. H. G. M. Williamson, "The Origins of Israel: Can We Safely Ignore the Bible?," in *The Origin of Early Israel—Current Debate: Biblical, Historical, and Archaeological Perspectives; Irene Levi-Sala Seminar, 1997* (ed. Shmuel Ahituv and Eliezer D. Oren; Beer-Sheva: Ben-Gurion University of the Negev Press, 1998), 141–51.

as to the number of revisions discerned, the perspectives of the ancient editors, and the settings in which they worked. Does Joshua contain extensions of pentateuchal sources, or is it wholly of Deuteronomistic composition? Is Joshua a unified exilic composition with postexilic supplementation, or did some form of the book exist earlier? Or was it wholly the result of postexilic scribal activity? Must we remain tied to hypotheses positing Deuteronomistic redaction at all? Proponents of all these positions are easily found. This critical discord certainly complicates naively treating these texts as direct historical testimony, but all the same, insufficient warrant exists for excluding, a priori, the possibility that the texts convey substantial perceptions of the period they describe. This diversity of models does not invalidate the practice of criticism, but it does caution the historian to see them in heuristic rather than in exclusionary functions.

An analogy from archaeology provides a warning. Archaeological tells are composed of layer upon layer of the debris of human occupation. Many feet and dozens of layers below the surface, one finds Early Bronze Age remains, with material from as late as the medieval or even modern eras on top. Nevertheless, archaeologists know that a scrupulous survey of the surface will turn up material from all the periods contained in the mound, typically roughly proportional to the scope of occupation for the respective periods buried below. The earlier material has a way of percolating to the top so that the surface debris, though many centuries later than the lowest levels and the result of complex processes of soil displacement, still discloses to the discerning excavator much of what lies beneath. Textual material is even more likely, on the "surface," to preserve ancient testimony simply because however much earlier traditions might be reframed and recontextualized, they are also reused and re-presented rather than being wholly obliterated. The popular term "rewritten Bible" creates a false impression of the nature of the process. As a result, the surface level of the text still offers the discerning reader significant insight into earlier testimony and certainly leaves open the need to explore carefully potential connections between the text and archaeological findings from its putative historical world. However venerable the models of the texts' compositional history, dating, and genre may be, their speculative nature demands that the critical reader be prepared to revise them, perhaps drastically, in light of unanticipated connections between the texts and archaeological findings. Thus the famous axiom of nineteenth-century scholarship that a text provides evidence not of the period it narrates but only of the period in which it was written represents a simplistic reductionism.

What about the literary genres employed in the texts? The fact that they are "not historical" in the modern sense is rather meaningless, since almost no texts produced in the Bronze and Iron Ages can be said to be "historical" in the modern sense. Yet historians still work with the Neo-Assyrian royal inscriptions even though they are a literary genre known to be transparently propagandistic and known as well to have been redacted (rewritten) many times. Egyptian inscriptions, though written to serve principally as celebrative proclamations of the divine pharaoh's glory, still serve historians seeking to write a history of ancient Egypt.[10] Scholars of the works of Homer have long noticed how the later form of his epics and their nature as transmitted narratives did not prevent them from conveying important historical information.[11] For example, the second prize in the funeral games of Patroclus, coming right after "women sashed and lovely," was a large plug of pig iron (*Iliad* 23.260). This prize is hard to imagine as drawing a crowd in the mid- to late first millennium BCE, when Homer wrote. However, it fits in the early Iron Age. As Baruch Halpern has demonstrated in his scrupulously critical siftings of several texts from the Historical Books, discerning critical interpretation will grasp both the antiquarian seriousness and the political and religious intentions of the ancient writers, all the while weighing the literary artifice employed by the narrators.[12] More to the point, Koert van Bekkum has analyzed Joshua 9–11 with a view to exploring the extent to which the "monologues" of text and artifact may be related one to another. These form a true dialogue in which, with both voices competently heard, "there is no considerable distance between story and history."[13] This is simply the job of the historian of ancient civilizations. Even given the difficulties, the complete exclusion of the Bible from attempts to describe Israel's appearance in Canaan seems to be an extreme and misplaced use, even an abuse, of critical scholarship. To echo Williamson, we are indeed not safe to ignore the Bible, especially since it remains the only extended textual account of Israel's origins of any kind.

Examining the role of the Bible in historical reconstruction requires discerning that in each instance the scholar is comparing interpretations. Exegesis of the Bible is compared to inferences drawn from the limited results of excavation.

10. See Kenneth A. Kitchen, "The Victories of Merneptah, and the Nature of Their Record," *JSOT* 28 (2004): 259–72.

11. See Edwin M. Yamauchi, "Historic Homer," *BAR* 33, no. 2 (2007), 28–37, 76. See also, more modestly, Trevor Bryce, *The Kingdom of the Hittites* (Oxford: Oxford University Press, 2005), 357–71, which is in the spirit of the dated but still useful treatment by G. S. Kirk, "The Homeric Poems as History," in *The Middle East and the Aegean Region, c. 1380–1000 BC* (vol. 2.2 of *The Cambridge Ancient History*; 3rd ed.; Cambridge: Cambridge University Press, 1975), 820–50.

12. Baruch Halpern, *The First Historians: The Hebrew Bible and History* (San Francisco: Harper & Row, 1988), esp. 266–80.

13. Koert van Bekkum, *From Conquest to Coexistence: Ideology and Antiquarian Intent in the Historiography of Israel's Settlement in Canaan* (CHANE 45; Leiden: Brill, 2011), 592.

As noted above, the biblical texts themselves reveal a more complex account of Israel's arrival in Canaan than usually is admitted. It shows that the standard picture often is a caricature. The first casualty of the critical sifting of the biblical presentation is its distinctive chronological structure. At the least this embraces the era from the exodus to the dedication of the temple, though connections both earlier and later also appear. This chronology can neither be followed with slavish literalism nor rejected as entirely fanciful, precisely due to the complexity of the genres and compositional processes lying behind them. These data bear summary and consideration.

Following the exodus, Israel sojourned in the wilderness forty years, during which time, the text claims, everyone over the age of twenty died except for Joshua and Caleb. By implication, these two men were older than twenty; hence, their survival is a divinely granted exception. In Joshua 14:6–12 Caleb declares that forty-five years have passed since that time, implying that the narrative in Joshua 1–14 spans, nominally, five years. The time covered in Joshua 15–24 is not stated, but the text says that Joshua died at the age of 110 (Josh. 24:29). This number is conspicuous for being the same age that Joseph attained when he died, and for being ten years less than Moses's age at his death. In addition, interpreters note that 110 years was an Egyptian typological number for a full life. Therefore, this number might not imply an absolute chronology.[14] The text nowhere indicates when Joshua was born or his age when Yahweh decreed the death of the exodus generation; thus Joshua's age at the beginning of the conquest remains an estimate. The canonical narrative places him no younger than twenty when the spies went out and so at least sixty at the beginning of the Joshua narrative, sixty-five at the point of Caleb's request, leaving forty-five more years until Joshua's death, if the figure of 110 functions literally. Though fraught with interpretive hazards and imprecisions, this information is necessary to any attempt to conceptualize and evaluate how the material understands the time frame of its story.

The sole outlier in the chronology of the conquest narrative remains the reference to the Philistine pentapolis in Joshua 13:2–3. This implicitly places the advanced old age of Joshua at a time after the establishment of the Philistines in these cities, taken normally as around 1175 BCE. This text alone in the conquest tradition speaks of the Philistines, whose absence from the rest of the Joshua narrative is conspicuous if the text in fact was substantially composed at a later time when the Philistines stood as the literary and cultural foil for highlighting Israel's distinct identity.

14. Discussions of this point all depend on Jozef M. A. Janssen, "On the Ideal Lifetime of the Egyptians," *OMROL* 31 (1950): 33–41.

However provisional, connections between this internal chronological scheme and events in external history challenge the interpreter's discernment. The famous notation in 1 Kings 6:1 that the temple dedication occurred 480 years after the exodus has led, with the helpful synchronism establishing the temple dedication in 966 BCE, to the claim for "the biblical date" of the exodus at 1446 BCE. The figure of 480 years, however, seems suspiciously round and typologically pregnant, reminiscent of the *Distanzangaben* of other ancient Near Eastern texts.[15] In addition, carefully compiling the chronological notes between the exodus and 1 Kings 6:1, allowing for overlapping where indicated, produces a total of over 557 years, plus at least two periods of unknown duration. Another, possibly more fruitful starting point is the note in Exodus 12:40–41 that the exodus took place 430 years after Jacob entered Egypt. If this occurred under the Hyksos, which is a reasonable assumption, it would date his entry to the late 1700s BCE and yield an exodus in the early thirteenth century BCE. A converging line of reasoning would date the destruction of Hazor by fire, if attributed to Israel (per Josh. 11), via an Egyptian inscription from Hazor to the 1230s BCE.[16] Allowing five years for the events of Joshua 1–14 (cf. Josh. 14:6–12) places entry into the land at about 1240–1235 BCE. Taking forty years of wilderness wandering at face value places the exodus at about 1280–1275 BCE, converging with the date estimated on the basis of Exodus 12:40–41. The Egyptian pharaoh Merneptah campaigned in Canaan, and in an inscription datable to the last decade of the thirteenth century BCE, he claims to have annihilated "Israel."[17] Again, allowing enough time for Israel to settle in the land and perhaps even to begin losing its grip, and allowing for the forty years in the wilderness, returns one to the early thirteenth century BCE for the exodus.

Following Merneptah, Egyptian control over Canaan deteriorated as Egypt came into increasing conflict with the Sea Peoples, among whom were the Philistines, who ultimately settled the southern coast of Canaan around 1175 BCE.[18] Shortly afterward, Egypt made one final attempt to regain its

15. For the idea of *Distanzangaben*, or stereotypical periods employed in ancient chronologies, see Julian Reade, "Assyrian Kinglists, the Royal Tombs of Ur, and Indus Origins," *JNES* 60 (2001): 1–29.

16. Kenneth A. Kitchen, "An Egyptian Inscribed Fragment from Late Bronze Hazor," *IEJ* 53 (2003): 20–28. The alternative attempt to link the destruction of Hazor to Judg. 4–5 fails primarily because a close reading of Judg. 4–5 cannot support any claim for Deborah and Barak carrying the battle north to Hazor. For summary and literature, see Lawson G. Stone, *Joshua, Judges, Ruth* (ed. Philip W. Comfort; CorBC 3; Carol Stream, IL: Tyndale, 2012), 250–53; Hawkins, *How Israel Became a People*, 113–15.

17. James K. Hoffmeier, "The (Israel) Stela of Merneptah," *COS* 2:6.40–41.

18. Itamar Singer, "Egyptians, Canaanites, and Philistines in the Period of the Emergence of Israel," in *From Nomadism to Monarchy: Archaeological and Historical Aspects of Early Israel* (ed. Israel Finkelstein and Nadav Na'aman; Jerusalem: Israel Exploration Society, 1994), 282–338;

hold on Canaan and, on its failure, withdrew abruptly in about 1150 BCE. The arrival of the Philistines and the reference to the Philistine pentapolis in Joshua 13:2–3 constitute the one anachronism in the chronology sketched above and based on the biblical materials. Closer inspection of the passage suggests that it could be an interpolation or even an explanatory gloss by a later editor. The peculiar note about Ekron being "counted as Canaanite" suggests perhaps both a recollection of the towns as Canaanite and the recognition of their later identity as Philistine. Merneptah's notice at the end of the thirteenth century and the death of Joshua around 1190 BCE could then mark the transition from Israel's "appearance" in Canaan to the process of its expansion and social definition, which continued all the way up to the formation of the state at the end of the IA1.

The reasonable, if not exact, connections between the admittedly difficult biblical chronological framework and the admittedly tentative connections with external history yield a chronological structure firm enough to be testable but not sufficiently exact to justify dogmatism. On this scheme, the exodus occurred around the beginning of the reign of Ramesses II, who came to the throne in about 1279 BCE, possibly shortly before his famous campaign at Kadesh (ca. 1274 BCE). In his eighth regnal year (1271) Ramesses seems to have found it necessary to traverse the Sinai and maneuver in force in the Transjordan, including action in Edom and Moab up to the area of Jericho. This would place Ramesses in the vicinity of the wilderness wandering of the Israelites after the exodus.[19] Israel's "appearance" in Canaan would have occurred around 1240–1230 BCE. Just as Merneptah's assault on Israel demarcates roughly the end of the period of Israel's "appearance" in Canaan, with the arrival of the Philistines, crises now begin to arise around Israel's need to consolidate and expand through the rest of the IA1. The campaign of Merneptah in 1209, notwithstanding his exaggerations, would have represented a major setback to the tribes seeking to consolidate their hold. The additional arrival of the Philistines (ca. 1175 BCE) would set the stage for the crisis that would catalyze Israel's full state formation. Despite its vulnerabilities, this provisional framework, seeing the period around 1240–1175 BCE as the era of Israel's appearance in Canaan, seems workable.

Lawrence Stager, "Biblical Philistines: A Hellenistic Literary Creation?" in *"I Will Speak the Riddles of Ancient Times": Archaeological and Historical Studies in Honor of Amihai Mazar* (ed. Aren Maeir et al.; Winona Lake, IN: Eisenbrauns, 2006), 2:285–374.

19. See Kenneth A. Kitchen, "Some New Light on the Asiatic Wars of Ramesses II," *JEA* 50 (1964): 47–70. Debate continues, of course, as to the nature of "Moab" at this time as scholars continue to struggle with this very fragmentary text.

The Extrabiblical Evidence

Having noted the general thrust of the biblical material, the methodological issues deriving from the compositional dynamics that produced the biblical text, and the peculiar nature of the chronological data for the Israelite settlement in Canaan, we now must attend to the historical-cultural horizon within which the settlement occurred. Discussions of Israelite origins often fuse this issue with the question of Israel's social structure and expansion in Canaan through the IA1. They essentially dissolve the "conquest" and the "period of the judges" into one historical frame and posit a single phenomenon of Israel's settlement. That the biblical writers distinguish Israel's establishment in the land from its later crises of consolidation bears notice and corresponds as well to a striking feature of the region's history.

The LBA/IA1 Transition: The Perfect Storm

The most conspicuous result of the foregoing chronological analysis is the position of Israel's appearance in Canaan at the LBA/IA1 transition, which stands exactly between the proposed era of the conquest and the period of Israel's tribal community. A significant amount of biblical material, from the career of Moses to the death of Saul, takes the end of the LBA and the following IA1 as its narrative world. Studies of Israel's emergence in Canaan at the LBA/IA1 transition often note the social disarray of Canaan but fail to place it in the context of the larger, dramatic changes occurring in the entire eastern Mediterranean region.[20] The Bronze Age made a messy exit from the stage of history in what has been called "arguably the worst disaster in ancient history, even more calamitous than the collapse of the western Roman Empire."[21] Many urban centers from Mycenae to Emar and as far south as

20. The most important treatments of the general transition include William A. Ward and Martha Sharp Joukowsky, eds., *The Crisis Years: The 12th Century B.C.; From beyond the Danube to the Tigris* (Dubuque, IA: Kendall/Hunt, 1989); Mario Liverani, *Prestige and Interest: International Relations in the Near East ca. 1600–1100 BC* (SHANE 1; Padova: Sargon, 1990); Robert Drews, *The End of the Bronze Age: Changes in Warfare and the Catastrophe ca. 1200 B.C.* (Princeton: Princeton University Press, 1993); Seymour Gitin with Amihai Mazar and Ephraim Stern, eds., *Mediterranean Peoples in Transition: Thirteenth to Early Tenth Centuries BCE; In Honor of Professor Trude Dothan* (Jerusalem: Israel Exploration Society, 1998); Oliver Dickinson, *The Aegean from Bronze Age to Iron Age: Continuity and Change between the Twelfth and Eighth Centuries BC* (London: Routledge, 2007); Marc Van de Mieroop, *The Eastern Mediterranean in the Age of Ramesses II* (Oxford: Blackwell, 2007); Christoph Bachhuber and R. Gareth Roberts, eds., *Forces of Transformation: The End of the Bronze Age in the Mediterranean; Proceedings of an International Symposium Held at St. John's College, University of Oxford, 25–26th March, 2006* (TANE 1; Oxford: Oxbow, 2010); Eric Cline, *1177 B.C.: The Year Civilization Collapsed* (Princeton: Princeton University Press, 2014).
21. Drews, *End of the Bronze Age*, 3.

Gaza fell in flames.[22] The Mycenaean palace culture disintegrated, Troy fell, the Hittite Empire vaporized, Ugarit and Cyprus collapsed, Emar burned, and farther east the once-vibrant Assyrian power contracted sharply while the last Kassite king of Babylon fled to Susa. Egypt emerged least damaged but soon saw its control of Canaan evaporate.[23] The level of disruption varied, with the northern Levant recovering most rapidly as the "neo-Hittite" kingdoms took root in surviving or newly reoccupied sites.[24] Still, historians rightly term this transition "the catastrophe" or "the great collapse."[25] The decades on either

22. Jonathan N. Tubb, ed., *Palestine in the Bronze and Iron Ages: Papers in Honour of Olga Tufnell* (ULIAOP 11; London: University of London Institute of Archaeology, 1985); W. H. Stiebing, *Out of the Desert? Archaeology and the Exodus/Conquest Narratives* (Buffalo, NY: Prometheus Books, 1989); Ahimai Mazar, *Archaeology of the Land of the Bible: 10,000–586 B.C.E.* (ABRL; New York: Doubleday, 1990), 295–367; Michael G. Hasel, *Domination and Resistance: Egyptian Military Activity in the Southern Levant, ca. 1300–1185 B.C.* (PÄ 11; Leiden: Brill, 1998); Ann E. Killebrew, *Biblical Peoples and Ethnicity: An Archaeological Study of Egyptians, Canaanites, Philistines, and Early Israel, 1300–1100 BCE* (SBLABS 9; Atlanta: Society of Biblical Literature, 2005); Lester L. Grabbe, ed., *The Archaeology* (vol. 1 of *Israel in Transition: From Late Bronze II to Iron IIA [c. 1250–850 BCE]*; LHBOTS 491; London: T&T Clark, 2008); Paul Collins, *From Babylon to Egypt: The International Age, 1550–500 BC* (Cambridge, MA; London: Harvard University Press, 2008).

23. James Weinstein, "The Collapse of the Egyptian Empire in the Southern Levant," in Ward and Joukowsky, *Crisis Years*, 142–50; Singer, "Egyptians, Canaanites, and Philistines." Egyptian withdrawal from Canaan did not plunge Egypt into an immediate crisis but did stall its imperial aspirations. See Leonard H. Lesko, "Egypt in the 12th Century," in Ward and Joukowsky, *Crisis Years*, 151–56.

24. Matters seem less dire in northern Mesopotamia, suggesting, if not a "dark age," perhaps a "dusky" one. See Mario Liverani, "The Collapse of the Near Eastern Regional System at the End of the Bronze Age: The Case of Syria," in *Centre and Periphery in the Ancient World* (ed. Michael Rowlands, Mogens Larsen, and Kristian Kristiansen; NDA; Cambridge: Cambridge University Press, 1987). K. Lawson Younger Jr., "The Late Bronze/Iron Age Transition and the Origins of the Arameans," in *Ugarit at Seventy-Five: Proceedings of the Symposium "Ugarit at Seventy-Five," Held at Trinity International University, Deerfield, Illinois, February 18–20, 2005, under the Auspices of the Middle Western Branch of the American Oriental Society and the Mid-West Region of the Society of the Biblical Literature* (ed. K. Lawson Younger Jr.; Winona Lake, IN: Eisenbrauns, 2007), 131–74; Timothy P. Harrison, "Lifting the Veil on a 'Dark Age': Ta'yinat and the North Orontes Valley during the Early Iron Age," in *Exploring the Longue Durée: Essays in Honor of Lawrence E. Stager* (ed. J. David Schloen; Winona Lake, IN: Eisenbrauns, 2009), 171–84; J. David Hawkins, "Cilicia, the Amuq, and Aleppo: New Light in a Dark Age," *NEA* 72 (2009): 164–73; Timothy P. Harrison, "The Late Bronze/Early Iron Age Transition in the Northern Orontes Valley," in *Societies in Transition: Evolutionary Processes in the Northern Levant between Late Bronze Age II and Early Iron Age; Papers Presented on the Occasion of the 20th Anniversary of the New Excavations in Tell Afis, Bologna, 15th November 2007* (ed. Fabrizio Venturi; STO 9; Bologna: CLUEB, 2010), 83–102.

25. William F. Albright, "Syria, the Philistines, and Phoenicia," in *History of the Middle East and the Aegean Region, c. 1380–1000 B.C.* (vol. 2.2 of *The Cambridge Ancient History*; ed. I. E. S. Edwards, N. G. L. Hammond, and E. Sollberger; 3rd ed.; Cambridge: University Press, 1975), 507–36. On "the great collapse," see Peter M. M. G. Akkermans and Glenn M.

side of 1200 BCE demarcate a liminal era, a dangerous time, with an old world passing and a new, undefined one aborning.

Many forces converged in the collapse of the LBA, forming a "perfect storm" of interlocking cultural failures that swamped the entire region.[26] Contracting food supplies, resulting from a protracted drought, constituted the worst long-term stressor.[27] Food shortages in Anatolia and Mesopotamia necessitated control of other regions, most notably Syria, increasing tensions among the LBA states.[28] Although too much importance is often placed on the rise of iron technology, advanced metallurgy could not have hurt groups struggling for an edge. Advances in bronze casting and possibly ironworking necessarily figure in the military aspects of the LBA collapse.[29] The social and economic failure of the city-state, with the subsequent reversion to lineage-defined tribal communities, likely drove unrest among the have-not nonurban cultures at the end of the LBA.[30] Did Mother Nature take a role in the LBA collapse? Evidence has mounted supporting the suggestion that a period of unusually frequent and severe earthquakes marked the LBA/IA1 transition. Claims of a region-wide epidemic of some highly contagious killer disease have yet to

---

Schwartz, *The Archaeology of Syria: From Complex Hunter-Gatherers to Early Urban Societies (c. 16,000–300 BC)* (CWA; Cambridge: Cambridge University Press, 2003), 358–59.

26. Cline, *1177 B.C.*, 139–70.

27. William H. Shea, "Famine," *ABD* 2:771; Alan D. Crown, "Toward a Reconstruction of the Climate of Palestine 8000 B.C.–0 B.C.," *JNES* 31 (1972): 312–30; Barry Weiss, "The Decline of Late Bronze Age Civilization as a Possible Response to Climatic Change," *Climatic Change* 4 (1982): 172–98; Jehuda Neumann and Simo Parpola, "Climatic Change and the Eleventh-Tenth–Century Eclipse of Assyria and Babylonia," *JNES* 46 (1987): 161–82; Ronald L. Gorny, "Environment, Archaeology, and History in Hittite Anatolia," *BA* 52 (1989): 78–96; Harvey Weiss and Raymond S. Bradley, "What Drives Societal Collapse?," *Science* 291 (2001): 609–10; Brian Fagan, *The Long Summer: How Climate Changed Civilization* (New York: Basic Books, 2004), 169–88. Sing C. Chew, *The Recurring Dark Ages: Ecological Stress, Climate Changes, and System Transformation* (Lanham, MD: Altamira, 2007); Rafael Reuveny, "Climate Change-Induced Migration and Violent Conflict," *Political Geography* 26 (2007): 656–73; Eelco J. Rohling et al., "Holocene Climate Variability in the Eastern Mediterranean and the End of the Bronze Age," in Bachhuber and Roberts, *Forces of Transformation*, 2–5.

28. Albrecht Goetze, "The Struggle for the Domination of Syria," in Edwards, Hammond, and Sollberger, *History of the Middle East*, 1–20; Horst Klengel, *Syria, 3000–300 B.C.: A Handbook of Political History* (Berlin: Akademie Verlag, 1992), 100–180. For Syria, most recently, see D. Kaniewski et al., "Late Second-Early First Millennium BC Abrupt Climate Changes in Coastal Syria and Their Possible Significance for the History of the Eastern Mediterranean," *Quaternary Research* 74 (2010): 207–15; Trevor Bryce, *Letters of the Great Kings of the Ancient Near East: The Royal Correspondence of the Late Bronze Age* (London: Routledge, 2003), 131–36. On food shortages in Hatti and Syria, documented in contemporary correspondence, see Bryce, *Letters of the Great Kings*, 228–29.

29. See the review in Drews, *End of the Bronze Age*, 174–208.

30. Akkermans and Schwartz, *Archaeology of Syria*, 359.

win support.[31] The disruption of the LBA also saw significant movements and dislocations of people groups. Even after caveats against overusing migrations and invasions to explain culture change are registered, few can deny the impact of dramatic settlement shifts in the region.[32] Moreover, the Sea Peoples were not alone. They must be seen alongside other destabilizing groups, such as the northern Kaska people, who had long resisted Hittite rule and played a role in the fall of Hattusha. Likewise, the Arameans in the northern Fertile Crescent and Levant had put pressure on the traditional imperial powers. A notable interruption in seafaring beginning with early IA1 suggests a contraction or collapse in interregional trade, a factor on which the vitality of the LBA states depended.[33] Finally, although military tactics and technology do not tell the whole story, changes in warfare, particularly the emphasis on massed infantry, new types of body armor, short javelins, and the distinctive long, straight, double-edged cut-and-thrust Naue II type of sword certainly afforded an advantage in many cases.[34]

All these factors converged on a culture becoming steadily more brittle and hollow. In the LBA Mediterranean world system, the urban elites of Egypt, Babylonia, Assyria, Mitanni, Hatti, Elam, Syria-Palestine, and the Aegean interacted in a multileveled club, or "peer polity interaction," dependent on interregional exchange, communication, and interurban trade, especially in luxury goods. This arrangement risked becoming a "house of cards" susceptible to collapse.[35] Destructive policies toward local agriculturists and pastoralists, as well as dependence on other, often distant sources for vital staples,

31. See Amos Nur and Eric H. Cline, "Poseidon's Horses: Plate Tectonics and Earthquake Storms in the Late Bronze Age Aegean and Eastern Mediterranean," *JAS* (2000): 27, 43–63; see also Drews, *End of the Bronze Age*, 33–47. For the epidemic suggestion, see L. Walløe, "Was the Disruption of the Mycenaean World Caused by Repeated Epidemics of Bubonic Plague?," *OA* 24 (1999): 121–26. Less credible is the suggestion of a smallpox epidemic: Tom Slattery, *The Tragic End of the Bronze Age: A Virus Makes History* (New York: Writers Club Press, 2000).

32. See, most recently, Assaf Yasur-Landau, *The Philistines and Aegean Migration at the End of the Late Bronze Age* (Cambridge: Cambridge University Press, 2010); but see also the essays in Eliezer D. Oren, ed., *The Sea Peoples and Their World: A Reassessment* (Philadelphia: The University Museum, University of Pennsylvania, 2000). Ann Killebrew (*Biblical Peoples and Ethnicity*) distinguishes the Philistine presence in Canaan as a colonizing activity versus Egypt's presence for the sake of imperial extraction.

33. Ernst A. Knauf, "From Archeology to History, Bronze and Iron Ages with Special Regard to the Year 1200 B.C.E. and the Tenth Century," in Grabbe, *Archaeology*, 72–85.

34. Drews, *End of the Bronze Age*, 135–208.

35. Van de Mieroop, *Eastern Mediterranean*, 223–34; Bryce, *Letters of the Great Kings*, 1–54, 76–106, 223–31; Mazar, *Archaeology of the Land*, 287. For the house-of-cards model, see Joseph Tainter, *The Collapse of Complex Societies* (NSA; Cambridge: Cambridge University Press, 1988). On the political bonds, see Amanda H. Podany, *Brotherhood of Kings: How International Relations Shaped the Ancient Near East* (Oxford: Oxford University Press: 2010), 191–309.

jeopardized the LBA city-states. When, around 1250 BCE, urban centers in the eastern Mediterranean began suffering assaults by groups viewed by the urban rulers as "barbarians" employing new weapons and tactics, the city-states could not effectively respond. The wave of urban destructions finally burned out as Ramesses III halted the advance of the Sea Peoples around 1175 BCE. This cost Egypt its imperial presence in Canaan.[36] Canaan itself saw disruptive groups such as the Shasu, Apiru, and a range of chieftains, warlords, thugs, and highwaymen. In such a setting a tribal war leader like the character of Joshua, aspiring to settle territory already contested, seems right at home.

Documentary Evidence

The principal documentary evidence outside the Bible bearing on Israel's appearance in Canaan remains the Merneptah Stela, with a few other small notes possibly playing a role. Despite failed attempts to argue the contrary, the most well-grounded interpretation remains that the inscription mentions Israel in a line reading, "Israel is laid waste, his seed is not."[37] While the other proper names in the immediate context of this line are flagged by the Egyptian determinative for a city, the name "Israel" is distinctively flagged as a "people." Most readers infer from this that in Merneptah's perception, Israel is present in Canaan, identifiable as a "people," not associated with urban centers and not in sufficient control of the land, or at least not in control long enough to have rated a geographical determinative. This reduced status clashes, however, with the second clause, "his seed is not," denoting the damage that Merneptah claims to have done. Some suggest that the reference is to the destruction of agricultural produce, translating "seed corn," implying a settled, agrarian Israel. But in the Mednet Habu inscription, Ramesses III narrates his naval defeat of the Sea Peoples, declaring, "Their seed is not." Apparently the phrase is a figure of speech for total annihilation. Thus among all the peoples and towns of Canaan, Merneptah felt it necessary to affirm that he had totally annihilated one particular people group, the one named "Israel." One can only speculate why the pharaoh felt compelled to report publicly, in this monumental inscription, that he had annihilated Israel. Worth noting also is a fragmentary inscription on a column base from the time of Ramesses II, now in the Egyptian museum in Berlin, which features captive lists in which Ashkelon and Canaan are followed

---

36. See Singer, "Egyptians, Canaanites, and Philistines," 284–94.

37. See Michael G. Hasel, "Merneptah's Reference to Israel: Critical Issues for the Origin of Israel," in *Critical Issues in Early Israelite History* (ed. Richard S. Hess, Gerald A. Klingbeil, and Paul J. Ray; BBRSup 3; Winona Lake, IN: Eisenbrauns, 2008), 47–59; J. Hawkins, *How Israel Became a People*, 76–80.

by a broken name-ring which can plausibly be restored as "Israel" once the archaizing spelling tendencies of such inscriptions is accounted for.[38] Lastly, notice should be taken of two captive lists found on column bases at the Soleb temple of Amenhotep III (1390–1352) and a copy at the Amarah West temple of Ramesses II. Both identify one captive group as "Yhwˁ (in) the land of the Shasu." While the name "Yhwˁ" might be a place name, it represents exactly the way the Hebrew divine name would appear in hieroglyphic. Moreover, names of deities and their domains sometimes overlap, leading many scholars to associate these inscriptions with Israel.[39] If these connections stand, then allusions to Israel or Yahweh may be pushed back at least to the time of Ramesses II if not much earlier, to the pre-Amarna period. While the documentary extrabiblical evidence for Israel's existence is limited, it appears nevertheless that a "people" called "Israel," living in Canaan, and a God named "Yahweh" were known in the Egyptian sphere of influence no later than Merneptah and probably much earlier. It remains to be seen how this information fits into a general narrative of the Israelites' possession of the land of Canaan.

Of Cities, Kings, and Campaigns

The book of Joshua reports assaults by Israelite forces against urban rulers in Canaan. The common perception, represented in a chart by Dever, is that every city that Joshua claims Israel defeated should display a destruction layer and would have shown evidence of Israelite occupation following the destruction.[40] Since evidence for these destructions and subsequent Israelite occupation is often lacking, scholars have regularly dismissed the stories in Joshua as unhistorical. The case of Jericho illustrates the problems involved most poignantly. On the surface, Joshua 6 narrates a city with a king and walls, which collapse. Then the Israelites slaughter the inhabitants and burn the city. The earliest excavations of Tell es-Sultan (Old Testament Jericho) by Ernst Sellin and Carl Watzinger did find evidence of a fortified city that was completely destroyed. However, they dated the destruction to around 1550 BCE, far too early to be Joshua's city. John Garstang excavated the city in the 1930s and argued that the destroyed city fell around 1400 BCE and was Joshua's city. He described the fortifications in detail and even conjectured the location of Rahab's house. The debate that followed culminated in further excavations of the site by Kathleen Kenyon, who concluded that the city's fall

38. Manfred Görg, "Israel in Hieroglyphen," *Biblische Notizen* 106 (2001): 21–27.

39. For example, Donald B. Redford, *Egypt, Canaan and Israel in Ancient Times* (Princeton: Princeton University Press, 1992), 272–73.

40. Dever, *Who Were the Early Israelites?*, 56–57.

occurred indeed in 1550 BCE, and that very little remained of any LBA site at Jericho. Importantly, she found only traces of LBA remains and that even Middle Bronze Age (MBA) remains were badly eroded and often constituted the top layer of the site. This seems to be a very unusual state of affairs, given that evidence did exist of some LBA settlement. Attempts by Bryant Wood to use Kenyon's data to redate the destruction to around 1400 BCE have not found a wide following, especially after a battery of radiocarbon dates definitively put the destruction of City IV at about 1550 BCE.[41]

Kenyon did not deny the biblical story's historicity, but she suggested that the severe erosion evident everywhere on the mound, as well as construction of a road across its southeast side, could well have obliterated evidence of an LBA settlement. Archaeologically aware visitors to Tell es-Sultan can observe the striking fact of MBA remains appearing at the surface layer of the mound in many places. Given the strategically vital nature of the site, with its spring and ready control of important highways and the Jordan River crossing, the idea that Tell es-Sultan sat uninhabited for centuries after 1550 BCE is almost inconceivable. In any event, no signs of a catastrophic destruction by fire of a fortified LBA citadel, datable to the fifteenth or thirteenth century BCE, have been found. Likewise, if et-Tell represents the correct location for Ai, the absence there of a significant LBA town (and the absence of signs of destruction) have also augured ill for the biblical narrative in the minds of many.

But have scholars been looking for the right things? Returning to the text of Joshua 6, Richard Hess has argued that we need not imagine a gigantic citadel, but that the LBA Jericho could well have been a much smaller city.[42] The fortifications could also have been remaining structures from the MBA city, perhaps reinforced in places. Even today one can observe imposing remains of the MBA and even Early Bronze Age walls. If they are impressive even today, surely they were available, and more impressive, in the LBA. Moreover, Jericho in the LBA need not have been a typical city. The location was ideal for a warlord to choose as a base of operations for raiding and pillaging along the important trade routes linking the lands east of the Jordan to the land of Canaan and for controlling the local populace by regulating access to the spring. The "king" of LBA Jericho could have been a typical Canaanite city "mayor," warlord, or outlaw quite at home in the hinterlands of Canaan in the LBA. However modest this view of Jericho seems, contrasted with the

41. Hendrik J. Bruins and Johannes van der Plicht, "Tell Es-Sultan (Jericho): Radiocarbon Results of Short-Lived Cereal and Multiyear Charcoal Samples from the End of the Middle Bronze Age," *Radiocarbon* 37, no. 2 (1995): 213–20.

42. Richard S. Hess, "The Jericho and Ai of the Book of Joshua," in Hess, Klingbeil, and Ray, *Critical Issues*, 33–46.

traditional picture, it would have posed a formidable challenge to migrating Israelites seeking entry into Canaan. Such a town also would not leave behind the kinds or amounts of destruction debris that one would expect of a larger and more complex city, and what debris remained could well have eroded. Thus the gap between what the text of Joshua 6 actually requires, especially seen in the context of the LBA Canaanite periphery, and what archaeological remains reveal—seems not as wide as has been traditionally claimed.

Similarly, the city of Ai poses initial resistance to connections with the biblical story. Some have therefore argued that the location itself should be reconsidered, nominating other sites in place of the traditional et-Tell.[43] For Joshua and the Israelites, the town was called "The Ruin." This suggests that it was not an imposing metropolis, but rather a previously occupied urban center that, like many LBA cities, had declined and served as a security salient for the nearby town of Bethel.[44] Again, a careful reading of the biblical narrative yields a more modest picture than the one so often made in the flannelgraph presentations of vacation Bible school. Such a picture also fits more readily with the archaeological evidence.

The site of Hazor presents a different picture than that of Jericho. The site has been thoroughly studied for several decades, and excavations remain active today under the direction of Amnon Ben-Tor. The upper city of Hazor evinces a terrific destruction by fire datable to the 1230s BCE by several lines of evidence, including an inscription that we noted earlier.[45] The debate centers on the identity of those who destroyed Hazor. The excavator has observed that the mutilation of proper names in cartouches on Egyptian inscriptions likely rules out Egyptians as the attackers. The date is too early for the Sea Peoples to have played a role. No remains associated with the Sea Peoples have been found in the LBA destruction layer of Hazor. Claims of decapitated Canaanite deities and vandalized sacred objects imply that Canaanites would not have destroyed the city, though possible conflict within the population of Hazor—that is, between the elites and the general populace—could have motivated the mutilation of some objects.[46] Such a process of elimination

43. Bryant G. Wood, "The Search for Joshua's Ai," in Hess, Klingbeil, and Ray, *Critical Issues*, 205–40.

44. See Hess, "Jericho and Ai."

45. Kitchen, "Egyptian Inscribed Fragment."

46. Amnon Ben-Tor, "The Sad Fate of Statues and the Mutilated Statues of Hazor," in *Confronting the Past: Archaeological and Historical Essays on Ancient Israel in Honor of William G. Dever* (ed. Seymour Gitin, J. Edward Wright, and J. P. Dessel; Winona Lake, IN: Eisenbrauns, 2006), 3–16; idem, "The Fall of Canaanite Hazor—The 'Who' and 'When' Questions," in *Mediterranean Peoples in Transition: Thirteenth to Early Tenth Centuries BCE* (ed. Seymour Gitin, Amihai Mazar, and Ephraim Stern; Jerusalem: Israel Exploration Society, 1998), 456–67.

Lawson Stone

Figure 4.2. Hazor cultic standing stone (Massebah)

leads some to the conclusion that Israel destroyed Hazor, as described in Joshua 11. This emphasizes the element of burning—a prominent feature of the destruction layer.

The possibility remains of an intraurban insurrection in which the people of Hazor rose against their own leadership and torched the acropolis.[47] Those destroyed cult sites eventually became scenes of religious activity characterized as "ruin cults." In these, according to Sharon Zuckerman, the occupants of the town recall the sacred function of a structure and so do not rebuild on it. Instead, they use the place as a site for certain religious rites.[48] Zuckerman does not explain how a population that had exploded in rage at their fleeing ruling elites, desecrating their cult statues and torching their buildings, would then reverse course and venerate those dilapidated sites in "ruin cults." The destruction of Hazor by outsiders with a strong revulsion toward the religious and political culture represented by Hazor as the "head of all those kingdoms" seems more probable.

47. Sharon Zuckerman, "Anatomy of a Destruction: Crisis Architecture, Termination Rituals and the Fall of Canaanite Hazor," *JMA* 20 (2007): 3–32.
48. Sharon Zuckerman, "The Last Days of a Canaanite Kingdom: A View from Hazor," in Bachhuber and Roberts, *Forces of Transformation*, 101–7; idem, "Ruin Cults at Iron Age I Hazor," in *The Fire Signals of Lachish: Studies in the Archaeology and History of Israel in the Late Bronze Age, Iron Age, and Persian Period in Honor of David Ussishkin* (ed. Israel Finkelstein and Nadav Na'aman; Winona Lake, IN: Eisenbrauns, 2011), 387–94.

The main objection to Israelites as the destroyers is simply that Israel as a community of farmers, shepherds, and peasants lacked the military capability to destroy a great citadel such as Hazor, a site covering over two hundred acres. Zuckerman actually provides the answer in noting that by the closing decades of the LBA, Hazor—like many of the urban centers destroyed in the LBA collapse, such as Hattusha and Ugarit—had entered a sharp decline, with fortifications in disrepair and monumental structures abandoned, underutilized, and poorly maintained. Some of these cities were all but abandoned when they finally met their doom.[49] Zuckerman points out that shortly before its final LBA destruction, rulers and principal defenders of Hazor seem to have evacuated the city. The evidence at Hazor suggests that, before leaving, the ruling elites occupying the acropolis ritually decommissioned cult sites and held what amounted to sociocultural funeral wakes, including the burial of cult objects, in recognition of their city's impending collapse. Evidence of IA1 "ruin cult" behavior, especially avoidance of rebuilding on erstwhile sacred sites, resonates with the biblical notion of *ḥērem*, in which certain destroyed cities became taboo, sometimes reinforced by a curse (see Josh. 6:17–19, 26). Thus nonprofessional fighters attacking and destroying a declining city, abandoned by its leaders and professional defenders, appears quite possible. The attackers might even have found allies in the populace left behind by their fleeing leadership.

Elements of Israelite Material Culture

The debate as to whether early Israel possessed a coherent material culture distinct from that of its rivals among the Canaanites and Philistines has run parallel to the larger debate about ethnicity and material culture in archaeology. Rather than define a set of "traits" or artifacts viewed as Israelite, Canaanite, or Philistine, scholars increasingly suggest that ethnic markers originate in those behaviors by which a group distinguishes itself from the threatening "other" encountered at the peripheries of its territory rather than at its heartland.[50] Such behaviors often generate a distinctive material

---

49. For example, Hattusha (see Bryce, *Kingdom of the Hittites*, 345–46).

50. See Elizabeth Bloch-Smith's nuanced use of the "meaningful boundaries" model of ethnicity in "Israelite Ethnicity in Iron I: Archaeology Preserves What Is Remembered and What Is Forgotten in Israel's History," *JBL* 122 (2003): 401–25. The model itself appears in Fredrik Barth, introduction in *Ethnic Groups and Boundaries: The Social Organization of Culture Difference* (ed. Fredrik Barth; Boston: Little, Brown, 1969), 7–38. For an application of this understanding to material culture, see Shlomo Bunimovitz and Zvi Lederman, "The Archaeology of Border Communities: Renewed Excavations at Tel Beth-Shemesh, Part 1: The Iron Age," *NEA* 72 (2009): 128–31.

culture, but the artifacts themselves do not signal ethnicity unless they signify self-differentiating behavior. This self-differentiation from a threatening
"other" provides a persuasive alternative account of the distribution of material culture previously explained solely in terms of chronological sequence
or spatial isolation, provided the people groups attach an identity value to
the elements of material culture involved (pottery, weapons, houses, etc.).
Certain features of material culture thus function as a kind of language or
code articulating a boundary between competing groups. Distinct Philistine
pottery, for example, could be perceived by non-Philistine cultural competitors as encoding the entire Aegean way of life, specifically as represented in
dietary practices. The avoidance of this pottery and its consequent absence
thus could become an ethnic marker without assuming the traditional "pots
and people" connection, depending on how the users (or avoiders) of these
artifacts viewed them.[51]

The archaeological features thought to indicate Israelite presence have included (1) the collared-rim storage jar, (2) the avoidance of painted pottery,
(3) the avoidance of imported pottery, (4) the absence or significant paucity
of pig bones in the faunal remains, and (5) the pillared house, in three- or
four-room variations. Avraham Faust has recently reviewed the objections to
seeing these features as signs of Israelite presence and has argued that, with a
carefully understood concept of ethnicity, and with a nuanced understanding of
the role of material culture in signifying identity, all these items remain useful
indices of Israelite presence. They also point to important elements of early
Israelite social ideology—namely, a valuing of egalitarianism and simplicity.[52]
If these aspects of material culture are used cautiously, the delineation of the
earliest Israelite settlement becomes possible.

Israelite Religious Remains

The culture of the early IA1 settlers in the hill country seems to have pre-
cluded public buildings such as temples. This renders identification of sites
devoted specifically to religious functions difficult for archaeologists, who must
rely on material culture for such determinations. Ralph Hawkins has reviewed
the literature and summarized the criteria for identifying cultic or sacred sites,
so that here only the most important or distinctive religious centers will be

---

51. See Shlomo Bunimovitz and Avraham Faust, "Chronological Separation, Geographical
Segregation, or Ethnic Demarcation? Ethnography and the Iron Age Low Chronology," *BASOR*
322 (2001): 1–10.

52. Avraham Faust, *Israel's Ethnogenesis: Settlement, Interaction, Expansion and Resistance*
(AAA; London: Equinox, 2006), 3–107. See also R. Hawkins, *How Israel Became a People*, 137–57.

considered.[53] First among all the locations with strong cultic functions for Israel in the IA1 is Shiloh (Tell Seilun). Israel Finkelstein's excavations confirmed the site's long history as a religious and administrative site before its apparent abandonment in the LBA. It revived as the new hill-country settlements around it began appearing. This reflects a level of planning and development beyond the scope of a merely localized center. In keeping with its descriptions in the biblical data, the storage facilities and structures on the site point to its role as a center for administration, storage, distribution, and religious activity. It does not reflect routine occupation. Likewise, Shiloh's fiery destruction in about 1050 BCE synchronizes with the biblical narrative, which does not directly report Shiloh's demise but certainly implies it.[54]

Another significant site for which cultic functions have been argued is a large structure excavated by Adam Zertal, located on Mount Ebal and overlooking the site of Shechem.[55] The large square structure is constructed of unworked fieldstones. It is dated by pottery and scarabs to the LBA/IA1 transitional era, with its corners aligned to the points of the compass. The structure lies behind a courtyard with pits filled with burnt animal bones in which donkeys, dogs, and pigs were not attested. It is located at a point reasonably associated with the statements about Mount Ebal in Deuteronomy 11:26–32; 27:1–8; Joshua 8:30–35. All this evidence and these considerations, very much suggesting that the site was cultic, led the excavator to imply very strongly that the structure might be the altar referred to in Joshua 8:30–35. This latter point inspired a vigorous debate in which alternatives (almost *any* alternatives) to the altar categorization were argued. If Zertal had not insinuated that the structure was the altar mentioned in Joshua 8:30–35, perhaps the debate might have unfolded differently.[56] A major objection to this structure being "Joshua's altar" is its invisibility from Mount Gerizim. That concern notwithstanding, whether the structure is "Joshua's altar" may be answered separately from the question of whether it is a cult site from the beginning of the settlement era, located near the place of an important ritual event spoken of in the Bible, with important markers of Israelite use. The structure need not have been "Joshua's altar" but could have been constructed after the Ebal-Gerizim ritual

53. Ralph K. Hawkins, *The Iron Age I Structure on Mt. Ebal: Excavation and Interpretation* (BBRSup 6; Winona Lake, IN: Eisenbrauns, 2012), 15–29; idem, *How Israel Became a People*, 175–88.

54. The most convenient summary is Israel Finkelstein's own, in "Seilun, Khirbet," *ABD* 5:1069–71.

55. The excavator's main publication is Adam Zertal, "An Early Iron Age Cultic Site on Mount Ebal: Excavation Seasons 1982–1987, Preliminary Report," *TA* 13–14 (1986–87): 105–65.

56. The point is very strongly implied in Adam Zertal, "Has Joshua's Altar Been Found on Mt. Ebal?," *BAR* 11, no. 1 (1985): 26–35, 38–41, 43.

to commemorate the event. Hawkins's extensive evaluation of all the proposed alternatives sifts through the debate, separating overstatement from reasoned argument, and concludes that this site is best understood as a cultic center, an altar that existed for a very short time at the end of the LBA and into the early IA1.[57] After a brief period of use, it was abandoned and carefully covered, as though respectfully retired. Until Zertal's final report appears, Hawkins has offered scholars and general readers the definitive study of the site.

The eastern hills of Manasseh also feature another type of site, possibly pointing to the religious activity of early Israel. Located just west of the Jordan River at the sites of Yafit, Massua, Bedhat es-Sha'ab, and farther west, el-Unuq on the southern bank of the Wadi Far'ah (N) are sites with several important commonalities. All these stone enclosures possess an elliptical shape. The stone walls appear mainly to serve demarcating, not defensive, functions. Each site has a large stone cairn at one end.

The site at Bedhat es-Sha'ab has been excavated and published most extensively and merits summary here.[58] One enters the enclosure, 169 x 88 meters in size, from the east on a pavement constructed with unshaped fieldstones placed on fill of earth and pottery, with the stones' flattest surfaces upward. One turns left to find a low double row of stones, carefully placed in connection with a prepared surface, a walkway of stone leading south, looping around a full 180 degrees before dividing into two branches almost exactly opposite the entry point. One branch opens left (westward) into the bleacher-like hillside; another leads right toward a four-sided enclosure in the center of the ellipse. The pathway does not continue, but a demarcation wall does extend northward, finally looping around and returning to the structure's entrance. At the north end, a large circular cairn of stones was surrounded by a pavement constructed like the entryway and the pathway. The excavators found animal bones of sheep, goats, and cattle, but only one donkey bone and no pig bones.

From pottery found both in the survey of the site and from underneath the stone pavements, the excavators concluded that the site was founded in the thirteenth or twelfth century BCE, continued in use during IA1 and, with decreasing intensity, through Iron Age II (IA2). It was abandoned in the eighth century BCE. The excavators argue that the site was cultic in nature, that the cairn likely was an altar, and that the pathway around the southern loop of the site was a processional road. In addition, the shape of the site, viewed

57. See R. Hawkins, *Iron Age I Structure*; a less technical summary appears in idem, *How Israel Became a People*, 184–88.

58. Adam Zertal and Dror Ben-Yosef, "Bedhat esh-Sha'ab: An Iron Age I Enclosure in the Jordan Valley," in Schloen, *Exploring the Longue Durée*, 517–29.

Lawson Stone

Figure 4.3. Bedhat es-Shaʿab

from the natural amphitheater created by the stepped slope of the hillside rising on the west, is that of a distinct footprint, or sandal shape. Hawkins has suggested that this footprint shape has religious significance, pointing to the large footprints carved into the threshhold of the temple at Ain Dara in Syria, also an LBA/IA1 site. He also notes the prominence of processional marching in the narrative of Jericho's fall, which presents a liturgical parade as the centerpiece of Israel's actions. Additionally, the use of the Hebrew term for "foot" (*regel*) to denote pilgrim festivals is suggestive. Its construction, a stone enclosure, also evokes the underlying sense of the term "Gilgal," or "circle." This implies that the word is not a proper name but rather the term for a kind of site, namely, a stone enclosure such as the ones described here. Hawkins concludes that the site could well have been an early Israelite cult and assembly site. Although the distinctive processional path found at Bedhat es-Shaʿab has not been found at the other sites, they all admit of a cultic interpretation.[59]

While it is possible to dispute many of the claims made about the sites discussed here, sites clearly do exist in the area of the earliest known Israelite settlement that possess features consistent with, even suggestive of, religious activities of the persons who settled in the area. The sites seem too large to have been constructed spontaneously but seem to represent the coordinated efforts of collaborating groups. Cult images have not been found in these areas, nor has any indication of a plurality of deities been found on any one

59. R. Hawkins, *Iron Age I Structure*, 118–22; idem, *How Israel Became a People*, 179–84. Hawkins suggests also that Mount Ebal is a sandal-shaped site.

site. Faunal remains have been consistent with Israelite practice, suggesting that a significant degree of communal organization and energy went into the creation of these cultic sites. Our LBA/IA1 settlers evidently had a simple religion, but one strongly felt.

Settlement Patterns

While early research into Israelite origins focused on urban destructions in its search of evidence for or against a military conquest, more recent archaeological research has turned to evidence of new villages appearing in the central highlands of Canaan beginning in about 1200 BCE. Finkelstein was among the first to compile a comprehensive review of such settlement surveys. However, the most extensive recent work has come from Zertal, whose published survey data provide information vital for all future assessments of this era.[60] A methodical survey of the areas traditionally assigned to Manasseh and Ephraim indicates a dramatic rise in new villages in the central highlands. Zertal has also argued from the evolution discernible in the cross-section of the typical cooking pot that the oldest of these new settlements appeared on the slopes just west of the Jordan, gradually moving westward. Settlements in the Judean hill country seem to have begun somewhat later. Zertal considers these new settlements as evidence for early Israel.[61] Other scholars have been less definitive, preferring terms like "proto-Israelite" or even avoiding any connections with Israel. Faust has argued in detail that the continuity of many important aspects of the material culture of these new settlements with the material culture of IA2 Israel supports the conclusion that most, if not all, of these new settlements provided the human and material culture that became the Israel known from IA2. Faust also notes that the cultural identity of IA2 Israel had already taken coherent shape in the early IA1, if not even earlier.[62]

The specific elements of this material culture will be discussed below, but here one observation demands attention. As mentioned above, the earliest Israelite settlement occurred on the eastern slopes of the Manassite hill country (west of the Jordan) and gradually expanded westward. From other archaeological surveys, it appears that, aside from the towns that served as

60. Adam Zertal, *The Manasseh Hill Country Survey* (2 vols.; CHANE 21.1–2; Leiden: Brill, 2004–2008).

61. Adam Zertal, "Israel Enters Canaan—Following the Pottery Trail," *BAR* 17, no. 5 (1991): 28–38, 42–47; idem, "'To the Land of the Perizzites and the Giants': On the Israelite Settlement in the Hill Country of Manasseh," in Finkelstein and Na'aman, *From Nomadism to Monarchy*, 47–69.

62. Avraham Faust, "How Did Israel Become a People? The Genesis of Israelite Identity," *BAR* 35, no. 6 (2009): 62–69, 92–94.

Egyptian administrative centers, the hill country of Canaan carried only a thin population. Thus the earliest Israelite settlements occurred in the center of the country.

The settlement data provoke another observation about the appearance of Israel in Canaan. On the one hand, the earliest settlement appears to have occurred peacefully as Israelites moved into thinly populated areas in the central hill country. On the other hand, the "conquest" traditions of the Bible narrate campaigns in the south (Josh. 10) and then north of the Jezreel Valley (Josh. 11). But both areas see new settlements only later in IA1. Thus the settlement data offer a concrete basis for analyzing the appearance of Israel in Canaan but stand in conflict with the "conquest" traditions, whether or not those traditions are considered historical in the first place. Even if the biblical narrative is regarded as historical, reconciling the conquest accounts with the archaeological settlement data poses a challenge.

A particular point of interest in assessing the Joshua narrative is the often-overlooked geographical notice in Joshua 1:4. This text puts particular interest on the northern limit of Joshua's commission, defined by reference to "the wilderness and this Lebanon," extending to "the great river, the river Euphrates," which is then further defined as "all the land of the Hittites." Why so scrupulous a definition of this northern frontier? The politics of the final decades of the LBA throw this text into relief. The territory denoted in Joshua 1:4 corresponds to the southern border of the LBA kingdom of Amurru, known from the Amarna letters of the fourteenth century BCE and, more important for this discussion, from the Hittite diplomatic correspondence of the twelfth century BCE. Amurru had inflicted headaches on Egypt since its king Aziru cleverly exploited his status as an Egyptian vassal to gain control of the region before betraying Egypt and allying with the Hittite king Shuppiluliuma. This brought territory formerly under Egyptian control into the Hittite orbit and ignited a century of conflict between Egypt and Hatti, the two great powers of the LBA. Ultimately the Battle of Kadesh and the subsequent treaty between Ramesses II of Egypt and Hattusili III of Hatti in 1258 BCE resolved the boundary dispute.[63] The divine delimitation of the conquest on the north kept the Israelites out of the region controlled by the Hittites, a border only clarified about twenty years before the Israelite entry. Treaty relations required a commitment to mutual defense as well as a promise to return fugitive slaves or rebels. This very provision was poignantly highlighted by a dispute between

---

63. See Itamar Singer, "A Concise History of Amurru," in *The Calm before the Storm: Selected Writings of Itamar Singer on the End of the Late Bronze Age in Anatolia and the Levant* (SBLWAWSup 1; Atlanta: Society of Biblical Literature, 2011), 197–242, esp. 211–13; Bryce, *Letters of the Great Kings*, 145–68.

The Amarna Texts

At the site of El Amarna in 1887, the first of 382 tablets inscribed in Akkadian cuneiform came to light in the ruins of the capital city of Akhenaten, Egypt's "heretic" pharaoh. This leader ruled in the mid-1300s BCE and is thought to have imposed a kind of monotheism on Egypt. After his death, his capital was abandoned as later pharaohs returned to traditional Egyptian capital cities. The tablets formed part of the archive of correspondence between the pharaoh and other great kings of the ancient Near East, as well as with vassal rulers in the Levant. Akkadian served as the universal diplomatic language, but letters from Canaan displayed linguistic features transparently drawn from the "Canaanite" dialect spoken in Canaan. At times Canaanite terms appear alongside their Akkadian counterparts.

The texts yield a wealth of information about how the great powers of the Late Bronze Age interacted with one another and especially how Egypt administered Canaan. In addition, the internal affairs of Canaan appear in bold relief as we "read their mail" and listen in on conspiracies, duplicities, protestations of loyalty, accusations of betrayal, and pleas for help against impending invasion. Cities such as Jerusalem, Gezer, and Shechem emerge as possessing scribes trained in cuneiform writing capable of conducting far-flung correspondence on a daily basis. In addition, the protestations and pleas of the city rulers inform us of how the pharaoh and the city rulers perceived their roles and responsibilities. As they discuss the threats faced, we learn of the practice of forced labor, of destabilizing groups such as the Apiru, and of hiring mercenaries. Descriptions include the theft of cattle and even of lowlanders held for ransom by highland peasants, the ransom ranging from thirty to one hundred shekels! These letters, dating as they do from a time prior to the Israelite settlement in Canaan, provide invaluable firsthand insights into life in the divided, violent, tempestuous territory that Israel claimed as its "promised land."

Ramesses II and Hattusili III over the latter's rebellious nephew, who apparently took refuge in Egypt. The Hittite king clearly expected the pharaoh to yield either the fugitive or a good explanation, at one point even threatening "another Kadesh."[64] Any penetration of the Israelites into Hittite territory could have triggered Egyptian demands that the Hittites act against Israel. Worse, it risked straining the treaty and reigniting the conflict between Egypt and Hatti, this time with Israel caught in the middle. The commission of Joshua seems aimed at preventing such a broadening of the conflict and possibly also

64. Bryce, *Letters of the Great Kings*, 86–93, 213–17. So important is this provision that, Bryce concludes, Urhi Teshub must have fled to Egypt before the treaty of 1258 BCE.

confines Yahweh's actions to the sphere of Egyptian hegemony. The latter point could imply a theological interest in the role of Egyptian domination, as though Yahweh's quarrel was only with Egypt, not with Hatti.

Toward a History of Israel's Possession of Canaan

Reviewing the diverse material bearing on the question of Israel's appearance in Canaan yields two questions. First, what are the basic building blocks of any responsible scholarly position that takes seriously both the biblical and the extrabiblical materials? Second and more controversial, is a linear account possible, a narrative of how a distinct community self-identified as "Israel" was established in Canaan, with self-defined boundaries distinguishing itself from the other groups competing for control of Canaan (i.e., the Canaanites, Egyptians, and Philistines)? Put differently, does our evidence allow moving beyond analyzing facts and factors to permit a sketch of this momentous transition?

Elements of a Reconstruction

Several observations provide a set of basic elements for sketching an account of the Israelite settlement of Canaan. These "facts and factors" become the foundation for any reconstruction. They form the dots that need to be connected.

First, Israel consisted of elements already resident within Canaan. This point is not as revolutionary as it seemed when George Mendenhall first proposed it. According to the biblical narrative, the ancestors of the Israelite nation lived in Canaan for centuries prior to the Egyptian sojourn. Indeed, New Kingdom Egypt deported a great many farmers and tradesmen from Canaan to Egypt, and to the Egyptians no significant difference between Canaanites and the ancestors of Israel would be discernible. They would speak the same language, share the same physical features, and likely share much material culture. Moreover, as practitioners of mixed agriculture and pastoralism, many cultural affinities would link the Israelites and Canaanite peasantry. So in Israelite settlements we should not expect to see the kind of distinct material culture that characterizes early Philistine sites. There, a heterogenous group colonized a region of Canaan, planting their Aegean culture on Canaanite soil. Indeed, a major part of the formation of Israel could be a process such as Dever sketches, in which the economic crisis triggered by the LBA collapse caused the repressed, socially, and economically marginalized rural populace to seek a different kind of life in the space created by the slipping of Egypt's grip and the infighting and confusion among the Canaanite city ruling elites.[65]

The book of Joshua surprisingly includes a number of stories implying that many in Israel derived from Canaan. The programmatic position of the Rahab story at the beginning of the Joshua narrative and the way the terminology used in her confession of faith (Josh. 2:9–11) reappears, with a different outcome, in the reports of how the kings of Canaan were conspiring against Israel (cf. 5:1; 9:1–3; 10:1–5; 11:1–5)—all this highlights the thematic importance of Rahab's inclusion in Israel.[66] Later biblical tradition names her in genealogical lists and identifies her as an ancestor of David and, ultimately, of Jesus. The story of the Gibeonite deception clearly describes the entry of an indigenous Canaanite group into the ranks of Israel (Josh. 9). "Foreigners" or "sojourners," along with "native-born" Israelites, made up Israel in the ceremony at Gerizim and Ebal and thus indicate not just presence but also some status in the covenant community. Inclusion in a ritual community implies a degree of social acceptance.

By the same token, the final speech at Shechem in Joshua 24 contrasts with Joshua's "Well Done, Mission Accomplished" speech in Joshua 23 by challenging the hearers to enter into covenant with Yahweh—to serve Yahweh—and warning them to put away foreign gods from their midst. Given the severity with which any deviation from the covenant was punished in the book, the only persons who might be in possession of non-Israelite cultic images would be elements of the Canaanite population who have affiliated with Israel but have not been fully assimilated or identified as "Israel." On this view, Joshua 24 becomes a revolutionary moment in which a new community is established. This community describes itself with the language of descent and kinship along with a shared narrative of the past. However, it is not composed of persons related by those ties, but rather united in covenant to the god Yahweh and to one another as fellow Israelites. The book of Joshua thus begins with the assimilation of a Canaanite prostitute and ends with a mass "Ellis Island" type of swearing-in ceremony in which many non-Israelites enter the covenant.

Second, the existence of certain distinctive features in the material culture of the new highland villages, even as they stand in continuity with the earlier Canaanite culture, points to an influence from outside the native Canaanite sphere. Something drives the differentiation. As Faust has argued, granting

---

65. Dever, *Who Were the Early Israelites?*, 167–89.

66. See Lawson G. Stone, "Ethical and Apologetic Tendencies in the Redaction of Joshua," *CBQ* 53 (1991): 25–36.

the similarity of the inventory of pottery forms in these villages to LBA Canaanite pottery, why then would Canaanite villagers suddenly begin to avoid painted and imported pottery? After all, if they are culturally continuous, why make any distinctions in pottery use? Even if a few collared-rim storage jars do appear in non-Israelite contexts, their overwhelming concentration appears in sites later emerging as Israel. If these are Canaanites, why do they evince this need for differentiation?[67] The evidence for pork avoidance, particularly at the boundaries between the Israelite settlements and Canaanite or Philistine communities, likewise points to a need for differentiation. But if the Israelites were merely Canaanites, why draw a line of difference?[68] Again, the pillared house, even if it did have some forerunners in LBA Canaan (which is not overwhelmingly clear), becomes strongly characteristic of communities that later constitute the Israelite and Judean states. What is the cultural energy that accounts for the need to differentiate these supposed "Canaanite" villages from Canaanite and Philistine neighbors?

Thus, the sharp increase in population in the highlands of Canaan in the early IA1 seems inadequately explained by appeals merely to prodigious reproductive activity or demographic shifts within Cisjordan (west of the Jordan). Nadav Na'aman, analyzing the Israelite settlement in the context of the end of the LBA in the eastern Mediterranean, noticed that all the documentary sources for the era indicate all the major regions witnessed a flux of different people groups moving through or to them. Speaking of the "unprecedented wave of migrations and profound demographic change in the entire region," Na'aman concludes,

> The overall picture emerging from the various sources does not corroborate the assumption that the Iron I settlement process was an internal Palestinian one, and that the inhabitants of the new settlements originated only from among the local Canaanite urban-rural-pastoral elements. . . . The scope and intensity of these events and the ensuing population movements do not fit reconstructions that separate a certain region from the entire Western Asiatic arena and isolate its micro-history from the overall historical developments of that time.[69]

67. Faust, *Israel's Ethnogenesis*, 41–70, 181–87.

68. Israel Finkelstein, "Pots and People Revisited: Ethnic Boundaries in the Iron Age I," in *The Archaeology of Israel: Constructing the Past, Interpreting the Present* (ed. Neil Asher Silberman and David Small; JSOTSup 237; Sheffield: Sheffield Academic Press, 1997), 227–30; Faust, *Israel's Ethnogenesis*, 35–40; R. Hawkins, *How Israel Became a People*, 152–55.

69. Nadav Na'aman, "The 'Conquest of Canaan' in the Book of Joshua and in History," in Finkelstein and Na'aman, *From Nomadism to Monarchy*, 246.

Scholars such as Anson Rainey and Adam Zertal have argued for the entry of a new population element from the east.[70] Many years ago Finkelstein observed that in the early stage of the settlement, the bulk of Israelite settlements clustered along the central watershed ridge and its slope eastward toward the Jordan.[71] If these groups traced their origins back to the highlands of Canaan, and if they are returning with a new religious and social ideology, then both cultural continuity and sharp points of differentiation, especially at points of contact with potentially stronger competitors in Canaan, are not only tolerable, but to be predicted.

Third, the archaeological data and even some of the biblical material point to the bulk of the earliest Israelite settlements appearing in the eastern zones of the tribal area designated for Manasseh.[72] Zertal, tracking the distribution of pottery, has suggested an initial settlement on the slopes west of the Jordan, where pastoralism and cereal cultivation would be most easily practiced. Settlement density shifted westward, however, up and over the watershed ridge and down onto the western slopes of the hill country, where the cultivation of olives and grapes became possible.[73] Rainey reviewed a range of cultural features, including linguistic data, also concluding that the earliest Israelite settlement came in the east, even in Transjordan, and moved west through the twelfth century BCE. This general consensus raises questions, however, for the biblical witness. As noted above, the inner biblical chronology suggests a mid- or late thirteenth century date for the military actions of the Israelites. It emphasizes actions in Benjamin first, then moves southward, and finally turns to the Galilee. Thus a historian interested in a dialogue between texts and archaeological research faces an intriguing challenge.

Fourth, despite current scholarly prejudice against "conquest" models, it is difficult to imagine any people group establishing a claim over Canaan, the scene of constant military clashes for the entire LBA, without any acts of warfare against the urban centers that controlled Canaan on behalf of Egypt. How could a group's putative annihilation merit notice in the inscription of an Egyptian pharaoh, Merneptah, if this group posed no formidable threat? In fact, urban destruction wrought by unforeseen "barbarian" groups conspicuously characterizes the end of the LBA throughout the eastern Mediterranean, including the Levant. Pharaonic inscriptions repeatedly speak of marching

70. Anson F. Rainey, "Whence Came the Israelites and Their Language?," *IEJ* 57 (2007): 41–64; Zertal, "'Land of the Perizzites.'"

71. Finkelstein, *Archaeology of the Israelite Settlement*, 324.

72. The main survey data are Finkelstein, *Archaeology of the Israelite Settlement*; Zertal, *Manasseh Hill Country*.

73. Zertal, "'Land of the Perizzites'"; idem, "Israel Enters Canaan."

against the Shasu, a pastoralist people in Canaan. The rise of the warlord Abdi-Ashirta in the high country around the Eleutheros Valley just north of Canaan, a region of mixed farming and pastoralism, provides a striking parallel. This man, without known status or portfolio, gathered up from the population a group composed of disenfranchised, desperate men, many of whom are known by the label *'apiru*, and carved out a kingdom and dynasty that became a vital swing vote in the shifting balance of power in the LBA Levant. Likewise, in the fourteenth century Shechem saw the rise of Labaya, another charismatic and conniving leader who forged a regional mini-empire before being assassinated by agents of Egypt. The end of the LBA featured such irregular or "outlaw" bands led by warlords, thugs, and tribal chieftains. In the firestorm that was the collapse of the LBA, is it really so unlikely that the Israelites did not toss a few brands into the burning?

Sketching a Narrative

Contemporary scholars have hesitated, understandably, to project a narrative of the process of Israel's appearance and possession of Canaan. This goes beyond simply inserting the facts and factors noted above into an existing model. It seeks to tell a story, one that accounts for as much data as possible. The exclusive focus on urban destructions, however important, often obscures other equally important features in the military narratives of the book of Joshua and often skews the reader's perspective. Several points about these "campaigns" typically escape serious notice.

First, the rhetoric of extreme destruction and annihilation of all life likely reflects the fixed idioms of ancient military jargon. K. Lawson Younger Jr., both in a monograph and in a focused study, has pointed out the pervasive use of a very stilted and stereotypical military language that should not be pressed in all its literal detail.[74] In essence, any decisive victory finds expression in the most extreme language of annihilation, even if followed almost immediately by statements of the tributes to be levied on the (presumably dead!) population. The actual killing of every single person in any ancient town or region poses an absolute logistical impossibility. Ancient armies lacked the mobility, communications resources, and weaponry to accomplish actual genocide. Indeed, modern concerns about genocide in the biblical texts mistakenly read these passages through the lens of the modern experience of actual genocide as well as the presence of the technology of warfare that could accomplish such

---

74. K. Lawson Younger Jr., *Ancient Conquest Accounts: A Study in Ancient Near Eastern and Biblical History Writing* (JSOTSup 98; Sheffield: JSOT Press, 1990); idem, "The Rhetorical Structuring of the Joshua Conquest Narratives," in Hess, Klingbeil, and Ray, *Critical Issues*, 3–32.

a terrible aim. But the ancients, for all their ferocity, possessed only knives, swords, arrows, spears, and rudimentary stone-hurling devices. They lacked the ability to slaughter all or even most of the occupants of a region. They also lacked the ability to prevent the escape of many. Most of the urban centers destroyed in the LBA seem to have been abandoned before their final capture and destruction. To make archaeological traces of near-apocalyptic destructions the standard for demonstrating the historicity of the Joshua narratives is to misunderstand the texts from their literary, theological, and historical perspectives.

Second, the book of Joshua actually stresses the killing of the "kings" far more strongly than the destruction of the cities themselves. The book does not report the Israelites attacking any Canaanite peasant villages or settlements or any encampments of pastoralists, an odd omission if the text really sought to report annihilation of the entire population. Only three cities are actually said to have been destroyed: Jericho, Ai, and Hazor (cf. Josh. 11:13). The list of towns in Joshua 12 does not claim that the towns were destroyed, or even assaulted. Reports of capture, not destruction, of Lachish, Eglon, Hebron, and Debir do appear in Joshua 10:29–39. These emphasize the killing of the city rulers. The list notwithstanding, Joshua 10 devotes its primary attention to the conspiracy of the five kings, their flight, imprisonment, and execution. Joshua 12 claims that "one king" in each town was killed. The kings of Canaan appear as the principal targets.

As the Amarna correspondence graphically illustrates, the city rulers served as the executive agents of Egypt in the administration of Canaan. Through a long process, as noted above, Ramesses II had finally settled his dispute with the Hittite Empire over their respective spheres of influence in the Levant. Relations between the pharaoh and Hatti remained warm. Thus Ramesses II sent physicians and medicines to the Hittite king and warmly invited Hattusili to visit Egypt. The pharaoh welcomed a second Hittite princess into his harem.[75] Certainly the pharaoh assumed Egypt's continued control over Canaan, reaching back at least to the time of Thutmose III, two centuries earlier. The killing of thirty-one city rulers in Canaan would have disrupted Egypt's system of command and control and drawn the attention of the pharaoh. Following the chronology above, the last city, Hazor, fell in about 1235 BCE. This was the forty-fourth year of Ramesses II, who invested the final years of his rule exploiting the peace attained with the Hittites to establish his cultural legacy within Egypt. In the last years of his reign, he increasingly delegated

---

75. Kenneth A. Kitchen, *Pharaoh Triumphant: The Life and Times of Ramesses II, King of Egypt* (Warminster, UK: Aris & Phillips, 1982), 73–95.

the major responsibilities to his heir designate, Merneptah. The latter ruler was already in his sixties and suffering from both crippling arthritis and severe dental problems.[76] Ultimately it fell to Merneptah to deal with any disruption of the Egyptian order in Canaan. The campaign reported in the Israel Stela may represent exactly such an action. The decimation of Egypt's administrative force in Canaan, not the actual securing of lands for direct settlement, could explain why Merneptah found it necessary to declare his annihilation of "Israel," an entity not yet even associated with a city or territory. In fact, if he dealt Israel a severe blow, the setback to the settlement process could be mirrored in the sudden decline noted in the book of Judges "after the death of Joshua" (cf. Judg. 1:1–3:6). The actions narrated in Judges 1 could point to Israelite attempts to regain what they had lost and to reestablish themselves.

Third, after the taking of Jericho and Ai, the book of Joshua reports two "campaigns." Quite apart from historical and archaeological concerns, these campaigns raise questions about the connection between the "conquest" and the actual Israelite settlement. A southern campaign, prompted by the attack of a conspiracy of kings against Israel's treaty partner, Gibeon, led to a sweep that captured important segments and intersections of the southern road system in Canaan (Josh. 9–10; esp. 10:29–43).

The northern campaign (Josh. 11) involved a rapid move through the central hill country and across the Jezreel Valley to attack the Canaanites at the Waters of Merom. The traditional location of Merom, the modern village of Meron in the Upper Galilee, seems an unlikely place for Canaanite war leaders to amass chariotry, which receives emphasis in the narrative (Josh. 11:4, 6, 9). The abrupt, precipitous hills and gullies of the region make a poor place for the mustering of large chariot forces. By contrast, the other locations in the story, such as Dor, Achsaph, Shimron, and Hazor, command access points between hills and valleys and make fit locales for chariots. So where might the Waters of Merom be located? Van Bekkum has compiled the evidence and options, concluding that "the 'waters of Merom' could be identfied with the rich spring of Nabi Shu'eib at the foothill of Tel Qarney Hittin, and Tel Qarney Hittin itself turns out to be Maron."[77] This location, the "Horns of Hittin," west of the Sea of Galilee, is a strategic one conducive to the use of chariots. On its southern shoulder are remains of an LBA fortress, destroyed in the thirteenth century BCE. Likewise, the text mentions Chinneroth, which probably denotes not the general region associated with the Sea of Galilee but rather the site

---

76. Ibid., 112.

77. Van Bekkum, *From Conquest to Coexistence*, 173–75. See also *NEAEHL* 2:452. See earlier, Nadav Na'aman, *Borders and Districts in Biblical Historiography* (JBS 4; Jerusalem: Simor, 1986), 126.

of Tel Kinrot. The tel possesses LBA and even more extensive IA1 Canaanite remains.[78] The towns of the northern campaign thus form a kind of fence that stretches from Dor across the western end of the Jezreel Valley to Achsaph (Tel Keisan). It continues eastward to Shimron, past the Horns of Hittin to Tel Kinroth, and thence to Hazor. This chain of cities formed a natural line with the Jezreel Valley, and with the Jordan Valley and Sea of Galilee to the east.

A difficulty arises with the observation that neither of the regions involved in these two campaigns evidences early Israelite settlement. The earliest, concentrated, and distinctive Israelite settlements appear in the hill country along the watershed ridge running through the territories of Ephraim and Manasseh. Paradoxically, the book of Joshua offers no narrative of conquest for the very region that saw the earliest and heaviest Israelite settlement. Twice Joshua and the Israelites travel in this region unimpeded, once to Mount Ebal in the area of Shechem, and then through the region on their way to the battle at the Waters of Merom. The Israelites have easy access to Shiloh, which serves as an administrative center, and also to Shechem, for the final covenant ceremony. No sign of resistance or danger arises in the narrative. So the text presents a "conquest" of regions not settled, and a settlement of regions not conquered. Joshua 17:14–18 is instructive on this point. When the Joseph tribes complain that they have insufficient space, Joshua does not censure their lack of faith or urge them simply to fight more enemies, but rather to clear the forests, which they did with a vengeance.[79] Joshua seems to accept the presence of Canaanite "chariots of iron" in the Jezreel and Beth Shean as an understandable deterrent to immediate expansion (v. 18b), though ultimately this challenge must be faced. In addition, the battles of the conquest come to an end at Hazor, which fell in about 1235 BCE, while the earliest settlements in the highlands appear to come somewhat later, closer to 1200 BCE. They are attested even later still for the more southerly and northerly regions. This very tension could almost serve as a sign of the debate surrounding the Israelite settlement. One set of data points to military action, another points to more peaceful settlement. Might these two phenomena be interrelated?

One possible scenario is to reconsider whether the battle narratives in Joshua actually intend to constitute a "conquest" at all. "Conquest" is not a term used in the biblical narrative, but rather is of modern manufacture. If the objective of the military action was to kill the city rulers, thus breaking up

78. Stefan Münger, Jürgen Zangenberg, and Juha Pakkala, in collaboration with Guy Bar-Oz et al., "Kinneret—An Urban Center at the Crossroads: Excavations on Iron IB Tel Kinrot at the Lake of Galilee," *NEA* 74 (2011): 68–90. See also *NEAEHL* 1:299–301; 5:1684–85.

79. On the deforestation, see Richard Hess, *Joshua: An Introduction and Commentary* (TOTC 6; Downers Grove, IL: InterVarsity, 1996), 260–61.

Egypt's administration of Canaan and possibly preventing reprisals from those cities at Egypt's behest, then it is impressive that most of the cities engaged form two "belts," one to the south and one to the north, of the main area of Israelite settlement, in which no fighting is reported. The possibility exists that the battles in the book of Joshua were aimed at creating militarily neutralized zones to the north and south of the main areas in which the Israelites initially settled. The main bulk of the Israelites could indeed have entered the land in the vicinity of the eastern entrance of the Wadi Far'ah, moving into the eastern slopes of the hill country of Ephraim and Manasseh, where the earliest settlement sites appear. The farmers and pastoralists built small, unwalled, and thus defenseless villages. If the local Canaanite peasantry in general were in sympathy with Israel, and if the hill country in fact was only thinly settled, then the entry of the tribes would have been a "peaceful infiltration." But they would remain vulnerable to attack and oppression by the same city rulers who had presided over Canaan's troubles for centuries and had depleted the highland regions through conscription. The battles reported in Joshua could be seen as two campaigns aimed primarily at neutralizing the ability of the city rulers to act against the new settlers. Certainly the book of Joshua reports the opposition to Israelite presence (cf. 5:1; 9:1; 10:1–5; 11:1–5, 19). The two campaigns in effect created a ring of fire, or firewall, protecting the new hill-country settlements. With the capture of Jericho and Ai, and with the alliance with Gibeon, these campaigns gave Israel control over important segments of the highway network in Canaan.

In addition, the neutralization of the Canaanite towns disrupted Egypt's administration of the area. This opened the way for expanding Israelite settlements beyond the hill country, where excavation and survey has revealed that Israelite settlement indeed came later. Though only a suggestion, this does cohere reasonably well with the text and what is known of the archaeological record.

The damage done to Egypt's administrative network in Canaan could not be immediately addressed by a pharaoh who, though the most powerful and grand king in Egyptian history, was now crippled by arthritis. He focused on his diplomatic ties. Ramesses II held important sites such as the coastal towns and Beth Shean. But in 1209 BCE Ramesses II's coregent and successor, Merneptah, campaigned in Canaan and reported a devastating blow struck against Israel. This defeat would constitute a body blow to the emerging nation hoping to cross the "ring of fire" and expand its holdings. Thus the early Israelites were thrown back into a weakened position, as found in the book of Judges. The collapse of Egyptian control over Canaan (ca. 1150 BCE) provided needed relief and allowed a brief recovery and resumption of settlement expansion. However, the resulting power vacuum spawned multilayered

The Hurrians

Unfamiliar to most students of the Old Testament, the Hurrians played an intriguing role in the ancient world. Documented as early as the third millennium BCE, the Hurrians come most strongly onto the stage of history in the Late Bronze Age (LBA). Having expanded westward as far as Anatolia and eastward to the Tigris, the Hurrians formed the unified state of Mitanni. In the peculiar peer-polity mode of LBA international relations, Mitanni functioned as a top-tier great power. The king of Mitanni interacted as a "brother" with the kings of Hatti and Egypt. Unfortunately, Mitanni remained ever under pressure from the Hittites in the west and the ambitious second-tier power, Assyria, in the east. After the collapse of Mitanni (ca. 1350 BCE), the erstwhile Mitannian territories came under the nearest dominant power, either the Hittites or the Assyrians. After the general collapse of the LBA (ca. 1200 BCE), many of the Neo-Hittite city-states in Syria lay within formerly Mitannian territory. Ethnic Hurrians appeared throughout the Levant, especially in Syria and Ugarit, where personal names, lexical texts, and literary and ritual texts testify to their influence.

For Canaan, the Amarna texts (from Egypt) suggest that the king of Jerusalem, ʿAbdi-Ḫeba, was Hurrian. Other stray Hurrian names appear in the Amarna letters. By the late 1400s BCE the Egyptians regularly referred to Canaan as "Kharu/Khuru-land" and sometimes identified prisoners from Canaan as "Hurrians." This Hurrian label reflects not the ethnicity of the captives, but rather Egyptian administrative terminology. In the important Israel Stela of Merneptah, the line "Canaan is plundered" is seen by many to be in parallel with the line "Hurru is become a widow." This exemplifies the tendency in Egypt to identify the two. In the Old Testament the Hebrew word ḥorî renders the term "Hurrian."

The Hurrians had a significant impact on the culture of the ancient Near East. Their technology in glassmaking, metallurgy, and weaponry possibly brought the distinctive LBA chariot into widespread use. Most famous is the Hurrian mastery of horse training. The manual of Kikkuli, a Hurrian horse trainer, served as a standard text for training warhorses. It describes practices still in use today.

The most detailed information about Hurrian culture derives from the personal and family archives unearthed in the north Mesopotamian city of Nuzi. The texts document adoptions, land transfers, lawsuits, and a host of other details of the culture. Some personal names in the Bible, such as "Sheshai," "Talmai," and "Piram," may best be analyzed as Hurrian. In the region of the southern Levant, evidence of Hurrian culture disappears after the tenth century BCE.

conflicts with Canaanites, raiders from Transjordan, and the Philistines, who had arrived in 1175 BCE and ultimately would provoke a crisis leading to the foundation of the Israelite state.

5

The Judges and the Early Iron Age

ROBERT D. MILLER II

Iron Age I (IA1) covers the years 1200–1000 BCE. This period began with the general situation in Canaan as had obtained in the (preceding) Late Bronze Age (LBA), but almost immediately there were changes. Just as Egypt dictated the policy and the future for Canaan in the LBA, so again changes in Egypt altered the situation in Canaan. Beginning in about 1200, Egypt became consumed with internal matters, with conflict between the king and the religious leaders. The Egyptians slowly lost control of Canaan, losing the last footholds by 1150. This allowed several different groups to expand in various parts of the country, for the most part living alongside one another without conflict.

As we will see from the Bible and archaeology, one can divide these communities into four groups, each of which will be discussed: the Canaanites, the Israelite clans, the Israelite nomads, and the Philistines. Our focus will be on the Israelite clans, for reasons to be explained shortly.

The Canaanite communities are simply the continuation of the LBA population: the same towns, only their mayors were now independent kings. All the cities on the Mediterranean coast and in the Jezreel Valley remained Canaanite, at least at the start of the Iron Age. The Canaanites controlled the coastal highway as well, along with a route up to Jerusalem. Jerusalem, then known as "Jebus," remained a Canaanite city, although it was surrounded on the north, east, and south by Israelites.

Other Canaanite cities include many from the LBA. Megiddo continued to be large and important, along with Taanach, Ibleam, Gezer, and others. A look at Megiddo shows some features of the Canaanite culture. A large collection of carved ivory works of art was found in IA1 Megiddo.[1] Some had been made in the LBA and simply kept by the owners. No one came around house to house and said, "The Late Bronze Age is over today." For the Canaanites, it never ended—the Egyptians had just disappeared. Aspects of an older and developed Canaanite culture can be seen from these carvings. The Canaanites had ivory, imported from Egypt; they had horses and likely camels. They had a large olive oil industry and traded with Lebanon and Cyprus. This, we will see, is completely different from the Israelites, who lived in the hills.

As discussed in the preceding chapter, no one is exactly sure how or even when the Israelites arrived in the hill country, but in the IA1 period the entire half of the West Bank from Jerusalem north (see details below) was more densely occupied than it had been in centuries—occupied by small villages belonging to the Israelites. This community formed the center of the stories in the biblical book of Judges.

The Book of Judges and the Bible's Treatment of the Early Iron Age

Since the time of the early Jewish rabbis, it has been recognized that the stories in the book of Judges might not be arranged chronologically.[2] Rather, the book arranges several disparate stories thematically to address two questions: How will reconstituted Israel conduct its affairs as a people of the covenant at home in Canaan? How will Israel be governed without a Moses or a Joshua to exercise leadership?

The book is framed by a question-and-answer repeated from chapter 1: "Who shall go up first for us to do battle?" The question is answered in 21:25: "In those days there was no king in Israel; all the people did what was right in their own eyes" (NRSV). In the closing chapters the question-and-answer pair occurs again, in reverse order, as Israel mobilizes for civil war: "In those days there was no king" (17:6). "Who shall go up first for us?" (20:18).

---

1. Itamar Singer, "Egyptians, Canaanites, and Philistines in the Period of the Emergence of Israel," in *From Nomadism to Monarchy: Archaeological and Historical Aspects of Early Israel* (ed. Israel Finkelstein and Nadav Na'aman; Jerusalem: Israel Exploration Society, 1994), 319.

2. For example, from Rabbi Jose ben Halafta's 160 CE *Seder Olam Rabbah* to the thirteenth-century CE Rabbi David Kimchi.

The thematic structure of the book is largely beyond the scope of this chapter, but some observations should be made as they pertain to the history of this period. Judges 1:1–3:6 forms a preface that precedes the introduction of the first "judge." The first chapter presents an unfinished conquest and a rather indecisive settlement of the Israelites in the "promised land." Judges 1 says that the tribes of Judah and Benjamin (and they alone) eliminated the Canaanite presence. Otherwise, initial success deteriorates into nearly disastrous straits (1:27–34).

The book then sets out a pattern in 2:11–19 that one might expect would be followed through the rest of the book. This pattern gives the impression of a sort of retributive theology. After every instance of seeking foreign gods, the Israelites are handed over to enemies until God raises a deliverer—a charismatic, nonhereditary, military leader whom we call by the rather inaccurate English term "judge." Prosperity during the career of the judge lasts only until a relapse into idolatry after the judge's death. If this actually were the pattern of all the ensuing stories—and it is not, as many scholars have pointed out—it would illustrate quite clearly what scholars have called the "Deuteronomistic theology": blessings of fertility and independence come to Israel when they obey the law, while defeat and servitude result from disobedience.[3] The theology of the book of Judges is quite a bit more sophisticated than this, as most modern commentaries will illustrate.[4]

In the remainder of the book, the judges are far from being the righteous deliverers envisioned in chapter 2; indeed, they come to typify the sins of their people. A good example is the cycle of stories about Gideon and his son Abimelech (Judg. 6–9), which opens the second part of the book of Judges. With the Gideon material, the progressive threefold deterioration of Israel (the theme of the book of Judges) takes place in earnest: the people decline into idolatry, violence, and immorality. After Gideon, it is a precipitous slide through Abimelech, Jephthah, Samson, and the carnage of chapters 17–21. The Gideon passages have been considered by some scholars to stand at the center of the overall structure of the book of Judges,[5] but in any case they constitute a turning point. Let us consider one story from this cycle in more detail, as it also illuminates the historical value of the book of Judges.

The story from Judges 9 takes place in Shechem. This is the story of Abimelech of Arumah (9:41). His name means, "My father is king," and his father

---

3. See, e.g., Gerhard von Rad, *Old Testament Theology* (trans. D. M. G. Stalker; 2 vols.; New York: Harper & Row, 1962–65), 1:327.

4. See, e.g., J. Clinton McCann, *Judges* (IBC; Louisville: Westminster John Knox, 2002), esp. 36; J. Alan Groves, *Judges* (THOTC; Grand Rapids: Eerdmans, forthcoming).

5. J. Paul Tanner, "The Gideon Narrative as the Focal Point of Judges," *BSac* 149 (1992): 150.

was Gideon, who had been a judge. After the death of Gideon, Abimelech tried to establish a kingdom at Shechem. He capitalized on his father's popularity and on the political and geographic centrality of Shechem. As a shrewd politician, he could use the Shechemites' natural tendency toward kingdom building to his own advantage.

It took three years for the people of Shechem to realize their mistake. Abimelech had no more respect for them than he did for his own brothers, whom he had previously murdered. A story of intrigue and bloodshed involving Abimelech and his followers from Arumah follows. The local inhabitants tried to escape Abimelech's fury by hiding in their temple, which became an inferno for those trapped inside when Abimelech ordered its destruction by fire. Following Abimelech's ruthless act in Shechem, he went on to another town. Again, the people took refuge in the tower of the city, and again Abimelech decided to destroy them by fire. However, an anonymous woman threw down a millstone that landed directly on the head of Abimelech.

The historicity of the events themselves is impossible to prove or disprove. As we will see from the archaeology, a scenario such as Abimelech's is perfectly likely for this period. The story gives an accurate image of the life of the Israelite clans: no real kings, just chiefs who always wanted to be more powerful. Its narrative also corresponds to the importance of Shechem in the IA1 and the basic geography of the city and its environs.

Some scholars have argued for substantial historicity of the events described, while others make no such assumptions.[6] This issue really applies to the study of Judges as a whole. Does historicity matter? For modern readers, this can be a serious obstacle to acceptance of the text. If the importance of the details in the narratives is still thought to be plausible, the text has as its message the story of a fundamentally meaningful world. However, as the twentieth-century philosopher Michael Polanyi showed, even if the narrative is implausible, it is still possible for our imagination to integrate the story's incompatible elements into a meaning—a meaning that is born and remains more intuitive than literal but nonetheless is not merely a subjectively personal meaning.[7] In the case of Abimelech, on the one hand, the story is "legend" only in that it is a religious narrative that treats the lives of great heroes. On the other hand, it is "historical" only in that its primary meaning is the plain meaning that the text had for its historical Israelite audience.

6. A. Graeme Auld, "Gideon: Hacking at the Heart of the Old Testament," *VT* 39 (1989): 259–60.

7. Michael Polanyi, *Meaning* (Chicago: University of Chicago Press, 1975), 158.

Figure 5.1. Iron I (?) temple at Tell-Balatah/Shechem

With the Enlightenment, biblical scholars found themselves moving rapidly toward the dawn of so-called higher criticism, where questions concerning historical context became very important. Even the Jewish philosopher Baruch Spinoza read Judges in terms of its references to ancient history and recognized the variance of the book's dating schema from that of Kings.[8] Under the impact of the historical-critical method, Judges invited an extension of source criticism from the Pentateuch, especially in Germany. "J," "E," and "D" were identified within Judges, along with independent sources. As the nineteenth century progressed, the rest of Europe and America also became involved in source-critical analyses of Judges. Notable examples of this trend were T. K. Cheyne's 1900 article on Judges in the *Encyclopaedia Biblica* and George Foot Moore's 1895 commentary.[9] In the mid-twentieth century the source- and redaction-critical enterprise moved to consideration of the place of the book in the larger Deuteronomistic History, as Martin Noth's 1953 construct of an overarching historical work from Joshua through Kings gained acceptance.[10] Robert Boling's still highly influential Anchor Bible commentary of 1975 addresses the precise extent of Deuteronomistic

8. Baruch Spinoza, *Tractatus theologico-politicus*, 128–37.

9. George Foot Moore, *A Critical and Exegetical Commentary on Judges* (ICC; Edinburgh: T&T Clark, 1895).

10. See the ET: Martin Noth, *The Deuteronomistic History* (JSOTSup 15; Sheffield: University of Sheffield, Department of Biblical Studies, 1981).

material, the stages of Deuteronomistic editing, and the nature of the pre-Deuteronomistic book.[11]

Throughout this period no critical work on Judges was complete without an extensive exploration of its chronology, both internally and in relation to the larger history of Israel. As archaeology led to the revision of "conquest" models for the rise of early Israel (see chap. 4 above), George Mendenhall and Norman Gottwald suggested new ways to understand the people's experience of oppression in the period of the judges.[12] The overthrow of city-state domination by an underclass of peasants and displaced persons was illustrated by the war against Jabin and Sisera in Judges 4–5. Judges as a whole provides substantial support for a gradual infiltration model for the emergence of Israel.

Studies in the 1980s and 1990s by James Flanagan and Gösta Ahlström combined archaeological evidence with critical analysis of the biblical text, thereby to propose reconstructions of the twelfth and eleventh centuries BCE.[13] At the same time, Philip Davies, Niels Peter Lemche, and Thomas Thompson argued that the biblical accounts of a "judges period" were historically unreliable constructs of postexilic authors and are best used only as sources for understanding that later time.[14]

Nevertheless, most scholars do not hesitate to critically compare the archaeology of IA1 Israel with the biblical text. The biblical text might provide valuable information about the history of early Israel, especially if by "history" we no longer mean just battles and rulers, but rather we include the lifestyles, economics, and culture of the people; it would be most difficult to prove that it does not. There is value, therefore, in the interpretive traditions of the ancient Israelites themselves. However, such information will always be inextricably bound with thick cultural concepts, intentions, and concerns of the author's own period and of many others before his time. For this reason, archaeology forms an all-important source for reconstructing the history of Israel in the period of the judges.

---

11. Robert Boling, *Judges: Introduction, Translation, and Commentary* (AB 6A; Garden City, NY: Doubleday, 1975).

12. George E. Mendenhall, "The Hebrew Conquest of Palestine," *BA* 25 (1962): 66–87; Norman K. Gottwald, *The Tribes of Yahweh: A Sociology of the Religion of Liberated Israel, 1250–1050 B.C.E.* (Maryknoll, NY: Orbis Books, 1979).

13. James Flanagan, *David's Social Drama: A Hologram of Israel's Early Iron Age* (JSOTSup 73; Sheffield: Almond, 1988); Gösta Ahlström, *Who Were the Israelites?* (Winona Lake, IN: Eisenbrauns, 1986); idem, *The History of Ancient Palestine from the Palaeolithic Period to Alexander's Conquest* (JSOTSup 146; Sheffield: Sheffield Academic Press, 1993).

14. Philip R. Davies, *In Search of "Ancient Israel"* (JSOTSup 148; Sheffield: Sheffield Academic Press, 1992); Niels Peter Lemche, *Ancient Israel: A New History of Israelite Society* (BibSem 5; Sheffield: JSOT Press, 1988); Thomas L. Thompson, *Early History of the Israelite People: From the Written and Archaeological Sources* (SHANE 4; Leiden: Brill, 1992).

Identification and Evaluation of Archaeological and Other Sources

First we must define what period and geographic range to consider archaeologically. We have already observed that along the Mediterranean coast and in the broad valleys of the Jordan and Jezreel there was no real break in material culture between the LBA and the IA1 period. If we turn to the highlands of Israel north of Jerusalem, many factors delimit a break at the end of the thirteenth century and place the highland sites within the twelfth–eleventh centuries. These factors include, but are not limited to, datable Egyptian scarabs, typological changes in objects such as axes, and the chronology of the rise of iron metallurgy. Even with the pottery, there is a discontinuity. In the Late Bronze Age II period (approximately 1400–1200 BCE) there are many well-formed shapes but little regional variation, while in IA1 there are a few coarse vessel types but with many regional variants.

It is also necessary to delimit the geographic scope of this archaeological discussion. Archaeologically, the distinct highland settlement appears to have occupied the highland area between Jerusalem and the Jezreel Valley. The "Judean" area south of Jerusalem, to which we will return, was sparsely inhabited, compared with the densely populated north-central hill country. This north-central region was bounded on the north by a line of Egyptian, Canaanite, and Philistine city-states running from Dor to Beth Shean (Dor, Jokneam, Megiddo, Taanach, Ibleam, Ophrah, Beth Shean), and on the south by a similar line from Gezer to Jerusalem, which exhibit material cultures distinct from the highland unit until the late eleventh century. A similar line can be drawn on the western edge, from Socoh to Aphek to Joppa. On the eastern edge, while it is assumed that the Jordan River was a sufficient boundary on topographic bases, there is also a similar line part of the way down the river from Beth Shean to Rehob to Hamath to Zarethan (Tell es-Saidiyeh) to Sukkoth.[15]

All these lines are of sites whose material culture is totally unlike that of the highlands. Lowland sites, most much larger than those of the highlands (e.g., Ekron/Tel Miqne, a fifty-acre site with fortifications more than three meters thick), have locally made Egyptian pottery forms (e.g., bowls found at Beth Shean), large amounts of Mycenaean pottery made on Cyprus (e.g.,

---

15. Herbert Donner, *Von den Anfangen bis zur Staatenbildungszeit* (vol. 1 of *Geschichte Volkes Israel und seiner Nachbarn in Grundzügen*; GAT 4.1; Göttingen: Vandenhoeck & Ruprecht, 1995), 139–40; Amihai Mazar, "The 11th Century in the Land of Israel," in *Cyprus in the 11th Century B.C.: Proceedings of the International Symposium Organized by the Archaeological Research Unit of the University of Cyprus and the Anastasios G. Leventis Foundation, Nicosia, 30–31 October 1993* (ed. Vassos Karageorghis; Nicosia: A. G. Leventis Foundation, University of Cyprus, 1994), 39–57.

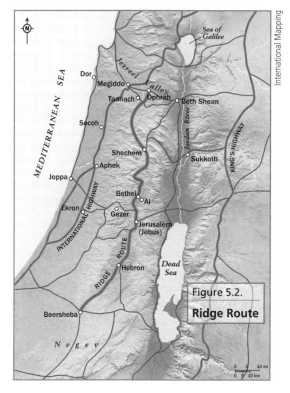

Figure 5.2.

Ridge Route

International Mapping

at Ophrah), incense stands, cuneiform tablets (e.g., one tablet from Taanach),[16] hieroglyphic door lintels (e.g., at Beth Shean), and unique pottery forms such as beer jugs (at Beth Shean, Timnah, etc.). The differences from the highlands are quite clear.[17]

There is more uniformity in the IA1 highland ceramic corpus than diversity: a few coarse vessel types. Granted, these are vessel types also found in the lowland assemblages, but many of the types found in the lowlands are simply missing in the highlands, and the percentages of forms are different. The homogeneity of this "hill-country complex," as William Dever calls it, is due both to a fairly closed trading system and to a single group sharing common stylistic elements. In Dever's terms, this is a unique "'archaeological assemblage,' usually typical of a socio-economic, cultural, or ethnic group," which defines and delimits this "Highland Ethnicity" that was early Israel.[18] Archaeologically, IA1 Israelites are the "insiders" who share regular commerce and who share styles.

It is a separate question whether the twelfth- and eleventh-century Israelite community was confined to the highlands. The greatest number of IA1 sites is found within this north-central hill country of Palestine. Areas such as Galilee remain less well understood for the IA1 period. The central part of lower Galilee, the tribal allotments of Zebulun and Naphtali, show new

---

16. In addition to sixteen LBA cuneiform texts and fragments, there is at least one IA1 cuneiform tablet: *TT*433, a receipt for a grain shipment (see *NEAEHL* 4:1432).

17. Ann E. Killebrew, *Biblical Peoples and Ethnicity: An Archaeological Study of Egyptians, Canaanites, Philistines, and Early Israel, 1300–1100 B.C.E.* (SBLABS 9; Atlanta: Society of Biblical Literature, 2005).

18. William G. Dever, "Archaeology and the Emergence of Early Israel," in *Archaeology and Biblical Interpretation* (ed. John R. Bartlett; New York: Routledge, 1997), 36, 42.

settlement patterns after a gap in occupation following the LBA. Farther east there is no IA1 occupation.[19]

South of Jerusalem the situation was quite different from the "highland settlement." Instead of many little villages—hundreds, really, in the north—there are a few largish towns, including Hebron, Beersheba, Beth Zur, and Debir, and many campsites. This thinly populated area seems to be evidence of a nomadic society, much like the West Bank south of Jerusalem was until the mid-1950s. It was Israelite at this time. There are enough similarities to the northern highlands and differences from everyone else to conclude this. In addition, it is the region that eventually becomes the most important for the stories of the Bible: over two-thirds of the stories recorded in the Old Testament that can be placed on a map occurred in the regions between Jerusalem and Beersheba. Yet it was a different kind of Israel than the highland chiefdoms—a kind of Bedouin Israel.

The book of Judges also seems to reflect this fact, that the real "Israel" of IA1 was the northern hill country. None of the stories, except that of Samson, takes place in the southern part of the land, and all the stories take place at least in part in the northern highlands.

The Archaeology of the Israelite Highlands

Between 1968 and 1972 all of the West Bank was explored by archaeological survey. In the last decades of the twentieth century, several archaeological surveys (especially surveys undertaken by Israel Finkelstein and Adam Zertal) reexamined these regions, particularly that half of the West Bank north of Jerusalem.[20] These archaeological survey data provide the greatest insights into the history of IA1 Israel.

Most of the cities Judges 1 identifies as Canaanite in IA1 turn out archaeologically to have been non-Israelite. These include Jerusalem, Beth Shean, Taanach, Dor, Ibleam, Megiddo, Gezer, and Aijalon (Judg. 1:21, 27–29, 34).

The map of the IA1 highland settlement reveals six distinct zones of occupation. There are two partly intertwined zones north of modern Nablus, one centered on Dothan, and the other around Tirzah. A large zone was centered

---

19. Raphael Frankel, *Settlement Dynamics and Regional Diversity in Ancient Upper Galilee: Archaeological Survey of Upper Galilee* (IAAR 14; Jerusalem: Israel Antiquities Authority, 2001), 55–56, 132; Zvi Gal, *Lower Galilee during the Iron Age* (trans. Marcia Reines Josephy; ASORDS 9; Winona Lake, IN: Eisenbrauns, 1992).

20. Israel Finkelstein, Zvi Lederman, and Shlomo Bunimovitz, *Highlands of Many Cultures: The Southern Samaria Survey; The Sites* (2 vols.; TAUIAM 15; Tel Aviv: Institute of Archaeology, Tel Aviv University, 1997); Adam Zertal, *The Manasseh Hill Country Survey* (2 vols.; CHANE 21.1–2; Leiden: Brill, 2004–2008).

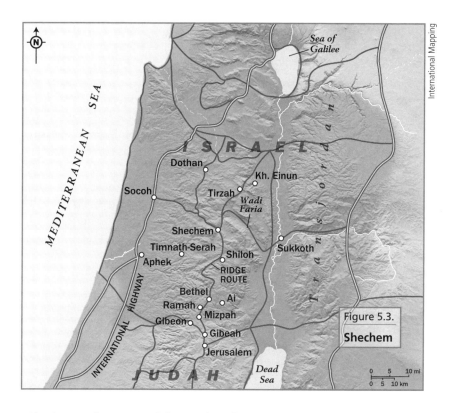

Figure 5.3.
Shechem

on Shechem in the center of the northern highlands. Another surrounds Shiloh farther south. To the west of this, a zone centers on Timnath-Serah, considered by the Bible to be the home and burial place of Joshua (Josh. 19:49–50; 24:30). Finally, there is a complex matrix of sites at the southern edge of the highlands in the tribal region of Benjamin: Gibeon, Mizpah, Ramah (Khirbet Raddanah), Gibeah, Ai, and Bethel.

Interesting correlations with the biblical text appear from this, along with some contradictions. Shiloh, Shechem, and the centers of Benjamin just listed that were politically important in IA1 are presented as such in the book of Judges (of course, the issues are complex, but here the point is merely to note this fact). Dothan and Tirzah, however, are not presented as significant in the period of the judges.

Beginning with the southern end of the highlands, the situation at the start of IA1, then, is one of multiple cities in Benjamin. Ai and Gibeon were much larger than the others, but the absence of a city wall at Ai militates against it being the local capital, and it seems unlikely that Gibeon controlled so many large sites far to its east. Probably all of these Benjaminite sites were

Robert D. Miller II

Figure 5.4. The site of Et-Tell, identified as Ai

administrative centers, each an independent, simple chiefdom.[21] The destruction of Gibeah at the end of the IA1, or more properly, about 1150 BCE, probably is echoed in Judges 20 in the Israelite civil war against Gibeah and Benjamin (also Hosea 9:9; 10:9).[22]

Northward, there was the Shiloh chiefdom.[23] The territory controlled from the walled city of Shiloh contains both subordinate towns administering territory and numerous villages directly supporting Shiloh. To the northwest of Shiloh, the towns now comprising the sites of Khirbet Sur and Khirbet Bir el-Kharayib controlled a small enclave, while the site of Baal-Shalishah was the administrative center for the entire eastern edge of Shiloh's territory. To the west of the Shiloh chiefdom was a smaller-scale polity centered on Timnath-Serah. Interestingly, neither of these polities appears to correlate at all with the supposed ancient roads from the highlands to the coast (to Aphek), one of which apparently ran from Gophnah to Rantis (Arimathea?) roughly along modern Highway 465, and another that ran from Shiloh along the Nahal Shiloh all the way to Aphek.

21. On the applicability of chiefdom models to IA1 Israel, see Robert D. Miller II, *Chieftains of the Highland Clans: A History of Israel in Twelfth and Eleventh Centuries B.C.* (Grand Rapids: Eerdmans, 2005).

22. Nancy L. Lapp, "Ful, Tell el-," *OEANE* 2:346.

23. Miller, *Chieftains*, esp. 97–103.

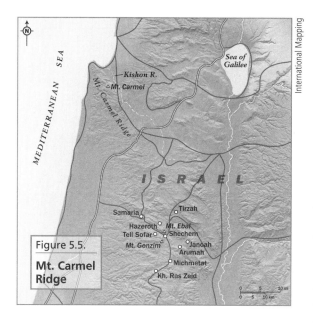

Figure 5.5.
Mt. Carmel Ridge

The people of the villages of this chiefdom were variously farmers, herders, and hunters. They supported the chieftains with oil, wine, and enough grain or meat to live on, and they provided items such as incense and resin to trade for alabaster, Philistine pottery, and other items. Such trade was extensive enough for the chiefdom to be using the Egyptian gold standard of weight.[24] Another means of tribute was the conscription of labor, the likes of which built the wall of Shiloh and pillared buildings on the west side of the city.

Despite its relatively small territory, Shiloh is the only chiefdom capital with evidence of large-scale interaction with other Israelite chiefdoms. Petrography shows that Shiloh was importing pottery from the domain of Tirzah in the twelfth century BCE and later from Shechem in the eleventh.[25] The books of Joshua and 1 Samuel hold that Shiloh was the residence of the ark of the covenant during this period (Josh. 18:1, 8–10; 19:51; 21:2; 22:9, 12; 1 Sam. 1–4). Perhaps the archaeological evidence attests to something that also is reflected in the biblical text's view of Shiloh. Shiloh was destroyed around 1050 BCE,[26] and this may be reflected in Psalm 78:60; Jeremiah 7:12, 14; 26:6. These texts seem to place a destruction of Shiloh on the heels of Israel's defeat by the Philistines at Ebenezer (1 Sam. 4).

To the north of the Michmetat and Beth Dagon sloughs was the largest chiefdom, Shechem. A broad east-west area south of the latitude of Mount Gerizim was administered by an extensive network of midsized towns. While a similar situation does not obtain north of Mount Ebal due to the proximity

---

24. A. Eran, "Weights from Excavations 1981–1984 at Shiloh," *ZDPV* 110 (1994): 151.

25. J. Glass et al., "Petrographic Analysis of Middle Bronze Age III, Late Bronze Age and Iron Age I Ceramic Assemblages," in *Shiloh: The Archaeology of a Biblical Site* (ed. Israel Finkelstein, Shlomo Bunimovitz, and Zvi Lederman; Tel Aviv: Institute of Archaeology, Tel Aviv University, 1993), 271–77.

26. Shlomo Bunimovitz, "Area C," in Finkelstein, Bunimovitz, and Lederman, *Shiloh*, 21.

of the Tirzah chiefdom, the area to the east and west of Shechem was full of tributary sites. Passing the large site of Tell Sofar, which guards the western end of the Nablus Pass, subsystems of sites were also administered far to the northwest along the Nahal Alexander road to the coastal plain. Only the region southwest of Mount Ebal is empty of IA1 sites. This is not a gap in the survey coverage; there are in fact no IA1 sites there. This leaves no sites along the supposed direct route from Shechem to the coast, following modern Highway 55. Shechem's subordinate administrative towns included Tell Sofar administrating the northwest; Khirbet Ras Zeid administrating the southwest; and Arumah administrating the southeast, Michmetat, Janoah, and Hazeroth (a town known from the Samaria ostraca). The southwestern extension controls the road from the Watershed Route (Shechem to Shiloh and beyond in both directions, following modern Highway 60) along the modern Trans-Samarian Road (Highway 505) to the coastal plain, and probably also a branch of the route that swings north along the Kanah River.

The villages of this vast chiefdom, built in cleared sections of the shrub thicket and maquis, could largely support themselves with cereal farming, primarily wheat. They did eat foods from other crops that they grew: lentils, chickpeas, and broad beans were ground up and made into something like falafel; barley and millet were grown primarily to make beer. Olive oil, flax, and other cash crops were moved as tribute from the villages of the thicket, maquis, and the wolds of the valleys at the southern edge of the chiefdom

Robert D. Miller II

Figure 5.6. Poor dwellings at Shechem East Gate

to the municipal centers. The economic prosperity of the elders of Shechem was not shared by all segments of society, however. While the chief lived in his house with a courtyard in central Shechem, just to the northeast the poor dwelt in huts at the old East Gate.

As an archaeological curiosity with the Shechem chiefdom, it seems that their city was uninhabited for a portion of IA1. The site was abandoned from 1125 to 1000 BCE.[27] This being the case, if one looks at the rest of the large towns in the Shechem chiefdom, there are none that, from exploration done so far, show any signs of serious enlargement in the eleventh century indicative of their having replaced Shechem as the regional center. There is a gap at Shechem, showing that the regional cohesion broke down in the eleventh century. Several smaller systems with centers at places such as Arumah, Michmetat, and Hazeroth were the result.

Practically speaking, this means that in the twelfth century there were nine subchief centers in the chiefdom of Shechem.[28] There must have been a successful rebellion in 1125, undertaken by one or more of the subchiefs. The only subchiefs powerful enough to succeed in such a rebellion would have been the ones at Ophrah, Khirbet Ras Zeid, and Arumah. These were the ones with the most strategic economic positions themselves and the most subordinate villages of their own. But the only one of these subchief capitals that was fortified was Arumah, making it the most likely one to have led the rebellion of 1125. One can only think of Judges 9, the story we previously examined of Abimelech of Arumah and his violent career in Shechem, which must bear some connection to these events.

The dense shrubland to the northeast of Shechem was the domain of Tirzah, a chiefdom that extended in all directions. This polity, unlike that of Shechem, contained one very large subordinate center, Khirbet Einun. All the sites around Einun are large by comparison with the rest of the Tirzah polity. Archaeological evidence shows that the elders at Tirzah traded with foreign groups for silver, iron, basalt, and Phoenician pottery.[29] This Tirzah domain was a land primarily of herders, those of the high maquis and thicket to the east, and those of the broad valley of Tirzah. Relations with foreign powers were at times more direct than for other Israelite chiefdoms, for while mountains barred the frontier with Beth Shean in the north, control of this valley was contested with the Canaanite city-state of Sukkoth, east of the Jordan.

27. J. D. Seger, "Shechem," *OEANE* 5:22.
28. Miller, *Chieftains*, 99–100.
29. Alain Chambon, *Tell el-Fâr'ah I: L'âge du fer* (Paris: ÉRCM 31; Paris: Éditions Recherche sur les civilisations, 1984), 20, 140.

Figure 5.7. Site of Dothan

To the northwest of Tirzah, across the Sanur Valley moors, was the chiefdom of Dothan. The city of Dothan lay on the moorland of the Dothan Valley, with its subordinate administrative centers far off into the surrounding thicket and maquis. The Dothan polity controlled the northern entry of the Watershed Route into the highlands. Beyond its control to the west, smaller polities of Israelites inhabited the thicket.

The interrelation between the elites of the highland Israelites resulted in the city of Shiloh importing most of its fancy pottery—jars, bowls, lamps— from the Tirzah chiefdom.[30] About the time Shechem was destroyed, Shiloh switched to importing these from one or more of the resultant simple chiefdoms of the Shechem region. Presumably, since this region was closer, it was more economical to do so, although the quality of pottery was inferior to the Tirzah products. Hostile relations with the centralized Shechem chiefdom in the twelfth century might have previously prevented import from Shechem. It is an open question whether this hints that predestruction Shechem was not Israelite; certainly, everything in the material culture of twelfth-century Shechem looks like the rest of the Israelite highlands.

Ancient Near Eastern Sources on Highland Israel

From IA1 Palestine itself, there are almost no epigraphic remains; the IA1 texts are minimal. The most significant is a supposed abecedary inscribed on a wheeled storage jar found at Izbet Sartah. It consists of five lines of

30. Glass et al., "Petrographic Analysis," 277.

eighty-three letters total, written left-to-right and epigraphically dated to the twelfth–eleventh centuries. Given the possibility that the inscription has no relation to Hebrew—Joseph Naveh thought it to be Greco-Canaanite Philistine, and there was abundant Philistine pottery on the site[31]—it is best to remove it from the discussion.

Other than this, there is a potsherd from an IA1 burial cave at Manahat inscribed with four letters and a potsherd inscribed "oil" from the tiny village of Khirbet Tannin near Tirzah.[32] The Ahilud Inscription from Khirbet Raddanah appears now to be a find without stratigraphy, quite possibly not from the IA1 period, and should not be considered.[33]

This is in marked contrast to the scribal cultures of the LBA and Iron Age II periods, and to continued non-Israelite scribal activity at neighboring Aphek, Beth Shemesh, and Taanach.[34] The most curious factor is the restriction of written texts to small, obscure sites: Izbet Sartah, Khirbet Tannin, and Manahat. It remains unclear why there are no inscriptions from Shechem, Dothan, Shiloh, Tirzah, Ai, Bethel, Gibeon, or Gibeah.

Other sources for independent information about the twelfth- and eleventh-century highland settlement are contemporary ancient Near Eastern records. But to put it bluntly, there is next to nothing relevant to this period of the highlands. There are at least four possible reasons why there are no documents in ancient Near Eastern sources about the IA1 hill country. First, there could have been "no one up there," but the archaeological analysis certainly has disproved this. Second, the only hegemonic power that might have extended its claim into that region, Egypt, was in fact incapable. Some hold that Egyptian control in the highlands may have collapsed even before the end of the reign

31. Joseph Naveh, "Some Considerations on the Ostracon from ʿIzbet Ṣarṭah," *IEJ* 28 (1978): 35. On the pottery, see Israel Finkelstein, *ʿIzbet Ṣarṭah: An Early Iron Age Site near Rosh Haʿayin* (BARIS 299; Oxford: British Archaeological Reports, 1985), 91.

32. Lawrence E. Stager, "Inscribed Potsherd from the Eleventh Century BC," *BASOR* 194 (1969): 45–52; André Lemaire, "Notes d'épigraphie nord-ouest sémitique," *Sem* 35 (1985): 14.

33. Zvi Lederman, "An Early Iron Age Village at Khirbet Raddana: The Excavations of Joseph Callaway" (PhD diss., Harvard University, 1999). One might also note 47 inscribed IA1 arrowheads on which, according to Richard S. Hess, 12 of the 54 names in the book of Judges are found ("Israelite Identity and Personal Names from the Book of Judges," *HS* 44 [2003]: 25–39; idem, "Arrowheads from Iron Age I: Personal Names and Authenticity," in *Ugarit at Seventy-Five: Proceedings of the Symposium "Ugarit at Seventy-Five," Held at Trinity International University, Deerfield, Illinois, February 18–20, 2005, under the Auspices of the Middle Western Branch of the American Oriental Society and the Mid-West Region of the Society of the Biblical Literature* [ed. K. Lawson Younger Jr.; Winona Lake, IN: Eisenbrauns, 2007], 113–29). The problem here is that these arrowheads are almost without exception from the antiquities market, and so the same difficulty as with the Raddanah Ahilud inscription obtains. Many of these arrowheads are no doubt ancient, but some of them may be modern forgeries.

34. Ryan Byrne, "The Refuge of Scribalism in Iron I Palestine," *BASOR* 345 (2007): 2–3.

of Rameses III (1186–1155).[35] Only a few items from later than Rameses IV (1155–1149) have surfaced in Canaan, all of them north in the Israelite territory. Yet an Egyptian text, Papyrus Anastasi III, shows that during the reign of Rameses III Egypt held a powerful grip on parts of Palestine in response to the Hittite conquest of Syria, particularly in the south of the country, the Jezreel Valley, and the Jordan Valley. We know that IA1 Canaan supplied Egypt with grain, wine, oil, slaves, and horses. Even in the highlands Egyptian power did not collapse until the end of the reign of Rameses III, and possibly not until the end of Rameses IV. Rameses IV seems to have held power of some sort in Galilee, the Jezreel Valley, Judah, and along the coast. A third possibility is that papyrus Egyptian records, contracts, and so on have not survived, or fourth, records did survive but have not been found. One of these last two possibilities seems most likely. Whichever of these reasons is correct, lacking direct records, we need to rely on archaeology and the Bible to fill in our history.

Summary of Historical Understanding

As we have seen, it is unlikely that archaeology or the Bible will be able to provide a political history of the events of the IA1 in Israel. Nevertheless, this should not be seen as an entirely unfortunate situation. "History" involves much more than rulers and battles, and what is nowadays called "social history" and "cultural history" tells us more about those aspects of ancient societies that the ancients themselves would have deemed important. What follows, then, is a synthesis of the archaeological and biblical evidence about the economies, lifestyles, and religion.

Society and Economy

Society in IA1 highland Israel was village-based. Small villages exploited economic niches variously of herding, cereal agriculture, and vine and olive horticulture (Judg. 9:27). These villages were on the hilltops; the large ones were merely towns of maybe four hundred people. They usually had no walls, simply clustering the houses together. They also had no domesticated horses or camels (19:3, 10) or much iron (4:13–14). They were using flint and bronze tools and weapons, especially slings—all in contrast to their neighbors.

The Israelites lived in nuclear families (Judg. 6:29–32), but often in clusters of houses around a common courtyard with their relatives. The average nuclear

---

35. Itamar Singer, "The Beginning of Philistine Settlement in Canaan and the Northern Boundary of Philistia," *TA* 12 (1985): 117.

family had two or three children who survived infancy. The house was made
of mud bricks, with a stone foundation and wood beams. Houses had three
or four rooms, and likely often sleeping quarters on the roof or a covered
roof loft (Judg. 3:20). The house of a moderately prosperous family might
have had a second story of wood—tamarisk or poplar or palm. The Israelites
raised sheep and goats (Judg. 13:15) and, less commonly, cattle for wool and
for dairy products, not meat. The herders took the animals out in the morn-
ing up to eight miles away from the village. But the hills were then heavily
vegetated with thick scrub. This included evergreen shrubs with short pine,
oak, and pistachio trees (no more than four meters high). Orchids, peonies,
lilies, and crocuses bloomed. Because one could not easily exploit sheep, the
settlers would burn off the brush, terrace the hillsides, and farm wheat as far
as an hour's walk from the town (Judg. 6:11). The wheat was used for everything: bread, macaroni, beer, animal food, straw baskets, straw mats. Barley
played an important but secondary role. And they did have orchards, as well,
on these terraces. Olives grew wild and were easily domesticated, and so olives
and grapes were prevalent.[36]

Archaeologists of the past century made much of the supposedly uniquely
Israelite "four-roomed house," although this turned out to be not at all unique
to IA1 Israel. Yet there is a standardized form in the IA1 highlands. Its ubiquity
is attested in examples at Dothan, Ai, and Ramah. This house form, which
allows each room to be entered directly from the main room, can be contrasted
with most LBA and lowland IA1 houses, in which each room is entered from
the previous one. Some scholars interpret this as allowing for ritual purity to
be maintained by isolating the impure in a given room, although the nature of
isolation could just as easily be based on gender as on (biblical) purity laws.
Moreover, it now seems clear that the large, first-floor room was a court for
the animals, whether it was covered or not. This central room may have been
partially open, although most food-processing and textile activities would
have required space outside the buildings, where most cooking ovens and
hearths have been found.

These little villages were partly self-sufficient, but not entirely so. There
was a sharing of risk and responsibilities to cope with local environmental
constraints and labor needs. They certainly were not egalitarian. Each larger
town had its rich and poor. There was likely a ruling family of town elders in
the larger towns. They had separate neighborhoods in the town (excavated

---

36. For fuller treatment, see Robert D. Miller II, "Modeling the Farm in Early Iron Age Israel,"
in *Life and Culture in the Ancient Near East* (ed. Richard E. Averbeck, Mark W. Chavalas, and
David B. Weisberg; Bethesda, MD: CDL Press, 2003), 289–310.

Figure 5.8. Four-roomed house at Iron I Dothan

examples include Bethel, Ai, Shechem). Their houses were larger, maybe with walled yards and paved courts, but not palaces. They likely wore distinctive clothing and intermarried with their own extended relatives or with elder families of other towns (possibly underlying Judg. 1:12–15; 12:9).[37]

If we bring together the archaeological data with information drawn from ethnographic analogy, including late premodern farming practices in the Levant, along with some information in a text from a period slightly later than IA1 known as the Gezer Calendar, we can even describe the regular farming practices of the Israelites, as follows.[38]

We can begin arbitrarily in December, when the plowing for alfalfa, broad beans, and chickpeas began, a task performed by the men. In January men performed the shallow plowing for cereal grains (wheat and barley), and both men and women sowed the cereals. Sowing of broad beans may have begun this early. In February, while sowing of cereals continued, men engaged in the second plowing. Sowing lentils and chickpeas at this stage was possible,

37. For full archaeological evidence and extended discussion, see Miller, *Chieftains*, esp. 73–75.

38. Lucian Turkowski, "Peasant Agriculture in the Judaean Hills," *PEQ* 101 (1969): 27–28, 101; Annelies Moors, "Gender Hierarchy in a Palestinian Village," in *The Rural Middle East: Peasant Lives and Modes of Production* (ed. Kathy Glavanis and Pandeli Glavanis; Birzeit: Birzeit University, 1989), 199; Richard T. Antoun, *The Arab Village: A Social Structural Study of a Transjordanian Peasant* (Bloomington: Indiana University Press, 1972), 10–12. On the applicability of this material and other complementary sources, see Miller, "Modeling the Farm," 289–310.

also. In March all the remaining legumes were sown, digging the olive trees and grapevines took place, and the men plowed for green fallow. April saw continuation of digging olives and vines and plowing for green fallow, with women weeding. Any remaining vegetables (onions, leeks, garlic, etc.) were then planted. In May the harvest begins, with both sexes first harvesting lentils, alfalfa, chickpeas, and broad beans, and by mid-May the barley was ready for harvest. Wheat was harvested in late May or early June. Men then begin the threshing, which could continue into August, when winnowing and vine tending began. Winnowing and vine tending continued into September. In October, both men and women harvested the vine and other fruits (e.g., apricots). The olive harvest covered late October and November.

Gender

Consider the foregoing calendar in terms of gender roles. In the winter men plowed for legumes, handled the second plowing, and plowed for green fallow. Men threshed the grain in the summer. Additional male tasks included house and cistern building and repair. While both men and women sowed cereals, lentils, chickpeas, and other legumes, as well as dug the vines and olives and participated in the harvest, the only agricultural role away from the village that was solely women's was the spring weeding. Roles more likely to take place at a distance from the residential compound were thus primarily for males. Where the Israelite communities relied in part on domesticated animals (and faunal remains from Shiloh, Ai, and other sites show that this was an important part of the economy), these were grazed on distant land up to nine miles away, usually by boys. Judging from bone artifacts, the hunting of deer and hare played a secondary but surely not insignificant role in the economic system. This too was a job for males.

Women's productive tasks involved keeping the home in order, caring for young children, tending gardens and small animals, producing textiles, and taking responsibility for food preparation and preservation.[39] These tasks, especially the last two, were very time-consuming and involved highly specialized technology and skills.[40] This productive work would have had to proceed largely unaffected by the significant proportion of women's lifespans taken up with childbearing.[41] The Bible's focus on men, therefore, should not so mask female agency as to merit the label "patriarchal." "Patrilineal," "patrilocal,"

---

39. Carol Meyers, "The Family in Early Israel," in *Families in Ancient Israel* (by Leo G. Perdue et al.; Louisville: Westminster John Knox, 1997), 25.

40. Ibid.

41. Ibid., 28.

and even "androcentric" may be accurate terms.[42] The former two are purely social, and the latter is only a postulate from the biblical data. However, a history of IA1 Israel cannot support nineteenth-century Western gender images.

Religion

Finally, we can take a look at religion. The book of Judges suggests that Israelite religion in this period was far from "orthodox." Only two priests are mentioned in the book (Micah in chaps. 18–19, Phinehas in chap. 20), and one of them (the former) is idolatrous. The ark of the covenant is ignored throughout the book until it makes a surprise appearance at the end, when Israel brings it out for their fight with fellow Israelites (20:27).

In addition to the worship of "Baals and Astartes" (2:13), in Judges 8:22–28 the judge Gideon created "an ephod and put it in his city, in Ophrah. All Israel whored after it there. It became for Gideon and for his family as a noose" (8:27). Gideon's creation of the ephod from melted-down spoils reminds the reader of the creation of the golden calf at Sinai (Exod. 32:2–4), made from spoils brought from Egypt. An "ephod" raises several other allusions. The nearest ephod story to the Gideon cycle is in 1 Samuel 14, where "the ephod," carried by the priest, is brought with the Israelites into battle during their revolt against the Philistines (14:3). In 1 Samuel 14:18 (LXX), Saul is said to be "the man who carried the ephod in Israel." Saul's ephod is not an instrument of idolatry, and it may be that Gideon's is also meant to worship God. However, ephods are only "made" here and in Judges 17:5, where it is clearly an idolatrous object. All ephods in the Old Testament are at best ambiguous and often problematic, except for Exodus 28–29; 39. Ephods are regularly connected with divination (1 Sam. 2:28; Hosea 3:4), and the latter reference includes the verb "to whore," as in Judges 8. The items listed in Gideon's spoil in Judges 8:26 likewise all have negative connotations. Rings are always negative (e.g., Exod. 32:2–3, where they are used in making the golden calf). Crescents and pendants are negative in Isaiah 3:18–19. Purple garments are acceptable when part of the official cult of God (Exod. 25–28; Num. 4; 2 Chron. 3) but otherwise are negative (Ezek. 27:7, 16; Esther 1:6; 8:15). Gideon's ephod becomes "as a noose," which is what foreign cults often are to Israel (Exod. 23; 34; Deut. 7; Josh. 23; Judg. 2; Ps. 106). And the verb "to whore" always indicates idolatry.

So we should not be surprised if the archaeology of the IA1 hill country reveals a religious mixed bag. There was very little in the way of permanent shrines in early Israel, if these existed at all. There is possible evidence for

---

42. Ibid., 34.

permanent altars (one on Mount Ebal has been the subject of some debate), for the sacrifice of sheep and goats, and for a ritual use of deer antlers. Incense burners were common (e.g., Ai and the so-called Bull Site). Their decoration suggests religious use, but we should not necessarily connect them with incense offering of "a pleasing odor to the LORD." It is equally possible that they were used (1) in divining and traditional healing; (2) to cleanse places, persons, or objects of negative spiritual energies; and (3) to invite benevolent spirits.[43]

There are abundant figurines from the Israelite highland villages (Ai, Bethel, Tirzah, Dothan, the Bull Site), although all are markedly small. They probably had religious or ceremonial significance and may have been used in many types of rituals. Humans, dogs, horses, and geese are represented, with a slight preference for female humans, but notably, no good evidence is found for bulls or calves other than two bull jugs from Dothan (in contrast to numerous bovine images from the following centuries).[44] Although it is possible that different people in different parts of IA1 Israel worshiped differently, the present data are too scanty to trace such diversity. If we assume that these figurines, plaques, and zoomorphic objects have religious significance,[45] and that at Ai, at least, the figurines can be linked to cultic installations,[46] then perhaps we have in this corpus of images a rough divine onomasticon, or "pantheon." But if so, it does not accord well with either a purely monotheistic cult or the aniconic traditions of the later biblical texts.[47] Nor does this list accord with Rameses III's mention of only Anat/Astarte and Baal among Levantine gods.[48]

43. See Robert D. Miller II, "A 'New Cultural History' of Early Israel," in *The Texts* (vol. 2 of *Israel in Transition: From Late Bronze II to Iron IIA [c. 1250–850 BCE]*; ed. Lester L. Grabbe; LHBOTS 521; London: T&T Clark, 2010), 186.

44. The famous "Bull" from the so-called Bull Site must be removed from discussion. It was not found by archaeologists but rather was a chance discovery by a soldier. See Amihai Mazar, "The Bull Site," *BASOR* 247 (1982): 27–42. Although the excavator always referred to the site as single-period IA1 (e.g., Mazar, "Bull Site"), an independent survey of the site found only 5 percent of the sherds collected to be IA1 (Adam Zertal, *Seker Har Menasheh* [in Hebrew] (2 vols.; Haifa: Haifa University Press, 1996), 2:169. Most of the sherds are Middle Bronze, and the bull would fit well stylistically into a Middle Bronze context (Israel Finkelstein, "Two Notes on Northern Samaria," *PEQ* 130 [1998]: 97).

45. This is standard operating procedure for archaeologists. See Colin Renfrew, "Archaeology of Religion," in *The Ancient Mind: Elements of Cognitive Archaeology* (ed. Colin Renfrew and Ezra B. W. Zubrow; NDA; Cambridge: Cambridge University Press, 1994), 48–49.

46. Miller, "'New Cultural History,'" 184.

47. The absence of any figurines from the Mount Ebal site is indication of an aniconic tradition, although one that features significant nonbiblical ritual use of antlers. See Robert D. Miller II, "Shamanism in Early Israel," *WZKM* 101 (2011): 309–42.

48. Eileen N. Hirsch, "Ramses III und sein Verhältnis zur Levante," in *Das Königtum der Ramessidenzeit: Voraussetzungen, Verwirklichung, Vermächtnis; Akten des 3. Symposions zur ägyptischen Königsideologie in Bonn 7.–9.6.2001* (ed. Rolf Gundlach and Ursula Rössler-Köhler; ÄAT 36.3; Wiesbaden: Harrassowitz, 2001), 223–27.

The catalog of burial evidence from the IA1 highland settlement is meager. Sufficient excavation has taken place now to say that it is too meager, and that more graves should have been found. If the dead were disposed of by exposure, bone scatters would have been found. This means that the main disposal method was simply burial of remains outside of settlements, without proper tombs. Some archaeologists believe that this attests to a societal value of simplicity. One suspects that this is drawn from the biblical text, but it is true that grave goods are indeed a metaphor for a particular kind of ideal and not biographical information about the deceased.[49] If not an "egalitarian ideal," we can at least conclude that the early Israelites had no mythos of a "great warrior."[50]

Philistines

Previously we identified three groups that populated the southern Levant in the IA1. These were the Canaanites, the settled Israelites of the northern highlands, and the Israelite tribes in Judah. The fourth group of people in IA1 did not actually arrive until this period was already under way. These were the Philistines. The arrival of the Philistines on the coastal plain was a significant development that would change the course of local history. One can call it an "arrival" because these people were definitely newcomers to the region. Their culture is unlike that of everyone else in the Holy Land. Egyptian records say that the Philistines came by sea at this time, were prevented by the Egyptian military from settling in Egypt, and instead settled in coastal Canaan (Papyrus Harris 1). For the next six hundred years they preserved their own culture. The Philistines had their own language (the Israelites and Canaanites spoke dialects of the same one) and their own art, and they brought the use of iron with them.

Most scholars conclude that the Philistines came from the area of Greece and the islands between Greece and Turkey. One class of evidence is their material culture. Their tombs are similar to the Mycenaean Greek style. Their "bichrome" pottery is Greek, with lots of Greek designs of birds, fish, and spirals. Their temples are Greek-style. No one wore suits of armor in the Near East before the Philistines, but the Greeks did. Even their names, as recorded in Egyptian documents and the Bible, reflect Greece and western Anatolia. For example, the giant Goliath, whom David kills, has a name that comes from the Lydian name "Alyattes."[51]

49. J. Whitley, "Objects with Attitude: Biographical Facts and Fallacies in the Study of Late Bronze Age and Early Iron Age Warrior Graves," *CAJ* 12 (2002): 217, 219–20, 223, noting examples of women and children buried with weaponry in ancient Greece.

50. Ibid., 227.

51. A connection first noted by G. A. Wainwright ("Some Early Philistine History," *VT* 9 [1959]: 79n3), and reinforced by a version of the name appearing in an inscription from the

Arameans

Aramean relations with Israel go back into the proverbial mists of Israelite prehistory. In 1961 the German scholar Martin Noth argued that Israel's own origins went back to "proto-Arameans" of the Middle Bronze Age (based on supposed references at Mari and biblical texts such as "My father was a wandering Aramean" [Deut. 26:5]). But now it seems that Arameans do not appear on the historical stage this early (Noth's particular thesis was disproven as early as 1964). The earliest Arameans appear on the desert fringe of northern Mesopotamia around 1400 BCE, and more likely the date should be two centuries later.[a]

After the Hittite Empire disintegrated in about 1200 BCE, Aramean groups swallowed up western Semitic tribes, gained the caravan routes, and formed two zones of Aramean concentration, one along the Khaibur River and another south of the Orontes, around Damascus. More seminomadic Arameans who crossed the Euphrates around 900 BCE conquered remaining Neo-Hittite states and assimilated the culture.[b]

The Aramaic language has the distinction of being the Semitic language spoken today with the longest continuous written tradition, spanning three millennia. The language of the Iron Age Arameans and of Aramaic passages in the Bible (Ezra 4:8–6:18; 7:12–26; Dan. 2:4–7:28; and a few other verses) belongs to the Old Aramaic stage.[c]

The heartland of the Philistine settlement was the Gaza Strip, but extending about twelve miles farther north than today: Gaza, Gath, Ashkelon. But within a generation or two they had extended their control northward along the coast almost as far as Mount Carmel, and across the Jezreel Valley to Beth Shean.[52] They conquered the Canaanite cities on the coast, built new cities, and dominated those in the Jezreel Valley. They prevented the expansion of the Israelites to the north and west. By the end of the IA1 period, they probably effectively ruled the Israelites as well. We might note the presence of forty-seven Philistine bichrome sherds at IA1 Mizpah—two painted kraters and other body sherds manufactured at Ashdod, but an additional six painted kraters of similar typology, along with more body sherds, made in Benjamin.[53] This

---

excavations at Gath. See Aren M. Maeir et al., "A Late Iron Age I/Early Iron Age II Old Canaanite Inscription from Tell eṣ-Ṣāfī/Gath, Israel," *BASOR* 351 (2008): 39–71.

52. Yuval Gadot, "Continuity and Change in the Late Bronze to Iron Age Transition in Israel's Coastal Plain: A Long-Term Perspective," in *Bene Israel: Studies in the Archaeology of Israel and the Levant during the Bronze and Iron Ages in Honour of Israel Finkelstein* (ed. Alexander Fantalkin and Assuf Yasur-Landau; CHANE 31; Leiden: Brill, 2008), 63–64.

53. Miller, *Chieftains*, 49–50.

Aramaic, with Canaanite, is a West Semitic language that by 800 BCE became the lingua franca of the Middle East. Examples of the geographic distribution of Aramaic documents in the late eighth century range from the Bukan Stela at ancient Mannea in northwestern Iran[d] to the Adon Papyrus from Egypt.[e] There is even a one-line Aramaic inscription on a seventh-century Olympian bowl from Greece.[f] From the sixth century BCE, the Aramaic script replaced the Old Hebrew script for writing Hebrew itself.[g]

a. K. Lawson Younger Jr., "The Late Bronze/Iron Age Transition and the Origins of the Arameans," in *Ugarit at Seventy-Five: Proceedings of the Symposium "Ugarit at Seventy-Five," Held at Trinity International University, Deerfield, Illinois, February 18–20, 2005, under the Auspices of the Mid-Western Branch of the American Oriental Society and the Mid-West Region of the Society of the Biblical Literature* (ed. K. Lawson Younger Jr.; Winona Lake, IN: Eisenbrauns, 2007), 133–34.

b. For detailed history, see Edward Lipiński, *The Aramaeans: Their Ancient History, Culture, Religion* (OLA 100; Leuven: Peeters, 2000).

c. For discussion, see Otto Jastrow, "Old Aramaic and Neo-Aramaic: Some Reflections on Language History," in *Aramaic in Its Historical and Linguistic Setting* (ed. Holger Gzella and Margaretha L. Folmer; VOK 50; Wiesbaden: Harrassowitz, 2008), 1–10.

d. Ingo Kottsieper, "Eine altaramäische Inschrift aus Bukān," in *Staatsverträge, Herrscherinschriften und andere Documente zur politischen Geschichte* (vol. 2 of *Texte aus der Umwelt des Alten Testaments*; ed. Michael Lichtenstein; Gütersloh: Mohn, 2005), 312–13.

e. Dirk Schwiderski, ed., *Texte und Bibliographie* (vol. 2 of *Die alt- und reicharamäischen Inschriften* [= *The Old and Imperial Aramaic Inscriptions*]; FSBP 4; Berlin: de Gruyter, 2004), 2.1.

f. Ibid., 336.

g. Klaus Beyer, *The Aramaic Language: Its Distribution and Subdivisions* (trans. John F. Healy; Göttingen: Vandenhoeck & Ruprecht, 1986), 10.

locally made Philistine pottery, along with pots from Philistia, was discovered in the middle of highland Israel. Two lines from the stories in the book of Judges about the judge Samson stand out in relation to this. One is a simple statement of fact in Judges 14:4: "At that time the Philistines had control of Israel." The other is a rhetorical question in Judges 15:11. The men of Judah pose it to Samson after he had upset the delicate status quo and fragile conditions of Philistine occupation. His actions were certain to bring Philistine reprisals unless Samson surrendered: "Do you not know that the Philistines are rulers over us?"

This brings us back to the Bible and the book of Judges. The history just presented here ends the IA1 with Philistine hegemony weighing heavy over Israel. The book of Judges likewise presents an "unconquest" scenario, not only politically, but also, more important, morally. This is the whole message of Judges: a steady unconquest story by which Israel becomes Canaan, a systematic decline into idolatry, immorality, and violence. That is the meaning of the offhand remark about Israel's religious capital in 21:12, "Shiloh in the territory of Canaan."

6

The Story of Samuel, Saul, and David

DANIEL BODI

The lives and times of Samuel, Saul, and David are to be placed in the last two-thirds of the eleventh century BCE for the first two characters; David also spans the first half of the tenth century. While Samuel, with his multifaceted role, marks the transition from the time of the judges to that of the first officially designated tribal leaders, Saul and David inaugurate what is traditionally perceived as first dynastic monarchies among the Hebrews.

Here the presentation of the biblical stories about these three characters will be followed by a comparative analysis of some of the elements found in these narratives, considering how these might be taken as authentic historical reminiscences of the customs and practices of the ancient Hebrew tribes.

This analysis will first include the presentation of the older historical-critical view concerning the narrative material found in the books of Samuel, where the stories bearing on these biblical characters are found. Second, I will suggest that the new approach of seeing the "house of Saul" pitted against the "house of David" should be preferred for comparative reasons. Indeed, two eighteenth-century-BCE Mari texts provide a historical analogy depicting the conflict between two clans, the Addu Benjaminites and the Līm Sim'alites, spanning three generations. Third, this chapter will explore why it is preferable to view Saul and David as tribal chiefs rather than as kings. Fourth, the launching of Saul's career as a warlord can be compared to a similar procedure in one Mari text. Fifth, David's rise to power will be compared to the pattern of seizing power in the ancient Near East as reflected in a series of texts (Zimrī-Līm from Mari, Idrimi from Alalaḫ, and the Apiru from Amarna).

The Biblical Accounts

Samuel

The prophet Samuel is also regarded as the last of the judges to rule the tribes of Israel. His Hebrew name, *šĕmû'ēl*, seems to have been derived from an original *šimuhū'il*, meaning "His name is God." It is not clear from which tribe he stemmed. According to 1 Samuel 1:1, he belonged to the tribe of Ephraim, while according to 1 Chronicles 6:33, he was of the tribe of Levi. He was born in Ramah. His mother, Hannah, one of Elkanah's wives, was initially barren and asked God to give her a son, vowing to dedicate him as a Nazirite. According to the Septuagint (LXX) and the Dead Sea Scroll (4QSamᵃ) versions of 1 Samuel 1:11, 22, Samuel was to abstain from alcoholic beverages and was not to cut his hair because he was a Nazirite.

In 1 Samuel 1:20 his name is explained as "asked of Yahweh," based on a wordplay with the root *šā'al* (to ask). This wordplay is seen as a redactional device anticipating his later role in the anointing of Saul, whom the people requested as a tribal leader.[1] It could also be an example of the so-called analogical or Babylonian hermeneutics, of the kind found in Genesis 11:9, where two different Hebrew roots, *bll* (to confuse) and *bbl* (Babylon), are brought together in order to highlight some inner connection perceived by the scribe or redactor. For the ancient scribes, it sufficed that two roots had just a single consonant in common to show that the meaning of one term was anticipated by the other.[2] After Hannah weaned Samuel, the priest Eli oversaw the boy's upbringing at the tabernacle at Shiloh (1 Sam. 1). This fulfilled Hannah's vow. While Samuel was still a boy, serving in the temple, God called him to become a prophet (1 Sam. 3).

A major Philistine victory over the Israelites resulted in the capture of the ark of the covenant, the death of Eli, and the transfer of the priesthood from Shiloh (1 Sam. 4). Samuel acted as a traditional judge by mustering the tribes

---

1. Matitiahu Tsevat, "Die Namengeburg Samuels und die Substitionstheorie," *ZAW* 99 (1987): 250–54.

2. For a discussion and numerous examples of such hermeneutics in the Hebrew Bible, see Daniel Bodi, *Israël et Juda: À l'ombre des Babyloniens et des Perses* (ÉAHA; Paris: De Boccard, 2010), 177–207.

at Mizpah and leading the Israelites to victory at Ebenezer. He continued to serve as judge from his home in Ramah. Each year he administered justice within a circuit encompassing Bethel, Gilgal, and Mizpah (1 Sam. 7).

In his old age he appointed his own sons, Joel and Abijah, as judges serving at Beersheba. Like Eli's sons, they became corrupt, perverting justice and taking bribes (1 Sam. 8:1–3). Moreover, the tribal elders challenged Samuel's leadership. They preferred to have a king to lead them into battle against the Philistines. While initially resisting the pressure (1 Sam. 8:11–18), Samuel received divine guidance to give in to their demands (1 Sam. 8:22). According to 1 Samuel 9:1–10:16, he secretly anointed Saul as *nāgîd* (leader)—literally, "the one who stands in front" (9:16; 10:1 [also called *melek* in 15:1]). This suggests that the term *melek* (king) had a particular meaning in ancient Hebrew that developed after Saul became Israel's leader. Even while anointing Saul, Samuel warned the people about the potential dangers associated with this institution (1 Sam. 9–12).

Before long, a breach developed between Samuel and Saul, when the latter decided to offer sacrifices before battle (1 Sam. 13), something that was not his prerogative. This split became final when Saul later broke the taboo of the *ḥērem* and spared the life of the Amalekite king Agag. Samuel killed Agag and returned to Ramah. He rejected Saul, refusing to have any further dealings with him (1 Sam. 15). Samuel's final act was to anoint David in private as the next tribal leader of Israel (1 Sam. 16). Samuel retired to his home at Ramah, where he died and was buried.

This happened after Saul began trying to kill David because the king saw David as a dangerous political rival (1 Sam. 25:1; 26:2). The night before the battle with the Philistines, at Gilboa, Saul decided to visit a necromancer at Endor. Yahweh no longer communicated to the king through dreams, Urim, or prophets. A desperate Saul tried to summon the advice of Samuel's ghost (28:4–7). By contrast, David, who also kept a teraphim in his house (19:16), possibly for divinatory purposes,[3] gained ready response to his multiple divine inquiries (1 Sam. 22:10, 13, 15; 23:2, 4; 30:8; 2 Sam. 2:1; 5:19, 23).

Modern critical assessments of Samuel tend to ascribe limited historical value to the various traditions about him. The chief arguments against their historicity are these: (1) the "legendary" character of some of the narratives, such as the story of his infancy; (2) the fact that Samuel is depicted in such a diversity of roles (seer, prophet, judge, war leader, national leader, priest); and (3) the problem of aligning these various roles with the supposed literary

---

3. Daniel Bodi, *The Michal Affair: From Zimri-Lim to the Rabbis* (HBM 3; Sheffield: Sheffield Phoenix Press, 2005), 26n88 (bibliography).

sources (*Traditionsgeschichte*) or orally transmitted traditions (*Überlieferungs-geschichte*).[4] Some of these problems could be elucidated by extrabiblical comparative data.

Although there is little certainty about the sources utilized in Samuel, the problem is compounded by how the books of Samuel deal mostly with the conflict between the house of Saul and the house of David. Samuel is an initial catalyst and mediator in this conflict. In contrast to historical-critical and tradition-historical studies, attempting to disentangle the various sources underlying 1 Samuel and determine what is pre-Deuteronomistic and what belongs to the various Deuteronomistic redactions, literary critics propose to read the final Hebrew Masoretic Text as a coherent narrative, focusing on its literary merits. Applying "close reading" of the stories by looking for narratological features of the text such as plot, chiastic arrangement, repetition of key words, parallels of situations, contrasts, and ambiguity, some scholars have produced detailed and insightful analysis of the main events and protagonists in the books of Samuel.[5]

Saul

Saul, son of Kish, of the tribe of Benjamin, was the first tribal leader of ancient Israel. His Hebrew name, *šā'ûl*, means "asked [of God]," and his story occupies most of 1 Samuel 9–31. Saul rose to kingship as a response to a political crisis in Israel. Under the pressure of the militarily superior Philistines, descendants of the Sea Peoples, who settled in the Palestinian coastal plain more than a century earlier, the oppressed Israelites came to the conclusion that only a common tribal warlord could bring about their deliverance. The coastal cities of Ashdod, Ashkelon, and Gaza, with the inland cities of Ekron and Gath, were the major Philistine population centers, forming a pentapolis. The Philistines had iron weapons before the Israelites did and imposed a monopoly on iron sword production (13:19–22). They also effectively employed chariots and heavy infantry on the battlefield. The defeat experienced by the Israelite tribes at Aphek, including the loss of the ark (1 Sam. 4), showed that old patterns of leadership were ineffective.

Three narratives record how Saul came to be a leader of the tribes in Israel. The first recounts how Samuel reluctantly and secretly anointed Saul in the land

---

4. George W. Ramsey, "Samuel," *ABD* 5:954–57.

5. Robert Alter, *The David Story: A Translation with Commentary of 1 and 2 Samuel* (New York: Norton, 1999); idem, *The Art of Biblical Narrative* (New York: Basic Books, 1981); Meir Sternberg, *The Poetics of Biblical Narrative: Ideological Literature and the Drama of Reading* (Bloomington: Indiana University Press, 1985).

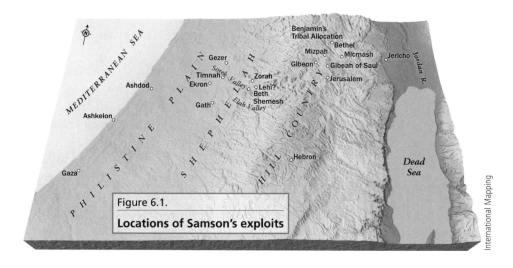

Figure 6.1.

Locations of Samson's exploits

of Ziph (1 Sam. 9:27–10:1). The mention of asses in this context is significant, the donkey being a royal symbol among seminomadic tribes as in eighteenth-century-BCE Mari. The second (10:17–24) describes the choice of Saul by lot from among the elders of Israel. The third manner in which Saul became tribal leader occurred when Jabesh-gilead was besieged by Nahash the Ammonite, and the Israelites sought his leadership (1 Sam. 11). Saul seized the opportunity and mustered the Israelite tribes with a symbolic act. He cut a pair of oxen into pieces, which he sent to the various tribes. This enrollment technique seems to be typical of the seminomadic tribes as attested in a Mari document. Following the victory over the Ammonites, a religious ceremony at Gilgal confirmed the appointment of Saul as king (11:14–15).

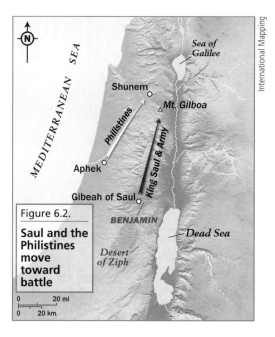

Figure 6.2.

Saul and the Philistines move toward battle

The separate narratives concerning how Saul became leader of the Israelite tribes are viewed as the product of different traditions combined in the existing

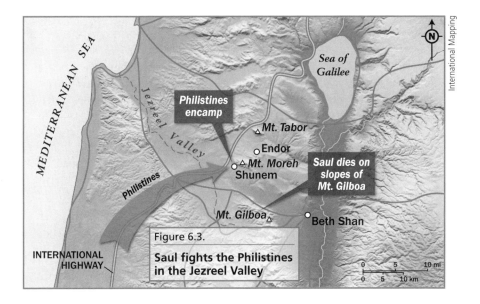

Figure 6.3.

Saul fights the Philistines in the Jezreel Valley

account.[6] These divergent traditions are perceived as reflecting ambivalence concerning the new institution of tribal kingship.[7] Some studies on the figure of Saul in 1 Samuel attempt to see how the various images of Saul may be complementary.[8]

The end of Saul's career is marked by his severe conflict with the old prophet Samuel and with his political rival, David. On three occasions, one of them posthumously, the prophet Samuel remonstrated with Saul for disobeying the terms of his appointment. The number "three" carries the mark of a definitive seal on Saul's failed rule. The first time Saul did not wait for Samuel, but arrogated to himself the right to offer sacrifices at Gilgal (1 Sam. 13:7–10). On the second occasion Saul disobeyed when he did not destroy all of Amalek. Samuel condemned him with the adage, "To obey is better than sacrifice, and to hearken

6. Diana Vikander Edelman, *King Saul in the Historiography of Judah* (JSOTSup 121; Sheffield: JSOT Press, 1991); idem, *"Saul ben Kish in History and Tradition,"* in *The Origins of the Ancient Israelite States* (ed. Volkmar Fritz and Philip R. Davies; JSOTSup 228; Sheffield: Sheffield Academic Press, 1996), 142–59; Nadav Na'aman, "The Pre-Deuteronomistic Story of King Saul and Its Historical Significance," *CBQ* 54 (1992): 638–58; Eben Scheffler, "Saving Saul from the Deuteronomist," in *Past, Present, Future. The Deuteronomistic History and the Prophets* (ed. Johannes C. de Moor and Harry F. van Rooy; OtSt 44; Leiden: Brill, 2000), 263–71.

7. Karel van der Toorn, "Saul and the Rise of Israelite State Religion," *VT* 43 (1993): 519–42; Simcha S. Brooks, "From Gibeon to Gibeah: High Place of the Kingdom," in *Temple and Worship in Biblical Israel* (ed. John Day; LHBOTS 422; London: T&T Clark, 2005), 40–59.

8. Sarah Nicholson, *Three Faces of Saul. An Intertextual Approach to Biblical Tragedy* (JSOTSup 339; Sheffield: Sheffield Academic Press, 2002); Barbara Green, *How Are the Mighty Fallen? A Dialogical Study of King Saul in 1 Samuel* (JSOTSup 365; Sheffield: Sheffield Academic Press, 2003).

Khirbet Qeiyafa Ostracon

The Khirbet Qeiyafa Ostracon was found in 2008 in the Shephelah, in a site identified with Shaʿaraîm (Two Gates) on account of the two gates found in the remains of the Elah fortress (Josh. 15:36; 1 Sam. 17:52). It has been interpreted differently by a variety of scholars, and no definitive agreement has been reached yet on the way the inscription should be read (from right to left, or from left to right).[a] The Elah fortress and the inscription—considered to be the oldest text in Paleo-Hebrew, at this stage indistinguishable from a Canaanite script—are important and interpreted by some scholars as indications of first steps taken toward state administration in 1000 BCE Judah. According to Émile Puech, the Khirbet Qeiyafa Ostracon represents the earliest known text relating to the establishment of some form of administration of the Israelite society, likely referring to the installation of the first king, Saul.[b] Carbon 14 dating places the potsherd at the end of the eleventh to the beginning of the tenth century BCE. However, the five-line text of the ostracon, written in ink on a potsherd, is badly abraded and cannot be deciphered with certainty. Puech reads the inscription from left to right rather than in the more common Hebrew direction of right to left. He sees in it the concluding section of an administrative document and proposes the following reading of the inscription:

Michael Netzer/Wikimedia Commons

Figure 6.4. Khirbet Qeiyafa Ostracon

than the fat of rams" (15:22).[9] Samuel publicly rejected Saul as ruler over Israel. When Saul tore Samuel's robe, Samuel declared that God had torn away Saul's rule over Israel (15:28). Samuel rebuked Saul the third and last time in the story of the medium of Endor (1 Sam. 28). This forbidden consultation filled the cup of Saul's inconsequential rule and double standard and foretold his doom.

From the viewpoint of the editor/redactor of the Deuteronomistic History,[10] the institution of kingship in Israel was a tragic enterprise, doomed from its beginning. In the protracted conflict between Saul and David, the story of Michal

9. Scripture translations in this chapter are by the author.
10. This refers to the person or persons responsible for parts of Deuteronomy and virtually all of Joshua, Judges, 1–2 Samuel, and 1–2 Kings.

1. *l' t'šq : w'bd ͏ʾ⌐l⌐ : l : ⌐b⌐zh*	Do not oppress, and serve God: l: . . . despoiled him/her.
2. *špṭ* (?) *wbk 'lm⌐n⌐* (?) *šlṭ*	The judge and the widow wept; he had the power
3. *bgr. wb'll . qṣm*(?) *yḥd :*	over the resident alien and the child, he eliminated them together.
4. *'⌐d⌐m wśrm ysd mlk :*	The men and the chiefs/officers have established a king.
5. *ḥm <ššm> 'bdm : mdrt .*	He marked 60 [?] servants among the communities/habitations/generations.

The potsherd would be all that is left from a copy made for the purpose of memorizing a message coming from elsewhere, being a copy of an administrative circular letter coming from a hierarchically superior person (king or minister of the central administration). Puech finds that the text contains all the essentials that the biblical texts mention in respect to the changes introduced by Saul: (1) the need for judges who will not oppress the foreigner and those less fortunate (e.g., the widow and the orphan), and a need for those who will protect them from abuse of the kind that Samuel's sons practiced over the weak; (2) the installation of a king; (3) the existence of servants who serve the king; (4) the injunction not to oppress, but to serve God; and, most important, (5) the designation of a new monarch not through a succession on the throne but rather through election by the people and the officers. For Puech, the text announces the installation of a centralized royal administration, and it makes this announcement to a distant frontier province. If this reading and interpretation are correct, the Khirbet Qeiyafa Ostracon would be the only archaeological artifact referring to Israel's first king and the earliest extrabiblical indication of the establishment of the Israelite monarchy. This text certainly merits attention and requires further research.

a. Gershon Galil, "The Hebrew Inscription from Khirbet Qeiyafa/Neta'im," *UF* 41 (2009): 193–242.
b. Émile Puech, "L'Ostracon de Khirbet Qeiyafa et les débuts de la royauté en Israël," *RB* 17 (2010): 162–84, esp. 171.

plays an important role. It criticizes Israel's monarchy.[11] It exposes abuses and the merciless power struggle that the monarchy generated in Israelite society. The redactor uses the story of the tragic fate of the royal princess Michal as a mirror that blends the figures of Saul, her father, and David, her husband. The account demonstrates opportunistic behavior on the part of both men.

David

The biblical account of David's life is found in 1 Samuel 16–31; 2 Samuel; 1 Kings 1–2; 1 Chronicles 11–29. David was the second tribal leader of Israel,

11. Bodi, *The Michal Affair*, 144.

whose reign is traditionally dated from about 1000 to 962 BCE. His name in Hebrew, *dāwid*, is etymologically related to *dôd* (beloved), close to "Jedidiah" (beloved of Yahweh), a name that Nathan gave to Solomon, David's son (2 Sam. 12:25). This is why Johann Stamm translates David's name with "Liebling" (beloved).[12] The root of the name is *dwd* (so *dāwid* or *dāwîd*). Baruch Halpern convincingly explains an alternative interpretation in which the name is understood as "(paternal) uncle," while remaining related to the meaning "beloved." The "paternal uncle," or *dwd*, is the family member responsible for burial when a household is without direct heirs (Amos 6:10: *dwdw*). He is the nearest relation to whom the incest taboo does not apply, which is the reason the term also denotes one's "beloved."[13] The priority should be given to the first meaning, however, since no text spells David's name as *dd*, the way "uncle" is sometimes written.[14]

David was the great-grandson of Ruth (from Moab) and Boaz, a man from the tribe of Judah. He was the youngest of Jesse's eight sons.[15] The name of his mother is not mentioned. The fact that David had a Moabite great-grandmother was deemed more important. When forced to flee Saul, David takes refuge with the king of Moab and seeks protection for his parents (1 Sam. 22:3–4). This is natural in view of David's Moabite origins through Ruth, the mother of Obed, Jesse's father. This fact has provoked lengthy discussions among rabbis in both Talmuds. The rabbis in the Jerusalem Talmud (*y. Sanh.* 2.3) argue that Nabal would have been a better royal candidate than David, with a better genealogy. This might have been prompted by Nabal's words in 1 Samuel 25:10: "Who is David? Who is the son of Jesse?" (cf. 1 Sam. 25:3). The rabbis in Babylon were aware of the objections raised by their colleagues in Palestine and provided a lengthy legal discussion in order to rehabilitate David (*b. Yebam.* 72b). Using a series of biblical quotes and establishing a very intricate relationship between different verses, they succeed in "deconstructing" the statement in Deuteronomy 23:3 and conclude that an Israelite is permitted to marry a Moabite or an Ammonite woman. Therefore David should be considered a full-fledged Israelite. Both historical-critical scholarship and rabbinic tradition agree in seeing David's marriage with Michal, the daughter of Saul, as an opportunistic move to enter the royal family of the first king.

---

12. Johann J. Stamm, *Beiträge zur hebräischen und altorientalischen Namenskunde* (ed. Ernst Jenni and Martin A. Klopfenstein; OBO 30; Freiburg: Universitätsverlag, 1980), 25.

13. Baruch Halpern, *David's Secret Demons: Messiah, Murderer, Traitor, King* (BIW; Grand Rapids: Eerdmans, 2001), 269.

14. Walter Dietrich, "*dāwīd*, *dôd* und *bytdwd*," *TZ* 53 (1997): 17–32.

15. See 1 Sam. 17:12. However, 1 Sam. 16:10; 1 Chron. 2:15 mention only seven sons, implying that David was the eighth, the number "seven" is conventional, as in the story of Idrimi.

There are two traditions about the way David entered Saul's court. One tradition says that he remained with Saul after his military exploit over the Philistine giant Goliath. In 1 Samuel 17:55–56 Saul does not know David's identity, and in 18:2 Saul takes David into his service. According to another tradition, David entered the service of Saul as a musician, and initially Saul "loved him a lot" (*wayye'ĕhābēhû mĕ'ōd*) (1 Sam. 16:21). This is the first occurrence of the term "love," which serves as a catchword. It appears at the beginning of Michal and David's relationship. In 1 Samuel 18:20 it is said that Michal loved (*'hb*) David. At this stage there was no hostility between Saul and David. Her father's initial love for David probably encouraged Michal in her own feelings toward the young man. The relationship between Saul and David soon deteriorated. Victim of a morbid jealousy, Saul foundered into insanity. At the beginning, however, David assumed a therapeutic role with Saul. "And whenever the evil spirit[16] from God was upon Saul, David took the lyre and played it with his hand" (16:23).

In the ancient Near East a person's sickness often is explained as an attack by an evil spirit or by the hand of a god. In Akkadian, for example, an epidemic is indicated by the expression *qāt ili* (the hand of god). In Mesopotamia the goddess of war and love, Inanna/Ishtar, was both revered and feared by the population on account of her unpredictability. She too was prone to murderous rage, as reflected in her warring exploits. A special cultic official (*gala*), who was both a priest and a singer in charge of lamentations, had an instrument on which he played appeasing music, and he chanted prayers and supplications in order to assuage the hot-tempered goddess.[17] This is an earlier example of music being used for therapeutic purposes. It is comparable to what David was doing with his lyre: trying to relieve Saul's tormented mind.[18]

Saul's dealings with David declined rapidly. Saul used the marriage settlement between his daughter Michal and David as a trap (*môqēš*) to cause his death (1 Sam. 18:21, 25).[19] Having failed to get rid of his would-be son-in-law, Saul then proposed to his son Jonathan that they both kill David (19:1). However, Jonathan and David formed an alliance (20:41–42). It appears from 1 Samuel 24:9 that there was a group at Saul's court that deliberately fomented trouble between Saul and David.

16. Septuagint: *pneuma ponēron*.

17. Samuel N. Kramer, "BM 29616: The Fashioning of the *gala*," *AcSum* 3 (1981): 1–9.

18. Rivkah Harris, "Inanna-Ishtar as Paradox and a Coincidence of Opposites," *HR* 30 (1991): 261–78, esp. 266n26.

19. Incidentally, the irony of their transaction is caught by the modern Hebrew meaning of the term *môqēš*, which refers to a military antipersonnel land mine.

Being pursued by Saul with an army of three thousand (1 Sam. 24:2), David became an outlaw and vagabond—a prime example of the *'apiru* rebel and mercenary. David gathered around him a motley group of six hundred warriors: "everyone who was in distress, and everyone who was in debt, and everyone who was discontented" (22:2 NRSV). He became their leader. Reckoning that Saul's superior forces would one day catch up with him, David opted to place his life in the hands of the Philistine king Achish, who received him as a vassal and granted him Ziklag as a dwelling place (27:1–7). David served as personal bodyguard of the Philistine warlord (28:2). Achish commanded him and his men to accompany the Philistine army into battle against Israel (28:1; 29:1). When the other Philistine warlords protested the wisdom of this decision, David returned to Ziklag and was spared the final confrontation with Saul and his compatriots. At Mount Gilboa the Philistines defeated Israel, and Saul perished on the battlefield together with his sons Jonathan, Abinadab, and Malchishua (1 Sam. 31:2).

David can be viewed as having reigned in two places: first in Hebron for a period of seven years and six months, and then in Jerusalem for thirty-three years (2 Sam. 5:4–5; 1 Chron. 3:4; 29:27). According to the biblical record, he was thirty when he began to reign, and he died at the age of seventy-one (1 Kings 2:11). Most of the latter part of David's reign was marred by dire events precipitated by David's assassination of his elite officer, Uriah the Hittite. David took Uriah's beautiful wife, Bathsheba, for himself.

Absalom's revenge for his sister's rape and his coup d'état against David, his father, are described in great detail in 2 Samuel 13–15. Thus David suffered divine retribution for his misdeeds.

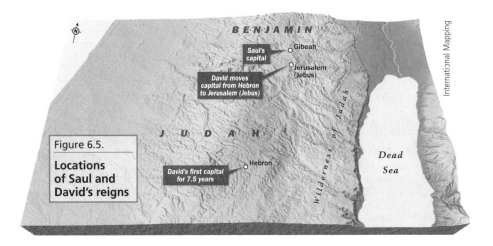

Figure 6.5.

Locations of Saul and David's reigns

David appears as a man with one deep personality flaw: he was a "ladies' man." There are four circumstantial narratives about prominent women who played a role in his life: Michal, Abigail, Bathsheba, and Abishag. Female figures who appear in the David narrative often play a significant role as catalysts of change, revealing a significant and sometimes dark side of his personality. The Babylonian Talmud (*b. Sanh.* 21a) says, "David had four hundred children, all born of captive women taken as concubines by the king because of their beauty." Indeed, the study of David's numerous relationships with women allows us to gain insight into his character.[20]

Critical Issues

The House of Saul Pitted against the House of David

The historical-critical study of biblical narratives in the books of Samuel dealing with the careers of Saul and David proposes two ways of viewing the relationship between these two tribal chiefs: (1) the older interpretative model identified "David's Rise to Power" and the "Throne Succession Narrative"; (2) the newer model, which I prefer for comparative reasons, is to view this relationship as "The House of Saul Pitted against the House of David."

According to the older historical-critical approach, the composition of the narratives in the books of Samuel was explained by the "fragmentary hypothesis," implying that it grew out of a series of originally independent units—a "History of David's Rise to Power," an "Ark Narrative," a "Throne Succession Narrative," and an "Appendix"—which were joined together to produce the work.[21]

The narrative of David's "Rise to Power" stretches from 1 Samuel 15 to 2 Samuel 5.[22] With sober realism the text describes the devious ways by which a poor shepherd becomes a warrior in the service of Saul and eventually a tribal chief. At the root of David's rags-to-riches story would be an original

---

20. For an analysis of David's relationships with Michal, Abigail, Bathsheba, and Abishag, see Adele Berlin, "Characterization in Biblical Narrative: David's Wives," *JSOT* 23 (1982): 69–85.

21. J. Alberto Soggin, *Introduction to the Old Testament: From Its Origins to the Closing of the Alexandrian Canon* (trans. John Bowden; Philadelphia: Westminster, 1976), 189–94 (§3, "Independent Units"), as well as all major introductions by the previous generation of scholars.

22. Jakob H. Grønbaek, *Die Geschichte vom Aufstieg Davids (1 Sam. 15–2 Sam. 5): Tradition und Komposition* (trans. Hanns Leister; ATDan 10; Copenhagen: Prostant apud Munksgaard, 1971); Rolf A. Carlson, *David, the Chosen King: A Traditio-Historical Approach to the Second Book of Samuel* (trans. Eric J. Sharpe and Stanley Rudman; Stockholm: Almqvist & Wiksell, 1964); Joachim Conrad, "Zum geschichtlichen Hintergrund der Darstellung von Davids Aufstieg," *TLZ* 97 (1972): 321–32.

narrative that some scholars place at the end of the tenth or at the beginning of the ninth century BCE.[23] The freedom that the narrator retains in respect to the main protagonists, Saul and David, remains unique in the literature of the ancient Near East. It continues and develops into what is traditionally called the "Throne Succession Narrative" (2 Sam. 9–20; 1 Kings 1–2). Leonhard Rost formulated the hypothesis of the Throne Succession Narrative, arguing for the existence of a unified document now found in 2 Samuel 6:16, 20–23; 7:11b, 16; 9–20; 1 Kings 1–2.[24] Otto Kaiser dates the composition of this narrative in the eighth–sixth centuries BCE.[25] Here the often-tragic family events of the house of David are subject to a detailed and circumstantial description. A series of crimes are committed, provoking crises that radically undermine David's rule and maintain a persistent questioning on how to resolve the succession of the aging king. In fact, the institution of tribal kingship entails the question of dynasty. Through dramatic confrontations between the sons and their father, the issue of succession is heightened.

Both Gerhard von Rad and Martin Noth followed Rost's position. For them, the Throne Succession Narrative formed one of the earliest historical writings in the world and became a precursor of the Deuteronomistic History in its use of the retribution principle or the chain of cause and effect.[26]

Rost's analysis was shared by a great number of scholars for about fifty years before his postulated unity of the Throne Succession Narrative was seriously questioned and eventually abandoned. Walter Dietrich[27] showed that the negative assessment of David's act in 2 Samuel 11:27b ("The thing . . . was evil in the eyes of Yahweh" [wayyēra' haddābār . . . bĕ'ênê yhwh]) reflects the characteristic Deuteronomistic negative evaluation formula for the reigns

23. Otto Kaiser, "David und Jonathan," *ETL* 66 (1990): 281–96. According to Tryggve Mettinger, the narrative of David's rise to power stems from the time of the schism (*King and Messiah: The Civil and Sacral Legitimation of the Israelite Kings* [ConBOT 8; Lund: Gleerup, 1976], 38–41).

24. Leonhard Rost argued for a continuous story formed by a skillful joining of independent traditions to recount the history of the succession to David's throne. See his *Die Überlieferung von der Thronnachfolge Davids* (BWANT 42; Stuttgart: Kohlhammer, 1926); ET, *The Succession to the Throne of David* (trans. Michael D. Rutter and David M. Gunn; HTIBS 1; Sheffield: Almond, 1982).

25. Otto Kaiser, "Beobachtungen zur sogenannten Thronnachfolgeerzählung," *ETL* 64 (1988): 5–20.

26. Gerhard von Rad, "The Beginning of Historical Writing in Ancient Israel," in *The Problem of the Hexateuch, and Other Essays* (trans. E. W. Trueman Dicken; London: Oliver & Boyd, 1966), 166–204; idem, *Old Testament Theology* (trans. D. M. G. Stalker; 2 vols; New York: Harper & Row, 1962–1965), 1:312–16; Martin Noth, *The Deuteronomistic History* (JSOTSup 15; Sheffield: JSOT Press, 1981), 55–56.

27. Walter Dietrich, *Prophetie und Geschichte: Eine redaktionsgeschichtliche Untersuchung zum deuteronomistischen Geschichtswerk* (FRLANT 108; Göttingen: Vandenhoeck & Ruprecht, 1972), 127–32.

of various kings of Israel and Judah in 1–2 Kings. Furthermore, the motif of a judgment on the king being passed on to the next generation, found in 2 Samuel 12:14, corresponds to the analogous motif found in 2 Kings 21:20. In the nineteenth century Friedrich Schwally[28] argued that Nathan's intervention (in 2 Sam. 11:27b–12:15a) was a literary fiction added secondarily to an original story because the image of Nathan as a guardian of public morality was incompatible with the image of a scheming prophet as found in 1 Kings 1. Moreover, a prophet defending Solomon would not condemn a union that brought about his birth. Building on Schwally's work, Walter Dietrich, Ernst Würthwein, and Timo Veijola[29] questioned the authenticity of the unit describing Nathan's audience with David, characterizing it as secondary. The older story in 2 Samuel 11:2–27a + 12:15b–25 lacks any explicit ethical evaluation of David's behavior, leaving the impression that this is the way kings act, and therefore no further comment is needed. Nathan's audience with David is reminiscent of later prophetic materials, such as 1 Kings 20:35–42; Isaiah 5:1–7; Jeremiah 3:1; Haggai 2:10–14. However, in the light of new data on Amorite precursors of the ideology of divine retribution and the ethical demands of Amorite prophets on their tribal chieftains, this traditional historical-critical position needs to be more nuanced. As I have shown elsewhere, both for the Bensim'alite (e.g., Zimrī-Līm) and the Benjaminite (e.g., Hammurabi) Amorite chieftains, this kind of behavior was unacceptable.[30] Why should it have been otherwise for the ancient Hebrew tribal chiefs?

On the one hand, some scholars no longer consider the Throne Succession Narrative as a piece of historiography but rather as a narrative of a particular genre composed for "serious entertainment."[31] On the other hand, recent research has shown that we do not have an account of "David's Rise to Power."

---

28. Friedrich Schwally, "Zur Quellenkritik der historischen Bücher," *ZAW* 12 (1892): 153–61. He perceived the narrative of Absalom's conspiracy in 2 Sam. 15 as a continuation of 11:27.

29. Ernst Würthwein, *Die Erzählung von der Thronfolge Davids: Theologische oder politische geschichtsschreibung?* (ThSt 115; Zurich: Theologischer Verlag, 1974), 19–30. According to Würthwein, the divine condemnation of David and his monarchy constitutes the thematic unity of 2 Sam. 12. Timo Veijola, "Salomo—der erstgeborene Bathshebas," in *Studies in the Historical Books of the Old Testament* (ed. J. A. Emerton; VTSup 30; Leiden: Brill, 1979), 230–50, esp. 233–34.

30. Daniel Bodi, *The Demise of the Warlord: A New Look at the David Story* (HBM 26; Sheffield: Sheffield Phoenix Press, 2010), 72–74. On Hammurabi as a Benjaminite, see Dominique Charpin, *Hammu-rabi de Babylone* (Paris: Presses universitaires de France, 2003), 43.

31. R. N. Whybray, *The Succession Narrative: A Study of II Sam. 9–20 and I Kings 1 and 2* (SBT 9; London: SCM, 1968); Peter R. Ackroyd, "The Succession Narrative (So-Called)," *Int* 35 (1981): 383–96; David M. Gunn, *The Story of King David, Genre and Interpretation* (JSOTSup 6; Sheffield: JSOT Press, 1989), chap. 2; Gillian Keys, *The Wages of Sin: A Reappraisal of the "Succession Narrative"* (JSOTSup 221; Sheffield: Sheffield Academic Press, 1996).

Rather, the narrative deals with rivalry between two houses fighting for tribal supremacy: the house of Saul pits itself against that of David. In this newer view of traditional material, the narrative ends not with the establishment of a new capital in the City of David, but rather with Nathan's prophecy in 2 Samuel 7 bearing on the future of the Davidic dynasty.[32]

The Conflict between Two Houses: The Mari Historical Analogy

This newer way of seeing the narratives about Saul and David, as a conflict between two clans, finds a fitting historical analogy in two Mari texts. The Amorite view of history can be reconstructed from the eighteenth-century-BCE Mari text (ARM I 3), a letter sent by Yasmaḫ-Addu to the god Nergal.[33] This document describes the power struggle between two Amorite clans, the Benjaminite Addu clan pitted against the Bensim'alite Līm clan.[34] As in the Hebrew tradition, so also among the Amorites, the winning clan is similarly presented in the light of the hermeneutical principle of divine retribution. In this text the ruler of Mari, Yasmaḫ-Addu, recapitulates the historical events related to the protracted conflict between two reigning dynasties: the members of the Līm clan (Yagid-Līm, Yaḫdun-Līm, Sūmū-Yamam) against the Addu clan (Ilā-Kabkabū, Šamšī-Addu, Yasmaḫ-Addu). The former were the ancient rulers of Mari and belonged to the Bensim'alite, or northern Amorite, tribes. The latter were part of the Benjaminite, or southern, tribes. The end of the power struggle between these two clans is reflected in the prophetic letter relating the message of the god Adad from Aleppo to the last ruler of Mari, Zimrī-Līm (A. 1968). The god Adad is more than just a local ba'al, a master and lord over a single city. His influence stretches beyond the city of Aleppo in northern Syria, as he claims to have given the rule over Mari, on the banks of the Euphrates, to the warlord who revered him. These Mari documents represent a veritable philosophy of history with an ideology based on the

32. Jacques Vermeylen, "La maison de Saül et la maison de David: Un écrit de propagande théologico-politique de 1S 11 à 2S 7," in *Figures de David à travers la Bible: XVIIe congrès de l'ACFEB, Lille, 1er–5 septembre 1997* (ed. Louis Desrousseaux and Jacques Vermeylen; LD 177; Paris: Cerf, 1999), 34–74, esp. 53; idem, *La loi du plus fort: Histoire de la rédaction des récits davidiques de 1 Samuel 8 à 1 Rois 2* (BETL 154; Leuven: Peeters, 2000).

33. Daniel Bodi, "Les différents genres de la correspondence divine," *Ktèma* 33 (2008): 245–58. This article tries to bring greater precision in defining the genre of the letters to the gods, something that is less than clear in Beate Pongratz-Leisten, *Herrschaftswissen in Mesopotamien: Formen der Kommunikation zwischen Gott und König im 2. und 1. Jahrtausend v. Chr.* (SAAS 10; Helsinki: Neo-Assyrian Text Corpus Project, University of Helsinki, 1999), 202–9 ("'Échange de letters avec les dieux' in der Mari-Zeit").

34. Daniel Bodi, "The Retribution Principle in the Amorite View of History: Yasmaḫ-Addu's Letter to Nergal (ARM I 3) and Adad's Message to Zimrī-Līm (A. 1968)," *ARAM* (forthcoming).

operation of divine retribution. The view of history as the outworking of a retributive principle is common to all the major cultures of the Mediterranean shoreline. It is found in Mesopotamia in several epochs (from the Legend of Narām Sîn to the Poem of Erra), in the Hurrian-Hittite text concerning the fall of Ebla, in Egypt, in Greece, and in the Hebrew historiographic tradition. The Mari evidence comes from the Northwest Semitic domain to which the Hebrews belonged. It could therefore be considered a precursor of the theological historiographic genre, reflecting an ideology that anticipates the one attributed to the redactor of the Deuteronomistic History. This hermeneutical principle is a common ancient Near Eastern way of interpreting history. It is one that the Hebrew tradition shares and adapts to its own use.

The motif of repeating evil acts of one's father is shared by the Amorites and the Hebrews. In the Mari letter to the god Nergal, as a punishment for the sacrilege that Yaḥdun-Līm committed, his son Sūmū-Yamam rebelled against his father and took his throne. In the case of David, his son Absalom (2 Sam. 15–18) rebelled against him as a consequence of the divine retribution for the crime that David committed against Uriah the Hittite. The Mari text further states something very important. It accuses Sūmū-Yamam of acting in the same manner as his ancestor, of walking in a perverse manner like his father. One phrase in the text decries the guilty behavior carried forward from one generation to the next: "Sūmū-Yamam continued to act exactly like his father Yaḥdun-Līm and with his hands did outrageous/improper things" (*Sūmū-Yamam qātam* [*š*]*a abī-*[*š*]*ū-ma* (7') *Yaḥdun-Līm irṭ*[*u*]*b i*[*t*]*eppuša-am* (8') *u lā šināti ina qātī-š*[*u īpuš*]*-ma*, ARM I 3 [6']). Here, the Akkadian uses the idiomatic expression *qātam ša abī-šu-ma irṭub iteppuša-am*: "to continue to act according to the hand of his father" or "in the same way as his father."[35] The corresponding Hebrew expression is "to walk in one's father's ways." In 1 Samuel 8:3, 5 the sons of the old prophet Samuel are said *not* to have walked in their father's ways (*wĕlōʾ-hālĕkû bānāyw bidrākāyw*).[36]

In the so-called Deuteronomistic evaluation of Israelite kings, this phrase corresponds to the statement "He walked in the way of his father/of Jeroboam." In 1 Kings 22:53 (52 ET) it is said that Ahaziah, son of Ahab, "walked in the way of his father [*wayyēlek bĕderek ʾābîw*], in the way of his mother,

---

35. *Rat/ṭābu*, "to proceed to do something, to begin an activity; [Old Assyrian], Mari, Rimah, [Boghazkeui]" (*CAD* R 217); Wolfram Freiherrn von Soden (*Akkadisches Handwörterbuch*, 3 vols. [Wiesbaden: Harrosowitz Verlag, 1965–81], 963) connects it with Hebrew *rdp* (to pursue). *Qātu*, "in idiomatic [and] . . . adverbial uses" meaning "the same way" (*CAD* Q 193–94). Here the same way as his father; *lā šināti*, "improper actions or words, falsehoods " (*CAD* Š/3, 40).

36. The Qere is in the plural, followed by *Targum Pseudo-Jonathan*, the Syriac, and the Vulgate versions. The Kethib is in the singular, followed by the Septuagint.

and in the way of Jeroboam." In 2 Kings 21:21 Amon, son of Manasseh, "walked in all the way in which his father walked" (*wayyēlek bĕkol-hadderek 'ăšer-hālak 'ābîw*).[37]

After the reversal of fortunes with the capture of Mari by Zimrī-Līm, at the end of his fifteen-year reign, the descendants of the Benjaminite Addu clan sought refuge with Hammurabi of Babylon, an Amorite ruler who was also of the Benjaminite stock, and who finally burned and buried Zimrī-Līm's city of Mari.

The motif of committing a sacrilegious act that triggers divine retribution is another feature that ARM I 3 shares with the Hebrew tradition. Yagid-Līm committed a perjury, but Sūmū-Yamam also committed a sacrilegious act. Instead of reconstructing a temple of the god Nergal, he refurbished it as a dwelling for one of his numerous wives.[38] In the biblical traditions one finds the cultic offenses of Saul for which he lost his rule.

Thus ARM I 3 (9') reads, "Your temple which former kings made, he destroyed and made it into a house for his wife. (10') Upon finding (this) out you called him to account and his servants (11') killed him." The embezzlement angered the god Nergal, so that Sūmū-Yamam's servants assassinated him.[39] Notice that here we are not given the real political or family reasons why Sūmū-Yamam was assassinated. The text offers only ideological, religious reasons.

The power struggle between the Bensim'alite Līm-clan and the Benjaminite Addu-clan continued until the time of the last ruler of Mari, Zimrī-Līm. By leading military campaigns and fighting against Išmē-Dagān, the son of Šamšī-Addu I, Zimrī-Līm continued the conflict and rivalry between the two dynasties. This rivalry resembles the one that occurred seven centuries later between two Hebrew tribal chieftains, David of the tribe of Judah and Saul of the tribe of Benjamin. The first Hebrew tribal chieftain and warlord, Saul, lost his reign on account of a hubristic act. As he was awaiting Samuel's divine instructions on how to deal with the invading enemy, he began to grow impatient. With all eyes on him, Saul precipitously went ahead and made a sacrifice to Yahweh, something beyond his prerogatives. He was chosen to be a *nāgîd* (leader), not a *kōhēn* (priest). The tribal prophet, Samuel, returned,

---

37. See also 1 Kings 15:3 (Abijam in Judah); 15:26 (Nadab in Samaria); 15:34 and 16:2 (Basha in Samaria); 16:19 (Zimri of Samaria); 16:25–26 (Omri in Samaria); 16:31 (Ahab in Samaria); 22:43 (Jehoshaphat in Judah).

38. In the case of Solomon, the biblical tradition accuses him of having done something similar. In addition to constructing the temple of Yahweh, he built numerous cultic sites for his wives and concubines, and they beguiled him into worshiping their gods, divinities other than Yahweh.

39. As noted by Georges Dossin, "Archives de Sûmum-Iamam, roi de Mari," *RA* 64 (1970): 17–44, esp. 18.

rebuked Saul for committing a sacrilegious act, and prophesied that Yahweh would raise up another leader, from another clan, in his place (1 Sam. 13:6–14).[40]

This Mari letter is important as one of the earliest statements in the Northwest Semitic cultural area that hubristic acts lead to tragedy and demise. Such an ideology continues to Herodotus's *Histories* in the Greek milieu of the fifth century BCE. More than a millennium before the Greek historian, the Northwest Semites incorporated the theological principle of retribution into their view of history.

Now that the various military conflicts between the Amorite tribes are better known, it has become increasingly evident that these tribes paid great attention to the ethnic and clan background of their chieftains, something similar to the Hebrew traditions. This fact might shed some light on the conflict between David and Nabal in 1 Samuel 25 and the lengthy rabbinic discussion in the Talmud (*y. Sanh.* 2.3), where the rabbis argue that Nabal would have been a better royal candidate than David in view of the latter's Moabite extraction.[41] Among the Amorites the tribal rulers were chosen only from local royal or leading houses, even if the locals had divergent opinions about who was the best candidate to assume leadership. When an outsider, like Qarnī-Līm from Andarig, managed to seize power, and when he eventually lost his rule, his entire family was massacred in order not to leave a single member of that race and clan to challenge the position of the truly local one.[42] The extermination of Saul's descendants sparked accusations in David's time. Shimei, a member of Saul's clan, publicly reviled David, calling him a "man of blood" (2 Sam. 16:7–8). The threat of killing everyone down to the child or the dog "who urinates against the wall" (*maštîn běqîr*) occurs in contexts of exterminating or threatening to exterminate an entire dynasty or a ruling clan. David uses it in 1 Samuel 25:22 in his encounter with Nabal. It occurs in the context of turbulent dynastic successions in Israel (1 Kings 14:10; 21:21; 2 Kings 9:8).[43]

---

40. But David too would reap divine retribution on account of assassinating Uriah the Hittite in order to take away his wife, Bathsheba. See Bodi, *Demise of the Warlord*.

41. For the presentation of the discussion, see Bodi, *The Michal Affair*, 29–31; cf. Deut. 17:15: "You may not put a foreigner [*nkry*] over you, who is not your brother." Both Talmuds dedicate lengthy discussions to demonstrating that David, even with his Moabite origin and the prohibition in Deut. 23:3, was permitted to rule over Israel (*b. Yebam.* 72b; *y. Sanh.* 2.3). See Gary N. Knoppers, "The Davidic Genealogy: Some Textual Considerations from the Ancient Mediterranean World," *Transeu* 22 (2001): 35–50.

42. Jean-Marie Durand, "Assyriologie: L'Étude de la société et du peuplement du Proche-Orient au XVIIIe siècle av. notre ère," *ACF* 104 (2003–2004): 817–59, esp. 831.

43. Shemaryahu Talmon and Weston W. Fields, "The Collocation *mštyn bqyr w'šwr w'zwb* and Its Meaning," *ZAW* 101 (1989): 85–112, esp. 88. The authors argue that the expression *mštyn bqyr* refers to Saul's adviser, whom Nabal hosted in the upper room.

The ancient Hebrews share with the Amorite tribes similar ideology based on divine retribution and radical attitudes in their fights for dynastic successions.

The jewel of the Mari documentation is the spectrum of West Semitic semi-nomadic tribes that it presents, ranging from the fully nomadic to those in the process of becoming sedentary. For example, one Mari letter (ARMT 8 11) mentions the division of the Bené Awin clan into two groups: the already-sedentary ones, who settled in the city of Appan (*wašbût Appan*) (line 5), and the nomads *ḫibrum ša nawêm* (those transhumant in the steppe) (line 21). Moreover, the writers of the Mari documents frequently used societal concepts foreign to contemporary Mesopotamian society. Having no linguistic equivalents for these in standard Akkadian, they were occasionally obliged to use West Semitic loanwords that are often familiar to us from the Hebrew.[44]

Saul and David as Tribal Chiefs instead of Kings

Saul and David are traditionally dated to the end of the eleventh and the beginning of the tenth centuries BCE.[45] A few words should be said, however, about the "Low Chronology" espoused by the Tel Aviv archaeologist Israel Finkelstein. The archaeological evidence for the Iron Age walls, gates, and other major structures in Jerusalem, Gezer, Megiddo, and Hazor, as well as the general demographic picture of Jerusalem and Judah as interpreted by Finkelstein, calls for a reevaluation of the biblical depiction of Saul, David, and Solomon and their achievements. The archaeological strata in Gezer, Megiddo, and Hazor, which the high chronology usually ascribed to the so-called period of the united monarchy, are dated to the ninth century BCE.[46] They are inter-

44. On Mari Akkadian *ummātum* (ethnic group) and Hebrew *'ummôt* in Gen. 25:16; Num. 25:15; Ps. 117:1, see Michael Streck, *Das amurritische Onomastikon der altbabylonischen Zeit, 1: Die Amurriter. Die onomastische Forschung, Orthographie und Phonologie, Nominalmorphologie* (AOAT 271; Münster: Ugarit-Verlag, 2000), 82–124 (§1.93); Abraham Malamat, "*Ummātum* in Old Babylonian Texts and Its Ugaritic and Biblical Counterparts," *JAOS* 11 (1979): 527–36, esp. 533; idem, *Mari and the Early Israelite Experience* (Oxford: Oxford University Press, 1989), 33, with a list of forty Amorite words corresponding to Hebrew, such as the Akkadian *nawûm* and Hebrew *nāweh* (pasture) as a place where nomads pitch tents. On Mari *ga'um* or *gāyum* (clan) and Hebrew *gōy*, see Ephraim A. Speiser, "'People' and 'Nation' of Israel," *JBL* 79 (1960): 157–63. On Mari *ḫibrum ša nawīm* (transhumant people of the steppe) and Hebrew *ḥeber* (nomadic families roaming together), see Abraham Malamat, "Mari and the Bible: Some Patterns of Tribal Organization and Institution," *JAOS* 82 (1962): 143–50, esp. 145; Oswald Loretz, "Der juridische Begriff *niḫlatum/nḥlt/naḥālāh* 'Erbbesitz' als amurritisch-kanaanäische Hintergrund von Psalm 58," *UF* 34 (2002): 453–79.

45. Mordechai Cogan, "Chronology," *ABD* 1:1002–11; Edelman, "Saul ben Kish"; van der Toorn, "Saul and the Rise."

46. Israel Finkelstein, "The Archaeology of the United Monarchy: An Alternative View," *Levant* 28 (1996): 177–87; idem, "State Formation in Israel and Judah: A Contrast in Context, a Contrast in Trajectory," *NEA* 62 (1998): 35–52; Israel Finkelstein and Neil Asher Silberman,

preted as architectural achievements of the northern kingdom of Israel under the Omride dynasty, not under Solomon. Moreover, the archaeological finds in Jerusalem are considered to be meager, calling into question its supposed status as the capital city of a state comprising Israel and Judah. Finkelstein's analysis of the archaeological data from Jerusalem shows that the settlement of the tenth century BCE was no more than a small, poor highland village, without monumental construction.[47] Basing his study on topographical surveys of the hill country of Judah to the south of Jerusalem, Finkelstein concludes that it was rather sparsely populated in the tenth–ninth centuries BCE and seems to have attained a more substantial position only in the late eighth century.[48] On that ground, the idea of the united monarchy and the roles of David and Solomon are relegated to the genre of legends, unsubstantiated by any plausible archaeological or historical facts. Finkelstein applied the same approach to Nehemiah's Jerusalem. Since not a single stone of the wall that Nehemiah supposedly rebuilt in the fifth century BCE was found in archaeological excavation, Finkelstein holds Nehemiah 3 to be a figment of the scribe's imagination, with no historical reality.

Concerning Saul, Finkelstein holds that the biblical story reflects, in the main, some northern oral traditions about the Saulides. Israelite refugees brought these south to Judah in the late eighth century BCE, after the fall of the northern kingdom. They were then redacted to serve the royal ideology of the Jerusalem dynasty.[49] For example, 2 Samuel describes the death of Saul in the battle on Mount Gilboa against a Philistine army. It records how the citizens of Beth Shean, the ancient Egyptian stronghold in the valley, displayed

---

The Bible Unearthed: Archaeology's New Vision of Ancient Israel and the Origin of Its Sacred Texts (New York: Free Press, 2001); idem, *David and Solomon: In Search of the Bible's Sacred Kings and the Roots of Western Tradition* (New York: Free Press, 2006). Finkelstein accepts the historicity of David, however, and dates much of the Hebrew Bible before the Hellenistic period.

47. Israel Finkelstein, "The Rise of Jerusalem and Judah: The Missing Link," *Levant* 33 (2001): 105–15; David Ussishkin, "Solomon's Jerusalem: The Text and the Facts on the Ground," in *Jerusalem in Bible and Archaeology: The First Temple Period* (ed. Andrew G. Vaughn and Ann E. Killebrew; SBLSymS 18; Atlanta: Society of Biblical Literature, 2003), 103–11.

48. Israel Finkelstein and Neil Asher Silberman, "Temple and Dynasty: Hezekiah, the Remaking of Judah and the Rise of the Pan-Israelite Ideology," *JSOT* 30 (2006): 259–85. They write, "In a few decades in the late eighth century Jerusalem grew in size from c. 6 to c. 60 hectares and in population from around 1,000 to over 10,000 (estimated according to 200 inhabitants per hectare)" (265).

49. Israel Finkelstein, "The Last Labayu: King Saul and the Expansion of the First North Israelite Territorial Entity," in *Essays on Ancient Israel in Its Near Eastern Context: A Tribute to Nadav Na'aman* (ed. Yairah Amit et al.; Winona Lake, IN: Eisenbrauns, 2006), 171–87. Finkelstein writes, "In fact, Saul and the Saulides may compare better with Labayu than do the Omrides. Both Saul and Labayu established a large territorial entity in the highlands; both seem to have attempted to expand into lowlands; and both failed to do so" (179).

his corpse on their walls. In this revisionist view, the record reflects an ancient memory of a battle against an Egyptian army. A later redaction attributed to the Philistines the role of Egypt in the story.

Using the same interpretive principle as Finkelstein, based on the a priori that "if something is not found by archaeology, it means it did not exist in spite of what the written sources say," Nadav Na'aman shows the flaws of this approach by taking it *ad absurdum* with respect to an earlier Jerusalem. According to the five Amarna letters written by ʿAbdi-Ḫeba, king of Jerusalem, in the mid-fourteenth century BCE, the city was a highland stronghold that dominated a pastoral population in the hill country and the Shephelah. Yet in Jerusalem there is almost no archaeological evidence dating to the fourteenth century. Should one, therefore, affirm that the Amarna letters from Jerusalem and other archaeologically unattested cities from that period represent imaginative scribal exercises in letter writing?[50] According to Na'aman, one should avoid systematically disregarding written sources in favor of a supposed scientifically superior archaeological method. The relationship between the two should not be viewed as being either-or.[51]

Without entering into a discussion of Finkelstein's interpretation of archaeological data and of his dating of the Gezer, Megiddo, and Hazor "Solomonic remains"[52] or of Solomon's smelting activities,[53] his forceful statement should

50. Nadav Na'aman, "The Contribution of the Amarna Letters to the Debate on Jerusalem's Political Position in the Tenth Century BCE," *BASOR* 304 (1996): 17–27. The same point was made in Na'aman's lecture at the Society of Biblical Literature annual meeting in Boston on November 23, 2008.

51. Conscious of the problem, Finkelstein launched a new research project dealing with the beginnings of Israel with a team of collaborators, using various methods based on advanced technology that can detect and examine evidence not immediately spotted by the human eye. The project, under the direction of Israel Finkelstein and Steve Weiner, is called "Reconstructing Ancient (Biblical) Israel: The Exact and Life Sciences Perspective" and is sponsored by the European Research Council.

52. For a critique of Finkelstein's chronology, see Amihai Mazar, "Iron Age Chronology: A Reply to I. Finkelstein," *Levant* 29 (1997): 157–67; idem, "Jerusalem in the 10th Century BCE: The Glass Half Full," in Amit et al., *Essays on Ancient Israel*, 255–72. For a more positive assessment of David's times, see Nadav Na'aman, "Sources and Composition in the History of David," in Fritz and Davies, *Origins of the Ancient Israelite States*, 170–86.

53. Thomas E. Levy et al., "Reassessing the Chronology of Biblical Edom: New Excavations and 14C Dates from Khirbat en-Nahas (Jordan)," *Antiquity* 302 (2004): 865–79; Thomas E. Levy and Mohammad Najjar, "Edom and Copper: The Emergence of Ancient Israel's Rival," *BAR* 32, no. 4 (2006): 24–35, 70. Levy, of the University of California–San Diego, working with Najjar, of Jordan, excavated an ancient copper-production center at Khirbat en-Nahas (ruins of copper) down to virgin soil, through more than six meters of industrial smelting debris (slag). The 2006 dig uncovered new artifacts, and with them a new set of radiocarbon dates placing the bulk of industrial-scale production at Khirbat en-Nahas in the tenth century BCE. It remains to be determined who actually controlled the copper industry there. It may have been David and

in any case be heeded. The use of the term "monarchy" is a misnomer and should be abandoned when talking of Saul, David, and Solomon. It reminds us of European monarchies and seems inadequate to describe the ancient reality of Hebrew tribes. Therefore, in describing the reigns of these rulers, it seems more appropriate to use the expressions "tribal chieftain" or "warlord," which better describe their position among the ancient Israelite tribes. In other words, the domains that they governed may more precisely be described as "chiefdoms" rather than full-scale "states."

Finkelstein understands the terms *melek* (king), *bêt* (temple), and *hêkāl* (palace) in a way that does not correspond to their usage by seminomadic populations. Already the Amorite seminomadic tribes used the corresponding Akkadian terms in their own manner. First, although Zimrī-Līm, the Sim'alite sheikh and warlord from Mari, calls himself *šarrum dannum* (strong king), he is historically and politically a minor figure when compared to his Benjaminite contemporary, Hammurabi of Babylon. Hammurabi created an empire. In terms of historical importance and accomplishment, Zimrī-Līm cannot compare with Hammurabi. Nevertheless, he uses the same designation for himself. Second, even a relatively modest town such as Talḫayum in northern Syria (located between the Ḫabur and the Sārum Rivers) designates the ruler's dwelling with the term é-kál-lam$_x$(NAM) and é-kál-lam$_x$(LAM) (= *ekallum*, "palace").[54] The term does not stand for any architecturally major building or construction but simply for the house in which the town's ruler lived. At the time of Zimrī-Līm's influence in northern Syria, the region between the Euphrates and the Ḫabur Rivers was just a conglomerate of small states, always fighting among themselves. A series of princes, who often were kin and led by a warlord, ruled. Many of them were ambitious. They might conquer a fortified city and just as quickly lose it. Such tribal leaders, who succeeded in acquiring a local throne, proclaimed themselves *šarrum* (king) from their *ekallum* (palace). Third, in one Mari tablet, on "Nomadic Life," a sheikh designates his tent with the Akkadian term *bītum* (house) (A.1146, l. 17).[55] Fourth, even

---

Solomon, or perhaps regional Edomite leaders, or even the Egyptians, since Egyptian objects have been found in situ. The Bible places Solomon's smelting activities in the lower Jordan region, where he had copper *nḥšt* utensils smelted in clay molds (1 Kings 7:46). For Israel Finkelstein's viewpoint, see his article "Khirbat en-Nahas, Edom and Biblical History," *TA* 32 (2005): 119–25.

54. For the transliterated cuneiform text, see Jean-Marie Durand, *Documents épistolaires du Palais de Mari, 2* (LAPO 17; Paris: Cerf, 1998), 271, letter [A. 2417], no. 607, lines 6–1, 30–36, 42–47; also Jean-Marie Durand, "Les anciens de Talḫayum," *RA* 82 (1988): 97–113.

55. Pierre Marello, "Vie nomade," in *Florilegium marianum: Recueil d'études en l'honneur de Michel Fleury* (ed. Jean-Marie Durand; NABU 4; Paris: SEPOA, 1992), 115–25. For a new translation, see Jean-Marie Durand, *Les documents épistolaires du palais de Mari* (3 vols.; LAPO 16–18; Paris: Cerf, 1997–2000), 1:146–51.

when archaeology finds specific artifacts that may indicate beyond doubt a certain turn of events, the historical reality as reflected in texts might indicate the opposite. This may necessitate a modification of the archaeological interpretation. A notorious example is the Marriage Stela found in the rock temple of Rameses II in Abu Simbel in Nubia. The stela presents Ḫattušili III together with his daughter standing before Pharaoh Rameses II, who sits between two divinities.[56] The Akkadian letters of the Egyptian-Hittite correspondence indicate that the Hittite king never set foot in Egypt.[57] In this particular case independent textual evidence is superior to the archaeological data.

One important contribution made by the Mari documents is the light that they shed on the importance of the donkey as a royal symbol among Northwest Semitic tribes. Baḫdi-Līm, a high official from Mari, specifically advises the warlord and tribal chieftain Zimrī-Līm to enter the city of Mari riding on a donkey and not on a horse: "You are king of the Ḫaneans [= seminomads] and, only secondarily, king of the Akkadians. May my lord not ride on horses! Let it be only in a chair (drawn by) mules that my lord may ride and honor his royal head!" (ARM 6 76:20–24).[58] The donkey seems to have a particular symbolic relationship with the chiefs of the seminomadic tribes. The opposition that this statement establishes between the Ḫaneans and the Akkadians probably reflects nomadic and sedentary populations. The donkey is also the paramount symbol of royalty in the Hebrew tradition. The journey to trace the missing donkeys, or the future kingship, takes Saul and his servant on a tour of four subregions of Mount Ephraim: Shalishah, Shaalim, Benjamin, and Zuph (1 Sam. 9:3–5). They come to the home of a famous seer, subsequently identified as Samuel (9:6, 15–27). Their travels take them throughout the same territory that Samuel is said to have covered in his annual sanctuary circuit in 1 Samuel 7:15–17: Bethel, Gilgal, Mizpah, and Ramah, his home. There is an implication that Saul has toured the borders of his future kingdom.

In the episode of Absalom's revolt in 2 Samuel 16, Ziba, the servant of Mephibosheth, met David with a couple of donkeys (v. 1). They were saddled and carried two hundred loaves of bread, a hundred bunches of raisins, and a hundred summer fruits. David was fleeing Jerusalem on foot. Offering them

56. Kurt Bittel, "Bildliche Darstellungen Ḫattušili III in Ägypten," in *Kaniššuwar: A Tribute to Hans G. Güterbock* (ed. Harry A. Hoffner Jr. and Gary M. Beckman; AS 23; Chicago: Oriental Institute of the University of Chicago, 1986), 39–48.

57. Elmar Edel, *Die ägyptisch-hethitische Korrespondenz aus Boghazköi in babylonischer und hethitischer Sprache* (2 vols.; ARWAW 77; Opladen: Westdeutscher Verlag, 1994).

58. Jean R. Kupper, *Correspondance de Baḫdi-Lim, préfet du palais de Mari* (ARM 6; Paris: Imprimerie Nationale, 1954), 108–9; see also the new interpretation of this passage (ARM 6 76:20–21) by Dominique Charpin, "Un souverain éphémère en Ida-Maraṣ: Išme-Addu d'Ašnakkum," *MARI* 7 (1993): 165–91, esp. 170n36.

to David, Ziba said, "The donkeys are for the king's household to ride on" (v. 2). In so doing, Ziba betrayed his master, Mephibosheth, the last descendant from the house of Saul and a potential rival of David. He deprived the disabled Mephibosheth of the opportunity to display his loyalty in a time of political crisis. Thus Ziba prevented Mephibosheth from showing mercy as David had shown to this son of Jonathan. In this incident the donkey plays the double role of Ziba's allegiance to David and of a nomadic symbol of David's legitimate kingship.[59] In the Song of Deborah the chiefs of Israel are said to "ride on tawny asses" (Judg. 5:10). Using the same royal symbol of a donkey, Zechariah 9:9–10 announces the coming of the Messiah in the following terms: "Lo, your king comes to you triumphant and victorious, humble [ʿny] and riding on an ass, on a colt, the foal of an ass. I will cut off the chariot from Ephraim and the war horse from Jerusalem." In this context the donkey symbolizes peace, while the horse stands for war and more generally refers to foreign oppressors: Assyrians, Egyptians, and Greeks. This peaceful meaning of the donkey is present already among the eighteenth century BCE Amorites, who sacrifice a donkey in their peace treaties. Two Mari tablets designate the animal sacrificed in a peace treaty as "the donkey of peace."[60]

Matthew's Gospel picks up Zechariah's prophecy and applies it to Jesus's entry into Jerusalem riding on a donkey, followed by a colt (Matt. 21:2–7; John 12:14–15). In light of the foregoing Amorite parallels, it is not certain that the choice of a donkey for a ride expresses the modesty and humility of the messianic king. The sense of the Hebrew term ʿny used in Zechariah 9:9 should be reconsidered. Modern translations are influenced by the Greek *praÿs* and Latin *mitis* (débonnaire, good, gentle) used in Matthew 21:5. The sense of the root ʿny, however, is different. The term stands for respectful submission of the human to the divine. This attitude expresses piety and deference of the king toward the divine world, common to the ancient Near Eastern world. The biblical reworking of this concept applies it to all humans: the blessed

59. Elena Cassin, "Le droit et le tordu I," in *Le semblable et le différent: Symbolisme du pouvoir dans le Proche-Orient ancien* (Paris: Découverte, 1987), 50–71, esp. 53–54.

60. For the Amorite expression "donkey of peace" (*anše ḫa-a-ra-am ša sa-li-mi-im*), see Jean-Marie Durand, *Archives épistolaires de Mari I* (ARM 26; Paris: Éditions Recherche sur les Civilisations, 1988), 174–75, no. 39, lines 13–14: (13) [*ni-iš*] dingir-meš *za-ak-ra-a-ni*[*-im*] (14) *ù* anše *ḫa-a-ra-a*[*m*] *ša sa-li-m*[*i-im*] *bi-ri-it mu-t*[*e*]*-ba-al lu-u*[*q-tú-ul*] "Swear the oath of the gods so that I may kill the donkey of peace with Muti-Abal"; Dominque Charpin, "Une campagne de Yahdun-Lîm en Haute-Mésopotamie," in *Florilegium marianum: Recueil d'études à la mémoire de Maurice Birot* (ed. Dominique Charpin and Jean-Marie Durand; NABU 3; Paris: SEPOA, 1994), 177–200, esp. 188 text. A.1098: 21–23: (21) *ù a-na a*[*b*]*-bé-e i-da-ma-ra-aṣ*ᵏⁱ *ù* [*a-du-na*]*-*ᵈIM *šu-pu-ur-ma* (22) *a-na ṣe-ri-ka li-*[*i*]*l-li-ku-nim-ma* (23) *ḫa-a-ra-am ša sa-li-mi-im qú-tu-ul-ma it-ti-šu-nu i-ša-ri-iš du-b*[*u*]*-ub* "Write to the 'fathers' of Ida-Maraṣ and of Aduna-Addu, so that they may come to you: kill the donkey of peace and speak frankly with them."

are those who accept God's superiority and consequently God's representative on earth: the king. The humility that the Hebrew text implies stands not for poverty and modesty but rather for obedience. The people accept a just and legitimate submission to their king just as the latter submits to God's authority. In this sense, the king is the depository of divine rule and power, and a warrant of peace. Being accepted by all, he is able to restore order. His mission of pacification is illustrated by him riding on a donkey in contrast with the more warlike aspect of riding on a horse. The Semitic kingship is neither modest nor poor, but peaceful and triumphant.

Another feature common to the Amorite and the Hebrew traditions is the anointing with the oil of victory. The act of anointing the king is attested in Ebla and in the Amorite, the Hittite, the Amarna, and the Hebrew traditions (1 Sam. 10:1 [Saul]; 16:13 [David]), but not in Mesopotamia proper.[61] In 1 Kings 1:38, when he is proclaimed as David's official successor, Solomon is made to ride on "king David's mule," and Zadok the priest anoints him.

Saul and a Mari Text

One Mari text throws light on the practice mentioned in 1 Samuel 11:5–7, in connection with Saul when he mustered the tribal levy enjoining various Hebrew tribes to take part in a military campaign. The Ammonite incident is an independent tradition usually considered to be one of the oldest and most authentic about Saul. The fact that Saul was prompted for military action by the "spirit of God" connects his experience to that of the judges Othniel, Gideon, Jephthah, and Samson. The attack of Nahash on Jabesh-gilead and Saul's response to it culminated in a public proclamation of Saul's tribal leadership at Gilgal. Saul was behind the plow in the field with a yoke of oxen. When the messenger brought the news to him about the outrage done to the Israelites in Jabesh-gilead by the Ammonite King Nahash, "(Saul) took a yoke of oxen, and cut them in pieces and sent them throughout all the territory of Israel by the hand of messengers, saying, 'Whoever does not come out after Saul and Samuel, so shall it be done to his oxen!' Then the dread of Yahweh fell upon the people, and they came out as one man" (v. 7). The Song of Debrorah shows that a good turnout of the tribes in time of crisis was not easily achieved (Judg. 5:15–17).

The symbolic act of dismembering the oxen may be regarded as a kind of conditional curse: may the oxen of anyone who does not respond to the summons suffer the same fate. The cutting up of a yoke of oxen and using

---

61. Sophie Lafont, "Le roi, le juge et l'étranger à Mari et dans la Bible," *RA* 92 (1998): 161–81; idem, "Nouvelles données sur la royauté mésopotamienne," *RHDFE* 73 (1975): 473–500.

their pieces to summon Israel to war, threatening dissenters with reprisals, corresponds to a similar practice in Mari text ARM 2 48.[62] The Mari parallel suggests that the threat might have been more direct, implying that the people themselves, not their oxen, would be slain. The practice of dismembering an animal to levy the troops seems to have had its origin in covenant making, which often involved dismemberment of animals accompanied by an oath: "May I suffer the fate of these animals if I am not true to the terms of this agreement!" There seems to be a correspondence between dismembered pieces of an animal and the dismembered human body, as confirmed by the grim incident of the Levite's concubine who was dismembered in Judges 19:29. Pieces of her body were sent to various Israelite tribes, thereby summoning them to punish the Benjaminites. In ARM 2 48 Baḫdī-Līm, a servant of Zimrī-Līm, has difficulties in levying troops among the Hanean nomadic tribes. To summon the recalcitrant nomadic tribes, a criminal taken from a prison was decapitated, and his head was paraded through several towns. Seeing what happened to that man, the Hanean tribes would respond in fear to the summons to join the military campaign.[63]

David and the Pattern of Seizing Power in the Ancient Near East

David as a leader of a troop of ʿapiru mercenaries seems to follow the manner of taking power in the ancient Near East since the Middle Bronze Age, the time of the tribal leader and warlord. Consider the Amorite Zimrī-Līm in the eighteenth century BCE, Idrimi of Alalaḫ in the mid-fourteenth century BCE, and ʿAbdi-Aširta of Amurru and Rib-Addi of Byblos, also in the fourteenth century BCE. In their struggle to seize power or recover their lost power, these warlords led troops of mercenaries called ḫapiru/ʿapiru. In the Iron Age as well, during his conflict with Saul, David followed the sociopolitical pattern of seizing power, a model well established in the ancient Near East. Indeed, prior to David, several warlords and petty Levantine kings had recourse to this pattern of sociopolitical action when confronted with a similar problem: they avail themselves of the ʿapiru mercenaries in their power struggle.

62. Cuneiform text: Charles-François Jean, *Lettres* (ARM 2; Paris: Librairie orientaliste P. Geuthner, 1941), plate LXII, no. 48; transliteration and translation: *Lettres diverses* (ARM 2; Paris: Imprimerie Nationale, 1950), 102–3; translation and commentary: Durand, *Les documents épistolaires*, 2:176–77; preliminary study: Gerhard Wallis, "Eine Parallele zu Richter 19,29ff und 1 Samuel 11,5ff aus dem Briefarchiv von Mari," *ZAW* 64 (1952): 57–61.

63. P. Kyle McCarter Jr., *1 Samuel: A New Translation with Introduction, Notes, and Commentary* (AB 8; Garden City, NY: Doubleday, 1980), 203; Robert Polzin, "HWQYʿ and Covenant Institutions in Israel," *HTR* 62 (1969): 227–40.

Mari Text ARM 2 48	
1. *a-na be-lí-ia*	To my lord
2. *qí-bí-ma*	say:
3. *um-ma Ba-aḫ-di-li-im*	Thus Baḫdī-Līm
4. (*ÌR*)*warad-ka-a-ma*	your servant.
5. *iš-tu* (*UD*)*ūmu 5 KAM i-na ḫa-da-nim*	Five days since the appointed time
6. *Ḫa-na^meš ú-qa-a ù Ṣa-bu-um*	(that) I wait for the Ḫanean-nomads but the troop
7. *ù-ul i-pa-aḫ-ḫu-ra-am*	does not gather together.
8. *Ḫa-na^meš iš-tu na-wi-im ik-šu-dam-ma*	The Ḫanean-nomads arrived from the pastureland
9. *ù ina li-ib-bi a-la-ni-ma wa-aš-bu*	but dwell in the midst of towns
10. *1–šu 2–šu a-na li-ib-bi a-la-ni*	Once, twice to the midst of towns
11. *á[š]-ta-pa-ar-ma <li>-id-ku-ni-iš-šu-nu-ti*	I have sent so that they may be levied
12. *ù ú-ul ip-ḫu-ru-nim-ma*	but they didn't gather together.
13. *ù a-di* (*UD*)*ūmu 3 KAM ú-ul ip-ḫu-ru-nim-ma*	And if in three days they (still) don't get together,
14. *i-na-an-na šum-ma lib-bi be-lí-ia*	now, if my lord agrees
15. *1* ^lube-el ar-nim i-na ne-<pa>-ri-im li-du-ku-m[a]*	let them execute a criminal in the workhouse
16. *qa-qa-as-sú li-ik-ki-su-ma*	let them cut his head off
17. *ù bi-ri-it a-la-ni-e*	and between the towns,
18. *a-di Ḫu-ud-nim^ki ù Ap-pa-an^ki*	up to Ḫudnum and Appān,
19. *li-sa-ḫi-ru aš-šum ṣa-bu-um i-pa-al-la-aḫ-ma*	let them tour in order that the troops may become fearful
20. *[ar-ḫ]í-iš i-pa-aḫ-ḫu-ra-am*	and quickly gather here
21. *[a-na] ṭe₄ em ḫa-ma-ti-im*	(so that) according to the urgent order
22. *[ša] be-lí u-wa-e-ra-an-ni*	which my lord gave me,
23. *[a]r-ḫi-iš ge-er-ra-am*	rapidly the military campaign
24. ⌈*a**⌉-*ṭà-ar-ra-du*	I may expedite.

THE ḪAPIRU/ʿAPIRU

In his conquest for power, David may be perceived as a *ʿapiru* warlord. The Mari texts present such *ʿapiru* as troublemakers often associated with pulling off a political coup. The Akkadian verb **ḫabārum*, in the G-stem preterite *iḫbur*, means "to leave one's home, hometown, or homeland." One unpublished text (A. 1977) states, "This man, having packed his belongings, left [*iḫbur*] for Carchemish (with king) Aplahanda."[64] In the D-stem *ḫubburum* means "to

---

64. Jean-Marie Durand, "Assyriologie: Le Problème des *ḫabiru*," ACF 105 (2004–2005): 563–84, esp. 570.

Line 3: The name "Baḥdī-Līm" means "my support is the clan." See Michael Streck, *Das amurritische Onomastikon der altbabylonischen Zeit* (AOAT 271; Münster: Ugarit-Verlag, 2000), 323, 343 ("Mein Rückhält ist Līm").

Lines 5–6: "the appointed, convened time," *ḫadānu*; *uqqâ* D-stem present 1cs from *qu''u, quwwû, qummû, qubbû* D-stem, a transitive verb meaning, "to await, wait for, wait on someone." See D. Bodi, "Akkadian and Aramaic Terms for a 'Favorable Time' (*ḫidānu, adānu,* and *'iddān*): Semitic Precursors of Greek *kairos*?" in *Time and History in the Ancient Near East* (Proceedings of the 56th Rencontre Assyriologique Internationale at Barcelona 26–30 July 2010; ed. L. Feliu, J. Llop, A. Millet Albà, and J. Sanmartín; Winona Lake, IN: Eisenbrauns, 2013): 47–56.

Lines 7, 20: *ipaḫḫur-am* G-stem present 3ms.

Line 11: Restituting <*li*>, following Jean-Marie Durand, *Les documents épistolaires du palais de Mari* (3 vols.; LAPO 16–18; Paris: Cerf, 1997–2000), 2:177n368.

Lines 12–13: *ipḫurū-nim-ma* G-stem (u/u) preterite 3mpl + *nim* ventive + enclitic *-ma*; *ipḫur/ipaḫḫur* from *paḫāru*, "to gather."

Line 14: *bēl arnim*, "criminal," lit., "lord, master of crime"; *nupūru* CAD N/2, 341, *nubūru, nepāru, nurpāru*, "workhouse, ergasterion"; *lidūkū-ma*, "let them execute, kill."

Line 16: *qaqqassu likkisū-ma* root *nakāsum*, "to cut, fell," G (i/i) G-stem preterit 3mpl; *ikkis/inakkis*.

Line 18: "up to Ḫudnum and Appān"; the first place name is rendered "région en plateau" by Durand (*Les documents épistolaires*, 2:177na). This is a Bensim'alite village near Mari. The root of this toponym, *'dn*, probably is related to the city of Hadnā in no. 601 and to the Assyrian territory of Bīt 'Adīni, which gave its name to the garden of Eden. Appān (Le Cap, or "the summit") is a Bensim'alite city in the region north of Mari, facing the Benjaminite region of Mišlān.

Line 19: vocalize *lisaḫḫirū*, AHw, 1006 D, "herumwenden, abwenden," "abgeschalgene Kopf durch die Orte herumwenden" (in the G-stem the thematic vowel would be u/u *ishur/isahhur*), and here the thematic vowel is (i), hence it is a D-stem.

Line 24: *aṭarradu* represents a subordinative/subjunctive always dependent on *aššum* in line 19. In line 19 *ipallaḫ-ma* and in line 20 *i-pa-aḫ-ḫu-ra-am* with a ventive, the coordinated previous verbs are usually according to the Mari usage in the indicative.

make someone leave, to drive away," as in ARM I 60:22: *ṣa-b[u-u]m šu-ú da-ba*-bà*-am li-iḫ-še-eḫ ṣa-ba-am ša-a-ti ḫu-ub-bi-ir* (if the troop wishes to talk idly, make that troop leave).[65]

This usage and etymology identify the *ḫapiru* primarily as a people who are politically exiled. The Ugaritic (*'prm*) and Egyptian (*'pr.w*) usages of the term indicate that the root should most probably be *'-p-r* with an initial *'ayin* and with the second root consonant /p/ rather than /b/.[66] This in turn would confirm the link with "dust," *eperum* (<*ḫaparum), Hebrew *'āpār*, and would tend to exclude any etymological link with the Hebrew term *'ibrî* (derived from the verb *'ābar*, "to cross over"—i.e., the river, meaning crossing the Euphrates).[67]

65. Durand, *Les documents épistolaires*, 2:402n110 (*dabābum*, "talk, [idle] speech"; *ḫašāḫu*, "to desire, wish for").

66. Oswald Loretz, *Habiru-Hebräer: Eine sozio-linguistische Studie über die Herkunft des Gentiliziums 'ibrî vom Appelativum ḫabiru* (BZAW 160; Berlin: de Gruyter, 1984). The administrative texts from Ugarit in the Akkadian language use the logogram ^{lú}SA.GAZ^{meš} with the translation of the same administrative entries (lists of taxes) in the Ugaritic alphabetic script as *'prm* in plural.

67. See EA 141.1–5, letter of Ammunira from Beirut to the Pharaoh: "Man from Beirut, your servant and dust: gloss *a-pa-ru* at your feet" (= *'aparu*).

In Genesis 14:13 Abram the "Hebrew" (*'ibrî*) is rendered with *peratēs* in the Septuagint, from *peran* (from across, from beyond). George Mendenhall's equation of the *'apiru* with the Hebrews, on which basis he argues that *'apiru* and "Israelite" are "practically synonymous," is today abandoned.[68] As pointed out by Manfred Weippert, Mendenhall lays "too great an emphasis on the voluntary nature of the existence of the *'apiru*. It seems to me that entry into this category of classless individuals must normally, as the texts seem to indicate between the lines, have been experienced as a misfortune. . . . External pressure is the cause, not free choice."[69]

Already Edouard Dhorme had placed the term *'apiru* in connection with Hebrew *'āpār* (dust), suggesting that the word meant "the dusty ones" or "those covered with dust" on account of their nomadic movement across the steppe.[70] Instead of Dhorme's somewhat romantic explanation, at the origin of this term Jean-Marie Durand sees a reference to a rite whereby the one who had to go into exile from his hometown or homeland would take a bit of dirt from his hearth or dust from the floor of his home.[71] Moreover, there are a number of biblical and ancient Near Eastern texts that describe the role of dust in different rites of mourning. It could suggest the sadness of the return to the original dust from which one was created, or the severing of links with a city by shaking the dust off one's feet. Inversely, keeping a bit of dust from one's home could signify keeping some links with one's place of origin despite being exiled. This suggestion is indirectly confirmed with David's dethronement in his home, the City of David, by his son Absalom. While fleeing, David meets a Benjaminite, Shimei. Shimei throws dust on David, the fugitive (2 Sam. 16:13: *wĕ'ippar bĕ'āpār* [dusting him with dust]). With this symbolic gesture, Shimei adds to David's opprobrium as one rejected by the

---

68. George E. Mendenhall, "The Hebrew Conquest of Palestine," *BA* 25 (1962): 66–87, esp. 71; idem, *The Tenth Generation: The Origins of the Biblical Tradition* (Baltimore: Johns Hopkins University Press, 1973), 140. For a critical review of Mendenhall, see Jack M. Sasson, review of George E. Mendenhall, *The Tenth Generation: The Origins of the Biblical Tradition*, *JBL* 93 (1974): 294–96.

69. Manfred Weippert, *Die Landnahme der israelitischen Stämme in der neuren wissenschaftlichen Diskussion: Ein kritischer Bericht* (FRLANT 92; Göttingen: Vandenhoeck & Ruprecht, 1967); ET, *The Settlement of the Israelite Tribes in Palestine: A Critical Survey of Recent Debate* (trans. James D. Martin; SBT 21; London: SCM, 1971), 66.

70. Edouard Dhorme, "Les Habirou et les Hébreux," *RH* 78 (1954): 256–64, esp. 261.

71. Jean-Marie Durand, "Assyriologie: Le Problème des *habiru*," *Annuaire du Collège de France* 105 (2004–2005), 571; Jean Bottéro, "Les Habiru, les Nomades et les Sédentaires," in *Nomads and Sedentary Peoples: XXX International Congress of Human Sciences in Asia and North Africa* (ed. Jorge Silva Castillo; México, D.F.: Colegio de México, 1981), 89–107; Jeffrey Szuchman, ed., *Nomads, Tribes, and the State in the Ancient Near East: Cross-Disciplinary Perspectives* (OIS 5; Chicago: Oriental Institute of the University of Chicago, 2009).

community. The same symbolic gesture is found among the Amorites in a Mari text (A. 2071:14–15)[72] where the corresponding expression occurs, *eperam ina qaqqadī-šu inappaṣū-ma* (they will throw dust on his head). In context, this act indicates the community's rejection of that person.

The *'apiru* were outlawed people who had fled their sovereigns. They had no lands. Instead, they wandered in groups as marauders or rented their services as mercenaries to warlords throughout the Fertile Crescent. Rather than an ethnic term, the word identified a social class of uprooted ones, outcasts isolated from their families, clans, and homelands. Thus they came together to look for other means of economic survival.[73]

There are three elements in Zimrī-Līm's conquest of power over Mari that resemble the rise of David.[74] First, as already described above, there was the conflict between two houses. Zimrī-Līm belonged to the Lim Sim'lite clan that fought against the Addu Benjaminites. A second resemblance is the practice of taking the wives of the vanquished adversary. A third manner in which Zimrī-Līm's rise resembles David's attainment of kingship in the books of Samuel is the heterogeneous nature of Zimrī-Līm's army.

Taking the Wives of the Vanquished Predecessor

One Mari text (A. 4636) gives the list of women found in Yasmaḥ-Addu's "harem" (i.e., palace ladies) now in Zimrī-Līm's hands, once he took over the city of Mari.[75] In the list are daughters of several predecessors associated with Mari: Yaḥdun-Līm, Ḥadni-Addu, and Sumu-Yamam. It shows that most of the women who were in the service of Yasmaḥ-Addu stayed in Mari and continued their life in the service of the next occupant of the palace, Zimrī-Līm. They preserved the same order of enumeration, implying the same degree of importance and the same internal hierarchy. It is possible that, after Yasmaḥ-Addu left the Mari palace, the gates of the city of Mari were opened to the new ruler, Zimrī-Līm.[76] The transfer of power from one owner of Mari to another included acquisition of the predecessors' palace women.

72. Durand, *Archives épistolaires*, 538. The verb *napāṣu* (*CAD* N/1, 285) (G u/a) *ippuṣ/inappaṣ* in this case means "to hurl."

73. Daniel E. Fleming, *Democracy's Ancient Ancestors: Mari and Early Collective Governance* (Cambridge: Cambridge University Press, 2004), 95–100; idem, "Prophets and Temple Personnel in the Mari Archives," in *The Priests in the Prophets: The Portrayal of Priests, Prophets and Other Religious Specialists in the Latter Prophets* (ed. Lester L. Grabbe and Alice Ogden Bellis; JSOTSup 408; London: T&T Clark, 2004), 44–64.

74. Dominique Charpin and Jean-Marie Durand, "La prise de pouvoir par Zimri-Lim," *MARI* 4 (1985): 293–343.

75. Jean-Marie Durand, "Les dames du palais de Mari à l'époque du royaume de Haute-Mésopotamie," *MARI* 4 (1985): 385–436, esp. 431.

76. Charpin and Durand, "La prise de pouvoir," 323.

This resembles two moments in David's career. First, in 1 Samuel 25, after the death of Nabal, a rich farmer from Carmel in the vicinity of Hebron, David took over Nabal's wife, Abigail, and probably his lands. Second, in 2 Samuel 12:8 Nathan reminds David of what he had already received from Yahweh's hand: "And I gave you your master's house, and your master's wives into your lap, and gave you the house of Israel and Judah." This verse is the only reference in the Hebrew Bible to David's taking Saul's wives. The Hebrew expression "and I gave [wā'ettĕnâ] . . . your master's wives into your lap [wĕ'et-nĕšê 'ădōnêkā bĕḥêqekā]," referring to Saul's wife and a concubine now in David's possession, has a parallel in the Amorite Akkadian found in Mari documents. Yasmaḫ-Addu uses the idiomatic expression "to place (a woman) in someone's lap" (ana sūnim nadānum) about a princess from Qaṭna who was added to his already-large harem. It forms an exact equivalent of the Hebrew phrase.[77] In both cases the expression is used of tribal chieftains and their wives. The capture of harems between tribal chiefs is a standard practice in the act of seizing power.

THE HETEROGENEOUS CHARACTER OF ZIMRĪ-LĪM'S AND DAVID'S ARMIES

The army of Zimrī-Līm with which he conquered Mari shows a high degree of heterogeneity. It was composed of mer'um, the "chief of pasture," (derived from the root r'y, "to pasture, graze") and of "palace servants" designated under the term "conscripts," as if he had to mobilize every person available. In the Epic of Zimrī-Līm the "chiefs of pasture" were requisitioned when Zimrī-Līm ordered his chief officer to mobilize the sheikhs so that they might also bring along their Hanean seminomadic warriors. Thus these "chiefs of pasture" would join his military campaign.[78] In his conquest of power, Zimrī-Līm had to rely on hired hands and 'apiru warriors.

In respect to David, one finds a similar heterogeneous army. In 1 Samuel 22:2 the narrator reports, "Everyone who was in distress, and everyone who was in debt, and everyone who was discontented gathered to him; and he became captain over them. And there were with him about four hundred men." The troop of 'apiru warriors mentioned in Mari documents may have had thirty, fifty, eighty-five, or as many as four hundred men.[79]

---

77. Jack M. Sasson, "About 'Mari and the Bible,'" RA 92 (1998): 97–123, esp. 107.
78. Charpin and Durand, "La prise de pouvoir," 327.
79. Michaël Guichard, "Un David raté ou une histoire de habiru à l'époque Amorite: Vie et mort de Samsī-Erah, chef de guerre et homme du people," in Le jeune héros: Recherches sur la formation et la diffusion d'un thème littéraire au Proche-Orient ancien; Actes du colloque organisé par les chaires d'Assyriologie et des Milieux bibliques du Collège de France, Paris, les 6 et

The Seizing of Power by Idrimi from Alalaḫ in the Mid-Fourteenth Century BCE

In 1939 the English archaeologist C. Leonard Woolley found a statue dating from the mid-fourteenth century BCE in a niche of a destroyed temple; this was in Alalaḫ, modern Tell Atchana, in the Orontes region. On account of World War II, the first publication of the inscription, by Sidney Smith, had to wait until 1949.[80] Amir Fink, however, has reinvestigated the records and results of the old excavations at Tell Atchana. He has argued that Woolley missed the stratigraphy of the locus where the statue was found in 1939. By the time Woolley returned to the site after World War II, in 1946, his misinterpretation could no longer be corrected because much of the physical record was no longer there to be reexamined.[81] Therefore the statue most probably was smashed and buried at the moment of the Hittite conquest of Alalaḫ, in the mid-fourteenth century BCE, at the transition from Level IV to Level III.

The story of Idrimi from Alalaḫ is written in a particular kind of Akkadian full of Northwest Semiticisms akin to the Amarna Akkadian.[82] As told in the inscription, the seizing of power by Idrimi is presented according to the same pattern of relying on the ʿapiru warriors. When Idrimi, son of Ilu-ili-ma, was young, a bad thing happened (maybe a revolt or Hurrian pressure from Mitanni) that caused his family to flee Ḫalab (Aleppo), his paternal and ancestral home (bīt abīya [line 3]), and seek refuge with his mother in Emar, on the Euphrates.[83] Alone among his brothers, though he was the youngest,

---

7 avril 2009 (ed. Jean-Marie Durand, Thomas Römer, and Michael Langlois; OBO 250; Fribourg: Academic Press; Göttingen: Vandenhoeck & Ruprecht, 2011), 29–93, esp. 37, with references.

80. Sidney Smith, The Statue of Idri-mi (OPBIAA 1; London: British Institute of Archaeology in Ankara, 1949), 14–23. See also Willam F. Albright, "Some Important Recent Discoveries: Alphabetic Origins and the Idrimi Statue," BASOR 118 (1950): 11–20. Albright compared Idrimi to biblical Joseph.

81. Eva von Dassow, State and Society in the Late Bronze Age: Alalaḫ under the Mittani Empire (SCCNH 17; ed. David I. Owen and Gernot Wilhelm; Bethesda, MD: CDL Press, 2008), 31; Amir Fink, "Where Was the Statue of Idrimi Actually Found? The Later Temple of Tell Atchana (Alalakh) Revisited," UF 39 (2007): 161–245; idem, Late Bronze Age Tell Atchana (Alalakh): Stratigraphy, Chronology, History (Oxford: Archaeopress, 2010).

82. Shlomo Izre'el, "The Amarna Letters from Canaan," CANE 2:2411–19, esp. 2412; Richard Hess, "Alalakh Studies and the Bible: Obstacle or Contribution?," in Scripture and Other Artifacts: Essays on the Bible and Archaeology in Honor of Philip J. King (ed. Michael D. Coogan, Cheryl Exum, and Lawrence E. Stager; Louisville: Westminster John Knox, 1994), 199–215; idem, "Canaan and Canaanite in Alalakh," UF 31 (1999): 225–77.

83. Benno Landsberger, "Assyrische Königsliste und 'Dunkeles Zeitalter,'" JCS 8 (1954): 47–73; Jussi Aro, "Remarks on the Language of the Alalakh Texts," AfO 17 (1954–1956): 361–65. Matitiahu Tsevat, "Alalakhiana," HUCA 29 (1958): 109–35; A. Leo Oppenheim, "The Story of Idrimi, King of Alalakh," ANET 557–58; George Giacumakis, The Akkadian of Alalakh (JLSP 59; The Hague: Mouton, 1970); Edward L. Greenstein and David Marcus, "The Akkadian Inscription of Idrimi," JANESCU 8 (1976): 59–96.

Idrimi decided to recover his patrimony. Just like David, who was the youngest of Jesse's seven sons (1 Chron. 2:15; but cf. 1 Sam. 16:10), Idrimi was the youngest son, whose ambitions surpassed those of his older brothers. This literary motif occurs again in the Assyrian inscriptions of Esarhaddon, who affirms, *ša aḫḫê-ya rabūti aḫū-šunu ṣeḫru anāku* (Of my older brothers, I was their youngest brother).[84]

Idrimi left his brothers in Emar and set forth, accompanied by his horse, chariot, and driver, to recover his lost power. He sought refuge with the Sutû warriors. Crossing the desert, he arrived at the city of Ammiya in northern Canaan. There he found compatriots and people from Ḥalab (Aleppo) and its western territories: Mukiš, Niya, and Ama'e. These different groups of people recognized him as the son of one of their former lords. They joined him in his goal to regain lost power. There, with a group of the *'apiru* men, Idrimi spent seven years until, through divination (i.e., observing the flight of birds), he determined that the storm-god Addu favored his quest.

Idrimi built ships. Together with his mercenaries and *'apiru* warriors, he set out for Mukiš, the territory of Alalaḫ, and regained power over the city.[85] On his arrival at Mount Ḥazi (= Mount Cassius), the people of Niya, Ama'e, Mukiš, and Alalaḫ welcomed him and made a treaty with him. However, Parattarna, king of the Hurrians, opposed Idrimi. After seven years Idrimi sent an embassy to Parattarna. He mentioned his ancestor's service to Parattarna's ancestors and provided the latter with numerous gifts. The king of the Hurrians was finally persuaded. Idrimi swore fealty as a vassal and became king of Alalaḫ.

Idrimi attacked seven fortified towns in the Ḥatti territory, taking many captives and much booty. With the spoils from his campaigns, Idrimi built himself a house fit for a king. Furthermore, he spread the wealth among his soldiers, family, friends, and subjects. If inhabitants of his realm had no home, he settled them in appropriate dwellings. He attended to the worship of the gods of Alalaḫ. He put his son Addu-nirari in charge of these duties. Idrimi also used some of the captured booty to build himself "a throne equal to the throne of other kings" (line 81) in Alalaḫ.

When speaking of the Idrimi Inscription, A. Leo Oppenheim compared it to the story of David: "All this seems to me to bespeak the existence of a specific literary tradition, totally different in temper and scope from that of the ancient Near East; of this tradition we have known only the later, far more substantial but equally admirable, fruits in the narrative of certain sections

---

84. Riekele Borger, *Die Inschriften Asarhaddons, Königs von Assyrien* (AfOB 9; Graz: Weidner, 1956), 40 (A 18).

85. Giorgio Buccellati, "La 'carriera' di David a quelle di Idrimi re di Alalac," *BO* 4 (1962): 95–99; Niels Peter Lemche, "David's Rise," *JSOT* 10 (1978): 2–25, esp. 12.

of the Book of Genesis and especially in the story of King David—another *document humain.*"[86]

Idrimi's success confirmed the divine favor that he had received through auguries and other omens. For Idrimi, as for David, personal triumph confirmed his divine election. Similarly, after David killed one hundred Philistines and brought the proof to Saul, the latter interpreted David's success as an indication that "Yahweh was with David" (1 Sam. 18:27–28).

Moreover, the narrative of Idrimi's seizing power is punctuated with the figure "seven." He stays seven years with the ʿapiru warriors. After seven years the god Addu becomes favorable to him. The Hurrian king is hostile to Idrimi yet another seven years. In the seventh year Idrimi launches fruitful negotiations with his adversary. Idrimi fills his treasury with the spoils gathered from seven Hittite cities. With the booty he decides to build a palace. David is the youngest of the seven sons of Jesse. He stays seven years in Hebron before he manages to conquer a Jebusite fortress. By despoiling the Jebusites, he appropriates their city for himself and it becomes his own City of David. He also accumulates the necessary material for building a sanctuary. The number "seven" is conventional in the Idrimi and David stories.[87] David does something similar when he establishes political support groups with the elders of Judah by offering them presents from the part of the spoil he collected during his numerous raids (1 Sam. 30:26–31).

For Edward Greenstein, "The lengthy narrative of Idrimi's adventures in obtaining and securing his throne is unlike any Mesopotamian text and has its closest parallels in the Egyptian Story of Sinuhe and the biblical stories of Jacob, Joseph, Moses, Jephthah, David, and Nehemiah; the many parts of the inscription display remarkable recurrence of motifs and key terms."[88]

THE SEIZING OF POWER BY ʿABDI-AŠIRTA OF AMURRU

In the fourteenth century BCE the Egyptian Empire dominated the Levant up to the borders of the Hittite kingdom of Mitanni. It was a period of political trouble and upheavals in the region where the two empires met. While the Assyrians and the Babylonians maintained good relations with Egypt, the Hittites in these times became sufficiently powerful to attract the Amorites to their side. The region between the two empires favored the power struggle of

---

86. A. Leo Oppenheim, review of Sidney Smith, *The Statue of Idri-mi, JNES* 14 (1955): 200.

87. Various aspects of Idrimi's career, such as the number "seven," have been analyzed by Mario Liverani, *Myth and Politics in Ancient Near Eastern Historiography* (ed. Zainab Bahrani and Marc Van de Mieroop; Ithaca, NY: Cornell University Press, 2004).

88. Edward L. Greenstein, "Autobiographies in Ancient Western Asia," *CANE* 4:2421–32, esp. 2425.

petty chiefs and princes of Canaan and Amurru. In this context of adverse political parties and conflicts, the city lords appealed to a class of warriors, designated as ^{lú}GAZ^{meš} or ^{lú}SA.GAZ^{meš}. They could overturn the local potentates and take control of the cities, while encouraging local populations to rebel against their overlords.[89]

Among the Amarna letters, the largest correspondence comes from Rib-Hadda of Byblos, one of the vassals of the pharaoh, whose city is located in northern Canaan and who was a rather verbose correspondent. One must admit, however, that in some of these letters we might be dealing with the stylistic device of hyperbole. Moreover, some city leaders write the pharaoh and use the term 'apiru as a slur, presenting cities that they dislike as being full of 'apiru and their leaders as having gone over to the 'apiru. The value of the historical information should, therefore, be judged independently for each letter.

The correspondence of northern vassals of the pharaoh is generally divided into three periods: the first and second periods, where the letters from Rib-Hadda predominate, and a third, post-Rib-Hadda period. The letters EA 68–95 belong to the first period, when 'Abdi-Aširta of Amurru (EA 60–62) appears as Rib-Hadda's principal enemy during the reign of Pharaoh Amenophis III. The letters EA 101–138 and 363 belong to the second period, when 'Abdi-Aširta was succeeded by his sons and especially by Aziru, while Amenophis IV was pharaoh.[90] We are interested in this second period.

The Amarna letters describe the intrigues and conflicts of kinglets and princes against the warlords and the ^{lú}GAZ^{meš}. William Moran translates this logographic reading by 'apiru, a term referring to outlaws whom the princes and city lords designate as their principal enemies.[91] The land of Amurru is located north of Byblos, in the mountain region between the Mediterranean coast and the Orontes Valley. The region was covered with forests and was unsuitable for agriculture. The warlords in that region were 'Abdi-Aširta and his sons, among whom Aziru became the chief warlord after the death of his father. The letters of Rib-Hadda of Byblos inform us that some inhabitants of the city of Byblos and of Ammiya (already mentioned in Idrimi's account above) joined the ^{lú}GAZ^{meš} ('apiru) and were in league with the Amurru enemies, who sought more power. The people from Amurru recruited local farmers,

---

89. Izre'el, "Amarna Letters from Canaan," esp. 2411.

90. On 'Abdi-Aširta and Aziru, the rulers of Amurru, see Yuval Goren, Israel Finkelstein, and Nadav Na'aman, "The Expansion of the Kingdom of Amurru according to the Petrographic Investigation of the Amarna Tablets," *BASOR* 329 (2003): 2–11.

91. William L. Moran, ed. and trans., *The Amarna Letters* (Baltimore: Johns Hopkins University Press, 1992); Marvin Chaney, "Ancient Palestinian Peasant Movements and the Formation of Premonarchic Israel," *Palestine in Transition: The Emergence of Ancient Israel* (ed. David Noel Freedman and David Frank Graf; SWBA 2; Sheffield: Almond, 1983), 39–90.

the *hupšu*, and encouraged them to rebel against their chiefs and lords. The correspondence of Rib-Hadda reflects the power struggle for control of the region in this northern part of the land of Canaan.[92]

According to a series of letters (e.g., EA 74, 76, 79, 82, 84), the warlord 'Abdi-Aširta of Ammuru (*ammuru* means the "west" in Akkadian and stands for the coastal area along the Mediterranean as seen by the peoples living in the east, in Mesopotamia)[93] appealed to the *ʿapiru* mercenaries and gave the Amurru region an important position among the city-states of the Levant.[94]

In EA 76.17–29 Rib-Hadda writes to the pharaoh, describing the military action of 'Abdi-Aširta: "He has just gathered together all the Apiru against Šigata [and] Ampi, and [h]e himself has taken these two cities. [*I s*]*aid*, 'There is no place where [me]n can enter against him. He has seized [. . .]. . . . , [so] send me [a garris]on of 400 men *a*[*nd* x pairs of h]orses with all speed.'"

The figure of four hundred men is reminiscent of the number of men in David's troop about to attack Nabal's domain: "About four hundred men went up after David, while two hundred remained with the baggage" (1 Sam. 25:13).

Another letter (EA 71.16–22) reveals the composition of 'Abdi-Aširta's troops: "What is 'Abdi-Aširta, servant and dog, that takes the land of the king for himself? What is his auxiliary force that it is strong? Through the Apiru his auxiliary force is strong!" In 1 Samuel 24:15 David addresses Saul referring to himself as a dog: "After whom has the king of Israel come out? After whom do you pursue? After a dead dog! After a flea!" (ESV).

Geographically even closer to David, Lab'ayu from Shechem together with his sons, and with the help of the Apiru mercenaries, transformed their city (located at the center of the land of Canaan) into a powerful stronghold (EA 244: Lab'ayu about to seize Megiddo; EA 246.6: the sons of Lab'ayu have paid money to the Apiru mercenaries and the Sutean nomads in order to fight against Biridya the ruler of Megiddo; EA 243.21: "And the warring of the Apiru in the land is seve[re]").

The Apiru attract entire villages or groups from city-states who join their ranks (EA 74.21, 36; 76.33–37; 77.28; 79.10, 20, 26; 81.13; 104.52–54; 111.17–21;

---

92. Gösta W. Ahlström, "Administration of the State in Canaan and Ancient Israel," *CANE* 1:587–603, esp. 589.

93. Georges Dossin considered the god Amurru as being specifically Canaanite ("Amurru, dieu cananéen," in *Symbolae biblicae et mesopotamicae: Francisco Mario Theodoro de Liagre Böhl dedicatae* [ed. M. A. Beek et al.; SFSMD 4; Leiden: Brill, 1973], 95–98, esp. 96). On the religion of the Amorites, see Jean-Marie Durand, "La religion amorrite en Syrie à l'époque des Archives de Mari," in *Mythologie et religion des Sémites occidentaux* (ed. Gregorio del Olmo Lete; OLA 162; Leuven: Peeters, 2008), 161–722.

94. Horst Klengel, *Mittel- und Südsyrien* (vol. 2 of *Geschichte Syriens im 2. Jahrtausen v. u. Z.*; Berlin: Akademie Verlag, 1969), 247–50 ("Abdiaširta und die Ḫāpiru").

116.37).[95] Occasionally entire regions join the Apiru (EA 104.51–53; 144.24–26.29; 272.10–17; 273.12–14; 290.12). Not only the lower social classes join their ranks; some rulers also join (EA 148.41–43). The Apiru are involved in military attacks and threaten the security of cities, and the goal of their attacks is to snatch control of the cities from the local rulers and take them away from the Egyptian lordship (EA 68.13, 17, 18; 73.29, 33; 75.10; 76.33–37; 83.16–18; 85.71–79; 87.21; 90.24; 91.4, 24; 104.51; 118.37–39; 127.20; 185; 186; 207.21; 215.13–15; 243.20; 288.36–38; 366.12, 21). They plunder lands and regions (EA 286.56; 313.5; 318.11). The Apiru also hire their military services to various local kinglets and fight for the political causes of the latter (EA 76.17; 132.19–21; 195.27; 246.5–10). The kinglets reward the Apiru for the services rendered by giving them lands (EA 287.31; 289.21–24).

Conclusion

The historical study of the period of Samuel, Saul, and David must consider the events, notions, ideologies, circumstances, and processes reflected in the biblical narrative. This is true whether they appear as brief anecdotes, conventional descriptions, stock literary motifs, or schematic representations. Moreover, later compilation, composition, and redaction do not rule out the preservation of earlier material useful for historical studies. "In this respect it has to be borne in mind that tangible, realistic elements, even if found in anachronistic descriptions or frameworks, (may) reflect realities on which they were modeled."[96] The narratives about these figures, despite legendary claims by some scholars, seem to reflect authentic historical reminiscence of a stage when ancient Israelite seminomadic chieftains were slowly becoming sedentary, adopting urban mores and lifestyle.[97]

---

95. Wolfgang Zwickel, "Der Beitrag der Ḫabiru zur Entstehung des Königtums," *UF* 28 (1996): 751–66. The author interprets the Jephthah story in Judg. 10:6–12:7 and that of David against Nabal in 1 Sam. 25 in light of the behavior of *ḫabiru/'apiru* groups of mercenaries as reflected in Amarna texts. David's 400 + 200 men would be one such group.

96. Zecharia Kallai, "Biblical Narrative and History: A Programmatic Review," *WZKM* 96 (2006): 133–57, esp. 137; Joe Uziel and Itzhaq Shai, "Iron Age Jerusalem: Temple-Palace, Capital City," *JAOS* 127 (2007): 161–70.

97. For a summary of the historical and archaeological discussion with all the necessary bibliographic references related to the issue of the united monarchy, see Gary N. Knoppers, "The Vanishing Solomon: The Disappearance of the United Monarchy from Recent Histories of Ancient Israel," *JBL* 116 (1997): 19–44; idem, *The Reign of Solomon and the Rise of Jeroboam* (vol. 1 of *Two Nations under God: The Deuteronomistic History of Solomon and the Dual Monarchies*; HSM 52; Atlanta: Scholars Press, 1993).

7

United Monarchy

Archaeology and Literary Sources

STEVEN M. ORTIZ

The persons of David and Solomon have captured the imagination of many individuals. From their portrayal as the Hollywood hero or villain to earlier works of art such as Michelangelo's *David*, artists have been drawn to the vivid stories of these kings of the united monarchy. The exploits of the battlefield and the intricacies of palace life have been foundational for many sermons and Bible studies as examples of great leadership or the danger of women. The psalms attributed to David and the proverbs attributed to Solomon (as well as Song of Songs and Ecclesiastes) are biblical texts that have provided comfort and insight to many Jews and Christians. These have contributed to larger-than-life personas of the main kings during this period. One of the ironies is that while the biblical texts and the archaeological record contain many details concerning this period of Israelite history, there has been much debate concerning the nature of this period. The biblical texts contain many images: from the battle exploits and palace intrigue of David, to the wealth, splendor, and wisdom of Solomon. One of the problems for the historian is to remove the layers of tradition as well as misperceptions of these two kings. Many students of the biblical text come to this period with contemporary reconstructions that are erroneous.

The Biblical Portrait of David and Solomon

David: Transition from Shepherd Boy to King

The biblical account presents numerous episodes in the life of David, some of which have been identified as legendary by critical scholarship. While specific stories would have developed their individual literary structures and later be woven into the larger account preserved in the canon of Scripture, there is no reason to doubt that the general story line is based on actual events. The accounts can be verified reasonably by correlating them with archaeological data and anthropological theory. With the death of Saul and his sons, various issues emerged regarding the stability of the new Israelite polity. Out of this complex period, David emerges and builds up the kingdom of Israel into the greatest kingdom that Israel had ever known. During the vacuum created by the weakness of the world powers of the age, smaller powers were vying for control of the southern Levant (e.g., Edom, Moab, Aram, Philistia, Israel). Although Saul was actually the first king of the united monarchy, he never fully unified the tribes internally but only as a loose tribal confederation, principally held together by the Philistine threat, which kept the tribes united against a common enemy.

It was one thing to be a military leader under Saul's hegemony; it was another for David to become the political leader of this confederacy. The short- and long-term goals of David can be summed up in one word: control. David needed to control the people and control the land. These two factors have a symbiotic relationship. If you control the land (e.g., trade and communication routes, agriculture/herding lands), you control the population; if you control the population (e.g., they submit to your leadership), you control the land. The highest priorities for David involved the establishment of his kingship, his reputation, and his support. He then had to formulate both a domestic and a foreign policy.

David was quickly able to learn from Saul's mistakes and to identify the best way to control the population. One of the main things that David established was a new concept for the tribes: a high view of kingship. Each tribe had given allegiance to its tribal chief and patriarch, but now their loyalty was to the crown. The Israelite monarchy was new, and there was still an underlying tension of tribal authority. Now the authority was being placed in the king (monarchy) and not the tribal structure. David held that Yahweh established David's kingship; the king was God's anointed. He maintained this view within the political arena since he had a high view of the position, regardless of Saul's actions toward him. David would not kill Saul (1 Sam. 24:1–7; 26:1–12), but he did kill those who harmed God's anointed (2 Sam. 1:1–15). He publicly mourned for Saul (1:11–12, 17–27).

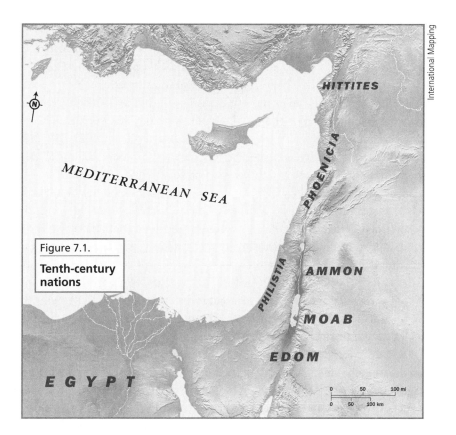

Figure 7.1.

Tenth-century nations

With David's rise to power, one issue that emerged was how a shepherd boy from Bethlehem could become a king. David had built his reputation long before he came to the throne. Naturally, in any tribal culture a man's reputation is first established militarily. David showed that he was capable as a military leader (1 Sam. 17; 18:30; 19:8; 23:1–14; 30:1–20). Perhaps more unique was his reputation in the political arena. David was one of Saul's right-hand men (22:14). David was very wise and made key connections in government—that is, within the house of Saul. David became a close friend of the heir to the throne, Jonathan (18:1–5; 1 Sam. 20), and also married into the house of Saul through Michal (18:1–29).

A third aspect of his reputation is moral. The biblical accounts highlight several decisions made by David to illustrate that he acted in such a manner that nothing could be named against him. Examples include not harming God's anointed, Saul (1 Sam. 24:1–7; 26:1–12); accepting Abigail's advice not to act rashly against her husband, Nabal (25:23–35); public mourning of Saul and Jonathan (2 Sam. 1:11–12, 17–27); public mourning of Abner (3:31–38); and kindness to Saul's household (2 Sam. 9). In a summary account of David's accomplishments, it is stated that he "administered justice and righteousness for all his people" (2 Sam. 8:15).[1] This appears contradictory because the biblical text also records many of David's sins. It hints that the public perception of David was that of a man of moral character, particularly in contrast to Saul. Nevertheless, this is a literary feature and purposefully used by the biblical author to contrast the two men in the book of Samuel. Three accounts depicting his character are (1) his acceptance of Abigail's advice concerning Nabal (1 Sam. 25:23–35); (2) his public mourning of Saul's death (2 Sam. 1); and (3) his maintenance of clean hands during the civil war and the events that followed (2 Sam. 2–4).

David needed to establish support among the southern tribes first. He did this by protecting the southern tribes from the Amalekites to the south. He also subdued Philistine hostility by cunningly establishing a base of fighting men at Ziklag in Philistine territory. It was a natural step to establishing his first capital at Hebron, where he won the support of this region. He had a harder time gaining support from the north. It did not happen until after the civil war, when the northern leadership fell apart (2 Sam. 2:12–4:12). He reclaimed Michal, Saul's daughter, as his wife (3:13) and showed kindness to Mephibosheth of the house of Saul (2 Sam. 9).

David's domestic policy was twofold: (1) bring security to the tribes against the Philistine threat (2 Sam. 5:17–25); and (2) unite the tribes by creating new images of unity. David chose a neutral capital in the center of the country, which belonged neither to the southern nor to the northern tribes. The capture of Jebusite Jerusalem and establishment of it as the capital was the next domestic policy after security. He then moved the ark of the covenant to Jerusalem (2 Sam. 6) and stated his desire to build a temple (2 Sam. 7) as a central place of worship that belonged to the state, not to a particular tribe.

David's foreign policy likewise was twofold: conquer and control. David dominated the southern Levant by either conquering or subduing as vassals those polities adjacent to Israel or those polities that controlled important communication and trade routes. We have a summary of this in Chronicles, generally moving from west to east: Philistines (1 Chron. 18:1); Aram-Zobah and Moab (18:2–3); northern Transjordan Plateau, Hammath (18:10); Aram-Damascus (18:5–6); Edom (18:12–13); and Ammon (19:10–19). With the complete conquest and subjugation of these polities, all David had to do was control his kingdom. There were three groups: (1) Israel; (2) the conquered kingdoms considered tributary kingdoms (Edom, Moab, Ammon, Aram-Damascus, Aram-Zobah), some with Israelite governors appointed over them (2 Sam. 8:6, 14); and (3) vassal kings and

---

1. Scripture translations in this chapter are by the author.

Moab

Moab was one of three Iron Age kingdoms in Transjordan, located between Ammon to the north and Edom to the south. The territory was situated on the high plateau immediately east of the Dead Sea. Its political borders expanded and contracted throughout its history. Moab occupied the al-Kerak Plateau with its southern border at the Zered River (Wadi Hasa) and its northern border at the Arnon River (Wadi Mujib), although at its height it expanded north up to the Madaba Plateau.

The biblical account is ambiguous, as it reflects supportive and hostile relationships with Israel. Moab was hostile toward the Israelite migration through the region (Num. 21–24) as well as the various Israelite dynasties of Saul, David, and later the Omrides (e.g., 1 Sam. 14:47; 2 Sam. 8:2; 2 Kings 3). Yet Ruth is a Moabite in the lineage of David, and Solomon had Moabite women in his harem and built a shrine for their deity, Chemosh (1 Kings 11:1, 7, 33). Moab became a vassal state of the Assyrians (eighth and seventh centuries BCE).

Archaeological investigations show that there was a decline in settled life during the Middle and Late Bronze Ages (ca. 2000–1300 BCE). Several sites have been excavated that are providing data on the history of Moab (e.g., Dhiban, Khirbet Mudaynah al- Mu'rrajeh, Tell Hesban, Madaba, Tall al-Umayri, Tell Jalul, Khirbet Iskander, and Khirbet al-Mudayna on Wadi ath-Thamad). Perhaps the most famous find is the Mesha Inscription, a basalt monument discovered at Dhiban. It is a Moabite text of thirty-four lines that dates to the mid-ninth century BCE and reports King Mesha's victory over Israelite oppressors (cf. 2 Kings 3).

states required to accept David's hegemony (Philistia, northern Transjordan, Gesher the king of Hammath, and Hiram the king of Tyre).

The biblical text reflects the transition from tribe to state in early Israel. The major Israelite settlement was in the north. Saul, a Benjaminite, came from the more populous north, while David remained in the south. As we will see, little archaeological investigation has been done in Judah in comparison to the hills of Ephraim and Manasseh. Nevertheless, a picture of a more sparsely settled countryside emerges, as attested in the biblical account. David's initial settlement was at Hebron, in the south. He did not unite the north and south until the open civil war and the overthrow of the northern kingdom, with its various assassinations and coups.

Solomon

The biblical account of Solomon (1 Kings 1–11), in contrast to David, focuses on the administration of the monarchy versus establishing the kingship and the social transformation from a confederacy of chiefdoms. Whereas the biblical texts concerning David focus on his righteousness, the accounts of Solomon emphasize his wisdom. A summary of the biblical accounts of Solomon describes his wisdom, wealth, marriage to foreigners, and building projects (most important, the temple). The biblical author summarizes Solomon's reign thus: "King Solomon was greater than all the kings of the earth in riches and in wisdom. All the earth sought the presence of Solomon, to hear the wisdom that God had put in his heart" (1 Kings 10:23–24).[2] This summary is authentic insofar as the united monarchy reflects a period of Israel's greatest influence and power during the tenth century and its dominance in the southern Levant. While this text also emphasizes God's blessing on the nation under the rule of Solomon, later tradition has taken this summary out of its tenth-century context of the southern Levant. The tenth-century Israelite state enjoyed hegemony and honor from the nations as described, but it was a fragile and short-lived situation. Within a generation the kingdom divided, reflecting the geopolitical realities.

Solomon established a strong military, but there are no accounts of his military cunning or of any battles. He maintained a strong army, with horses and chariots that were established in "chariot cities" (1 Kings 9:17–19). Solomon built his kingdom not on military achievements but rather on diplomatic activity through the ancient Near Eastern policy of treaties and alliances, which included marriages (the pharaoh's daughter as well as Moabite, Ammonite, Edomite, Sidonian, and Hittite marriages [1 Kings 11:1]). Solomon's reign was dominated by building projects, particularly the king's palace and Yahweh's temple. This is typical dynastic activity of ancient Near Eastern kings. These building projects required the king to utilize corvée labor. The abuse of corvée labor was the downfall of Solomon's son Rehoboam.

Biblical and Historical Sources

Biblical Texts

One of the underpinnings in reconstructing the united monarchy is to read between the lines of the various biblical texts. There is no single book of the Bible that is dedicated to this period of Israelite history. The accounts of David and Solomon are found in three major sources: the books of Samuel, the book of 1 Kings, and the books of Chronicles. In addition, a number of psalms and

---

2. While the initial accounts provide a positive summary of Solomon's inauguration, reading between the lines exposes an account of palace intrigue for his kingship (1 Kings 1–2).

proverbs found in the canonical books are connected to these kings or at least their reigns. One problem for the biblical historian is that the united monarchy played such an important theological role for later Israelite history that this has added a layer of imagery and motifs onto the actual events during this period. The theology of messianism, kingship, God's kingdom, Zion, and temple (e.g., Jerusalem) had naturally grown into such major themes in the biblical text that the actual founding individuals and events must be excavated from these motifs.

The sources for reconstructing the united monarchy are found basically in 1 Samuel 8–1 Kings 11, as well as parallels in 1 Chronicles 11–2 Chronicles 9. The accounts in the books of Samuel and Kings belong to the so-called Deuteronomistic History. Scholars have identified "sources" within the corpus such as the Throne Succession Narrative (more precisely known as the Court History), temple construction, the Ark Narrative, the Rise and Fall of Saul, the Rise of David, and Nathan's Oracle.

The book of Samuel is a popular narrative that explains how the dynasty of David was established. It focuses on a contrast between the failed leadership of Saul and the leadership and character of David. The books represent a transition from the role of Samuel as the last of the judges to the development of a political leader, a king. One of the major accounts found in the book of Kings is the construction of the temple. Because of the theological significance of God's temple, its construction and description take a prominent place in the text. Historians often place a greater emphasis on the "discovery" of the temple in the archaeological record. Biblical scholars also erroneously assume that the temple played a larger role in the daily life of the common Israelite. The author of Chronicles provides the basis for the use of various sources in writing his history of the accounts of David and Solomon. The Chronicler references the records of Samuel the seer, the records of Nathan the prophet, and the records of Gad (1 Chron. 29:29). So it is apparent that the biblical texts reflect a tradition of coalescing sources such as accounts, battles, and administrative documents to create a unified account.[3]

Historical Texts

There are very few extrabiblical texts that date to the period of the united monarchy. We have two Egyptian campaigns of the Twenty-Second Dynasty:

---

3. For an example of the growing reception history of the united monarchy, see William M. Schniedewind, *Society and the Promise to David: The Reception History of 2 Samuel 7:1–17* (Oxford: Oxford University Press, 1999).

Siamun and Shishak.[4] While
the extent of these cam-
paigns is debated, it is clear
that the early dynasties of
the Third Intermediate period of Egypt tried to reestablish control of the southern Levant. Neither of these
sources mentions the reign of
David or Solomon, although it
is possible to reconstruct Egyp-
tian-Israelite relations based on
the campaigns (see below). Recent
analysis by Kenneth Kitchen has proposed that there might
be geographical references to the "heights of David" in the
northern Negev region.[5]

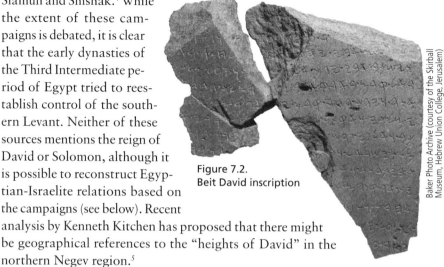

Figure 7.2.
Beit David inscription

Baker Photo Archive (courtesy of the Skirball
Museum, Hebrew Union College, Jerusalem)

Although it is not contemporary with the united monarchy,
archaeologists have discovered a major inscription from Tel Dan that refers to
the house of David. The Tel Dan Stela, bearing an inscription of the "house
of David," was a victory stela of the Aramean king Hadad, who brags about
defeating the house of David. This victory stela is dated to the ninth century and was found in pieces as part of a pavement for the entrance into the
city of Dan. Although from a later century, the stela demonstrates that the
Arameans of the ninth century BCE remembered the Davidic dynasty of an
earlier era. More specifically, it has put to rest any theory that David was not
a historical figure.[6]

Methodological Approaches

Bible historians are well aware of the pitfalls of attempting to reconstruct the
history of David and Solomon by separating the actual events from the biblical

4. See Kenneth A. Kitchen, "Egyptian Interventions in the Levant in Iron Age II," in
*Symbiosis, Symbolism, and the Power of the Past: Canaan, Ancient Israel, and Their Neighbors
from the Late Bronze Age through Roman Palaestina; Proceedings of the Centennial Sympo-
sium, W. F. Albright Institute of Archaeological Research and American Schools of Oriental
Research, Jerusalem, May 29/31, 2000* (ed. William G. Dever and Seymour Gitin; Winona Lake,
IN: Eisenbrauns, 2003), 113–32.

5. Kenneth A. Kitchen, "A Possible Mention of David in the Late Tenth Century BCE, and
Deity *Dod as Dead as the Dodo?," *JSOT* 76 (1997): 29–44.

6. In addition, the Mesha Inscription has a reference to David. See André Lemaire, "'House
of David' Restored in Moabite Inscription," *BAR* 20, no. 3 (1994): 30–37.

imagery that reflects more theological themes. The united monarchy has come under considerable debate. Some scholars assume that the imagery around the first kings of Israel is based solely on hyperbole and later prophetic schools creating theological constructs. Some deny that David and Solomon were actual historical figures, contending rather that they were myths or legends created by the biblical authors. The debate led scholars to define "rules of evidence" as the focus shifted to discussions of historiography and the nature of history writing. This attempt to define "objective" criteria for evaluating the sources has led to using social science methods. Three areas of research have been dominant in the attempts to reconstruct the united monarchy: (1) the historicity of the biblical texts, (2) the archaeological data, and (3) the use of anthropological models for analyzing the text and archaeological data. These are not mutually exclusive, but certain assumptions and issues are associated with each one.

Biblical Text / Historical Data

The biblical authors did not intend to write a systematic history of ancient Israel. The texts dealing with this period of history do not define or present the accounts in such fashion, and the term "united monarchy" is not used by the biblical authors. David's rise to kingship is found in the books of Samuel, and it is mostly in contrast to the first king, Saul. Solomon was not the firstborn son in the dynastic line, and there is little information regarding the relationship between Solomon and David. We know more about David's relationships with Saul and his son Jonathan, and the relationship between David and Solomon's mother, than about David's relationship with Solomon. The majority of the historical texts devoted to Solomon's reign are actually about the construction of the temple.

Historians sometimes assume that such important kings as David and Solomon would leave an imprint on other historical sources. But this logically flawed reasoning assumes a false premise in order to argue against David and Solomon being actual persons of history. For the later Israelite and Judean kings of the ninth and eighth centuries, we have many names in texts as well as inscriptions.[7] The lack of historical texts and inscriptions in the archaeological record for David and Solomon is a simple fact that the historian must accept. This lacuna is easily understood when the nature of the tenth century is placed within its historical and geographical context. Since the major world powers of the Mediterranean axis did not invade ancient Palestine, there were

---

7. See Mordechai Cogan, *The Raging Torrent: Historical Inscriptions from Assyria and Babylonia Relating to Ancient Israel* (Jerusalem: Carta, 2008).

Ammon

The Ammonites inhabited the northern Central Transjordanian Plateau from the later part of the second millennium BCE until the end of the Iron Age II. The name of their state was "Ammon," and their capital was Rabbath-Ammon (modern-day Amman). Of the Transjordan polities during the biblical period, more is known of the Ammonites due to extensive archaeological research.

The political and geographical boundaries shifted throughout their history. They were centered around Rabbath-Ammon, but extending as far north as the Jabbok River (Wadi Zarqa), as far south as the Arnon River (Wadi Mujib), and from the Jordan Valley in the west to the desert in the east.

The Ammonites allied with the Amalekites to help the Moabite king defeat and subjugate Israel (Judg. 3:12–14; 10:6–18). Jephthah defeated the Ammonites (Judg. 11:33), as did Saul (1 Sam. 11:11) and David (2 Sam. 8:12). Solomon married the Ammonite Naamah, whose son Rehoboam became king (1 Kings 14:21, 31). This marriage represents the tribal relations between Ammon, Gilead, Gad, Rueben, and the half-tribe of Manasseh.

The Ammonites became dominant in the Iron Age IIB (eighth–seventh centuries BCE), as they were able to control the major trade routes from the south up to Assyria. They are mentioned in the annals of Assurbanipal, Tiglath-pileser III, and Sennacherib.

no typical accounts of battles and tribute to be recorded. The archaeological record rarely reveals inscriptions of kings of ancient Palestine (this is true for Philistia, Edom, Ammon, Moab, Aramean states, etc.).[8]

The nature of the biblical texts and the lack of collaborating documentation in historical records have prompted a trend in biblical studies to question whether the biblical text can be used for reconstructing a history of the united monarchy. There are two schools of thought within this trend. The first, as evidenced by the writings of Philip Davies, Niels Peter Lemche, and Thomas Thompson, questions whether there is any historicity in the biblical accounts. In regard to David and Solomon, they conclude that the events describing Israel's development of the monarchy are created to provide the Jewish people with a "glorious past." This group, referred to as the Copenhagen School, has been labeled as nihilist and minimalist.[9]

8. For a fuller discussion of the flaws in such arguments based on a lack of references to David and Solomon in Egyptian and Assyrian sources, see Kenneth A. Kitchen, *On the Reliability of the Old Testament* (Grand Rapids: Eerdmans, 2003), 88–91.

9. It appears that "minimalist" has become the best term, possibly by default, and is the term used here. See Philip R. Davies, *In Search of "Ancient Israel"* (JSOTSup 148; Sheffield: Sheffield

The second group consists of those scholars who attempt to analyze the biblical narrative and separate historical events from later tradition. The assumption is that the biblical writers had an agenda when recounting the events associated with the rise of the united monarchy. Some have viewed it as the natural outcome of the desire to place the monarchy in a positive light, while others conclude that the writers tried to deceive their audience by distorting any negative event regarding the monarchy.[10] The result of this scholarship promotes an unflattering view of the biblical account of David and represents the influence of minimalist trends within biblical studies. There appears to be a new trend to popularize these critical views of the historicity of the rise of the monarchy.

Archaeological Data

William F. Albright began study of the archaeology of David and Solomon. The Albright model has been the dominant paradigm in biblical archaeology. Albright developed the current ceramic stratigraphy for the study of sites in Syria-Palestine based on his excavations of Tell Beit Mirsim. Today the dating of almost all archaeological strata is based on the principles underlying ceramic seriation. Albright associated the adoption of red-slip burnished pottery with the united monarchy. Hence, cultural horizons with this ceramic trend were dated to the tenth century BCE.

Yigael Yadin's excavations at Hazor further developed the archaeology of the united monarchy. Yadin noticed that the gate systems at Megiddo and at Hazor were very similar. Recalling the text of 1 Kings 9:17–19 (Solomon's building projects), he associated the gate systems with a common architect and hence a central authority. Yadin went back to Megiddo and Hazor and isolated monumental features that he associated with Solomon, notably Palace 6000 and Palace 1723 at Megiddo. He also went to the old Gezer excavation reports and postulated a third Solomonic gate erroneously identified as a Hellenistic Tower.[11] William Dever reexcavated Gezer and unearthed the city that is associated with Solomon.[12] He found that Yadin's intuitions were

Academic Press, 1992); Niels Peter Lemche, *Ancient Israel: A New History of Israelite History* (BibSem 5; Sheffield: JSOT Press, 1988); Thomas L. Thompson, *Early History of the Israelite People: From the Written and Archaeological Sources* (SHANE 4; Leiden: Brill, 1992).

10. Steven L. McKenzie, *King David: A Biography* (Oxford: Oxford University Press, 2000); Baruch Halpern, *David's Secret Demons: Messiah, Murderer, Traitor, King* (BIW; Grand Rapids: Eerdmans, 2001); Israel Finkelstein and Neil Asher Silberman, *The Bible Unearthed: Archaeology's New Vision of Ancient Israel and the Origin of Its Sacred Texts* (New York: Free Press, 2001).

11. Yigael Yadin, "Solomon's City Wall and Gate at Gezer," *IEJ* 8 (1958): 80–86.

12. For a summary of the Gezer excavations, see Steven Ortiz and Samuel Wolff, "Guarding the Border to Jerusalem: The Iron Age City of Gezer," *NEA* 75 (2012): 4–19.

correct. Yadin's association of the three-chambered gates of the Iron Age with the Solomonic building projects became the model for traditional biblical archaeology, making a one-to-one correlation between the biblical text and archaeological data.

In the early 1990s the debate over the stratigraphy of the Iron Age was initiated with an article by Gregory Wightman, who proposed a redating of stratigraphy associated with the tenth century, particularly the Solomonic levels.[13] Wightman's proposals were not accepted, as John Holladay and Ron Tappy independently addressed the relevant issues.[14] Wightman's redating was again proposed by Israel Finkelstein's "Low Chronology" paradigm. This has dominated archaeological discussion for the last decade.[15] The Low Chronology proposes that the conventional ceramic chronology that archaeologists have been using for dating strata in the southern Levant is off by nearly one hundred years. This would push cultural horizons that had been dated to the tenth century forward into the ninth century BCE. While the Low Chronology debate has identified some simplistic reconstructions, its greatest contribution has been to sharpen the use of archaeology in biblical reconstructions. Ironically, more biblical scholars than archaeologists have jumped on the Low Chronology bandwagon. Although Finkelstein has been influential, the majority of field archaeologists are not swayed by his chronological reinterpretations. The Low Chronology was popular when first proposed, but recent excavations continue to support the conventional chronology (e.g., Hazor, Rehov, Edom, Tel Gezer, Tel Beth Shemesh, Khirbet Qeiyafa; and Philistine sites such as Ashkelon, Tel-Miqne-Ekron, Tel es-safi, and Gath). In addition, methodological shortcomings of the Low Chronology have been identified.[16]

13. Gregory J. Wightman, "The Myth of Solomon," *BASOR* 277–78 (1990): 5–22.

14. John S. Holladay, "Red Slip, Burnish, and the Solomonic Gateway at Gezer," *BASOR* 277–78 (1990): 23–70; Ron E. Tappy, *The Archaeology of Israelite Samaria* (HSM 44; Atlanta: Scholars Press, 1992).

15. For a fuller discussion, see Steven Ortiz, "Deconstructing and Reconstructing the United Monarchy: House of David or Tent of David? (Current Trends in Iron Age Research)," in *The Future of Biblical Archaeology: Reassessing Methodologies and Assumptions; The Proceedings of a Symposium, August 12–14, 2001 at Trinity International University* (ed. James K. Hoffmeier and Alan R. Millard; Grand Rapids: Eerdmans, 2004), 121–47; idem, "The Archaeology of David and Solomon: Navigating the New Methods and Madness," in *Do Historical Matters Matter to Faith? A Critical Appraisal of Modern and Postmodern Approaches to Scripture* (ed. James K. Hoffmeier and Dennis R. Magary; Wheaton: Crossway, 2012), 497–516.

16. See Raz Kletter, "Chronology and United Monarchy: A Methodological Review," *ZDPV* 120 (2004): 13–54; Amihai Mazar, "Iron Age Chronology: A Reply to I. Finkelstein," *Levant* 29 (1997): 157–67; Steven M. Ortiz, "Does the Low Chronology Work? A Case Study of Qasile X, Gezer X, and Lachish V," in *"I Will Speak the Riddles of Ancient Times": Archaeological and Historical Studies in Honor of Amihai Mazar on the Occasion of His Sixtieth Birthday* (ed.

Anthropological Models

In an attempt to unite the text with the archaeology, scholars have turned to the use of anthropological models. This has been very productive, as patterns found throughout human social structure are clearly seen in the biblical accounts. Many theories have been adopted to explain the united monarchy, but the issues are now coalescing around three areas: (1) Iron Age state formation, (2) kinship and kingship, and (3) urbanization and social stratification.

The united monarchy is best viewed as a secondary state within the southern Levant. This is typical for the Iron Age II period, as many other secondary states were formed during this period (e.g., Aramea, Philistia, Edom).[17] One of the classic paradigms is the evolution from a chiefdom to a state society.[18] This simplistic paradigm has been questioned in the larger field of anthropology, but there is still some relationship between state development and a chiefdom social structure. The question for social scientists is how states are formed. Sophisticated models address center and periphery and the collapse of states. These studies have led scholars to develop the concept of "secondary states" (states that develop in the collapse or vacuum of primary states). The small states of the southern Levant, to which the united monarchy belonged, were formed during the end of the Iron Age I period as the larger Late Bronze Age states collapsed (e.g., Egyptian New Kingdom, Mitanni, Mycenae, and Hittites).[19]

One of the catalysts for state formation in the history of the Middle East is the underlying tribal organization that still underpins the states of this region.[20]

Aren M. Maeir and Pierre de Miroschedji; Winona Lake, IN: Eisenbrauns, 2006), 587–612; idem, "Deconstructing and Reconstructing the United Monarchy."

17. Alexander H. Joffe, "The Rise of Secondary States in the Iron Age Levant," *JESHO* 45:4 (2002): 425–67; Kletter, "Chronology and United Monarchy"; Dan Master, "State Formation Theory and the Kingdom of Ancient Israel," *JNES* 60 (2001): 117–31. As a contrary position of state formation in the southern Levant, Israel Finkelstein proposes that the state started in the ninth century BCE, with the catalyst being the westward expansion of the Assyrian Empire ("A Great United Monarchy? Archaeological and Historical Perspectives," in *One God—One Cult—One Nation: Archaeological and Biblical Perspectives* [ed. Reinhard G. Kratz and Hermann Spieckermann; BZAW 405; Berlin: de Gruyter, 2010], 3–28).

18. Frank S. Frick, *The Formation of the State in Ancient Israel: A Survey of Models and Theories* (SWBA 4; Sheffield: Almond, 1985).

19. This was a complex process that took over one hundred years to develop. The Israelite tribes were a loose tribal confederacy that did not crystallize into a state until the united monarchy.

20. For a fuller discussion of this phenomenon in recent history, see Philip S. Khoury and Joseph Kostiner, eds., *Tribes and State Formation in the Middle East* (Berkeley: University of California Press, 1990). For a succinct analysis of state formation for the Transjordan region, see Randall W. Younker, "The Emergence of the Ammonites," in *Ancient Ammon* (ed. Burton Macdonald and Randall W. Younker; SHCANE 17; Leiden: Brill, 1999), 189–218.

Several scholars have noted that the rise of the Davidic state fits the pattern found in many Middle Eastern cultures. This is a secondary state formed in the vacuum created by primary states where the social organization is based on tribal chiefdom patterns of social organization. Some of these scholars have proposed models of secondary state formation. Alexander Joffe has presented the most comprehensive model incorporating anthropological theory.[21] Lawrence Stager has offered a model that incorporates the kinship model of a patrimonial kingdom.[22] This is supported by the biblical text describing how David and Solomon organized the kingdom based on established tribal structures of the earlier period. Other anthropological models focused on kinship, social stratification, and the role of the temple.

Conclusion: Uniting the Biblical Text and Archaeological Data

Several basic questions face the archaeologist studying the united monarchy. Can archaeology shed light on the transition from a tribal society to the centralized rule of a monarchy? Does the archaeological record reflect the existence of a mighty kingdom as described in the biblical sources? Does the archaeological record reflect the internal development of the kingdom from Saul until the time of Solomon? The question today is not "Has archaeology proved that David and Solomon existed?" Rather, it is "What was the nature of the united monarchy?" Even with the lack of nonbiblical historical sources for the united monarchy, and the nature of the narrative genre that we find in the biblical texts, scholars have been able to coalesce the biblical accounts with the archaeological record and provide a fairly robust historical reconstruction of the united monarchy.[23] When the layers of biblical tradition and the theological paradigms are removed, archaeologists have been able to reconstruct the kingdoms of David and Solomon.[24]

21. Joffe, "Rise of Secondary States."

22. Lawrence E. Stager, "The Patrimonial Kingdom of Solomon," in Dever and Gitin, *Symbiosis*, 63–74.

23. For an excellent discussion of how archaeologists create incorrect historical reconstructions of the biblical text, see Ziony Zevit, "The Davidic-Solomonic Empire from the Perspective of Archaeological Bibliology," in *Birkat Shalom: Studies in the Bible, Ancient Near Eastern Literature, and Postbiblical Judaism Presented to Shalom M. Paul on the Occasion of His Seventieth Birthday* (ed. Chaim Cohen et al.; 2 vols.; Winona Lake, IN: Eisenbrauns, 2008), 1:201–24.

24. Gabriel Barkay, "The Iron Age II–III," in *The Archaeology of Ancient Israel* (ed. Amnon Ben-Tor; New Haven: Yale University Press, 1992), 302–73; John S. Holladay, "The Kingdoms of Israel and Judah: Political and Economic Centralization in the Iron IIA-B (ca. 1000–750 BC)," in *The Archaeology of Society in the Holy Land* (ed. Thomas E. Levy; New York: Facts on File, 1995), 368–415; Amihai Mazar, *Archaeology of the Land of the Bible: 10,000–586 B.C.E.* (ABRL; New York: Doubleday, 1990), 368–402.

The United Monarchy: A Synopsis of Recent Research

Geopolitical Context

The southern Levant is situated between major powers and is a vital bridge connecting major communication and trade routes. It is part of the eastern Mediterranean littoral that joined Egypt and Mesopotamia. The emergence of the united monarchy occurred during major shifts in the eastern Mediterranean and specifically the southern Levant. On the international scene there was the thirteenth-century BCE collapse of the Eastern Mediterranean. This produced major migrations of peoples and destruction of sites. Two of the best-known migrations were the Sea Peoples, of which the Philistines were a part, and the Israelites. The collapse of these major states (e.g., Egyptian New Kingdom, the Hittite state, Mycenae) had created a power vacuum. Two north-south routes, the traditional Via Maris (International Coastal Highway) and the highway along the Transjordan Plateau, were major thoroughfares in the ancient Near East. In addition, there were two major east-west routes. The broad Jezreel Valley linked the two north-south highways in the north, and the Negev desert linked them between Gaza and the Edomite territory in the south. These four routes and the topography of the southern Levant created interaction spheres where the intersections became valuable points of power that states wanted to control.

During the Iron Age I–II transition (ca. 1100–1000 BCE) both the southern and the northern Levant (e.g., Lebanon and Syria) experienced the growth of various secondary states. While this development was not unilateral, or caused by a single variable, historians can document the political gamesmanship that occurred as various polities grew into secondary states and vied for control of the land bridge—more specifically, the two major north-south routes and the two east-west routes. The biblical account of the rise of Saul and the diminishment of the prophet Samuel illustrates this period. As the Philistines were becoming a dominant force in the southern Levant, the Israelites demanded a "king" to organize the tribes into a similar polity. Saul was unable to bring state development about, but he was able to organize the Israelite tribes into a larger tribal confederacy. It was not until David that the political transformation occurred, although it was still based on a fragile social organization and tribal allegiance.

The Philistines were the first polity to capitalize on controlling the major routes, especially since they already occupied an important section of the major coastal route. While the biblical texts of Samuel focus on the expansionist policies of the Philistines to the east (i.e., where the Israelite tribes were centered), archaeology is able to provide a larger window into this period. By the eleventh century BCE the Philistines already had major urban centers throughout the southern coastal plain (e.g., Ashdod, Gath, Ekron, Ashkelon,

Edom

Edom is located north of the Gulf of Aqaba and east of the Jordan Valley (Wadi Arabah). Its northern border is the Zered River (Wadi Hasa). Some biblical texts hint that the Edomites occupied territory west of the Arabah in the Negev Highlands (Num. 20:16; 34; Josh. 15:1). The name means "red" and perhaps refers to the reddish stone and soil prevalent in the region. The region is well known for the Nabatean kingdom and the infamous city of Petra. The early history of Edom (also called "Mount Seir") is associated with the patriarchal stories of Esau settling in this region as well as a list of kings who ruled the land (Gen. 36).

Edom becomes prominent in the biblical text as the "king of Edom" refused to permit the Israelites safe passage through their land (Num. 20:14–21). Saul fought them (1 Sam. 14:47), and David had a major campaign against them (2 Sam. 8:13–14). King Hadad of Edom was an adversary to Solomon (1 Kings 11:14–21). Hadad had to flee to Egypt, illustrating that Solomon had gained the upper hand and was able to acquire the port of Ezion-geber, in the heart of Edomite territory. Edom was a vassal of Judah but gained its freedom in the ninth century BCE (2 Kings 8:20–22). The biblical texts and archaeological data show that Edom was able to extend west across the Arabah into the Negev during the eighth–sixth centuries BCE (e.g., Tel Aroer, Tel Ira, Tel Malhata, Horvat Qitmit, and En Hatzeva).[a]

Archaeological investigation has shown this region to be sparsely populated.[b] Scholars debate whether there was sedentary occupation before the eighth century. Major sites are Tawilan, Busayra (Bozrah), Feifeh, Tall al-Khalayfi, and Khirbet an-Nahas.[c] Recent excavations by Thomas Levy at Khirbet en-Nahas have revolutionized current thinking on the settlement processes of Edom. Based on carbon 14 dating, he dates a major copper-smelting industry and the evidence for monumental buildings to the tenth century BCE. The results are still tentative, but it appears that there is archaeological evidence for a state-level society in the southern plateau of Jordan.[d]

a. Itzhaq Beit-Arieh, "The Edomites in Cisjordan," in *You Shall Not Abhor an Edomite for He Is Your Brother: Edom and Seir in History and Tradition* (ed. Diana Vikander Edelman; SBLABS 3; Atlanta: Scholars Press, 1995), 33–40.

b. Larry Herr and Mohammad Najjar, "The Iron Age," in *Jordan: An Archaeological Reader* (ed. Russell B. Adams; London: Equinox, 2008), 311–34.

c. Burton MacDonald, *East of the Jordan: Territories and Sites of the Hebrew Scriptures* (ASORB 6; Boston: American Schools of Oriental Research, 2000), 185–86.

d. Thomas E. Levy et al., "Lowland Edom and the High and Low Chronologies: Edomite State Formation, the Bible and Recent Archaeological Research in Southern Jordan," in *The Bible and Radiocarbon Dating: Archaeology, Text and Science* (ed. Thomas Levy and Thomas Higham; London: Equinox, 2005), 129–63.

and perhaps Gaza).[25] Although the biblical text does not mention it, they were also expanding into the Negev, with several smaller occupation sites allowing them to control the southern trade route from Arabia to the coast.

While the importance of Transjordan is implied by the reference to the "King's Highway" (Num. 20:17; 21:22), references to state polities do not occur until later historical periods. Recent archaeological work in Edom has demonstrated that during the tenth century there was a large-scale copper mining industry at Khirbet en-Nahas in the Feinan region, east of Wadi Arabah in Jordan. A large citadel and administrative buildings are dated by the excavators to the tenth century BCE. Thomas Levy has postulated that Edom was a centralized polity in the tenth century BCE, with an intensive trade network.[26]

It seems unlikely that the isolated western highlands would produce a territorial state to compete with the Philistines and the polities in Transjordan, but this is what took place. The geographical diversity of the territory of the united monarchy should be recognized. The southern tribe of Judah was confined to the central hill country and bordered by desert regions to its south and east. It competed with the Philistines for control of the fertile Shephelah between the hill country and the coast. The northern tribes were intermingled with various cultural and political influences (e.g., Phoenicians, Arameans) as they occupied Galilee and the hill country of Samaria. It was no small task to unite the people of both the northern and the southern regions into a common polity. The united monarchy was short-lived: its eventual breakup occurred soon after Solomon's reign.

Egypt and Israel during the Tenth Century BCE

The biblical texts portray the rise of David and Solomon as a local event between the polities of the southern Levant, but there is some hint of outside political involvement. Many scholars have addressed the relationship between the united monarchy and Egypt.[27] The united monarchy corresponds chronologically with the Twenty-First and Twenty-Second Dynasties of Egypt. While

25. Trude Dothan, "Initial Philistine Settlement: From Migration to Coexistence," in *Mediterranean Peoples in Transition: Thirteenth to Early Tenth Centuries BCE* (ed. Seymour Gitin, Amihai Mazar, and Ephraim Stern; Jerusalem: Israel Exploration Society, 1998), 148–61.

26. Thomas E. Levy et al., "Reassessing the Chronology of Biblical Edom: New Excavations and 14C Dates from Khirbat en-Nahas (Jordan)," *Antiquity* 302 (2004): 865–79.

27. Paul S. Ash, *David, Solomon and Egypt: A Reassessment* (JSOTSup 297; Sheffield: Sheffield Academic Press, 1999); Kenneth A. Kitchen, *The Third Intermediate Period in Egypt, 1100–650 B.C.* (2nd ed.; Warminster, UK: Aris & Phillips, 1986), 272–312; Karol Myśliwiec, *The Twilight of Ancient Egypt: First Millennium B.C.E* (trans. David Lorton; Ithaca, NY: Cornell University Press, 2000), 27–67.

the later part of this period in Egyptian history has many synchronisms with Assyrian and biblical history, the beginning of the period has been difficult to reconstruct. Egypt was weak during the Twenty-First and Twenty-Second Dynasties, but two kings were able to mount campaigns: Siamun of the Twenty-First Dynasty and Sheshonq I of the Twenty-Second Dynasty.

There are some references to Egyptians or Egypt in the Bible that relate to the period of the united monarchy. Most of these are brief mentions in the context of larger accounts. For example, there is the lone Egyptian found by David's men when they were returning to Ziklag after a raid by the Amalekites (1 Sam. 30:11). There is also the mention of a Cushite in David's army (2 Sam. 18:19–31). One of David's mighty men is ascribed status by killing "an Egyptian, an impressive man" (2 Sam. 23:20–22).

The following two accounts demonstrate that Egypt served as a shelter for political refugees or enemies of the state at the time of the monarchy. After David conquered Edom (1 Kings 11:14–22), Hadad, from the Edomite royal house, fled to Egypt. He was treated well by the pharaoh, who gave him a sister of Queen Tahpenes as a wife. After David's death, Hadad returned to Edom and becomes an adversary of Solomon. The second incident occurred during Solomon's reign as Jeroboam I also fled to Egypt to escape Solomon's attempt to kill him. This would have been when Shoshenq I was pharoah. Eventually Jeroboam returned to rule the northern kingdom after the death of Solomon.

The texts that provide the most enigmatic reference to the role of Egypt and the united monarchy relate to Solomon's reign. The first is the conquest of Gezer by the pharaoh and his gift of Gezer to Solomon as a dowry. Solomon built a palace for the princess, and she moved from the "city of David" to her house (1 Kings 3:1; 7:8; 9:16, 24; 11:1; 2 Chron. 8:11). The second is the reference to trade relations between Solomon and Egypt, specifically horses and chariots from Egypt (1 Kings 10:28; 2 Chron. 1:17; 9:28). On the surface these texts present conflicting accounts of the relation between the united monarchy and Egypt.[28] It appears that a weakened Egypt had a foreign policy that adapted previous policies from the earlier New Kingdom dynasties to the reality of secondary states emerging in what was once its northern frontier.

The dominant view among scholars is that the pharaoh should be identified as Siamun, the sixth king in the Twenty-First Dynasty.[29] The question naturally

---

28. For a discussion of the history of interpreting these texts, reflecting editing and later redactions, see William M. Schniedewind, "Excavating the Text of 1 Kings 9: In Search of the Gates of Solomon," in *Historical Biblical Archaeology and the Future: The New Pragmatism* (ed. Thomas E. Levy; London: Equinox, 2010), 241–49.

29. For a summary, see Steven M. Ortiz, "Solomon's Egyptian Father-in-Law: A Reassessment of Egyptian Activity Based on Recent Archaeological Discoveries," *NEASB* 56 (2011): 25–32.

arises as to what this pharaoh was doing in the southern Levant when supposedly the united monarchy had dominion. Several historical reconstructions
have been proposed.[30] Abraham Malamat states that Siamun's conquest of
Gezer as a wedding gift to Solomon led to the first peace treaty between
Egypt and the united monarchy, with Solomon being the dominant player in
this treaty.[31] He proposes that the Twenty-First Dynasty was weak and thus
had to form alliances with smaller states, unlike the New Kingdom when the
southern Levant contained client states of the pharaoh. Some have proposed
that David and Solomon had Egyptian officials at their court;[32] others claim
that Solomon was influenced by Egyptian administrative practices.[33]

Kitchen proposes that there was an alliance between Egypt (Twenty-First
Dynasty) and Israel. This was a political alliance between Siamun and Solomon
aimed at subduing the Philistines' control, serving both parties as Siamun
"established suzerainty over Philistia (levying tribute on its rich cities), while
Solomon gained an important city that guarded the pass up to his capital."[34]
André Lemaire suggests that Solomon's kingdom probably came under the
sphere of influence of the Twenty-First Dynasty.[35] There have been some who
postulate that there was no contact or minimal contact between Egypt and
the southern Levant during the Twenty-First Dynasty. Those who hold to this
view doubt the historicity of the account of an Egyptian campaign in Syria-
Palestine, and even more so that of the marriage of an Egyptian princess to
Solomon.[36] A recent, more radical view proposed by Israel Finkelstein and
Neil Asher Silberman claims that this is part of temple propaganda during
Josiah's reform or the exilic period.[37]

There is a marked contrast between Egyptian presence in the Late Bronze
Age and the Iron Age. The distribution of the limited Egyptian finds is

30. See discussion in Ash, *David, Solomon and Egypt*, 15–18.

31. Abraham Malamat, "Aspects of the Foreign Policies of David and Solomon," *JNES* 22
(1963): 1–17; idem, "The First Peace Treaty between Israel and Egypt," *BAR* 5, no. 5 (1979): 58–61.

32. Roland de Vaux, "Titres et fonctionnaires égyptiens à la cour de David et de Salomon,"
RB 48 (1939): 394–405; Aelred Cody, "Le titre égyptien et le nom proper du scribe de David,"
RB 72 (1965): 381–93.

33. Donald B. Redford, "Studies in Relations between Palestine and Egypt during the First
Millennium B.C.," *JAOS* 93 (1973): 3–17.

34. Kitchen, *Reliability of the Old Testament*, 110.

35. André Lemaire, "Salomon et la fille de Pharaon: Un problem d'interprétation historique,"
in Maeir and de Miroschedji, *"I Will Speak the Riddles,"* 699–710.

36. Donald B. Redford, *Egypt, Canaan, and Israel in Ancient Times* (Princeton: Princeton
University Press), 1992; J. Alberto Soggin, *An Introduction to the History of Israel and Judah*
(trans. John Bowden; 2nd ed.; Valley Forge, PA: Trinity Press International, 1993); Ash, *David,
Solomon and Egypt*.

37. Israel Finkelstein and Neil Asher Silberman, *David and Solomon: In Search of the Bible's
Sacred Kings and the Roots of the Western Tradition* (New York: Free Press, 2006).

concentrated along the coast or in the Jezreel Valley.[38] This is especially true of the Egyptian pottery forms and of the Egyptian influences on some Philistine pottery forms.[39] Recently Stefan Münger has shown, based on the distribution of scarabs, that Siamun had ventured all the way up the coast to Tel Dor.[40] Unlike the Late Bronze Age, there are no Egyptian structures (e.g., palaces and temples) during the Iron Age, but there is evidence of Egyptianizing elements in the material culture, particularly along the coast. It is clear that while Egypt had no hegemony over the southern Levant, there was some contact. Perhaps the best illustration is an eleventh-century-BCE Egyptian tale in the Report of Wenamun.[41] This shows that although there was trade and contact, Egypt was weak and had no political or military presence in the area.

Settlement Planning: Towns to Cities, Hierarchy, Urbanization

There is no reference in the Bible to David's political organization beyond his army and the unification of the tribes under the capital of Jerusalem. His conquests of the Philistines and the Transjordan tribes demonstrate that there was a rational plan to secure the major trade routes of the coastal highway and the Transjordanian Plateau. It is during Solomon's reign that we get an idea of an organizational structure to the kingdom. We have two references to planned administration. The first is Solomon's districts. The second is a small reference tucked away in a summary statement regarding Solomon's building projects. It is mentioned in 1 Kings 9:15 that he rebuilt Jerusalem and the cities of Hazor, Megiddo, and Gezer. No explanation is given as to why these cities were chosen, but it is easy to see that Solomon was fortifying key cities to guard the major communication routes. Gezer now served as the forward guard in the Aijalon Valley, farther west than the fortress that was at Khirbet Qeiyafa.[42]

Analyses of settlement hierarchy, demographics, and settlement distribution can easily determine the nature of an ancient society. Archaeological surveys and excavations have well documented the process of Iron Age urbanization in the western highlands. Surveys of the hill country have shown that several small villages and towns dominated the Ephraim and Manasseh hills. Finkelstein

---

38. Ash, *David, Solomon and Egypt*, 93.

39. Trude Dothan, *The Philistines and Their Material Culture* (New Haven: Yale University Press, 1982), 172–85.

40. Stefan Münger, "Egyptian Stamp-Seal Amulets and Their Implications for the Chronology of the Early Iron Age," *TA* 30 (2003): 66–82.

41. Miriam Lichtheim, "The Report of Wenamun," in *The New Kingdom* (vol. 2 of *Ancient Egyptian Literature: A Book of Readings*; Berkeley: University of California Press, 1973), 224–30; idem, "The Report of Wenamun," *COS* 1.41.

42. Ortiz and Wolff, "Guarding the Border."

has proposed that the urban planning across the span of the Iron Age demonstrates pastoralists inhabiting circular settlements that eventually evolve into the city plan of the Iron Age II.[43] Site hierarchy distributions show that there was a structural imposition across the landscape that can be attributed only to a state level of societal development.

Demographics are very difficult to determine in ancient societies. Most of the data comes from statistical modeling of surface sherds from surveys. Various studies by Avi Ofer and Gunnar Lehmann have postulated from seven thousand to twenty thousand people living in Judah.[44] Amihai Mazar estimates that this number is the basic threshold for a state, and with the additional territories of the north and some from Transjordan added to Judah's area, it is more than enough to be considered a territorial state.[45] This demographic data is reasonable for social scientists working with ancient cultures, but it is usually seen as too low for biblical scholars who assume that it should be a larger amount, probably based on contemporary estimates of territorial states.[46] Unfortunately, people come to the biblical text and the archaeological data with modern constructs imposed upon ancient demographics.

Often also misunderstood is the biblical assertion that Solomon "ruled over all the kingdoms from the River to the land of the Philistines and to the border of Egypt" (1 Kings 4:21). A superficial reading of the biblical text would imply that the territory extended from modern-day Iraq to modern-day Egypt. However, the idiom refers to controlling the land bridge between Egypt and Mesopotamia. The text refers to ruling over all the kingdoms (e.g., vassal relationships) and not territorial expansion. Another biblical idiom is "from Dan to Beersheba" (2 Sam. 24:2; 1 Kings 4:25). It refers to the whole of Israel and provides a more accurate picture of the territorial boundary of the united

43. Israel Finkelstein, *The Archaeology of the Israelite Settlement* (trans. D. Saltz; Jerusalem: Israel Exploration Society, 1988).

44. Avi Ofer, "'All the Hill Country of Judah': From a Settlement Fringe to a Prosperous Monarchy," in *From Nomadism to Monarchy: Archaeological and Historical Aspects of Early Israel* (ed. Israel Finkelstein and Nadav Na'aman; Jerusalem: Israel Exploration Society, 1994), 92–122; Gunnar Lehmann, "The United Monarchy in the Countryside: Jerusalem, Judah and the Shephelah during the Tenth Century B.C.E.," in *Jerusalem in Bible and Archaeology: The First Temple Period* (ed. Andrew G. Vaughn and Ann E. Killebrew; SBLSymS 18; Atlanta: Society of Biblical Literature, 2003), 117–64.

45. Amihai Mazar, "Archaeology and the Biblical Narrative: The Case of the United Monarchy," in Kratz and Spieckermann, *One God—One Cult—One Nation*, 29–58. See also David Ussishkin, "Archaeology of the Biblical Period: On Some Questions of Methodology and Chronology of the Iron Age," in *Understanding the History of Ancient Israel* (ed. H. G. M. Willliamson; PBA 143; Oxford: Oxford University Press, 2007), 131–41.

46. David W. Jamieson-Drake, *Scribes and Schools in Monarchic Judah: A Socio-Archaeological Approach* (JSOTSup 109; Sheffield: Almond, 1991).

Casemate Walls

Casemate walls are defensive city walls constructed of two parallel walls, with the space between them divided by partitions forming rooms (casemates). These walls are usually thinner than solid city walls. They are characteristic of Iron Age fortifications from the tenth century to the end of the eighth century BCE. Although their beginnings had been dated to the time of Solomon (e.g., Hazor Stratum X, Gezer 8 [VII]), recent excavations at Khirbet Qeiyafa demonstrate that they originated earlier. There are two types: freestanding and integrated. Integrated casemates use the casemate as both a defensive exterior wall and as part of a dwelling. Tell Beit Mirsim and Qeiyafa are integrated casemates. Some of these casemates probably were filled in with rubble to support a later wall system built above them (e.g., Hazor VIII and Samaria, both from the ninth century BCE).

monarchy, stretching from the Huleh Basin in the north (with the conquered Canaanite cities of Hazor Stratum X–IX and Tel Dan Stratum IV) to the Negev (Beersheba Stratum VI and Stratum V). One of the settlement shifts that archaeology has been able to add to the biblical data is the fifty or so fortified enclosures and small settlements of the central Negev highlands (probably associated with the "heights of David" in the Sheshonq I Inscription). Most of these are small settlements or isolated farmsteads close to water sources (e.g., oasis, water beds), where some desert agriculture can be used. They usually were located on hills within sight of each other. Most were twenty-five to seventy meters in diameter. Some had a row of casemate rooms surrounding a large central courtyard with a narrow entrance.

The Iron Age II witnessed shifts in the nature of the settlements. Several sites (e.g., Hazor, Kinneret, Beth Shean, Tel Rehov, Megiddo, Yoqne'am, Tel el-Far'ah north, Beth Shemesh, Tell Beit Mirsim, Lachish, and Beersheba) had major changes indicating processes of urbanization that continued to grow until the eighth century BCE.[47] A recent study of the Iron Age strata in the southern part of the country (e.g., Shephelah, coast, Judean hills, and Negev) has revealed that the major fortified sites were instituted in the late tenth century. The archaeologists conclude that the state originated in the southern region rather than the Judean hills.[48] The recent work at Jerusalem, Beth Shemesh, and Khirbet Qeiyafa negate this view.[49] It is more accurate

47. Judah may have continued this urbanization process until the seventh century, esp. Jerusalem and sites in the Shephelah.

48. Ze'ev Herzog and Lily Singer-Avitz, "Redefining the Centre: The Emergence of State in Judah," *TA* 31 (2004): 209–44.

49. Eilat Mazar, *The Palace of King David: Excavations at the Summit of the City of David; Preliminary Report of Seasons 2005–2007* (trans. Ben Gordon; Jerusalem: Shoham Academic

to interpret the center at Jerusalem and the outlying areas as the periphery of the Judean urban expansion. Westward expansion is seen on the coastal plain. Two Philistine sites on the Yarkon Basin, Aphek and Tel Qasile, were destroyed at the end of the Iron Age I (tenth century).[50] In addition, the major Philistine city of Ekron experienced destruction and a depopulation of the city that forced a contraction from a fifty-acre Iron Age I site down to a ten-acre settlement.[51]

These settlement patterns and control of the Yarkon River Basin, occupation in the Negev, and expansion into the Judean Shephelah put the Philistine dominance during the Iron Age I in check and coincide with the foreign policies of the early Israelite state as discussed above. Other patterns discerned in the archaeological record are site hierarchy and interaction spheres. The biblical texts contain administrative documents suggesting that there were such policies at least as early as the Solomonic reign. This is particularly true of 1 Kings 4 and Solomon's administrative districts.[52] It is clear that the districts—based on natural topography, ecozones, and tribal districts—are centered on a city, possibly used as a redistribution and taxation city.

SETTLEMENT HIERARCHY

There are four types or tiers of cities: (1) capital cities (e.g., Jerusalem and Samaria); (2) major administrative centers (e.g., Lachish and Hazor); (3) secondary administrative cities (e.g., Beersheba); and (4) provincial towns. The specific tier of the city would influence the amount of funds and labor invested into the city planning by the crown.

Capital cities include Samaria and Jerusalem. Little is known of the overall plan of Jerusalem.[53] Much more is known about Samaria, albeit the

Research and Publication, 2009); idem, *Discovering the Solomonic Wall in Jerusalem: A Remarkable Archaeological Adventure* (Jerusalem: Shoham Academic Research and Publication, 2011); Shlomo Bunimovitz and Zvi Lederman, "The Iron Age Fortifications of Tel Beth-Shemesh: A 1990–2000 Perspective," *IEJ* 51 (2001): 121–48; Yosef Garfinkel and Saar Ganor, eds., *Excavation Report 2007–2008* (vol. 1 of *Khirbet Qeiyafa*; Jerusalem: Israel Exploration Society, 2009).

50. Pirhiyah Beck and Moshe Kochavi, "Aphek (in Sharon)," *NEAEHL* 1:69; Moshe Kochavi, Pirhiyah Beck, and Esther Yadin, *Aphek-Antipatris I: Excavation of Areas A and B; The 1972–1976 Seasons* (Tel Aviv: Emery and Claire Yass Publications in Archaeology of the Institute of Archaeology, Tel Aviv University, 2000), 17–18.

51. Seymour Gitin, "Philistia in Transition: The Tenth Century BCE and Beyond," in Gitin, Mazar, and Stern, *Mediterranean Peoples in Transition*, 162–83.

52. See Richard S. Hess, "The Form and Structure of the Solomonic District List in 1 Kings 4:7–19," in *Crossing Boundaries and Linking Horizons: Studies in Honor of Michael C. Astour on His 80th Birthday* (ed. Gordon D. Young, Mark W. Chavalas, and Richard E. Averbeck; Bethesda, MD: CDL Press, 1997), 279–92.

53. Even with the new excavations by Eilat Mazar (*Palace of King David* and *Discovering the Solomonic Wall*), we still do not have a plan of the royal acropolis.

Figure 7.3. Beersheba city plans

ninth-century-BCE city. The city consisted of two parts: a large rectangular royal acropolis and a lower city. The acropolis, approximately four acres and surrounded by a wall 1.6 meters thick, was surrounded by a casemate wall in the first half of the ninth century BCE. The city of Jezreel was built utilizing a similar plan. Ahab had a royal residence here (1 Kings 21). Capital cities are designed as two-part cities consisting of a royal enclosure and the rest of the city. A well-organized orthogonal city plan is evident.

Major administrative centers are cities in which a majority of the settlement plan is devoted to public complexes. These are usually orthogonal units within the overall plan. Cities with this type of city plan are Megiddo (Strata V [VA–IVB], VIB, IVA) and Lachish (Strata IV III). Ze'ev Herzog proposes that Hazor (Strata X–IV), Gezer, and Tel Dan also had similar plans.[54] These cities are planned according to the peripheral principle. The public buildings usually are in a central location (acropolis) and built according to the orthogonal plan. They are different from the plans of capital cities in that the public area is incorporated into the private area of the city. Secondary administrative centers, according to Herzog, are similar to royal fortresses. There is only one

54. Ze'ev Herzog, "Settlement and Fortification Planning in the Iron Age," in *The Architecture of Ancient Israel: From the Prehistoric to the Persian Periods; In Memory of Immanuel (Munya) Dunayevsky* (ed. Aharon Kempinski and Ronny Reich; Jerusalem: Israel Exploration Society, 1992), 250.

that fits this model: Beersheba. The administrative areas and private residential quarters are integrated and have no distinct separation. Several settlements may be defined as provincial towns. The key examples are Tell Beit Mirsim and Tell en-Naṣbeh. Provincial towns have few or no public structures. Most of the city is occupied by private dwellings.

In addition to settlement hierarchy, surveys reveal a system of major cities surrounded by forts. Adam Zertal has studied the Samaria region and has found fourteen forts that guarded access to the city of Samaria. Other forts have been found in the Judean hills and the Negev highlands. Most of these forts date to the later Iron Age, and so it was assumed that this type of settlement originated after the united monarchy. This changed with the discovery of Khirbet Qeiyafa, which is a single site with two large gates and a casemate fortification encircling the settlement. It is a fortified center situated above the Elah Valley. Its vantage point in the Judean hills overlooks the site of the traditional battle between the Israelites and Philistines, as recounted in the David-and-Goliath military account (1 Sam. 17). The site dates to the tenth century and appears to have been a forward post during the united monarchy.

City Plans

There are basically two types of plans for the typical Israelite city. The first is the orthogonal plan. It is based on the square, using right angles. This is a well-planned and organized city scheme, not utilized frequently in the southern Levant. It requires extensive labor (e.g., leveling and quarrying) to build it from the traditional oval, mound-shaped site. The orthogonal plan was usually employed for a capital city. Sometimes it was used only for the acropolis, or in an administrative section of the city, such as a palace. The number of orthogonal Iron Age II settlements is small.[55] Herzog observes that there is a "greater use of monumental building techniques (ashlars, proto-Aeolic capitals, carved window balustrades, etc.)."[56]

The other city plan is the oval-shaped pattern of the peripheral and radial city layout. The peripherally organized settlement is the simplest plan. It is organized within a city wall that was built around an Israelite city according to the contour and topographic features of the typical tel. The city is designed in radiating or concentric rings inside the city wall. Sometimes both plans are incorporated into a city, with a section or acropolis having an orthogonal plan within the radial plan of the city, as in Lachish.

55. Ibid., 247.
56. Ibid.

PUBLIC BUILDINGS AND FORTIFICATIONS

Large public works are diagnostic features of a state-level society. Evidence of monumental architecture dating to the tenth century BCE is found throughout ancient Palestine in the form of large public buildings, fortifications, palaces, water systems, and monumental ornamentation. A typical Israelite city consisted of public and domestic parts. The city contained a fortification wall (solid or casemate) connected to a gate complex of several chambers. These chambers contained four to six cells with towers. During the later Iron Age (eighth century BCE) a secondary wall line was added to the fortification system.

Several large, magazine-type buildings have been found dating to the tenth century BCE, including a series of long rows of rooms used for storage. These buildings usually are associated with gate complexes or palaces. They have cobbled flagstone surfaces with several rows of pillars supporting a superstructure, hence the common nomenclature "pillared buildings." One of the debates surrounding the archaeology of the united monarchy is the identification of tripartite pillared buildings as either storehouses or stables. Most scholars now acknowledge that these were multifunctional.[57] The earliest examples are found along the coast in the eleventh century BCE (Qasile and Abu Hawam). This structure becomes common during the ninth century BCE, as they are found at Megiddo, Lachish, Hazor, Tel el Ḥesi, and Beersheba. Regardless of the functional interpretation of these structures, they demonstrate a socioeconomic behavior (both quality and quantity) found only in state-level societies. Jeffrey Blakely has studied these pillared buildings in their spatial context and notes that they match the description of Solomon's districts as delineated in 1 Kings 4:4–19. Thus they confirm the borders of the united monarchy as described in the text and capitalize on the location of trade routes.[58]

PALACES

Evidence of central authority and monarchial rule occurs in royal architectural elements. Several palaces have been excavated.[59] At Megiddo two palaces were excavated that date to the tenth century BCE.[60] David Ussishkin postulated that the Syrian *bit-hilani* palace was the prototype for Solomon's palace

---

57. Paul Z. Gregor, "A Tripartite Pillared Building in Transjordan," *ADAJ* 53 (2009): 9–19; Larry G. Herr, "Tripartite Pillared Buildings and the Market Place in Iron Age Palestine," *BASOR* 272 (1988): 47–67.

58. Jeffrey A. Blakely, "Reconciling Two Maps: Archaeological Evidence for the Kingdoms of David and Solomon," *BASOR* 327 (2002): 49–54.

59. For example, Megiddo, Samaria, Hazor, Lachish, Ramat Raḥel, Jerusalem.

60. All the other palaces so far excavated date to the eighth–seventh centuries BCE.

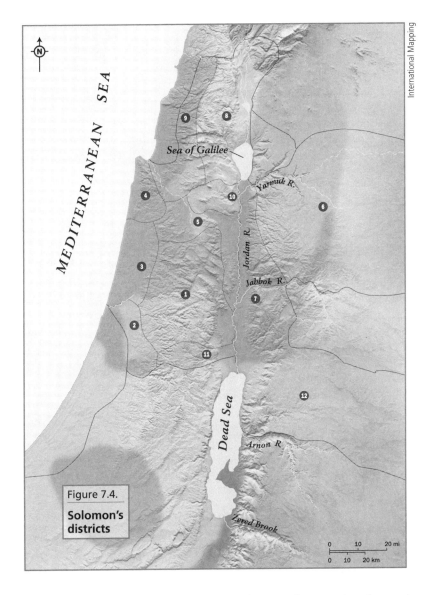

Figure 7.4.

Solomon's districts

as described in the Bible and the Megiddo palaces.[61] They consist of a portico, throne room, and a great hall. This view has recently been modified as it has become clear that the southern Levant had its own tradition of large palace structures. Ilan Sharon and Anabel Zarzecki-Peleg, based on the Hazor palace,

61. David Ussishkin, "King Solomon's Palace and Building 1723 in Megiddo," *IEJ* 16 (1966): 174–86.

Tripartite Pillared Buildings

Tripartite pillared buildings are a well-known architectural feature of Iron Age administrative structures. They are rectangular buildings with two rows of pillars placed longitudinally to form three long halls. These buildings are usually found with flagstone surfaces in the side halls and a beaten earth surface in the central hall. They were discovered at the following sites: Hazor, Tell Abu Hawam, Tel Kinneret, Ein-Gev, Tell Hadar, Tell Hadid, Megiddo, Tell Qasile, Tell el-Hesi, Lachish, Gezer, Beth Shemesh, Timnah, Beersheba, Tel Malhata, Masos, Tall Jalul, Khirbet al-Mudayna, and perhaps Gibeon. The structures are located in public areas and are usually grouped together. There has been a debate as to whether they were used for stables (e.g., Megiddo, Lachish) or storehouses (Beersheba, Hazor, and Beth Shemesh). Other proposals are bazaars/marketplaces, customs houses, tax-collection centers, and industrial complexes. It is probable that they were multipurpose buildings that served different needs of the government.

have defined the palatial architecture of the Iron Age Levant as Lateral-Access Podium structures.[62] These are associated with other public structures (usually pillared buildings) in an enclosure that is set apart in the city. Such buildings are smaller than the *bit-hilani* palaces in northern Syria and usually are square versus the broadhouse of the *bit-hilani*. Gunnar Lehmann and Ann Killebrew have proposed that a better definition is a Central Hall Tetra-Partite Residency.[63] Although a majority of these palaces date after the tenth century BCE, it is clear that they represent a local tradition that originated earlier.

In addition to monumental buildings, proto-Aeolic capitals have been found throughout ancient Palestine during the Iron Age. Large capitals are evidence of palatial structures and are only found associated with monumental public buildings. Proto-Aeolic capitals[64] have been found at Hazor, Megiddo, Samaria, Jerusalem, and Ramat Rahel.

Centralization: Capital

When discussing the kingdom of David and Solomon, we must address the capital city of Jerusalem. It is accurate to recognize that there is little archaeological

62. Ilan Sharon and Anabel Zarzecki-Peleg, "Podium Structures with Lateral Access: Authority Ploys in Royal Architecture in the Iron Age Levant," in *Confronting the Past: Archaeological and Historical Essays on Ancient Israel in Honor of William G. Dever* (ed. Seymour Gitin, J. Edward Wright, and J. P. Dessel; Winona Lake, IN: Eisenbrauns, 2006), 145–67.

63. Gunnar Lehmann and Ann E. Killebrew, "Palace 6000 at Megiddo in Context: Iron Age Central Hall Tetra-Partite Residencies and the *Bit-Hilani* Building Tradition in the Levant," *BASOR* 359 (2010): 13–33.

64. Over thirty have been found to date. See Yigal Shiloh, *The Proto-Aeolic Capital and Israelite Ashlar Masonry* (Qedem 11; Jerusalem: Israel Exploration Society, 1979).

data excavated in Jerusalem that can be associated with the united monarchy. This presents a major problem for those who hold to the historicity of the Davidic monarchy, especially since Jerusalem has been extensively excavated.[65] We must ask, what has caused this pattern in the archaeological record? Critics attribute the paucity of the archaeological record to fictional recollections of David and Solomon. This interpretation of the archaeological record does not account for the nature of the archaeology of Jerusalem and demonstrates a naive understanding of the problems of interpreting such archaeological data.

The archaeology of Iron Age Jerusalem presents several difficulties. First, Jerusalem is a living city. People are now dwelling on the site of the ancient city, which allows only for selected areas to be excavated. Second, Jerusalem is a sacred city. Third, the Iron Age (and Bronze Age) city was built on the crest of the eastern hill, with the Tyropoean Valley to the west and the Kidron Valley to the east. Since the city was rebuilt throughout history and the site was continuously occupied on the crest of the hill, the amount of Iron Age occupation that remains in situ is minimal. Another factor to consider is that each new city destroyed the city beneath it in order to get to bedrock. This produces complicated stratigraphical problems for the interpretation of the archaeological record. The so-called problem of Jerusalem is due largely to the lack of preservation of the archaeological record—not that the city did not exist during the tenth century BCE. Any interpretation of the archaeology of Jerusalem as it relates to David and Solomon must take into account the complexity of Jerusalem's archaeology.[66] In spite of these difficulties of obtaining archaeological data from Jerusalem, recent excavations have produced some evidence of the tenth century BCE. Joe Uziel and Itzhaq Shai have noted that one of the problems in reconstructing the development of Jerusalem is a modern paradigm, or perception, that the ancient city of Jerusalem should be large. They posit that first the center appears (e.g., capital-temple palace) and then the urban development. Hence we should see a trajectory from a nucleus (city center) to urbanization, instead of the other way. This is the pattern of growth that we see in Iron Age Jerusalem, as Jerusalem grows from a centralized capital and religious center in the tenth century to a large urban city in the eighth century BCE.[67]

65. There were three major excavations: the City of David by Yigal Shiloh, the Southern Wall by Benjamin Mazar, and the Jewish Quarter by Nahman Avigad—all sponsored by the Hebrew University of Jerusalem.

66. Jane M. Cahill, "Jerusalem at the Time of the United Monarchy: The Archaeological Evidence," in Vaughn and Killebrew, *Jerusalem in Bible and Archaeology*, 13–80; E. Mazar, *Palace of King David*.

67. Joe Uziel and Itzhaq Shai, "Iron Age Jerusalem: Temple-Palace, Capital City," *JAOS* 127 (2007): 161–70.

Economics

The biblical text refers to Solomon's wealth, particularly the descriptions of the temple with gold-plated walls and golden furniture and vessels (1 Kings 6:20–22, 28, 30, 32, 35; 7:48–50). In addition, several passages describe the various contents of trade, caravans, gifts, and tribute (1 Kings 9:11, 28; 10:2, 10, 14). The book of Kings also mentions that Shishak (Shesqonq I) "carried off the treasures of the temple of the LORD and the treasures of the royal palace. He took everything, including all the gold shields Solomon had made" (1 Kings 14:26). Alan Millard has noticed that the descriptions in the biblical text are comparable to other descriptions in ancient Near Eastern texts as well as archaeological data, particularly the New Kingdom of Egypt (fifteenth–thirteenth centuries BCE) and the Neo-Assyrian Empire of the ninth–seventh centuries BCE.[68] Granted, a small territorial state in the southern Levant cannot be compared to large empires such as Assyria and Egypt; hence many scholars assume that the descriptions are a small kingdom's attempt to use hyperbole or later writers' attempts to falsify descriptions or copy royal descriptions of wealth from the later Neo-Assyrian and Babylonian periods.[69]

John Holladay has addressed the royal economy of ancient Israel, particularly during the eighth century BCE, and has compared Hezekiah's tribute in relation to the Neo-Assyrian typology and history of tribute extraction.[70] He calculated that Judah was well positioned to take advantage of the various trade spheres (e.g., Phoenicia in the north and the Arabian Caravans in the south). Holladay analyzed texts from the Archives of the Royal Inscriptions of Mesopotamia and concluded that tolls of ninth-century-BCE camel caravans from the south were a major economic source of wealth for eastern African, Arabian, and the Indian Ocean economies.[71] Although Holladay analyzed a period later than the united monarchy, it can be postulated that this economic activity started during the tenth century BCE, and the biblical descriptions of Solomon's wealth reflect this reality. This is based on a trajectory of the economy as demonstrated by the control of these trade routes. It is also supported by the presence of a large-scale copper mining industry in Edom during the tenth century BCE. Thomas Levy has proposed that Edom was a centralized

68. Alan R. Millard, "King Solomon in His Ancient Context," in *The Age of Solomon: Scholarship at the Turn of the Millennium* (ed. Lowell K. Handy; SHCANE 11; Leiden: Brill, 1997), 30–53.

69. For an example of this type of reasoning, see Hermann Niemann, "The Socio-Political Shadow Cast by the Biblical Solomon," in Handy, *Age of Solomon*, 252–99.

70. John S. Holladay, "Hezekiah's Tribute, Long-Distance Trade, and the Wealth of Nations, ca. 1000–600 BC: A New Perspective," in Gitin, Wright, and Dessel, *Confronting the Past*, 311–31.

71. Ibid., 326–27.

polity with an extensive trade network, based on his excavations at Khirbet en-Nahas in the Feinan region, east of Wadi Arabah in Jordan.[72]

Military

The biblical account contains many references to military battles, particularly involving David. In addition, David had a standing army and his "mighty men" (2 Sam. 20:7; 23:8, 17; 1 Chron. 11:11, 19). Solomon created a force of fourteen hundred chariots that were stationed in Jerusalem and in various "chariot cities" (1 Kings 9:19; 10:26). Most of the biblical references to the military concern later kings of Judah and Israel. Archaeologists have found tenth-century remains of stables (Megiddo, Lachish, Jezreel). A recent monograph by Deborah O'Daniel Cantrell has demonstrated that ancient Israel had a robust equestrian component to its military and state.[73] She defines the various compounds throughout Iron Age cities as "horse-related architecture" and reports "training facilities, such as Megiddo, with stables for 450 horses; the Jezreel fortress with its huge enclosed courtyard; and Lachish with its courtyard, chambered gates, and stables were in fact processing thousands of horses, only some of which required stabling at any given time."[74] Her work has conclusively shown that the Megiddo stables are part of a major chariot city that originated in the Late Bronze Age and remained active until the Neo-Assyrian period.

Temple

Some scholars are quick to point out that there is no archaeological evidence for the temple of Solomon. This argument betrays a naive assumption about the archaeological data. We have no archaeological evidence of Herod's temple, but no scholar seriously doubts its existence. Although there is no archaeological evidence for Solomon's temple, archaeological research provides a methodological paradigm to address the archaeological realia of the temple's description in the biblical texts. Archaeologists can look at the evolution and development of temples throughout the ancient Near East. They can make comparisons between the temple built by Solomon and other cultic

---

72. Thomas E. Levy et al., "Lowland Edom and the High and Low Chronologies: Edomite State Formation, the Bible and Recent Archaeological Research in Southern Jordan," in *The Bible and Radiocarbon Dating: Archaeology, Text and Science* (ed. Thomas Levy and Thomas Higham; London: Equinox, 2005), 129–63.

73. Deborah O'Daniel Cantrell, *The Horsemen of Israel: Horses and Chariotry in Monarchic Israel (Ninth–Eighth Centuries B.C.E.)* (HACL 1; Winona Lake, IN: Eisenbrauns, 2011).

74. Ibid., 9.

Figure 7.5. Remains of Ain Dara temple . . .

. . . and side rooms.

structures found in excavations. Several temples have been excavated from the Early Bronze Age to the Roman period in Syria-Palestine. When one compares these temples, the description of Solomon's temple corresponds with cultic structures of the Iron Age I/II transition.

Perhaps the most common comparison has been between Solomon's temple and the Tayanat temple found in Syria.[75] Recently renewed investigations have found a similar temple at Ain Dara, also in Northern Syria. The published excavation report of the Ain Dara temple shows closer parallels to the biblical description of Solomon's temple.[76] As the corpus of ancient Near Eastern temples continues to grow, evidence strongly suggests that, based on a comparative analysis of temple architecture, the temple of Solomon fits well in a tenth-century BCE architectural tradition of tripartite temples.

Daily Life

Recent research on social transformations in the lives of the ancient Israelites will benefit our understanding of the development of the ancient Israelite state. Scholars tend to forget that a state was not just a group of elites who acted on the stage of history, but rather the totality of the individuals. Questions that are difficult to answer include these: If you were a local farmer in the hill country of Judah or Samaria, did you consider yourself to be a participant in the monarchy or a subject of the crown? What about ethnic and political identification? If you were a Hittite and part of David's military, was your allegiance to David, to the crown, or to your tribe? Social identification is difficult to discern in the historical record and more so in the material culture.

The biblical text reveals that kinship played an important role in the administration of the monarchy.[77] One of the basic components has been the *bêt 'āb* (house of the father) as the source of identity within the tribal society.[78] While the monarchy retained a kinship-based organization, a socially stratified society developed. In addition, we see various administrative positions that occur only in the context of a state level of society (e.g., "son of the king," servant of the king, scribe, and adviser to the king). A major monograph analyzed

75. See David Ussishkin, "Building IV at Hamath and the Temples of Solomon and Tell Tayanat," *IEJ* 16 (1966): 104–10; Timothy Harrison, "Neo-Hittites in the North Orontes Valley: Recent Investigations at Tell Tayinat," *JCSMS* 2 (2008): 59–68.

76. See John M. Monson, "The Temple of Solomon: Heart of Jerusalem," in *Zion, City of Our God* (ed. Richard S. Hess and Gordon J. Wenham; Grand Rapids: Eerdmans, 2004), 1–22.

77. Carol Meyers, "Kinship and Kingship: The Early Monarchy," *OHBW* 165–205; Stager, "Patrimonial Kingdom of Solomon."

78. J. David Schloen, *The House of the Father as Fact and Symbol: Patrimonialism in Ugarit and the Ancient Near East* (SAHL 2; Winona Lake, IN: Eisenbrauns, 2001).

the biblical text and the archaeological data (mostly epigraphic) and found nineteen titles that were either status or function related.[79]

DOMESTIC HOUSES

A new house type also appears at sites in the hill country: the four-room dwelling. It is commonly called the "Israelite four-room house" because it appears so frequently in the western highlands. Shlomo Bunimovitz and Avraham Faust have proposed that the spatial patterning of the four-room house represents a unique Israelite worldview.[80] While domestic structures have been used to define ethnicity (especially Philistine versus Israelite), household archaeology is becoming more sophisticated in the use of data and interpretations that go beyond ethnic identification.[81] Some studies illustrate the shift from a rural settlement to a town community and the related kinship structures of extended family as well as household economic activity.[82]

LITERACY

One of the typical features associated with a state is a bureaucracy complete with writing. Two questions arise regarding the state in ancient Israel: Where are the state documents? What was the level of literacy? Some scholars question the existence of the united monarchy because there is a lack of inscriptions from tenth century BCE. Perhaps the most influential monograph is David Jamieson-Drake's *Scribes and Schools in Monarchic Judah*. He reports that the majority of archaeological finds associated with state bureaucracy (e.g., bullae, seals, and inscriptions) become significant in number only in the eighth century BCE.[83] Hence the state must have originated after the tenth century BCE, he concludes.[84]

Yet from the biblical texts we see much statecraft: diplomacy, districts, taxation, military lists, and so on. This evidence implies a robust documentation

79. Nili Sacher Fox, *In the Service of the King: Officialdom in Ancient Israel and Judah* (HUCM 23; Cincinnati: Hebrew Union College Press, 2000).

80. Shlomo Bunimovitz and Avraham Faust, "Building Identity: The Four-Room House and the Israelite Mind," in Dever and Gitin, *Symbiosis*, 411–23.

81. Assaf Yasur-Landau, Jennie R. Ebeling, and Laura B. Mazow, eds., *Household Archaeology in Ancient Israel and Beyond* (CHANE 50; Leiden: Brill, 2011).

82. See, in ibid., Aaron J. Brody, "The Archaeology of the Extended Family: A Household Compound from Iron II Tell en-Naṣbeh" (237–54); Yuval Gadot, "Houses and Households in Settlements along the Yarkon River, Israel, during the Iron Age I: Society, Economy, and Identity" (155–81); Avraham Faust, "Household Economies in the Kingdoms of Israel and Judah" (255–73).

83. Jamieson-Drake, *Scribes and Schools*.

84. Amihai Mazar has noted that the ninth century BCE holds no more inscriptions than the tenth century BCE, yet this is the period when most minimalists claim the state started in ancient Palestine ("The Spade and the Text: The Interaction between Archaeology and the Israelite History Relating to the Tenth–Ninth Centuries BC," in *Understanding the History of Ancient Israel* [ed. H. G. M. Williamson; PBA143; Oxford: Oxford University Press, 2007]: 143–71).

system for the state. Chance finds from later Iron Age II periods show that ostraca were abundant as sources preserving writing. The excavations at the City of David in Jerusalem found a room full of bullae, hinting that a majority of the documentation was written on perishable materials.[85] And the likelihood of finding writing dating to the tenth century would be difficult. The question of literacy is also debated. Two inscriptions, the Gezer Calendar and the Tel Zayit abecedary, provide evidence of writing.[86] The controversial Khirbet Qeiyafa Ostracon can now be added to this list.[87] This will remain an open question. It is clear that during the divided monarchy there was functional literacy. The question is how early this appeared in ancient Israel.[88]

Conclusion

The united monarchy will continue to be debated among scholars. Many come to the investigation of this period with preconceived notions of a state, sometimes using models and traits of modern Western states. Contributing to these misperceptions are later biblical motifs that viewed this time period as a golden age. But on the whole, the archaeology and literary sources provide enough data for the historian to reconstruct the nature of the united monarchy with a reasonable degree of accuracy.

This was a unique period in Israelite history, where a single king was able to coalesce multiple tribes into a unified political force. Solomon's son Rehoboam would eventually lose this fragile coalition that lasted, at most, seventy-five years. A simple portrait shows that David strategically used a kinship-based culture, key conquests, and control of major interaction spheres. He established a political and spiritual center with the capital and temple at Jerusalem. This laid the groundwork for Solomon to focus on the maintenance of the new kingdom and the oversight of trade routes and vassals. The kingdom was strategically placed between the world powers of the ancient Near East. Solomon took advantage of the control of trade. The biblical text attributes the expansion to God's plan while pointing out the strengths and failures of these leaders.

---

85. Nahman Avigad, *Hebrew Bullae from the Time of Jeremiah: Remnants of a Burnt Archive* (Jerusalem: Israel Exploration Society, 1986).

86. Ron Tappy and P. Kyle McCarter, eds., *Literate Culture and Tenth-Century Canaan: The Tel Zayit Abecedary in Context* (Winona Lake, IN: Eisenbrauns, 2008).

87. Haggai Misgav, Yosef Garfinkel, and Saar Ganor, "The Ostracon," in Garfinkel and Ganor, *Excavation Report 2007–2008*, 243–60.

88. Richard S. Hess, "Questions of Reading and Writing in Ancient Israel," *BBR* 19 (2009): 1–9.

8

The Biblical Prophets in Historiography

James K. Mead

What contribution can the biblical prophets make to the writing of a history of Israel? The thesis of this chapter is that the prophetic stories and speeches in the Hebrew Bible give us a historically reasonable, though incomplete, portrait of the ministry and message of those individuals who claimed to speak God's word to his people. To the extent that the biblical prophets worked in contexts and conveyed messages that bear some similarity to those of the wider ancient Near Eastern world in the second and first millennia BCE, we may incorporate prophetic literature as part of our evidence in laying a foundation for a history of Israel. I will address the pertinent information in biblical texts, describe what we can know of prophecy in the wider ancient Near Eastern context, discuss issues that arise from an analysis of these sources, and briefly summarize the nature of our current historical understanding.

Israelite Prophecy and the Biblical Text

My thesis holds in tension two important claims about reconstructing a historically accurate portrait of biblical prophecy in its ancient context: the existence of a sufficient amount of reliable evidence within the Bible and the incomplete nature of this evidence, which disallows an exhaustive portrait.

This tension should make us cautiously optimistic as we begin our exploration of the topic at hand. Although there is certainly not the amount of data that we would like to possess, there is far more information in the Bible about prophecy than there is about, for example, family life in ancient Israel or the precise nature of Israelite wisdom schools. Thus we may proceed with an examination of the terms that biblical authors used to identify prophets before we consider a basic description of their ministry and message in the biblical literature.

Prophetic Titles and Terms

The individuals whose names are associated with the "Latter Prophets" of the Hebrew Bible clearly had precursors whose words were never collected into documents that made their way into the biblical canon. If we take Amos and Hosea in the latter half of the eighth century BCE to be the earliest of the "canonical prophets," who were some of the important predecessors, and by what titles were they known during and earlier than the divided monarchy? In what follows I will focus on the titles and reserve comment about their historical usage in the subsequent discussion of biblical literature. For the sake of style and consistency, I will employ the words "prophet," "prophetic," and "prophecy" even though it will be clear that the variety of terms had their genesis and usage in different historical locations and periods.[1]

A term associated with one of the earliest expressions of prophetic activity in ancient Israel is "seer" (*rō'eh*). The judge Samuel (1 Sam. 7:15–17) is called a "seer" in both the dialogue and the narration of 1 Samuel 9, where Saul and his servant need guidance to find the family's missing donkeys. Both Saul and his servant and Samuel himself use "seer" as a prophetic title (vv. 11, 18–19), a connection that the biblical narrator makes for the reader: "Formerly in Israel, anyone who went to inquire of God would say, 'Come, let us go to the seer'; for the one who is now called a prophet was formerly called a seer" (v. 9). The literary context also repeatedly connects this title to "man of God" (vv. 5–10), discussed below. In addition to using *rō'eh* for Samuel (1 Chron. 9:22; 26:28; 29:29), the Chronicler identifies Hanani by this title (2 Chron. 16:7, 10).[2] Based on the common Hebrew root for seeing, *rō'eh* evokes the

---

1. David L. Petersen, *The Prophetic Literature: An Introduction* (Louisville: Westminster John Knox, 2002), 6.

2. David Petersen points out that this use of "seer" for Hanani is "a noteworthy exception" to postexilic literature's consistent use of the term *nābî'* (prophet) for "intermediaries," his general word for all persons who fulfilled these functions ("Prophet, Prophecy," in vol. 4 of *The New Interpreter's Dictionary of the Bible* [ed. Katherine Doob Sakenfeld; Nashville: Abingdon, 2009], 623).

ability to sense knowledge unavailable to the common person who seeks God's insight and wisdom.

Another Hebrew term occurring with similar frequency is *ḥōzeh*, also translated as "seer" in several English versions. The limited frequency and lack of a well-developed literary context make it difficult to distinguish *ḥōzeh* from *rō'eh*, since both Hebrew roots can refer to physical sight and mental or spiritual perception. However, whereas the biblical record associates *rō'eh* almost exclusively with Samuel, both narratives and the canonical prophets apply the title *ḥōzeh* to different individuals: Gad (2 Sam. 24:11), Iddo (2 Chron. 9:29), Jehu or Hanani (19:2),[3] and Amos (Amos 7:12). A general reference in the Deuteronomistic History to "every seer" (2 Kings 17:13 [in parallel with the word "prophet"]) may include other persons beyond the known individuals above.

In a different vein from the above terms' focus on seeing, the title "man of God" (*'îš hā'ĕlōhîm*) is less specific but far more frequent than *rō'eh* and *ḥōzeh*. The Deuteronomistic History refers to major figures such as Moses (Deut. 33:1; Josh. 14:6), Samuel (1 Sam. 9:8), Elijah (1 Kings 17:18; 2 Kings 1:9–13), and Elisha (2 Kings 4:7 [+ 29x]) by the "man of God" title; there is also the lesser-known Shemaiah (1 Kings 12:22) and three unnamed figures (1 Sam. 2:27; 1 Kings 13:1; 20:28). Special attention may be given to the "man of God" from Judah (1 Kings 13), who indicts Jeroboam's cultic innovations by proclaiming divine judgment on Jeroboam as well as on the priests he appointed and the altar he built. His particular oracle about the priests and the altar (vv. 2–3) is set apart for special attention later in this story (vv. 31–32) and when it is fulfilled under King Josiah (2 Kings 23:15–18). Moreover, like Moses, Elijah, and Elisha, this anonymous man of God is associated with a miraculous event, the withering and healing of Jeroboam's hand (1 Kings 13:4–6). The multiple associations of persons called "man of God" with miracles, indictment of leaders, and predictive fulfillment reflect the variegated nature of at least this type of prophetic ministry.

Finally, among all of these terms, the term "prophet" itself (*nābî'*) has the greatest frequency and the widest range of canonical occurrences. These individuals are designated as "prophet" by God, a human character, or a biblical author: Abraham (Gen. 20:7), Aaron (Exod. 7:1), Miriam (Exod. 15:20), Moses (Deut. 18:15), Deborah (Judg. 4:4), an unnamed prophet (Judg. 6:8), Samuel (1 Sam. 3:20), Gad (1 Sam. 22:5), Nathan (2 Sam. 7:2; 1 Kings 1:22), Ahijah (1 Kings 11:29), an old prophet of Bethel (13:11), Jehu (16:7), one hundred prophets of the Lord (18:13), 450 prophets of Baal (18:22),

---

3. The Hebrew construct form is somewhat ambiguous: the NRSV and NJPS render the Hebrew phrase as "Jehu son of Hanani the seer," and the NIV as "Jehu the seer, the son of Hanani."

Elijah (19:16), an unnamed prophet (20:13), four hundred prophets in Ahab's court (22:6), Micaiah (22:8), the "companies of prophets" (lit., "sons of prophets") (2 Kings 2:3; 4:38; 6:1), Elisha (6:12), Jonah (14:25), Isaiah (19:2), and Huldah (22:14). We also have these canonical prophets: Jeremiah (1:5), Ezekiel (2:5), Hosea (9:8), Habakkuk (1:1), Haggai (1:1), and Zechariah (1:1). One could add Amos to this list in spite of his denial of a prophetic vocation (7:14), given the way he refers to his divine commission to "prophesy" (7:15).

It is not enough, of course, simply to list places where the prophetic title occurs, since its meaning must be understood in relation to its root verb, "to prophesy" (nābā'), which carries the primary sense of divine "calling" (passively), though human "calling" on divine beings (actively) has also been proposed.[4] When the approximately one hundred occurrences of the verb are considered, we realize that biblical authors often described prophetic activity in unflattering terms. To be sure, the list in the previous paragraph suggests that the title was employed for persons who served the cause of some god other than the Lord of Israel, but how they conduct their prophetic activity is also judged poorly. Moses warns the people not to "heed the words of those prophets" who entice Israel to worship other gods (Deut. 13:2–3), and later he clarifies that "prophets" prove themselves false when their predictions fail to happen (18:21–22). In the Historical Books the frenzied physical activity of the prophets of Baal—"limping," self-laceration, and loud cries to Baal—leaves a vivid impression on the reader (1 Kings 18:26–29) in contrast to Elijah's deliberate action and eloquent prayer (18:30–37). A few chapters later Micaiah ben Imlah mocks the disingenuous unanimity of Ahab's court prophets (22:6, 15), and King Jehoshaphat instinctively senses that the court prophets are not genuine prophets "of the LORD" (22:7). A final example is Jeremiah's word from the Lord, which groups certain false "prophets" with diviners, dreamers, soothsayers, and sorcerers (Jer. 27:9).

In consideration of the diverse contexts in which "seer," "man of God," and "prophet" are used, scholars have debated the existence of an overarching category that might correlate the biblical data. With an emphasis on the content of their speeches, Patrick Miller states, "One of the primary definitions of the prophetic role . . . is that of *messenger*. Both formally and conceptually, the prophetic oracle is a message, not simply from the deity but from the divine world, from the divine assembly where the decrees of God are set forth and

---

4. For an overview of the linguistic information, see Pieter A. Verhoef, "Prophecy," *NIDOTTE* 4:1067–78. For a careful defense of the active meaning, in light of ancient Near Eastern evidence, see Daniel E. Fleming, "The Etymological Origins of the Hebrew *nābî*': The One Who Invokes God," *CBQ* 55 (1993): 217–24.

transmitted."[5] In contrast to this opinion, John Greene claims that biblical authors did not, apart from isolated cases, employ "messenger" language to describe the prophets.[6] Given the different roles, experiences, and messages of the prophets, David Petersen suggests that "the one element common to all prophets" is that "they functioned as intermediaries between the human and the divine worlds. They could represent humans to God (Amos 7:2) or God to humans (Amos 5:4)."[7] While this may be true, it is difficult to argue that this concept is unique to prophets, since other officials in ancient Israel "mediated" the relationship between God and humans in governance (kings) or religious ceremonies (priests). On balance, therefore, the term "prophet" still seems to be the most useful category, insofar as it avoids confusion with other persons who delivered messages or represented God, and it has the advantage of being the eventual word of choice among biblical authors.[8] To be sure, there can be confusion here because the modern definition of prophecy tends to focus only on prediction, but the Septuagint, New Testament, and other Greek literature chose *prophētēs* "because it rendered an idea that was close enough to what they thought a *nābî'* was."[9]

Development of Prophetic Ministry in Narratives and Speeches

Having gained some awareness of the range of titles for prophetic individuals, we move on to the biblical presentation of prophets and prophecy. The biblical data could be organized in several ways, but one helpful approach is in terms of the developing portrait of prophecy from just before the monarchy (mid-eleventh century BCE) to the postexilic era (late fifth century BCE). A variety of historical, political, and socioreligious factors influenced prophets' relationships with society and its leaders, their organization or independence, their forms of speech and writing, and the main thrust of their message to Israel.

5. Patrick D. Miller, "The World and Message of the Prophets," in *Old Testament Interpretation: Past, Present, and Future; Essays in Honor of Gene M. Tucker* (ed. James Luther Mays, David L. Petersen, and Kent Harold Richards; Nashville: Abingdon, 1995), 101.

6. John T. Greene, *The Role of the Messenger and Message in the Ancient Near East* (BJS 169; Atlanta: Scholars Press, 1989), 260–65. For general background on the function of two particular ancient Near Eastern messengers, West Semitic *mal'āk* and Akkadian *mār šipri*, see Samuel A. Meier, *The Messenger in the Ancient Semitic World* (HSM 45; Atlanta: Scholars Press, 1988).

7. Petersen, *Prophetic Literature*, 7.

8. Martti Nissinen, "What Is Prophecy? An Ancient Near Eastern Perspective," in *Inspired Speech: Prophecy in the Ancient Near East: Essays in Honor of Herbert B. Huffmon* (ed. John Kaltner and Louis Stulman; JSOTSup 378; London: T&T Clark, 2004), 18–19.

9. Ibid., 19.

First, the development of prophecy correlates with the existence of monarchy in Israel. To be more precise, the phenomenon of prophecy saw its greatest activity and influence during the divided kingdoms, with gradual development up to that time and gradual decline afterward. Of course, prophetic activity existed long before Israel was ruled by kings, though we should not pour the full range of prophetic status and function into early canonical uses, as if Abraham, called *nābî'* in Genesis 20:7, acted like an Elijah or Isaiah. A more significant place to see the beginnings of prophetic activity is the first Old Testament verbal use of *nābā'*, in Numbers 11:25, when the spirit of God enabled elders standing near the tent of meeting to "prophesy." Of course, these "prophets" appear to have no particular message or function beyond their experience of the spirit, which probably is why Moses wished "that all the LORD's people were prophets" (Num. 11:29). There is, however, a long historical gap between this event and the rise of Samuel's leadership, with the "prophetess" Deborah (Judg. 4:4) and an unnamed prophet in the Gideon cycle (Judg. 6:8) being the exceptions. Indeed, "the word of the LORD was rare" during Eli's priesthood at Shiloh (1 Sam. 3:1), but Samuel, who will anoint and advise King Saul, becomes a "trustworthy prophet of the LORD" who lets "none of [Samuel's] words fall to the ground" (3:19–20).

The prophetic narratives and the speeches in the Prophetic Books highlight different ways in which prophets connect with kings and people. In the Deuteronomistic History prophetic activity gradually increases in the united monarchy, at first focused in Samuel and Nathan, but then continued with numerous individuals sent by God with messages for kings. However, the book of Kings mentions only Jonah (2 Kings 14:25) and Isaiah among the canonical prophets (2 Kings 18:13–20:19 //Isa. 36–39), instead introducing men such as Ahijah and Jehu, who have no official connection to King Jeroboam (1 Kings 11:29–39) or King Baasha (16:7), and large groups of prophets who appear to serve Ahab as yes-men (22:6). The Deuteronomistic writers also give a central place to the stories about Elijah and Elisha, thus making the prophetic presence and word the true authority during the divided monarchy.[10] Indeed, in literary terms, these two prophets form the centerpiece of the monarchic narrative: Solomon to Ahab (1 Kings 1–16); Elijah and Elisha during the Omride and Jehu dynasties (1 Kings 17–2 Kings 13); and the eventual downfall of Israel and Judah (2 Kings 14–25).[11] Elijah and Elisha have a multifaceted ministry, serving wealthy and poor families, members of the companies of prophets,

---

10. See James K. Mead, "Elijah," *DOTHB* 249–54; idem, "Elisha," *DOTHB* 254–58.
11. Robert L. Cohn, "The Literary Structure of Kings," in *The Book of Kings: Sources, Composition, Historiography, and Reception* (ed. Baruch Halpern and André Lemaire; VTSup 129; Leiden: Brill, 2010), 107–22.

and advising (or confronting) kings in times of war and revolution. Apart from the appearance of Isaiah and Huldah during the reigns of Hezekiah and Josiah, respectively, the historical narratives give the impression that there was not significant prophetic activity in the last century of the divided monarchy, mentioning prophets' work only in general terms (2 Kings 17:13).

For their part, the canonical Prophetic Books present what feels like another world, occasionally alluding to specific kings and historical circumstances, but more often than not presenting the prophets' oracles with little or no contextual information. Nevertheless, the final form of several Prophetic Books immediately calls attention to the Israelite or Judean kings during whose reigns the prophet worked (Isa. 1:1; Jer. 1:2; Ezek. 1:2; Hosea 1:1; Amos 1:1; Mic. 1:1; Zeph. 1:1; for non-Israelite monarchs, see Hag. 1:1; Zech. 1:1). Thus the biblical canon explicitly ties prophecy to the existence of the monarchy. Yet the content of the prophets' speeches reached far beyond the interests of kings. There are, of course, cases where a prophet confronts or counsels a king—Isaiah with Ahaz (Isa. 7) or Hezekiah (Isa. 36–39); Jeremiah with Jehoahaz (Jer. 22)—but these are notable exceptions that confirm the general impression of distance between prophets and kings. Rather, the prophets turn their sights on the many injustices committed by the wealthy leaders and on the rampant idolatry among the population. The content of these prophetic critiques will be discussed below, but suffice it to say that "princes" (Isa. 1:23), "kings," and officials (Jer. 1:18) are not far from the mind of the prophets.

Second, the development of prophecy is characterized by different types of prophetic roles or groups. Scholars often speak of three primary categories of biblical prophets. The first category includes those associated with the cultic life of Israel, as evidenced by Samuel's relationship with the tabernacle at Shiloh (1 Sam. 3:1–2, 21) and his knowledge of "the band of prophets" from a shrine near Gibeath-elohim (1 Sam. 10:5–13). A different kind of connection with the religious cult arises where some prophets are members of priestly families, such as Jeremiah (Jer. 1:1) and Ezekiel (Ezek. 1:3). A second category, which we have already noted, includes prophets supported by the royal court. Although the large group at Ahab's palace seems to be a mouthpiece for his policies and plans, someone like Nathan advised King David concerning the temple (2 Sam. 7) but also freely challenged David's behavior (2 Sam. 12). A third category of association is represented by Elisha's company of prophets, who possibly were his students (2 Kings 6:1) and may have participated in various forms of ministry to members of the group (4:38–44). These categories can be otherwise expressed, such as Isaiah's reference to his "disciples" (Isa. 8:16).

Third, the development of prophecy witnessed increasing frustration over the covenant failure of leaders and people. Not only was the monarchy the occasion for the greatest incidence of prophecy, but also it was the setting wherein Israel and Judah lost their covenant moorings. The canonical prophets gave their greatest attention to two topics, and most of their speeches gravitate to one or both of these concerns: Israel's unfaithfulness to the God of the covenant (especially idolatry) and Israel's disobedience to the social expectations of the covenant (especially injustice). One reads only a few verses in the text of Isaiah before encountering, "I reared children and brought them up, but they have rebelled against me. . . . Ah, sinful nation, people laden with iniquity, offspring who do evil, children who deal corruptly, who have forsaken the LORD" (Isa. 1:2b, 4a). This opening set of oracles continues with admonitions about justice: "Learn to do good; seek justice, rescue the oppressed, defend the orphan, plead for the widow" (1:17). The book of Jeremiah has similar concerns as it begins: "I will utter my judgments against them, for all their wickedness in forsaking me; they have made offerings to other gods, and worshiped the works of their own hands" (Jer. 1:16). Of course, these books do not contain only judgment speeches: strains of hope and comfort are heard throughout. But the good news of salvation that they offer presupposes either immediate repentance or impending judgment: "Seek the LORD and live, or he will break out against the house of Joseph like fire, and it will devour Bethel, with no one to quench it" (Amos 5:6). As a general pattern, the canonical prophets tend to cluster words of hope and salvation toward the end of their books. For example, Ezekiel's messages of hope (chaps. 33–48) clearly are dated after the fall of Jerusalem in 586 BCE (33:21).[12]

Fourth, the development of prophecy is characterized by a gradual move from basically independent, spoken oracles to well-developed literary forms. Both the Historical Books and the canonical prophets identify prophetic speech with the introductory formula "Thus says the LORD" (*kōh-'āmar yhwh*), carrying through from the earliest expressions with Joshua (Josh. 24:2), to Elijah (2 Kings 1:6) and Elisha (2 Kings 3:16), up to and including almost all the canonical prophets. What surely began with the spoken word is sooner or later written down for posterity's sake (Isa. 8:1, 16; Jer. 36:2; 45:1). On a larger scale, the content of the canonical prophets reveals oral-to-literary progression. Isaiah's collected oracles are often difficult to connect to their historical or even surrounding literary context; the same is true of other eighth-century prophets: Hosea, Amos, and Micah. A century later, Jeremiah's prophecies are increasingly contextualized, having more narrative and public biography

12. I have used classic designations for types of oracles, such as those in Claus Westermann's *Basic Forms of Prophetic Speech* (trans. Hugh Clayton White; Philadelphia: Westminster, 1967). One can also identify greater diversity beyond oracles of "judgment" and "salvation" (Petersen, "Prophet, Prophecy," 638–41).

than Isaiah and his older contemporaries. Later still is Ezekiel's exilic mode of communication, recording his visionary experiences and symbolic acts in narrative form, anchored to their context with a formulaic reference to the date. Haggai's postexilic messages are likewise written prosaically and dated to the reign of Darius I (Hag. 1:1; 2:1, 10). There are, of course, exceptions to this scheme, such as the exilic oracles of Second Isaiah, Malachi's disputations, or the apocalyptic portions of Zechariah 1–6. As for the noncanonical prophets, there were clearly oral traditions about Elisha, as evidenced by Gehazi's recollections to the king (2 Kings 8:4–5) and Jehoshaphat's knowledge of Elisha as a true prophet of the Lord (3:12). While there is much debate over the literary process (e.g., was there ever an independent "prophetic record"?), at some point these oral forms were committed to writing and placed within the Historical Books.[13]

Summary

The biblical evidence for prophecy has introduced us to dozens of individuals, most of whom were men, though a few prominent women also served as prophets. Although the canonical Prophetic Books may give the impression that prophecy was dominated by a few great individuals, we know that there were many prophets in various types of formal and informal associations. Throughout the monarchical era, prophets were known for their mediation of the divine word, but it is safe to say that their role shifted from a primary focus on advising or confronting kings to one that addressed a wider audience with messages about idolatry and injustice. Finally, even though most prophetic oracles spoke God's judgment on Israel, Judah, and the nations, the Prophetic Books generally move toward oracles of hope and salvation.

Israelite Prophets in the Ancient Near Eastern Context

This essay contends that the aforementioned data from the Hebrew Bible present a reasonable portrait of prophecy in part because the ancient Near Eastern context contains evidence of similar phenomena. Not only do we learn of persons who served prophetic functions, but also the texts themselves contain messages that addressed royalty and often related to the religious cultus. Coming alongside these data is a great deal of information about other religious practices (e.g., magic, divination) traditionally related to prophecy.

---

13. See Antony Campbell, *Unfolding the Deuteronomistic History: Origins, Upgrades, Present Text* (Minneapolis: Fortress, 2000).

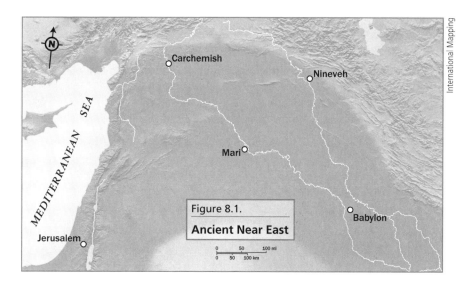

Figure 8.1.

Ancient Near East

Ancient Near Eastern Prophetic Texts

Four groups of sources shed light on prophetic experience in the ancient Near East: Mari letters, Neo-Assyrian prophecies, West Semitic texts, and miscellaneous sources.

THE MARI LETTERS

Following the excavation of the royal archive at Mari (Tell Ḥāriri on the upper Euphrates River) in the 1930s, scholars published hundreds of cuneiform tablets in stages over several decades.[14] There are about fifty letters that contain prophetic texts, most of which concern Zimri-Lim, the king of Mari (ca. 1774–1760).[15] The diverse data may be organized by prophetic titles, their setting and phenomena, and the content of their messages.

Almost all the prophetic Mari letters are sent from, or in reference to, persons primarily known by one of two titles. The most common prophetic

14. For background information on Mari, see Jean-Claude Margueron, "Mari (Archaeology)," *ABD* 4:525–29; Jean-Marie Durand, "Mari (Texts)," *ABD* 4:529–36. For a helpful review of scholarly work in the 1980s and 1990s, see André Lemaire, "Traditions amorrites et Bible: Le prophétisme," *RA* 93 (1999): 49–56.

15. Here all citations of ancient Near Eastern texts are from Martti Nissinen, Choon-Leong Seow, and Robert K. Ritner, *Prophets and Prophecy in the Ancient Near East* (ed. Peter Machinist; SBLWAW 12; Atlanta: Society of Biblical Literature, 2003). For other translations of the Mari letters, see J. J. M. Roberts, *The Bible and the Ancient Near East: Collected Essays* (Winona Lake, IN: Eisenbrauns, 2002), 157–253; Wolfgang Heimpel, *Letters to the King of Mari: A New Translation, with Historical Introduction, Notes, and Commentary* (MC 12; Winona Lake, IN: Eisenbrauns, 2003).

Prophecies in the Mari Letters (ARM 26 213)

The prophecies in the Mari letters were primarily addressed to Zimri-Lim, an eighteenth-century-BCE king of Mari. The following excerpt (ARM 26 213) is representative of the basic literary and structural elements described in this chapter. Some key concepts are the connection of the prophetic experience to the temple, the mention of phenomena, the god's interest in threats to the king, and the attestation of the prophecy with symbols.

> A letter from Šibtu to Zimri-Lim concerning an internal threat to his throne:
> Spe[ak] to my lord: Thus Šibtu, your servant:
> The pala[ce] is well.
> In the temple of Annunitum, three days ago, Šelebum went into [a] trance (immaḫḫu) and said:
> > "Thus says Annunitum: Zimri-Lim, you will be tested in a revolt! Protect yourself! Let your most favored servants whom you love surround you, and make them stay there to protect you! Do not go around on your own! As regards the people who would tes[t you]: those pe[ople] I deli[ver up] into your hands."
> Now I am sending the hai[r and the fringe of the garment] of the assi[nnu] to [my lord].

title at Mari was *muḫḫum* (fem. *muḫḫutum*), from the Akkadian root meaning "to become ecstatic." The ecstatic nature of their behavior is not actually described in the letters, though in one case there is a symbolic act of eating a lamb before delivering the prophecy (ARM 26 206).[16] The second title, the *āpilum* (fem. *āpiltum*), a term meaning "one who answers," was so named apparently because such a person gave answers to inquirers. The proper name of an *āpilum* is often given, as are the deities with whom they were associated (e.g., Adad, Dagan, Šamaš, Marduk) or the temples where they spoke oracles. Three other titles (*assinnu, qammatum, nabû*) appear only a few times in total. There are no particular identifying characteristics for *assinnu* and *qammatum*, so their precise meaning is debated, but the occurrence *nabi ša* (plural form of *nabû*) obviously sparked interest among scholars who previously found no evidence of that prophetic title outside of the Hebrew Bible.[17] In the Mari letter these prophets are Hanaeans (seminomadic tribesmen) who are asked

16. The Mari letters are published in many collections, and Nissinen, Seow, and Ritner (*Prophets and Prophecy*) use the traditional designation "ARM," for *Archives Royales de Mari* (ed. Georges Dossin; Paris: Librairie orientaliste Paul Geuthner, 1978). A few Mari letters cited below are identified with their registration numbers preceded by the letters "A" and "M."

17. In addition to the study cited above (Fleming, "Etymological Origins"), see Daniel E. Fleming, "*NĀBÛ* and *MUNABBIĀTU*: Two New Syrian Religious Personnel," *JAOS* 113 (1993): 175–83. In response to Fleming's work, John Huehnergard raises questions about the function

to "deliver an oracle for the well-being of [Zimri-Lim]" (ARM 26 216:8–9). The final category refers to prophets not given any title and who thus may have been private persons rather than professional prophets.

The setting and phenomena are connected, insofar as the letters generally report the occasion out of which the revelatory message arose and the means by which it was delivered. At Mari many revelations took place in temple settings, often indicated by phrases such as "In the temple of Ḫišamitum, a [pr] ophet called Iṣi-aḫu arose and said . . ." (ARM 26 195:5). If a dream occurs outside the temple precincts, it is simply reported as being told to the letter writer by the recipient of revelation: "Iddin-ili, the priest of Itur-Mer has had a dream. He says . . ." (ARM 26 238:4). Still other dream texts indicate no context (e.g., ARM 26 235), and for all of these reports there is no extended information about what induced the dream itself. Prophets generally just report the revelation that they received, though in two cases a servant named "Shibtu" makes an inquiry of a prophet and then reports the results to Zimri-Lim (ARM 26 207; 26 212).

An extremely important issue at Mari was the authentication of prophecy. Sometimes this is implicit in the letter, such as when the prophet repeats the dream to shift responsibility to the letter writer (ARM 26 235). In other cases, one prophet may corroborate the message of another (A 1121:46–48), or a prophet may report a dream only after experiencing it a second time on the next day: "This is what he saw: 'Thus sa[ys God]: You [pl.] may not bu[ild] this ruined house again! . . .' On the da[y] he had this dream, he did not te[ll] anybody. The next day, he had the same dream again" (ARM 26 234:1', 7'). In yet another case, the writer herself made a second inquiry to confirm the report (ARM 26 212:10'). More often, however, at the close of a letter an author will state something like, "Now I have sent a lock of his head and his garment hem to my lord" (ARM 26 215:22). These tokens of authenticity might not be necessary if the letter writer deems the prophet already trustworthy (ARM 26 233:50), but the king might also have other types of divination performed as confirmation (A 1121:13). William Moran has suggested that all of these symbols of confirmation seem "calculated to keep both the professionals and the laity from airing their inspirations too casually and to make them strictly accountable for giving them public expression."[18]

In regard to the content of their messages, the extant letters present a basic structure in which the prophetic messages were couched, with expected

---

of prophetic personnel at Emar, but his argument does not effectively refute Fleming's linguistic analysis ("On the Etymology and Meaning of Hebrew NĀBÎ'," ErIsr 26 [1999]: 88*–93*).

18. William L. Moran, "New Evidence from Mari on the History of Prophecy," *Bib* 50 (1969): 25.

variations and exceptions: (1) designation of the subject by profession or name; (2) the place of the prophecy; (3) a verb indicating that the prophet "arose" to speak; (4) a formulaic expression to introduce direction quotations, such as "Speak to my Lord: Thus [prophet's name] your servant"; and (5) the quotation itself.[19] The content of the messages covers two broad areas: cultic concerns and political/military matters. Concern for temples and cultic activity arises when a deity such as Dagan asks why Zimri-Lim has not sent messengers to his temple, promising that victory will come if he were to do so (ARM 26 233:23–39). The king may be asked to provide certain offerings: "Gather all the consecrated portion and [let it] be taken to the temple of Adad [in] Aleppo" (ARM 26 194:16–17 [see ARM 26 221:7–18]). In a graphic description the king hears how seriously the Temple of Annunitum has been neglected, such that the writer is living in excrement and urine (ARM 26 198:13'–14'). The king's political and military policies are not completely separated from the cultic concerns above, but the two areas share a complex interrelationship. A letter from Nur-Sîn reminds Zimri-Lim that Adad "restored [the king] to his ancestral throne," and if the king offers his estate to Adad, the deity promises to "give him throne upon throne, house upon house, territory upon territory, city upon city. I shall give him the land from the rising of the sun to its setting" (A 1121:13–28). The servant Šibtu relates a prophecy from an *assinnu* about the impending threat of Babylon's ruler, but Zimri-Lim is assured, "My lord will see what God will do to this man: You will capture him and stand over him. His days are running short, he will not live long" (ARM 26 212:1'–9'). Sometimes the god directly addresses another nation with judgment: "Babylon, what are you constantly doing? I will gather you into a net and. . . . The dwellings of the seven accomplices and all their wealth I give in the hand of Zimri-L[im]" (ARM 26 209:6–14).

NEO-ASSYRIAN PROPHECIES

The second-largest set of prophetic texts from the ancient Near East was discovered during the mid-nineteenth century in the royal archives of Nineveh. The thousands of cuneiform tablets that were found contain treaties, royal records, literary texts, divination and astrology, and prophetic texts. Eleven tablets of oracles were published by Simo Parpola in 1997 and contain records of the prophecies themselves as well as collections of rewritten and edited oracles, a phenomenon that makes this corpus different from that of Mari. There are twenty-nine oracular texts and fragments, mostly addressed by the goddess Ištar of Arbela to Esarhaddon (681–669 BCE), and a few to his son

19. Ibid.

and successor, Assurbanipal (668–627).[20] In light of the much smaller corpus, we may focus our attention on the content of the prophecies.[21]

The primary impression we get from the Neo-Assyrian prophecies is the divine focus on the stability of the king's throne, especially from the threat of domestic and foreign enemies. Prophets called *raggimu* (fem. *raggintu*) delivered oracles in the voice of the goddess herself, using language such as "I am Ištar of Arbela" or "I am the Lady of Arbela."[22] Many of the messages begin with the words "Fear not," before going on to address the potential cause of fear, namely, the king's enemies: "I am the great Lady, I am Ištar of Arbela who throws your enemies before your feet. . . . I will flay your enemies and deliver them up to you. I am Ištar of Arbela, I go before you and behind you" (SAA 9 1.1.11′–24′). Usually the "enemy" (sg. or pl.) is nondescript, but in a few messages the goddess specifies places such as the Elamite or Mannean kingdoms (SAA 9 2.4.12′–15′), or she implies that the enemy is internal: "These traitors conspired against you" (SAA 9 3.3:10). With enemies vanquished, Ištar assures Esarhaddon of the everlasting nature of his throne: "I will give endle[ss] days and everlasti[ng] years to Esarhaddon, my king" (SAA 9 1.6.11′–14′).

A second major concern, underlying the first, is the relationship of the goddess to the king. Ištar's interest in the king borders on intimacy and affection. Seeing herself as "yo[ur] great midwife . . . [and] excellent wet nurse," she confesses, "[I] keep thinking of [you], I have loved yo[u] great[ly]! I hold you by yo[ur] curl in the great heavens" (SAA 9 1.6.15′–18′, 22′–28′). In other oracles the goddesses "incessantly bestow their love [upon] Assurbanipal" (SAA 9 9.4–5); "I rejoice over Esarhaddon, my king! Arbela rejoices!" (SAA 9 1.3.11′–12′). She also seems to fulfill a role of representing the other gods to the king and vice versa: "Sixty Great Gods are still standing around you; they have girded your loins" (SAA 9 1.4.25′–26′). Her commitment to Esarhaddon began while he was still prince by protecting him in the "Palace of Succession" (SAA 9 1.2.33′). An "oracle of peace" speaks about the "covenant tablet" brought

20. For greater detail, see the introduction to "Nineveh Oracles" in Nissinen, Seow, and Ritner, *Prophets and Prophecy*, 97–101; Karel van der Toorn, "Mesopotamian Prophecy between Immanence and Transcendence: A Comparison of Old Babylonian and Neo-Assyrian Prophecy," in *Prophecy in Its Ancient Near Eastern Context: Mesopotamian, Biblical, and Arabian Perspectives* (ed. Martti Nissinen; SBLSymS 13; Atlanta: Society of Biblical Literature, 2000), 71–87.

21. The edition on which Nissinen depends is Simo Parpola, *Assyrian Prophecies* (SAA 9; Helsinki: Neo-Assyrian Text Corpus Project, University of Helsinki, 1997).

22. The prophetic title derives from "the verb *ragāmu*, 'to shout, to proclaim'" (Nissinen, Seow, and Ritner, *Prophets and Prophecy*, 7).

Ištar and Esarhaddon

The theme of protecting the king from enemies dominates the Neo-Assyrian prophecies. A representative selection highlights the close relationship the goddess Ištar has with Esarhaddon (681–669 BCE). She reassures him of her commitment and protection, so that he need not fear any enemies.

> [I am the Lady of Arb]ela! [Esarhaddon], whose bosom [Ištar] of Arbela has filled with favor: You could rely on the previous word I spoke to you, couldn't you? Now you can rely upon the later words, too!
>
> Praise me! When the daylight declines, let torches flare! Praise me before them! Fear and trembling I will banish [fr]om my palace. You shall eat safe food; you shall drink safe water; you shall live in safety in your palace. Even your son and grandson will exercise kingship in the lap of Ninurta.
>
> By the mouth of La-dagil-ili, a man from Arbela. (SAA 9 1.10)

to the palace and read to the king (SAA 9 3.3.26–32), which Martti Nissinen calls "the document of the covenant between the supreme god and the king."[23]

Third, the goddess shows concern for the welfare of the religious cult in a few oracles, sometimes merely alluding to the need for offerings (SAA 9 2.3.21'–27'). But one oracle makes the temple a major focus, when Ištar chides Esarhaddon for apparently neglecting to bring offerings: "What have [yo]u, in turn, given to me? The [fo]od for the banquet is no[t there], as if there were no temple at all! My food is wi[thhe]ld from me, my drink is with[he]ld from me!" (SAA 9 3.5.25–30).

WEST SEMITIC TEXTS

A much smaller corpus of extrabiblical prophecy comes from Syria-Palestine, with a selection of fragmentary texts that nonetheless witness to the activities of prophets.[24] The most important of these is inscribed on a now broken plaster inscription dated to the eighth century BCE and discovered at Deir ʿAllā in modern-day Jordan. Scholars have attempted to reconstruct the fragments, grouping them in two "combinations" that relate a prophecy of Balaam, well known from the biblical account in Numbers 22–24. In spite of the significant interpretive challenges posed especially by Combination II, the inscription provides some important insights for our topic. First, Balaam is introduced in Combination I as a "seer of the gods" (line 1: ḥzh ʾlhn), corroborating the

23. Ibid., 121, note j.

24. For introduction, transliteration, and translation of these texts, see Choon-Leong Seow, "West Semitic Inscriptions," in Nissinen, Seow, and Ritner, *Prophets and Prophecy*, 201–18.

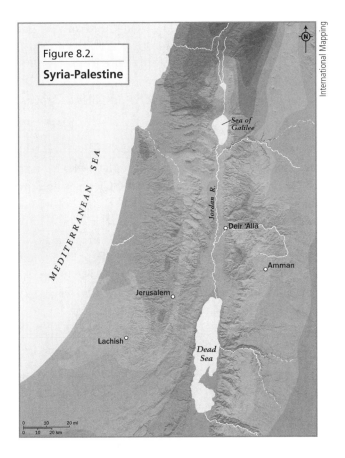

Figure 8.2.

Syria-Palestine

term (*ḥōzeh*) that we saw in several biblical texts. Second, a divine "assembly" (line 6: *mw'd* = Heb. *mô'ēd*) decrees judgment on the earth, evoking not only biblical texts of cosmic destruction but also the role of the divine assembly in confirming the authenticity of prophets (1 Kings 22:19–23; Jer. 23:22). Third, the "vision" recounted in Combination II (line 16), though fragmented, refers to the "king" (lines 15, 18: *mlk*) apparently as an object of punishment.

Five other texts mention the existence of prophets, with brief allusions to their work or messages. An Ammonite inscription from the ninth century BCE appears to be a partial oracle of the god Milcom, warning of divine punishment on the king's enemies. The Zakkur Stela recounts an eighth-century-BCE military victory over Aram that was connected with a divine assurance: "Baalshamay[n] answered me, [and] Baalshamayn [spoke] to me [thr]ough seers and through visionaries, [and] Baalshamayn [said], 'F[e]ar not, for I have made [you] king, [and I who will st]and with [you], and I will deliver you from all [these kings . . .]'" (lines 11–14). Finally, three of the famous Lachish ostraca (3, 6, 16) are letters written just before the destruction of Jerusalem in 586 BCE and contain reference to "the prophet" (*hnb'* = *hannabî*).[25] According to Choon-Leong Seow, "Apart from these six texts, there are no other West Semitic inscriptions that indisputably concern prophets and their activities."[26]

MISCELLANEOUS SOURCES

We need note only briefly other materials that relate to prophetic activity, though they do not necessarily identify the prophets who were involved with the messages. A number of second-millennium-BCE omen texts from Babylon report anomalies in nature, especially unusual births, to predict particular outcomes for a king's reign or a nation's economic prosperity.[27] Two oracles of the goddess Kititum offer guidance and direction to King Ibalpiel of Eshnunna, a contemporary of Zimri-Lim from a rival city-state.[28] Although Egyptian culture does not contribute literary evidence to our discussion, scholars mention the Report of Wenamun, a priest from Thebes who comes to Egypt in the eleventh century, influenced in part by an oracle from an ecstatic at Byblos.[29]

Ancient Near Eastern Prophecy and Contextual Considerations

Before moving on to the important assessment of issues in the historiography of the prophets, it is appropriate to consider the ancient Near Eastern evidence within its own context because we cannot simply lump together prophecy at eighteenth-century Mari with that of seventh-century Nineveh. Karel van der Toorn calls attention to four contrasting areas (purpose of written records, prophetic persons, cultic contexts, and depiction of the gods) between these two major collections, with the overarching difference being "transcendence." He states, "In the Old Babylonian conception, the gods inhabit this world. . . . By Neo-Assyrian times, the gods have their proper habitat in heaven."[30] Given the vast time span between these collections, therefore, van der Toorn cautions that we should be as sensitive to their differences as we are to their commonalities.[31] Along these lines, I call attention to three considerations.

25. The word "prophet" does not appear on ostracon 6 but is conjectured to complete line 5, though some scholars have suggested the word could be "official[s]" (ibid., 217, note b).

26. Ibid., 201.

27. See Nissinen, Seow, and Ritner, *Prophets and Prophecy*, 189–92.

28. See ibid., 93–95.

29. See Robert K. Ritner, "Report of Wenamon," in Nissinen, Seow, and Ritner, *Prophets and Prophecy*, 219–20.

30. Van der Toorn, "Mesopotamian Prophecy," 86.

31. Ibid., 87.

First, there is the broad phenomenological question of divination and sha-manism, a topic that will remain important when comparing Israelite prophecy to its ancient Near Eastern counterparts. Some scholars have argued that all prophetic phenomena be understood in light of more comprehensive catego-ries. It is true that the Mari letters refer to the king's use of methods such as extispicy (the study of anomalies in animal organs, especially livers) to verify a prophetic word. But the original prophetic oracles came through dreams and visions, not divination. A similar challenge exists when applying the concept of shamanism to the Mesopotamian literature. Although differing greatly across cultures, shamanism is about establishing "means of contact with the supernatu-ral world by the ecstatic experience of a professional and inspired intermediary, the shaman."[32] Using the methods of cultural anthropology, Lester Grabbe has argued that the ancient Mesopotamian prophets were "spirit mediums rather than shamans in the classic sense," by which he means that most of the Mari and Assyrian prophets involuntarily received their messages, whereas "the main characteristic of the shaman is that he or she is a master of the spirits."[33] All of this is to say that even outside of biblical literature we should not lose the distinctive aspects of prophecy in an effort to place it under the broadest pos-sible categories. The fact is that ancient Near Eastern prophecy had its own features that were not, strictly speaking, the same as traditional shamanism.

Second, there is the sociological question of prophets' relationships to royal authority. It should come as no surprise that, given their provenance in royal archives, almost all of the prophecies at Mari and Nineveh relate to kings. It is entirely possible that prophets from both locations and time periods com-municated oracles to private citizens, but these would not make their way into official correspondence. Mari texts include administrative lists of clothing, animals, silver, and other products given to prophets, in some cases explaining that the gifts are for delivery of oracles or other services (ARM 25 142:12–15; M 11436:1–6). This scant evidence is more than we have from Neo-Assyrian texts, but in any case we cannot simply assume that the royal subject matter of the oracles and letters means that these prophets completely depended on the king for their livelihood. Moreover, the fact that the Mari prophets oc-casionally challenged the king indicates that they were not kept on retainers merely to tell the king what he wanted to hear.

Third, there is the matter of literary history. The extrabiblical sources did not undergo the same processes of redaction and canonization that we associate

---

32. Åke Hultkrantz, quoted in Lester Grabbe, "Ancient Near Eastern Prophecy from an Anthropological Perspective," in Nissinen, "What Is Prophecy?," 17.
33. Ibid., 18.

with the biblical prophets, but the Neo-Assyrian prophecies reveal some re-writing and editing, whereas the Mari letters do not. Nissinen describes the two kinds of tablets used for prophecies: (1) horizontal tablets containing individual oracles as "immediate records of a prophetic performance," few of which make their way into the archives; and (2) larger, vertical tablets on which several prophecies were arranged. "In this phase, not only editorial selection and stylization of the oracles takes place, but prophecy is [also] reused in a new situation and finally becomes a part of written tradition transcending specific historical situations and retaining its relevance in changing circumstances."[34]

Major Issues in the Study of Israelite Prophets and Prophecy

This look at biblical and ancient Near Eastern prophecy leads to an assessment of the data in terms of several compelling challenges. We may isolate three major areas, acknowledging that they form intersecting lines that complicate the portrait of prophecy in the wider biblical world: (1) prophetic phenomena and experience in its social context, (2) cross-cultural prophetic influence in the ancient Near East, and (3) prophecy in its literary and theological development. Since my goal has been to ask whether there is reliable historical information about prophets and their work, I will make that the primary focus of discussion.

The Challenge of the Prophetic Phenomena in Its Social Context

Scholars continue to debate two aspects of prophetic phenomena: the nature of the experience itself—how prophets received and communicated their oracles—and the social contexts that informed and shaped the prophetic experience.

The Bible primarily depicts prophetic phenomena as receiving visions and oracles that formed the basis for what prophets spoke and wrote to God's people. Ancient Near Eastern prophetic texts reveal striking affinities with the dominant biblical portrait. In spite of the differences in time and location (see below on cross-cultural influence), there certainly is enough similarity to suggest that the Bible's portrait of prophetic phenomena is historically reasonable. Some of the more important affinities include the following.

First, there is the association of prophecy with ecstatic experience. In 1 Samuel 10 ecstatic modes of prophesying are described, and the book of Ezekiel relates several intense visionary experiences (e.g., 1:4–28; 8:2–11:24). Although

---

34. Nissinen, "Nineveh Oracles," 97–98.

the Bible does not emphasize ecstasy as the major mode of prophecy, it does offer a witness that such things did occur. The *muḥḥum* prophets of Mari were so named apparently because of their ecstatic behavior, even though the texts offer little in the way of specifics. Second, there is the communication of divine messages. Both major collections of Mesopotamian prophecy record messages from gods to people, sometimes laying stress on the details of the report (Mari) or on the oracle itself as divine speech (Nineveh). Likewise, the Bible indicates that prophets spoke on behalf of God to the people, even though there is variation in the way such oracles are presented in the canonical form of biblical books. Third, there is the existence of some common prophetic titles. The Mari letters focus mainly on *āpilum* and *muḥḥum* prophets, but they attest the Semitic root, *nb'*, which was the Bible's primary title. Closer to the Israelite context was the root *ḥzh*, which appears at Deir ʿAllā and in the biblical presentation of "seers." For all three of these affinities, the differences and distinctive emphases are significant, but the common phenomena suggest historical reliability of the biblical presentation.

Recently, however, some scholars have questioned the Bible's sharp divide between the practices of divination and prophecy. Frederick Cryer suggests that as part of the ancient Near East, Israel was a "magic society."[35] He sees the concept of the Urim and Thummim (Exod. 28:30) as a "late catch-all invention designed to symbolize the entire practice of cultic divination" and regards the casting of lots in Joshua 7 and 1 Samuel 10 as two cases where "juridical divination is wedded to extended sequences of enquiries."[36] "The Deuteronomistic and Priestly strictures against certain forms of divination," Cryer argues, are presented not as "a blanket prohibition of the practice of divination, but as a means of restricting the practice to those who were 'entitled' to employ it."[37] Ann Jeffers concurs with this basic argument, claiming that in spite of the condemnation of magicians, diviners, and mediums in Deuteronomy 18:9–13, the reality was far more complex; the categories of prophecy and divination cannot be sharply distinguished.[38] In a similar vein, Anne Marie Kitz states, "The Hebrew Bible may not necessarily dismiss the efficacy of divination per se, but rather any human attempt, unaided by Yahweh alone, to interpret the implications of divine activity."[39] The biblical

---

35. Frederick H. Cryer, *Divination in Ancient Israel and Its Near Eastern Environment: A Socio-Historical Investigation* (JSOTSup 142; Sheffield: JSOT Press, 1994), 324.

36. Ibid.

37. Ibid, 327.

38. Ann Jeffers, *Magic and Divination in Ancient Palestine and Syria* (SHCANE 8; Leiden: Brill, 1996), 1.

39. Anne Marie Kitz, "Prophecy as Divination," *CBQ* 65 (2003): 24.

and extrabiblical prophetic texts, however, actually contain little attestation of magical activity. Whatever may be the semantic range of terms for divination, when prophecy is actually recorded at places such as Mari, Nineveh, and Israel, the focus is on the spoken and written word rather than on prophetic technique. This focus on the orality of the message may explain the biblical authors' reticence to go behind the oracles. The Bible's matter-of-fact references to divination show that there was no attempt to "cover up" divination, while its official condemnation of the practice implies that there was a major difference between prophecy and divination in the minds of biblical authors.

With regard specifically to the social contexts of the prophetic phenomena, we saw how biblical prophetic ministry developed over the course of Old Testament history, with prophets (individually and in groups) working within the royal court. Here too the affinities with ancient Near Eastern sources are unmistakable, especially in terms of connections with kingship at Mari and Nineveh, though their precise social arrangements are unknown. J. J. M. Roberts wisely points out that "the prophetic word was only one element in the mix that resulted in particular royal decisions," with counselors, diplomats, and military advisers playing major roles; at Mari and in Israel, "the prophetic word often conflicted inconveniently with the other determining factors in royal policies."[40] For their part, biblical prophets gradually took on a greater role as covenant intermediaries, condemning Israelite society for its idolatry and injustice while also promising restoration after judgment. Although social and religious issues are present in the other cultures, the nature of these covenant-based critiques is quite distinctive.

Robert Wilson's classic study of the social location of biblical prophecy called attention to its frequent "peripheral" role; that is, some of the prophets come from outside the centers of power.[41] However, Petersen argues that because of their typically urban setting and connections with the monarchy, "there is considerable evidence for thinking that the prophets were not impoverished or members of a lower class. Instead, they articulate values that involve concern for those who might be oppressed by powerful groups or structures in Israelite and Judahite society."[42] In all of this, we must keep in mind that our major source of data is the biblical record itself, such that any historical

---

40. J. J. M. Roberts, "Prophets and Kings: A New Look at the Royal Persecution of Prophets against Its Near Eastern Background," in *A God So Near: Essays on Old Testament Theology in Honor of Patrick D. Miller* (ed. Brent A. Strawn and Nancy R. Bowen; Winona Lake, IN: Eisenbrauns, 2003), 346.

41. Robert R. Wilson, *Prophecy and Society in Ancient Israel* (Philadelphia: Fortress, 1980).

42. Petersen, *Prophetic Literature*, 13.

reconstruction of the social setting will be dependent on what models and methods are used to interpret the biblical prophets.

The Question of Cross-Cultural Prophetic Influence

The discovery and investigation of ancient Near Eastern parallels to biblical literature eventually resulted in the scholarly use of anthropology and cross-cultural research to highlight the continuity and similarity between all ancient Near Eastern religious experiences.[43] What, then, are we to make of the nature of the connection between Israelite prophecy and its ancient Near Eastern counterparts?

I have argued that common prophetic phenomena suggest the historical plausibility of the Bible's basic presentation of prophets, their behavior, and their message. But this is not the same as drawing lines of direct historical causation or even indirect cultural influence. While some of the early publications comparing the Mari letters to biblical prophecy hinted at possible literary influence, the consensus for the past twenty years has been to think more in terms of analogous collections. Given what he calls the "temporal and geographical gap between the Mari texts and early Israel," Herbert Huffmon maintains that "it clearly is not a matter of direct continuity"; instead, he sees a "phenomenological background for biblical prophecy, both in cultic and non-cultic forms."[44] That being said, there are striking similarities in the way Neo-Assyrian prophets and Second Isaiah tell people to "fear not" because there will be divine intervention to bring about a change in circumstances. Indeed, Nissinen argues that these phrases in the Assyrian and Israelite collections are "historically, ideologically, and institutionally related."[45] But even if at this point we cannot demonstrate that Israelite prophets knew these other sources and/or consciously drew on them, the historical question is, rather, how the reasonableness of the ancient Israelite portrait of prophecy contributes to an accurate reconstruction of Israel's history. Thus, in spite of the millennium between Mari and the earliest biblical prophets, the common phenomena at least suggest the reasonable likelihood of the biblical presentation.

43. See Thomas Overholt, *Channels of Prophecy: The Social Dynamics of Prophetic Activity* (Minneapolis: Fortress, 1989); idem, *Prophecy in Cross-Cultural Perspective: A Sourcebook for Biblical Researchers* (SBLSBS 17; Atlanta: Scholars Press, 1986).

44. Herbert B. Huffmon, "The Expansion of Prophecy in the Mari Archives: New Texts, New Readings, New Information," in *Prophecy and Prophets: The Diversity of Contemporary Issues in Scholarship* (ed. Yehoshua Gitay; SBLSS; Atlanta: Scholars Press, 1997), 17.

45. Martti Nissinen, "Fear Not: A Study on an Ancient Near Eastern Phrase," in *The Changing Face of Form Criticism for the Twenty-First Century* (ed. Marvin A. Sweeney and Ehud Ben Zvi; Grand Rapids: Eerdmans, 2003), 160.

The Challenge of Prophecy in Its Literary and Theological Development

The historical issues that I have been exploring are not, of course, completely separable from those of a literary and theological nature. As literature, the prophetic narratives and canonical books are subject to the same critical methods that scholars have applied to other parts of the Bible. Thus a major challenge to a thesis of historical probability is the charge that prophetic literature derives not from a time close to the prophets but rather from much later in Israel's history. Ehud Ben Zvi and Diana Edelman edited a volume titled *The Production of Prophecy: Constructing Prophecy and Prophets in Yehud* (2009), which proposes just such an idea. In her essay there, Edelman contends that the Prophetic Books "are the constructions of the past by Persian-era literati in which the justice of Yahweh was communicated by a small faithful, prophetic minority, justifying Yahweh's destruction of Jerusalem and its polity for great sins committed."[46] The charge that some or much of the Old Testament is an imperially motivated project is not new, but it poses a direct challenge to the historiography of prophets. Nevertheless, there are serious problems with this approach. First, the textual evidence from ancient Near Eastern prophecy witnesses to the antiquity of prophetic phenomena also seen in the Bible, suggesting that the canonical prophets are not the stuff of later literary invention. Second, a hypothetically Persian-era work would betray too many subtle linguistic features that, while having the feel of something archaic, would at best be only archaistic in nature.

There is, to be sure, room for later literary activity among scribes and tradents of the canonical texts, but Nissinen seems to overstate the difference between the "concrete phenomenon" of prophecy and "its literary interpretation" when he says that the latter may be "historically and literally rooted in ancient Hebrew prophecy" but "is no longer representative of the 'authentic' prophetic phenomenon."[47] The matter of later literary handling of the Prophetic Books and narratives may highlight the larger canonical integrity of those sources because what is historically reasonable is not completely divorced from the prophets' theological interests. Their content is grounded in the covenantal claims of Israel's God as expressed in the narratives and legal materials of the Torah. The prophets' central activity of criticizing idolatry, injustice, and unfaithful leadership is exactly what we should expect from literature that reflects the conditions and concerns of the later monarchical

---

46. Diana Vikander Edelman, "From Prophets to Prophetic Books: The Fixing of the Divine Word," in *The Production of Prophecy: Constructing Prophecy and Prophets in Yehud* (ed. Ehud Ben Zvi and Diana Vikander Edelman; London: Equinox, 2009), 42.

47. Nissinen, "What Is Prophecy?," 31.

era. Hence, the question of what is historically probable is augmented by the theological interests of the prophets themselves.

Israelite Prophecy and History: The State of the Discipline

The foregoing discussion points to areas of significant agreement among scholars. First, Israelite prophecy shared the same kinds of phenomena found in other ancient Near Eastern cultures, from the titles used by some prophets and the types of phenomena that they experienced to their shared speech forms and similar subject matter. Second, within this common milieu, Israelite prophecy was clearly distinctive in ways that are completely consistent with Israel's historical, geographical, and cultural setting. Biblical prophets not only shared a dynamic relationship with the monarchy; they also addressed society at large and focused on covenantal fidelity more than on outward, ritual behavior. Third, the historical reliability of the biblical portrait of prophecy cannot be completely separated from Israel's unique processes of theological reflection, literary production, and its community's choices about canonization.

For the time being, matters have reached something of a plateau because it has been decades since the last major discovery that yielded comparative prophetic literature. Nevertheless, there certainly are avenues of scholarly research, particularly along two lines, one external and the other internal to the Bible. The comparative picture can be filled out and fine-tuned as scholars attend to the broader cultural background provided by royal archival data as well as artifacts and literary sources. That is, just as "historical Jesus" studies have been advanced by the study of first-century Galilee, so also we can extend our understanding of the world of ancient Near Eastern prophets. With respect to the Bible itself, literary and theological interpretation of the prophetic texts and messages can inform the historical quest. When theories of late dating, for example, challenge traditional views, scholars must do the meticulous work of linguistic analysis to probe the consistency between the data and the purportedly late literary setting. Together, these areas of agreement and avenues of future research can contribute to the foundation for a historically informed, culturally sophisticated, and theologically sensitive approach to the Prophetic Books and prophetic phenomena in ancient Israel.[48]

---

48. The collection of essays, *Prophets, Prophecy, and Ancient Israelite Historiography*, edited by Mark J. Boda and Lissa M. Wray Beal (Winona Lake, IN: Eisenbrauns, 2013), was published too late for me to incorporate its insights into this chapter.

9

Late Tenth- and Ninth-Century Issues

Ahab Underplayed? Jehoshaphat Overplayed?

KYLE GREENWOOD

What had once been a league of twelve tribes, and then a united monarchy, quickly turned to two competing kingdoms in the late tenth century BCE. After the reign of Solomon the kingdom of Israel split into northern Israel and southern Judah. Although the theological and political interests lie primarily in the southern kingdom, the biblical narrative proceeds to trace the parallel histories of both political entities.

The biblical history of Israel and Judah is derived from two distinct sources: the so-called Deuteronomistic History and Chronicles.[1] Whereas the Deuteronomistic History was completed during the Babylonian exile (2 Kings 25:27–30), Chronicles was edited during the Persian period, after Cyrus issued his famous decree in 539 BCE (2 Chron. 36:22–23). As such, it is not surprising that these two histories were written from competing perspectives.

---

1. For an overview of the nature of these sources, as well as exemplary summaries of the scholarship on each, see Martin J. Selman, "Chronicler's History," *DOTHB* 157–61; Sandra Richter, "Deuteronomistic History," *DOTHB* 219–30.

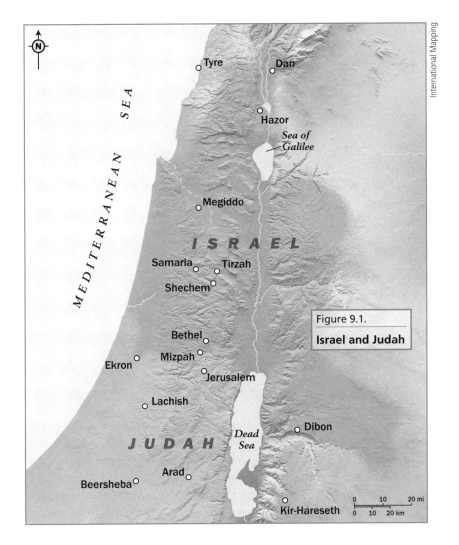

Figure 9.1.

Israel and Judah

According to Rodney Duke, there are three significant differences between Chronicles and Kings.[2] First, Kings focused on the consequences of sin, while Chronicles attempted to account for both curses and blessings, offering an explanation for successes as well as failures. Second, the Deuteronomistic Historian emphasized idolatry as the chief sin in Israel and Judah. For the Chronicler, however, the most important act of unfaithfulness was failure to seek the Lord, especially in the temple. In other words, "One could say that the whole ritual system symbolized the maintenance of the creational

2. Rodney K. Duke, "Chronicles, Book of," *DOTHB* 171–72.

distinction between that which was holy and that which was unholy for the purpose of sustaining an unpolluted relationship with God."[3] Third, for the Deuteronomist, sins were cumulative, thus sealing the fate of future generations (e.g., 2 Kings 23:26–27). This was not the case with the Chronicler, for whom restoration was possible through humility and seeking Yahweh (2 Chron. 7:14).

Two more points may be added to Duke's three distinctions between Chronicles and Kings. The first is that Chronicles has a general disinterest in the activities of northern kings. For example, Kings allots over six chapters to the northern king Ahab (1 Kings 16–22), but Chronicles covers the events of Ahab's life in one chapter (2 Chron. 18). It is nearly reversed for the southern king Jehoshaphat, who is given two chapters and one verse in Kings (1 Kings 15:24; 22; 2 Kings 3) and five chapters in Chronicles (2 Chron. 17–21). Moreover, Jehoshaphat's alliances with his northern contemporaries made him susceptible to prophetic rebuke (2 Chron. 19:1–3; 20:35). The second point is that Chronicles lacks the Elijah/Elisha cycle, which is prominently featured in the Deuteronomistic History. These five variances underscore the ideological perspectives from which the two historians operated.

Late Tenth-Century Historical Issues

The united monarchy came to a sudden halt with the conclusion of Solomon's reign. According to the biblical record, there were two underlying causes of its collapse, one theological, the other political. The theological cause is found only in the account provided by the Deuteronomistic Historian. Because Solomon built altars to foreign deities and offered sacrifices to those gods, the Lord determined to tear a portion of the kingdom from the Davidic line (1 Kings 11:1–13). The political reason for the collapse is recorded by both the Deuteronomistic Historian and the Chronicler. When Solomon established his administration, he appointed Adoniram as foreman of corvée labor, which was used during the construction of the temple and palace (1 Kings 4:6; 5:14).[4] After Solomon's death, both Kings and Chronicles report that the kingdom's subjects demanded a lighter load from their new king. After consulting the elders, then his peers, Solomon's son Rehoboam decided to increase the labor rather than decrease it (1 Kings 12:11; 2 Chron. 10:11). At this, the northern ten tribes seceded from the union. What was once the united kingdom of Israel had now dissolved into

---

3. Ibid., 172.

4. On the issue of forced labor in the construction of the temple, see Kyle R. Greenwood, "Labor Pains: The Relationship Between David's Census and Corvée Labor," *BBR* 20 (2010): 467–78.

Late Tenth- and Ninth-Century Monarchs

Israel	Judah	Aram	Assyria
Jeroboam (931/30–910/9)	Rehoboam (931/30–913)		
	Abijah (913–911/10)		
Nadab (910/9–909/8)	Asa (911/10–870/69)		Adad-nirari II (911–891)
Baasha (909/8–886/85)			Tukulti-Ninurta II (890–884)
Elah (886/85–885/84)		Bar-hadad I (885–870)	Assurnasirpal II (883–859)
Zimri (885/84)			
Tibni (885/84–880)			
Omri (*885/84–880*; 880–874/73)			
Ahab (874/73–853)	Jehoshaphat (*872/71–870/69*; 870/69–848)	Hadadezer (870–842)	Shalmaneser III (858–824)
Ahaziah (853–852)	Jehoram (*853–848*; 848–841)		
Joram (852–841)	Ahaziah (841)		
Jehu (841–814/13)	Athaliah (841–835)	Hazael (841–806)	Shamshi-Adad V (823–811)
Jehoahaz (814/13–798)	Jehoash/Joash (835–796)		Adad-nirari III (810–783)

Overlapping reigns and coregencies appear in italics. Dates for Judean and Israelite kings are from Edwin R. Thiele, *The Mysterious Numbers of the Hebrew Kings: A Reconstruction of the Chronology of the Kingdoms of Israel and Judah* (3rd ed.; Grand Rapids: Eerdmans, 1983), 217.

two separate kingdoms, Judah and Israel. Rehoboam continued to rule Judah from its capital in Jerusalem. Jeroboam became the first king of the northern kingdom, Israel, establishing his throne in Shechem (1 Kings 12:25).

Late Tenth-Century Biblical History

The details of the early divided monarchy are recounted in 1 Kings 12–15 and 2 Chronicles 10–14. For the biblical historian, the contrasting perspectives of these two accounts are most interesting. Whereas the primary interest of the historian in 1 Kings lies in condemning the northern kingdom through Jeroboam, the Chronicler focuses his attention on the reign of his southern counterpart, Rehoboam. The ideological rationale is apparent in that the Deuteronomistic Historian sees in Jeroboam's idolatry the beginning of a downward retributive spiral, from which Israel would never recover. The historian begins his account of the divided monarchy with Jeroboam placing golden calves at the northern and southern borders of Israel, citing Aaron verbatim (Exod. 32:4): "your gods . . . who brought you out of the land of Egypt" (1 Kings 12:28). As the king once chosen to counteract Solomon's apostasy (11:34), Jeroboam soon became the standard by which all future royal apostasy would be measured (e.g., 15:26, 34).

Whereas the historian of 1 Kings focused on the religious rebellion of Jeroboam, the Chronicler attended to the pious political and personal achievements of Rehoboam.[5] In terms of piety, Rehoboam had intended to invade Israel and reclaim the northern territory, but he paid heed to the Lord's command and called off the campaign (2 Chron. 11:1–4). Politically, Rehoboam demonstrated success in numerous building projects (11:5–12) and winning the support of the priests and Levites (11:13–17). Personally, the first king of the southern kingdom obtained numerous wives and concubines, who bore him scores of offspring (11:18–23).

Shishak's Raid

According to both the Deuteronomist (1 Kings 14:25–26) and the Chronicler (2 Chron. 12:2–4), Pharaoh Shishak besieged Jerusalem in the fifth year of Rehoboam's reign. Although the identity of biblical Shishak is technically uncertain,[6] most historians surmise that Shishak is one and the same with Pharaoh Shoshenq I, the founder of the Twenty-Second Dynasty of Egypt.[7] Aside from a complementary chronology, two pieces of epigraphic evidence support this conclusion. First, Shoshenq left a record of the itinerary of his campaign, an inscription at the southern entrance to the temple of Amon at Karnak.[8] Although the inscription has its challenges, its partially obstructed list of several dozen conquered Levantine cities demonstrates his military presence there in the late tenth century. Among the more prominent cities in the list are (in order of appearance) Gaza, Gezer, Beth Shean, Gibeon, Megiddo, Penuel,

---

5. For a summary of the varying biblical accounts of Rehoboam and Jeroboam, see Scot McKnight, "Rehoboam," *DOTHB* 838–40. See also Gary N. Knoppers, "Rehoboam in Chronicles: Villain or Victim?," *JBL* 109 (1990): 423–40.

6. See Kevin A. Wilson, *The Campaign of Pharaoh Shoshenq I into Palestine* (FAT 2/9; Tübingen: Mohr Siebeck, 2005); Kenneth A. Kitchen, review of Kevin A. Wilson, *The Campaign of Pharaoh Shoshenq I into Palestine*, *JSS* 54 (2009): 274–76; Troy Leiland Sagrillo, "Šīšaq's Army: 2 Chronicles 12:2–3 from an Egyptological Perspective," in *The Ancient Near East in the 12th–10th Centuries BCE: Culture and History; Proceedings of the International Conference Held at the University of Haifa, 2–5 May, 2010* (ed. Gersho Galil et al.; AOAT 392; Münster: Ugarit-Verlag, 2012), 425–50.

7. Leo Depuydt, "Egypt, Egyptians," *DOTHB* 243.

8. Kenneth A. Kitchen, *The Third Intermediate Period in Egypt, 1100–650 B.C.* (2nd ed.; Warminster, UK: Aris & Phillips, 1986), 287–302; Benjamin Mazar, "Shishak's Campaign to the Land of Israel," in *The Early Biblical Period: Historical Studies* (ed. Shmuel Ahituv and Baruch A. Levine; Jerusalem: Israel Exploration Society, 1986), 139–50.

Tirzah, and Arad. Second, a stela fragment bearing Shoshenq's name has been unearthed at Megiddo. Although it was found in an excavation dump, not in situ, it does little to undermine the biblical position that an Egyptian pharaoh campaigned during the reign of Rehoboam. In fact, for J. Maxwell Miller and John Hayes, "The reference to Sheshonq/Shishak's campaign (1 Kings 14:25), and the fact that the narrators placed it in an approximately accurate chronological context, is further indication that they had at least some grasp of the chronology of events going back to the beginning of the period of the separate kingdoms."[9]

The significance of Shishak's raid rests most prominently in the establishment of the chronology of the late tenth and early ninth centuries. If Shishak destroyed the cities, as suggested in his temple inscription, then the destruction layers at places such as Megiddo and Arad may be dated to the late tenth century. If, however, Shishak merely marched through the countryside, leaving the cities unscathed, then another explanation must be found for these destruction layers. Given the biblical attestation of an Egyptian military plundering (1 Kings 14:26; 2 Chron. 12:4) alongside Shishak's inscription and stela fragment, the evidence is quite compelling that Shishak's Levantine campaigns resulted in the destruction layers attributed to the late tenth century.[10]

Ninth-Century Historical Issues

Although the prophetic voices of Elijah and Elisha dominate the Deuteronomistic narrative, the political interests of both Israel and Judah also play a vital role. This is particularly true as these new kingdoms relate to each other amid competing powers such as Aram, Moab, Phoenicia, and Assyria. In Israel the major political figures include Omri, Ahab, Joram,[11] and Jehu, while in Judah the key royal personalities include Asa, Jehoshaphat, and Ahaziah.

9. J. Maxwell Miller and John H. Hayes, *A History of Ancient Israel and Judah* (2nd ed.; Louisville: Westminster John Knox, 2006), 241.

10. On the significance of Shishak's raid on late tenth-century destruction levels, see Amihai Mazar, "The Debate over the Chronology of the Iron Age in the Southern Levant: Its History, the Current Situation, and a Suggested Resolution," in *The Bible and Radiocarbon Dating: Archaeology, Text and Science* (ed. Thomas E. Levy and Thomas Higham; London: Equinox, 2005), 13–28.

11. In the northern kingdom J(eh)oram, the son of Ahab, was the brother and successor of Ahaziah, the king of Israel; in the southern kingdom, Ahaziah was the son and successor of Jehoram, the king of Judah. Occasionally the biblical authors spell the name of Jehoram of Israel as "Joram" in order to avoid confusion with Judah's king. The succession in Israel is Ahab, Ahaziah, J(eh)oram; in Judah it is Jehoshaphat, Jehoram, and Ahaziah. In this chapter

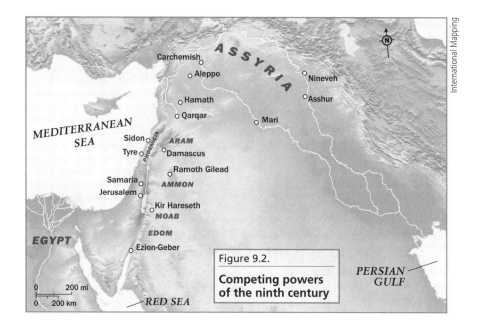

Figure 9.2.

**Competing powers
of the ninth century**

The biblical account of ninth-century events is recorded in 1 Kings 16–2 Kings 13 and 2 Chronicles 16–24. Although the Prophetic Books (particularly Amos and Hosea) allude to conditions initiated in the ninth century, they make no direct reference to the period. Extrabiblical evidence is available from inscriptions from Tel Dan, Moab, Aram, and Assyria. In addition to the various textual data, there is significant archaeological evidence from Arad, Dan, Hazor, Lachish, Megiddo, Mizpah, and Samaria.

Ninth-Century Biblical History

Whereas the Chronicler focuses on the reign of Asa in Judah (2 Chron. 16), the Deuteronomistic Historian presents the start of the ninth century as one of severe instability in Israel (1 Kings 16:8–24). Following the revolt of Baasha at the end of the tenth century, Zimri revolted against Baasha's son Elah. A popular uprising propelled Omri to the head of Zimri's army; with the support of the masses, Omri initiated a coup d'état against the royal household. Conceding defeat, Zimri committed suicide by burning his own palace while

---

"Jehoram" refers to the king of Judah, while "Joram" applies to the Israelite son of Ahab. On the view that Jehoram and Joram were the same monarch ruling a reunited kingdom, see Miller and Hayes, *History of Ancient Israel and Judah*, 320–23. For a text-critical explanation for the alternate spellings, see Emanuel Tov, *Textual Criticism of the Hebrew Bible* (3rd rev. and exp. ed.; Minneapolis: Fortress, 2012), 35.

he cowered inside. Omri retained the regency by successfully resisting Tibni's move for the vacant throne. Thus began the Omride dynasty, which dominates the narrative of the northern kingdom for the next fourteen chapters of the books of Kings.

Little account is given concerning the particulars of Omri's twelve-year reign, other than the fact that he moved Israel's capital from Tirzah to Samaria, where he purchased a hill from the town's namesake, Shemer (1 Kings 16:24). Omri's son Ahab succeeded him and ruled Israel for twenty-two years. According to the Deuteronomist, Ahab's exogamous marriage with the Phoenician princess Jezebel resulted in the ascendancy of Baalistic syncretism, beginning with the construction of a Baal temple in the capital city (16:29–32). The focus of the Deuteronomist's account, therefore, is the antagonistic relationship between the house of Omri and Yahwistic orthodoxy, represented at various junctures by the prophetic office and the Davidic dynasty.

In addition to the theological issues at the fore in the biblical account, exterior forces began to involve themselves in both states' political survival. The most prominent of these forces was Aram. Three encounters with Aram are recounted in the closing chapters of 1 Kings. The first such affair is found in 1 Kings 20:1–25, which details a military coalition led by Ben-Hadad. According to the historian, Ben-hadad demanded tribute from Ahab, who readily consented. However, when the coalition increased the demand to include Ahab's wives and children, Ahab reneged. Rather than waiting for Ben-hadad's assault, Ahab initiated an attack and defeated the Damascus forces. Despite the setback, Ben-hadad was able to muster another army of equal size to engage Israel in a second conflict (20:26–43). Shortly thereafter Aram invaded the Israelite camp at Aphek. Whereas Aram's army filled the land, Israel's army was "like two little flocks of goats" (20:27). Nonetheless, Ahab's forces prevailed once again. For the next three years conflict ceased between these two rival kingdoms. Finding an ally in Jehoshaphat, the newly crowned king of Judah, Ahab sought to reclaim Ramoth-gilead from Aramean possession (1 Kings 22:1–40; 2 Chron. 18:1–34). This third conflict ended in the demise of Ahab and the defeat of the Israel-Judah alliance.

Jehoshaphat's reign receives mixed reviews in the two biblical histories. The Chronicler's portrait of his accomplishments is much more embellished than that found in 1 Kings. In Chronicles, Jehoshaphat had firm control over Judah and commanded a military whose forces were stationed "in all the fortified cities of Judah" (2 Chron. 17:2). Furthermore, the entire land of Judah, as well as Philistines and Arabs, brought him tribute in the form of silver and livestock (17:5, 11). He built fortification cities and amassed a military of over a million strong (17:14–18).[12] In a sort of epilogue on Jehoshaphat's career, the Chronicler notes that not everything that Jehoshaphat touched turned to gold. Although there is no condemnation for his alliance with Ahab, the Chronicler admonishes Jehoshaphat for forming an alliance with Ahab's son Ahaziah. Thus, when Jehoshaphat embarked on a new shipbuilding enterprise based in Ezion-geber, it was inevitable that the project ultimately would fail (1 Kings 22:48; 2 Chron. 20:36–37).

After the brief interlude of foreign affairs with Moab (see "The Moabite War of 2 Kings 3" on pp. 306–7 and 313–15), the historian once again resumes the situation between Israel and Aram, while the episode is not recorded by the Chronicler. The Deuteronomistic Historian fails to mention the name of "the king of Israel," although the narrative sequence assumes the king to be Joram. Nonetheless, in 2 Kings 6:8–23 a mob of mercenary Arameans were turned away from the northern city of Dothan. Later the king of Israel prepared a diplomatic feast for Aram, after which "the Arameans no longer came raiding into the land of Israel" (6:23). However, in the very next scene Ben-hadad of Aram besieged Samaria, which was suffering from a severe famine (6:24–25), causing its inhabitants to resort to cannibalism. Conditions were so severe that four lepers risked their lives to defect to the Arameans. Hearing what they thought to be the advancement of the Hittite and Egyptian armies, the Arameans fled their camps (7:6). The lepers reported this news to Joram, who mustered his forces and plundered the Arameans (7:15).

When Jehoram succeeded his father, Jehoshaphat, he apparently entered into a marriage alliance with Israel by marrying Athaliah, Ahab's daughter. The alliance continued into the reign of Jehoram's son Ahaziah. This Israel-Judah alliance under Joram and Ahaziah, respectively, engaged Hazael at Ramoth-gilead. According to the Deuteronomist, Joram was wounded in battle. The fact that the alliance was more than political is suggested by Ahaziah's journey to Jezreel to visit the injured Joram (2 Kings 8:29; 2 Chron. 22:6).

One of the Israelite officers at Ramoth-gilead was Jehu, who was anointed by Elisha to eradicate the house of Ahab. Both biblical historians recount how Jehu killed Ahaziah (2 Kings 9:27; 2 Chron. 22:9) and his family (2 Kings 10:14;

---

12. This number is based on the number assigned to each of the five military commanders, ranging from 180,000 to 300,000 warriors per leader. However, archaeological evidence suggests a ninth-century Judean population of approximately 250,000 (Joseph Blenkinsopp, "Ahab of Israel and Jehoshaphat of Judah: The Syro-Palestinian Corridor in the Ninth Century," *CANE* 2:1309–19). Perhaps it is better to read *'elep* here as a military unit rather than "thousand." See also Francis I. Andersen, "Israelite Kinship Terminology and Social Structure," *BT* 20 (1969): 36.

2 Chron. 22:8). The Deuteronomist's account also reports on Jehu's execution of Joram (2 Kings 9:24), the remainder of Ahab's family in Samaria (10:11, 17), and all the worshipers of Baal (10:25). According to the historian, it was during his reign that "the LORD began to trim off parts of Israel" (10:32), a possible reference to the Assyrian incursion under Adad-nirari III. As predicted by Elisha in 2 Kings 8:12, Hazael of Aram had seized Israel's land assets east of the Jordan.

Following Ahaziah's death, his mother, Athaliah, assumed control of the throne and killed all the legitimate heirs (2 Kings 11:1–3; 2 Chron. 22:10–12), with the lone exception of Ahaziah's infant son Joash, whose aunt preserved his life. With the help of the priest Jehoida, Joash assumed the throne at the age of seven (2 Kings 11:21; 2 Chron. 23:1–15). Among his accomplishments as king was the renovation of the temple in Jerusalem (2 Kings 12:4–16; 2 Chron. 24:4–14). During his reign, however, Hazael extended his control to the west of the Jordan (2 Kings 12:17; 2 Chron. 24:23–24). Although "the LORD gave Israel a savior" from Aramean oppression (2 Kings 13:5), Hazael emaciated Israel's military to a meager fifty horsemen, ten chariots, and ten thousand foot soldiers (2 Kings 13:7). Meanwhile in Jerusalem, Joash capitulated to Aram and looted the temple treasuries to pay tribute. The payoff succeeded: Hazael relented his attack on Jerusalem and returned to Aram (2 Kings 12:18). According to the historian, Joash died in a royal conspiracy, presumably led by his own servants (2 Kings 12:21; 2 Chron. 24:25–26).

The Deuteronomistic Historian's account of the events of ninth-century Israel and Judah concludes with a final assessment of Israel's international affairs. By this time, Moab was making annual forays into Israelite territory, and Aram continued to oppress Israel during the entirety of the reign of Joash's father, Jehoahaz (2 Kings 13:22; 2 Chron. 24:23–24). When Hazael died, the fortunes turned in Israel's favor. Joash was able to beat back Hazael's successor, Ben-hadad, three times and recover cities that had been lost to Aram during the preceding reigns (2 Kings 13:25).

Extrabiblical Textual Evidence

During the ninth century, the number of texts related to the history of ancient Israel and Judah surges. In some cases, the extrabiblical textual evidence explicitly refers to characters or events of the Old Testament. In others, the texts merely allude to the events of the biblical account or reflect the conditions of the period.

Tel Dan Inscription

The Tel Dan Inscription, erected in the ninth century and written in Old Aramaic, is most notable for containing the earliest known reference to the Davidic dynasty.[13] Celebrating the defeat of Israel, this monumental inscription recounts how the king, at the command of Hadad, successfully defeated the king of Israel.[14] Furthermore, it recounts earlier campaigns by Israel into Aramean territory during the reign of that king's predecessor.

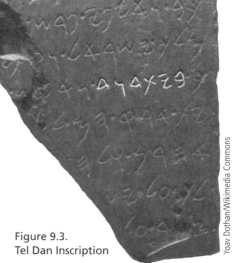

Two significant issues relating to the inscription itself require us to treat certain judgments regarding its details as somewhat speculative. First, the royal sponsor of the monument is not named in the text. Second, the names of Israel's kings

Figure 9.3.
Tel Dan Inscription

Yoav Dothan/Wikimedia Commons

Joram and Ahaziah must be reconstructed due to the fragmentary nature of that portion of the monument. Nonetheless, a general consensus has emerged regarding these problems.[15] With respect to the former, the monument's provenance suggests that the anonymous king was an Aramean monarch, most likely Hazael.[16] With respect to the latter, no viable challenge has been offered to the reconstruction of Joram and Ahaziah as the two kings originally mentioned in the stela.[17]

---

13. Alan R. Millard, "The Tell Dan Stele," *COS* 2:39.161–62; Brian B. Schmidt, "Tel Dan Stele Inscription," in *The Ancient Near East: Historical Sources in Translation* (ed. Mark W. Chavalas; Malden, MA: Blackwell, 2006), 305–6.

14. On the propagandistic function of the iconography on ancient Near Eastern stelae, see Christoph Uehlinger, "Neither Eyewitnesses, nor Windows to the Past, but Valuable Testimony in Its Own Right: Remarks on Iconography, Source Criticism and Ancient Data Processing," in *Understanding the History of Ancient Israel* (ed. H. G. M. Williamson; PBA 143; New York: Oxford University Press, 2007), 173–228.

15. For a cogent defense of the reconstruction, see William M. Schniedewind, "Tel Dan Stela: New Light on Aramaic and Jehu's Revolt," *BASOR* 302 (1996): 79–80.

16. Larry G. Herr, "The Iron Age II Period: Emerging Nations," *BA* 60 (1997): 140.

17. Ingo Kottsieper, "The Tel Dan Inscription (*KAI* 310) and the Political Relations between Aram-Damascus and Israel in the First Half of the First Millennium B.C.E.," in *Ahab Agonistes: The Rise and Fall of the Omri Dynasty* (ed. Lester L. Grabbe; LHBOTS 421; London: T&T Clark, 2007), 105–34.

Old Aramaic

Aramaic is one of many languages in the Semitic family, which also includes Akkadian, Arabic, Hebrew, Phoenician, and Ugaritic. Aramaic itself is divided into three main branches, each with further limbs extending from the Semitic trunk. West Aramaic includes Nabataean, Palmyrene, Jewish Palestinian, Samaritan, and Christian Palestinian. East Aramaic includes Syriac, Babylonian Aramaic, and Mandean. Old Aramaic consists of Imperial Aramaic (also known as Classical Aramaic), Biblical Aramaic, and Old Aramaic proper.

In the strictest sense, Old Aramaic refers to the language preserved in ancient inscriptions from Damascus, Hama, Arpad, and Samʾal, dating in the tenth–seventh centuries BCE. The rise of the language's namesake, the Arameans, resulted in its widespread dissemination. Due to the alphabetic nature of its script, the language eventually became the lingua franca in the ancient Near East.[a]

Some of the most important ancient Near Eastern texts were written in Old Aramaic and have demonstrable significance due to their connection to the Old Testament. These include the Tel Dan Inscription, the Zakkur Stela, and the Melqart Stela. In addition to these, the Sefire Treaty Inscriptions provide extrabiblical evidence and context for covenant blessings and curses. The Deir ʿAllā Inscription shows strong affinities with Numbers 22–24. Two other inscriptions, the Zincirli Inscription (Hadad Inscription) and the Tell Fekhariyah Inscription (also known as the Hadad-Yithʿi Inscription), are important for their contributions to linguistic studies.[b]

a. W. Randall Garr, *Dialect Geography of Syria-Palestine, 1000–586 B.C.E.* (Philadelphia: University of Pennsylvania Press, 1985); Stephen A. Kaufman, "Languages (Aramaic)," *ABD* 1:176–78.
b. Joseph A. Fitzmyer, "The Inscriptions of Bar-Gaʾyah and Matiʿel from Sefire," *COS* 2.82:213–17; Baruch A. Levine, "The Deir ʿAllā Plaster Inscriptions," *COS* 2.27:140–45; Alan R. Millard, "Hadad-Yithʿi," *COS* 2.34:153–54; K. Lawson Younger Jr., "The Hadad Inscription," *COS* 2.36:156–58.

Mesha Stela

The Moabite Stela of King Mesha was composed as a dedicatory inscription to the Moabite deity Kemosh.[18] It commemorated the defeat of Omri's son and the construction of Qarhoh, the sanctuary of Kemosh. According to the inscription, Omri had seized the Moabite territory of Medeba, which stayed under Israelite control into the reign of Omri's son. However, with the help of Kemosh, Mesha defeated Israel, regained control over Medeba, and rebuilt Qarhoh, using Israelite prisoners to supply the labor.[19]

18. Klaas A. D. Smelik, "The Inscription of Mesha," COS 2:23.137–38; Brian B. Schmidt, "Moabite Stone," in Chavalas, *Ancient Near East*, 311–16.
19. A second ninth-century inscription from Moab was discovered in 2012 by Chang-Ho Ji at Khirbet Ataruz, known as Atarot in the Mesha Inscription as the land conquered by King

Zakkur Stela

In response to his military successes against the Aramean coalition led by Bar-hadad, King Zakkur of the Hittite city-states Hamath and Lu'ash erected a victory stela dedicated to the god Baal-shamayn.[20] Although Zakkur is not mentioned in the Old Testament, the events described in the text correspond to the political conditions of the late ninth or early eighth century. With Assyria's westward expansion, especially under Adad-nirari III, Aram became preoccupied with self-preservation rather than expansionistic imperialism. The Deuteronomist possibly alludes to these very conditions in 2 Kings 13:5: "Therefore the Lord gave Israel a savior, so that they escaped from the hand of the Arameans."

Hazael Booty Inscriptions

Four brief dedicatory inscriptions from the late ninth century refer to "our lord Hazael" and provide extrabiblical evidence, however scant, for the reign of Hazael of Damascus.[21] Two inscriptions were written on bronze horse pieces. Two others were written on ivory. Although the texts, unfortunately, provide no useful details regarding the types or quantities of tribute received by Hazael, they do indicate Hazael's status as a sovereign conqueror.

Melqart Stela

The Melqart Stela, discovered north of Aleppo, contains a relief of the god Melqart along with a brief Aramaic dedicatory inscription from Bar-hadad of Aram.[22] Due to its brevity, it contains no useful information other than the king's name.

Mesha. The cult pedestal on which the inscription is etched was unearthed in a temple complex. Although the inscription itself does not contain any direct historical information, it seems to confirm the historical milieu from which the Mesha Inscription arose. The inscription is currently being analyzed by P. Kyle McCarter, Christopher Rollston, and Stefan Wimmer and is scheduled for publication in late 2014 or early 2015. Rollston has posted a preliminary report of the inscription at http://www.rollstonepigraphy.com/?p=631, titled, "The Ninth Century 'Moabite Pedestal Inscription' from King Mesha's Ataruz: Preliminary Synopsis of an Excavated Epigraphic Text and its Biblical Connections."

20. Alan R. Millard, "The Inscription of Zakkur, King of Hamath," COS 2:35.155; Scott Noegel, "Zakkur Inscription," in Chavalas, Ancient Near East, 307–11. For an accessible and thorough treatment on the Hittites, see Billie Jean Collins, The Hittites and Their World (SBLABS 7; Atlanta: Society of Biblical Literature, 2007).

21. Alan R. Millard, "The Hazael Booty Inscriptions," COS 2:40.162–63.

22. Wayne T. Pitard, "The Melqart Stela," COS 2:33.152–53; idem, "The Identity of the Bir-Hadad of the Melqart Stela," BASOR 272 (1988): 3–21. "Bir-hadad" is an alternate spelling of "Bar-hadad."

Luwian

Spoken throughout southern and western Anatolia, Luwian was the language of the Hittite Kingdom.[a] The remaining remnants of that long-dead language are preserved in two different scripts. Cuneiform Luwian dates to approximately 1650–1200 BCE, while Hieroglyphic Luwian dates to approximately 1200–700 BCE. Its ultimate demise was likely a result of two factors: Assyrian destruction of Neo-Hittite states, and the introduction of the less cumbersome alphabetic scripts into Anatolia and Syria. As an Indo-European language, Luwian is not related to any of the Semitic languages, such as Hebrew, Aramaic, and Akkadian.[b]

As far as Hittitologists are aware, Cuneiform Luwian dates to the founding monarch of the Hittite kingdom, Hattusili I, in about 1650 BCE. The first texts were found in modern Boğazköy, the site of the ancient Hittite capital, Hattusha. Cuneiform Luwian receives its name because it uses the same wedge-shaped writing style as Mesopotamian cuneiform. In all likelihood, Hittite scribes borrowed the script from scribes in northern Syria, but adapted the script to the language of Hattusha.

With the discovery of the Karatepe Inscription in 1946, decipherment of Hieroglyphic Luwian gained much firmer footing.[c] Dating to the late eighth or early seventh century, this Hieroglyphic Luwian–Phoenician bilingual inscription contains the longest extant text for either language. In typical monumental inscription fashion, the royal sponsor Azatiwata extols his greatness for building a fortress and being a pious warrior.[d] However interesting the contents of the inscription may be, the greater value in this monument was its significance for decoding Hieroglyphic Luwian.[e]

a. H. Craig Melchert, ed., *The Luwians* (HO 68; Leiden: Brill, 2003).
b. H. Craig Melchert, "Indo-European Languages of Anatolia," *CANE* 4:2151–59; John Huehnergard, "Languages (Introduction)," *ABD* 4:155–70.
c. John David Hawkins, "Karkamish and Karatepe: Neo-Hittite City-States in North Syria," *CANE* 2:1295–1307.
d. John David Hawkins, "Azatiwata," *COS* 2.21:124–26; K. Lawson Younger Jr. "The Azatiwada Inscription," *COS* 2.31:148–50; Edward L. Greenstein, "Autobiographies in Ancient Western Asia," *CANE* 4:2421–32.
e. John David Hawkins, *Inscriptions of the Iron Age, Part I* (vol. 1 of *Corpus of Hieroglyphic Luwian Inscriptions*; UISK 8; Berlin: de Gruyter, 2000); Annick Payne, *Iron Age Hieroglyphic Luwian Inscriptions* (SBLWAW 29; Atlanta: Society of Biblical Literature, 2012).

Royal Inscriptions of Shalmaneser III

The most extensive extrabiblical evidence from the ninth century has no parallel account in either the Deuteronomistic History or the Chronicler. Under the reign of Ashurnasirpal, Assyria reemerged as the Neo-Assyrian

Empire. From 853 to 838 BCE Shalmaneser III formally adopted a foreign policy of western expansionism, in which the "long-range aims were to profit from the wealth of the Levant and to add Egypt to the Neo-Assyrian empire."[23] His exploits are recorded in numerous inscriptions, including the Kurkh Monolith Inscription, Ashur Clay Tablets, Calah Bulls, Marble Slab Inscription, Kurba'il Statue, Black Obelisk, Ashur Basalt Statue, and Black Stone Cylinder.[24]

The various royal inscriptions of Shalmaneser recount the monarch's most notable military campaigns into the region of Aram, which took place in regnal years six, ten, eleven, fourteen, eighteen, and twenty-one. It is well known that Tiglath-pileser I (1115–1077 BCE), during the tail end of the Middle Assyrian period, made forays into Aram, but with little success. Although he bragged about having crossed the Euphrates twenty-eight times to defeat the Arameans, the fact that he was compelled to return so frequently is a strong indicator that his campaigns were not as successful as he would have us believe.[25] Although Shalmaneser was not the first Assyrian king to venture into Aramean territory, he was the first to face a contingent of allied forces—the so-called Damascene Coalition—in his westward campaigns.

Three points emerge as especially important in founding the history of ancient Israel and Judah. First, in his Basalt Statue, Shalmaneser refers to Hazael of Damascus as the "son of a nobody," a term used in the ancient Near East to refer to an illegitimate ruler. Shalmaneser's use of this derogatory epithet corresponds to the biblical account, in which Hazael usurped the throne from Ben-hadad (2 Kings 8:15). Second, Hazael's predecessor is named "Hadadezer" (^{d}Adad-idri) in the Assyrian texts rather than "Ben-hadad" as he is called in the biblical text. Moreover, whereas the Deuteronomist attributes Ben-hadad's death to Hazael, the Basalt Statue simply states that Hadadezer died. Third, during his sixth regnal year Shalmaneser encountered a coalition of Levantine forces led by Hadadezer of Damascus, Irhuleni of Hamath, and Ahab the Israelite (*Sir'alāia*). Especially noteworthy regarding this coalition is that Israel is ascribed more chariots (two thousand) than either Aram or Hamath (twelve hundred each), and is nearly equal to Assyria's chariot force of 2,002. Furthermore, Israel's ten thousand troops are equal to the number

23. A. Kirk Grayson, "Shalmaneser III and the Levantine States: The Damascus Coalition," *JHS* 5, art. 4 (2004): 5, http://www.jhsonline.org/Articles/article_34.pdf.

24. K. Lawson Younger Jr., "Kurkh Monolith," "Annals: Aššur Clay Tablets," "Annals: Calah Bulls," "Annals: Marble Slab," "Kurba'il Statue," "Black Obelisk," "Aššur Basalt Statue," "Black Stone Cylinder," "The Die (Pūru) of Yahli," *COS* 2.113A–I:261–72; Brent A. Strawn, "Shalmaneser III," in Chavalas, *Ancient Near East*, 289–93.

25. Kyle Greenwood, "Campaigns of Tiglath-pileser I against the Arameans and Babylonia," in Chavalas, *Ancient Near East*, 156–57.

attributed to Hamath and Irqata, and they are outnumbered only by Damascus (twenty thousand). Fourth, during his eighteenth regnal year Shalmaneser received tribute from Jehu (*Ia-ú-a*) from the house of Omri (*Bīt Ḫumri*), which included silver, gold, tin, and Jehu's royal scepter.

Royal Inscriptions of Adad-nirari III

Adad-nirari III continued the westward expansionist policies of his predecessor, though his annals do not reflect the same level of dominance. Although the evidence points to an early eighth-century date for both the Tell Rimah Stela and the Calah Orthostat Slab,[26] their pertinence for ninth-century history is readily apparent. Adad-nirari III came to power around 805 BCE and was seen by King Jehoahaz of Israel as one who would release Israel from Aramean domination. However, the rulers from whom Assyria received tribute included those from Hatti, Amurru, Mari, Damascus, Tyre, Sidon, Edom, and Phoenicia. The Tell Rimah Stela even mentions Joash (*Iu'asu*) "the Samarian."[27] The fact that the Judean king is mentioned as a Samarian may be evidence of Judah's status as a vassal to Israel in these waning years of the Omride dynasty. Israel viewed Assyria as a savior at the end of the ninth century, but it would not be long before that perception required modification.

Archaeological Evidence

During the fifth year of Rehoboam's reign, Pharaoh Shishak invaded the Levant, leaving layers of destruction in his wake. However, Israel and Judah not only survived the incursion of 925 BCE but also, archaeological data suggest, thrived in its aftermath.[28] Although the ninth century has left significant evidence pointing to a period of prosperity and growth for both kingdoms, the record shows a more robust centralized government in the northern kingdom.[29]

26. K. Lawson Younger Jr., "Tell Al Rimah Stela," "Calah Orthostat Slab," *COS* 2.114F–G: 275–77.

27. On the identification of *Iu'asu* as Joash, see Mordechai Cogan and Hayim Tadmor, *II Kings: A New Translation with Introduction and Commentary* (AB 11; Garden City, NY: Doubleday, 1988), 145.

28. For a brief account of the complexities of dating Shishak's raid, see Amihai Mazar, "The Spade and the Text: The Interaction between Archaeology and Israelite History Relating to the Tenth–Ninth Centuries," in Williamson, *Understanding the History*, 149–50.

29. For a concise summary of archaeological evidence for this period, see Edward F. Campbell, "A Land Divided: Judah and Israel from the Death of Solomon to the Fall of Samaria," *OHBW* 219–21, 225–26.

Northern Kingdom

Building activity in the northern kingdom increased substantially during this period. Among the most notable constructions was the new capital at Samaria. Although construction of the palace at Samaria may have begun during the reign of Omri, his brief reign suggests that it was likely completed, if not completely built, during Ahab's rule. The Samarian acropolis, with its enclosures and strongholds, "formed a defensive line on the slopes of the mountains of Samaria and defended the main passes from the coastal plain to the center of the mountains."[30] The construction style found at Samaria seems to have served as a prototype for other Israelite architecture, particularly at Beth Shean, Megiddo, and Hazor.[31] The use of Phoenician ashlar-style masonry in these sites may indicate a Phoenician influence on Israelite architecture.[32] The most significant archaeological find from Samaria is an extensive cache of carved ivories that probably were inlays for lavish furniture and likely are the background for 1 Kings 22:39; Amos 6:4.[33] The Samarian ivories, along with evidence of olive oil production in the Samarian region and the discovery of ornamented jewelry in both Samaria and Megiddo, point to a period of royal luxury in the northern kingdom.[34]

Whereas Samaria was established during the Omride dynasty, Megiddo had been populated since about 6000 BCE.[35] During the united monarchy Megiddo had functioned primarily as a civilian administrative center. Following its destruction by Pharaoh Shishak, the Omride kings made significant architectural changes, suggesting its transformation into a military garrison.[36] An Omride, probably Ahab, built a twelve-foot-wide offset-inset wall to encompass the city, as well as an elaborate water system that allowed for safe access within the confines of the fortress.[37] Two complexes of horse stables are the most sensational find. At one time, this complex was thought to have belonged to Solomon.[38] Deborah Cantrell and Israel Finkelstein have countered with

---

30. Shimon Dar, "Samaria (Archaeology of the Region)," *ABD* 5:928. See also Ron Tappy, "Samaria," *OEANE* 4:465.

31. See Kathleen Kenyon, *Archaeology in the Holy Land* (3rd ed.; New York: Praeger, 1970), 277.

32. See B. S. J. Isserlin, *The Israelites* (Minneapolis: Augsburg Fortress, 2001), 123.

33. Eleanor Ferris Beach, "The Samaria Ivories, Marzeah, and Biblical Texts," *BA* 55 (1992): 130–39; Herr, "Iron Age II," 141; Harold A. Liebowitz, "Ivory," *ABD* 3:584–87.

34. Kenyon, *Archaeology in the Holy Land*, 277.

35. Israel Finkelstein and David Ussishkin, "Back to Megiddo: A New Expedition Will Explore the Jewel in the Crown of Canaan/Israel," *BAR* 20, no. 1 (1994): 28.

36. See Yigael Yadin, "New Light on Solomon's Megiddo," *BA* 23 (1960): 62–68.

37. Finkelstein and Ussishkin, "Back to Megiddo," 43.

38. P. L. O. Guy, *New Light from Armageddon: Second Provisional Report (1927–29) on the Excavations at Megiddo in Palestine* (OIC 9; Chicago: University of Chicago Press, 1931), 37–48.

an eighth-century date, suggesting that Hazael, and not Shishak, destroyed Megiddo around 835 BCE.[39] The preponderance of evidence, however, seems to favor a ninth-century date, with Ahab being the likely architect of the stables.[40] In any case, Cantrell provides ample evidence that Megiddo served as an equine training center from the fifteenth century until the eighth century.[41] Based on the size of the two complexes, it has been estimated that the stables could have accommodated approximately 450–480 horses and 50–100 chariot teams.[42] Megiddo's stables probably did not represent the entirety of Israel's chariot forces. It is highly likely that Israel's equine program was facilitated in other centers, such as Hazor, Dan, Kinrot, Beth Shean, and Bethsaida.[43] If this is the case, it may account for the large chariot force mentioned in the Kurkh Monolith Inscription of Shalmaneser III.

Another Israelite city that had undergone significant changes during this period is Hazor. During the ninth century Hazor's architectural footprint doubled in size.[44] The remains of Stratum VIII likely date to Ahab, whose archaeological contributions include a citadel 70 x 80 feet in size, a large administrative complex, a pillared storehouse, and a "marvelously engineered water system," resembling the one found at Megiddo.[45]

Two other northern cities deserve brief mention. In Dan extensive construction began in the tenth century, presumably under the authority of Jeroboam I. The most prominent finds in this area were a *bāmâ* (shrine) and a four-horned altar, suggesting that Dan functioned as an active cultic center during this period (see 1 Kings 12:30).[46] Dan's cultic importance continued into the ninth

---

39. Deborah O'Daniel Cantrell, "Stable Issues," in *Megiddo IV: The 1998–2000 Seasons* (ed. Israel Finkelstein, David Ussishkin, and Baruch Halpern; 2 vols.; TAUIAM 24; Tel Aviv: Emery and Claire Yass Publications in Archaeology of the Institute of Archaeology, Tel Aviv University, 2006), 2:630–42; Deborah O'Daniel Cantrell and Israel Finkelstein, "A Kingdom for a Horse: The Megiddo Stables and Eighth Century Israel," in Finkelstein, Ussishkin, and Halpern, *Megiddo IV*, 2:643–65. See also the discussion on the Low Chronology by Steven Ortiz in chap. 7 of the present volume.

40. Yadin, "New Light," 68; Israel Finkelstein and Amihai Mazar, *The Quest for the Historical Israel: Debating Archaeology and the History of Early Israel* (ed. Brian B. Schmidt; SBLABS 17; Atlanta: Society of Biblical Literature, 2007), 171; David Ussishkin, "Megiddo," *OEANE* 3:467.

41. Deborah O'Daniel Cantrell, *The Horsemen of Israel: Horses and Chariotry in Monarchic Israel (Ninth–Eighth Centuries B.C.E.)* (HACL 1; Winona Lake, IN: Eisenbrauns, 2011), 113.

42. Graham I. Davies, "King Solomon's Stables: Still at Megiddo?," *BAR* 20, no. 1 (1994): 45–49; David Ussishkin, "Megiddo," *ABD* 4:677.

43. Cantrell, *Horsemen of Israel*, 112.

44. Yohanan Aharoni, *The Archaeology of the Land of Israel: From the Prehistoric Beginning to the End of the First Temple Period* (trans. Anson F. Rainey; Philadelphia: Westminster, 1982), 242.

45. Amnon Ben-Tor, "Hazor," *OEANE* 3:1–5; William G. Dever, "Qedah, Tell El-," *ABD* 5:578–81; Yigael Yadin, "Hazor," *EAEHL* 2:489.

46. Avraham Biran, "Dan (Place)," *ABD* 2:15.

century as well, as evidenced by the expansion of the *bāmâ*.[47] Additionally, this was the site of the famed Tel Dan Inscription. Even though Jeroboam I had relocated Israel's capital to Tirzah, Shechem remained an administrative center, particularly for tax collection.[48] The destruction of Stratum IX appears to have occurred in two phases, one that correlates to Ben-hadad's invasion in 856, the other fitting the raids under Hazael around 810.[49]

Southern Kingdom

The invasions by Shishak in 925 BCE left an indelible mark on the Judean landscape. This massive destruction, however, merely demonstrates the constructive productivity of Judah's ninth-century kings, most notably Asa and Jehoshaphat. One such city whose ruins testify to Judah's fortitude was Arad. Although the last mention of Arad as a place name is Judges 1:16, its importance to the southern kingdom is evident in the archaeological record. Following Shishak's tenth-century raids, the fortress underwent significant modifications. The solid fortress wall was replaced by a sawtooth casemate wall. The new gate was flanked by two massive towers. Furthermore, a water collection system with two large cisterns was installed.[50] Besides the renovations in the defense infrastructure, the ninth-century changes included restoration to the temple complex. Not only was the temple repaired, but also its sanctuary was enlarged, possibly to align with the increased standard of the royal cubit from 45 to 52.5 centimeters.[51] The size of the new altar, 5 x 5 cubits, corresponds to the specifications given in Exodus 27:1. Since the dating of Stratum X is not known precisely, both Asa and Jehoshaphat are viable candidates for the construction. Further, the destruction may have occurred during the reign of Jehoram (2 Chron. 21:8–10, 16–17) or with Hazael's invasion of Judah during the reign of Joash (= Jehoash; 2 Kings 12:17–18).[52]

It has already been mentioned that Ezion-geber was notable during Jehoshaphat's reign as a port city. During this period the port was fortified "with massive double walls and elaborate city gates,"[53] and the construction style at

---

47. David Ilan, "Dan," *OEANE* 2:109; Avraham Biran, "Dan, Tel," *EAEHL* 1:320.

48. Lawrence E. Toombs, "Shechem (Place)," *ABD* 5:1184.

49. Edward F. Campbell and James F. Ross, "The Excavations of Shechem and the Biblical Tradition," *BA* 26 (1963): 22.

50. Ze'ev Herzog et al., "The Israelite Fortress at Arad," *BASOR* 254 (1984): 1–34.

51. Yohanan Aharoni, "The Israelite Sanctuary at Arad," in *New Directions in Biblical Archaeology* (ed. David Noel Freedman and Jonas C. Greenfield; Garden City, NY: Doubleday, 1971), 28–44.

52. Dale W. Manor and Gary A. Herion, "Arad," *ABD* 1:334.

53. Meier Lubetski, "Ezion-Geber," *ABD* 2:724.

Lawson Stone

Figure 9.4. Arad

Ezion-geber is similar to that at Arad.[54] Its destruction may very well comport with the Edomite revolt as depicted in 2 Kings 8:20–22.

Although there are few intriguing finds throughout the southern Levant, evidence of ninth-century construction is possible in other locations. In Mizpah we find evidence of a new wall, a massive tower, and an increase in the number of buildings, all of which may date to the ninth century.[55] The dating of Stratum IV at Lachish is less certain and may date to Rehoboam, Asa, or Jehoshaphat.[56] Construction at Jerusalem was minimal during this period.

Historical Issues of Ninth-Century Israel and Judah

It becomes readily apparent that the biblical record does not always comport with the extrabiblical evidence. Moreover, the biblical text is not always consistent with itself in some respects. Before these issues can be resolved with any degree of satisfaction, it will be helpful to briefly review the most pressing issues raised from a historical study of ninth-century Israel and Judah. While several minor issues could be addressed, the remainder of this chapter

54. Aharoni, *Archaeology*, 249.
55. Ibid., 243.
56. David Ussishkin, "Lachish," *ABD* 4:120–21.

turns to an investigation of the most critical issues raised from a historical analysis of the data.

Aramean Wars (1 Kings 20; 22:1–40)

Aram faced the Israelite forces three times in the closing chapters of 1 Kings. The first battle occurred at Samaria and is reported in 1 Kings 20:1–24, with Ahab proving victorious over Ben-hadad. The second battle (1 Kings 20:26–34) took place at Aphek and also resulted in an overwhelming defeat of the Aramean king Ben-hadad at the hand of Ahab. In the third and final battle (1 Kings 22:1–40) Ahab requested the assistance of Jehoshaphat in recapturing Ramoth-gilead from an anonymous Aramean king. The expedition was disastrous for Ahab, who died in the conflict.

The Kurkh Monolith Inscription of Shalmaneser III provides important contextual information because it explicitly names "Ahab, the Israelite" among the leaders of the Damascene Coalition at the Battle of Qarqar in 853 BCE. The date of the battle coincides with the final years of Ahab's reign (874/873–853). The challenge, however, is that the Assyrian evidence paints a slightly different picture. First, according to the Kurkh Monolith Inscription, the Aramean king who was contemporary with Ahab was Hadadezer (^{d}Adad-idri), not Ben-hadad. Second, 1 Kings 20:27 describes Ahab's military "like two little flocks of goats," whereas Aram's troops "filled the country." However, in the Assyrian annals Israel and Aram have comparably sized forces. Aram's chariotry numbered twelve hundred, while Israel's numbered two thousand; Aram's troops totaled twenty thousand, Israel's ten thousand. Third, whereas the Bible consistently depicts Aram and Israel as enemies, Shalmaneser's inscription considers them allies in the Damascene Coalition. Finally, there is an apparent internal discrepancy in 1 Kings 22 in the manner in which Ahab died. Did he die at the hand of the Aramean king (1 Kings 22:37), or did he die peacefully (1 Kings 22:40)?

The Moabite War of 2 Kings 3

According to Nadav Na'aman, there are five historical problems with the account of 2 Kings 3 in relation to the Mesha Stela:

1. It is unlikely that Joram would have participated in a campaign against Moab after the death of his father, Ahab.
2. The author inserted into the account the name of the pious king Jehoshaphat in the place of the sinful king Joram.
3. The mention of an Edomite king is an anachronism, reflecting conditions of a later author.

4. During the Omride dynasty Aram and Israel were allies against Assyria, not mutual enemies.

5. In the biblical account the capital of Moab is given as Kir-hareseth, whereas the Mesha Inscription states that it was Dibon, then Qarhoh.[57]

In addition to Na'aman's objections, Lester Grabbe has noted two more contradictions. First, in the Old Testament, Mesha was a vassal of Ahab, whereas in the Moabite inscription Mesha was a vassal of Ahab and Omri. Second, in the biblical account Mesha rebelled after Ahab's death, but in the inscription Mesha rebelled during Ahab's lifetime.[58]

Jehu's Revolt

According to the biblical record, Jehu was given the prophetic mandate to destroy the entire house of Ahab (2 Kings 9–10). Naturally, this directive included Ahab's son Joram, but it also included Ahaziah, the son of Athaliah, a granddaughter of Omri (2 Kings 8:26). According to the Bible, Jehu is venerated because he annihilated the house of Omri. However, in the Tel Dan Inscription, Hazael takes credit for the royal assassination. On the one hand, the Tel Dan Inscription confirms the assassination of Joram and Ahaziah; on the other hand, they disagree markedly on the details.

Dominant Kingdom

Does the Bible underplay Ahab? Does it overplay Jehoshaphat? Both kings are given heavy consideration by the biblical authors. Whereas the "Book of Kings records more about Ahab than any other Northern monarch,"[59] the "Chronicler devotes almost as many words to Jehoshaphat (101 verses) as he does to Hezekiah (117 verses)."[60] However, the portrayal of these respective kings diverges greatly. For both the Deuteronomist and the Chronicler, there is little for which the house of Omri could be commended. As J. Alberto Soggin succinctly notes, "With very few exceptions, the biblical texts have nothing but negative comments to make about Omri and his son Ahab."[61] By contrast,

57. Nadav Na'aman, "Royal Inscription versus Prophetic Story: Mesha's Rebellion according to Biblical and Moabite Historiography," in Grabbe, *Ahab Agonistes*, 164–65.

58. Lester L. Grabbe, "Are Historians of Ancient Palestine Fellow Creatures—or Different Animals?," in *Can a "History of Israel" Be Written?* (ed. Lester L. Grabbe; JSOTSup 245; Sheffield: Sheffield Academic Press, 1997), 25.

59. Hayyim Angel, "Hopping between Two Opinions: Understanding the Biblical Portrait of Ahab," *JBQ* 35 (2007): 3.

60. Gary N. Knoppers, "Reform and Regression: The Chronicler's Presentation of Jehoshaphat," *Bib* 72 (1991): 500.

61. Soggin, *History of Israel and Judah*, 213.

Jehoshaphat's shortcomings, if mentioned at
all, are heavily glossed, such that in 1–2 Kings
"one is struck by the lack of commentary
on, or evaluation of, Jehoshaphat's treaty
with Ahab, his abortive shipbuilding venture, and his refusal of a maritime treaty
with Ahaziah."[62] Moreover, the portrayal
of the Jehoshaphat of Chronicles is even
more positive, prompting only a mild prophetic rebuke for his pact with Ahab at
Ramoth-gilead (2 Chron. 18:1–19:3).[63] In
other words, for the Chronicler, the most
glaring blemish in Jehoshaphat's portfolio
was his brief association with Ahab.

The extrabiblical evidence, however,
tells a different story. Although Ahab and
the Omrides are mentioned in Shalmaneser's annals, the Mesha Inscription, and
the Tel Dan Inscription, "the sources for
Jehoshaphat's reign are restricted to the
biblical record."[64] Furthermore, although the
archaeological record indicates some marked
improvements in Judah's architecture during

Paterm/Wikimedia Commons

Figure 9.5.
Mesha Stela

Jehoshaphat's reign, it pales in comparison to the engineering exploits of his
northern counterpart. Beyond the visible evidence of construction feats in
this period, the ninth century also shows a distinct difference in the economic
viability and the political independence of these neighboring kingdoms.

Evaluation of the Evidence

Aramean Wars

According to the historical record, Aram-Damascus had four kings during
the ninth century. Bar-hadad I ruled during the first quarter of the century,
followed by Hadadezer, who ruled during the middle of the ninth century. Bar-
hadad II succeeded Hadadezer and ruled only briefly before Hazael usurped

---

62. Knoppers, "Reform and Regression," 503.
63. Gary N. Knoppers, "Jehoshaphat's Judiciary and 'The Scroll of YHWH's Torah,'"
JBL 113 (1994): 59–80.
64. Kenneth C. Way, "Jehoshaphat," *DOTHB* 531–34.

the throne in approximately 844/842 BCE.[65] As previously stated, the biblical record names Ben-hadad (the Hebrew form of Bar-hadad, meaning "son of the god Hadad") as the Aramean king contemporary with Ahab, while the Assyrian annals name Hadadezer as Ahab's ally in the Damascene Coalition.

The customary approach for many biblical historians is to privilege the Assyrian sources. To synchronize the Assyrian and biblical sources, then, the texts pertaining to the Aramean wars must be dated to a later period. This position is best summarized by Grabbe: "An explanation of the biblical picture has become widely accepted in scholarship: 1 Kings 20–22 contains material from the later Jehu dynasty (e.g., 2 Kings 13) which has been mistakenly assigned to the reign of Ahab."[66] Simon De Vries, however, thinks that these accounts, particularly 1 Kings 22, fit better with Joram's reign.[67] In both cases, the inclination is to assert that the biblical writers were more likely to identify the kings of Aram correctly than to situate their own kings with accuracy.

While the historian may have theological reasons for manipulating historical details to serve his agenda, it is not necessary to suggest so in this case. Due to the prevalence of the name "Ben-hadad" in both the Aramean and biblical texts, it is quite likely that the name was a dynastic throne name.[68] This suggestion is supported by Amos 1:4, in which "Ben-hadad" is in parallel with "Hazael." If Hazael may be known as Ben-hadad, it stands to reason that Hadadezer likewise may be called "Ben-hadad" by the Deuteronomist. In fact, the throne name may be preferable for the biblical authors, who are less acquainted with the Aramean monarchs than with their own.

Besides the obvious disparity in the size of Ahab's army between 1 Kings and Shalmaneser's inscriptions, Na'aman asks, "Is it really feasible that the kingdom of Israel by itself had at its disposal a chariot force equal in strength to that of the Assyrian Empire at the height of its greatness under Shalmaneser III?"[69] Citing Hayim Tadmor's observation that Shalmaneser's account of the Battle of Qarqar contains at least ten scribal errors,[70] Na'aman suggests

---

65. Wayne T. Pitard, *Ancient Damascus: A Historical Study of the Syrian City-State from Earliest Times until Its Fall to the Assyrians in 732 B.C.E.* (Winona Lake, IN: Eisenbrauns, 1987), 145.

66. Lester L. Grabbe, *Ancient Israel: What Do We Know and How Do We Know It?* (London: T&T Clark, 2007), 47. See also Nadav Na'aman, "The Northern Kingdom in the Late Tenth–Ninth Centuries BCE," in Williamson, *Understanding the History*, 408.

67. Simon J. De Vries, *1 Kings* (WBC 12; Dallas: Word, 1985), 269.

68. Donald J. Wiseman, *1 and 2 Kings: An Introduction and Commentary* (TOTC 9; Downers Grove, IL: InterVarsity, 1993), 176.

69. Nadav Na'aman, "Ahab's Chariot Force at Qarqar," in *Ancient Israel and Its Neighbors: Interaction and Counteraction* (vol. 1 of *Collected Essays*; Winona Lake, IN: Eisenbrauns, 2005), 9.

70. Hayim Tadmor, "Que and Musri," *IEJ* 11 (1961): 144–45n10.

that "the number 200 is much more suitable to the reality of that period than the number 2,000."[71] For him, it is inconceivable that Israel's chariot force would equal that of Assyria's at its peak with two thousand chariots. Cantrell, however, is not so hasty to dismiss the Assyrian numbers.[72] First, she notes the improbability of multiple sources having virtual agreement. Second, Israel possessed the land and labor resources to support between five thousand and ten thousand horses. Likewise, based on his assessment of Assyrian "Horse Lists," Frederick Fales concludes that the Assyrian numbers probably reflect a fairly accurate account of the coalition's chariot forces.[73]

Another suggestion to account for the size of Israel's chariotry in Shalmaneser's annals is that the number given in the Assyrian sources may represent not only Israel's forces but also those of its vassals: Judah, Moab, and Edom.[74] Furthermore, it should be remembered that both the Assyrian and biblical accounts were written with a specific rhetorical intent. For the Assyrians, it speaks well of the king to have defeated a large army. It would be expected for Shalmaneser to embellish the size of the enemy for propagandistic purposes. The biblical text has a similar rhetorical objective. Its purpose is to show that Yahweh is sovereign over both the mountains and the lowlands. With Yahweh at the vanguard, Israel cannot be defeated, regardless of the disproportionate armies. Nonetheless, it appears as though Ahab was quickly able to replenish his depleted forces from nearby Jezreel and Beth Shean.[75] Thus in 1 Kings 20:15 Ahab's army is seven thousand strong, a force comparable to the ten thousand listed in the Kurkh Monolith Inscription, especially if one allows for the expected exaggeration on the part of Shalmaneser.[76] Moreover, unlike the idiomatic phrase "like two little flocks of goats" in 20:27, the number in 20:15 represents what appears to be an actual register of troops, accounting for the usual treatment of numbers in the biblical texts.[77]

---

71. Na'aman, "Ahab's Chariot Force," 9.

72. Cantrell, *Horsemen of Israel*, 118n20.

73. Frederick Mario Fales, "Preparing for War in Assyria," in *Économie antique: La guerre dans les economies antiques* (ed. Jean Andreau, Pierre Briant, and Raymond Descant; EAH 5; Saint-Bertrand-de-Comminges: Musée d'archéologie départmental, 2000), 52–53.

74. André Lemaire, "Hebrew and West Semitic Inscriptions and Pre-Exilic Israel," in *In Search of Pre-exilic Israel: Proceedings of the Oxford Old Testament Seminar* (ed. John Day; JSOTSup 406; London: T&T Clark, 2004), 366–85; Brad E. Kelle, "What's in a Name? Neo-Assyrian Designations for the Northern Kingdom and Their Implications for Israelite History and Biblical Interpretation," *JBL* 121 (2002): 643.

75. Cantrell, *Horsemen of Israel*, 119.

76. K. Lawson Younger Jr., "Neo-Assyrian and Israelite History in the Ninth Century: The Role of Shalmaneser III," in Williamson, *Understanding the History*, 255.

77. John W. Wenham, "Large Numbers in the Old Testament," *TynBul* 18 (1967): 19–53; Alan R. Millard, "Large Numbers in Assyrian Royal Inscriptions," in *Ah, Assyria . . . : Studies in*

Since the Assyrian annals of Shalmaneser list Ahab, alongside Hadadezer of Damascus and Irhuleni of Hamath, it is often said that the biblical account regarding enmity between Aram and Israel must relate to a post-Omride period. Edward Lipiński's assessment has become the veritable consensus on the issue: "The stories of I Kings 20 and 22 do not belong to the time of Ahab, who appears instead as an ally of Hadadezer in the royal inscription of Shalmaneser III (858–824). The chronology of the Bible and its use of older sources referring to this period are extremely problematical."[78] However, this valuation may attribute too much weight to a single line in the Assyrian inscription. Wayne Pitard ascribes the absence of Israel in Shalmaneser's later annals to the simple fact that Hadadezer remained the dominant member of the coalition,[79] while both J. Alberto Soggin and Siegfried Horn argue that Shalmaneser's continued attacks on the Damascene Coalition merely demonstrate a persistent alliance between Israel and Aram.[80] It may also be the case, though, that Israel's absence from these later annals suggests that the alliance with Israel had dissolved shortly after the Battle of Qarqar.[81] As V. Philips Long suggests, "There is nothing improbable in the notion that Ahab first joined Aram in opposing an Assyrian threat, but then, when that threat was removed, turned against his former ally."[82] In fact, we have evidence of a similar situation occurring between Mari and Ekallatum, who allied themselves with Elam only to become hostile toward each other once the threat dissipated.[83] Long's suggestion is not without merit. First, the Tel Dan Inscription states, "The king of Israel entered previously in my father's land" (lines 3–4). While "the king" may refer to Joram, whom Hazael claims to have killed, it may also refer to Ahab, since Joram is mentioned by name in lines 7–8. Second, 1 Kings 22:1 states that three years had passed since Aram

---

Assyrian and Ancient Near Eastern Historiography Presented to Hayim Tadmor (ed. Mordechai Cogan and Israel Eph'al; ScrHier 33; Jerusalem: Magnes, 1991), 213–22.

78. Edward Lipiński, *The Aramaeans: Their Ancient History, Culture, Religion* (OLA 100; Leuven: Peeters, 2000), 375.

79. Pitard, *Ancient Damascus, 130.*

80. Soggin, *History of Israel and Judah,* 220; Siegfried Horn, "The Divided Monarchy: The Kingdoms of Judah and Israel," in *Ancient Israel: From Abraham to the Roman Destruction of the Temple* (ed. Hershel Shanks; rev. ed.; Washington, DC: Biblical Archaeology Society, 1999), 146.

81. William W. Hallo, "From Qarqar to Carchemish: Assyria and Israel in the Light of New Discoveries," *BA* 23 (1960): 34–61, esp. 40.

82. V. Philips Long, "How Reliable Are Biblical Reports? Repeating Lester Grabbe's Comparative Experiment," *VT* 52 (2002): 371.

83. Wolfgang Heimpel, *Letters to the King of Mari: A New Translation, with Historical Introduction, Notes, and Commentary* (MC 12; Winona Lake, IN: Eisenbrauns, 2003), 128–31. See also Richard S. Hess, review of Wolfgang Heimpel, *Letters to the King of Mari, DJ* 8 (2005), http://www.denverseminary.edu/article/letters-to-the-king-of-mari.

and Israel had last engaged each other in battle, suggesting that the alliance with Aram was brief. Finally, neither the Hebrew text nor the Septuagint demands that 1 Kings 20–22 be read in historical sequence. The Septuagint does not separate the three battles with the story of Naboth's vineyard (1 Kings 21). Furthermore, the Hebrew account of these three battles begins with an inverted syntax, in which the subject precedes the verb. This syntactic feature may indicate several situations, but the likely possibilities include (1) to indicate contrast, (2) to indicate a change of subject, or (3) to express anterior time.[84] In either case, the syntax suggests a break from the previous narrative, which seems to complement the ancient Near Eastern evidence rather than contradict it.[85]

In 1 Kings 22 we have what look like two opposing conclusions to Ahab's life. According to verse 37, Ahab died and was buried in Samaria; in verse 40, however, Ahab "slept with his ancestors." According to J. Maxwell Miller, this phrase "appears elsewhere in his history only in the cases of those kings who died a natural death."[86] De Vries presses the implications by stating that the phrase "has to mean that he died in peace and honor, and therefore cannot apply to the king of v. 37."[87] The argument, then, is that both verses cannot refer to the same king. However, there appear to be two notable exceptions to the use of this phrase. The first is found in the demise of Ahaziah, who perished in a manner quite similar to Ahab (2 Kings 9:27–28). Having been pierced by an arrow from Jehu's men, Ahaziah died and was buried "with his ancestors" (9:28). The second is seen in the account of Azariah/Uzziah, who, though struck with leprosy for committing cultic offenses, nonetheless "slept with his ancestors" (15:7). Thus, it may be argued that leprosy does not permit a natural death, or at least not an honorable death. Therefore, Azariah did not die with peace and honor. In reality, the absence of the phrase "slept with his ancestors" seems to be an indication that the king died as a result of a palace coup,[88] either at the hands of humans or of God. Since Ahab died in neither fashion, and because he was an ally with the pious Jehoshaphat, it is not surprising that Ahab was buried in Samaria and "slept with his ancestors."

84. Ronald J. Williams, *Hebrew Syntax: An Outline* (2nd ed.; Toronto: University of Toronto Press, 1976), 96–97; Bill T. Arnold and John H. Choi, *A Guide to Biblical Hebrew Syntax* (Cambridge: Cambridge University Press, 2003), 169–70.

85. See Long, "How Reliable Are Biblical Reports?," 371.

86. J. Maxwell Miller, "The Elisha Cycle and the Accounts of the Omride Wars," *JBL* 85 (1966): 445. See also Marsha White, "Naboth's Vineyard and Jehu's Coup: The Legitimation of a Dynastic Extermination," *VT* 44 (1994): 66–76, esp. 72.

87. De Vries, *1 Kings*, 269.

88. See, e.g., Elah (1 Kings 16:10), Zimri (16:18), Tibni (16:22), Joram (2 Kings 9:24), Ahaziah (9:27), and Jezebel (9:33).

Moabite War Clarified

According to André Lemaire, "The historical interpretation of the Mesha Stela is fraught with a prioris that have obscured its historical interpretation in the past because of overhasty references to the Bible on two points: dating and wars."[89] Lemaire even maintains that 2 Kings 3 and the Mesha Inscription do not recount the same events. Furthermore, T. Raymond Hobbs asserts that a harmonization of these two texts is impossible.[90] By contrast, Frank Moore Cross and David Noel Freedman are more optimistic, saying, "The two sources give supplementary accounts of the conflict, which resulted in the independence of Moab."[91] Anson Rainey concurs, viewing the two narratives as complementary accounts of the same historical event.[92] Although differences clearly emerge between the two accounts, the minor inconsistencies do not make it necessary to drastically alter its placement in the biblical narrative.

Among Na'aman's five objections to the historian's account of the Moabite war (see "The Moabite War of 2 Kings 3" on pp. 306–7), several are readily resolved. In fact, his first and fourth objections are addressed either directly or indirectly in the previous section. These two objections rest on the assumption that "the story about the campaign of the three kings against Moab was composed in Judah quite late,"[93] due, in part, to the premise that Edom did not develop into a kingdom until the eighth century.[94] However, this premise does not coincide with recent archaeological excavations at the Edomite fortress at Khirbat en-Nahas. Using both radiocarbon and isotope dating methods, Thomas Levy and Mohammad Najjar have confirmed "that during the mid-ninth century BCE, the gatehouse and probably the fortress ceased to have a military function, but they were part of large-scale metal production activities at the site."[95] There is strong evidence to suggest that Edom participated in metallurgical activities as early as the fifteenth–thirteenth centuries BCE. It now appears that copper production during the Iron Age allowed Edom to

---

89. André Lemaire, "West Semitic Inscriptions and Ninth-Century BCE Ancient Israel," in Williamson, *Understanding the History*, 288.

90. T. Raymond Hobbs, *2 Kings* (WBC 13; Dallas: Word, 1985), 40.

91. Frank Moore Cross and David Noel Freedman, *Early Hebrew Orthography: A Study of the Epigraphic Evidence* (AOS 36; New Haven: American Oriental Society, 1952), 40.

92. Anson F. Rainey and R. Steven Notley, *The Sacred Bridge: Carta's Atlas of the Biblical World* (Jerusalem: Carta, 2006), 203–5.

93. Na'aman, "Royal Inscription," 164.

94. John R. Bartlett, "Edom," *ABD* 2:287–95; Kenneth G. Hoglund, "Edomites," in *Peoples of the Old Testament World* (ed. Alfred J. Hoerth, Gerald L. Mattingly, and Edwin M. Yamauchi; Grand Rapids: Baker, 1994), 335–47.

95. Thomas E. Levy and Mohammad Najjar, "Edom and Copper: The Emergence of Ancient Israel's Rival," *BAR* 32, no. 4 (2006): 32.

thrive during the ninth century. While this does not prove an Edomite kingdom, it certainly bolsters the likelihood.

The remaining inconsistencies posited by Na'aman require a more detailed engagement. The first is the presence of Jehoshaphat, even though his death is recorded at the end of 1 Kings. This problem was not lost on translators of the Septuagint, who read "Ahaziah" in place of "Jehoshaphat." The suggestion, then, is that the original version did not contain Jehoshaphat's name, but had been inserted into the account because of his piety.[96] However, in every case in which the Hebrew text mentions "king of Judah," it also provides the king's name, Jehoshaphat. This is not so with Joram. His name appears only twice (2 Kings 3:1, 6), while the phrase "king of Israel" occurs six times, and "king over Israel" occurs once more. If redactors replaced Joram's name with Jehoshaphat's, they were not very thorough in doing so. In any case, 2 Kings 3:4, like 1 Kings 20 and 22, is introduced by a noun clause, indicating that the regular narrative flow is being disrupted in some manner. Either it is introducing a shift in scene (from Samaria to Moab), or it is introducing a shift in chronology. If the latter, then Jehoshaphat's name would be an indication that this chapter is a flashback to the final year of Jehoshaphat, the same year in which Joram ascended to the throne in Israel, around 848 BCE. This might also explain the political situation as described in 2 Kings 3:5. The most opportune time for a vassal to rebel against his sovereign is at the death of the sovereign's strong leader. Furthermore, the prompt action taken by Joram in 2 Kings 3:6 might support his recent ascension.

The final objection raised by Na'aman is that in Kings the capital of Moab is given as Kir-hareseth, whereas the Mesha Inscription states that it was Dibon, then Qarhoh. Erasmus Gass notes the presence of five place names mentioned in the Bible or the Mesha Inscription, all located in Moabite territory.[97] In support of Na'aman, Gass concludes that the archaeological evidence does not support a city of capital proportions in ancient Kir-hareseth.[98] However, it should be noted that the biblical text never claims that Kir-hareseth was the capital city of Moab, only that it was among the cities destroyed by the Israelites. If, however, "Kir-hareseth" did refer to Moab's capital, it may have been used as a derogatory term for Moab's capital, given the preponderance of city names prefixed with "Kir-" in that region.[99] Alternately, Rainey asserts

96. Steven L. McKenzie, *The Trouble with Kings: The Composition of the Book of Kings in the Deuteronomistic History* (VTSup 42; Leiden: Brill, 1991), 97.

97. Erasmus Gass, "Topographical Considerations and Redaction Criticism in 2 Kings 3," *JBL* 128 (2009): 65–84.

98. Ibid., 75.

99. Ibid.

that Moab had two capital cities: Dibon, the northern capital, and Kir-hareseth, the southern capital.[100]

Grabbe's two concerns deserve brief attention. It is true that the usual sense of *bnh* (his son) in line 6 of the Mesha Inscription would refer to Omri's eldest biological child. However, as is well known, "son" may also refer to any descendant. In this case, it is just as likely that "his son" refers not to Ahab but rather to Joram, another descendant from the house of Omri. In this light, lines 6–7 coincide nicely with the historical conditions of 2 Kings 3:5–6, 27. According to the biblical text, after Ahab's death the vassal Mesha rebelled against Joram, king of Israel. According to the Mesha Inscription, Omri's "son" determined to oppress Moab once again, but Mesha "enjoyed his sight and that of his house. And Israel perished utterly forever."[101] Although the two texts diverge considerably on the details, the outcome is similar. In typical royal fashion, Mesha's stela pronounces an overwhelming victory over his foes. Although 2 Kings 3:27 does not concede complete annihilation for Israel, it does record defeat at the hands of Mesha. Thus, if we account for the rhetorical agendas of each text, it seems just as likely that the Mesha Inscription and 2 Kings 3 recount the same event as not.

Jehu's Revolt

The issues surrounding Jehu's revolt are rather straightforward. The Deuteronomistic Historian claims that Jehu, by virtue of prophetic decree, assassinated King Ahaziah of Judah, King Joram of Israel, and Joram's seventy sons. The Tel Dan Inscription tells a similar story with a different protagonist. In it, Hazael killed seventy kings, King Joram of Israel, and King Ahaziah of Judah. The basic events are in conformity: Joram and Ahaziah were assassinated. But assassinated by whom?

Before the discovery of the Tel Dan Inscription, Michael Astour suggested that a pro-Assyrian faction supported Jehu's revolt.[102] He argued that Jehu killed Joram and Ahaziah in an effort to quell the anti-Assyrian revolt and to appease Shalmaneser III. The evidence suggests, however, that Shalmaneser III's primary interest after the dissolution of the Damascene Coalition was Hazael of Aram, not Israel. Furthermore, it seems rather unlikely that Jehu's political supporters would demand tribute shortly thereafter, as depicted in the Black Obelisk.

100. Rainey and Notley, *Sacred Bridge*, 205.
101. André Lemaire, "'House of David' Restored in Moabite Inscription," *BAR* 20, no. 3 (1994): 30–37.
102. Michael C. Astour, "841 B.C.: Assyria's First Invasion of Israel," *JAOS* 91 (1971): 388.

This reference to Jehu as a "son of Omri" in the Black Obelisk has led to some interesting speculation with respect to Jehu's revolt. While Na'aman considers the phrase "an apparent contradiction,"[103] Tammi Schneider suggests that Jehu was actually a member of the Omride dynasty.[104] Likewise, Lipiński wonders how Jehu could have killed the last of the Omride kings, given his status as a "son of Omri."[105] In reality, all these speculations are unnecessary. First, Shalmaneser may have been unaware of the change in dynastic rule in the minor western state of Israel. Second, the Assyrians used the phrase "son of" for multiple purposes, including offspring, descendant, subordinate, citizen, or member of a group.[106] Israel Eph'al has argued that "son of Omri" is one of three designations for Israel's kings, its kingdom, and its citizens.[107]

A third suggestion is that Jehu may have served as an agent of Hazael.[108] Thus, while Jehu may have initiated this genocidal act, perhaps Hazael authorized it. This hypothesis works especially well if, in fact, Israel was a vassal of Aram during the reign of Hazael, as Pitard contends.[109] It also fits with the prophetic oracle of 1 Kings 19:17, in which the Lord says to Elijah, "Whoever escapes from the sword of Hazael, Jehu shall kill; and whoever escapes from the sword of Jehu, Elisha shall kill." In other words, Hazael may have left some of his bidding to Jehu. This bloody coup d'état is also likely behind Hosea 1:4: "And the LORD said to him, 'Name him Jezreel; for in a little while I will punish the house of Jehu for the blood of Jezreel, and I will put an end to the kingdom of the house of Israel.'" Although the Deuteronomistic Historian looked favorably on Jehu for his acts of violence, the eighth-century prophet Hosea could look back only in horror.

Dominant Kingdom

The subtitle of this chapter asks whether Ahab is underplayed or Jehoshaphat is overplayed in the Old Testament. These are fair questions. Both Kings and Chronicles depict Jehoshaphat in a mostly positive light, while Ahab's portrayal is mostly negative. The theological basis for this treatment is obvious.

---

103. Nadav Na'aman, "Jehu Son of Omri: Legitimizing a Loyal Vassal by His Lord," in *Ancient Israel and Its Neighbors: Interaction and Counteraction* (vol. 1 of *Collected Essays*; Winona Lake, IN: Eisenbrauns, 2005), 13–15.

104. Tammi Schneider, "Rethinking Jehu," *Bib* 77 (1996): 100–107.

105. Lipiński, *The Arameans*, 380.

106. *CAD* M/1, 308.

107. Israel Eph'al, "The Samarian(s) in the Assyrian Sources," in Cogan and Eph'al, *Ah, Assyria*, 36–45.

108. Schniedewind, "Tel Dan Stela," 85.

109. Pitard, *Ancient Damascus*, 151.

On the one hand, Ahab's marriage with the Phoenician princess Jezebel gave an official endorsement to Baalism and paved the way for religious persecution in the north, especially against the prophets of Yahweh. Jehoshaphat, on the other hand, was the righteous king who twice requested to inquire of a prophet of the Lord before battle (1 Kings 22:7; 2 Kings 3:11). The Chronicler saw an even more pronounced divide between the two kings. Only one chapter (2 Chron. 18) is devoted to Ahab's reign and reports his death at Ramoth-gilead. Jehoshaphat, by contrast, "had great riches and honor" (18:1), initiated religious and judicial reforms (19:3–11),[110] offered an elaborate public prayer prior to the Moabite conflict (20:5–13), and "walked in the way of his father Asa and did not turn aside from it" (20:32). In both Kings and Chronicles the oracle against Ahab by Elijah is vindictive and demeaning (1 Kings 21:19), while the prophetic admonitions uttered against Jehoshaphat for his misgivings were but mild rebukes (2 Chron. 19:1–3; 20:37).

The extrabiblical evidence, however, paints a different picture. First, unlike ninth-cenury Judah, the Omride dynasty is present not only in several ancient Near Eastern texts; it also is a dominant player in international affairs. In both the Tel Dan Inscription and the Mesha Inscription, the Omrides oppressed their foreign enemies. In fact, the oppression was severe enough to warrant later retaliation by Hazael and Mesha. The Kurkh Monolith Inscription names Ahab, the Israelite, among the three chiefs of the Damascene Coalition.

Second, Ahab's building accomplishments have been well documented. According to Brad Kelle and Brent Strawn, "Archaeology has shown that during the Omride period impressive cities that functioned as administrative centers were built, and further suggests the emergence of a fully developed territorial state in Israel, defined by sophisticated organization, a standing army and international trade."[111] Ahab either constructed or completed the palace complex at Samaria, which held a cache of ivory carvings. At Megiddo, he was responsible for the construction of horse stables and the intricate water delivery system. At Hazor, Ahab built an impressive citadel and a water system similar to the one at Megiddo. Ahab also constructed a fortification wall.

Third, the Omrides's political prowess is also well attested. Herbert Parzen summarizes these accomplishments as follows: (1) they made peace with Judah for the first time since the united monarchy; (2) the marriage alliance with Jezebel solidified peaceful and profitable relations with Phoenicia; (3) they placated Damascus; (4) they conquered Moab; and (5) they formed alliances

110. For a critical treatment of Jehoshaphat's reforms, see Bernard S. Jackson, "Law in the Ninth Century: Jehoshaphat's 'Judicial Reform,'" in Williamson, *Understanding the History*, 369–97.

111. Brad E. Kelle and Brent A. Strawn, "History of Israel 5: Assyrian Period," *DOTHB* 463.

with Phoenicia and Damascus, opening commercial routes to the coast and Syria.[112] The Omrides, especially under Ahab, played an integral part in Syria-Palestine during the ninth century.

The extrabiblical portrait of Jehoshaphat is not as flattering, as incomplete as it may be. There is no record of Jehoshaphat outside the biblical texts. In fact, the only two ninth-century Israelite or Judahite kings mentioned in any extrabiblical text are Jehu in the Black Obelisk of Shalmaneser III, and Joash in the Tell Rimah Stela of Adad-nirari III. In both cases, they have the dubious distinction of being kings who paid tribute to Assyria. While Jehoshaphat was involved in some impressive construction projects at Arad, Ezion-geber, and Mizpah, his architectural achievements were neither as extensive nor as widespread as those of his northern counterpart.

From a purely historical perspective, the biblical text does overplay Jehoshaphat and underplay Ahab. Of course, since the so-called Historical Books of the Old Testament are not purely historical narratives, this should come as no surprise. The authors of Kings and Chronicles had a theological agenda that superseded the historical record. This does not mean that they were uninterested in actual human history; rather, they were more concerned with an accurate theological history.[113] Their very purpose for writing was not to show how humans were involved in history, but to show how God was at the center of it.

---

112. Herbert Parzen, "The Prophets and the Omri Dynasty," *HTR* 33 (1940): 70.
113. McKenzie, *Trouble with Kings*, 79.

10

Eighth-Century Issues

*The World of Jeroboam II, the Fall of Samaria,
and the Reign of Hezekiah*

SANDRA RICHTER

Israel's eighth-century-BCE world is reported in the histories found in the books of Kings and Chronicles as well as in the writings of the prophets Hosea, Amos, Micah, and Isaiah. Here we find a portrait of Israel and Judah at the height of their urban development and state formation, played out against the backdrop of an enduring kinship-based culture.[1] On the international scene we are told first of Aram and then of Assyria as dominating and directing Israel's fate, with the ultimate demise of the divided monarchy's golden age attributed to the expansion of the Neo-Assyrian Empire. This portrait as presented in the biblical text is confirmed and illuminated by an extraordinary

---

1. On Israel's kinship-based society, see Roland de Vaux, *Ancient Israel: Its Life and Institutions* (trans. John McHugh; London: Darton, Longman & Todd, 1961); Leo G. Perdue et al., *Families in Ancient Israel* (Louisville: Westminster John Knox, 1997); Philip J. King and Lawrence E. Stager, *Life in Biblical Israel* (LAI; Louisville: Westminster John Knox, 2001); Avraham Faust, *The Archaeology of Israelite Society in Iron Age II* (trans. Ruth Ludlum; Winona Lake, IN: Eisenbrauns, 2012).

Figure 10.1.

Eighth-century world

breadth of archaeological and epigraphic evidence. Archaeologically, Israel and Judah's political and cultural zenith is illustrated by an unprecedented number of settlements and expanse of land under exploitation. Many smaller finds indicate the affluence and influence of the northern kingdom in the first half of the century; a bonanza of recovered material culture demonstrates the impact of Hezekiah's rebellion against the Neo-Assyrian Empire in the second half. Epigraphically, a profusion of foreign and domestic inscriptions preserve and expand our understanding of Judah and Israel's experience in this century. As a result, we can approach the task of reconstructing the eighth century with great historiographic confidence. As Baruch Halpern attests, "There is not much doubt that the archaeological record of the 8th–6th centuries comports in almost every particular with the general political picture that we derive from epigraphs and the biblical record, critically regarded."[2]

2. Baruch Halpern, "The State of Israelite History," in *Reconsidering Israel and Judah: Recent Studies on the Deuteronomistic History* (ed. Gary N. Knoppers and J. Gordon McConville; SBTS 8; Winona Lake, IN: Eisenbrauns, 2000), 556. Halpern (ibid., 545–57) states that the Deuteronomistic History preserves a very accurate picture of the international arena in the eighth century, placing Israel and Judah in contact with Assyria and Aram, naming the Assyrian and Aramean monarchs of the day as well as their sons and assassins. The Chronicler, although by design

This century may be divided into two distinctive periods. The first half (800–745 BCE) is characterized by the wealth and influence of Jeroboam II and Uzziah's allied kingdoms. The second half (745–700 BCE) is dominated by the rise of the Neo-Assyrian Empire, the collapse of the northern kingdom, and Hezekiah's reign in the south.

Chart of the Kings

Israel		Judah		Assyria	
Jehoahaz	814/13–798	Joash	835–796	Adad-nirari III	810–783
Jehoash	798–782/81	Amaziah	796–767		
Jeroboam II	793/92–782/81; 782/81–753	Uzziah	792/91–767; 767–740/39	Tiglath-pileser III	744–727
Zechariah	753–752				
Shallum	752				
Menahem	752–742/41	Jotham	750–740/39; 740/39–732/31		
Pekahiah	742/41–740/39				
Peka	752–740/39; 740/39–732/31	Ahaz	735–732/31; 732/31–716/15	Shalmaneser V	727–722
Hoshea	732/31–723/22			Sargon II	722–705
		Hezekiah	729–716/15; 716/15–687/86	Sennacherib	705–681
		Manasseh	697/96–687/86; 687/86–643/42		
		Amon	643/42–641/40		
		Josiah	641/40–609		
		Jehoahaz	609		
		Jehoiakim	608–598		
		Jehoiachin	598–597		
		Zedekiah	597–586		

Overlapping reigns and coregencies appear in italics. Dates for Judean and Israelite kings are from Edwin R. Thiele, *The Mysterious Numbers of the Hebrew Kings: A Reconstruction of the Chronology of the Kingdoms of Israel and Judah* (3rd ed.; Grand Rapids: Eerdmans, 1983), 217.

First Half of the Eighth Century (800–745 BCE)

In the first half of the eighth century, Israel and Judah enjoyed a level of cooperation with each other and their neighbors such that they were able to control the critical trade routes connecting the Levant to Egypt and the East.

---

only reporting on the southern kingdom, "follows to the letter the chronological statements of Kings and does not change its data even when they collide with his theological tenets" (Sara Japhet, *I & II Chronicles: A Commentary* [OTL; Louisville: Westminster John Knox, 1993], 17).

A stable agricultural economy in the north and mineral resources in the south resulted in exceptional economic prosperity for both.[3] Internationally, the eighth century opens with Aram-Damascus dominating central Syria (2 Kings 12:18–19; 2 Kings 13:3–5, 22–25; 2 Chron. 24:23–25). But under Jehoahaz and Joash, per the prophecies of Elisha, Israel rebounds against the subjugation by its northern neighbor (2 Kings 13:14–25). Aram-Damascus's previous access to lower Galilee, Jezreel, and the Sharon plain is curtailed by means of three strategic Israelite victories, and the repatriation of the Gadites and Reubenites throughout the northern Transjordan begins (cf. 1 Chron. 5:16–26). It is probable that these successes are largely the result of Adad-Nirari III's conquest of Damascus in 796, perhaps the "deliverer" predicted in 2 Kings 13:3–5, 22–25.[4]

The Northern Kingdom

The following decades saw great successes for the northern kingdom. With the yoke of Aram-Damascus broken by the rod of Assyria, and Assyria itself experiencing a time of great weakness and withdrawal, the stage was set for Jeroboam II's ascension to the throne.[5] First as coregent with his father, Jehoash (793), and then as sole monarch (782), Jeroboam II transformed Israel's international standing by restoring the ancient boundaries "from the entrance of Hamath as far as the Sea of the Arabah," recovering Damascus and Hamath, and regaining almost full control over the Transjordan (2 Kings 14:25–28; cf. 1 Chron. 5:9–17; Amos 6:13–14).[6] Thus Jeroboam II's forty-one-year reign stands as the high-water mark for the northern kingdom economically and militarily. And although the Deuteronomic Historian is more than a bit con-

---

3. Edward F. Campbell, "A Land Divided: Judah and Israel from the Death of Solomon to the Fall of Samaria," *OHBW* 207.

4. Anson F. Rainey and R. Steven Notley, *The Sacred Bridge: Carta's Atlas of the Biblical World* (Jerusalem: Carta, 2006), 215; see also K. Lawson Younger Jr., "Saba'a Stela," COS 2.114E:274–75; idem, "Tell al Rimah Stela," COS 2.114F:275–76.

5. Aram dominated the northern Levant throughout most of the ninth century. Adad-nirari III's (810–783) successful campaign interrupted this reality long enough to free the northern kingdom from Aram's expansion into its territories. But the period following was one of decline in Assyria. The reigns of Shalmaneser IV (782–773), Ashur-dan III (772–755), and Ashur-nirari V (754–745) were marked by domestic revolt and mortal conflict with the expanding nation of Urartu. As a result, all energy was directed toward controlling ambitious provincial leaders and defending the borders of Assyria's heartland. Western campaigns evaporated, and the northern kingdom was freed to expand and prosper. See Marc Van de Mieroop, *A History of the Ancient Near East, ca. 3000–323 BC* (2nd ed.; Malden, MA: Blackwell, 2007), 240–48; William W. Hallo, "From Qarqar to Carchemish: Assyria and Israel in the Light of New Discoveries," *BA* 23 (1960): 41–44; Michael Roaf, *Cultural Atlas of Mesopotamia and the Ancient Near East* (New York: Facts on File, 1990), 158–76.

6. Scripture translations in this chapter are by the author.

flicted over such an evil but successful king (2 Kings 14:23–29), and although Hosea and Amos repeatedly decry his pitiless abuse of the voiceless in Israel, all identify Jeroboam II as the most politically successful king in the history of the northern kingdom.

Samaria: Its Ostraca and Ivories

Jeroboam II's capital was the third and most illustrious of the northern kingdom, Samaria. Built by Omri in 876 BCE, the fortified site was situated strategically in the heart of fertile agricultural land, astride the western branch of the National Highway, with direct access to the Jezreel Valley.[7] Here we find Israelite monumental architecture at its best. Brilliantly engineered, the raised central summit of Samaria's acropolis was utilized only for buildings related to royal function. The stonework of these buildings (including Ahab's "Ivory House") is renowned for its superior quality—beautifully dressed and set dry (i.e., without mortar) in header-stretcher design with outstanding precision. It has long been assumed that the Israelites acquired these skills from the Phoenicians.[8]

The Samaria ostraca, excavated in the western acropolis of Omri's city, are hailed as the most significant collection of inscribed documents from Israel and stand as an important early testimony to Israelite literacy. These also speak to the wealth and influence of Jeroboam II's kingdom. More than one hundred such potsherds inscribed with black ink have been excavated, sixty-three with legible Hebrew inscriptions. The typical formula is: "In the [Xth] year, from [place name] to [personal name], a jar of old wine/fine oil."[9] The years named are regnal years: the ninth, tenth, and fifteenth, and the assumption is that these are the years of Jehoash and Jeroboam II.[10] Although these notations clearly reflect some sort of governmental transaction involving shipments of the luxury items of virgin oil and vintage wine from various

---

7. Lawrence E. Stager, "Shemer's Estate," *BASOR* 277–78 (1990): 93–107; David A. Dorsey, *The Roads and Highways of Ancient Israel* (LBNEA; Baltimore: Johns Hopkins University Press, 1991), 140–44, 165.

8. See Nahman Avigad, "Samaria (City)," *NEAEHL* 4:1300–1303; Ron E. Tappy, "Samaria," *DOTHB* 855; King and Stager, *Life in Biblical Israel*, 22.

9. For transliteration and translation of all of the ostraca, see Sandra Landis Gogel, *A Grammar of Epigraphic Hebrew* (SBLRBS 23; Atlanta: Society of Biblical Literature, 1998), 6.1.21; see also Shmuel Ahituv, *Echoes From the Past: Hebrew and Cognate Inscriptions from the Biblical Period* (trans. and ed. Anson F. Rainey; Jerusalem: Carta, 2008), 258–312.

10. Anson Rainey (Rainey and Notley, *Sacred Bridge*, 221–22) offers a solution for the missing eleventh–fourteenth years. He claims that Jeroboam II came to the throne in 793 as coregent with his father, Jehoash, who had begun to reign in 798. Hence, Jeroboam II's tenth year is his father's fifteenth, and all the ostraca may come from the same two-year period.

settlements in the tribal inheritance of Manasseh to the royal household, there is significant debate as to their nature and function. Most have concluded that the ostraca are tax receipts, ostensibly communicating that the ancestral houses in the region were paying early and often for the extravagances of the eighth-century kings.[11] Anson Rainey mounts a convincing alternative: the recipients of the shipments ("to [personal name]") are actually members of the ancestral houses themselves, who were now serving as governmental appointees residing in the capital city and supporting themselves by means of their patrimonial estates outside the city.[12] All of the ostraca had been discarded (excavated from a fill beneath the floor of the "Ostraca House"). As incoming foodstuffs typically were identified by means of an inscription or clay bulla attached to the containing jar, and contemporary cuneiform evidence indicates that this information had to be collected before being finalized on papyrus ledgers, therefore Rainey argues that the Samaria ostraca are not tax receipts but "scratch-pad notations" discarded after the final ledger was tallied. Hence, the recipients of the shipments are not tax collectors but "servants of the crown" who are receiving supplies from their family estates.[13] His theory maintains the portrait of an affluent eighth-century royal city, "peopled by the king's retinue and mulcting the neighboring countryside,"[14] but answers a number of previously unaddressed questions. Not the least of these is why the ostraca were discarded and remained in the royal city if they were indeed receipts. The sherds upon which the notes are written come from vessels belonging to Samaria's stratum IV or V, and there is no paleographic distinction between those from the ninth, tenth, and fifteenth years; hence the relative date for all is set in the first quarter of the eighth century.

Of particular interest is the window that the Samaria ostraca provide into the societal evolution of the northern kingdom. Most would argue that by now Israel is an "advanced agrarian society" in which large landholders (one being the throne) were buying up tracts of land from smaller landholders,

11. Frank Moore Cross, *Canaanite Myth and Hebrew Epic: Essays in the History of the Religion of Israel* (Cambridge, MA: Harvard University Press, 1973), 222n11. Yigael Yadin countered that the *lāmed* prefixed to the personal name is possessive, and therefore the personal name represents the sender, not the tax collector (Avigad, "Samaria (City)," 1304).

12. These individuals are spoken of in the literature as the "*l*-men" because in Hebrew "to [personal name]" is written by affixing the Hebrew preposition *lāmed* to the beginning of a person's name (see Rainey and Notley, *Sacred Bridge*, 221–22). Stager is of a similar opinion, seeing these persons "not as bureaucratic officials such as tax collectors from various administrative districts around Samaria but as notables representing various clans in and about the capital" (*Life in Biblical Israel*, 313–14).

13. Rainey offers Mephibosheth (2 Sam. 9:7–13) as a case in point: he eats "at the king's table" but still is expected to subsidize his own support (cf. 1 Sam. 8:14).

14. Campbell, "Land Divided," 234.

Lawson Stone

Figure 10.2. An example of the Samaria ivories

and a cycle had begun in which the peasantry was losing possession of their ancestral lands. In other words, the kinship structure so essential to Israelite society was disintegrating under the pressures of urbanization and monarchy. As Avraham Faust summarizes, "The vast majority of the population was composed of small, poor farmers who had been dispossessed of their lands and were in a constant state of impoverishment and became hired staff employed in the royal economy."[15] But the Samaria ostraca temper these perceptions.[16] To our surprise, these eighth-century ostraca rehearse the same clan names attributed to Manasseh in Numbers 26:30–33 and Joshua 17:1–6, thus demonstrating that land given to the clans of Manasseh during the settlement remained in the hands of their descendants until this time. Apparently, even in Jeroboam II's urbanized and stratified monarchy, clan identity was still foundational to economic and social organization.[17]

The Samaria ivories further illustrate the wealth and international character of Jeroboam II's kingdom. Named by Nahman Avigad as "the most important collection of miniature art from the Iron Age discovered in Israel," these were first excavated on the royal acropolis, on the floor of Ahab's courtyard north of the Ostraca House.[18] Subsequent expeditions unearthed many more: ivory plaques and hundreds of ivory fragments throughout the royal quarter. The largest concentration of pieces came from the rubbish

15. Faust, *Archaeology*, 14.

16. De Vaux, *Ancient Israel*, 68–83; Lawrence E. Stager, "The Finest Olive Oil in Samaria," *JSS* 28 (1983): 241–45; J. David Schloen, *The House of the Father as Fact and Symbol: Patrimonialism in Ugarit and the Ancient Near East* (SAHL 2; Winona Lake, IN: Eisenbrauns, 2001), 165; Oded Borowski, *Agriculture in Iron Age Israel* (Boston: American Schools of Oriental Research, 2002), 26.

17. Faust, *Archaeology*, 13–27; Carol Meyers, "Kinship and Kingship: The Early Monarchy," *OHBW* 200–201.

18. Avigad, "Samaria (City)," 1304–5.

deposit of the Ivory House. The diverse collection may be distinguished as two main groups: (1) plaques carved in high relief, the background being generally pierced or open, with sphinxes, lions, bulls, and human figures predominating; and (2) plaques carved in low relief, decorated with insets of precious stones, colored glass, and gold foil. Syrian, Egyptian, and especially Phoenician influence is evident throughout. Many of the plaques have letters in Hebrew script. The ivories were most likely used as inlays in the palace furniture of the Israelite kings.[19]

The Prophetic Critique by Amos and Hosea

Amos preaches during the reign of Jeroboam II, "two years before the earthquake" (Amos 1:1).[20] Although he was a native southerner and a farmer, his target audience was Samaria, the capital of the Northern Kingdom. Hence, the prophet's oracles are full of allusions to and descriptors of Israel's eighth-century world. Aram-Damascus, the "house of Hazael," and Ben-hadad are specifically condemned because of their harsh treatment of Gilead during Hazael's conquest in the latter part of the ninth century (Amos 1:3–5). Philistia is condemned (cf. 2 Chron. 21:16–17), and Phoenicia, Edom, Ammon, and Moab are specified as well (Amos 1:6–2:3). Clearly this prophet is "fully informed about the political and military events of the late ninth to early eighth centuries BCE."[21]

Amos is fully informed regarding the northern kingdom's cult sites at Bethel and Dan as well. As Frank Moore Cross rehearses in *Canaanite Myth and Hebrew Epic*, one of the "grand bundle of themes" in the Deuteronomistic History is Jeroboam I's act of treason in his appointment of alternate centers of worship at his northern and southern borders.[22] His motivation was to maintain the integrity of his political schism by instituting a religious

---

19. Ibid., 1306.

20. Although we have no direct epigraphic record of this quake, the archaeological record of such an event in the first half of the eighth century is significant. The quake apparently was "strong enough to become paradigmatic of massive catastrophe, . . . a colloquial standard of comparison" (David Noel Freedman and Andrew Welch, "Amos's Earthquake and Israelite Prophecy," in *Scripture and Other Artifacts: Essays on the Bible and Archaeology in Honor of Philip J. King* [ed. Michael D. Coogan, Cheryl Exum, and Lawrence E. Stager; Louisville: Westminster John Knox, 1994], 189). See also William G. Dever, "A Case-Study in Biblical Archaeology: The Earthquake of ca. 760 BCE," *ErIsr* 23 (1992): 27–35*; Philip J. King, *Amos, Hosea, Micah: An Archaeological Commentary* (Philadelphia: Westminster, 1988), 21. Josephus conflates Amos 1:1; Zech. 14:5; 2 Chron. 26:16–21 in order to link this seismic benchmark to the story of Uzziah's sacrilege resulting in his leprosy (Freedman and Welch, "Amos's Earthquake," 189–90); cf. Zech. 14:5.

21. Rainey and Notley, *Sacred Bridge*, 222.

22. Cross, *Canaanite Myth*, 278–81.

schism, for, "if this people go up to offer sacrifices in the house of Yahweh at Jerusalem, then the heart of this people will return to their lord, to Rehoboam king of Judah; and they will kill me and return to Rehoboam king of Judah" (1 Kings 12:27). Hence, in the ancient sacred spaces at Bethel and Dan, Jeroboam initiated a syncretized form of Yahwism that adopted the cultic symbol of the northern territory's indigenous deity (Baal), a non-Levitical and voluntary priesthood (1 Kings 12:31; 13:33), and a new holy calendar,[23] all while claiming to embrace the orthodoxy of Sinai.[24] But with Jeroboam I's proclamation, "Behold your gods, O Israel, who brought you up from the land of Egypt!" (1 Kings 12:28), the Deuteronomistic Historian registers his opinion. Just as Aaron had lead the people into apostasy at the foot of Mount Sinai with his golden calf (Exod. 32:4, 8), so too had Jeroboam I. The continuation and expansion of this northern religion is evident from excavations at Dan, which demonstrate that the sacred area was heavily utilized and augmented during Jeroboam II's reign.[25] And so Amos speaks:

23. Borowski (*Agriculture*, 43) argues that this new calendar followed the agricultural cycle in the north, whereas the Jerusalem calendar followed the agricultural cycle in the south.

24. In the literature it is often stated that the bull calves of Jeroboam I's sanctuary were not intended as images of Baal or any other deity but rather were "intended to represent the throne of the invisible God of Israel," and therefore that rather than intentional syncretism, Jeroboam I was simply embracing an older symbol of Yahweh in his attempt to centralize the cult in the north and legitimize his claim to kingship (King, *Amos, Hosea, Micah*, 96–97; cf. Otto Eissfeldt, "El and Yahweh," *JSS* 1 [1956]: 25–37; Cross, *Canaanite Myth*, 73–75n117). Cross argues, "It is wholly implausible that an insecure usurper, in the attempt to secure his throne and to woo his subjects would flout fierce Yahwists by installing a foreign or novel god in his national shrine" (*Canaanite Myth*, 75). But as Gary Knoppers counters, the calves of Aaron and Jeroboam I are without question viewed as foreign cult symbols in the biblical text ("Aaron's Calf and Jeroboam's Calves," in *Fortunate the Eyes That See: Essays in Honor of David Noel Freedman in Celebration of His Seventieth Birthday* [ed. Astrid B. Beck et al.; Grand Rapids: Eerdmans, 1995], 92–104). Moreover, Daniel Fleming has clarified that El is always identified epigraphically as "bull," and the "calf" is reserved for younger deities—e.g., Baal ("If El Is a Bull, Who Is a Calf? Reflections on Religion in Second-Millennium Syria-Palestine," in *Frank Moore Cross Volume* [ed. Baruch A. Levine et al.; Eretz-Israel 26; Jerusalem: Israel Exploration Society, 1999], 24–25). Hence, if the iconography of the northern kingdom belongs to Yahweh/El, it should be a bull. In an upcoming article I will argue that, although an insecure usurper would indeed hesitate to replace a national deity, religious history amply illustrates that syncretism is a standard response in regions exploited by a colonizing power. The northern kingdom seceded (or not, as some might argue) based on the exploitative policies of the southern kingdom, whose king was, of course, divinely commissioned by Yahweh. It is entirely reasonable, and far more representative of the biblical record, to conclude that, in its secession, the north embraced a syncretized form of traditional Yahwism that claimed the covenant at Sinai, rejected the manifest destiny of the Davidic dynasty, while embracing the deity of the indigenous population, Baal.

25. Avraham Biran, "Tel Dan: Biblical Texts and Archaeological Data," in Coogan, Exum, and Stager, *Scripture and Other Artifacts*, 11–15.

> But do not seek [*tidrĕšû*] Bethel,
>   do not enter [*tābō'û*] Gilgal!
> (To) Beersheba you shall not cross over [in order to worship].
> For Gilgal will certainly go into captivity,
>   and Bethel will become *'āwen*. (Amos 5:5)

The language here surely is an intentional allusion to Deuteronomy 12:5, where Yahweh's most fundamental directive in regard to Israelite worship is first expressed: Israel is to seek out (*drš*) and come to (*bw'*) one, and only one, central cult site, the one of Yahweh's choosing:

> But you shall seek [*tidrĕšû*]
>   the place in which Yahweh your God will choose
> out of all your tribes to place his name,
>   and there you will come [*ûbā'tā*]. (Deut. 12:5)[26]

The rebuke regarding the northern kingdom is clear: Bethel and Dan are illegitimate, and the cult emanating from these sites will ultimately be the grounds for implementing the covenant curse (2 Kings 17:7–18; cf. Deut. 28).

Amos's use of *'āwen* (iniquity) to describe Bethel is also significant. His contemporary Hosea often refers to Bethel (*bêt 'ēl*, "house of God") as *bêt 'āwen*, meaning "house of iniquity" (Hosea 4:15; 5:8; 10:5; cf. 6:8; 10:8; 12:11). Based on fifteen occurrences in the Psalter in which "makers of *'āwen*" are identified as idol makers, Francis Andersen and David Noel Freedman argue that Amos's and Hosea's pejorative rendering of "Bethel" is intended to censure the northern kingdom's cult site as not merely a "house of iniquity," but also as a "house of idols" (cf. Amos 3:24; 4:4; 5:5; 7:10, 13).[27]

The book of Amos's greatest fame arises from its critique of Israel's domestic sphere. Apparently the successes of Jeroboam II's kingdom had not filtered down to the citizens of the land; rather, wealth and influence had produced a self-indulgent ruling class whose affluence had been built on the backs of the voiceless. "Thus says Yahweh: For three transgressions of Israel, and for four I will not revoke punishment. Because they sell the righteous for money, and the needy for a pair of sandals" (2:6).

Amos is appalled at unfair trade practices, the marginalization of the poor (2:6–8; 5:11; 8:4–6), an unjust court system (5:10–12), and the lavish, immoral,

---

26. For more on Deut. 12:5, see Sandra Richter, *The Deuteronomistic History and the Name Theology: lĕšakkēn šĕmô šām in the Bible and the Ancient Near East* (BZAW 318; Berlin: de Gruyter, 2002), 45–49, 51–54, 58–59, 61–63.

27. Francis I. Andersen and David Noel Freedman, *Hosea: A New Translation with Introduction and Commentary* (AB 24; Garden City, NY: Doubleday, 1983), 372.

self-absorbed consumerism of the upper class (6:4–7). Amos knows all about the ivory ornamentation of Jeroboam II's palace, as well as the luxurious lifestyle of his courtiers, as reflected in the Samaria ostraca.

> Woe to those who are at ease in Zion,
> and to those who feel secure in the mountain of Samaria. . . .
> Those who recline on beds of ivory
> and sprawl on their couches. . . .
> Therefore, they will now go into exile at the head of the exiles,
> and the sprawlers' banqueting[28] will pass away. (6:1–7)

Ultimately, Amos mocks Jeroboam II's acclaimed military and economic achievements as irrelevant in light of his larger crimes against his Lord. Even the king's greatest achievement, the restoration of Israel's boundaries "from the entrance of Hamath as far as the Sea of the Arabah," is "Lo-debar" (lit., "not-a-thing") in the prophet's eyes (Amos 6:13–14). "'For this reason I am going to raise up a nation against you, O house of Israel,' declares Yahweh, the God of Hosts, 'and they will afflict you from Lebo-hamath to the brook of the Arabah.'" This new opponent can be none other than the rising Assyrian Empire, which eventually would subjugate this same expanse of territory that Jeroboam had so gloriously conquered.[29]

The prophet Hosea, a native northerner, also targets the crimes of the northern kingdom. He is placed by most in the final years of Jeroboam II through the fall of Samaria in 722 BCE. He appears to have firsthand information regarding the Syro-Ephraimite conflict in 734–732 BCE.[30] But unlike Amos, Hosea's focus is neither the international scene of the eighth century nor the social injustices of Jeroboam II's kingdom; his primary focus is the apostasy of the northern cult.

Like Amos, Hosea declares the cult centers at Bethel and Dan and the false religion practiced there as the ultimate betrayal of the Sinai covenant. Through Hosea Yahweh names his rival for Israel's affections, Baal. In the spirit of the covenant lawsuit[31] and with the emotion of a wounded spouse, Hosea gives

---

28. The infamous *marzea* festival surely is in view here. See Jonathan S. Greer, "A Marzea and a Mizraq: A Prophet's Mêlée with Religious Diversity in Amos 6:4–7," *JSOT* 32 (2007): 243–62; Robert E. Cooley and Gary Davis Pratico, "Gathered to His People: An Archaeological Illustration from Tell Dothan's Western Cemetery," in Coogan, Exum, and Stager, *Scripture and Other Artifacts*, 70–92.

29. Campbell, "Land Divided," 232; cf. Rainey and Notley, *Sacred Bridge*, 223. See also Amos 3:9–11.

30. King, *Amos, Hosea, Micah*, 25–26.

31. For an introduction to the *rîb* (lawsuit) in Israelite prophecy, see Richard N. Soulen and R. Kendall Soulen, *Handbook of Biblical Criticism* (3rd ed.; Louisville: Westminster John

voice to Yahweh's anger and grief as the northern kingdom's now unavoidable judgment draws near:

> Contend with your mother, contend!
> For she is not my wife,
> and I am not her husband!
> So that she may put aside her promiscuity from her face
> and her adultery from between her breasts,
> lest I strip her naked
> and make her like the day of her birth,
> lest I make her like the wilderness,
> like a parched land, and kill her with thirst! (2:2–3)

Unlike most of the writing prophets, however, Hosea's message is, in large part, his life. Hosea is commissioned, "Take for yourself a wife of harlotry, and have children of harlotry, for the land commits flagrant harlotry, forsaking Yahweh" (Hosea 1:2). Whether Gomer was a woman with a reputation for promiscuous behavior or was a woman professionally employed as a prostitute has been hotly debated over the years.[32] Regardless of how Gomer earned her reputation, in her tribal, patriarchal culture she was an outcast, unmarriageable. Yet Hosea takes her in marriage and fathers three children, thereby providing for her societal standing and financial security. The paradox here is fully intentional: Hosea is to Gomer as Yahweh is to the northern kingdom.

But like Israel, this young woman, who had gone from nothing to everything, repeats the crimes of her past, and Hosea finds his wife not only cheating on him but also apparently engaged in prostitution (2:12 [10 ET]). By chapter 3, Gomer is being forced into slavery. Yahweh's command comes a second time: "Go and love again a woman who is loved by a neighbor and commits adultery" (3:1). Thus, although the prophet has already given this woman a home, children, and probably his heart, he now finds himself in the public

---

Knox, 2001), 165; Helmer Ringgren, "רִיב," *TDOT* 13:473–79; James Limburg, "The Root *ryb* and the Prophetic Lawsuit Speeches," *JBL* 88 (1969): 291–304; G. Ernest Wright, "The Lawsuit of God: A Form-Critical Study of Deuteronomy 32," in *Israel's Prophetic Heritage: Essays in Honor of James Muilenburg* (ed. Bernhard W. Anderson and Walter Harrelson; New York: Harper, 1962), 26–67.

32. The modifier used in Hosea 1:2 to describe Gomer is *zĕnûnîm*, meaning the "status and practice of the *zônâ*"; *zônâ* means "women occasionally or professionally committing fornication" (*HALOT* s.v. "זוֹנָה" and "זְנוּנִים" [1:275–76]). Thus, Gomer's exact status is unclear. The text may be speaking proleptically of the time when Gomer will become unfaithful to Hosea, thereby making her a "wife of harlotry" and their children "children of harlotry." This too, however, is debated.

square, bidding on her freedom: "So I bought her for fifteen shekels of silver and a homer and a half of barley" (3:2).[33] The message to Israel is clear. The nation has repeatedly breached its vows to Yahweh. Yahweh will forgive. But this time he will discipline his wayward nation so severely that her appetite for other lovers will be obliterated and her yearning for Yahweh confirmed: "'And it will come about in that day,' declares Yahweh, 'that you will call me *'îšî* [my husband/man], and no longer will you call me *ba'lî* [my husband/lord]'" (2:18 [16 ET]). Here the judgment of exile is tempered by the promised restoration so critical to the covenant lawsuit form. And who is the rival to be eradicated? "He has rejected your calf, O Samaria, saying, my anger burns against them. . . . A craftsman made it, so it is not a god! Surely the calf of Samaria will be broken to pieces!" (8:5–6; cf. 13:1–3).

As predicted by the prophets, the eigthth century will not end as well in the north as it began. Rather, the long and successful reign of Jeroboam II will be followed by the brief and unsuccessful sojourn of his son Zechariah (six months, 753), who is assassinated by Shallum (one month, 752), who is assassinated by Menahem (752), who manages to hold his throne for ten years, in large part due to his willing submission to the rising Neo-Assyrian Empire. Meanwhile, Pekah is ruling in the Transjordan as Menahem's rival. And when Menahem's son Pekahiah ascends the throne in 741 BCE, Pekah assassinates him and claims the reunited kingdom for himself in 740 BCE. Pekah's reign will come to an end in the midst of the disastrous Syro-Ephraimite conflict when Hoshea, with Assyria's approval, assassinates Pekah in 732 BCE (2 Kings 15:30). Hoshea is left with only the central hill country.[34] The specter of the Neo-Assyrian Empire is now in full view, and the days of the northern kingdom are numbered.

The Southern Kingdom

A similar story unfolds in the first half of the eighth century in the south. Amaziah takes the throne in 796 BCE. He successfully campaigns against

---

33. The price that Hosea offers here for Gomer identifies this exchange as the sale of a slave. The homer contained ten ephahs, and so Hosea is offering fifteen ephahs of barley along with his silver money. According to 2 Kings 7:1, 16, 18, this amount of barley equates to fifteen silver shekels. Thus, Hosea's payment, although half in grain and half in silver, was equivalent to thirty shekels, the going price for a female slave (Lev. 27:4; cf. Exod. 21:32). See Sandra Richter, *The Epic of Eden: A Christian Entry into the Old Testament* (Downers Grove, IL: IVP Academic, 2008), 43–45; C. F. Keil and F. Delitzsch, *Minor Prophets* (vol. 10 of *Commentary on the Old Testament*; trans. James Martin; Peabody, MA: Hendrickson, 1989), 68–69; Andersen and Freedman, *Hosea*, 298–301.

34. Campbell, "Land Divided," 237–39; Rainey and Notley, *Sacred Bridge*, 228, 231–32.

Edom to the southeast (2 Chron. 25:13; cf. 2 Kings 8:20–22),[35] but in the process he triggers a conflict between north and south that ultimately results in northern aggression against a number of Judean border towns and the looting of Jerusalem (2 Chron. 25:5–10; 2 Kings 14:11–14). Although the text is not transparent on this point, apparently Amaziah himself is taken prisoner during this encounter and spends ten years in Samaria as Jehoash's prisoner.[36] Thus, according to Rainey, when "the people of Judah" replace Amaziah with young Uzziah/Azariah (referred to as "Azariah" in Kings and "Uzziah" in Chronicles), this inauguration actually precedes Amaziah's death by twenty-five years (2 Chron. 26:1; 2 Kings 14:21) and therefore puts Uzziah/Azariah on the throne in the years 792–740 BCE, an unprecedented fifty-two-year reign.[37]

Under Uzziah's leadership the south reaches its territorial and economic summit. The Chronicler goes into great detail regarding Uzziah's administrative, economic, and military successes (2 Chron. 26:1–15). His victories over the Philistines and Meunite[38] territories facilitate the expansion of grain production to the west, his "public works" projects in the Judean wilderness extend pastoralism in the east, and if Rainey is correct in his assessment of *bakkarmel* in 2 Chronicles 26:10, Uzziah shores up and expands royal viticulture in the south as well.[39] Hence, the three pillars of Judah's agricultural economy are refortified and expanded—an accomplishment well suited to the only person in the Bible ever spoken of as a "lover of the soil" (*'ōhēb 'ădāmâ*).[40] Of equal and perhaps greater economic significance is Uzziah's reclamation of the strategic port city of Elath, which results in Judah's complete control of the caravan trade routes from Arabia as far as Egypt and beyond.[41] As a result,

---

35. The Calah Orthostat Slab speaks of Edom as one of Adad-Nirari III's victims (K. Lawson Younger Jr., "Calah Orthostat Slab," *COS* 2.114G:276).

36. Rainey and Notley, *Sacred Bridge*, 217–18; cf. Mordechai Cogan and Hayim Tadmor, *II Kings: A New Translation with Introduction and Commentary* (AB 11; Garden City, NY: Doubleday, 1988), 155–59.

37. Amaziah will return to Jerusalem in 782 BCE (apparently an act of goodwill by the rising king, Jeroboam II), but his "emeritus" status will be terminated in 767 BCE when he is assassinated at Lachish (2 Chron. 25:27).

38. See Hayim Tadmor, "The Meunites in the Book of Chronicles in the Light of an Assyrian Document," in *"With My Many Chariots I Have Gone Up the Heights of the Mountains": Historical and Literary Studies on Ancient Mesopotamia and Israel* (Jerusalem: Israel Exploration Society, 2011), 793–804.

39. Rainey (Rainey and Notley, *Sacred Bridge*, 219) argues that this is not the Carmel mountain range belonging to the northern kingdom, but the hill country south of Hebron, which was considered agricultural "fringe" area during most of the monarchy (1 Sam. 25:2; Josh. 15:48–52, 55–57) (cf. Japhet, *I & II Chronicles*, 880).

40. See Borowski, *Agriculture*, 14, 19, 106.

41. First Kings 9:26–28 records the first Israelite utilization of Elath under Solomon. Israel apparently lost control of the port to Shishak/Shoshenq I in the late tenth century. Jehoshaphat

during his days Kadesh Barnea (a caravan station between Gaza and Elath) is rebuilt,[42] and farther south Kuntillet ʿAjrûd appears as well.

Uzziah's professional army (2 Chron. 26:11) and conscript militia (26:12–13) are equally impressive.[43] Unlike an earlier era in which a soldier provided his own weapons (e.g., 1 Sam. 13:19–23; 1 Chron. 12:1–2), Uzziah fully equips his men.[44] Yet, as Sara Japhet notes, Uzziah is no conquistador; rather, he seems to utilize his military primarily for the support and expansion of Judah's economy: "an efficient ruler, a diligent administrator and, in particular, a man of strong economic initiative, who brought his realm to prosperity and affluence."[45] Lastly, Uzziah fortifies a now weakened Jerusalem.

Uzziah's particular upgrade to Jerusalem's fortifications has engendered a great deal of discussion: "And he built in Jerusalem elaborately devised war machines [*ḥiššĕbōnôt maḥăšebet ḥôšēb*] to stand upon the towers and the corners in order to shoot with arrows and large stones" (2 Chron. 26:15).[46] The ingenuity and innovation involved in the creation of these apparatuses are communicated by the thrice-repeated root *ḥšb*, but the exact design and function of Uzziah's invention is debated. Many have argued that these devices cannot be catapults, since torsion-based catapults were unknown in Uzziah's day, while others argue that these are indeed catapults, indicating the late and nonhistorical nature of the Chronicler's report.[47] Yigael Yadin's classic treatment identifies these not as offensive machinery but rather as defensive accoutrements built atop the walls and towers of Jerusalem in order to offer additional coverage to soldiers as they launched arrows and large stones against their attackers. Yadin

---

attempted to resecure the port in the mid-ninth century but failed (1 Kings 22:47–48). Thus Uzziah's was a victory indeed (Paul H. Wright, "Ezion-geber," *DOTHB* 274–77; cf. Rainey and Notley, *Sacred Bridge*, 217–18). The obscure reference in 2 Kings 14:28 that speaks of Jeroboam II returning Damascus and Hamath to "Judah in Israel" might be "best understood as recovery of commercial access and treaty relationship with the two Syrian states" (Campbell, "Land Divided," 233).

42. ʿAin el-Qudeirat/Tell el-Quideirat's "Middle Fortress" (the second of three) typically is attributed to Uzziah. Heavily fortified, its function was to defend Judah's southern border. It was served by several round silos and a large internal cistern fed by an exterior spring (cf. 2 Chron. 26:10a) (Rudolph Cohen, "Kadesh-Barnea: The Israelite Fortress," *NEAEHL* 3:843–47; Dale W. Manor, "Kadesh-Barnea," *ABD* 4:2).

43. Simon J. De Vries, *1 and 2 Chronicles* (FOTL 11; Grand Rapids: Eerdmans, 1989), 356.

44. For a synopsis of Israel's weaponry and warfare methods, see King and Stager, *Life in Biblical Israel*, 224–46.

45. Japhet, *I & II Chronicles*, 884.

46. *HALOT*, s.v. "מַחֲשֶׁבֶת" (2:572); cf. "חוֹשֵׁב" (1:360) and "חִשְּׁבֹנוֹת" (1:361).

47. Jacob M. Myers, *II Chronicles: Introduction, Translation, and Notes* (2nd ed.; AB 13; Garden City, NY: Doubleday, 1973), 150; Peter Welten, *Geschichte und Geschichtsdarstellung in den Chronikbüchern* (WMANT 42; Neukirchen-Vluyn: Neukirchener Verlag, 1973), 113; Nicholas Sekunda, "The Might of the Persian Empire," in *The Ancient World at War: A Global History* (ed. Philip de Souza; London: Thames & Hudson, 2008), 72.

Kuntillet ʿAjrûd (Isolated Hill of Water Wells) is an extremely remote and isolated desert site. This is as true today as it was in ancient times. So why might the ruins of two lightly fortified, early eighth-century buildings, finished in plaster, with storage rooms still crowded with vessels, occupy this desolate hill? Stranger still, what is the source and meaning of the odd assortment of inscriptions and private artwork found here? The answer to these questions lies in the fact that Kuntillet ʿAjrûd stands at the crossroads of what once was a lucrative trade route between Gaza on the Mediterranean coast and the port city of Elath, and a track traversing the Sinai along the Wadi Quraiya. Moreover, as its name communicates, it has water.

Kuntillet ʿAjrûd, excavated by Zeʾev Meshel in three seasons between 1975 and 1976, is indeed unique. Having the features of both fortress and sacred space, it has been interpreted as a Judean fort, a scribal school, a pilgrimage site, and most compelling, a caravansary.[a] Much of the pottery excavated in this Negev site is of Israelite and Phoenician derivation, and the theophoric element of the inscribed names is characteristic of the northern Israelite dialect, showing that this southern site had sustained contact with the northern kingdom. Of the mix of architecture and artifacts unearthed at Kuntillet ʿAjrûd, the most sensational are the inscriptions and handwritten artwork. Here in this Judean/Israelite site we find inscriptions written to Baal, El, Yahweh of Samaria, Yahweh of Teman, and Asherah. And most intriguing, Yahweh is linked in word and possibly image with a consort, Asherah.[b]

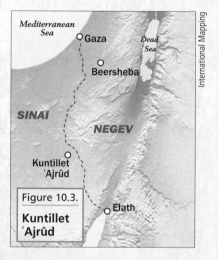

Figure 10.3. Kuntillet ʿAjrûd

As categorized by the excavator, the inscriptions at Kuntillet ʿAjrûd include letters incised on pottery vessels before firing, inscriptions incised on pottery vessels after firing, inscriptions incised on the rims of stone bowls, and ink-on-plaster inscriptions found both in situ and crumbled on the floor.[c] Those attracting the most notice come from two large storage jars (Greek *pithoi*) that are adorned with both texts and artwork. The inscriptions read:

> I bless you by Yahweh of Samaria and his Asherah. (Pithos A).[d]

> [. . .] to Yahweh of the Teman and his Asherah. And may he grant everything that he asks from the compassionate god [. . .] and may he grant according to his needs all that he asks! (Pithos B)[e]

> I bless you by Yahweh of Teman and his Asherah. May he bless you and keep you and may he be with my lord. (Pithos B)[f]

The first issue here is obvious: Yahweh is identified as having a consort, specifically the consort of El, the head of the Canaanite pantheon. Second, Yahweh is being localized in Teman (perhaps Edom [Amos 1:12]?) and Samaria. A third issue is the relationship between the artwork and the inscriptions. Both *pithoi* have elaborate and, as William Dever characterizes them, "exotic" painted scenes that demonstrate various classic Near Eastern themes.[g] None show any particular artistic talent. Rather, most scholars characterize the artwork as "graffiti," even "doodling."[h] There are three images in the mix, however, that overlap the inscription of Pithos A ("Yahweh of Samaria and his Asherah") and have stirred three decades of scholarly debate.

As depicted here, the scene shows two figures standing with arms linked, one male and one androgynous, while off to the right a seated figure is playing the lyre. The leading interpretation is that the two standing figures are the apotropaic Egyptian dwarf-god Bes, and the seated figure is either male and unrelated to the scene or female and possibly a depiction of Asherah.[i] Kyle McCarter, following Mordechai Gilula, identifies the standing figures as god and consort, and because of their bovine appearance, specifically as "the Yahweh of Samaria" and his consort, Asherah (cf. Hosea 8:5–6).[j] But most conclude, with Judith Hadley, that the inscriptions and the drawings are the work of many different hands and occasions, superimposed one upon the next, and therefore the inscription provides no commentary for the scene.[k] In sum, although perhaps not as sensational as some originally hoped, these inscriptions and images do make very clear that a mixture of Baalism, Yahwism, and the northern kingdom's particular Canaanite-Israelite syncretism were alive and well at this particular way station in the outback of Uzziah's trade network.

Figure 10.4. Kuntillet ʿAjrûd artwork

a. André Lemaire, *Les écoles et la formation de la bible dans l'ancien Israël* (OBO 39; Fribourg: Éditions universitaires; Göttingen: Vandenhoeck & Ruprecht 1981), 30; Zeʾev Meshel, "Horvat Teman," *NEAEHL* 4:1460–64; Rainey and Notley, *Sacred Bridge*, 224; Judith Hadley, "Some Drawings and Inscriptions on Two Pithoi from Kuntillet ʿAjrud," *VT* 37 (1987): 180–209; Richard S. Hess, "Yahweh and His Asherah? Religious Pluralism in the Old Testament World," in *One God, One Lord: Christianity in a World of Religious Pluralism* (ed. Andrew D. Clarke and Bruce W. Winter; 2nd ed.; Exeter: Paternoster; Grand Rapids: Baker Books, 1992), 13–42. See Zeʾev Meshel's final publication of the site, *Kuntillet ʿAjrûd (Horvat Teman): An Iron Age II Religious Site on the Judah-Sinai Border* (Jerusalem: Israel Exploration Society, 2012).

b. The debate regarding the third-masculine suffix on *'srt* (Asherah) has raged for decades. Does this actually indicate Yahweh and his Asherah, or is it Yahweh and his asherah pole or his sacred place? Anson Rainey concludes the debate in his typical style: "Suffice it to say that this is a common Ancient Near Eastern format for mentioning a deity and his consort. Furthermore, there is no valid grammatical rule against attaching a personal possessive pronoun to a proper name, especially that of a deity" (Rainey and Notley, *Sacred Bridge*, 224). Richard Hess offers an exhaustive study on the orthography of the goddess's name, arguing that other options do exist: (1) the "suffix" may be an archaic diptotic form, an interpretation that is supported by various Ugaritic and Arabic examples; or (2) the final *h* of the form may be "the preservation of a final -*a* vowel, already characteristic of the syllabic spellings of Asherah attested throughout the Late Bronze Age" ("Ashera or Asherata?," *Or* 65 [1996]: 217).

c. Meshel, "Horvat Teman," 1461.

d. P. Kyle McCarter, "Kuntillet ʿAjrud: Inscribed Pithos 1," *COS* 2.47A:171.

e. P. Kyle McCarter, "Kuntillet ʿAjrud: Inscribed Pithos 2," *COS* 2.47B:172.

f. Ibid.

g. William G. Dever, *Did God Have a Wife? Archaeology and Folk Religion in Ancient Israel* (Grand Rapids: Eerdmans, 2005), 163.

h. Rainey and Notley, *Sacred Bridge*, 224; Hadley, "Drawings and Inscriptions," 207.

i. See Hadley, "Drawings and Inscriptions"; for the classic treatment of these images, see Pirhiya Beck, "The Drawings from Horvat Teiman (Kuntillet ʿAjrud)," *TA* 9 (1982): 3–68; see also Dever, *Did God Have a Wife?*, 163–66.

j. P. Kyle McCarter, "Kuntillet ʿAjrud," *COS* 2.47:171; cf. Mordechai Gilula, "To Yahweh Shomron and His Asherah" (in Hebrew), *Shnaton* 3 (1978–1979): 129–37.

k. Hadley, "Drawings and Inscriptions," 207.

finds pictorial representation of these devices in the Lachish murals.[48] In a recent monograph, Israel Eph'al offers a third option. Eph'al observes that Assyrians and Babylonians referred to their various war machines (siege towers and battering rams in particular) with the somewhat vague Akkadian term *nēpēšû* (something manufactured, a machine). He notes that from the fifth century onward the Greeks used the term *mēchanai*, similarly (a general term for artillery devices and other engines of war that were used by attackers and defenders alike); and that the Septuagint translates Uzziah's "machines" with *mēchanas memēchaneumenas*; hence he concludes that Uzziah's inventions were indeed artillery devices, but that "the vague and undefined derivation of the terms used in the three languages suggests that they do not refer to a specific, well-defined weapon, but rather serve as a general term for siege and war engines." Therefore we can say nothing more regarding Uzziah's fame-producing military innovation.[49]

In sum, the contemporary and collaborative roles of Jeroboam II in the north and Uzziah in the south resulted in a time of unprecedented security and prosperity for both kingdoms. From the border of Egypt to the Central Orontes Valley, the first half of the eighth century BCE sees "a dynamic power center in the southern Levant" unrivaled in Israel's monarchy since the days of Solomon.[50]

But these days of influence and prosperity are short-lived. For "in the year that king Uzziah died" (Isa. 6:1), the kingdoms of Israel and Judah witness a power shift in the international scene that will alter the face of world history. The military challenges pass from the localized subjugation of Aram-Damascus via Hazael and trouble with Edom, to the worldwide subjugation of the Fertile Crescent under the Neo-Assyrian Empire. With the ascension of Tiglath-pilesar III in 745 BCE, the Assyrian kings push past their traditional western boundary (the western arm of the Euphrates) and set their rapacious eyes on the wealth of the Levantine states. The end result will be the collapse of the northern kingdom and a close call of such enormous proportions in the south that the tale goes down in infamy.

---

48. Yadin lists Lachish murals 431 and 434, which depict structures atop the city walls made of wooden frames holding defenders' shields and thereby creating a screen behind which the archers and warriors may stand to their full height and wield their weapons unencumbered (*The Art of Warfare in Biblical Lands in the Light of Archaeological Study* [trans. M. Pearlman; 2 vols.; New York: McGraw-Hill, 1963], 2:326). See also David Ussishkin, *The Conquest of Lachish by Sennacherib* (TAUIAP 6; Tel Aviv: Institute of Archaeology, Tel Aviv University, 1982), segments III–IV and enlarged photographs 103, 106.

49. Israel Eph'al, *The City Besieged: Siege and Its Manifestations in the Ancient Near East* (CHANE 36; Leiden: Brill, 2009), 100–102.

50. Rainey and Notley, *Sacred Bridge*, 218.

Last Half of the Eighth Century (745–700 BCE)

The Rise of the Neo-Assyrian Empire

A principal reason for the combined success of Jeroboam II and Uzziah's kingdoms in the first half of the eighth century was an attending period of internal disarray and external weakness in Assyria.[51] Thus, when Tiglath-pileser III took the throne in 745 BCE, his first task was to restructure his own internal provincial system in order to restrict the power of local, corrupt officials and to centralize power in the crown. The second task was territorial expansion. Toward this end, Tiglath-pileser III established the first fully professional standing army (complete with chariotry and cavalry) and turned his attention westward. The result was constant military activity throughout his reign and overflowing coffers at home.[52] For those in the path of expansion who chose to cooperate with the crown, a vassal relationship with Assyria was initiated. Here the local ruler retained his office but was charged with annual (often crippling) tribute. For those less cooperative, the local leader was stripped of his office (often executed) and replaced with someone of the emperor's choosing. For those least cooperative, the local government was obliterated, an Assyrian governor established, and the territory absorbed into the empire as a province.[53] This final stage saw exile—a strategy designed to strip the conquered nation of its will to rebel by relocating the bulk of its population elsewhere. In this fashion, national identity was lost, dissident factions were dissolved, and the new heterogeneous populace in both the old and the new territories was left with survival as its only objective and Assyria as its only lord. As attested by every epigraphic and visual resource available to us, the Neo-Assyrian Empire celebrated and propagated its reputation for unprecedented brutality. The goal was to instill a level of terror that intimidated opponents into early submission and a level of demolition that stripped the conquered of the agency to ever rise in defiance again.[54] And although Assyria perhaps did not initially

---

51. After Adad-Nirari's (810–783) victories in Syria, Assyria essentially disappeared from the international scene. See note 5 above.

52. Assyria was a society defined by war. As Van de Mieroop (*History of the Ancient Near East*, 229–30; cf. 252) details, the army itself provided the basic structure and administrative hierarchy of the society, and the king's commission was to wage war for Aššur's benefit. The second half of the eighth century saw a sequence of extremely capable leaders in Assyria: Tiglath-pileser III (745–727), Shalmaneser V (726–722), Sargon II (721–705), and Sennacherib (705–681). Hence, this era also saw many successful military campaigns.

53. See Benedikt Otzen, "Israel under the Assyrians," in *Power and Propaganda: A Symposium on Ancient Empires* (ed. Mogens Trolle Larsen; Mesopotamia 7; Copenhagen: Akademisk Forlag, 1979), 251–56.

54. One of Assyria's standard strategies involved the decimation of a besieged enemy's vineyards and orchards. The goal was to cripple the city for decades beyond the conflict. This

intend to absorb these foreign territories into the empire, the end result was full assimilation.

The Northern Kingdom

Due to its strategic position along the crossroads of the international highways, the northern kingdom encountered the expanding reach of the Neo-Assyrian Empire before Judah did. In his third regnal year, as reported in 2 Kings 15:19–26, Pul (Tiglath-pileser III) was drawn to the west by what he viewed as sedition among the western Syrian states, sedition that was endangering his trade network. In the list of resulting tribute reported in Tiglath-pileser's Iran Stela, a certain "Menahem the Samarian" is named as having voluntarily offered what Edward Campbell describes as a "breathtaking" tribute of one thousand talents of silver.[55] This deliberate acquiescence on Menahem's part brought peace to Israel for the

Baker Photo Archive (The British Museum)

Figure 10.5. Alabaster panel from the palace of Sennacherib portraying the execution of Judeans during the seige of Lachish.

---

strategy, and the threat of this strategy, were regularly communicated by text and image. See Sandra Richter, "Environmental Law in Deuteronomy," *BBR* 20 (2010): 355–76; Steven W. Cole, "The Destruction of Orchards in Assyrian Warfare," in *Assyria 1995: Proceedings of the 10th Anniversary Symposium of the Neo-Assyrian Text Corpus Project Helsinki, September 7–11, 1995* (ed. Simo Parpola and Robert M. Whiting; Helsinki: Neo-Assyrian Text Corpus Project, University of Helsinki, 1997), 29–40; Aren M. Maeir, Oren Ackermann, and Hendrik J. Bruins, "The Ecological Consequences of a Siege: A Marginal Note on Deuteronomy 20:19–20," in *Confronting the Past: Archaeological and Historical Essays on Ancient Israel in Honor of William G. Dever* (ed. Seymour Gitin, J. Edward Wright, and J. P. Dessel; Winona Lake, IN: Eisenbrauns, 2006), 239–43.

55. K. Lawson Younger Jr., "The Iran Stela," COS 2.117B:287; see the dating of the campaign by Rainey (Rainey and Notley, *Sacred Bridge*, 225–26). According to calculations by Campbell ("Land Divided," 237), as Menahem raised one thousand shekels by imposing fifty shekels per "mighty man of wealth," at least sixty thousand citizens would have had to contribute. This is three times the amount that Jeremiah had to pay for his family's field in Anathoth, no doubt creating opposition to Menahem and contributing to the successful conspiracy against Menahem's heir Pekahiah (see Rainey and Notley, *Sacred Bridge*, 220).

remainder of his reign. His son Pekahiah, however, is assassinated shortly after his ascension by anti-Assyrian Pekah, who conspires with Rezin of Damascus to throw off the yoke of Assyria (2 Kings 15:23–28). Pekah and Rezin make every attempt to convince Ahaz of Judah to join the resistance. When he refuses, they turn their forces against him, besieging Jerusalem and doing great harm in the southern reaches of the country (2 Kings 16:1–6; 2 Chron. 28:5–7; Isa. 7:1–2). According to the prophet Isaiah, this is the critical moment of challenge and promise for the southern kingdom. Will Ahaz trust in his God to bring "Immanuel" (lit., "God with us" [Isa. 7:14]), or will he trust in his own devices? Ahaz makes the wrong choice, rejecting the help of Yahweh and turning to Assyria for aid (2 Kings 16:7–9; 2 Chron. 28:16–21; Isa. 7–8). Isaiah responds, "Because these people have rejected the gently flowing waters of Shiloah [the irrigation aqueduct designed to water the royal gardens of the Kidron Valley][56] . . . , now, therefore, Yahweh is about to overwhelm them with the raging waters of the River [the Euphrates], even the king of Assyria" (Isa. 8:6–7). This is the turning point of First Isaiah. Ahaz the faithless willingly subjects Judah to God's enemy; it will be up to Hezekiah the faithful to deliver them.[57]

In response, Tiglath-pileser III campaigns to the Mediterranean coast and claims the port cities from Byblos to Gaza. Damascu falls in 732 BCE. Rezin is executed, and Pekah is assassinated by Hoshea (Tiglath-pileser claims credit).[58] The northern kingdom is subjugated as a constellation of Assyrian provinces, Hoshea is left with only the hill country (2 Kings 15:29–30; cf. Isa. 9:1), and much of what had been the ten northern tribes is deported (2 Kings 17:1–6; 1 Chron. 5:6, 25–26). The biblical account is confirmed by a number of detailed Assyrian descriptions of the same.[59]

Hoshea will remain loyal to Assyria while Tiglath-pileser lives. But shortly after the ascension of his heir, Shalmaneser V (726–722), Hoshea sees an opportunity for freedom and seeks help from the Saite dynasty of Egypt (2 Kings 17:4). This move costs Hoshea his throne and his citizenry their land.[60] A three-year Assyrian siege of Samaria ensues. Samaria is conquered.

56. See Yigal Shiloh, "Jerusalem," *NEAEHL* 2:710–11; King and Stager, *Life in Biblical Israel*, 217–18. Ronny Reich disputes the existence of such an aqueduct, having determined that neither his Channel I nor Channel II served this purpose (*Excavating the City of David: Where Jerusalem's History Began* [Jerusalem: Israel Exploration Society, 2011], 315, 318).

57. John N. Oswalt, *Isaiah: Chapters 1–39* (NICOT; Grand Rapids: Eerdmans, 1986), 192–229.

58. K. Lawson Younger Jr., "Summary Inscription 4," *COS* 2.117C:288.

59. For a meticulously researched synthesis of the Assyrian and biblical accounts of these conflicts, see Rainey and Notley, *Sacred Bridge*, 229–32. See also K. Lawson Younger Jr., "Israelites in Exile: Their Names Appear at All Levels of Assyrian Society," *BAR* 29, no. 6 (2003): 36–45, 65–66.

60. Campbell, "Land Divided," 239.

And with the 720 BCE follow-up campaign under Shalmaneser V's successor, Sargon II, 27,290 people are deported into the northeastern reaches of the empire, never to come home again.[61] Isaiah is vindicated (Isa. 7:3–9), and as his contemporary Micah (1:6–7) predicted, the ivory city of Samaria is left a "heap of ruins in the field."[62] The words of the Deuteronomistic Historian ring out in the broken silence:

> And so it was that the children of Israel sinned against Yahweh their God, the one who had brought them up from the land of Egypt, from under the hand of Pharaoh, king of Egypt. They feared other gods [ʾĕlōhîm ʾăḥērîm]. They walked in the customs of the nations whom Yahweh had driven out before the children of Israel. The children of Israel did things secretly that were not right against Yahweh their God. They built for themselves high places in all of their cities, from watchtower to fortified city. . . . Yahweh had warned Israel and Judah, through all his prophets, every seer, saying, "Turn from your evil ways and keep my commandments, my customs according to all the law which I commanded your fathers, and which I sent to you through my servants the prophets." But they did not listen, they stiffened their neck, . . . they abandoned all the commandments of Yahweh their God and made for themselves molten images, two calves, and made an Asherah and worshipped all the host of heaven and served Baal. . . . So Yahweh was very angry with Israel and removed them from his presence. None was left except the tribe of Judah. (2 Kings 17:7–18)

The warnings of Amos and Hosea are confirmed. Israel had repeatedly violated Yahweh's covenant, and the crimes of the kingdom had come home to roost. "The silence of the written sources for what followed in the north is deafening."[63]

The Southern Kingdom

With the death of Uzziah, the southern kingdom passes first to Jotham and then to Ahaz.[64] Jotham is highly commended by the Chronicler (2 Chron. 27:6); Ahaz is not. Not only does Ahaz willingly submit Judah to Assyrian

---

61. K. Lawson Younger Jr., "The Great 'Summary' Inscription" *COS* 2.118E:296; see idem, "The Fall of Samaria in Light of Recent Research," *CBQ* 61 (1999): 461–82.

62. Samaria will be rebuilt as an Assyrian provincial capital and repopulated by deportees from other regions within the empire. Sargon II claims in the Nimrud Prisms, "I repopulated Samerina [i.e., Samaria] more than before. I brought into it people from countries conquered by my hands. And I appointed my eunuch as governor over them. And I counted them Assyrians" (K. Lawson Younger Jr., "Nimrud Prisms D & E," *COS* 2.118D: 295–96).

63. Campbell, "Land Divided," 239.

64. Due to his affliction with a skin disease, Uzziah spent his final years in isolation (2 Chron. 26:16–23). Jotham's reign began during this period as coregent. It is quite possible that Jotham

vassalage but he also worships the gods of the nations. Unlike any Judean king before him, he "closed the doors of the house of God, and made altars for himself in every corner of Jerusalem" (2 Chron. 28:24; cf. 29:7; 2 Kings 16:10–16). The Deuteronomistic Historian reports that he also lost Elath (i.e., control of the southern trade routes) to the Arameans, who "have lived there to this day" (2 Kings 16:6). The review of Ahaz's reign is so negative that the Chronicler states that he was denied burial in the tombs of the kings of Israel (2 Chron. 28:25–27; cf. 2 Kings 16:20; Hosea 12:15 [14 ET]).[65]

Then comes Hezekiah (715–686). The early years of his reign are marked by economic success, rapid demographic growth, patronage of the arts, and an exceptional alliance with the priesthood resulting in unprecedented religious reform (2 Kings 18:3–6; 2 Chron. 32:27–28).[66] He is given the high-

---

preceded his father in death (Ralph W. Klein, *2 Chronicles: A Commentary* [ed. Paul D. Hanson; Hermeneia; Minneapolis: Fortress, 2012], 9).

65. Noting 2 Chron. 28:16, 21, 23, Japhet points out that Ahaz "repeatedly asks for help . . . but always from the wrong quarter. Instead of help comes ruin, because he does not turn to the one who alone can aid him, the 'God of his fathers'" (*I & II Chronicles*, 908).

66. The profile of Judah's cult in the eighth century BCE is greatly enhanced by excavations of the Judean fortress at Arad, where the only known Yahwistic temple discovered in Judah is found. A tripartite footprint, a large altar constructed according to the dictates of Exod. 20, at least one *maṣṣēbâ* still in use in the early eighth century, and two incense altars have been unearthed at this facility. Intriguing is the fact that at some point in the eighth century, after two phases of building, this sacred space was carefully dismantled and covered with what most have interpreted as a protective layer of soil. Yet the temple structure and its appurtenances show no signs of destruction. As a result, it has been theorized that Hezekiah ordered the retirement of this facility along with the sacred space at Beersheba as an expression of his religious reforms. Current evidence is such that this theory cannot be proven or disproven. See Ze'ev Herzog et al., "The Israelite Fortress at Arad," *BASOR* 254 (1984): 1–34; Amihai Mazar, "Temples of the Middle and Late Bronze Ages and the Iron Age," in *The Architecture of Ancient Israel: From the Prehistoric to the Persian Periods; In Memory of Immanuel (Munya) Dunayevsky* (ed. Aharon Kempinski and Ronny Reich; Jerusalem: Israel Exploration Society, 1992), 186; Yohanan Aharoni, "Arad: Its Inscriptions and Temple," *BA* 31 (1968): 2–32; Ze'ev Herzog, Miriam Aharoni, and Anson F. Rainey, "Arad—an Ancient Israelite Fortress with a Temple to Yahweh," *BAR* 13, no. 2 (1987): 16–35; Miriam Aharoni, "Arad," *NEAEHL* 1:75–87; cf. Mordechai Cogan, "Into Exile: From the Assyrian Conquest of Israel to the Fall of Babylon," *OHBW* 244–46; Anson F. Rainey, "Hezekiah's Reform and the Altars at Beer-sheba and Arad," in Coogan, Exum, and Stager, *Scripture and Other Artifacts*, 333–54. Also signficant to Hezekiah's reputation as a reformer are the hundreds of Judean pillar-based figurines that proliferated in Judah after the fall of Samaria in the late eighth century and the seventh century. These figurines, apparently mass-produced, depict a nude female with prominent breasts, either a simple pinched or carefully modeled head, and a separately mold-made base later attached to the body. Since their find sites are primarily domestic, and the number of recovered figurines reaches its peak at the end of the eighth and early seventh centuries (the exact era the Bible identifies with the reforms of Hezekiah), most have concluded that these figurines are an expression of domestic religion, or even a political ideology encouraging reproduction, that went either unnoticed or untouched by Hezekiah's reforms. See Dever, *Did God Have a Wife?*, 176–95; Raz Kletter, *The Judean Pillar-Figurines*

est commendation by the historians (2 Kings 18:3; 2 Chron. 29:2). Isaiah depicts him as the righteous foil of Ahaz (Isa. 36–37).[67] Indeed, throughout the Bible Hezekiah is portrayed as a reformer and a hero—a portrait that comes to us animated by more material culture than any other individual in biblical history.

Hezekiah, the "Poster Child" of Biblical Archaeology

The year was 705 BCE. Sargon II had been in power since 722 BCE and had proven himself "everywhere victorious" and every inch a "war-chief."[68] But shortly after the completion of his immense (and immensely lavish) palace Dûr-Sharrukîn, Sargon "went against Tabal and was killed in the war."[69] His son Sennacherib took his place. Under the oppressive policies of the Neo-Assyrian Empire, it was typical that an unexpected transition of power such as this would trigger revolt in the outlying provinces. The hope was that the new king would be too busy consolidating power at home to field an army against a far-distant uprising. Sennacherib's ascension was just such an opportunity. Prodded into action by Egypt, the rulers of the smaller Levantine states conspired and rebelled. Provoked by Merodach-baladan II of Babylon, Elam, the Aramean tribal groups, and all of Babylonia followed suit.[70] Hence, in the first year of his reign Sennacherib of Assyria found himself facing insurrection in every corner of his empire.

According to his annals, Sennacherib first pursued his own back door: "Like a mighty wild ox, I did not wait for my forces, nor did I hold back for the rear guard."[71] The new king besieged, conquered, and plundered his eastern vassals, and then turned westward.

The biblical writers are surprisingly restrained about the details of this epic event, but it is obvious that in taking his stand against Neo-Assyria, Hezekiah had placed his nation in mortal peril. If he and Judah were going to come out alive, he has a lot to do and a limited time in which to do it. He certainly will not attempt to meet his enemy on the field; rather, he will

---

and the Archaeology of Asherah (BARIS 636; Oxford: Tempus Reparatum, 1996); Ryan Byrne, "Lie Back and Think of Judah: The Reproductive Politics of Pillar Figurines" NEA 6 (2004): 137–51.

67. Dan Cole, "Archaeology and the Messiah Oracles of Isaiah 9 and 11," in Coogan, Exum, and Stager, Scripture and Other Artifacts, 53–69.

68. Georges Roux, Ancient Iraq (3rd ed.; London: Penguin Books, 1992), 314–15.

69. ARAB 2.855.

70. Mordechai Cogan, "Sennacherib's First Campaign: Against Merodach-Baladan," COS 2.119A:300–301.

71. Ibid., lines 16–19.

prepare for siege warfare by fortifying his primary urban centers against the blast to come. As 2 Chronicles 32:1–8 summarizes, Hezekiah updates fortifications (the casemate walls of an earlier generation will not withstand the Assyrian battering ram),[72] secures his water supply, and stockpiles food. He also reassures his populace that the resistance to come is worthwhile: "Be strong and courageous, do not fear or be dismayed because of the king of Assyria, nor because of all the multitude which is with him; for the one with us is greater than the one with him. With him is only an arm of flesh, but with us ['immānû] is Yahweh our God to help us and to fight our battles" (2 Chron. 32:7–8a).[73]

The preparations made by this Judean king are thoroughly documented via the archaeological and epigraphic record. In Hezekiah's Jerusalem we find the "Broad Wall," so named because of its unprecedented twenty-three-foot breadth, "designed to withstand the Assyrian battering rams."[74] The pottery sealed beneath the wall date it without question to 701 BCE.[75] The largest remaining section of the wall is 128 feet long, oriented northeast by southwest on the high ground of the ridge 900 feet west of the Temple Mount. Although its path has been debated, the excavators agree that this wall originally connected to the Temple Mount farther north and served to extend David's city slightly south, thus encircling the newly expanded western residential suburb of the city and securing Hezekiah's reservoir within (2 Kings 20:20).[76] The

---

72. See King and Stager, *Life in Biblical Israel*, 231–47; cf. Andrew G. Vaughn, *Theology, History, and Archaeology in the Chronicler's Account of Hezekiah* (SBLABS 4; Atlanta: Scholars Press, 1999).

73. There is a long-standing debate as to how many confrontations there were between Hezekiah and Sennacherib. Those arguing for two gather their evidence from the biblical record that seems to reflect both Hezekiah's victory (the "B" source: B1 = 2 Kings 18:17–19:9a and 19:36–37; and B2 = 2 Kings 19:9b–35) and defeat (the "A" source: 2 Kings 18:13–16). But since both the Bible and Sennacherib claim only one campaign, the differing tones in the biblical text surely are better read as compiled perspectives on the same encounter. For a synopsis, see Michael D. Coogan, *A Brief Introduction to the Old Testament: The Hebrew Bible in Its Context* (Oxford: Oxford University Press, 2009), 278–80; cf. Mordechai Cogan, "Sennacherib's Siege of Jerusalem," *COS* 2.119B:302; William H. Shea, "Sennacherib's Second Palestinian Campaign," *JBL* 104 (1985): 401–18; Richard S. Hess, "Hezekiah and Sennacherib in 2 Kings 18–20," in *Zion, City of Our God* (ed. Richard S. Hess and Gordon J. Wenham; Grand Rapids: Eerdmans, 2004), 23–41.

74. Amihai Mazar, *Archaeology of the Land of the Bible: 10,000–586 B.C.E.* (ABRL; New York: Doubleday, 1990), 420.

75. Shiloh et al., "Jerusalem," 2:704–7; Reich, *Excavating the City of David*, 312.

76. Nahman Avigad asserts that the Broad Wall is best understood as having encircled the new reservoir in "an area that henceforth would be within the city walls" (Shiloh et al., "Jerusalem," 708). See also John Rogerson and Philip R. Davies, "Was the Siloam Tunnel Built by Hezekiah?," *BA* 59 (1996): 138–49; Reich, *Excavating the City of David*, 114–15, 314; King and Stager, *Life in Biblical Israel*, 213–23, 231–34.

150 acres enclosed by this wall tripled the area of the previous city, testifying to the "artificial" expansion of the population that surely resulted from the influx of refugees fleeing the collapse of the northern kingdom.[77] As Avigad states, the wall "was erected with sufficient urgency to sacrifice houses in its way."[78] As Isaiah protests, "Then you saw that the breaches in the wall of the city of David were many, and you collected the waters of the lower pool. Then you counted the houses of Jerusalem, and you tore down houses to fortify the wall. And you made a reservoir between the two walls for the waters of the old pool" (Isa. 22:9–11).

Hezekiah also attended to his water supply. The Gihon spring had been Jerusalem's perennial water supply for millennia. Unfortunately, its point of issue stands halfway down the slope of the Ophel. Hence, protecting it had been a perennial problem as well. Ronny Reich and Eli Shukron have unearthed a massive Middle Bronze fortification system surrounding the spring and an equally massive underground reservoir designed to store its water inside the ancient city. These discoveries establish that earlier theories regarding Warren's Shaft as the point of access to the spring from within the city were in error.[79] As excavations continue, a principal question is why this fortification system went out of use (apparently by the eighth century), and why Hezekiah thought it necessary to make "the pool and the conduit" in order to "bring water into the city" (2 Kings 20:20).[80]

Nevertheless, Hezekiah's Tunnel discovered in 1838 by Edward Robinson and the Siloam Tunnel Inscription discovered in 1880 confirm that Hezekiah is indeed responsible for this most ambitious of all the Iron Age water systems. The tunnel extends 533 meters (1,748 feet), through solid rock, underneath the city of Jerusalem. The channel was cut with a perfect average gradation of .6 millimeters per meter, with a difference in elevation between the beginning of the tunnel and the southern exit of only 32 centimeters. As the excavators report, this sort of precision is "indeed remarkable, even by modern-day

77. Reich, *Excavating the City of David*, 313. See also Ronny Reich and Eli Shukron, "The Urban Development of Jerusalem in the Late Eighth Century B.C.E.," in *Jerusalem in Bible and Archaeology: The First Temple Period* (ed. Andrew G. Vaughn and Ann E. Killebrew; SBLSymS 18; Atlanta: Society of Biblical Literature, 2003), 209–18.

78. Nahman Avigad, "Excavations in the Jewish Quarter of the Old City, 1969–1971," in *Jerusalem Revealed: Archaeology in the Holy City, 1968–1974* (ed. Yigael Yadin; trans. Rafi Grafman; Jerusalem: Israel Exploration Society, 1975), 43–44.

79. Ronny Reich, "Light at the End of the Tunnel: Warren's Shaft Theory of David's Conquest Shattered," *BAR* 20, no. 2 (1999): 22–33, 72.

80. See Reich, *Excavating the City of David*, 142–213. The "streams outside the city" that Hezekiah speaks of sealing up were likely the irrigation outlets of the Siloam Channel, understood to have been created during Solomon's day to water his royal garden in the Kidron Valley; cf. King and Stager, *Life in Biblical Israel*, 215–18; see also n. 56.

standards."[81] The challenges of light and oxygen alone would have been enormous, but the fact that two teams of rock cutters worked from opposite ends of the channel is nearly inconceivable. The advanced skills necessary to complete this project have often been juxtaposed with the apparently senseless, circuitous route of the tunnel itself (see fig. 10.6). The conundrum was solved when Yadin's geological consultant Dan Gill weighed in on the discussion. Demonstrating that the ancient city of Jerusalem is situated atop a naturally occurring karstic system of channels and

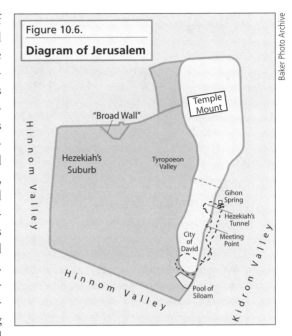

Figure 10.6.

Diagram of Jerusalem

Baker Photo Archive

shafts, he pointed out that the elevation of the ceiling of Hezekiah's Tunnel is quite irregular, a feature completely inconsistent with a shaft constructed by human hands.[82] His conclusion was that the objective of Hezekiah's engineers was not to cut a virgin path through the limestone beneath Jerusalem but to follow the preexisting, serpentine path of naturally occurring karsts, clearing, connecting, and grading them such that the water could flow freely from outside the city to inside the city. For "why should the kings of Assyria come and find abundant water?" (2 Chron. 32:4).

Sennacherib's plan of attack proceeded down the Levantine Coast first, where he successfully confronts the Phoenician, Philistine, and Egyptian forces. Next he turned up into the hill country of Judah. Of necessity, Sennacherib's first target is Judah's most formidable citadel, Lachish, the administrative center for the Shephelah region and the guardian of the roads leading up into Judah's heartland. Sequential excavations have demonstrated that the city was heavily fortified with a double wall (the outer wall being a state-of-the-art inset-offset

81. Dan Gill, "The Geology of the City of David and Its Ancient Subterranean Waterworks," in *Various Reports* (vol. 4 of *Excavations at the City of David*, by Yigal Shiloh; ed. Donald T. Ariel et al.; Qedem 35; Jerusalem: Institute of Archaeology, Hebrew University of Jerusalem, 1996), 1–28, esp. 20.

82. Ibid. See also Dan Gill, "How They Met: Geology Solves Long-Standing Mystery of Hezekiah's Tunnelers," *BAR* 20, no. 4 (1994): 20–33, 64.

The Siloam Tunnel Inscription

Baker Photo Archive (Istanbul Archaeological Museum)

Figure 10.7. Siloam Tunnel Inscription

The Siloam Tunnel Inscription was first discovered in 1880 by some local boys during an afternoon swim at the pool of Siloam, just south of the Old City of Jerusalem. Scouting about inside an old tunnel adjoining the pool, the boys found some strange letters engraved in the wall about twenty-five feet inside the opening. One of the boys thought it wise to inform his teacher at the mission school, Conrad Schick. Being conversant in issues of archaeology and epigraphy, Schick decided to investigate. What he found was a partially submerged, multilined, Old Hebrew inscription on a prepared and "framed" surface.[a]

Since what we now know to be Hezekiah's Tunnel had been discovered more than forty years earlier, it would follow that this text must be the monumental inscription installed to celebrate Hezekiah's eighth-century engineering marvel. But because everyone at the time assumed that ancient Jerusalem was contained within the sixteenth-century Ottoman walls that still surround the Old City, no one had yet realized that the seemingly insignificant Arab/Yemenite village of Silwan and its small reservoir just south of the Old City had once been the Ophel of David's famous citadel. But when Schick pursued the boys' discovery, the identity of this debris-laden water tunnel became paramount. Could this indeed be the royal waterworks system of Hezekiah?

wall designed to resist the Assyrian battering ram), an exceptionally large and complex gate system, a fortified central administrative building, enough armament and personnel to mount a defensive siege ramp within the city, a sizeable stockpile of food, and what has been identified as a chariotry training facility second only to Megiddo.[83] Even so, Lachish was no match for the Assyrian war

83. Deborah O'Daniel Cantrell, *The Horsemen of Israel: Horses and Chariotry in Monarchic Israel (Ninth–Eighth Centuries B.C.E.)* (HACL 1; Winona Lake, IN: Eisenbrauns, 2011), 9, 85, 126–27.

The inscription commemorates in stone the moment when Hezekiah's two rock-cutting teams, working from opposite ends of the tunnel, successfully converged. The emotion in the inscription is palpable. And atypical for monumental inscriptions known from the ancient Near East, this one celebrates the heroic deeds of the laborers, not the king:

> . . . the tunneling through. And this was the manner of the tunneling through. While . . . the quarrying axe, each to its companion, and while there remained three cubits [to be cut through] . . . the voice of a man called to his fellow, for there was a fissure [split/overlap] in the rock from the south to the north. . . . So at the moment the tunnel was driven through the quarrymen hewed, each man toward his fellow, axe against axe; then the water flowed from the spring to the reservoir for 200,000 cubits, and 100 cubits was the height of the rock over the head of the quarrymen.[b]

Over the decades, the elegant script of the Siloam Tunnel Inscription has become the keystone of First Temple epigraphy. Its late eighth-century provenance has been established via the disciplines of paleography, historical linguistics, and archaeology, and it has therefore become a benchmark against which all other preexilic Northwest Semitic inscriptions are assessed.[c]

a. Unfortunately, once discovered, the inscription suffered the fate of many artifacts. It was hacked out of the wall for sale to a wealthy collector in Jerusalem, doing great damage to the inscription and destroying the prepared medium of display (see Reich, *Excavating the City of David*, 33–35).

b. Translation from Jo Ann Hackett et al., "Defusing Pseudo-Scholarship: The Siloam Inscription Ain't Hasmonean," *BAR* 23, no. 2 (1997): 41; see also K. Lawson Younger Jr., "The Siloam Tunnel Inscription," *COS* 2.28:145–46.

c. In 1996 John Rogerson and Philip Davies of the University of Sheffield published an article claiming that the script of this prominent piece was actually intentionally archaized second-century script from the Hasmonean dynasty (John Rogerson and Philip R. Davies, "Was the Siloam Tunnel Built by Hezekiah?," *BA* 59 [1996]: 138–49). Because of the visibility and potential influence of the article, these claims were met with an immediate and crushing response. In a collaborative publication, Frank Moore Cross, Jo Ann Hackett, André Lemaire, P. Kyle McCarter Jr., and other leading epigraphists refuted Rogerson and Davies's claims point by point, confirming via multiple disciplines the late eighth-century date of the inscription (Hackett et al., "Defusing Pseudo-Scholarship"; cf. Ronald S. Hendel, "The Date of the Siloam Inscription: A Rejoinder to Rogerson and Davies," *BA* 59 [1996]: 233–37; Jane M. Cahill, "A Rejoinder to 'Was the Siloam Tunnel Built by Hezekiah?,'" *BA* 60 [1997]: 184–85).

machine. Alluded to in the Bible and the Taylor Prism, this conquest is graphically illustrated in the archaeological remains (2 Kings 18:14, 17; Isa. 36:2, 8).[84] In the wreckage were hundreds of what David Ussishkin named "royal Judean storage jars," now broadly known as *lamelek* ("belonging to the king") jars. The latter name is due to the royal stamps that the jars bear on one or more of

84. For a detailed treatment of the excavations and remains at Lachish, see Ussishkin, *Conquest of Lachish*. For a full translation of the Taylor Prism, see Mordechai Cogan, "Sennacherib's Siege of Jerusalem," *COS* 2.119b:302–3.

Lawson Stone

Figure 10.8 The Lachish panels recovered from the palace of Sennacherib, illustrating in detail the seige of Lachish in Judah.

their loop handles.[85] Neutron activation analysis has shown that these storage jars came from a centralized source, confirming that Hezekiah was stockpiling food at his strategic cities for the eventuality of siege. This is more than enough independent evidence to validate the Bible's claims about the confrontation at Lachish but, incredibly, the battle also comes to us illustrated by means of actual images of the conflict.

In Sennacherib's "Palace without Rival," completed in Nineveh in 694 BCE (excavated by Austin Henry Layard in 1845–1847), the Assyrian king installed twelve marble orthostats depicting the siege of Lachish in detail. The friezes portray the battle diachronically, with the Assyrian forces attacking, the citizens of Lachish defending, soldiers carrying off booty and torturing prisoners, exiles departing the city, and Sennacherib himself (identified by his own inscription) enthroned in his military camp outside the city receiving tribute. These panels have been a gold mine of data for the study of Assyrian and Judean weapons and warfare, as well as certain details of domestic life in Judah otherwise un-available. Here the overwhelming force of the Assyrian military, its devastating

85. Two types of emblems are known: the first portrays a four-winged scarab, the second a winged sun-disc. Each has *lĕmelek* written across the top, and one of four towns (Hebron, *mmšt*, Ziph, Socah) across the bottom in Old Hebrew Script (Ussishkin, *Conquest of Lachish*, 45; see also Philip J. King, "Why Lachish Matters," *BAR* 31, no. 4 [2005]: 36–47).

methods, and the anguish of the vanquished is etched in stone—as is a fully illustrated guide to the archaeological remains of Lachish Level III.

Lastly, we have Sennacherib's own account of his assault on Hezekiah's kingdom in column 4 of the Taylor Prism:

> But as for Hezekiah, the Jew, who did not bow in submission to my yoke, forty-six of his strong walled towns and innumerable smaller villages in their neighborhood I besieged and conquered by stamping down earth ramps and then by bringing up battering rams, by assault of foot-soldiers, by breaches, tunneling and sapper operations. I made to come out from them 200,150 people, young and old, male and female, innumerable horses, mules, donkeys, camels, large and small cattle, and counted them as the spoils of war. He himself I shut up like a caged bird within Jerusalem, his royal city.[86]

Notice that although Sennacherib claims to have attacked and humiliated "Hezekiah the Jew," he does not claim to have conquered Jerusalem. Rather, as the biblical historians report, Jerusalem was spared. Thus Sennacherib, who in his day conquered the world, did not conquer Jerusalem. The brief addendum to the account in 2 Kings drives the historian's theological point home: whereas Yahweh was able to defend his man in Jerusalem against the greatest superpower of that day, Nisroch the god of Assyria was unable to defend his man in his own temple against his own sons (19:36–37). And so the epic tale closes with this unequivocal declaration: "O Yahweh, the God of Israel, who is enthroned above the cherubim, you are God, you alone" (19:15).

But the price of Hezekiah's resistance was formidable. Lachish and its western province were leveled and ceded to Philistia, their agricultural support systems decimated, and much of their populace deported.[87] Thus, although Hezekiah goes down in biblical history as one of the monarchy's greatest heroes, the seventh century in Judah will open with tremendous loss.[88] Much will need to be regained and rebuilt if Judah is ever to rise again.

---

86. Ussishkin, *Conquest of Lachish*, 17. Widespread destruction is corroborated by 2 Kings 18:13; Isa. 36:1; Mic. 1:13–16, as well as by excavations at Tel Halif, a prominent mound in the foothills of Judah. See Oded Borowski, "In the Path of Sennacherib," *BAR* 31, no. 3 (2005): 24–35; also Mordechai Cogan, "Sennacherib's Siege of Jerusalem," *COS* 2.119B:302–3, esp. 303.

87. See note 53 above.

88. Bill Arnold notes the preponderance of occurrences of the Hebrew verb *bṭḥ* ("to trust") in the narratives involving Hezekiah as the explanation for his heroic portrayal in the Bible. "Trust is at the root of Hezekiah's opposition to idolatry (2 Kings 18:4–5), his observance of Mosaic law (2 Kings 18:6) and his attitudinal disposition of dependence on Yahweh for deliverance (2 Kings 18:30)" ("Hezekiah," *DOTHB* 412).

11

Judah in the Seventh Century

From the Aftermath of Sennacherib's Invasion to the Beginning of Jehoiakim's Rebellion

BRAD E. KELLE

The seventh century BCE constituted the last full century of existence for the Iron Age kingdom of Judah. This period began in earnest with the reign of Manasseh (697/696–643/642), although the precise ending of Hezekiah's reign remains debated (see below). It included the reigns of Amon (643/642–641/640), Josiah (641/640–609), Jehoahaz II (609), and most years of Jehoiakim (609–598).[1] The last few decades in biblical scholarship have witnessed a new appreciation for the ancient sources related to seventh-century Judah, which has given this period a new significance for the study of ancient Judean history.[2] Recently scholars have reexamined the relevant sources and considered new

1. In keeping with the conventions of this volume, dates for Judah follow Edwin R. Thiele, *The Mysterious Numbers of the Hebrew Kings: A Reconstruction of the Chronology of the Kingdoms of Israel and Judah* (3rd ed.; Grand Rapids: Eerdmans, 1983).
2. See Megan Bishop Moore and Brad E. Kelle, *Biblical History and Israel's Past: The Changing Study of the Bible and History* (Grand Rapids: Eerdmans, 2011).

350

evidence, using methods that have moved the seventh century (and Manasseh's reign in particular) to the forefront of discussion.[3]

Biblical Sources for Seventh-Century Judah in General

The Old Testament Historical Books contain two overlapping accounts of Judean history in the seventh century BCE as a whole: 2 Kings 21:1–25:30 and 2 Chron. 33:1–36:21. The Kings account is generally considered part of the Deuteronomistic History (see below). Additionally, at least some of the speeches attributed to certain writing prophets belong to this period, even if the final forms of their books come from a later era. Overall, the biblical texts portray a sequence of events for the reign of each king, including various internal social conflicts and external wars, and a variety of cultic activities undertaken by kings and people. Yet the Old Testament writers consistently cast Judah's history in light of their theological understanding of Israel's existence as the people of Yahweh.

As the introductory chapter to this book indicates, the use of the biblical sources in particular is complicated by developments in the study of Israel's Scriptures in recent decades. In keeping with the discussion provided in the introduction, at the outset of this chapter we may identify some factors for consideration that apply to all the biblical sources related to the period under consideration here. The Deuteronomistic History (Joshua–2 Kings) is generally considered to be a larger historiographical composition that originated in a first edition, perhaps as early as the time of Hezekiah or Josiah, and continued to be supplemented in various ways throughout subsequent years.[4] The Chronicles account postdates that of Kings, likely originating in the sixth century BCE, with perhaps later editorial additions. The biblical texts related to the seventh century BCE attribute some of their material to earlier sources, such as the "Book of the Annals of the Kings of Judah" (e.g., 2 Kings 21:17). The existence, nature, and content of these sources remain uncertain, yet such references represent the biblical writers' consciousness of their own selectivity in the material presented. With regard to the Old Testament prophetic texts, the effort to distinguish between the prophets' original words and the supplements of later redactors remains an issue for the use of

---

3. See esp. the collected essays in Lester L. Grabbe, ed., *Good Kings and Bad Kings: The Kingdom of Judah in the Seventh Century BCE* (LHBOTS 393; London: T&T Clark, 2005).

4. See Moshe Weinfeld, *Deuteronomy and the Deuteronomic School* (Oxford: Clarendon, 1972); Frank Moore Cross, *Canaanite Myth and Hebrew Epic: Essays in the History of the Religion of Israel* (Cambridge, MA: Harvard University Press, 1973), 274–89; Richard D. Nelson, *The Double Redaction of the Deuteronomistic History* (JSOTSup 18; Sheffield: JSOT Press, 1981).

these texts, yet historians have traditionally looked to the prophetic literature as a supplement to Kings. The Prophetic Books also include narratives that contain historiographical materials, some of which overlap with materials in 2 Kings (e.g., Jer. 39; 52).

These considerations suggest that while historians need not assume an essentially skeptical stance relative to the Old Testament's presentations, they must also avoid overinterpreting the biblical text as though it were a historical account whose primary purpose was to transmit historical detail. Most historians proceed by examining the biblical texts in dialogue with available archaeological and extrabiblical textual data. This additional data for seventh-century Judah includes material remains and artifacts, as well as Assyrian and Babylonian inscriptions and local and occasional documents such as letters, ostraca (inscribed potsherds), seals, and seal impressions. The result is often, as in this chapter, a mostly politically oriented history focused on major events, kings, wars, and related effects on the kingdom as a whole. As noted in the introduction to this book, however, students of history now seek to benefit from broader perspectives in archaeological study, new types of archaeological data, and greater consideration of sociological and anthropological research—all of which potentially yield insights into topics such as the daily life of common people in ancient Judah, the dynamics of economic and social systems, and the impact of physical environment and climate.

The Reigns of Manasseh and Amon

The Biblical Presentation

The biblical portrayals of Manasseh (2 Kings 21:1–18; 2 Chron. 33:1–20) and Amon (2 Kings 21:19–26; 2 Chron. 33:21–25) are sparse, largely passing over the first half of the seventh century BCE except to theologize about the kings' apostate practices. The prophetic literature explicitly attributes no surviving prophetic voices to the years from about 700 to 640 BCE, a period that covers the reigns of Manasseh (697/696–643/642 BCE), Amon (643/642–641/640), and the initial years of Josiah. According to the main historiographical account in 2 Kings 21, Manasseh inherited the throne at the age of twelve and reigned for fifty-five years—the longest of any Judean monarch. He inherited a kingdom in dire straits following the earlier invasion by the Assyrian emperor Sennacherib. The account, however, focuses almost exclusively on internal religious aspects, identifying Manasseh as the worst king in Judah's history. The texts tell how he sponsored apostate and idolatrous forms of worship (2 Kings 21:1–9), practices that may be reflected in later prophetic criticisms of the people's adoption of foreign customs (e.g., Zeph. 1:4–9). The biblical texts also depict a violent reign that featured the sacrifice of the king's own son and the shedding of much innocent blood (2 Kings 21:16). The account in 2 Chronicles 33 differs from the inward focus of the Kings account in only one respect: it includes an episode (2 Chron. 33:10–17) in which Manasseh is taken captive to Babylon by Assyrian forces, repents before Yahweh, and returns to Jerusalem to amend his ways and carry out a religious reform and building projects. In both accounts Manasseh is succeeded by Amon, whose brief depiction is once again primarily dedicated to describing his two-year reign as the continuation of Manasseh's religious apostasy (2 Kings 21:19–26; 2 Chron. 33:21–25). Both the Kings and Chronicles accounts describe a palace coup in which Amon was assassinated by his officials, after which the "people of the land" placed his son Josiah on the throne (2 Kings 21:23–24; 2 Chron. 33:24–25).

The assessment of the biblical sources for the eras of Manasseh and Amon largely reflects the general evaluation of the biblical sources for the seventh century as a whole (see discussion above). The accounts are part of larger compositions that have complex (and still somewhat unclear) editorial histories and whose presentations are shaped by particular theological aims. More important, the theological concerns of the biblical writers and editors yield sources that are narrow in their scope, presenting information predominantly related to internal social and religious affairs, with only passing references to broader historical happenings (and referring readers elsewhere, such as the "Book of the Annals of the Kings of Judah" [2 Kings 21:17, 25], for historical details). The one potential exception is the report in 2 Chronicles 33:10–17.

Toward the goal of a fuller picture of seventh-century Judean history, scholars pursue several primary questions regarding the reigns of Manasseh and Amon: (1) What was the nature of the aftermath of Sennacherib's invasion and the beginning of Manasseh's rule? (2) Did the bulk of Manasseh's reign constitute a time of recession or recovery for Judah within the Assyrian Empire? (3) To what extent did Assyrian power influence Judah's political and religious practices? (4) What can be known about the context of Amon's assassination and Josiah's subsequent accession? In general, interpreters must begin with the recognition that the nonbiblical historical evidence for Manasseh and Amon is just as sparse as the biblical descriptions, if not more so.[5] Although Manasseh's reign overlapped the zenith of Assyrian power and activity, his name appears in Assyrian inscriptions only in lists, without any significant

---

5. For a survey of the historical sources, see J. Maxwell Miller and John H. Hayes, *A History of Ancient Israel and Judah* (2nd ed.; Louisville: Westminster John Knox, 2006), 421–37.

detail. Additionally, the evidence from archaeology for this period, while abundant in many ways, remains complex. It is particularly difficult to distinguish which archaeological finds should be associated with the early seventh century (during Manasseh's time) and which belong to the latter part of the century (during Josiah's reign), and this difficulty is often the source of varying historical reconstructions.

The Aftermath of Sennacherib's Invasion and the Beginning of Manasseh's Reign

The timing and circumstances of the beginning of Manasseh's rule have been the source of debate. As noted above, the biblical texts simply state that Manasseh succeeded his father, Hezekiah, when he was twelve years old and reigned for a total of fifty-five years (2 Kings 21:1; 2 Chron. 33:1). Various attempts to correlate the chronological information within the book of Kings, however, have led some scholars to conclude that Manasseh's rule began as a coregency with Hezekiah, at least for the first decade or so of the seventh century. Edwin Thiele's chronology, used in this volume, represents the coregency view.[6] By working backward from the date of the first capture of Jerusalem attested in the Babylonian Chronicle as 597 BCE and following the biblical figures given for the reigns of the Judean kings from Hezekiah to Jehoiachin, Thiele concludes that the numbers require a coregency of ten or eleven years at some point during that era. In his view, Manasseh provides the most likely possibility for the needed coregency. Hence, Thiele proposes that Manasseh reigned as a coregent from 697/696 to 687/686 BCE and as sole ruler from 687/686 to 643/642, and that the ten-year coregency was included in the biblical total of fifty-five years.[7]

Many historians follow this reconstruction, but one should acknowledge that it results from particular configurations of (and assumptions about) the biblical data (especially the chronological figures in 2 Kings).[8] Assyrian inscriptions offer no help on this question other than the fact that they do not mention Hezekiah's death in conjunction with Sennacherib's invasion in 701 BCE—an absence of evidence from which the conclusion of a coregency does not necessarily follow.[9] Additionally, the biblical texts never report a coregency for

---

6. Thiele, *Mysterious Numbers*, 173–74.

7. Ibid., 174, 217, 219.

8. See discussion in Andrew G. Vaughn, *Theology, History, and Archaeology in the Chronicler's Account of Hezekiah* (SBLABS 4; Atlanta: Scholars Press, 1999), 8–13.

9. This is the case even though Sennacherib's inscriptions do record the death of other kings involved in the campaign of 701. Contrast the assertion by Anson F. Rainey and R. Steven Notley that the Assyrian silence concerning Hezekiah's death constitutes "strong testimony"

any monarch in Israelite and Judean history, raising the question of whether this is the proper way to explain the conflicting data that emerges from the regnal years and synchronisms assigned to the various kings. The hypothesis of a coregency for Manasseh's first ten years of rule may be correct, but the available evidence does not allow it to be proven conclusively, and other reconstructions seem equally plausible.[10]

Whether or not one hypothesizes a coregency, the most pressing historical question is the condition of the kingdom of Judah at the beginning of the seventh century BCE. The preceding chapter in this volume discussed the evidence for the Assyrian invasion in 701 BCE and its possible impact on Judah's people, economy, and territory. The present discussion will highlight only some key examples that possibly shed light on the situation in Judah during Manasseh's early years, and the reader should consult the preceding chapter for a fuller treatment. The biblical texts place Manasseh's accession and early years in the aftermath of Sennacherib's invasion of Judah, implying but not stating outright that Manasseh inherited (whether as coregent or sole ruler) a greatly reduced kingdom in dire economic and political straits. The first category of other available sources—the Assyrian inscriptions of Sennacherib—seems to confirm this picture. According to Assyrian records, Sennacherib captured forty-six walled towns and their associated villages, captured or exiled 200,150 Judeans, increased the kingdom's vassal payments, and gave away substantial portions of Judean territory to Philistine control, resulting in the creation of refugees and the reduction of resources.[11] Even if the Assyrian claims are exaggerated,[12] the evidence suggests significant devastation, death, and deportation, especially in western and southwestern Judah. Notable here is the convergence between some archaeological evidence from Philistia and the Assyrian inscriptions' claim that Sennacherib removed portions of

---

that Hezekiah did not leave the throne in the years immediately following 701 BCE (*The Sacred Bridge: Carta's Atlas of the Biblical World* [Jerusalem: Carta, 2006], 245).

10. For example, John H. Hayes and Paul K. Hooker, *A New Chronology for the Kings of Israel and Judah and Its Implications for Biblical History and Literature* (Atlanta: John Knox, 1988), 80–83.

11. *COS* 2.199: 300–303; *ANET* 287–88; Sarah C. Melville, "Oriental Institute Prism: Campaigns in Babylonia and Judah," in *The Ancient Near East: Historical Sources in Translation* (ed. Mark W. Chavalas; Malden, MA: Blackwell, 2006), 346–47. See also Riekele Borger, *Babylonisch-Assyrische Lesestücke* (3 vols.; Rome: Pontifical Biblical Institute, 1963), 1:75. For discussion of the Sennacherib texts related to 701 BCE, see Anson F. Rainey, "Manasseh, King of Judah, in the Whirlpool of the Seventh Century BCE," in Kinattūtū ša dārâti: *Raphael Kutscher Memorial Volume* (ed. Anson F. Rainey; TAUIAP 1; Tel Aviv: Institute of Archaeology, Tel Aviv University, 1993), 147–64.

12. See Marco De Odorico, *The Use of Numbers and Quantifications in the Assyrian Royal Inscriptions* (SAAS 3; Helsinki: Neo-Assyrian Text Corpus Project, University of Helsinki, 1995).

Judah's territory and gave them to several Philistine kings, including Padi, king of Ekron.[13] Archaeological data from ancient Ekron (Tel Miqne) indicate significant growth in the years following 701 BCE, including the development of a substantial olive oil industry (see below)—growth that presumably is linked to Sennacherib's transfer of the relatively fertile land of the Shephelah (a primary "breadbasket" for Judah consisting of valleys and foothills to the south and west of Jerusalem) to Padi's control.[14]

Other archaeological data from Judah supplements the picture of a state reduced, if not devastated. Surveys of sites in the Shephelah, for instance, indicate that 85 percent of the eighth-century BCE settlements were abandoned and not resettled throughout the next century.[15] Overall, the survey data points to a decrease in the built-up area of the Shephelah by the end of the seventh century, to less than one-fourth of its size in the eighth century, with a near total lack of Judean settlements in the western part of the area.[16] Similarly, archaeological evidence from the Judean hills indicates that some sites south of Jerusalem (e.g., Ramat Raḥel) suffered destruction in 701 BCE but were later rebuilt, although the pottery evidence for settlement at particular sites is difficult to pinpoint to precise eras.[17] Perhaps the parade example of destruction in the aftermath of Sennacherib's invasion is the city of Lachish in the Shephelah. The initial destruction of this fortified city is attested in both archaeological remains from the site and a pictorial relief of the Assyrian siege of the city, on the wall of Sennacherib's palace in Nineveh.[18]

13. COS 2.199:300–303; ANET 287–88.

14. See Seymour Gitin, "Tel Miqne-Ekron in the 7th Century BC: City Plan Development and the Oil Industry," in Olive Oil in Antiquity: Israel and Neighbouring Countries from the Neolithic to the Early Arab Period (ed. David Eitam and Michael Heltzer; SHANE 7; Padova: Sargon, 1996), 167–96, 219–43.

15. See Yehuda Dagan, "The Shephelah during the Period of the Monarchy in Light of Archaeological Excavations and Surveys" (MA thesis, Tel Aviv University, 1992); see also Avraham Faust, "Settlement and Demography in Seventh-Century Judah and the Extent and Intensity of Sennacherib's Campaign," PEQ 140 (2008): 168–94; Israel Finkelstein, "The Archaeology of the Days of Manasseh," in Scripture and Other Artifacts: Essays on the Bible and Archaeology in Honor of Philip J. King (ed. Michael D. Coogan, Cheryl Exum, and Lawrence E. Stager; Louisville: Westminster John Knox, 1994), 169–87.

16. Dagan, "Shephelah," 259–60, map 7; Vaughn, Theology, History, and Archaeology, 25.

17. See Yohanan Aharoni, Excavations at Ramat Raḥel, Seasons 1961 and 1962 (SAr 6; Rome: Center for Semitic Studies, 1964); Avi Ofer, "'All the Hill Country of Judah': From a Settlement Fringe to a Prosperous Monarchy," in From Nomadism to Monarchy: Archaeological and Historical Aspects of Early Israel (ed. Israel Finkelstein and Nadav Na'aman; Jerusalem: Israel Exploration Society, 1994), 92–122; Vaughn, Theology, History, and Archaeology, 32–45.

18. See David Ussishkin, The Conquest of Lachish by Sennacherib (TAUIAP 6; Tel Aviv: Tel Aviv University Institute of Archaeology, 1982); idem, The Renewed Archaeological Excavations at Lachish (1973–1994) (5 vols.; TAUIAM 22; Tel Aviv: Emery and Claire Yass Publications in Archaeology of the Institute of Archaeology, Tel Aviv University, 2004).

A final set of data that point to a dire situation in Judah during the opening years of the seventh century comes from the perspective of social history. Several biblical and extrabiblical sources related to taxation, tribute, and the storage and distribution of commodities suggest that the preceding century had witnessed a shift in Judean social dynamics that involved the intensification, if not emergence, of an economically stratified society. Various texts within the Old Testament Historical Books, as well as some prophetic critiques, hint that Judean kings practiced tax collection within an overall system of debt, taxation, and corvée labor (e.g., 2 Kings 15:20; 23:33–35; Amos 2:6–7; Mic. 2:1–2).[19] Within this kind of system, wealthy landowners in general, and the royal house in particular, had various means of collecting land and resources for themselves in a manner that caused poor farmers to fall increasingly into debt slavery.[20] In the case of Hezekiah's actions in the late eighth century, much of the taxation and consolidation served to prepare for the Assyrian invasion in 701 BCE and thus sustained at least some segments of Judah's population during that time.[21] During the aftermath of Sennacherib's subjugation of Judah, however, these kinds of economic practices of royal taxation and consolidation became an increasingly destructive force within Judean society. Whatever the precise calculations involved, the initial years of Manasseh's rule (as coregent or otherwise) involved the external pressure of increased vassal payments to a foreign empire that drew the resources gained by taxation away from Judah, reduced the kingdom's available resources, and exacerbated the economic burden on the lower classes.

Manasseh, Judah, and the Assyrian Empire in the Seventh Century

A second significant historical question for the first part of the seventh century BCE broadens to inquire about the status of Judah under Manasseh after the initial decade of the 690s BCE. The major historical questions concern how the kingdom functioned within the larger political and religious context of the Assyrian Empire and its western activities during this time and whether the remainder of the first half of the seventh century witnessed any kind of significant domestic political, social, or economic recovery in Judah.

As noted above, the main biblical texts (with the exception of 2 Chron. 33:10–17) portray Manasseh's activities as inwardly focused on religious affairs,

19. See Richard S. Hess, "Taxes, Taxation," *DOTHB* 950–54; Daniel C. Snell, "Taxes and Taxation," *ABD* 6:338–40.
20. See Nili Sacher Fox, *In the Service of the King: Officialdom in Ancient Israel and Judah* (HUCM 23; Cincinnati: Hebrew Union College Press, 2000).
21. Hess, "Taxes, Taxation," 953.

having no significant intersection with the larger events of the Assyrian Empire and involving no substantial domestic building within Judah. This portrayal tacitly identifies Manasseh as a long-term loyal Assyrian vassal, who reigned over a kingdom that remained politically and economically marginal, if not depressed, throughout his years. This impression led many twentieth-century scholars to conclude that any significant political or economic recovery in Judah took place only during the reign of Josiah, in the second half of the seventh century.

When one examines the available extrabiblical evidence for the reign of Manasseh, some elements strengthen the impression gained from the biblical portrayal, while other data suggest that the terse, theologically focused account obscures significant domestic developments and recovery that occurred during this era. The most important extrabiblical textual evidence is the corpus of Assyrian royal inscriptions and other similar texts related to the reigns of the Assyrian emperors Sennacherib (705–681), Esarhaddon (681–669), and Ashurbanipal (669–627). There are few (and merely passing) references to Manasseh and Judah in the Assyrian texts, but they generally reinforce the impression that Manasseh ruled as a loyal vassal within the shadow of the empire's activities in the west. The Assyrian Eponym Chronicles, or "*limmu* lists," preserve a year-by-year account in which each year is named after a key Assyrian official (Akk. *limmu*). Each entry records some condition or event that transpired that year, or the location of the army at the end of the year. The main canon of lists seems to have begun with the reign of Shalmaneser III in 858 BCE and provides good coverage through 649; several fragmentary copies of different lists can be used to extend coverage down to 612.[22] However, none of the entries for the years overlapping Manasseh's reign lists the location of the Assyrian army or any significant event.

As for the Assyrian royal inscriptions, Sennacherib's records do not indicate any further campaigns in Syria-Palestine between the invasion of Judah in 701 BCE and his assassination in 681.[23] An older theory had advanced the notion that Sennacherib conducted a second invasion of Judah in the early 680s. This theory was largely based on textual analysis of the invasion accounts in 2 Kings 18:17–19:37 (// Isa. 36) and the assumption that the Ethiopian ruler Tirhaka (Taharqa), who is mentioned in the context of Sennacherib's invasion

---

22. Alan R. Millard, *The Eponyms of the Assyrian Empire 910–612 BC* (SAAS 2; Helsinki: Neo-Assyrian Text Corpus Project, University of Helsinki, 1994), 72.

23. *COS* 1.137:467–68; 2.199E:305; Melville, "Oriental Institute Prism." See also Eckart Frahm, *Einleitung in die Sanherib-Inschriften* (AfOB 26; Vienna: Institut für Orientalistik der Universität Wien, 1997).

in 2 Kings 19:9, did not ascend the throne until 690.[24] Some recent proponents of the theory also attempted to redate some of Sennacherib's royal inscriptions to the years following 701.[25] Reassessments of Egyptian chronology, however, have demonstrated the likelihood that Taharqa was in fact a young man who could have served as a high-ranking officer in 701.[26] Likewise, new considerations of the relevant Egyptian and Assyrian material, as well as the archaeological data from destruction layers at Lachish, call into question the support for the older theory.[27] The Assyrian texts indicate that in the early seventh century Sennacherib faced a significant rebellion in Anatolia and Babylon, and his annals record successive campaigns to Anatolia in 696 and 695, as well as military action against Babylon that intensified beginning in 694 and culminated with the sack of Babylon in 689.[28]

One important factor that shaped Assyrian policy in the first part of the seventh century BCE was the activity of the Cushite pharaohs of the Twenty-Fifth Dynasty in Egypt. Indirect evidence from some Egyptian and Assyrian texts suggests that Taharqa (690–664) engaged in subversive diplomatic and commercial activities within Syria-Palestine (perhaps especially with Tyre and other coastal cities) during the period when Sennacherib was occupied in Anatolia and Babylonia.[29] In the years after Esarhaddon succeeded Sennacherib on the Assyrian throne in 681, Assyrian royal inscriptions attest to a series of campaigns directed against Egypt.[30] In 679 Esarhaddon's inscriptions report that he marched in a show of force to the Egyptian border and moved against Cyprus, Sidon, and Tyre. After a campaign against Sidon and other imperial activities,

---

24. See, e.g., William F. Albright, "The Chronology of the Divided Monarchy of Israel," *BASOR* 100 (1945): 16–22; John Bright, *A History of Israel* (4th ed.; Louisville: Westminster John Knox, 2000), 298–309.

25. William H. Shea, "Sennacherib's Second Palestinian Campaign," *JBL* 104 (1985): 410–18.

26. Kenneth A. Kitchen, *The Third Intermediate Period in Egypt, 1100–650 B.C.* (2nd ed.; Warminster, UK: Aris & Phillips, 1986), 383–87; Anson F. Rainey, "Taharqa and Syntax," *TA* 3 (1976): 38–41.

27. Frank J. Yurco, "The Shabaka-Shebitku Coregency and the Supposed Second Campaign of Sennacherib against Judah: A Critical Assessment," *JBL* 110 (1991): 35–45; Vaughn, *Theology, History, and Archaeology*, 8–10.

28. *COS* 2.199:305; Sarah C. Melville, "The Bavarian Inscription: The Destruction of Babylon," in Chavalas, *Ancient Near East*, 349.

29. An inscription from Karnak, e.g., may refer to tribute collected from kingdoms in the Levant (see Pascal Vernus, "Inscriptions de la troisième période intermédiaire (I)," *BIFAO* 75 [1975]: 1–66; Anthony J. Spalinger, "The Foreign Policy of Egypt Preceding the Assyrian Conquest," *ChrEg* 53 [1978]: 22–47; Rainey and Notley, *Sacred Bridge*, 245–46). Additionally, Esarhaddon mentions Taharqa's subversive influence in a description of his conflict with Tyre (Earle Leichty, *The Royal Inscriptions of Esarhaddon, King of Assyria (680–669 BC)* [RINP 4; Winona Lake, IN: Eisenbrauns, 2011]; Rainey and Notley, *Sacred Bridge*, 246). No Egyptian texts from Taharqa's reign, however, mention any military campaigns into Syria-Palestine.

30. *ANET* 289–94.

Baker Photo Archive (Pergamon Museum, Berlin)

Figure 11.1. Stela of Esarhaddon with Taharqa and Ba'alu of Tyre before him

in 674 Esarhaddon fully invaded Egypt but suffered defeat—an occasion absent from the Assyrian annals but preserved in the Babylonian Chronicles.[31] In 671, however, after subduing Tyre, Esarhaddon successfully invaded Egypt, defeated Taharqa, and captured Memphis.[32] Two years later (669), Esarhaddon campaigned again in Egypt to subdue a resurgent Taharqa, but he fell ill and died on the way.[33] His son Ashurbanipal succeeded him and continued the campaign, and Assyrian texts state that he compelled vassal kings in the west to provide troops and ships.[34] By 664, Ashurbanipal recaptured Memphis from the new Ethiopian king, Tantamani, and destroyed Thebes (cf. Noamon [= Thebes] in Nah. 3:8).[35]

In the course of these events, Manasseh is mentioned by name in two Assyrian royal inscriptions, but only in passing as a part of lists. Just before Esarhaddon's unsuccessful invasion of Egypt, Assyrian annals name "Manasseh king of the city of Judah" as one of twenty-two western vassals who provided building materials for Esarhaddon's newly planned palace.[36]

A decade later, Ashurbanipal's inscriptions identify Manasseh merely as one of the western kings who contributed troops to the Assyrian invasion of Egypt after 669.[37] Although not explicitly related to Manasseh or Judah, the Vassal

31. See *ANET* 302; Bill T. Arnold, "The Neo-Babylonian Chronicle Series," in Chavalas, *Ancient Near East*, 411; A. Kirk Grayson, *Assyrian and Babylonian Chronicles* (TCS 5; Locust Valley, NY: Augustin, 1975; repr., Winona Lake, IN: Eisenbrauns, 2000), 84.

32. See *ANET* 293; Arnold, "Neo-Babylonian Chronicle Series," 411; Grayson, *Assyrian and Babylonian Chronicles*, 85.

33. Arnold, "Neo-Babylonian Chronicle Series," 411.

34. See *ANET* 294; Sarah C. Melville, "Apology and Egyptian Campaigns," in Chavalas, *Ancient Near East*, 363–65.

35. See *ANET* 295–97.

36. *ANET* 291.

37. *ANET* 294. Miller and Hayes (*History of Ancient Israel and Judah*, 435) also propose that an Assyrian list of annual tribute from Syro-Palestinian states dates to the time of Manasseh (see *ANET* 301). The list mentions tribute received from "the inhabitants of Judah."

Treaty of Esarhaddon that sought to guarantee the succession of Ashurbani-pal is relevant. Since Esarhaddon himself had struggled against his brothers to secure the throne,[38] in the late 670s he required his vassals to submit to a special loyalty oath designed to safeguard his son's accession.[39] Esarhaddon's concerns and actions point to a significantly heightened Assyrian supervision and control of vassal kingdoms during the first part of the seventh century BCE. Taken together with these concerns and the evidence for extensive Assyrian military campaigns in the region, the references to Manasseh in Assyrian texts suggest that the Judean king reigned as a loyal Assyrian vassal who was no more than a bit player in larger political realities. For some historians, the cumulative weight of the evidence points to the conclusion that the biblical presentation of Manasseh's reign is an accurate reflection of a time that had little, if any, political, social, or economic significance for Judah.[40]

Given the evidence of heavy Assyrian activity and the biblical focus on Manasseh's religious deeds, scholars have considered a related historical question concerning Judean religion during this era. As noted above, 2 Kings in particular gives a thoroughgoing negative portrayal by telling how Manasseh sponsored apostate and idolatrous forms of worship (2 Kings 21:1–9). Some interpreters have explained these descriptions as reflecting Assyrian imposition of their religious practices on vassals like Manasseh,[41] but others contend that the available evidence does not support such a conclusion.[42] Perhaps some of the evidence for domestic developments under Manasseh (to be discussed below) moves beyond these polar alternatives. Manasseh's propagation of nonorthodox worship, while possibly reflecting Assyrian influence, may represent the cosmopolitan religion of a culturally integrated setting, with the voluntary incorporation of religious elements from various cultures and the revival of older, nonexclusivistic, Yahwistic practices from the time before Hezekiah's reforms.[43] The practices

---

38. *ANET* 289–90.

39. Sarah C. Melville, "The Succession Treaty of Esarhaddon," in Chavalas, *Ancient Near East*, 355–56.

40. A recent example of this trend is the comprehensive history volume by Iain W. Provan, V. Philips Long, and Tremper Longman III, *A Biblical History of Israel* (Louisville: Westminster John Knox, 2003), 274–75. Their reconstruction of Manasseh's time simply mirrors the biblical presentation of the period as insignificant, as they describe Manasseh's five-decade reign in a single paragraph.

41. As, e.g., Hermann Spieckermann, *Juda unter Assur in der Sargonidenzeit* (FRLANT 129; Göttingen: Vandenhoeck & Ruprecht, 1982).

42. J. W. McKay, *Religion in Judah under the Assyrians, 732–609 BC* (SBT 26; Naperville, IL: Allenson, 1973); Mordechai D. Cogan, *Imperialism and Religion: Assyria, Judah, and Israel in the Eighth and Seventh Centuries B.C.E.* (SBLMS 19; Missoula, MT: Scholars Press, 1974).

43. See Richard S. Hess, *Israelite Religions: An Archaeological and Biblical Survey* (Grand Rapids: Baker, 2007), esp. 330–32. See also Jacob Milgrom, "The Nature and Extent of Idolatry

Figurines

Archaeologists have discovered a significant quantity of figurines, both anthropomorphic and zoomorphic, in Israel and Judah from the tenth–sixth centuries BCE. Especially notable are more than eight hundred small female figurines discovered primarily in private homes. The figurines commonly feature a molded head, cylindrical body, and hands supporting the breasts. The female figurines may constitute evidence in considering the biblical references to religious activities during Manasseh's reign. Some interpreters see them as potential indicators of goddess worship (perhaps of Asherah, whether in connection with Yahweh worship or otherwise) in domestic settings or "nonofficial" religion. However, the female figurines are made of clay rather than the valuable materials normally used for statues of deities, and they seem to have been mass-produced in a manner suggesting that their production was somehow state-sponsored.[a] Connection with goddess worship exceeds the conclusions available from the evidence, and perhaps the female figurines were symbols of female fertility, used by women in conjunction with pregnancy, child rearing, or nourishment. Even so, their connection to the religious practices during Manasseh's reign remains to be fully determined.

a. See Richard S. Hess, *Israelite Religions: An Archaeological and Biblical Survey* (Grand Rapids: Baker Academic, 2007), 308–12.

associated with Manasseh in 2 Kings 21 feature Canaanite-Phoenician deities, such as Baal and Asherah, as well as astral deities related to Assyrian and Aramean practices.[44] Potentially, then, the religious deeds described in the biblical texts reflect not the imposition of Assyrian practices but rather Manasseh's efforts to establish commercial relations with Tyre that were expressed in terms of shared cultic activities.[45]

The only biblical text suggesting that Manasseh did not conduct himself as a subservient and loyal Assyrian vassal throughout his reign is 2 Chronicles 33:10–17. As described above, this passage recounts an episode in which Manasseh was taken captive by the Assyrians, brought in chains to Babylon, humbled himself before the Lord (see the apocryphal Prayer of Manasseh), and returned home to institute Yahwistic reforms and some building projects.

---

in Eighth-Seventh Century Judah," *HUCA* 69 (1998): 1–13; Lynn Tatum, "Jerusalem in Conflict: The Evidence for the Seventh-Century BCE Religious Struggle over Jerusalem," in *Jerusalem in Bible and Archaeology: The First Temple Period* (ed. Andrew G. Vaughn and Ann E. Killebrew; SBLSymS 18; Atlanta: Society of Biblical Literature, 2003), 291–306.

44. Mordechai Cogan, "Into Exile: From the Assyrian Conquest of Israel to the Fall of Babylon," *OHBW* 255.

45. McKay, *Religion in Judah*, 20–27; Rainey and Notley, *Sacred Bridge*, 246.

Other than the reference to Babylon, the text provides no specific chronological or historical details to locate this event. Thus the historical value of this tradition remains debated. At one level, the text reflects the common motif of a bad king who amends his ways, and it might have been created by the biblical writer to justify the long reign of an otherwise evil king.[46] Even so, the presence of a known literary motif does not necessarily discredit the tradition's historical value. Scholars have proposed a number of anti-Assyrian rebellions that occurred throughout the ancient Near East during Manasseh's reign as potential backgrounds for Judean participation in a revolt that would render understandable the actions described in the text. Foremost among the theories is the proposal that the tradition reflects a political act set in the context of Manasseh's rebuilding of Jerusalem and a major rebellion in Babylon by Ashurbanipal's brother in 652–648 BCE.[47] In the aftermath of Ashurbanipal's defeat of this rebellion, the Assyrian king remained at Babylon and dealt with the treasonous allies that had supported his brother.[48] Given the geographical detail in 2 Chronicles 33:11 that the Assyrians brought Manasseh to "Babylon," perhaps the Judean king was arrested and interrogated, along with other western rulers, to establish his loyalty before being ultimately returned to his throne. Still, there is no other evidence for Manasseh's involvement in any of these events. The story does not appear in 2 Kings, and as previously noted, Manasseh consistently appears in Assyrian texts as a loyal vassal. It is possible to argue that the story in 2 Chronicles 33:10–17 arose from a specific historical event that took place in Babylon near the midpoint of the seventh century. Yet the tradition is not historically verifiable with the evidence presently available.

Beyond the extrabiblical textual sources, the other key evidence for reconstructing the status of Judah within the Assyrian Empire in the first half of the seventh century comes from archaeological data related to the domestic situation in the land under Manasseh. The preceding discussion has already

---

46. See Miller and Hayes, *History of Ancient Israel and Judah*, 436–37; Ernst L. Ehrlich, "Der Aufenthalt des Königs Manasse in Babylon," *TZ* 21 (1965): 281–86; William Schniedewind, "The Source Citations of Manasseh: King Manasseh in History and Homily," *VT* 41 (1991): 450–61.

47. See esp. Rainey's arguments in Rainey, "Manasseh, King of Judah," 147–64; Rainey and Notley, *Sacred Bridge*, 249–50. For Ashurbanipal's inscriptions related to the revolt, see *ANET* 297–98. For others who maintain the possibility of historicity under various scenarios, see Cogan, "Into Exile," 254; Bright, *History of Israel*, 311; Bustenay Oded, "Judah and the Exile," in *Israelite and Judaean History* (ed. John H. Hayes and J. Maxwell Miller; OTL; Philadelphia: Westminster, 1977), 455. For details of the so-called Great Rebellion by Shamash-shum-ukin, see J. A. Brinkman, *Prelude to Empire: Babylonian Society and Politics, 747–626 B.C.* (OPBF 7; Philadelphia: The Babylonian Fund, University Museum, 1984), 93–104; Bill T. Arnold, *Who Were the Babylonians?* (SBLABS 10; Atlanta: Society of Biblical Literature, 2004).

48. *ANET* 298–300.

Figure 11.2. Ashurbanipal

mentioned the archaeological indications of significant reduction and destruction throughout Judean territory in the west and southwest at the outset of
Manasseh's reign. The primary question, however, is whether there is archaeological evidence for significant political, social, and economic recovery and
perhaps expansion in the later years of Manasseh's reign. On this point, one
finds considerable divergence among current historical reconstructions. One
of the main causes of such divergence is the difficulty in precisely correlating
archaeological data with narrow eras within the same century (e.g., precisely
establishing whether data from a site come from the first half of the seventh
century under Manasseh or from the second half under Josiah). Additionally,
today's main reconstructions differ over the chronology for Iron Age Judah
into which they place the various data.

The primary evidence under consideration centers on archaeological data
for building and development in the seventh century BCE within the areas of
the Shephelah, Negev (Beersheba Valley), Judean hills south of Jerusalem, and
the Judean desert east of Jerusalem.[49] There is a consensus that the Shephelah
experienced no significant recovery throughout the seventh century.[50] However,
with regard to the Negev, ceramic and other evidence indicates the rebuilding

49. For overviews, see Vaughn, *Theology, History, and Archaeology*, 19–79; Finkelstein,
"Archaeology of the Days of Manasseh."

50. See the survey in Dagan, "Shephelah." See discussion in Vaughn, *Theology, History, and
Archaeology*, 22–32; Finkelstein, "Archaeology of the Days of Manasseh."

of various sites and some Judean forts.[51] Some interpreters attribute these remains to the early seventh century and the activity of Manasseh,[52] while others restrict them to the last days of Manasseh's reign at the earliest.[53] Likewise, archaeological data indicate a steady settlement in the Judean hills, with the erection of some forts and farmhouses around Jerusalem, as well as new developments in the Judean desert to the east. Once again, however, archaeologists differ on the chronological assessment of the evidence and whether these developments should be attributed to Manasseh.[54]

The more traditional view that emerged from some of the assessments given above has been that the general situation of reduction and depression continued throughout all but perhaps the very last portion of Manasseh's reign, with significant change occurring only in the later part of the seventh century under Josiah.[55] In recent years, however, new assessments, often working from revised chronologies for the material remains of Iron Age Judah, have proposed a new reconstruction of the evidence. In keeping with some of the dating given above, this reconstruction proposes that the first half of the seventh century in Judah featured the rebuilding and development of local urban and production centers and renewed participation in the commerce of the Assyrian Empire, leading some current scholars to conclude that the time of Manasseh was the peak of settlement and development in the history of the southern kingdom.[56] The most fully developed arguments for this view appear in the works of Avraham Faust and Israel Finkelstein.[57] By relying especially on settlement, demographic, and

51. For a compilation of the data, see Vaughn, *Theology, History, and Archaeology*, 45–58.

52. Itzhaq Beit-Arieh, "Tel-ʿIra and Ḥorvat ʿUzzah: Negev Sites in the Late Israelite Period" (in Hebrew), *Cathedra* 42 (1987): 34–38; Itzhaq Beit-Arieh, ed., *Tel ʿIra: A Stronghold in the Biblical Negev* (TAUIAM 15; Tel Aviv: Emery and Claire Yass Publications in Archaeology of the Institute of Archaeology, Tel Aviv University, 1999); Israel Finkelstein and Nadav Na'aman, "The Judahite Shephelah in the Late 8th and Early 7th Centuries BCE," *TA* 31 (2004): 60–79.

53. Rainey and Notley, *Sacred Bridge*, 247; Lily Singer-Avitz, "'Busayra Painted Ware' at Tel Beersheba," *TA* 31 (2004): 80–89; Vaughn, *Theology, History, and Archaeology*, 50.

54. See Ofer, "'All the Hill Country of Judah,'" 92–121; Finkelstein, "Archaeology of the Days of Manasseh"; Lester L. Grabbe, "The Kingdom of Judah from Sennacherib's Invasion to the Fall of Jerusalem: If We Only Had the Bible . . . ," in Grabbe, *Good Kings and Bad Kings*, 82–89.

55. For example, Rainey and Notley, *Sacred Bridge*, 245–50.

56. For summaries, see Ehud Ben Zvi, "Prelude to a Reconstruction of the Historical Manassic Judah," *BN* 81 (1996): 31–44; Ernst A. Knauf, "The Glorious Days of Manasseh," in Grabbe, *Good Kings and Bad Kings*, 173. For a challenge to this view, see Nadav Na'aman, "When and How Did Jerusalem Become a Great City? The Rise of Jerusalem as Judah's Premier City in the Eighth–Seventh Centuries BCE," *BASOR* 347 (2007): 21–56.

57. See Finkelstein, "Archaeology of the Days of Manasseh"; Faust, "Settlement and Demography"; Avraham Faust and Ehud Weiss, "Judah, Philistia, and the Mediterranean World: Reconstructing the Economic System of the Seventh Century B.C.E.," *BASOR* 338 (2005): 71–92; idem, "Between Assyria and the Mediterranean World: The Prosperity of Judah and Philistia in the Seventh Century BCE in Context," in *Interweaving Worlds: Systemic Interactions in Eurasia,*

cultural data for particular regions, they propose that Judah came to participate in an integrated local economic system centered in Philistia, with different areas as specialized zones of production for commodities such as vineyards and wine (Ashkelon and coastal plain), olive oil (inner coastal plain and Shephelah), grain (Judean highlands), and sheep/goat raising (Judean desert). The port of Ashkelon was the heart of the system, as the production zones were organized toward the Mediterranean for maritime trade with the Phoenicians.[58] For proponents of this reconstruction, evidence for participation in the regional economic system dovetails with the data discussed above that may indicate expansion and recovery in parts of Judah in the early to mid-seventh century BCE.

Supplemental archaeological data used to bolster this reconstruction come in various forms from both inside and outside Judah. Within Philistia, excavations have revealed substantial development and expansion, especially at Ekron (Tel Miqne). Most important, there is evidence of a large olive oil industry at Ekron (likely holding a monopoly over oil production after formerly Judean territories in the Shephelah had been given to Philistia by Sennacherib) as well as a winery at Ashkelon.[59] Within Judah, scholars point to the use of Judean shekels in foreign markets,[60] an increase in written material such as seals, bullae,[61] and the continued use and possibly production of the *lmlk*-stamped jars[62]—all perhaps evidence of political, social, and economic recovery during this time. Even so, nearly every assessment of data within this recovery view can be challenged, and debate over the proper reconstruction of life in Judah during Manasseh's reign remains open.

The Reign of Amon

Whatever the proper reconstruction of Judah during the first half of the seventh century BCE, Manasseh's reign ended with his death in 643/642

7th to 1st Millennia BC (ed. Toby C. Wilkinson, Susan Sherratt, and John Bennett; Oakville, CT: Oxbow, 2011), 189–204.

58. For a survey of different production zones and their development, see Faust, "Settlement and Demography," 172–80.

59. See Avraham Faust, "The Interests of the Assyrian Empire in the West: Olive Oil Production as a Test-Case," *JESHO* 54 (2011): 62–85. See also Trude Dothan and Seymour Gitin, "Miqne, Tel," *OEANE* 4:30–35; Nadav Na'aman, "Ekron under the Assyrian and Egyptian Empires," *BASOR* 332 (2003): 81–91. For the winery at Ashkelon, see Faust and Weiss, "Between Assyria and the Mediterranean World," 190.

60. See Cogan, "Into Exile," 254.

61. See Grabbe, "Kingdom of Judah," 102.

62. See Oded Lipschits, Omer Sergi, and Ido Koch, "Royal Judahite Jar Handles: Reconsidering the Chronology of the *lmlk* Stamp Impressions," *TA* 37 (2010): 3–32; A. Douglas Tushingham, "New Evidence Bearing on the Two-Winged *LMLK* Stamp," *BASOR* 287 (1992): 61–65; but cf. Vaughn, *Theology, History, and Archaeology*, 85–167.

Figure 11.3. *lmlk*-stamped jar

according to the traditional chronology. The biblical accounts give only the minimal information that Manasseh's son Amon ruled for two years (643/642–641/640), was assassinated in a palace coup, and was succeeded by Josiah, who was placed on the throne by the "people of the land" (2 Kings 21:19–26; 2 Chron. 33:21–25). The two biblical accounts differ only in whether they assume a previous repentance and religious reform by Manasseh (only in 2 Chron. 33:10–17). Historians have precious little to go on concerning any larger historical realities associated with these descriptions. Perhaps the coup that overthrew Amon represented an anti-Assyrian move that was precipitated by a broad but short-lived western uprising attested in some Assyrian texts from the time.[63] The nature and constitution of the group called "the people of the land," who earlier had participated in the overthrow of Queen Athaliah, remain debated. The various biblical references to the group suggest that it possessed some judicial authority and military strength (perhaps aristocratic landowners), with a decidedly pro-Assyrian, pro-Davidic, anti-Egyptian bent to its politics.

The Reigns of Josiah and Jehoahaz II

The Biblical Presentation

The primary biblical presentations of Josiah (2 Kings 22:1–23:30; 2 Chron. 34:1–35:27) depict him as the ideal king, ruling in unmatched obedience to Yahweh. According to the main historiographical accounts, Josiah inherited the

63. Hayes and Hooker, *New Chronology*, 82. See previously, Abraham Malamat, "The Historical Background of the Assassination of Amon, King of Judah," *IEJ* 3 (1953): 26–29.

Hebrew Inscriptions and Seals

Numerous Hebrew inscriptions have been discovered from the areas of Iron Age Israel and Judah, some of which date to the seventh century BCE. With few possible exceptions, these are not royal or monumental inscriptions but rather local and occasional documents such as personal or official correspondence, receipts, legal agreements, or identifications on jars or other vessels. One category of Hebrew inscriptions is seals—engraved gemstones or rings, perhaps worn around the neck or on the finger and used to impress a person's identification into a lump of soft wax or clay to bind the strings around a rolled-up document (e.g., Gen. 38:18, 25; Exod. 28:11, 21; 1 Kings 21:8).[a]

Hebrew inscriptions also appear on bullae—the dried lumps of clay or wax that were impressed with seals and have survived from the documents to which they were originally attached. Several hundred such bullae in the seventh–sixth centuries BCE have been collected.[b] Some of the Hebrew seals and bullae are inscribed with personal names that also appear in the Old Testament. The most intriguing example is a bulla engraved with the identification "Berechiah [Baruch], son of Neriah, the scribe" (cf. Jer. 36:4–32), although this bulla was not found in an excavation, and the identification remains debated.

Other Hebrew inscriptions appear on ostraca—broken pieces of pottery containing ink writings or engravings. Ostraca typically record simple transactions or correspondence. For example, an archive of ostraca from the Judean city of Arad contains some Hebrew inscriptions from the late seventh to early sixth century BCE that are associated with the commander of the Judean military garrison.[c] Additionally, over a thousand storage jars discovered in various places throughout Judah are inscribed with a winged emblem, the Hebrew phrase *lmlk* (for/belonging to the king), and the name of one of four regional supply cities. These likely served as part of a royal supply system that existed in the eighth century. Overall, the localized and occasional nature of the Hebrew inscriptions on seals, bullae, ostraca, and other materials makes them significant for some specific questions (e.g., levels of literacy), but limits their usefulness for broader historical reconstruction.

a. See Shmuel Ahituv, *Echoes from the Past: Hebrew and Cognate Inscriptions from the Biblical Period* (trans. and ed. Anson F. Rainey; Jerusalem: Carta, 2008); P. Kyle McCarter Jr., *Ancient Inscriptions: Voices from the Biblical World* (Washington, DC: Biblical Archaeology Society, 1996).

b. See Nahman Avigad, *Bullae and Seals from a Post-Exilic Judean Archive* (Qedem 4; Jerusalem: Institute of Archaeology, Hebrew University of Jerusalem, 1976).

c. For the original publication, see Yohanan Aharoni, *Arad Inscriptions* (trans. Judith Ben-Or; ed. Anson F. Rainey; JDS; Jerusalem: Israel Exploration Society, 1981).

throne at the age of eight (with the help of the "people of the land" [2 Kings 21:24]) and reigned for thirty-one years (641/640–609 BCE). As in the cases of Manasseh and Amon, the biblical accounts focus almost exclusively on internal religious elements, providing a lengthy and detailed description of an extensive religious reform carried out by Josiah in conjunction with the discovery of a "book of the law" in the temple (2 Kings 22:8; 2 Chron. 34:14). The texts credit Josiah with validating the discovered book, sponsoring a covenant-making ceremony for the people, purging the temple and land of apostate elements and priests, closing outlying sanctuaries, and celebrating a special Passover festival. The king even extended this reform into the territories of Manasseh and Ephraim (specifically Bethel and Samaria) in the former northern kingdom (2 Kings 23:15, 19; 2 Chron. 34:6, 33; 35:17–18). The only explicit link between the biblical portrayals and the wider historical realities of the ancient Near East in the second half of the seventh century BCE appears in the descriptions of Josiah's death. Both Kings and Chronicles connect his death to an encounter with Pharaoh Neco II at Megiddo. While 2 Kings 23:29 contains only a vague statement that Neco killed Josiah, 2 Chronicles 35:20–24 presents Josiah as mounting a military challenge to the campaigning pharaoh that resulted in the Judean king's death. After the death of Josiah, the biblical texts state that the "people of the land" (see above) placed his son Jehoahaz II on the throne (2 Kings 23:31–34; 2 Chron. 36:1–3). The biblical sources for his reign are brief but include significant historical claims. He ruled for only three months (609 BCE) before being deposed, imprisoned at Riblah, and finally deported to Egypt by Pharaoh Neco II. After imposing a punitive tribute on Judah, the pharaoh placed Jehoiakim (Eliakim) on the throne in Jerusalem as an Egyptian vassal.

In addition to the main historiographical sources for this era, scholars have associated various prophetic texts with the time period and religious activities of Josiah. After an absence of prophetic sources explicitly related to the years between 700 and 640 BCE, the superscriptions of the books of Jeremiah and Zephaniah place some of the preaching of both prophets in the reign of Josiah, although neither book seems to explicitly mention Josiah's reform. Additionally, similarities in superscriptions and other elements lead some scholars to conclude that an initial collection of books that would later grow into the Book of the Twelve (the Minor Prophets) was first produced during Josiah's time.[64] From this perspective of later editing, some scholars identify a high number of references to Josiah's reform, even in books not explicitly associated with his time.[65] Alongside this primary religious focus, some prophetic texts refer to larger political occurrences, even if in a veiled

---

64. James Nogalski, *Literary Precursors to the Book of the Twelve* (BZAW 217; Berlin: de Gruyter, 1993).

65. For example, Marvin A. Sweeney, *King Josiah of Judah: The Lost Messiah of Israel* (Oxford: Oxford University Press, 2001).

manner (e.g., Jer. 22:10–11 and the death of Josiah; the book of Nahum and the fall of Nineveh).

The issues to be considered in the assessment of the biblical sources for Josiah and Jehoahaz II are the same as those enumerated previously for the texts related to Manasseh and Amon (see discussion above). One added element for the biblical texts for this era, however, concerns the larger historiographical composition of the Deuteronomistic History. As noted in the discussion of general seventh-century-BCE sources, this composition has been understood as a literary unity driven primarily by theological interests. In light of the overwhelmingly positive portrayal of Josiah, as well as some other literary elements, the case has been made that a first version of the Deuteronomistic History was put together in the reign of Josiah, followed by later editing phases.[66]

Scholars pursue several historical questions for this era that arise directly or indirectly from the biblical presentation: (1) What were the historical realities of religious reform in Judah in the second half of the seventh century? (2) What was the status of Judah under Josiah within the larger political context of Syria-Palestine? (3) What were the circumstances of Josiah's death and the short-lived rule of Jehoahaz II?

Religious Reform in Seventh-Century BCE Judah

In considering the historical sources for the extensive religious reform depicted in the biblical texts, one should first note that the accounts in Kings and Chronicles differ significantly. In 2 Kings 22–23 the reform is identified as a single movement that occurred during Josiah's eighteenth year (623/622). But 2 Chronicles 34–35 describes the reform as a multistage process that began in Josiah's eighth year, gained speed in his twelfth year with the elimination of high places, and came to a head in his eighteenth year with the purification of the Jerusalem temple and related actions. There is no clear way to resolve the differences between the biblical sources other than conjecture based on the possible theological interests of the Deuteronomistic History and Chronicler's account.[67] Additionally, at different points in each biblical account, the discovery of "the book of the law" plays a key role in the reform. In 2 Kings 22:8 its discovery occurs in Josiah's eighteenth year and provides the impetus for the entire reform; in 2 Chronicles 34:14 the book's discovery occurs after the first part of

---

66. Cross, *Canaanite Myth*; Nelson, *Double Redaction*; Weinfeld, *Deuteronomy*; Thomas Römer, *The So-Called Deuteronomistic History: Sociological, Historical and Literary Introduction* (London: T&T Clark, 2006).

67. See, e.g., Sara Japhet, *I & II Chronicles: A Commentary* (OTL; Louisville: Westminster John Knox, 1993), 117–20.

the reform has taken place and provides the impetus for the covenant renewal and Passover celebration. Beyond the Old Testament, no concrete historical sources exist to directly evaluate this element of the biblical presentation. Since the early nineteenth century, the scholarly consensus has identified Josiah's lawbook with some form of Deuteronomy, and the historical discussion has largely centered on questions concerning the date and structure of that book.[68]

Whatever position one adopts on the preceding issues, some limited sources exist for considering the general historical reality of Josiah's reform, especially the biblical depictions of the destruction of outlying sanctuaries and the extension of the reform into the territories of the former northern kingdom. A large quantity of Hebrew personal names appear in extrabiblical texts (ostraca, seals, etc.) from this period. These names are uniformly Yahwistic in a way that differs from what one finds in similar evidence among Judah's neighbors such as Ammon. Likewise, the dozens of available late Iron Age Hebrew inscriptions such as those from Arad and Lachish acknowledge and identify only Yahweh as Judah's God.[69] Such references do not constitute direct evidence for a reform in Judah in the second half of the seventh century BCE, but the worship of a single deity, if confirmed by these sources, often favors the kind of cultic centralization that stands at the center of Josiah's actions. Historians also consider archaeological evidence from certain cultic sites. In general, there is a lack of archaeological evidence for Josiah's reported actions, so firm conclusions are difficult to reach. Some scholars have linked Josiah with the evidence of a horned altar from Beersheba (see 2 Kings 23:8) that was dismantled and subsequently reused in a later construction,[70] but the archaeological context more clearly associates it with Hezekiah's reforms.[71] Similarly, excavations have revealed the remains of a cultic shrine at Arad, with an altar that was dismantled and buried in a later fill.[72] Once again, the archaeological stratum seems to associate this action with Hezekiah, but some interpreters observe that the data is insufficient to establish the chronology with certainty.[73]

68. See, in the present volume, chap. 3, "Covenant and Treaty in the Hebrew Bible and in the Ancient Near East." The identification of the lawbook with Deuteronomy goes at least back to Wilhelm M. L. de Wette, who argued that this version of Deuteronomy was not discovered in the temple but was written during Josiah's time (*Beiträge zur Einleitung in das Alte Testament* [1806–1807; repr., Hildesheim: G. Olms, 1971]).

69. See Hess, *Israelite Religions*, 269–90, 349–50.

70. Yigael Yadin, "Beer-sheba: The High Place Destroyed by King Josiah," *BASOR* 222 (1976): 5–17.

71. See Vaughn, *Theology, History, and Archaeology*, 47n112. Earlier, see Yohanan Aharoni, "The Horned Altar of Beer-sheba," *BA* 37 (1974): 2–6.

72. Vaughn, *Theology, History, and Archaeology*, 48–49.

73. See David Ussishkin, "The Date of the Judaean Shrine at Arad," *IEJ* 38 (1988): 142–57; Oded Borowski, "Hezekiah's Reform and the Revolt against Assyria," *BA* 58 (1995): 148–55.

Only indirect evidence from the general historical situation is available concerning the possible extension of Josiah's reforms into the northern territories. During this time, these territories existed as Assyrian provinces. If one follows the suggestion in Chronicles that Josiah began these activities in his twelfth year (2 Chron. 34:3), then perhaps the king was able to carry out the actions during the decline in Assyrian power just prior to the death of Ashurbanipal in 627 BCE (see below).[74] With the exception of the description of Bethel, however, the biblical accounts about Josiah's activities in the north seem general and editorial in nature.[75] On the whole, the evidence for Josiah's northern activities, as with that for his particular moves within Judah, permits few firm conclusions for the question of the historical realities showing religious reform in the second half of the seventh century. Yet one can hardly consider this topic apart from the related question of Judah's overall status within the region at the time.

The Status of Judah within Syria-Palestine

The historical question about Josiah's reign that has generated the most attention is the status of Judah within Syria-Palestine in the second half of the seventh century BCE. For the better part of the twentieth century, a main trend within historical scholarship interpreted Josiah's reign not only as a time of religious reform but also as a period in which Judah experienced renewed territorial expansion and political hegemony in the Levant—perhaps the greatest period of autonomy for Judah since the time of David.[76] Josiah, so the theory went, was able to annex territories in the former northern kingdom and establish Judean dominance over the bulk of Syria-Palestine. Historical scholarship since the 1980s, however, has produced substantial challenges to the older view, and the status of Judah in the second half of the seventh century has witnessed some of the most dramatic reassessments in the field.[77]

Before turning to the available sources related to Judah's status, we note the broader developments concerning the Assyrian Empire that form the background for this question. The second half of the seventh century BCE saw the demise of Assyrian rule in conjunction with the reemergence of Babylonia and Egypt. The Assyrian royal annals do not extend beyond 639 BCE, and

---

74. Rainey and Notley, *Sacred Bridge*, 256.

75. See Graham S. Ogden, "The Northern Extent of Josiah's Reform," *ABR* 26 (1978): 26–34; Miller and Hayes, *History of Ancient Israel and Judah*, 459.

76. For example, Bright, *History of Israel*, 316; J. Alberto Soggin, *A History of Israel: From the Beginnings to the Bar Kochba Revolt, AD 135* (trans. John Bowden; London: SCM, 1984), 257.

77. See Nadav Na'aman, "The Kingdom of Judah under Josiah," *TA* 18 (1991): 3–71; idem, "Josiah and the Kingdom of Judah," in Grabbe, *Good Kings and Bad Kings*, 189–247.

the few Egyptian texts for this period are focused mostly on internal political happenings.[78] The major source is the Babylonian Chronicles, a partial chronological record that gives a year-by-year account of the king's major military actions, with minimal editorial bias.[79] However, the relevant extant portions cover only the periods from 626–623 and 616–594, with a gap between 623 and 616. The sources indicate that Assyria maintained relative stability between 641 and 627, although the latter years of Ashurbanipal's reign saw increasing conflicts to the north, and firm control over other parts of the empire began to erode. The turning point came with Ashurbanipal's death in 627: shortly thereafter Nabopolassar wrested Babylon away from Assyrian control.[80] When the Babylonian Chronicles resume after the aforementioned missing tablets, they indicate that Nabopolassar had complete control of Babylonia by 616, actively engaging in military conflict against Assyria.[81] Over the next few years the Babylonian Chronicles record a series of conflicts involving the Assyrians (supported by the Egyptians), the Babylonians, and the Medes.[82] In 614 the Medes captured the city of Ashur and formed an alliance with Nabopolassar. In 612 the new alliance destroyed the Assyrian capital of Nineveh (cf. the biblical prophetic book Nahum). Sometime in 610 Pharaoh Neco II succeeded Psammetichus I (664–610) and marched northward through Syria-Palestine to join forces with the remnant of the Assyrian army at Haran. After a series of attacks and counterattacks, the Babylonians and Medes defeated the Assyrian-Egyptian force, marking the end of the Assyrian Empire.[83]

Against this background, the question of Judah's status under Josiah revolves primarily around the sources related to two items: (1) the possible expansion of Judean presence and hegemony at various sites in the Levant, and (2) the probable time when Egypt replaced Assyria as the dominant force in Syria-Palestine. Sources are limited for the first item, with no Assyrian, Babylonian, or Egyptian annalistic texts that refer to circumstances in Judah and

78. See Kitchen, *Third Intermediate Period*; Anthony J. Spalinger, "Egypt, History of (3d Intermediate-Saite Period [Dyn. 21–26])," *ABD* 2:353–64.

79. The Babylonian Chronicles are not a single composition but rather a genre of texts. See Arnold, "Neo-Babylonian Chronicle Series," 407–26; Grayson, *Assyrian and Babylonian Chronicles*; Jean-Jacques Glassner, *Mesopotamian Chronicles* (ed. Benjamin R. Foster; SBLWAW 19; Atlanta: Society of Biblical Literature, 2004).

80. *COS* 2.121:307; Grayson, *Assyrian and Babylonian Chronicles*, 88; Arnold, "Neo-Babylonian Chronicle Series," 411–12.

81. See Grayson, *Assyrian and Babylonian Chronicles*, 90–96; Arnold, "Neo-Babylonian Chronicle Series," 412–15.

82. See Grayson, *Assyrian and Babylonian Chronicles*, 92–96; Arnold, "Neo-Babylonian Chronicle Series," 412–15. For historical discussion, see Arnold, *Who Were the Babylonians?*, 87–93.

83. See Brad E. Kelle, *Ancient Israel at War, 853–586 BC* (EH 67; Oxford: Osprey, 2007), 54.

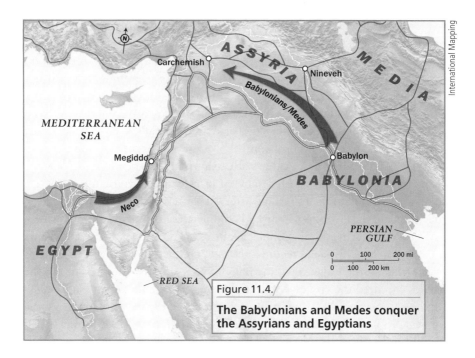

Figure 11.4.

The Babylonians and Medes conquer the Assyrians and Egyptians

only occasional inscriptional sources and archaeological evidence that can be configured in various ways. In spite of the popular scholarly theory that Josiah established political and territorial hegemony over portions of Syria-Palestine, the biblical texts do not make this claim. At best, they may imply it in their references to Josiah's actions against northern shrines (2 Kings 23:15, 19; 2 Chron. 34:6, 33) and inclusion of some groups from northern territories (2 Chron. 34:9; 35:17–18). Yet these references describe limited and focused actions, and the inclusion of northern groups found only in Chronicles is readily explainable in light of the larger theological interests of the book.

Other sources for assessing possible Judean expansion include Hebrew inscriptions found at Meṣad Hashavyahu, a small fortress on the southern Mediterranean coast.[84] Some scholars take these inscriptions as indicating a prominent Judean presence on the coast that suggests expansion and hege-mony.[85] Others, however, emphasize inscriptions that reveal the presence of Greeks at the fortress. Since Greeks were known to have served in the Egyptian

84. *ANET* 568. One Hebrew ostracon, e.g., contains the scribal recording of a complaint by a poor field-worker that his outer garment had been seized unfairly (cf. Amos 2:8). See Joseph Naveh, "A Hebrew Letter from the Seventh Century BC," *IEJ* 10 (1960): 129–39.

85. For a classic articulation, see Frank Moore Cross and David Noel Freedman, "Josiah's Revolt against Assyria," *JNES* 112 (1953): 56–58.

military, some scholars conclude that the settlement was more likely under Egyptian control, with Judean and Greek soldiers in Egypt's service.[86] There is also evidence for the construction of a seventh-century fort at Megiddo, as well as the fortification of the southern cities of Arad and Kadesh-Barnea, each with the presence of Hebrew inscriptions.[87] Perhaps these sites indicate a centralized royal building program with expanded reach into northern territory. Yet there is no direct evidence that Judeans built or occupied the fort at Megiddo, and most of the archaeological evidence for growth comes from the Negev, an area in which there was increasing Edomite settlement activity at the time.[88] In short, the inscriptional and archaeological evidence for possible Judean expansion is inconclusive, with the meaning of the evidence being largely dictated by the broader scenario into which it is placed.

At the heart of the broader scenario are the sources concerning the role and dominance of Egypt in the waning years of the Assyrian Empire. When does the available evidence suggest that Egypt gained control over the Levant, and does this allow for any period of Judean expansion and/or hegemony under Josiah that would lead one to interpret the local archaeological and inscriptional evidence in that manner? No Egyptian records refer directly to Judah, so historians primarily depend on the Babylonian Chronicles and related inscriptions that provide the general contours of Assyrian, Egyptian, and Babylonian actions in the final decades of the seventh century BCE. We may reasonably assume that such Egyptian hegemony, and thus any Judean resurgence, would have been impossible before Ashurbanipal's death in 627. Hence, throughout the first half of Josiah's reign (641–627) the presence of Assyrian governors in the northern territories likely rendered impossible any armed actions by Egypt or by a local Assyrian vassal kingdom like Judah. On the other end of the time frame, Egypt had clear control over Syria-Palestine and its territories by the time

86. Thus, e.g., Grabbe, "Kingdom of Judah," 87; Alexander Fantalkin, "Meẓad Ḥashavyahu: Its Material Culture and Historical Background," *TA* 28 (2001): 3–165. Inscriptions from Arad, a clearly Judean territory, also indicate the presence of Greeks without the necessary conclusion that the site must have been under Egyptian control. Perhaps the southern coastal location of Meṣad Hashavyahu makes Egyptian control more likely in that case, however.

87. *NEAEHL* 3:1023; Yohanan Aharoni, *Arad Inscriptions* (trans. Judith Ben-Or; ed. Anson F. Rainey; JDS; Jerusalem: Israel Exploration Society, 1981); Ze'ev Herzog et al., "The Israelite Fortress at Arad," *BASOR* 254 (1984): 1–34; Vaughn, *Theology, History, and Archaeology*, 49–58; Rainey and Notley, *Sacred Bridge*, 258. As noted in the discussion of Manasseh's reign, earlier twentieth-century scholarship often cited the *lmlk*-stamped jars as evidence of royal development and expansion under Josiah, but current scholarship since David Ussishkin's excavations at Lachish widely associate these jars with Hezekiah (see Vaughn, *Theology, History, and Archaeology*, 82–85).

88. For surveys of Negev sites that reflect Judean and/or Edomite settlement, see Vaughn, *Theology, History, and Archaeology*, 50–58.

of the Battle of Haran in 610, the context in which the Old Testament records Neco II's ability to move freely through Syria-Palestine and place a vassal king of his choosing on the Judean throne (2 Kings 23:31–35; 2 Chron. 36:1–4).

Is it possible that the Babylonian Chronicle's indications of Assyria's decline, Ashurbanipal's death, and Babylon's emergence (see above) reveal a window of time between 627 and 610 during which Judah was free from all but nominal imperial hegemony? As noted above, the Babylonian Chronicles have a gap between 623 and 616, so we do not know the circumstances that pertained throughout the region for nearly a decade after Ashurbanipal's death. If one follows the account of Josiah's reign in 2 Kings 22–23, the king begins his reforming activities in Judah and elsewhere in his eighteenth year (624), just a few years after Ashurbanipal died (but 2 Chron. 34:6–7 places the start of Josiah's moves into the north earlier, in his twelfth year). Assyria's increasing struggles with Babylon during these years certainly would have drawn Assyrian attention (and resources?) away from the western vassal kingdoms. Moreover, only when the Babylonian Chronicles resume in 616 do we find the first reference that places the Egyptian army (under Psammetichus I) on campaign in Mesopotamia to support the Assyrians against the Babylonians.[89] Although plagued by the gap in the Babylonian Chronicles, historians may speculate that Egypt's hegemony over the Levant was established only at this time, as the army would have marched unhindered through the land on the way to Mesopotamia in 616. Alternatively, given the isolated nature of the 616 reference, perhaps the first evidence of possible Egyptian control occurred even later, in 610, when the newly crowned Neco II marched to support the Assyrians at Haran.[90] If so, one may identify an even larger window of time for possible Judean expansion (ca. 627–610). The only inscriptional sources that imply treaty arrangements between Egypt and Syro-Palestinian kingdoms date from this time around 610. For instance, an inscription from Psammetichus I's fifty-second year (612) indicates the subordination and taxation of Phoenician cities,[91] and a letter to Egypt from a Philistine king named "Adon" implies a vassal arrangement, but its dating remains disputed.[92]

However, historians might interpret different evidence as indicating that Egypt replaced Assyria in the dominant role in Syria-Palestine very early on,

---

89. Grayson, *Assyrian and Babylonian Chronicles*, 91; Arnold, "Neo-Babylonian Chronicle Series," 414–15.

90. Grayson, *Assyrian and Babylonian Chronicles*, 96; Arnold, "Neo-Babylonian Chronicle Series," 414–15. For this view, see Rainey and Notley, *Sacred Bridge*, 258–59.

91. James H. Breasted, *Ancient Records of Egypt: Historical Documents from the Earliest Times to the Persian Conquest* (5 vols.; Chicago: University of Chicago Press, 1906–1907), 4:493–94.

92. *COS* 3.54:132–34.

perhaps even by cooperative design with Assyria at or before Ashurbanipal's death in 627.[93] Ashurbanipal's capture of Thebes in 664 had removed the anti-Assyrian Twenty-Fifth (Ethiopian) Dynasty and given control of Egypt to the Twenty-Sixth Saite Dynasty, reestablishing the cooperative relationship between Assyria and Egypt that had existed in the late eighth century BCE.[94] For much of his rule, Psammetichus I operated as an Assyrian ally. Given that background, perhaps Assyria withdrew from the west in agreement with its Egyptian allies and thus Judah was subservient to Egypt throughout virtually the entire second half of Josiah's reign. Although royal inscriptions provide no help, some potential evidence can be marshaled. A much later reference by Herodotus (*Hist.* 2.157) may suggest that Psammetichus moved into Syria-Palestine and besieged Ashdod as early as the late 640s or early 630s, but no Egyptian or Assyrian texts confirm this action. A multitude of Egyptian artifacts (e.g., scarabs, amulets) have been found with some significant distribution throughout the coastal plain and as far north as Arvad.[95] A few recent studies have offered more speculative attempts that take evidence for Egyptian treaty relations elsewhere in Syria-Palestine, connect it with the meager evidence available for Judah, and propose that Egypt established a formal vassal relationship with Judah, at least by the latter portion of Josiah's rule.[96] Bernd Schipper proposes that Psammetichus I used Greek mercenaries centered at Meṣad Hashavyahu to establish a system of vassal kingdoms in Syria-Palestine.[97] He also conjectures that certain texts suggest regular Judean vassal payments to Egypt. A stela of Psammetichus I mentions districts with royal overseers that channel tribute to Egypt, and most notably, a newly published Hebrew ostracon from the seventh century contains the references "in the thirtieth year" (presumably referring to Josiah, given the length of the reign) and "to the pharaoh" (presumably a designation for tribute).[98] These proposals are extremely speculative, but Neco II's act of deposing and appointing Judean kings immediately after Josiah's death clearly implies Egyptian control of Judean royal affairs, at least from that point forward.

---

93. Na'aman, "Kingdom of Judah under Josiah"; Donald B. Redford, *Egypt, Canaan, and Israel in Ancient Times* (Princeton: Princeton University Press, 1992), 430–69.

94. See Kenneth A. Kitchen, "Egypt, History of (Chronology)," *ABD* 2:325; Miller and Hayes, *History of Ancient Israel and Judah*, 446.

95. See Bernd U. Schipper, "Egypt and the Kingdom of Judah under Josiah and Jehoiakim," *TA* 37 (2010): 200–229.

96. See esp. ibid.; so also Na'aman, "Kingdom of Judah under Josiah."

97. For a survey of his evidence, see Schipper, "Egypt and the Kingdom of Judah," 212–20.

98. Ibid., 213–17. Schipper acknowledges that many elements related to this ostracon remain in question.

Given the difficulty of aligning the disparate evidence for the status of Judah in the second half of the seventh century BCE, no single, clear interpretation presents itself. The biblical texts make no significant claims beyond religious reformation. The other available sources do not substantiate the notion of political autonomy and expansion by Josiah, but neither do they preclude it. Some current interpreters will leave open the possibility of renewed Judean political and territorial hegemony under Josiah; others will consider such a scenario implausible; still others will seek mediating positions. In any case, scholars' conclusions will largely depend on how they weigh the evidence for the degree and timing of Egypt's hegemony over the Levant in the years leading up to the final demise of Assyria in 610.

The Death of Josiah and the Rule of Jehoahaz II (609 BCE)

A final historical question for this era concerns the circumstances of Josiah's death and the short-lived rule of Jehoahaz II (609). No direct sources other than the Old Testament are available. As described above, however, the accounts in 2 Kings 23:29 and 2 Chron. 35:20–24 are vague and difficult to reconcile. Both attribute Josiah's death to the newly crowned Pharaoh Neco II and place it in the context of his campaign to support the Assyrians at Haran (ca. 610/609), as reported in the Babylonian Chronicles. Scholars traditionally have favored the depiction in 2 Chronicles 35:20–24 that Josiah opposed the campaigning Egyptian army in battle, but this conclusion rests largely on assumptions about Josiah's power and status.[99] Perhaps the reference by Herodotus (*Hist.* 2.159.2) to some Syrian opposition to Neco near Gaza (cf. Jer. 47:1) makes the notion of attempted military intervention plausible, but any scenario remains largely speculative. In any case, the Babylonian Chronicles indicate that the Egyptians ultimately withdrew southward from Haran.[100] In this context, the Old Testament reports that Neco II deposed the new Judean king Jehoahaz II, whom the "people of the land" had placed on the throne after Josiah's death, and replaced him with the Egyptian appointee Jehoiakim (2 Kings 23:30–34).

The Reign of Jehoiakim

The Biblical Presentation

The historiographical depictions of Jehoiakim's eleven-year reign (2 Kings 23:34–24:7; 2 Chron. 36:5–8) are highly telescoped, providing only passing

99. So, e.g., Bright, *History of Israel*, 324.
100. Grayson, *Assyrian and Babylonian Chronicles*, 95–96; Arnold, "Neo-Babylonian Chronicle Series," 414–15.

comments about a number of events that occurred during his rule (609–598 BCE). The Chronicles account is especially brief. It mentions only the king's beginning and end, differing markedly on the last point from what is described in Kings. According to the Kings account, Neco II placed Jehoiakim on the throne as an Egyptian vassal, and the new king immediately taxed Judah to give a required payment to Egypt (2 Kings 23:34–35). At an unspecified subsequent time, Jehoiakim abandoned his initial loyalty to Egypt in favor of submission to Nebuchadnezzar of Babylon, who had come into the area (24:1). Just three years later, however, Jehoiakim rebelled against Babylonia, and the imperial reprisal included attacks from surrounding kingdoms against Jerusalem (24:2). With only the additional explanation that these events were divine punishment for the earlier actions of Manasseh (24:3–4), 2 Kings 24:6–7 reports that Jehoiakim died and was succeeded by his son Jehoiachin. There follows a final notice that Egypt intervened no further in Syria-Palestine, and the region was firmly under Babylonian control. The main biblical accounts exhibit tension on the nature of Jehoiakim's demise, as 2 Chronicles 36:6 says that Nebuchadnezzar captured Jehoiakim and deported him to Babylon.

The Prophetic Books also contain texts related to Jehoiakim's reign. Various passages throughout Jeremiah (e.g., 22:13–23; chaps. 25–26; 35) depict internal division within Judah over the proper course of action at the time, as well as Jehoiakim's vacillation among different political stances. The book of Habakkuk may also reflect the transitional phase during the rise of the Babylonians and its effect on local kingdoms. The most confusing reference is in Daniel 1:1–2, which attributes a siege of Jerusalem to Nebuchadnezzar in Jehoiakim's third year (606/605).

The events related to the reign of Jehoiakim extend slightly beyond the seventh-century BCE scope of this chapter. The present discussion will focus on the available sources for what occurred down through 600 BCE—the events that set in motion the historical realities that would culminate in the early sixth century. Given the terse nature of the biblical depictions, historians examine the available sources related to two primary questions for Jehoiakim's reign: (1) What were the circumstances of Jehoiakim's initial loyalty to Egypt and subsequent submission to Babylonia between 609 and 604? (2) What were the circumstances of Jehoiakim's rebellion against Babylonia and its initial effects between 604 and 600?

Jehoiakim's Initial Loyalty to Egypt and Subsequent Submission to Babylonia

As noted above, the biblical texts report that Neco II placed Jehoiakim on the throne in 609 BCE with the demand of vassal payment (2 Kings 23:34–35).

We know little about events related to Judah over the next few years, but a significant amount of evidence for larger historical happenings is available from the Babylonian Chronicles, as well as some other inscriptions and archaeological data.[101] Overall, nothing suggests that Jehoiakim wavered from being an obedient Egyptian vassal from 609 to 605. During this period, the Babylonian army (under Nabonidus, 625–605) campaigned primarily to the north but vied with Egypt for dominance over Syria-Palestine.[102] Some sources, such as an Aramaic letter to Neco II (probably from the king of Ekron) and the evidence of Greeks at Meṣad Hashavyahu, may testify to Egypt's dominance at this time, but their date and significance remain disputed (see above).

The turning point came in 605, when the Babylonian Chronicles record that the crown prince Nebuchadnezzar II (alternatively, "Nebuchadrezzar," as in Jer. 39:1) defeated the forces of Neco II at Carchemish after subduing most of the surrounding territory (see also Jer. 46:1–2).[103] This victory effectively established Babylonian dominance in the area and drove the Egyptians out of Syria-Palestine.[104] The biblical texts put Jehoiakim's break with Egypt and submission to Babylonia in the context of these events, but they give neither the timing nor the circumstances of that change (2 Kings 24:1). Babylonian military actions recorded in the Babylonian Chronicles may fill in some of the details. During the subsequent period of 605 to 601, the Babylonian Chronicles report that Nebuchadnezzar, who ascended the throne shortly after the Battle of Carchemish, marched throughout Syria-Palestine, collected tribute from various rulers, and converted the many smaller kingdoms in the region into Babylonian vassals.[105] Perhaps the decisive moment came in 604, when the Babylonian Chronicles seem to indicate that Nebuchadnezzar destroyed the Philistine coastal stronghold of Ashkelon, although the precise reading of the place name is debated.[106] Archaeological evidence bolsters this interpretation and attests to further destruction at other Phi-

101. For a survey, see Rainey and Notley, *Sacred Bridge*, 260–63.

102. See accounts of conflicts in Grayson, *Assyrian and Babylonian Chronicles*, 98; Arnold, "Neo-Babylonian Chronicle Series," 415. See Arnold, *Who Were the Babylonians?*, 89–91; David Vanderhooft, *The Neo-Babylonian Empire and Babylon in the Latter Prophets* (HSM 59; Atlanta: Scholars Press, 1999), 23–33.

103. COS 1.137:467–68; Grayson, *Assyrian and Babylonian Chronicles*, 98–99; Arnold, "Neo-Babylonian Chronicle Series," 415–16.

104. See Grayson, *Assyrian and Babylonian Chronicles*, 99.

105. For a summary of Nebuchadnezzar's campaigns, see Israel Eph'al, "Nebuchadnezzar the Warrior: Remarks on His Military Achievements," *IEJ* 53 (2003): 178–91.

106. Grayson, *Assyrian and Babylonian Chronicles*, 100; Arnold, "Neo-Babylonian Chronicle Series," 416–17.

listine cities across the following years, perhaps also reflected in accounts in the Babylonian Chronicles.[107]

This clear and violent establishment of Babylonian dominance in southern Syria-Palestine after 604 probably created a tense, internal choice within Judah. Biblical texts give the impression of a stressful and divisive situation, with much of the political leadership seemingly committed to remaining loyal to Egypt, while prophets such as Jeremiah advocated submission to Babylonia and criticized the king for misguided policies (see Jer. 22:13–19; 26:1–24; Hab. 1–2). Note, for instance, Jeremiah's reference (36:9) to the proclamation of a national fast called in Jehoiakim's fourth year (604). These Babylonian victories likely provided the final impetus for Jehoiakim to switch his loyalty to the Babylonians, although significant reservations and anti-Babylonian sentiments likely remained among Judah's leadership. The only biblical text that suggests a different course of events is the confusing reference in Daniel 1:1–2 to a siege of Jerusalem by Nebuchadnezzar in Jehoiakim's "third year." Perhaps this date is a deliberate bending of historical memories in line with the book's genre as survival/refugee literature,[108] but it may also reflect a different calendar (Tishri to Tishri) in which Jehoiakim's third year would be 605, the date of the Babylonian victory at Carchemish.[109] However, no extrabiblical evidence attests such a siege of Jerusalem at that time.

Jehoiakim's Rebellion against Babylonia

The Old Testament gives a terse statement that Jehoiakim rebelled against Nebuchadnezzar three years after he had pledged his loyalty but provides no insight concerning how and why (2 Kings 24:1). If the aforementioned chronology of Jehoiakim's submission to Babylonia is correct, the year was 601 BCE. The Babylonian Chronicles for Nebuchadnezzar's campaigns may reveal the circumstances. Just a few years after Nebuchadnezzar established hegemony in Syria-Palestine, the Babylonian Chronicles record that in 601 the Babylonian army tried to invade Egypt. The text reports that the Babylonians were repelled, and Nebuchadnezzar retreated to Babylon for the duration of the following year.[110] No Egyptian sources record the battle. Yet perhaps the reference in Jeremiah 47:1 to Neco II's attack on Gaza reflects an Egyptian

107. Again, the precise place names for Babylonian targets are difficult to determine in some cases. See Rainey and Notley, *Sacred Bridge*, 263.

108. Daniel L. Smith-Christopher, "The Book of Daniel," in vol. 7 of *The New Interpeter's Bible* (ed. Leander E. Keck; Nashville: Abingdon, 1996), 19–152, esp. 19–45.

109. Rainey and Notley, *Sacred Bridge*, 262.

110. Grayson, *Assyrian and Babylonian Chronicles*, 101; *ANET* 564; Arnold, "Neo-Babylonian Chronicle Series," 417. See Herodotus, *Hist.* 2.159.

resurgence into Syria-Palestine at that time, bolstered by this victory and the Babylonian withdrawal from the region. If so, Babylonia's perceived weakness, along with Egypt's apparent resurgence, likely led Jehoiakim to enter into open rebellion against Nebuchadnezzar in about 600.

The beginning of the Babylonian response to Judah's rebellion takes us to the end of the seventh century BCE. Sources do not provide any details of the campaign prior to the Babylonians' arrival at Jerusalem in 597 BCE (see the next chapter). The only suggestive piece of data is the reference in 2 Kings 24:2 that forces from several surrounding kingdoms, perhaps auxiliary forces in the service of Nebuchadnezzar, moved against Judean territory. Hebrew ostraca discovered at the fortified Judean stronghold of Arad preserve correspondence that may be related to Judean military actions and allude to Edomite encroachment into the Negev at this time (see Obadiah). Whatever the details, 2 Kings places Jehoiakim's death prior to the Babylonian siege of Jerusalem. Although 2 Chronicles differs (see above), it may be a textual corruption. In the Babylonian Chronicles, subsequent entries concerning the Jerusalem siege do not mention Jehoiakim.[111] Even so, this siege to come in the early sixth century will mark the culmination of things set in motion by Jehoiakim's actions.

---

111. See Rainey and Notley, *Sacred Bridge*, 260–61.

12

Sixth-Century Issues

The Fall of Jerusalem, the Exile, and the Return

PETER VAN DER VEEN

The Destruction of Jerusalem and Its Effects

The biblical narratives (2 Kings 25:1–21; Jer. 39:1–18; 52:4–8) relate how Jerusalem and the only surviving cities of Judah, Lachish and Azekah (Jer. 34:7) were captured and burned to the ground in King Nebuchadnezzar's nineteenth regnal year, and how Jerusalem's population was taken into exile to Babylon (586 BCE). Some biblical texts also mention that Edomite (auxiliary?) troops played their part in this momentous event of Judahite history (Ezek. 35:5; Obad. 13; 1 Esd. 4:45). As in 597, when Jerusalem had been besieged by the Neo-Babylonians for the first time, it was mainly the elite population and the skilled workers who were exiled to Babylon. The small numbers are telling. In that year (586) only 832 people seem to have been taken into exile. A few years later, in 582 BCE, in the course of a razzia, an additional 745 people of Judah were taken captive. At that time the Chaldeans crushed a rebellion

I wish to thank Mr. R. M. Porter for checking the English text and for making helpful suggestions.

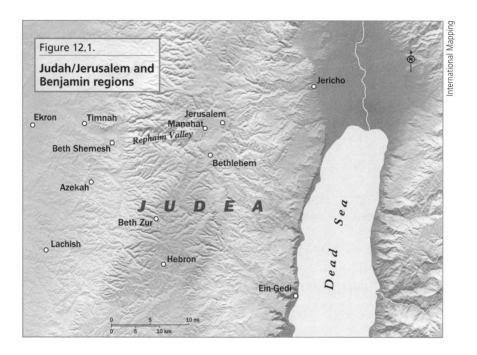

Figure 12.1.

Judah/Jerusalem and Benjamin regions

International Mapping

in Transjordan and annexed Ammon and Moab (cf. Jer. 52:28–30). Jeremiah 52:30 mentions some 4,600 Jews who had been deported.[1] The razzia may have occured as a reaction to the murder of Gedaliah, the son of Ahikam. He had been appointed governor at Mizpah by the Babylonians after the fall of Jerusalem (2 Kings 25:22–24; Jer. 40:5–6). Gedaliah had been a member of the former pro-Babylonian party in Jerusalem, while his father and grandfather had been prominent state officials under King Josiah and King Jehoiakim (cf. 2 Kings 22:8, 12).[2] As governor, Gedaliah ordered the remaining inhabitants of the land, as well as returning refugees, to work the fields and plantations for the Chaldeans (2 Kings 25:12; Jer. 40:6–12; 52:16). Gedaliah's tenure, however, was short-lived: he was murdered by rebels. Aided by King Baalis of Ammon (Jer.

1. This number seems to be contradicted by the larger number of ten thousand deportees reported in 2 Kings 24:14 right after the first siege, in 597 BCE. Oded Lipschits suggests that this number could include the total number of deportees in 597, 586, and 582 BCE (*The Fall and Rise of Jerusalem: Judah under Babylonian Rule* [Winona Lake, IN: Eisenbrauns, 2005], 59–60). These included the seven thousand soldiers and workmen referred to in 2 Kings 24:16, as well as the 3,023 people mentioned in Jer. 52:28. Although no satisfactory answer can be found at present, a total of some ten thousand to fourteen thousand (if all numbers are added up) deportees would still represent a rather small percentage of the overall population. According to current population estimates (see below), this grand total would amount to only 10–13 percent of the Judean population at the end of the monarchy.

2. For a general summary, see Robert Althann, "Gedaliah (Person) 2–5," *ABD* 2:923–24.

40:14), the assassins sought to install Ishmael, the son of Nethaniah, as king over Judah (Jer. 41:1–18). In fear of an imminent Babylonian revenge, several Judeans fled to Egypt prior to the razzia (see Jer. 42–44), despite warnings by Jeremiah not to return to the land of the ancient Israelite sojourn (Jer. 43:1–7). According to several prophetic oracles, the king of Babylon would come to punish the Jewish exiles in Egypt (e.g., Jer. 44:14, 27–28), and he would also overcome the pharaoh and his Nile Valley kingdom (e.g., Jer. 46:13–26; Ezek. 29:1–21; 30:1–19).[3] Subsequently, Jews seem to have settled in various towns within Lower Egypt (e.g., in Tahpanes/Tell Daphneh, Migdol/Tell Kedua, Noph/Memphis), in Patros (in Upper Egypt [Jer. 44:1]), and on the isle of Elephantine (called "Syene" in Isa. 49:12; Ezek. 29:10; 30:6). At Elephantine Jewish settlers[4] would build a temple for Yahweh.[5] Likewise, Jews also settled in other countries throughout the eastern Mediterranean world (Jer. 40:11–12).

Consequently, while only a minority of Judeans went into exile to Babylon, a certain number eventually departed to seek shelter elsewhere and start a new life. During their dispersion, some would adapt to a new life setting, while others preferred an existence in semi-isolation to observe Jewish religious rites and stay true to their ethnic conventions. Some of them eventually would return to their homeland during the reign of the Achaemenid kings Cyrus the Great (Ezra 1–6) and his immediate successors.

But what can be said about those who did not go into exile and stayed behind within the boundaries of the Neo-Babylonian province of Judah/Yehud? Jeremiah had advised the Judeans to stay and submit to Neo-Babylonian rule (Jer. 42:10–11). No mention is made of further governors at Mizpah after the

---

3. While the pharaoh Apries/Hophra (589–570) lost his throne during a rebellion instigated by his successor, Amasis (570–526), Nebuchadnezzar appears to have sought to restore Apries's reign in 569 or 567 BCE. Although cuneiform inscriptions refer to an invasion of Egypt by the Babylonians, the invasion does not appear to have had a lasting effect. Amasis alludes to an invasion by Asiatics, who had come in support of Apries. See *ANET* 308; Veysel Donbaz, "Some Late Babylonian Texts Gleaned from the Assur Collection," in *Historiography in the Cuneiform World* (vol. 1 of *Proceedings of the XLVe Recontre Assyriologique Internationale*; ed. Tzvi Abusch et al; Bethesda, MD: CDL Press, 2001), esp. 167, 173–74; Elmar Edel, "Amasis und Nebukadrezar II," *GM* 29 (1978): 13–20.

4. It is not certain when the first settlers arrived. However, according to *Let. Arist.* 13, Judean soldiers were stationed in Egypt as mercenary troops of Pharaoh Psamtek I (664–610) or Psamtek II (595–589). On this, see Bezalel Porten, "Settlement of the Jews at Elephantine and the Arameans at Syene," in *Judah and the Judeans in the Neo-Babylonian Period* (ed. Oded Lipschits and Joseph Blenkinsopp; Winona Lake, IN: Eisenbrauns, 2003), 459; also Dan'el Kahn, "Judean Auxiliaries in Egypt's Wars against Kush," *JAOS* 127 (2007): 507–16. On the settlement of Jewish settlers on the Isle of Elephantine, see Porten, "Settlement of the Jews," 451–70. The Rubensohn Letter 1 confirms that the Jewish temple was constructed prior to the Persian invasion in 525 BCE, when pharaohs still ruled Egypt (Porten, "Settlement of the Jews," 454, 456).

5. Isa. 19:19 refers to an altar that was to be built for Yahweh in the land of Egypt.

The Babylonians and Babylon

The Babylonians. The most powerful ruler of the Neo-Babylonian Empire was Nebuchadnezzar II (604–560). While his father, Nabopolasser (625–605), lay on his
deathbed, the crown prince Nebuchadnezzar fought with the Egyptians over the
sovereignty of Syria. Once the battle was won at Carchemish in 605, he brought
Syria and Palestine (Hatti-Land) to its knees. Nevertheless, in the succeeding years
the Babylonians encountered rebellion in many parts of the empire. The conquest
of Tyre alone would take no less than thirteen years. Despite some considerable
effort and military losses, their intended conquest of Egypt in 601 and the actual
invasion of Egypt in 569 (or 567?) would prove to be mostly ineffective. Nevertheless, Nebuchadnezzar was a mighty king, and he caused widespread devastation
in Syria-Palestine. His major building works in Mesopotamia would perpetuate
his fame. He was succeeded by his ephemeral son Avel-Marduk (561–560), his
son-in-law Nerglissar (559–556), and the latter's young son Labashi-Marduk (556).
The latter was killed in a conspiracy, and Nabonidus (555–539) took the throne.
Nabonidus's mother had served as high priestess of Harran. Harran's chief deity
was the moon-god Sin, to whom Nabonidus would construct important temples
there and at Ur. This "act of rebellion" against Marduk, the chief god of Babylon,
would discredit him before the priesthood of Marduk. Although the annexation
of Edom brought him fame, his popularity within Babylon decreased steadily. He
left the government in the hands of his son Belshazzar (also known from the book
of Daniel) for almost ten years, while he himself took up residence at Tayma in

murder of Gedaliah, but there is no reason to doubt that the Neo-Babylonians
continued to control this region so close to the northern border of Egypt.[6]
Does archaeology reveal evidence of continued settlement, and if so, can we
estimate the number of people who remained in the land of Judah? While
the majority of earlier scholars believed that the country was basically left
"empty" after the fall of Jerusalem, more recently others have countered the
empty-land concept, arguing that the theory is basically founded on myth and
cannot be supported by archaeological evidence.[7]

6. See Oded Lipschits, "Nebuchadrezzar's Policy in 'Hatti-Land' and the Fate of the
Kingdom of Judah," *UF* 30 (1999): 483–84. David Vanderhooft argues that the Neo-Babylonians
refrained from appointing other governors at Mizpah (*The Neo-Babylonian Empire and Babylon
in the Latter Prophets* [HSM 59; Atlanta: Scholars Press, 1999], 104–10). Neither the biblical
narratives nor archaeological evidence support a strong Babylonian interest in the region (but
see the discussion below, esp. on Tell en-Naṣbeh and Ramat Raḥel).

7. For several useful essays on the concept of the exile, see Ehud Ben Zvi and Christoph
Levin, eds., *The Concept of Exile in Ancient Israel and Its Historical Contexts* (BZAW 404;
Berlin: de Gruyter, 2010).

Saudi Arabia. During his reign the Persian king Cyrus II (559–530) conquered the Median capital Ecbatana (553), the region of Asia Minor (547/46), and finally the empire and city of Babylon itself (539).

Babylon. For its Jewish citizens, Babylon represented both cosmopolitan attitudes and a religion totally at odds with their own beliefs. The state deities Marduk (patron deity of Babylon) and Nabu (the Borsippan god of writing) apparently had brought military prowess and economic prosperity. Babylon experienced its cultural zenith during the sixth century BCE. Besides other temples and shrines dedicated to the chief deities of Babylon, the most imposing structure was the Etemenanki ziggurat, which comprised seven stories; the topmost level reached a height of 295 feet. Although the tower had been originally constructed during the Old Babylonian period, it was Nabopolassar and his son Nebuchadnezzar who renovated and embellished it. Nebuchadnezzar resided at several palaces, for instance at the northern and southern citadels, as well as at his summer palace, the northern perimeter of the city. The main palace (the southern citadel) contained five courtyards, which were encompassed by many small rooms. The throne room was located to the south of the third courtyard and could be entered through a monumental gateway. In the subterranean storerooms of this palace, food-ration lists were uncovered in which King Jehoiachin of Judah and his sons are mentioned. An imposing causeway led through the Ishtar Gate into the central city. The shrine built for the New Year's celebration (Akitu festival) was located in the northern part of the city. During this festival Marduk was annually reappointed as king of the gods, while a statue of Nabu was brought in procession from the nearby city of Borsippa.

"The Myth of the Empty Land" Theory

Hans Barstad, contrary to the former mainstream position of a large-scale abandonment of Judah,[8] has argued that life continued after the fall of Jerusalem and that the "Empty Land" position was basically a myth created by a small community of zealous Zion-oriented Jews who later returned from Babylon.[9] Thereby they sought to establish the belief that their restoration

8. The "Empty Land" or "Babylonian Gap" view, as based on archaeology, has followers such as Ephraim Stern ("The Babylonian Gap: The Archaeological Reality," *JSOT* 28 [2004]: 273–77). For an overview, see Oded Lipschits, "Shedding New Light on the Dark Years of the 'Exilic Period': New Studies, Further Elucidation, and Some Questions Regarding the Archaeology of Judah as an 'Empty Land,'" in *Interpreting Exile: Displacement and Deportation in Biblical and Modern Contexts* (ed. Brad Kelle, Frank R. Ames, and Jacob L. Wright; SBLAIL 10; Atlanta: Society of Biblical Literature, 2011), 81–82.

9. A more extreme position was already held by Charles C. Torrey, who denied both the exile and the return of the Jews. See Torrey, *The Composition and Historical Value of Ezra-Nehemiah* (BZAW 2; Giessen: J. Ricker, 1896), 51–65; idem, *The Chronicler's History of Israel:*

was a special miracle worked by Yahweh.[10] Hence the period after the destruction of Jerusalem and its temple became characterized as a time of "national humilation, filled with gloom and despair."[11] Barstad believes that the very concepts of exile and return stem from the Bible itself (especially so from the ideological and propogandistic views presented in the books of Chronicles, Ezra, and Nehemiah), as well as from later Jewish historians such as Flavius Josephus. Although Jerusalem was indeed destroyed by the Babylonians and some Jews undoubtedly were carried into exile, according to Barstad, this painful event was clearly not the momentous catastrophe pictured by the biblical writers.[12] Barstad suggests that archaeology supports the idea that Judah's society continued to function after the siege of Jerusalem, with peasants, artisans, traders, as well as village elders and cultic personnel in place. He also argues that several sources within the Hebrew Bible (including both prosaic and poetic texts) were written during this time period, not only in Babylon but also, and perhaps especially so, within Judah itself.[13]

It should be said, however, that the idea that large numbers of Judahites remained in the land is no recent innovation by scholars proposing a "myth of the empty land." It can also be found in the Bible (e.g., 2 Kings 25:22–26).[14] Even so, is the view supported by archaeological evidence?

Chronicles-Ezra-Nehemiah Restored to Its Original Form (New Haven: Yale University Press, 1954). The phrase "myth of the empty land," as employed by Hans Barstad (see next note), was adopted by him from Robert P. Carroll, "The Myth of the Empty Land," in *Ideological Criticism of Biblical Texts* (ed. David Jobling and Tina Pippin; Semeia 59; Atlanta: Scholars Press, 1992), 79–93.

10. Hans M. Barstad, *The Myth of the Empty Land: A Study in the History and Archaeology of Judah during the "Exilic" Period* (SO 28; Oslo: Scandinavian University Press, 1996). For a recent update by Barstad, see "The Myth of the Empty Land," in *History and the Hebrew Bible: Studies in Ancient Israelite and Ancient Near Eastern Historiography* (FAT 61; Tübingen: Mohr Siebeck, 2008), 90–117; see also idem, "After the 'Myth of the Empty Land': Major Challenges in the Study of Neo-Babylonian Judah," in Lipschits and Blenkinsopp, *Judah and the Judeans in the Neo-Babylonian Period*, 3–20. Although Barstad is one of the leading proponents of this view, he does not stand alone. For a list of adherents, see Barstad, *History and the Hebrew Bible*, 92–94. Lisbeth Fried argues that the biblical narratives on the destruction of Jerusalem and the subsequent exile and restoration share common ground with ancient Near Eastern ideologically animated history-writing patterns that deal with the same themes ("The Land Lay Desolate: Conquest and Restoration in the Ancient Near East," in Lipschits and Blenkinsopp, *Judah and the Judeans in the Neo-Babylonian Period*, 21–54.

11. Barstad, *History and the Hebrew Bible*, 91.

12. Ibid., 109.

13. Ibid., 95.

14. Ibid., 99–102.

The Archaeological Evidence

Barstad lists several towns where continued settlement is attested during the exilic period. These sites, however, are located mainly to the north of Jerusalem, in the former Benjamin district.[15] Lack of destruction levels and evidence of continued occupation at Tell el-Ful (Stratum IIIB),[16] Tell en-Naṣbeh/Mizpah (Stratum II),[17] el-Jib/Gibeon,[18] Beitin, and in several burial caves in that region seem to support this picture.[19] In fact, this concurs with the biblical narrative (2 Kings 25:22–30; Jer. 39:11–41:18), which relates that this area remained settled after the fall of Jerusalem. At that time the main administrative center of the Neo-Babylonian province had moved from Jerusalem to Mizpah, in the Benjaminite region. The biblical text relates that Gedaliah

15. Even Barstad's most recent list of towns where life continued is generally restricted to work done by him in preparation of his 1996 monograph, as he himself admits. See Barstad, "After the 'Myth of the Empty Land,'" 6.

16. See, e.g., Nancy L. Lapp, ed., *The Third Campaign at Tel el-Fûl: The Excavations of 1964* (AASOR 45; Cambridge, MA: American Schools of Oriental Research, 1981), 39–62. See also Israel Finkelstein, "Tell el-Ful Revisited: The Assyrian and Hellenistic Periods (with a New Identification)," *PEQ* 143 (2011): 106–18.

17. For a recent summary, see Jeffrey R. Zorn, "Tell en-Naṣbeh and the Problem of the Material Culture of the Sixth Century," in Lipschits and Blenkinsopp, *Judah and the Judeans in the Neo-Babylonian Period*, 413–47.

18. Gibeon and its great pool are also referred to in Jer. 41:12, 16. Among other items, so-called *mwsh* jar handles were found in the winery and in pits in the northwestern sector of the site, which shows that the town indeed flourished during the sixth–fifth centuries BCE. Lipschits also dates the *gb'n gdr* jar handle inscriptions, found in and near the great water pool, to the sixth century BCE, but his late date (followed by several scholars) has now been queried by me on the basis of stratified evidence (Peter G. van der Veen, "An Inscribed Jar Handle from Ras el-'Amud: A New Reading and an Absolute Date," *KUSATU* 11 (2010): 109–21, esp. 115–18). Surprisingly, Lipschits ignores this evidence in "Shedding New Light," 80.

19. It is primarily by comparison with diagnostic pottery types from other sites in Benjamin (e.g., Tell el-Ful) that the same conclusions can be reached for the sixth-century date of Beitin. On this material, see Cindy L. Van Volsem, "The Babylonian Period in the Region of Benjamin (586–538 BCE)" (MA thesis, Institute of Holy Land Studies, 1987), 90–140, esp. 90–95. For updated summaries of the pottery evidence, see Lipschits, *Fall and Rise of Jerusalem*, 192–206, 237–49; Peter G. van der Veen, "The Final Phase of Iron Age IIC and the Babylonian Conquest: A Reassessment with Special Emphasis on Names and Bureaucratic Titles on Provenanced Seals and Bullae from Israel and Jordan" (PhD diss., University of Bristol, 2005), 10–20, 64–68, now in press at Ugarit Verlag as AOAT 415 (2014); Kirsi Valkama, "What Do Archaeological Remains Reveal of the Settlements in Judah during the Mid-Sixth Century BCE?," in Ben Zvi and Levin, *Concept of Exile*, 39–59, with detailed literature. Gabriel Barkay reports that much material from this period was found in burial caves at Tel Gibea, Tell el-Ful, and Jericho, and to the south in the vicinity of Jerusalem at Bethany, Sharafat (Mount Herzl), Ketef Hinnom, and Betar. Some material was also found in the Judean highlands—e.g., at Beth Shemesh. See Gabriel Barkay, "The Redefining of Archaeological Periods: Does the Date 588/586 BCE Indeed Mark the End of the Iron Age Cultures?," in *Biblical Archaeology Today* (ed. Avraham Biran and Joseph Aviram; Jerusalem: Israel Exploration Society, 1993), 108.

ordered the country folk to work on the oil and fruit plantations, as well as in the vineyards, on behalf of their Neo-Babylonian overlords (Jer. 40:11–12). A detailed study of the material culture, specifically the ceramic traditions of the Benjamin region during this period, was made by Cindy Van Volsem.[20] Sixth-century building activity is attested at Tell en-Naṣbeh, which, as most scholars believe, is biblical Mizpah.[21] While the excavators did not carefully distinguish between the Iron Age strata, Jeffrey Zorn was able to identify a separate stratum dating from the Neo-Babylonian period through to the early Persian period.[22] The orientation of this Iron Age III stratum is different from its Iron Age II predecessor and is characterized by large structures, including Mesopotamian-style residences (including a "courtyard-style building" also attested at Megiddo) and very large four-room buildings (averaging about 130m²). While the plan of this stratum appears to have been consciously modified to suit its new administrative purpose, its pottery could be assigned to the period under discussion. Several other finds also confirm the foreign nature of this stratum. A bronze circlet with a Neo-Babylonian inscription,[23] an ostracon with a fragmentary Mesopotamian name/inscription (probably written in Hebrew),[24] "bathtub" coffins, "wedge- and circle-impressed sherds," and stamped "Mozah jar handles" were found.[25] A seal of a royal minister named "Ya'azanyahu" was also found[26] and may be related to one of Gedaliah's officers (see below).

20. Van Volsem, "Babylonian Period." See also Oded Lipschits, "The History of the Benjamin Region under Babylonian Rule," *TA* 26 (1999): 155–89; idem, *Fall and Rise of Jerusalem*, 192–206, 237–49; van der Veen, "Final Phase of Iron Age IIC," 10–20, 64–68; Ephraim Stern, *Archaeology of the Land of the Bible: The Assyrian, Babylonian, and Persian Periods, 732–332 B.C.E.* (ABRL; New York: Doubleday, 2001), 321–26; Charles E. Carter, *The Emergence of Yehud in the Persian Period: A Social and Demographic Study* (JSOTSup 294; Sheffield: Sheffield Academic Press, 1999).

21. Alternatively, Mizpah has been identified with the site of Nebi Samwil, but its occupational history does not match biblical Mizpah. See Yitzhak Magen and Michael Dadon, "Nebi Sawil" (in Hebrew), *Qadmoniot* 118 (1999): 62–77. On the problems of this site, see Zorn, "Tell en-Naṣbeh," 413n1.

22. Unfortunately, Zorn's PhD dissertation ("Tell en Naṣbeh: A Re-evaluation of the Architecture and Stratigraphy of the Early Bronze Age, Iron Age and Later Periods" [University of California, Berkeley, 1993]) has not been published. But see his website: http://www.arts.cornell.edu/jrz3/pdf_files_of_collected_works.htm, with further literature. See also Zorn, "Tell en-Naṣbeh," 413–47.

23. The reading remains uncertain, but David Vanderhooft and Wayne Horowitz suggest that the circlet contains the name of the dedicator and that of a divine ruler ("The Cuneiform Inscription from Tell en-Naṣbeh: The Demise of an Unknown King," *TA* 29 [2002]: 318–27).

24. See André Lemaire, "Nabonidus in Arabia and Judah in the Neo-Babylonian Period," in Lipschits and Blenkinsopp, *Judah and the Judeans in the Neo-Babylonian Period*, 292–93.

25. Zorn, "Tell en-Naṣbeh," 433–40; van der Veen, "Final Phase of Iron Age IIC," 16–20.

26. This seal was found in a late Roman grave. However, the excavators believed that the tomb had been recut and that its original date was confirmed by late Iron Age pottery. For a summary, see van der Veen, "Final Phase of Iron Age IIC," 11–16.

International Mapping

Figure 12.2.

Jerusalem and Benjamin, Judah regions

Barstad also postulates that Jerusalem had remained settled after 586 BCE, and that destruction, though violent, was not widespread.[27] Although Ezekiel 33:24 indeed refers to inhabitants "living in these ruins," Jerusalem archaeology appears to contradict Barstad's position, as evidence of conflagration and destruction, as well as of siege warfare, has been uncovered in almost every part

27. Barstad, *History and the Hebrew Bible*, 104–17. A similar minimalist view is expressed by Ronny Reich, who argues that evidence of Babylonian destruction within the City of David is limited only to discoveries by Yigal Shiloh and Eilat Mazar in Area G (*Excavating the City of David: Where Jerusalem's History Began* [Jerusalem: Israel Exploration Society, 2011], 317). This is not true, however, as evidence of destruction was also found in Shiloh's Area E, and was found by Kathleen M. Kenyon, somewhat to the north of Shiloh's area (*Digging Up Jerusalem* [London: Benn, 1974], 170–71). Besides several arrowheads that appear to be related to the siege of the city, this area contained destruction debris, which clearly overlies Persian period structures. See also Kathleen M. Kenyon, *Royal Cities of the Old Testament* (London: Barrie & Jenkins, 1971), 148–50. Most recently, see Margreet L. Steiner, *The Settlement in the Bronze and Iron Ages* (vol. 3 of *Excavations by Kathleen M. Kenyon in Jerusalem, 1961–1967*; CIS 9; London: Sheffield Academic Press, 2001), 93, 105 (also figs. 6.17, 6.23, 6.60), 114. The current excavations at the Givati Car Park have so far not yielded evidence of the Neo-Babylonian period, as Iron Age strata have not been studied in detail (personal communication with Doron Ben-Ami, March 2012).

of the city—that is, in the City of David,[28] on the Ophel,[29] and on the Western Hill.[30] Oded Lipschits concludes, "The destruction of Jerusalem at the beginning of the 6th century is one of the prominent archaeological finds to appear in the many years of excavation of the city, and evidence of it has been unearthed all over the city at the twilight of the First Temple period."[31]

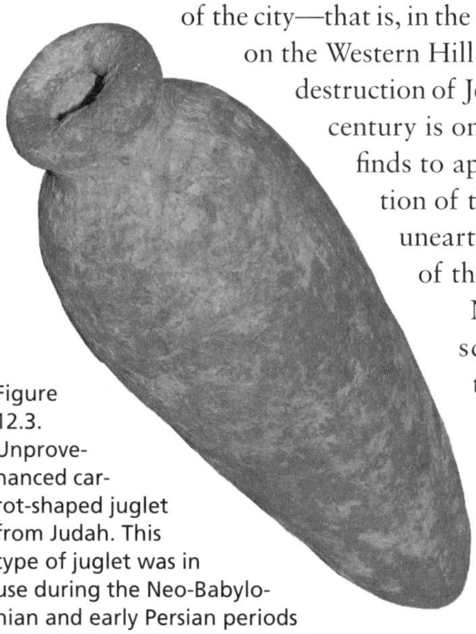

Nevertheless, evidence of some squatter occupation from after the destruction does exist.[32] Gabriel Barkay refers to typical late sixth-century BCE pottery found in the Armenian Garden, as well as "wedge-impressed pottery" uncovered on the Western Hill and underneath the Redeemer Church in the Christian Quarter. Wedge-impressed pottery was even

P. van der Veen

Figure 12.3. Unprovenanced carrot-shaped juglet from Judah. This type of juglet was in use during the Neo-Babylonian and early Persian periods in Judah, sixth–fifth century BC.

28. Evidence of destruction was esp. uncovered in the excavations of Yigal Shiloh in Stratum 10 of Areas E and G. See Yigal Shiloh, *1978–1982, Interim Report of the First Five Seasons* (vol. 1 of *Excavations at the City of David*; Qedem 19; Jerusalem: Institute of Archaeology, Hebrew University of Jerusalem, 1984), 18–19; idem, "Judah and Jerusalem in the Eighth–Sixth Centuries BCE," in *Recent Excavations in Israel: Studies in the Iron Age Archaeology* (ed. Seymore Gitin and William G. Dever; AASOR 49; Winona Lake, IN: Eisenbrauns, 1989), 102–3; Yigal Shiloh et al., "Jerusalem," *NEAEHL* 2:709. This evidence was confirmed recently by Eilat Mazar, who excavated the summit above Area G.

29. See Eilat Mazar, "The Royal Quarter of Biblical Jerusalem: The Ophel," in *Ancient Jerusalem Revealed* (ed. Hillel Geva; Jerusalem: Israel Exploration Society, 1994), 68–72; idem, *Discovering the Solomonic Wall in Jerusalem: A Remarkable Archaeological Adventure* (Jerusalem: Shoham Academic Research and Publication, 2011), 147. She states, "Indeed, the final phase of the fortified complex suffered an immense fire and heavy destruction, leaving complete pottery vessels, typical of the late First Temple Period, crushed within the ash-filled layer."

30. See, e.g., Nahman Avigad, *Discovering Jerusalem* (Nashville: Nelson, 1983), 54; Hillel Geva, ed., *Jewish Quarter Excavations in the Old City of Jerusalem: Conducted by Nahman Avigad, 1969–1982* (4 vols.; Jerusalem: Institute of Archaeology, Hebrew University of Jerusalem, 2008), 1:158.

31. Oded Lipschits, "Judah, Jerusalem and the Temple 586–539 B.C.," *Transeu* 22 (2001): 132.

32. For such evidence, see Barkay, "Redefining of Archaeological Periods," 107–8. Like Hans Barstad, Barkay also argues that there was "no gap in the history of Jerusalem during the Babylonian period" (107), but his view cannot be maintained in the light of the overwhelming evidence of destruction in various parts of the city, and as he himself admits, "The destruction of the City of David in Jerusalem was probably total." That destruction evidence in the City of David and on the Ophel is most naturally explained by how the siege was primarily targeted against the city's elite.

found in the City of David.[33] The date of the wedge-impressed pottery is debated. Based on its occurence in late sixth- and fifth-century BCE strata in the Tayma region in Saudi Arabia, this pottery may be connected with the resettlement of Jerusalem after the exile, in the late sixth century BCE.[34] Two Neo-Babylonian bullae were recently uncovered on the eastern slope of the City of David in a thick layer of destruction debris from the Babylonian siege.[35] On both of these a priest is depicted in front of the cult symbols of Marduk and Nabu, the chief deities of Babylon and Borsippa.[36] Rich tombs at Ketef Hinnom and at Mamilla also appear to have been in use at this time, but it is far from certain if the owners actually continued to live in or near the city's ruins.[37]

While destruction was decisive at the more prominent Judean sites such as Lachish (Stratum II), Khirbet et-Tabaqa/Beth Zur (Stratum III), Tell Batash/Timnah (Stratum II),[38] and Tel Goren/En-Gedi (Stratum V),[39] recent excava-

33. Ibid. See also Jeffrey R. Zorn, "Wedge- and Circle-Impressed Pottery—an Arabian Connection," in *Studies in the Archaeology of Israel and Neighboring Lands in Memory of Douglas L. Esse* (ed. Samuel R. Wolff; SAOC 59; Chicago: Oriental Institute of the University of Chicago, 2001), 689.

34. Zorn, "Tell en-Naṣbeh," 693–95. Zorn suggests an Arabian connection for this pottery and relates it to spice and frankincense trade.

35. See Eilat Mazar, *The Palace of King David: Excavations at the Summit of the City of David; Preliminary Report of Seasons 2005–2007* (trans. Ben Gordon; Jerusalem: Shoham Academic Research and Publication, 2009), 78–79. The debris also contains foreign and local arrowheads that likely date from the Babylonian siege. The pottery in the debris spans the period from the late Iron Age to the early Persian period (late sixth–fifth centuries BCE). Also found was a seal of a person called "Shlomit" with worshipers flanking the altar of Sin of Harran, but its date is not clear (ibid.).

36. This type of seal was in use by Neo-Babylonian officials as early as about 600 BCE, and it remained in use until the early fifth century BCE under Achaemenid rule. Although a sixth-century date seems preferable, these seal impressions could also date from after 538. See Richard L. Zettler, "On the Chronological Range of Neo-Babylonian and Achaemenid Seals," *JNES* 38 (1979): 257–70; van der Veen, "Final Phase of Iron Age IIC," 153, 216–18.

37. In principle, they could also have lived at Mizpah or Ramat Raḥel, while they wished to be buried with their ancestors near the former capital, hoping that Yahweh would soon restore the city to its former splendor. On the Ketef Hinnom and Mamilla excavations, see two essays, both in Geva, *Ancient Jerusalem Revealed*: Gabriel Barkay, "Excavations at Ketef Hinnom in Jerusalem," 85–106; Ronny Reich, "The Ancient Burial Ground in the Mamilla Neighbourhood, Jerusalem," 111–18, esp. 116.

38. Although some scholars have suggested that Timnah could have been destroyed as early as 603–601 BCE, there exists no positive evidence for this. Even the destruction of nearby Philistine Ekron may have occurred much later (possibly as late as 570 BCE). See Peter J. James, "Dating Late Iron Age Ekron (Tel Miqne)," *PEQ* 138 (2006): 85–97.

39. The latter seems to have served as a royal production center of balsam/perfume. Uniform buildings, courtyards with a great number of barrel-shaped vats, mortars, and ovens seem to confirm this. There is reason to believe that this site was destroyed only in 582 BCE during the subsequent razzia against Judah. A gloss by Rabbi Joseph on Jer. 52:6 (*b. Šabb.* 26a) states that

tions at Ramat Raḥel, south of Jerusalem, prove that the site was not
destroyed. Life went on during the
entire period under discussion. The
main citadel, built during the late
seventh century BCE, continued to
function as an administrative center,
while the place around the citadel
was turned into a well-watered garden, with springs and cisterns.[40] Lipschits suggests that the site became
an administrative center during both
the Neo-Babylonian and subsequent
Achaemenid periods, which he believes is confirmed by the quantity
of stamped jar handles from that

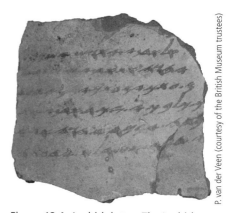

Figure 12.4. Lachish letter. The Lachish
letters found in the gate area of Lachish
stratum 2 describe the political circumstances in Judah on the eve of the Babylonian invasions in 586 BC.

period. Excavations at the site yielded many royal jar handles from the time
of Hezekiah and Manasseh (the so-called *lmlk* jar handles)[41] and from the
final years of the Judahite monarchy (the so-called rosette jar handles); yet
jar handles with lion stamps from the Neo-Babylonian period, as well as with
typical Persian period impressions naming officials and the province of Yehud,
were also uncovered in remarkable quantities.[42] Lipschits assumes that Ramat
Raḥel functioned as Judah's principal fiscal center, where taxes were collected.[43]

---

vinedressers and tenant farmers were left in the country by Nebuzaradan in 586 BCE. They
served as balsam gatherers at places such as En-Gedi. See John N. Graham, "'Vinedressers
and Plowmen': 2 Kings 25:12 and Jeremiah 52:16," *BA* 47 (1984): 55–58. On En-Gedi, see also
Peter G. van der Veen and François Bron, "Arabian and Arabizing Epigraphic Finds from the
Iron Age Southern Levant," in *Unearthing the Wilderness: Studies on the History and Archaeology of the Negev and Edom in the Iron Age* (ed. Juan Manuel Tebes; ANESSup 45; Leuven:
Peeters, forthcoming).

40. See Oded Lipschits et al., "Palace and Village, Paradise and Oblivian: Unraveling the
Riddles of Ramat Raḥel," *NEA* 74 (2011): 2–49. The site of Tall al-Umayri in Transjordan seems
to have fulfilled a similar administrative function as Ramat Raḥel under Neo-Babylonian and
Achaemenid rule. See Larry G. Herr, "Wine Production in the Hills of Southern Ammon and
the Founding of Tall al-'Umayri in the Sixth Century B.C.," *ADAJ* 39 (1995): 121–25.

41. An early seventh-century BCE date for some of the royal jar handles was first proposed by
George M. Grena, *LMLK—a Mystery Belonging to the King* (Redondo Beach, CA: 4000 Years
of Writing History, 2004), 333–38. See Peter G. van der Veen, "Arabian Seals and Bullae along
the Trade Routes of Judah and Edom," *JERD* 3 (2009): 33–34.

42. Note, however, that the attribution of the lion jar handles to the Neo-Babylonian period
is not accepted by all, and that they may date to the Persian period also. Most recently, see David
Ussishkin, "*Lmlk* Seal Impressions Once Again: A Second Rejoinder to Oded Lipschits," *AntOr*
10 (2012): 13–24, with relevant literature.

43. Lipschits, "Shedding New Light," 73.

J. Schweinsberg

Figure 12.5. Area of the Ramat Raḥel palace courtyard excavated by the author in 2006. The site continued to exist right through the time of the Babylonian exile.

The nearby Rephaim Valley (its main production center was located at Rogem Ganim),[44] with its terraces and alluvial soil, served as an ideal place for extensive well-planned agricultural activity under a centralized Judean administration during the Neo-Babylonian and Achaemenid periods.[45] Several small sites with farms and installations (e.g., at Khirbet er-Ras, near Manaḥat) appear to be related to the same agricultural enterprise.[46] Additional sites in Benjamin, the Valley of the Rephaim, and other parts of central Judah have yielded pottery from this period. The absence of de-

44. Besides typical pottery of the late Iron Age and Persian periods, both lion and Yehud stamps were also discovered at Rogem Ganim (ibid., 69n38). Work in the Rephaim Basin was carried out by, among others, Gilead Cinamon, and its results were assembled in his 2004 MA thesis for the University of Tel Aviv: "The Tumuli South-West of Jerusalem and Their Significance to the Understanding of Jerusalem's Countryside in the Iron Age II" (personal communication with Gilead Cinamon, 2005–2006).

45. Oded Lipschits and Yuval Gadot, "Ramat Raḥel and the Emeq Rephaim Sites—Links and Interpretations," in *New Studies in the Archaeology of Jerusalem and Its Region: Collected Papers* (ed. David Amit and Guy D. Stiebel; 2 vols.; Jerusalem: Israel Antiquities Authority, 2008), 2:88–96.

46. Lipschits, "Shedding New Light," 70. These sites include Khirbet er-Ras, Beit Safafa, Manaḥat, Givat Massuaḥ, and a cave near the Holyland Hotel in Jerusalem. Some thirty-five winepresses and multiple plastered tanks and caves for storage were uncovered.

struction layers suggests that these settlements existed throughout the sixth century BCE.[47]

The Population of Judah

Based on extensive fieldwork and the estimation of settled dunams in Judah from before the fall of Jerusalem and during the Persian period, Lipschits suggests that population numbers in Judah had drastically dropped from around 108,000 before 586 BCE to around 30,125 during the fifth century BCE.[48] Including the areas of Benjamin, the Jerusalem environs, northern and southern Judean hills, the Shephelah, the Beersheba Valley, and the western coast of the Dead Sea, he concludes that there was a 69.3 percent decrease of settled area between the late monarchic and Persian periods.

Judah's Southern Borders with Edom

Judah's southern border is directly related to the history of late Iron Age Edom.[49] Edomite assaults are already attested near Arad around 700 BCE (Arad Letter 40). However, both Edomite and North Arabian influxes in the area increased under the Neo-Assyrian rulers of the early seventh century BCE. While the Neo-Assyrian monarchs employed Arab sheikhs to oversee the trading networks in the Negev and Sinai deserts and to assist with camel transportation, it seems likely that local Edomites were involved.[50] The discovery of Edomite pottery[51] at various sites in the Sinai and in the northern Negev,[52]

47. Avraham Faust, "Judah in the Sixth Century B.C.E.: A Rural Perspective," *PEQ* 135 (2003): 37–53, esp. 39–43.

48. Oded Lipschits, "Demographic Changes in Judah between the Seventh and the Fifth Centuries BCE," in Lipschits and Blenkinsopp, *Judah and the Judeans in the Neo-Babylonian Period*, 363–66. See also Lipschits, *Fall and Rise of Jerusalem*, 149–84, 258–71. Lipschits has recently raised the population number during the Persian period to about forty thousand ("Shedding New Light," 78).

49. See, e.g., Itzhaq Beit-Arieh, "The Edomites in Cisjordan," in *You Shall Not Abhor an Edomite for He Is Your Brother: Edom and Seir in History and Tradition* (ed. Diana Vikander Edelman; SBLABS 3; Atlanta: Scholars Press, 1995), 33–40. For an update on the Edomite culture in the Negev, see Tebes, *Unearthing the Wilderness*.

50. It seems likely that the Assyrians did not distinguish carefully between North Arabians and Edomites (personal communication with Wolfgang Zwickel, March 2012).

51. For a detailed description of this pottery, see van der Veen, "Final Phase of Iron Age IIC," 208–12, 236–40. For a general summary, see Stern, *Archaeology of the Land of the Bible*, 288–92.

52. For a summary, see Diana V. Edelman, *The Origins of the "Second" Temple: Persian Imperial Policy and the Rebuilding of Jerusalem* (BW; London: Equinox, 2005), 253–65.

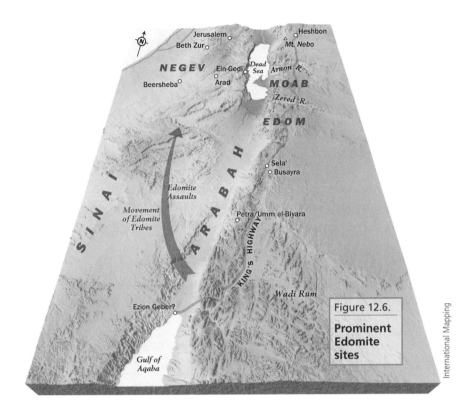

Figure 12.6.

Prominent Edomite sites

International Mapping

as well as Edomite cultic implements[53] and other small finds (including seals and ostraca),[54] appears to confirm the increasing presence of Edomites in the region. By around 600 BCE, Edom had become a major threat to Judah's southern strongholds. Witness the repeated complaints in Arad Letters 21 and 24. Several prophetic passages relate that the Edomites had penetrated into southern Judah, and that they had attacked Judean refugees on their way to Egypt after the fall of Jerusalem (e.g., Ezek. 35:5; Obad. 14; 1 Esd. 4:45).[55]

While Judah became a Neo-Babylonian province in 586 and Ammon and Moab in 582, Edom remained a vassal of Babylon until 553/552, when the Neo-Babylonian monarch Nabonidus (555–539) conquered and annexed it. A

53. As, e.g., at En Ḥazeva and Ḥorvat Qitmit. For a summary, see Stern, *Archaeology of the Land of the Bible*, 279–88. See also Piotr Bienkowski and Leonie Sedman, "Busayra and Judah: Stylistic Parallels in the Material Culture," in *Studies in the Archaeology of the Iron Age in Israel and Jordan* (JSOTSup 331; Sheffield: Sheffield Academic Press, 2001), 310–25.

54. Stern, *Archaeology of the Land of the Bible*, 270–73.

55. Yet Jer. 40:11 reports that some Jews also found shelter in Edom. See also Beth Glazier-McDonald, "Edom in the Prophetical Corpus," in Edelman, *You Shall Not Abhor an Edomite*, 23–32.

campaign against Edom is indeed attested in the Nabonidus Chronicle,[56] while a weathered rock relief at Sela ʿ (about one mile northwest of Busayra) probably depicts this king.[57] Not later than in the reign of the Achaemenid king Cambyses II (530–522), Arab kings ruled the area. According to Herodotus (*Hist.* 3.88), Cambyses recognized Arab rule in the region in appreciation for the services that the Arab king had granted during the Achaemenid invasion of Egypt in 525 BCE. These circumstances were going to have lasting effects on Judah's economic role in the region, with the important Negev trade routes now firmly in foreign hands.[58] The southern borders of the Neo-Babylonian and Achaemenid province of Judah (Yehud) had moved well to the north of the Negev, possibly near the Judean sites of Beth Zur and En-Gedi.[59]

Epigraphic Finds

As I have discussed elsewhere, some epigraphic finds from the period under discussion seem to name "exilic" personages known from the Bible.[60] Three

---

56. Paul-Alain Beaulieu, *The Reign of Nabonidus, King of Babylon, 556–539 B.C.* (YNER 10; New Haven: Yale University Press, 1989), 166; see also John Lindsay, "The Babylonian Kings and Edom," *PEQ* (1976): 23–39; van der Veen, "Final Phase of Iron Age IIC," 218–21.

57. Stephanie Dalley and Anne Goguel, "The Sela ʿ Sculpture: A Neo-Babylonian Rock Relief in Southern Jordan," *ADAJ* 41 (1997): 169–76; Fawzi Zayadine, "Le relief néo-babylonien à Sela ʿ près de Tafeleh: Interprétation historique," *Syria* 76 (1999): 83–90; Lemaire, "Nabonidus in Arabia." Nevertheless, straightforward evidence of destruction at the major Edomite sites is (still) lacking. For example, the late Iron Age stratum at Busayra ("Integrated Stage 3") existed at least until 300 BCE, as seems evident from stratified Attic ware. See Piotr Bienkowski, ed., *Busayra Excavations by Crystal-M. Bennett, 1971–1980* (BAMA 13; Oxford: Oxford University Press, 2002), 477. A bulla from late Iron Age Umm el-Biyara (Petra), stamped with the Neo-Babylonian state symbols of Marduk and Nabu, also confirms that Edom lay within the Neo-Babylonian sphere of influence. As the bulla had been attached to cloth, it is likely that it served to seal fiscal commodities. See Peter G. van der Veen, "The Seal Material," in *Umm al-Biyara: Excavations by Crystal-M. Bennett in Petra, 1960–1965* (ed. Piotr Bienkowski; LSS 10; Oxford: Oxbow, 2011), 81–82.

58. On some of these rulers at the time of Nehemiah, see Edwin M. Yamauchi, *Persia and the Bible* (Grand Rapids: Baker Books, 1996), 268–70.

59. For a detailed description of the borders of Yehud, see Lipschits, *Fall and Rise of Jerusalem*, 206–10, with map 7; see also John W. Wright, "Remapping Yehud: The Borders of Yehud and the Genealogies of Chronicles," in *Judah and the Judeans in the Persian Period* (ed. Oded Lipschits and Manfred Oeming; Winona Lake, IN: Eisenbrauns, 2006), 67–89. But Edelman (*Origins of the "Second" Temple*, 269–70) is not convinced that the southern border of Judah had already moved so far north so early.

60. See Peter G. van der Veen, "Gedaliah ben Aḥiqam in the Light of Epigraphic Evidence (A Response to Bob Becking)," in *New Seals and Inscriptions, Hebrew, Idumean and Cuneiform* (ed. Meir Lubetski; HBM 8; Sheffield: Sheffield Phoenix Press, 2007), 55–70; idem, "Gedaliah's Seal Material Revisited: Some Preliminary Notes on New Evidence from the City of David," in *New Inscriptions and Seals Relating to the Biblical World* (ed. Meir Lubetski and Edith Lubetski;

Figure 12.7. Unprovenanced bulla of Gedaliah, the minister of the king. It is possible that this seal impression had been stamped by the official seal of Gedaliah the governor prior to the fall of Jerusalem, when the latter had served in the Judahite bureaucracy.

bullae (one provenanced and two unprovenanced) possibly refer to the Judean governor Gedaliah. The provenanced bulla names a certain Gedalyahu *'šr 'l-hbyt* (a "minister of the Royal House") and was found at Lachish. It could refer to the governor in a position that he might have held before the fall of Jerusalem, as some have suggested.[61] Two unprovenanced bullae of a Gedalyahu *'bd hmlk* ("servant of the king" or simply "courtier") have also been considered. However, the equation stands on shaky ground since the recent discovery of another bulla at the City of David that names a Gedalyahu *bn pšḥr* (son of Pashḥur).[62] Close examination of the palaeography appears to suggest that all these bullae were impressed by seals carved either by the same hand or by a very small group of engravers, around 590 BCE. It is therefore possible that all these seals refer to one and the same person, who served at the court of King Zedekiah (Jer. 38:1).[63]

Epigraphic evidence can be attributed with relative certainty to Gedaliah's enemy King Baalis of Ammon (Jer. 40:14). He is referred to on a provenanced jar stopper that contains Egyptian symbols (a four-winged scarab and lotus bud standards) and the inscription *lmlkm'wr 'bd b'lyš'* (belonging to Milkomur, the minister of Baalyisha).[64] It was found at the Ammonite site Tall al-Umayri (about 9.5 miles south of Amman).[65] Baalis is also referred to on his own (unprovenanced)

SBLABS 19; Atlanta: Scholars Press, 2012), 21–33. On these identifications, see also Lawrence J. Mykytiuk, *Identifying Biblical Persons in Northwest Semitic Inscriptions of 1200–539 B.C.E.* (SBLAB 12; Atlanta: Society of Biblical Literature, 2004); idem, "Corrections and Updates to 'Identifying Biblical Persons in Northwest Semitic Inscriptions of 1200–539 BCE,'" *Maarav* 16, no. 1 (2009): 49–132.

61. For a list of authors who have discussed this possibility, see van der Veen, "Gedaliah ben Aḥiqam," 55–56.

62. For the discovery of this bulla, see Mazar, *Palace of King David*, 68.

63. Note also that the honorific title "servant of the king" and the title "minister of the palace" were in use before the end of the Judahite monarchy. Continued use of these titles by the Neo-Babylonian state in the peripheries is not attested.

64. For a study of the palaeographic and iconographic details on the jar stopper, see van der Veen, "Final Phase of Iron Age IIC," 167–76; see also Jürg Eggler and Othmar Keel, *Corpus der Siegel-Amulette aus Jordanien: Vom Neolithikum bis zur Perserzeit* (OBO 25; Fribourg: Academic Press; Göttingen: Vandenhoeck & Ruprecht, 2006), 312–13, and fig. 4.

65. The palaeographic date, the archaeological findspot, and the lack of a like-named king in the unbroken royal line of Ammon (ca. 725–582 BCE) make the equation virtually certain.

R. Deutsch (courtesy of Robert Deutsch)

Figure 12.8. Unprovenanced seal of king Baalyasha (Baalis) of the sons of Ammon. This king supported the conspiracy against Gedaliah the governor, which led to his assassination.

seal that depicts a striding sphinx and contains a fragmentary inscription. It can be restored as [*l*] *b'lyš*[ ] *mlk b*[*n 'm*]*n* ([belonging to] Baalyish[a], king of the s[ons of Ammo]n).[66]

Another seal, possibly referring to a military commander of Gedaliah, was unearthed at Tell en-Naṣbeh/Mizpah. The inscription reads Ya'azanyahu *'bd hmlk* ("servant of the king" or "courtier").[67] The seal is finely engraved. Both the style of the letters and the rooster depicted in the bottom register suggest a date near 600 BCE.[68] Although the seal was unearthed in a late Roman tomb, evidence does exist that the seal could have predated its provenance. A Ya'azaniah (alternately, Jezaniah), a son of a Maacathite, served Gedaliah at Mizpah (2 Kings 25:23; Jer. 40:8).[69] Although this equation is possible, no certainty can be reached.

Moreover, two unprovenanced bullae refer to a certain Ishmael *bn hmlk* (son of the king). According to Barkay, this person could be Gedaliah's main assassin, who was of royal descent (2 Kings 25:25; Jer. 40:13–41:2).[70] Indeed, study of the title "son of the king" confirms that holders of that title were relatives of the royal bloodline but not necessarily sons of the ruling monarch. If these bullae are genuine, this identification is supported by the date of the letters and by the name and title of the individual.[71]

66. The unprovenanced seal was examined by Robert Deutsch, who kindly supplied me with high-resolution photographs and a plasticine impression of the original seal. Doubts previously expressed by Bob Becking could be resolved. See van der Veen, "Gedaliah ben Aḥiqam," 69–70; Robert Deutsch, "Seal of Baalis Surfaces," *BAR* 25, no. 2 (1999): 46–49, 66; idem, "An Ammonite Royal Seal," in *West Semitic Epigraphic News of the 1st Millennium* (ed. Robert Deutsch and Michael Heltzer; Tel Aviv: Archaeological Center Publications, 1999), 53–57. For Becking's critique, see "The Seal of Baalisha, King of the Ammonites: Some Remarks," *BN* 97 (1999): 14–17, esp. 14; idem, *From David to Gedaliah: The Book of Kings as Story and History* (OBO 228; Fribourg: Academic Press; Göttingen: Vandenhoeck & Ruprecht, 2007), 147–73.

67. For a detailed discussion of this seal, see van der Veen, "Final Phase of Iron Age IIC," 1–26.

68. Ibid., 5–10. A rooster can also be seen on late Iron Age pottery from Gibeon (7).

69. The seal bears the honorific title *'bd hmlk* (servant of the king). Possibly it was carved when Ya'azanyahu was still an official of king Zedekiah, as implied by Jer. 40:7–8.

70. Gabriel Barkay, "A Bulla of Ishmael, the King's Son," *BASOR* 290–91 (1993): 109–14. A second bulla was more recently published by Robert Deutsch, *Biblical Period Hebrew Bullae: The Josef Chaim Kaufman Collection* (Tel Aviv: Archaeological Center Publications, 2003), 56–57n32.

71. See Peter G. van der Veen, "Beschriftete Siegel als Beweis für das biblische Israel? Gedalja und seine Mörder par exemple (eine Antwort an Bob Becking)," in *Wort und Stein: Studien*

A jar handle from Tel Goren/En Gedi was previously believed to refer to the king of Babylon by his Aramaic title *mr'*, but this reading is no longer accepted.[72]

The World of the Babylonian Deportees

Several passages in the Old Testament (e.g., in Ezra, Esther, and Daniel) relate to the life of the exilic Jewish community in Mesopotamia. Some Jews appear to have suffered a great deal in their new pagan surroundings (e.g., Pss. 79; 137; Isa. 40:27). In their view, life according to the Torah could be observed only within the God-given land of Israel, under Yahweh's protectorate. There the temple would be rebuilt and its cult restored. Other Jews, however, adapted more quickly to the new circumstances. This is what the prophet Jeremiah had advised them to do (Jer. 29:1–23). For them and their descendants, a return to an "empty and ruined" homeland would be hard to accept.[73] Ezekiel relates that Jews had settled at Tel Abib on the banks of the Kebar River,[74] in the region of Nippur (Ezek. 1:1; 3:15).[75] The so-called Murashu archive of a Jewish banker and trading company (455–403) mentions some twenty-eight settlements near Nippur that were home to Jewish families.

Almost one hundred additional cuneiform tablets have recently been studied. These also refer to Jewish citizens at Mesopotamian sites (e.g., at *alu ša Našar* and *al-Yaḥudu*), probably located in the Babylon-Borsippa region.[76] The name *al-Yaḥudu* stands out because it translates "City of Judah." Since this town is located in Babylonia and therefore cannot be equated with Jerusalem

---

zur Theologie und Archäologie; Festschrift für Udo Worschech (ed. Friedbert Ninow; BEAM 4; Frankfurt: Peter Lang, 2003), 253–55.

72. Gabriel Barkay, "The King of Babylonia or a Judean Official?," *IEJ* 45 (1995): 46. While the date of this jar handle can be no later than about 640 BCE, the inscription found above a winged sun-disc most likely reads *nrt*, as I was able to ascertain in 2001. I disagree with Barkay's reading, *nr'* ("Nera"), since the final letter is quite clearly a *taw*. See van der Veen, "Arabian Seals and Bullae," 33–35.

73. Also Josephus, *Ant.* 9.9.

74. Kebar River probably is Nar Kabari, which possibly is identical with the *šatt en-Nil*. This canal branches off the west bank of the Euphrates at Babylon and flows into it again farther to the south, near Ur.

75. Other places mentioned in the Old Testament where exiles resided are Tel-melah (probably URU *Malaḥanu*), located near Nippur at the Purat-Nippur, Tel-harsha, Cherub, Addan, and Immer (Ezra 2:59), places whose locations are unknown. Exiles are also said to have lived at Casiphia (unknown) and Ahava (perhaps ancient Ahwaz/Khwadsha at the Uqnu River in the Elamite Pekod-district). See Ezra 8:17, 21.

76. For a summary on this corpus, see Laurie E. Pearce, "New Evidence for Judeans in Babylonia," in Lipschits and Oeming, *Judah and the Judeans in the Persian Period*, 399–411.

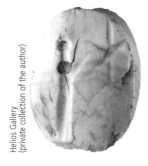

Figure 12.9. Unprovenanced official Neo-Babylonian stamp seal. The seal depicts a priest worshiping a star (sixth century BC).

(also called *al-Yaḥudu* in the Babylonian Chronicle of regnal year seven of Nebuchadnezzar), it is clear that it was meant to represent the "Babylonian Jerusalem."[77] One rendering of the latter name (URU *ša* LÚ *ia-a-ḫu-du-a-a*) emphasizes that its citizens came from Judah. The earliest texts within the new corpus date to regnal year thirty-three of Nebuchadnezzar (572).[78] Moreover, the so-called Weidner tablets (of regnal years ten through thirty-five of Nebuchadnezzar [595/594 and 570/569 BCE]), discovered in the southern citadel of Babylon, list monthly oil rations paid to a number of exiled foreign royals, citizens, and workmen. Among these we also find references to King "Ya'ukinu of Jakudu" (i.e., King Jehoiachin of Judah) and his sons.[79]

The First Returnees under Zerubbabel and Sheshbazzar

According to 2 Chronicles 36:22; Ezra 1:1–4; 6:1–5, King Cyrus of Persia (538–530) issued a decree during his first regnal year after the conquest of Babylon. The decree allowed the Jews to return home and rebuild the temple. Cyrus's friendly policy toward other nations and their gods is referred to on the so-called Cyrus Cylinder. It has often been quoted in support of the biblical text, although the inscription merely mentions peoples within Mesopotamia and Iran.[80] The first returnees came back under a governor named

77. This term was chosen by Francis Joannès and André Lemaire, "Trois tablettes cunéiformes à l'onomastique ouest-sémitique," *Transeu* 17 (1999): 26. Wilfred Lambert compares the name with "New York," "New Orleans," and the like ("A Document from a Community of Exiles in Babylonia," in Lubetski, *New Seals and Inscriptions*, 205). For further study of these new tablets, see Kathleen Abraham, "An Inheritance Division among Judeans in Babylonia from the Early Persian Period," in Lubetski, *New Seals and Inscriptions*, 206–21. According to Pearce ("New Evidence," 404), some five hundred different Jewish names could be read. She adds that out of perhaps six hundred persons, some 120 individuals bore names with theophoric elements composed of the divine name "Yahweh." See also Ran Zadok, *The Jews in Babylonia during the Chaldean and Achaemenian Periods according to Babylonian Sources* (SHJPLIMS 3; Haifa: University of Haifa, 1979).

78. The second-oldest tablet is from regnal year one of Amel-Marduk (561).

79. See Ernst F. Weidner, "Jojachin, König von Juda, in babylonischen Keilschrifttexten," in *Mélanges syriens offerts à Monsieur René Dussaud* (Paris: Geuthner, 1939), 2:923–35. Many of these tablets remain undeciphered and are kept in the Berlin Museum warehouse.

80. *ANET* 315–16. See also T. C. Mitchell, *The Bible in the British Museum: Interpreting the Evidence* (London: British Museum Publications, 1988), 83.

"Sheshbazzar" (Ezra 1:8, 11; 5:14).[81] Resettlement and building works on the temple were, however, hampered by drought (Hag. 1:9–11) and enmity with neighboring peoples (e.g., Ezra 3:3). During the second regnal year of King Darius I (520), at the time of the prophets Haggai and Zechariah, other Jewish exiles also returned home with their leader, Zerubbabel, the son or nephew of Shealtiel (1 Chron. 3:17, 19; Hag. 1:1, 14).[82] Although some scholars have suggested that these royal scions of the Davidic house could have enjoyed semi-independent status as vassal rulers at this time,[83] Nadav Na'aman has rightly argued that such a situation would not generally be in agreement with the overall policy of the early Achaemenid monarchs.[84] Although these men seem to have stirred the hopes of messianic expectations that God would soon restore the Davidic kingdom to Israel (Hag. 2:20–23; Zech. 8:1–8; 9:9–10), the influence of these governors must have been limited. The second temple was finally completed in 515 BCE.

Many scholars consider the biblical material in the book of Ezra to be late and unreliable, but others are willing to detect authentic information that could date back to the reign of Cyrus and his immediate successors. As Bob Becking correctly admits, few scholars so far have been willing to "bring in historical evidence as part of their discourse."[85] Nevertheless, this situation has improved during recent years.[86] For many scholars today, the concept of a grand return, as portrayed in Ezra 2 and Nehemiah 7, is as unacceptable as the idea of the "empty land" during the exilic period. Indeed, while population numbers in Judah drastically decreased after 586 BCE, these numbers did not substantially increase until the late Persian period. Despite some evidence of building activity at Jerusalem (albeit on a very small scale),[87] and at the main

81. This person probably was the same as Shenazzar, "a prince of Judah" and son of King Jehoiachin (1 Chron. 3:18).

82. On his pedigree, see Edelman, *Origins of the "Second" Temple*, 20–22.

83. So, e.g., André Lemaire, "Zorobabel et la Judée à la lumière de l'épigraphie (fin du VIe s. av. J.-C.)," *RB* 103 (1996): 48–57.

84. Nadav Na'aman, "Royal Vassals or Governors? On the Status of Sheshbazzar and Zerubabbel in the Persian Empire," *Henoch* 22 (2000): 35–44.

85. Bob Becking, "'We All Returned as One!': Critical Notes on the Myth of the Mass Return," in Lipschits and Oeming, *Judah and the Judeans in the Persian Period*, 5.

86. For some helpful recent volumes on the relevant period, see Lisbeth S. Fried, *The Priest and the Great King: Temple-Palace Relations in the Persian Empire* (BibJudSt 10; Winona Lake, IN: Eisenbrauns, 2004); Edelman, *Origins of the "Second" Temple*; Lipschits and Oeming, *Judah and the Judeans in the Persian Period*. For a slightly older book, but one still worth consulting, see Yamauchi, *Persia and the Bible*.

87. See esp. David Ussishkin, "The Borders and De Facto Size of Jerusalem in the Persian Period," in Lipschits and Oeming, *Judah and the Judeans in the Persian Period*, 147–66. But see also Oded Lipschits, "Persian Period Finds from Jerusalem: Facts and Interpretations," *JHS* 9 (2009): 1–30.

administrative centers of Ramat Raḥel and Mizpah (see above), resettlement
must have been slow and disappointing. This was especially true for those
who believed that God was about to restore Judah's former glory (Zech.
2:10–13; 10:10–12). Indeed, as I argued above, several cuneiform tablets (e.g.,
the Murashu archive from the reign of Darius II [423–405 BCE]) mention
Jewish citizens in Babylon and Persia and thus confirm that many Jews must
have preferred to remain "in exile," since life was more stable there.

Some inscribed evidence deserves mention here, as it relates to Zerububabel's
family members.[88] They are likely referred to in an unprovenanced archive of
bullae published by Nahman Avigad.[89] While most of the seal impressions
probably date to the fifth century BCE, one bulla may be from the late sixth
century. It belongs to a governor (*pḥw'*) Elnathan, who has been considered
to be the son-in-law of Zerubbabel. A seal (from the same archive) names a
woman called "Shelomit," who was the *'mt*, apparently of the same Elnathan.[90]
Although the word *'mh* can mean "maidservant," Eric Meyers has argued that
the connotation "woman of high standing" better fits the situation because
this female official signed documents in her own name, but with reference to
her husband, the governor.[91] She could well be the like-named daughter of
Zerubbabel, which would explain her high status (1 Chron. 3:19).[92] Finally, reference should also be made to another unprovenanced seal of a woman named
"Yehoyišma" (written in Paleo-Hebrew script) and her father, Šâwaššar'uṣur,
who bears a good Neo-Babylonian name written in late sixth-century Aramaic script. As has been argued, this person may well have belonged to the
early group of settlers who returned to their homeland at the end of the sixth
century BCE.[93]

88. Another member of this family, not referred to here, may be the fifth-century-BCE
Hananiah, named on stamped jar handles as an official of the province of Yehud. As has been
argued by some, he could have been another son of Zerubbabel (1 Chron. 3:19). A certain
Hananiah also held high positions in Jerusalem (Neh. 7:2–3). On this, see Edelman, *Origins of
the "Second" Temple*, 26–30.

89. Nahman Avigad, *Bullae and Seals from a Post-Exilic Judean Archive* (Qedem 4; Jerusalem: Institute of Archaeology, Hebrew University of Jerusalem, 1976).

90. Ibid., 11–13n14.

91. Eric M. Meyers, "The Shelomith Seal and the Judean Restoration—Some Additional
Considerations," *ErIsr* 18 (1985): 33–38. See also Rainer Kessler, "Die Sklavin als Ehefrau: Zur
Stellung der *'āmāh*," *VT* 52 (2002): 501–12.

92. On this pedigree, see Edelman, *Origins of the "Second" Temple*, 23, 30–31, with literature. A black seal inscribed with the same name was recently unearthed in the City of David in
debris from the Babylonian period. However, since no title or patronym is given, any identity
of persons must remain speculative. See Mazar, *Palace of King David*, 78–79.

93. Nahman Avigad and Benjamin Sass, *Corpus of West Semitic Stamp Seals* (Jerusalem:
The Israel Academy of Sciences and Humanities, 1997), 403n1071.

Imperial Aramaic

Imperial Aramaic (the Aramaic language spoken during the Neo-Babylonian period) was the official language used by the Persian administrative elite. It was introduced as the lingua franca of the empire during the reign of King Darius I. This unified language was the only means to cope with the international politics and correspondence of the vast Achaemenid Empire, which spread from Upper Egypt in the southwest, to Anatolia in the northwest, and eastward to the Indus Valley. Imperial Aramaic was formally standardized in both script and orthography. Because it was influenced by the Persian mother tongue of the Achaemenid monarchs, it proved to be a flexible language. Many documents were written in imperial Aramaic (e.g., some 15,000 to 30,000 tablets and fragments were uncovered at Persepolis), while fine pieces of literature, such as the famous Wisdom of Ahiqar, were composed in it. In Old Testament books from the Persian period, we encounter portions written in Imperial Aramaic, such as in the books of Ezra (4:8–6:18) and Daniel (2:4b–7:28).

The Rebuilding of the Temple as a Reliable Source

Many scholars have doubted the building report on the second temple in Ezra 1–6,[94] but Lisbeth Fried has recently argued that the story makes good sense in light of traditional ancient Near Eastern building inscriptions and alongside additional historical evidence from the period.[95] Once it is understood that the biblical writer simply rearranged the material that he had assembled from an existing bilingual building inscription (which, unfortunately, no longer exists), one can accept with relative certainty that building works had indeed begun under Cyrus. At that time the "former-times stone" (a stone taken from the first temple) was set aside during a traditional *kalû* celebration, and the old temple was ritually demolished through lamentation (Ezra 3:10a, 12; Zech. 7:1–3). Subsequently, Zerubbabel would have brought out this particular stone to incorporate it in the new temple during its final stages of completion (Zech. 4:7). While the first returnees would have brought with them the cultic vessels of the first temple (Ezra 1:9–11),[96] there is no reason to doubt that the second temple was indeed completed in the sixth regnal year of Darius I (515).

94. See, e.g., Lipschits, "Judah, Jerusalem," 141.
95. Fried, *The Priest and the Great King*, 156–77.
96. These would have been stored at the Esagil temple of Babylon.

13

Fifth- and Fourth-Century Issues

Governorship and Priesthood in Jerusalem

ANDRÉ LEMAIRE

The fifth and fourth centuries BCE were often considered obscure centuries in the history of ancient Israel. The historiographical tradition of the books of Ezra and Nehemiah posed many problems, the archaeology of this period was difficult to specify, and there were few inscriptions from this period that could be related to the Israelites. This state of the documentation improved somewhat for archaeology,[1] epigraphy,[2] and numismatics[3] during the last thirty

1. See Ephraim Stern, *Material Culture of the Land of the Bible in the Persian Period, 538–332 B.C.* (Warminster, UK: Aris & Phillips; Jerusalem: Israel Exploration Society, 1982); see also the following articles, all titled "Archéologie": J. Briend and J. Sapin, *Transeu* 1 (1989): 147–54; J. Sapin, *Transeu* 4 (1991): 103–11; J. Briend and J. Sapin, *Transeu* 10 (1995): 125–44; J. Sapin and J. Briend, *Transeu* 17 (1999): 89–110; J. Briend and J. Sapin, *Transeu* 24 (2002): 113–35; idem, *Transeu* 32 (2006): 163–83.

2. See André Lemaire, "Les inscriptions palestiniennes d'époque perse: Un bilan provisoire," *Transeu* 1 (1989): 87–106; see also the following articles by idem, all titled "Épigraphie": *Transeu* 4 (1991): 113–18; *Transeu* 10 (1995): 145–50; *Transeu* 17 (1999): 111–16; *Transeu* 24 (2002): 137–41; *Transeu* 32 (2006): 185–94.

3. See the following articles by J. Elayi and A. Lemaire, all titled "Numismatique": *Transeu* 1 (1989): 155–64; *Transeu* 4 (1991): 119–32; *Transeu* 10 (1995): 151–87; *Transeu* 17 (1999): 117–53; *Transeu* 25 (2003): 63–105; *Transeu* 33 (2007): 23–82.

years. Several books have tried a new synthesis,[4] but many problems and lacunae remain.[5] One of the difficulties for this period is to appreciate the relative importance of the relations between the people in the provinces of Yehud and Samaria, on the one hand, and the Diaspora, on the other. Both groups were living in the same Achaemenid and early Hellenistic Empires. Actually, it is impossible to understand Yehud during the Persian period without taking into account its relation with the Diaspora as shown by the personal story of the two main personages of this period: Nehemiah and Ezra. Furthermore, the books of Ezra and Nehemiah, which were one book, probably were written at the beginning of the Hellenistic period, at a time where there was no longer a governor of Yehud and when the high priests were the main Jewish authorities (see their list until Alexander in Neh. 12).[6]

Yehud in the Fifth Century BCE

We have very few documents for the history of the Yehud province at the beginning of the fifth century BCE. A few allusions by Nehemiah to the anterior situation seem to indicate that things were bad: "Those still remaining in the province who had survived the captivity were facing great trouble and reproach; the wall of Jerusalem was broken down, and the gates had been destroyed by fire" (Neh. 1:3).[7] Even if we take into account the aim of this description to justify the rebuilding of the wall, there probably was some basis

4. See Rainer Albertz, *From the Exile to the Maccabees* (vol. 2 of *A History of Israelite Religion in the Old Testament Period*; OTL; Louisville: Westminster John Knox, 1994), 437–533; Lester L. Grabbe, *The Persian and Greek Periods* (vol. 1 of *Judaism from Cyrus to Hadrian*; Minneapolis: Fortress, 1992), 27–220; Ernest-Marie Laperrousaz and André Lemaire, eds., *La Palestine à l'époque perse* (ÉABJ; Paris: Cerf, 1994); Reinhard G. Kratz, ed., *Religion und Religionskontakte im Zeitalter der Achämeniden* (VWGT 22; Gütersloh: Kaiser/Gütersloher Verlagshaus, 2002); Lester L. Grabbe, *Yehud: A History of the Persian Province of Judah* (vol. 1 of *A History of the Jews and Judaism in the Second Temple Period*; LSTS 47; London: T&T Clark, 2004); Oded Lipschits and Manfred Oeming, eds., *Judah and the Judeans in the Persian Period* (Winona Lake, IN: Eisenbrauns, 2006); Oded Lipschits, Gary N. Knoppers, and Rainer Albertz, eds., *Judah and the Judeans in the Fourth Century B.C.E.* (Winona Lake, IN: Eisenbrauns, 2007); Joseph Blenkinsopp, *Judaism, the First Phase: The Place of Ezra and Nehemiah in the Origins of Judaism* (Grand Rapids: Eerdmans, 2009); Daniel Bodi, *Israël et Juda: À l'ombre des Babyloniens et des Perses* (ÉAHA; Paris: De Boccard, 2010); Oded Lipschits, Gary N. Knoppers, and Manfred Oeming, eds., *Judah and the Judeans in the Achaemenid Period: Negotiating Identity in an International Context* (Winona Lake, IN: Eisenbrauns, 2011).

5. Diana Vikander Edelman, "Apples and Oranges: Textual and Archaeological Evidence for Reconstructing the History of Yehud in the Persian Period," in *Congress Volume: Helsinki 2010* (ed. Martti Nissinen; VTSup 148; Leiden: Brill, 2012), 133–44.

6. Grabbe, *Persian and Greek Periods*, 32.

7. Scripture translations in this chapter are by the author.

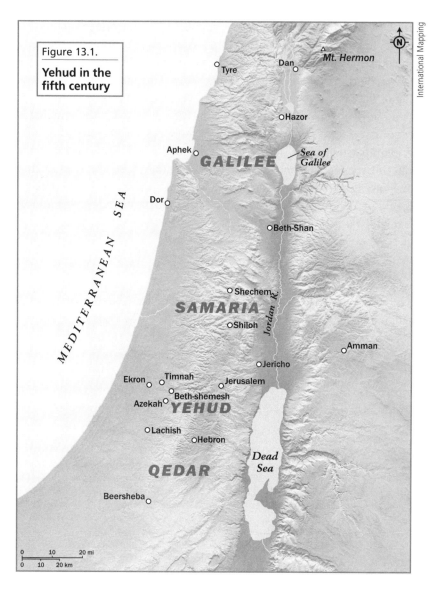

Figure 13.1.

Yehud in the fifth century

International Mapping

to this statement. Jerusalem was still an open city and, for this reason, could not be the capital of the province. The capital was at Mizpah after the fall of Jerusalem (2 Kings 25:22–26).

There were governors (*pĕḥôt*) at the head of the province, and they used "to lay a heavy burden on the people, exacting from them a daily toll of bread and wine to the value of forty shekels of silver. Their servants acted as tyrants toward the people" (Neh. 5:15). The names of some of these governors probably appear on several bullae published by Nahman Avigad.[8] A seal belonging to the same group and inscribed "belonging to Shelomit maidservant[9] of El-nathan the gov[ernor]" (no. 14) may help us to understand how the Judean governorship left the Davidic dynasty.[10] In fact, this Shelomit could well be Shelomit daughter of Zerubbabel, mentioned in 1 Chronicles 3:19. The governor Elnathan (bulla no. 5) would then be the son-in-law of Zerubbabel.[11] In this context the bulla inscribed "Yehud, Hananah" might belong to Hananiah the son of Zerubbabel and brother of Shelomit (1 Chron. 3:19), who might have been governor of Yehud before Elnathan. Other names of governors may appear on contemporary Yehud seal impressions, but their date is difficult to specify.[12] These Yehud stamps were probably connected with collecting taxes in kind, a system that went on well into the Hellenistic period. Ramat Raḥel/Beit-Hakerem could well have been used as a warehouse where these taxes were collected.[13]

The date of the mission of Nehemiah is indicated in his book as "the twentieth year" (Neh. 1:1) of King Artaxerxes. Most of the commentators agree that this Artaxerxes is Artaxerxes I. Thus the date would be 445 BCE. According to 1:11, Nehemiah was "king's cupbearer" in Susa, and he asked to be sent to Judah, to the city where his ancestors were buried, so that he might "rebuild it" (2:5). These indications make clear that Nehemiah was mainly concerned with Jerusalem, and that he wanted to make it again the capital of the province of Judah after some 142 years of the capital being at Mizpah. Probably by the use of forced labor, he restored the walls of Jerusalem (primarily its gates) in fifty-two days (6:15). Since Jerusalem was then depopulated,[14] he drew from the outlying villages "to bring one in every ten to live in Jerusalem" (11:1), especially priests and Levites. From that time onward,

---

8. Nahman Avigad, *Bullae and Seals from a Post-Exilic Judean Archive* (Qedem 4; Jerusalem: Institute of Archaeology, Hebrew University of Jerusalem, 1976). See also André Lemaire, "Das Achämenidische Juda und seine Nachbarn im Lichte der Epigraphie," in Kratz, *Religion und Religionskontakte*, 210–30, esp. 215–16.

9. Here "maidservant" (*'mt*) probably indicates the relation of a wife to her husband.

10. Bernard Gosse, "La disparition de la dynastie davidique," *Transeu* 39 (2010): 97–112, esp. 97–100.

11. André Lemaire, review of Nahman Avigad, *Bullae and Seals from a Post-Exilic Judean Archive*, *Syria* 54 (1977): 129–31; idem, "Populations et territoires de la Palestine à l'époque perse," *Transeu* 3 (1990): 31–74, esp. 34; see also Eric M. Meyers, "The Shelomith Seal and the Judean Restoration—Some Additional Considerations," *ErIsr* 18 (1985): 33–38.

12. Oded Lipschits and David Vanderhooft, "A New Typology of the Yehud Stamp Impressions," *TA* 34 (2007): 12–37; idem, *The Yehud Stamp Impressions: A Corpus of Inscribed Impressions from the Persian and Hellenistic Periods in Judah* (Winona Lake, IN: Eisenbrauns, 2011).

13. Lipschits and Vanderhooft, *Yehud Stamp Impressions*, 760–63.

14. On the problem of the population of Jerusalem during the Persian period, see Oded Lipschits, "Persian Period Finds from Jerusalem: Facts and Interpretations," *JHS* 9 (2011): 1–30.

Jerusalem again became the capital of the province of Judah. The Jerusalem temple apparently was used for collecting taxes in kind (10:37–39) as well as in silver ("yearly the third of a shekel" [10:32]).

In the context of this revival of Jerusalem, Nehemiah proclaimed economic measures for the whole population of the province.[15] He convinced the creditors to stop taking persons as pledges for debts and to give back to the debtors "their fields and vineyards, their olive groves and houses" (Neh. 5:11–12). This freeing of slaves and remission of debts was known during the First Temple period (Jer. 34:8–17; cf. Deut. 15:12–15),[16] as well as in the ancient Near East. However, it was always difficult to implement. Nehemiah himself claims to have given up the tax in kind, described as "the food/bread of the governor" (Neh. 5:14, 18).

After twelve years of governorship (Neh. 5:14), Nehemiah presented the report of his activity to Artaxerxes in Babylon in 433 (13:6). Parts of his report may have been reused in the book of Nehemiah. After some time, he may have returned to Jerusalem. The reforms attributed to him (Neh. 13) are essentially measures concerning the temple and the cult. They emphasize the role of the priests and the Levites. Their attribution to Nehemiah the governor is somewhat problematic. This may suggest that the chapter was reworked in a final redaction.

Epigraphic Evidence of the Late Fifth Century BCE

We do not know much about Yehud at the end of the fifth century BCE, after Nehemiah. We have only some information from Elephantine papyrus 30/31, a letter from "Yedanyah and his colleagues, the priests who are in Elephantine the fortress." They wrote to "Bagohi governor of Judah" (407).[17] The same letter mentions "Yehohanan the High Priest and his colleagues who are in Jerusalem," "Ostanes, the brother of Anani and the nobles of the Jews," as well as "Delaiah and Shelemiah, sons of Sanballat, governor of Samaria."

This reference to the sons of Sanballat probably indicates that Sin-uballiṭ/

15. See Kenneth D. Tollefson and H. G. M. Williamson, "Nehemiah as Cultural Revitalization: An Anthropological Perspective," *JSOT* 56 (1992): 41–68.

16. Bob Becking, "Drought, Hunger, and Redistribution: A Social Economic Reading of Nehemiah 5," in *The Historian and the Bible: Essays in Honour of Lester L. Grabbe* (ed. Philip R. Davies and Diana Vikander Edelman; LHBOTS 530; London: T&T Clark, 2010), 137–49.

17. Arthur E. Cowley, ed. and trans., *Aramaic Papyri of the Fifth Century B.C.* (Oxford: Clarendon, 1923), 108–22; Bezalel Porten and Ada Yardeni, *Textbook of Aramaic Documents from Ancient Egypt* (4 vols.; Jerusalem: Department of the History of the Jewish People, Hebrew University; Winona Lake, IN: Eisenbrauns, 1986–1999), 1:68–75.

Sanballat, the governor of Samaria and a contemporary of Nehemiah (Neh. 2:10, 19; 3:33 [4:1 ET]; 4:1 [7 ET]; 6:1–2, 5, 12, 14; 13:28), had recently died.[18] In Elephantine, Yedaniah did not yet know which son succeeded Sanballat. According to the later Wadi Daliyeh documents and the Samaria coins, the successor of Sanballat probably was Delaiah.[19] These Elephantine and Wadi Daliyeh documents complement Nehemiah 12:10–23 and allow us to specify somewhat the succession of the high priests in Jerusalem during the second half of the fifth century: Elyashib (Ezra 10:6; Neh. 12:10–11, 22–23), Yoyada (Neh. 12:10, 22), and Y(eh)ohanan (Ezra 10:6; Neh. 12:22–23; Elephantine).[20]

> ## High Priests in Jerusalem in Nehemiah 12
>
> Nehemiah 12:10–11: "Yeshua was the father of Yoyaqim, Yoyaqim the father of Elyashib, Elyashib the father of Yoyada, Yoyada the father of Yonatan, and Yonatan the father of Yaddua."
>
> Nehemiah 12:22: "The heads of the Levite and priestly families in the days of Elyashib, Yoyada, Yohanan, and Yaddua were recorded down to the reign of Darius the Persian."
>
> Verse 10: "Yonatan" must be corrected to "Yohanan," according to verse 22.
>
> Verse 22: "Darius" here is probably Darius III, the Persian king defeated by Alexander the Great.

Furthermore, one may note that the names of the two sons of Sanballat are clearly Yahwistic. Probably most of the population in the province of Samaria considered themselves Israelites. Recent excavations seem to have revealed that the first "Israelite" sanctuary on Mount Gerizim was built in the fifth century.[21] This Gerizim temple probably was built by Sanballat during Darius II's reign (424–405).[22] This is more likely than Darius III, as suggested by Josephus Flavius (*Ant.* 11.310).[23]

18. On Sanballat, see Siegfried Mittmann, "Tobia, Sanballat und die persische Provinz Juda," *JNSL* 26 (2000): 1–50, esp. 13–17; Jan Dušek, "Archaeology and Texts in the Persian Period: Focus on Sanballat," in Nissinen, *Congress Volume: Helsinki 2010*, 117–32.

19. See Jan Dušek, *Les manuscrits araméens du Wadi Daliyeh et la Samarie vers 450–332 av. J.-C.* (CHANE 30; Leiden: Brill, 2007), 602–5.

20. Ibid., 588.

21. Yitzhak Magen, Haggai Misgav, and Levanna Tsfania, *The Aramaic, Hebrew and Samaritan Inscriptions* (vol. 1 of *Mount Gerizim Excavations*; JSPub 2; Jerusalem: Israel Antiquities Authority, 2004), 3–6; Yitzhak Magen, *A Temple City* (vol. 2 of *Mount Gerizim Excavations*; JSPub 8; Jerusalem: Israel Antiquities Authority, 2008), 97–169.

22. Rainer Albertz, "The Controversy about Judeans versus Israelite Identity and the Persian Government: A New Interpretation of the Bagoses Story (*Jewish Antiquities* XI.297–301)," in Lipschits, Knoppers, and Oeming, *Judah and the Judeans in the Achaemenid Period*, 483–504, esp. 490.

23. Yitzhak Magen, "The Dating of the First Phase of the Samaritan Temple on Mount Gerizim in Light of the Archaeological Evidence," in Lipschits, Knoppers, and Albertz, *Judah and the Judeans in the Fourth Century B.C.E.*, 157–211; Dušek, *Les manuscrits araméens*, 603–4.

The Elephantine documents provide more than raw data about high functionaries in the province of Judah and Samaria toward the end of the fifth century. They are most important because they illuminate the life of a Judaean community in the Diaspora during that period. Most of the members of this community apparently were mercenaries in the Persian army. They probably were established in Elephantine from the seventh century and had built a temple to Yahô, their god. Their temple was destroyed during a riot in 410. In addition to the letters, we have contracts dealing with daily life (marriages, sales, wills, dowries, etc.).[24] To these may be added accounts and other lists[25] and ostraca.[26] All this documentation is written in Aramaic. Several papyri also contain some Aramaic literature, especially proverbs as well as the Novel of Ahiqar, probably used as reference literature in the local Aramaic school.[27] In this context, one may note that among 130 witnesses, only 5 did not write their own signatures.[28] The whole Achaemenid Empire used Aramaic as a written language, as at Elephantine. However, these Jewish mercenaries retained their ethnicity. They are labeled as "Judaeans" (YHDY'). Although they intermarried with the local populace,[29] their documents (ostraca as well as papyri) show that they kept their names, their religion (their god, "Yaho/Yaho Ṣeba'ot"), their temple,[30] their feasts (Shabbat, Passover, and Mazzot),[31] and their rituals (sacrifices, fasts, mourning, and purity).[32]

24. Porten and Yardeni, *Textbook of Aramaic Documents*, vol. 2.

25. Ibid., 3:72–281.

26. Ibid., 4:151–213; supplemented by Hélène Lozachmeur, *La collection Clermont-Ganneau: Ostraca, épigraphes sur jarre, étiquettes de bois* (MPAIBL 35; Paris: De Boccard, 2006); André Lemaire, review of Hélène Lozachmeur, *La collection Clermont-Ganneau: Ostraca, épigraphes sur jarre, étiquettes de bois*, *Transeu* 34 (2007): 177–83; idem, "Judean Identity in Elephantine: Everyday Life according to the Ostraca," in Lipschits, Knoppers, and Oeming, *Judah and the Judeans in the Achaemenid Period*, 365–73.

27. Porten and Yardeni, *Textbook of Aramaic Documents*, 3:22–71.

28. Ernst A. Knauf, "Elephantine und das vor-biblische Judentum," in Kratz, *Religion und Religionskontakte*, 179–88, esp. 182. Aramaic was also the main administrative language in Yehud. See David Vanderhooft, "*'el-mĕdînâ ûmĕdînâ kiktābāh*: Scribes and Scripts in Yehud and in Achaemenid Transeuphratene," in Lipschits, Knoppers, and Oeming, *Judah and the Judeans in the Achaemenid Period*, 529–44.

29. Hélène Nutkowicz, "Les mariages mixtes à Éléphantine à l'époque perse," *Transeu* 36 (2008): 125–39.

30. See Reinhard G. Kratz, "The Second Temple of Jeb and of Jerusalem," in Lipschits and Oeming, *Judah and the Judeans in the Persian Period*, 247–64.

31. See E. Gass, "Der Passa-Papyrus (Cowl 21¹)—Mythos oder Realität?," *BN* 99 (1999): 55–68.

32. Paul-Eugène Dion, "La religion des papyrus d'Éléphantine: Un reflet du Juda d'avant l'exil," in *Kein Land für sich allein: Studien zum Kulturkontakt in Kanaan, Israel/Palästina und Ebirnâri für Manfred Weippert zum 65. Geburtstag* (ed. Ulrich Hübner and Ernst A. Knauf; OBO 186; Freiburg: Universitätsverlag; Göttingen: Vandenhoeck & Ruprecht, 2002), 243–54; Reinhard G. Kratz, "Zwischen Elephantine und Qumran: Das Alte Testament im Rahmen des

The Elephantine documents, both the papyri and the ostraca, date essentially to the fifth century. They are clearly connected with the integration of Egypt within the Achaemenid Empire.[33] This Judaean community does not seem to have survived after the end of Persian domination in Elephantine, in 399[34] or 398.[35]

Diaspora in the Fifth Century BCE

Turning eastward to the Babylonian Diaspora, we see that it was more numerous than the Jewish presence in Egypt. It also played an important role for more than a millennium. For these Jewish communities in the early fifth century, we now have previously unpublished documentation: part of the so-called al-Yahudu Neo-Babylonian tablets dating from Nebuchadnezzar's 33rd regnal year (572) to Xerxes I's 9th regnal year (477). An initial group has been published by Francis Joannès and André Lemaire.[36] Kathleen Abraham has published additional texts.[37] The remaining documents are to be published by Laurie

---

antiken Judentums," in *Congress Volume: Ljubljana 2007* (ed André Lemaire; VTSup 133; Leiden: Brill, 2010), 129–46, esp. 140–43; Lemaire, "Judean Identity in Elephantine"; Bob Becking, "Yehudite Identity in Elephantine," in Lipschits, Knoppers, and Oeming, *Judah and the Judeans in the Achaemenid Period*, 403–19; Anke Joisten-Pruschke, *Das religiöse Leben der Juden von Elephantine in der Achämenidenzeit* (Göttinger Orientforschungen 3. Iranica, N.F. 2. Wiesbaden: Harrassowitz, 2008).

33. I. Kottsieper, "Die Religionspolitik der Achämeniden und die Juden von Elephantine," in Kratz, *Religion und Religionskontakte*, 150–78.

34. Bezalel Porten, *Archives from Elephantine: The Life of an Ancient Jewish Military Colony* (Berkeley: University of California Press, 1968); Porten and Yardeni, *Textbook of Aramaic Documents*, 4:234; Hélène Nutkowicz, "Éléphantine, ultime tragédie," *Transeu* 40 (2011): 185–98.

35. Pierre Grelot, *Documents araméens d'Égypte* (LAPO 5; Paris: Cerf, 1972) 59, 420–23; André Lemaire, "Recherches d'épigraphie araméenne en Asie Mineure et en Égypte et le problème de l'acculturation," in *Asia Minor and Egypt: Old Cultures in a New Empire* (ed. Heleen Sancisi-Weerdenburg and Amélie Kuhrt; AH 6; Leiden: Nederlands Instituut voor het Nabije Oosten, 1991), 199–206, esp. 199–201; idem, "La stèle araméenne d'Assouan (RES 438, 1806): Nouvel examen," in *Intertestamental Essays in Honour of Józef Tadeusz Milik* (ed. Zdzisław J. Kapera; QM 6; Kraków: Enigma, 1992), 289–304; idem, "La fin de la première période perse en Égypte et la chronologie judéenne vers 400 av. J.-C.," *Transeu* 9 (1995): 51–62, esp. 51–56.

36. Francis Joannès and André Lemaire, "Contrats babyloniens d'époque achéménide du Bît-Abi Râm avec une épigraphe araméenne," *RA* 90 (1996): 41–60; idem, "Trois tablettes cunéiformes à l'onomastique ouest-sémitique," *Transeu* 17 (1999): 17–34; Wilfred G. Lambert, "A Document from a Community of Exiles in Babylonia," in *New Seals and Inscriptions, Hebrew, Idumean and Cuneiform* (ed. Meir Lubetski; HBM 8; Sheffield: Sheffield Phoenix Press, 2007), 201–5.

37. Kathleen Abraham, "West Semitic and Judean Brides in Cuneiform Sources from the Sixth Century BCE: New Evidence from a Marriage Contract from Al-Yahudu," *AfO* 51 (2005–2006): 198–219; idem, "An Inheritance Division among Judeans in Babylonia from the Early Persian Period," in Lubetski, *New Seals and Inscriptions*, 206–21.

Pearce[38] and Cornelia Wunsch.[39] Laurie Pearce states, "The administrative and legal texts preserve details that facilitate a limited but supportable and consistent view of the status of the Judeans from the Babylonian perspective in the Neo-Babylonian and Achemenid periods."[40] Also, "The picture that emerges is that of a group of 'ethnically' homogenous state dependents, concentrated in a town named for their place of origin [āl-Yāhūdu]. Like their counterparts in the Murašû texts, Judeans at āl-Yāhūdu participated in economic activity in ways that indicate they were wholly integrated into the Babylonian state structure and practices."[41] This double aspect is clear from the fact that two of the three dēkû officials bear Yahwistic names: "These Judeans served in official capacities within their own community," according to Pearce.[42] "Documents from āl-Yāhūdu and surrounding towns provide a glimpse of the activities and status of Judean deportees to Babylonia from the time shortly after the start of the exile to the period in which the Murašû documentation begins."[43]

The Murashu archive[44] dates in the second half of the fifth century BCE (454–404). It is essentially a family archive of some 740 tablets recording business operations conducted by a Nippur family and their agents. Although members of the family paid visits to Susa and Babylon, they were essentially active around Nippur, with about one-third of the people having non-Baby-

38. Laurie Pearce, "New Evidence for Judeans in Babylonia," in Lipschits and Oeming, *Judah and the Judeans in the Persian Period*, 399–411; Laurie Pearce and Cornelia Wunsch, *Into the Hands of Many Peoples: Judeans and West Semitic Exiles in Mesopotamia* (CUSAS 18; Bethesda, MD: CDL Press, forthcoming).

39. Cornelia Wunsch, "Glimpses on the Lives of Deportees in Rural Babylonia," in *Arameans, Chaldeans, and Arabs in Babylonia and Palestine in the First Millennium B.C.* (ed. Angelika Berlejung and Michael P. Streck; Leipziger Altorientalistische Studien 3; Wiesbaden: Harrassowitz, 2013), 247–60; idem, *Judeans by the Waters of Babylon: New Historical Evidence in Sources from Rural Babylonia; Texts from the Schøyen Collection* (BabAr 3; Dresden: ISLET-Verlag, forthcoming).

40. Laurie Pearce, "'Judean': A Special Status in Neo-Babylonian and Achemenid Babylonia?," in Lipschits, Knoppers, and Oeming, *Judah and the Judeans in the Achaemenid Period*, 267–77, esp. 269.

41. Ibid., 271.

42. Ibid., 273.

43. Ibid., 274.

44. Guillaume Cardascia, ed. and trans., *Les archives des Murašû: Une famille d'hommes d'affaires babyloniens à l'époque perse (455–403 av. J.-C.)* (Paris: Imprimerie Nationale, 1951); Elias J. Bickerman, "The Babylonian Captivity," in *Introduction; The Persian Period* (vol. 1 of *The Cambridge History of Judaism*; ed. W. D. Davies and Louis Finkelstein; Cambridge: Cambridge University Press, 1984), 342–58; Matthew W. Stolper, *Entrepreneurs and Empire: The Murašû Archive, the Murašû Firm, and Persian Rule in Babylonia* (UNHAII 54; Leiden: Brill, 1985); idem, "Fifth Century Nippur: Texts of the Murašûs and from Their Surroundings," *JCS* 53 (2001): 83–132; Veysel Donbaz and Matthew W. Stolper, *Istanbul Murašû Texts* (UNHAII 79; Istanbul: Nederlands Historisch-Archeologisch Instituut, 1997).

Al-Yahudu Cuneiform Tablet (498 BCE)

1. 1 calf, two years old, white, the top of the huruppu . . . , which
3. Haraʾa, daughter of Talimmu,
6. sold to Neri-Yama, son of Ahu-yaqam,
4. for 23 shekels of white silver, ⅛th per shekel impure,
5. average quality, lacking the mark, as the fixed price.
11. Yahu-azari, son of Abdy-Yahu, accepts responsibility for future claims over
8. 1 calf, two years old, white, the top of the huruppu . . .
15. Haraʾa has received from Neri-Yama, and has been paid,
13. 23 shekels of white silver, ⅛th per shekel impure,
14. average quality, lacking the mark, the price of the calf.

Witnesses:

16. Yahu-azari, son of Tabshalammu
17. Nadabi-Yama, son of Sa(ssu)duqu
18. Nahhum, son of Yahu-azari
19. Bunene-ibni, son of Bel-kalamu
21. Abdu-Yahu, son of Shamaʾ-Yama
22. and the scribe: Anu-ahhe-iqisha, son of Ardi-Innin
23. Yahudu, month Tammuz, 19th day,
24. 24th year of Darius,
25. king of Babylon, king of the lands.[a]

Figure 13.2. The recto and obverse sides of the al-Yahudu tablet 1

a. Francis Joannès and André Lemaire, "Trois tablettes cunéiformes à l'onomastique ouest-sémitique," *Transeu* 17 (1999): 17–27; Wilfred G. Lambert, "A Document from a Community of Exiles in Babylonia," in *New Seals and Inscriptions, Hebrew, Idumean and Cuneiform* (ed. Meir Lubetski; HBM 8; Sheffield: Sheffield Phoenix Press, 2007), 201–5.

lonian names.[45] There is no indication that this family was a Judean/Jewish family. Only about 4 percent of the names are typically Jewish.[46]

45. Israel Ephʿal, "On the Political and Social Organization of the Jews in Babylonian Exile," in *XXI. Deutscher Orientalistentag: Vom 24. bis 29. März 1980 in Berlin* (ed. Fritz Steppat; ZDMGSup 5; Wiesbaden: Franz Steiner, 1983), 106–12, esp. 109.

46. Michael D. Coogan, "Patterns in Jewish Personal Names in the Diaspora," *JSJ* 4 (1973): 183–91; idem, "Life in the Diaspora: Jews at Nippur in the Fifth Century BC," *BA* 37 (1974): 6–12; idem, *West Semitic Personal Names in the Murašū Documents* (HSM 7; Missoula, MT: Scholars Press, 1976); Matthew W. Stolper, "A Note on Yahwistic Personal Names in the Murašû Texts," *BASOR* 222 (1976): 25–28.

Thus the picture is very different from the al-Yahudu archive. The Murashu archive suggests that the Jewish people are only a very small local minority. They do not form a distinct local enclave. These ordinary people, such as small landowners, petty officials, and witnesses, give Babylonian names to their children. They seem more or less assimilated into the general population of Babylonia. This assimilation[47] might provide the background for the reaction of the Jewish leaders (Nehemiah and Ezra) against intermarriage when they came back to the country of their ancestors.

The Mission of Ezra

The role and date of the mission of Ezra have been much discussed. In the present state of the books of Ezra and Nehemiah, both personages are presented as contemporary, but a detailed study of these books show that this presentation is artificial.[48] The story concerning Nehemiah was originally independent from the one concerning Ezra. In the book of Nehemiah, Ezra appears only in chapter 8. The mention of Nehemiah in Nehemiah 8:9 is missing in the Septuagint. Nehemiah 8–9 seems to have chronologically followed Ezra 7–10. Furthermore, the mention of Ezra in Nehemiah 12:26, 36 could well have been added by a final redactor.[49] In this context, one may date both leaders during the reign of an Artaxerxes: Ezra in the seventh year (Ezra 7:7) and Nehemiah in the twentieth year (Neh. 1:1). However, it might not be in the reign of the same Artaxerxes. Commentators propose two interpretations. Many commentators follow the presentation of the books of Ezra and Nehemiah and date the mission of Ezra in the seventh regnal year of Artaxerxes I (458).[50] Others date Ezra *after* Nehemiah, in the seventh year of Artaxerxes II (398).[51]

47. Ran Zadok, *The Earliest Diaspora: Israelites and Judeans in Pre-Hellenistic Mesopotamia* (PDRI 151; Tel Aviv: Diaspora Research Institute, Tel Aviv University, 2002), 57–61.

48. See, e.g., Sara Japhet, "Periodization and Ideology II: Chronology and Ideology in Ezra-Nehemiah," in Lipschits and Oeming, *Judah and the Judeans in the Persian Period*, 491–508, esp. 501.

49. Judson R. Shaver, "Ezra and Nehemiah: On the Theological Significance of Making Them Contemporaries," in *Priests, Prophets, and Scribes: Essays on the Formation and Heritage of Second Temple Judaism in Honour of Joseph Blenkinsopp* (ed. Eugene Ulrich et al.; JSOTSup 149; Sheffield: JSOT Press, 1992), 76–86.

50. See, e.g., H. G. M. Williamson, *Ezra, Nehemiah* (WBC 16; Waco: Word, 1985), xxxix–xliv; Joseph Blenkinsopp, *Ezra-Nehemiah* (OTL; Philadelphia: Westminster, 1988), 139–44.

51. Albin Van Hoonacker, "Néhémie et Esdras," *Le Muséon* 9 (1890): 151–84, 317–51, 389–401; idem, *Néhémie en l'an 20 d'Artaxerxès I: Esdras en l'an 7 d'Artaxerxès II; Réponse à un mémoire de A. Kuenen* (Leipzig: H. Engelcke, 1892); idem, "La question Néhémie et Esdras," *RB* 4 (1895): 186–92; H. H. Rowley, "The Chronological Order of Ezra and Nehemiah," in *The*

One can present several arguments in favor of this second historical dating:

1. Nehemiah 8 would date the official reading of the law brought by Ezra at least thirteen years after his arrival in Jerusalem. This gap is difficult to explain.
2. In his "memoirs" Nehemiah makes no reference to the law brought by Ezra.
3. When Ezra arrives in Jerusalem, the town has a city-wall (*gādēr* in Ezra 9:9) with many inhabitants (*qāhāl rab-mě'ōd* in Ezra 10:1).
4. Ezra is a contemporary of "Yehohanan son of Elyashib" (Ezra 10:6), who could well be the same as "Yehohanan the High Priest" in Elephantine papyrus 30/31 (see above). This text dates to 407 BCE. Yehohanan's father, Elyashib, would then have been high priest in the days of Nehemiah (Neh. 3:1; 13:28?).
5. More generally, the Elephantine papyri have no reference to the law brought by Ezra. To the contrary, apparently there was some hesitation about the date and the way to celebrate traditional Judean feasts.[52]

The political context of Ezra's mission in 398 would then be clear enough. It was a time when Egypt again became independent. Jerusalem and Samaria lay closer to the border of the Achaemenid Empire. However, the mission of Ezra is clearly different from that of Nehemiah.[53] Ezra was not sent as a governor. According to Ezra 7, Ezra was a priest and "a scribe learned in the law of Moses" (v. 6), who "devoted himself to the study and observance of the law of Yahweh and to teaching statutes and ordinances in Israel" (v. 10). It seems that his mission was to enact this law of Moses for all the Israelites "in the province of Beyond-Euphrates" (v. 25). From now on, the law of Moses would be also "the law of the king" for "all those who acknowledge the laws of your God" (v. 25). The people would be judged according to this law by appointed judges (v. 25). According to Nehemiah 8, the main public act of Ezra in Jerusalem was the public reading and explaining of this law of Moses.

Servant of the Lord, and Other Essays on the Old Testament (2nd ed.; Oxford: Blackwell, 1952), 135–68; Henri Cazelles, "La mission d'Esdras," *VT* 4 (1954): 113–40; George Widengren, "The Persian Period," in *Israelite and Judaean History* (ed. John H. Hayes and J. Maxwell Miller; OTL; Philadelphia: Westminster, 1977), 489–538, esp. 503–9; Japhet, "Periodization and Ideology II"; Dušek, *Les manuscrits araméens*, 591–93.

52. Pierre Grelot, "Le papyrus pascal d'Éléphantine et le problème du Pentateuque," *VT* 5 (1955): 250–65; idem, "La dernière étape de la rédaction sacerdotale," *VT* 6 (1956): 174–89; Lemaire, "La fin de la première période perse," 56–61.

53. For a comparison, see Reinhard G. Kratz, "Judean Ambassadors and the Making of Jewish Identity: The Case of Hananiah, Ezra, and Nehemiah," in Lipschits, Knoppers, and Oeming, *Judah and the Judeans in the Achaemenid Period*, 421–44.

The historical interpretation of Ezra's mission has been much discussed, and the authenticity of the "rescript of Artaxerxes" as presented in Ezra 7:11–26 much doubted.[54] However, comparison with the role of Udjahorresnet in Egypt[55] shows that Achaemenid authorities were concerned to have a written synthesis of the laws and customs of the country that they administered. Most of the commentators agree that this "law of Moses" probably was the synthesis of the Israelite traditions contained in the Pentateuch/Torah.[56] Actually, from this time until the decrees of Antiochus IV (167), the law of Moses seems to have been officially recognized by the Achaemenid and Hellenistic kings. Furthermore, this law does not mention "Jerusalem." Yet it was also accepted as the official reference in the province of Samaria, as shown by the Samaritan Pentateuch. In a way, this law of Moses became a kind of "constitution" for the Israelite people in Judah, Samaria, and the Diaspora. It became a reference text that was not to be changed. From that time onward, the reference to Scripture became explicit in the Israelite tradition.[57]

The Southern Levant in the Fourth Century BCE

With the independence of Egypt, the political situation of the fourth century became unstable. Thus several armies marched through the southern Levant. Several interventions of the new Egyptian pharaohs (Achoris, ca. 387; Tachôs, 359?) took place. Several military campaigns of the Persian army tried to retake Egypt (385–384; 373; 359 [?]; 351/350; 343–342).[58] This led to the 333/332 con-

---

54. Lester L. Grabbe, "What Was Ezra's Mission?," in *Second Temple Studies 2: Temple and Community in the Persian Period* (ed. Tamara C. Eskenazi and Kent H. Richards; JSOTSup 175; Sheffield: Sheffield Academic Press, 1994), 286–99; idem, "The 'Persian Documents' in the Book of Ezra: Are They Authentic?," in Lipschits and Oeming, *Judah and the Judeans in the Persian Period*, 531–70, esp. 551–55; Joseph Blenkinsopp, "Footnotes to the Rescript of Artaxerxes (Ezra 7:11–26)," in Davies and Edelman, *The Historian and the Bible*, 150–58.

55. See, e.g., Joseph Blenkinsopp, "The Mission of Udjahorresnet and Those of Ezra and Nehemiah," *JBL* 106 (1987): 409–21.

56. See, e.g., Erhard Blum, "Esra, die Mosetora und die persische Politik," in Kratz, *Religion and Religionskontakte*, 231–56.

57. Thomas Willi, "'Wie geschrieben steht'—Schriftbezug und Schrift: Überlegungen zur frühjüdischen Literaturwerdung im perserzeitlichen Kontext," in Kratz, *Religion und Religionskontakte*, 257–77; Joachim Schaper, "Torah and Identity in the Persian Period," in Lipschits, Knoppers, and Oeming, *Judah and the Judeans in the Achaemenid Period*, 27–38.

58. Damien Agut-Labordère, "Les frontières intérieures de la société militaire égyptienne: L'invasion de l'Égypte par Artaxerxès III à travers Diodore XVI.46.4–51.3," *Transeu* 35 (2008): 17–27; Pierre Salmon, "Les relations entre la Perse et l'Égypte du VIe au IVe s. av. J.-C.," in *The Land of Israel: Cross-Roads of Civilizations* (ed. Edward Lipiński; OLA 19; Leuven: Peeters, 1985), 147–68, esp. 159–60; Pierre Briant, *Histoire de l'Empire perse: De Cyrus à Alexandre* (Paris: Fayard, 1996), 664–94, 701–6, 733–38.

Baker Photo Archive (The Eretz Israel Museum)

Figure 13.3. A Yehud coin

quest of the Levant by Alexander.[59] Follow-ing his death, several Macedonian armies marched across the region during the wars of Alexander's successors.[60]

At about this time, Judah and Samaria started to develop their own coinage.[61] We may date this probably from about 380 BCE. The coins of Yehud have long been known.[62] Besides the legend "YHD" written in Aramaic or Paleo-Hebrew, they give us the name of two leaders: "Y(eho)hanan the priest" and "Yehiz-qiyah the governor." This coinage continued to be minted into the early Hellenistic period.[63] The mint of Samaria has come to light only during the past fifty years. It presents a great diversity of coins.[64] Besides the legend "Samaria," these coins give us several personal names, unfortunately without specifying their function. Both provincial coinages have only divisionary coins (drachma and below).

Besides a few stamps and ostraca found mainly in Jerusalem[65] and in Sa-maria,[66] the local documentation of this period is represented by fragmentary papyri and bullae. These were written in Samaria but discovered in a cave of Wadi Daliyeh, north of Jericho.[67] The papyri are mainly conveyances of slaves. One of the bullae, written in Paleo-Hebrew script, belongs to "[Dela?]yahu

59. Briant, *Histoire de l'Empire perse*, 848–59; Maurice Sartre, *D'Alexandre à Zénobie: Histoire du Levant antique IVe siècle avant J.-C.–IIIᵉ siècle après J.-C.* (Paris: Fayard, 2001), 44–52, 67–99.

60. Sartre, *D'Alexandre à Zénobie*, 99–110.

61. See Oren Tal, "Negotiating Identity in an International Context under Achaemenid Rule: The Indigenous Coinages of Persian-Period Palestine as an Allegory," in Lipschits, Knoppers, and Oeming, *Judah and the Judeans in the Achaemenid Period*, 445–59.

62. See Ya'akov Meshorer, *A Treasury of Jewish Coins from the Persian Period to Bar Kokhba* (Jerusalem: Yad ben-Zvi; Nyack, NY: Amphora, 2001), 1–21, plates 1–4.

63. See Haim Gitler and Catharine Lorber, "A New Chronology for the Ptolemaic Coins of Judah," *AJN* 18 (2006): 1–41.

64. See Ya'akov Meshorer and Shraga Qedar, *Samarian Coinage* (NSR 9; Jerusalem: Israel Numismatic Society, 1999).

65. Joseph Naveh, "Hebrew and Aramaic Inscriptions," in *Inscriptions* (vol. 6 of *Excavations at the City of David*, by Yigal Shiloh; ed. Donald T. Ariel et al.; Qedem 41. Jerusalem: Institute of Archaeology, Hebrew University of Jerusalem, 2000), 1–14, esp. 9–12.

66. George A. Reisner, Clarence S. Fisher, and David G. Lyon, *Plans and Plates* (vol. 2 of *Harvard Excavations at Samaria, 1908–1910*; HSS; Cambridge, MA: Harvard University Press, 1924), 247–48, plate 58; Salomo A. Birnbaum, "Sherds with Letters in Aramaic Script," in *The Objects from Samaria* (ed. John W. Crowfoot, Grace M. Crowfoot, and Kathleen M. Kenyon; Samaria-Sebaste 3. London: Palestine Exploration Fund, 1957), 25–33.

67. Mary J. W. Leith, *The Wadi Daliyeh Seal Impressions* (vol. 1 of *Wadi Daliyeh*; DJD 24; Oxford: Clarendon, 1997); Douglas M. Gropp, *The Samaria Papyri from Wadi Daliyeh*

son [of San]/ballat, governor of Samar[ia]." The names of several officials of
Samaria (governor, prefect, and judge) appear in these documents. The various
names on the bullae and on the coins, as well as the record of Josephus (*Ant.*
11), have led commentators to various reconstitutions of the governors' list for
Samaria and, indirectly, of the Jerusalem high priests. Thus Frank Moore Cross
proposed a list of the governors of Samaria and of the Jerusalem high priests,
arguing for several cases of papponymy (naming someone after a grandfather).[68]
However, this reconstruction is conjectural because it implies that names are
missing in the list in Nehemiah 12:22. In the context of a general study of the
Wadi Daliyeh documents, Jan Dušek, following James VanderKam,[69] preferred
to interpret the list of the high priests in Nehemiah 12:22 as complete with
Yohanan (about 410–370) and Yaddua (about 370–332). (Ha/'A)naniah would
have been governor of Samaria after Delayah son of Sanballat.[70]

According to Quintus Curtius Rufus, *Historiae Alexandri Magni* 4.8, 9–11
(see also the *Chronikon* of Eusebius and Jerome), Andromachos, the governor
of Samaria nominated by Alexander, was burned alive during a riot that took
place while Alexander was in Egypt. When Alexander returned to Samaria,
two or three hundred leading citizens tried to take refuge in the Mugharet Abu
Sinjeh of Wadi Daliyeh. Their title deeds were partly recovered as the Wadi Daliyeh papyri. These leading citizens apparently met their fate in this cave while
Alexander captured Samaria. He nominated Memnon as governor in place of
Andromachos. Perdiccas,[71] acting on Alexander's authority, installed a Macedonian colony in Samaria. This "elevation" of the status of Samaria probably led
to the development of Sichem (ancient Shechem),[72] as well as the development
of a town around the Gerizim temple.[73] Thus the Alexander campaign seems to
have had important and dramatic consequences for the population of Samaria.[74]

(vol. 2 of *Wadi Daliyeh*; DJD 28; Oxford: Clarendon, 2001), 1–116, plates i–xxxix; Dušek, *Les manuscrits araméens*.

68. See Frank Moore Cross, *From Epic to Canon: History and Literature in Ancient Israel* (Baltimore: Johns Hopkins University Press, 1998), 151–72, 173–202. For a modified view, see H. Eshel, "The Governors of Samaria in the Fifth and Fourth Centuries BCE," in Lipschits, Knoppers, and Albertz, *Judah and the Judeans in the Fourth Century B.C.E.*, 223–34.

69. James C. VanderKam, *From Joshua to Caiaphas: High Priests after the Exile* (Minneapolis: Fortress; Assen: Van Gorcum: 2004), 85–99.

70. Dušek, *Les manuscrits araméens*, 549, 584–91.

71. Sartre, *D'Alexandre à Zénobie*, 82.

72. Edward F. Campbell, *Text* (vol. 1 of *Shechem III: The Stratigraphy and Architecture of Shechem/Tell Balâṭah*; ASORAR 6; Boston: American Schools of Oriental Research, 2002), 311–13; Nancy L. Lapp, *Shechem IV: The Persian-Hellenistic Potttery of Shechem/Tell Balâṭah* (ed. Edward F. Campbell; ASORAR 11; Boston: American Schools of Oriental Research, 2008), 1–3.

73. Magen, "Dating of the First Phase," 183; idem, *A Temple City*, 1–93.

74. Adam Zertal, "The Pahwah of Samaria (Northern Israel) during the Persian Period: Types of Settlement, Economy, History and New Discoveries," *Transeu* 3 (1990), 9–30, esp. 15; Dušek, *Les manuscrits araméens*, 447–53.

The situation seems to have been different in Judah. There is a tradition about Alexander after his capture of Gaza. He is said to have met with the high priest Yaddua in Jerusalem. However, this appears to be a legend, whose historicity may be doubted, at least in the manner in which it is presented by Josephus (*Ant.* 11.329–339). Such a meeting of submission of Yaddua[75] (or would it have been Yehizqiyah the governor?)[76] to Alexander would not have been impossible on the plain near Antipatris, as proposed by the rabbinic tradition (*b. Yoma* 69a). In any case, there is no indication that Judah suffered from destruction at this time.

The papyrus of Ketef Jericho can be interpreted as an indication that the country did suffer later during the Diadochi wars (of Alexander's successors). This would have occurred in 312 BCE, when Ptolemy the son of Lagus took Jerusalem and deported inhabitants of Judaea and Samaria (*Let. Arist.* 3.12–13; Josephus, *Ant.* 13.4–7; *Ag. Ap.* 1.186).[77] Actually some two thousand Aramaic ostraca from Idumea reveal that the administration of Idumea, south of Judah, continued from the Persian to the Hellenistic period. There apparently was little change. Aramaic continued in use. Although not all these ostraca are published as yet, they seem to date essentially from 362 to 312 BCE.[78] The conquest and quick retreat of Ptolemy in the face of Antigonus and Demetrius in 312 apparently was accompanied by systematic destructions. The subsequent peace of 311 left the country quiet for ten years.[79]

Besides the coins and the stamps,[80] we have little direct information about Judah. From Elephantine papyri Cowley 30/31 and 32, we learn that "Baga-

75. Daniel R. Schwartz, "On Some Papyri and Josephus' Sources and Chronology for the Persian Period," *JSJ* 21 (1990): 175–99, esp. 187–88. Schwartz thinks that originally in this story there was a name different from "Yaddua."

76. This Yehizqiyah could have been interpreted later as a high priest, by Hecateus, as in Josephus, *Ag. Ap.* 1.187.

77. Hanan Eshel and Boaz Zissu, "Jericho: Archaeological Introduction," in *Miscellaneous Texts from the Judaean Desert* (by James Charlesworth et al.; DJD 38; Oxford: Clarendon, 2000), 3–20, esp. 11–12; Hanan Eshel, "Hellenism in the Land of Israel from the Fifth to the Second Centuries BCE in Light of Semitic Epigraphy," in *A Time of Change: Judah and Its Neighbours in the Persian and Early Hellenistic Periods* (ed. Yigal Levin; LSTS 65; London: T&T Clark, 2007), 116–24, esp. 122.

78. André Lemaire, *Collections Moussaïeff, Jeselsohn, Welch et divers* (vol. 2 of *Nouvelles inscriptions araméennes d'Idumées*; TranseuSup 9; Paris: Gabalda, 2002), 199–201. Bezalel Porten and Ada Yardeni propose to interpret the mentions of Alexander as referring to Alexander IV and not to Alexander III ("The Chronology of the Idumean Ostraca in the Decade or So after the Death of Alexander the Great and Its Relevance for Historical Events," in *Treasures on Camels' Humps: Historical and Literary Studies from the Ancient Near East Presented to Israel Eph'al* [ed. Mordechai Cogan and Dan'el Kahn; Jerusalem: Magnes, 2008], 237–49), but this proposition is not convincing (see Edward Anson, "Idumaean Ostraca and Early Hellenistic Chronology," *JAOS* 125 [2005]: 263–66).

79. Sartre, *D'Alexandre à Zénobie*, 105–6.

80. Oded Lipschits and David Vanderhooft, "Yehud Stamp Impressions in the Fourth Century BCE: A Time of Administrative Consolidation?," in Lipschits, Knoppers, and Oeming, *Judah and the Judeans in the Achaemenid Period*, 75–94.

vahya/Bagôhi" was governor of Yehud in about 407 BCE and perhaps at the beginning of the fourth century BCE. Another governor of Judah, "Yehizqiyah the governor," is known from Judean coins. However, these are difficult to date precisely (ca. 380–332). Are these two governors the only ones before Alexander (as proposed by Lisbeth Fried)?[81] It is impossible to be certain.[82] It is possible, however, to know something about the fourth-century administration of Judah by comparing it to documented evidence in the neighboring provinces of Samaria and Idumea. As in Samaria, there probably were a governor, a prefect, and judges. Actually, the existence of these judges is supposed by the mission of Ezra (Ezra 7:25). As in Idumea, the collection of taxes probably was under the responsibility of a "treasurer" (gnzbr). The poll tax apparently consisted of a half shekel (Exod. 30:13; 38:26).[83] That would be two-fourths of a shekel,[84] or two drachmas.[85] There were also land taxes paid in kind (grain, oil, wine, etc.) that were collected in storerooms.[86] In Judah these storerooms may have been connected with the temple in Jerusalem and/or with a site such as Ramat Raḥel. Many stamped jars have been found there. To collect these land taxes, the Aramaic ostraca from Idumea show, the collector (GB'/Y) had to use a cadastre of sorts. The various fields were registered with a certain quantity of grain.[87] Furthermore, these ostraca probably present lists of workers for the corvée labor (see hălāk in Ezra 4:13, 20; 7:24). The practice of an imperial corvée during the Achaemenid period seems now to be confirmed in Aramaic leather manuscripts from Afghanistan dated to the fourth century.[88]

The Aramaic ostraca from Idumea also give us some light on the cultural composition of the local population. Although one must be careful

81. Lisbeth Fried, "A Silver Coin of Yohanan Hakkohen," *Transeu* 26 (2003): 65–85, esp. 85.

82. André Lemaire, "Administration in Fourth-Century B.C.E.: Judah in Light of Epigraphy and Numismatics," in Lipschits, Knoppers, and Albertz, *Judah and the Judeans in the Fourth Century B.C.E.*, 53–74, esp. 54.

83. The poll tax was only "one third of a shekel" at the time of Nehemiah (Neh. 10:32).

84. In abbreviation: *R II*, as written on a few ostraca from Idumea and on the Ketef Jericho papyrus.

85. André Lemaire, "Taxes et impôts dans le sud de la Palestine (IVᵉ s. av. J.-C.)," *Transeu* 28 (2004): 133–42, esp. 139–40; idem, "Administration," 58–60.

86. "The storeroom of Makkedah" is mentioned several times in the Aramaic ostraca from Idumea.

87. Lemaire, "Administration," 56.

88. Shaul Shaked, "De Khulmi à Nikhšapaya: Les données des nouveaux documents araméens de Bactres sur la toponymie de la région (IVᵉ siècle av. n. è.)," *CRSAIBL* 147, no. 4 (2003): 1517–35; idem, *Le satrape de Bactriane et son gouverneur: Documents araméens du IVᵉ s. avant notre ère provenant de Bactriane* (Persika 4; Paris: De Boccard, 2004), 28–32; Joseph Naveh and Shaul Shaked, *Aramaic Documents from Ancient Bactria (Fourth Century BCE)*. From the Khalili Collections (London: The Khalili Family Trust, 2012).

Papyrus Cowley 30 (407 BCE)

(1) To our lord Bagohi governor of Judah, your servants Yedaniah and his colleagues the priests who are in Elephantine the fortress. (2) May the God of Heaven seek after the welfare of our lord abundantly at all times, and grant you favor before king Darius . . .

(8) . . . Naphaina led the Egyptians with the other troops. They came to the fortress of Elephantine with their weapons (9) broke into that Temple, demolished it to the ground, and the stone pillars which were there—they smashed them. Moreover, it happened (that) (10) they demolished 5 stone gateways built of hewn stone, which were in that Temple. And their standing doors, and the (11) the bronze hinges of those doors, and the cedarwood roof—all of (these) which with the rest of the fittings and other (things) which (12) were there—all (of these) they burned with fire. But the gold and silver basins and (other) things which were in that Temple—all (of these) they took (13) and made their own. And during the days of the king(s) of Egypt our fathers had built that Temple in Elephantine the fortress and when Cambyses entered Egypt (14) he found that Temple built. And they overthrew the temples of the gods of Egypt, all (of them), but one did not damage anything in that Temple. (15) And when this had been done (to us), we with our wives and our children were wearing sackcloth and fasting and praying to YHW the Lord of Heaven (16) who let us gloat over that Vidranga. The dogs removed the fetter from his feet and all goods which he had acquired were lost. And all persons (17) who sought evil for that Temple, all (of them), were killed and we gazed upon them. Moreover, before this—at the time that this evil (*Verso*: 18) was done to us—we sent a letter (to) our lord, and to Yehohanan the High Priest and his colleagues the priests who are in Jerusalem, and to Ostanes the brother of ʿAnani and the nobles of the Judeans. They did not send us a single letter . . .

(29) . . . Moreover, we sent all the(se) words in our name in one letter to Delaiah and Shelemiah sons of Sanballat governor of Samaria. (30) Moreover, Arsames did not know about this which was done to us at all. On the 20th of Marheshvan, year 17 of king Darius.[a]

a. Bezalel Porten and Ada Yardeni, *Textbook of Aramaic Documents from Ancient Egypt* (4 vols.; Jerusalem: Department of the History of the Jewish People, Hebrew University; Winona Lake, IN: Eisenbrauns, 1986–1999), 1:71.

in working with onomastics, it seems that most of the names were Edomite (with the name of the god Qôs), or North Arabic (especially with the ending –W), or common West Semitic. West Semitic names with the theonym YHW, YH, or YW were only a minority, less than 5 percent. This is true even though there was apparently a "temple of Yahô" (ostracon AL 283)

Wadi ed-Daliyeh Samaria Papyrus A (335 BCE)

(1) On the twentieth of Adar, the second year (of Arses), the accession year of [D]arius, the king, in Samar[ia the citadel, which is in Samaria the province.] (2) [Hananiah son of Beyadel sold] a certain Yehohanan son of Sheilah, this slave of his, without defect, [to Yehonur son of Laneri for 35 shekels of silver,] (3) the stipulated price, the full price. [Th]is sum of 35 sh(ekels) Hananiah [has received from Yehonur. . . . He will be a slave] (4) of his and of his sons after him in perpetuity. Yehonur has authority over the [said] Yeh[ohanan in perpetuity. . . . And this bond] (5) they concluded between them: If I, Hananiah son of Beyadel [enter into litigation with you, Yehonur . . . , or if someone else enters into litigation with you,] (6) Yehonur, or with your sons after you, I Hananiah, and my sons after me [will clear (the slave) . . . or, if I change (what is written) on this bond, which I concluded] (7) with you, you Yehonur, in these terms, [and say] to you, you Yehonur, [that 'Yehohanan, this slave, I did not sell you, and the sum of 35 shekels] (8) I have not received from you, then, the sum of 35 shekels, which [you, Yehonur,] gave [me, I, Hananiah, will return to you and will give it.] (9) And afterward, I, Hananiah, am liable; [I] will pay you, you Yehonur, [and your sons after you 7 silver minas of silver. . . . You will take possession of] (10) 7 silver minas of silver without litigation and without liabilities. Over the said Yehohanan [I, Hananiah,] do not [have authority. But you, Yehonur, (and your sons] after you [have authority] (11) as stipulated in this bond <which> they concluded between them be[fore PN. . . . The witnesses who] (12) affix their seals are trustworthy.

Douglas M. Gropp, *The Samaria Papyri from Wadi Daliyeh* (vol. 2 of Wadi Daliyeh; DJD 28; Oxford: Clarendon, 2001), 35; Jan Dušek, *Les manuscrits araméens du Wadi Daliyeh et la Samarie vers 450–332 av. J.-C.* (CHANE 30; Leiden: Brill, 2007), 118.

in Makkedah.[89] The situation seems quite different in Samaria, where the Yahwistic names in the Wadi ed-Daliyeh papyri are by far the dominant group. There the common West Semitic names follow in number, with only a few Aramaic, Akkadian, Phoenician, Persian, Edomite, Egyptian, and North Arabic names.[90] This situation probably was similar to the one in Judah. This is supported by the onomastics of the books of Ezra and Nehemiah,[91]

89. André Lemaire, "Nouveau temple de Yahô (IVᵉ s. av. J.-C.)," in *"Basel und Bibel": Collected Communications to the XVIIth Congress of the International Organization for the Study of the Old Testament, Basel 2001* (ed. Matthias Augustin and Hermann Michael Niemann; BEATAJ 51; Frankfurt: Peter Lang, 2004), 265–73.

90. Ran Zadok, "A Prosopography of Samaria and Edom/Idumea," *UF* 30 (1998): 781–828, esp. 781–85; Dušek, *Les manuscrits araméens*, 486–95.

91. See Paul-Alain Beaulieu, "Yahwistic Names in Light of Late Babylonian Onomastics," in Lipschits, Knoppers, and Oeming, *Judah and the Judeans in the Achaemenid Period*, 245–66, esp. 255–56.

the very few Yehud ostraca and seal impressions, and the Ketef Jericho papyrus. As far as we know, Judea, Samaria, and Idumea each had at least one temple of Yahô. Temples of other deities are only attested in Idumea (ostracon AL 83).[92]

Thus the fifth–fourth centuries BCE were a time of revival. Jerusalem emerged as capital of Yehud, due to the efforts of Nehemiah. The synthesis of the Israelite traditions was brought to the community of Yehud by Ezra. Both came from the eastern Diaspora, whose influence did not cease with Alexander. Indeed, the growing importance of the Jewish high priest and the loss of a local governor may have been the major political change that the young Greek conqueror introduced.[93]

92. On sanctuaries of other deities in Palestinian provinces, see Jens Kamlah, "Zwei nordpaläs-tinische 'Heiligtümer' der persischen Zeit und ihre epigraphischen Funde," ZDPV 115 (1999): 163–90; Oren Tal, "Achaemenid to Greek Rule: The Contribution of Achaemenid-Ptolemaic Temples of Palestine," Transeu 36 (2008): 165–83.

93. VanderKam, From Joshua to Caiaphas, 99–123.

14

The Hellenistic Period

Literary Sources

Within the Jewish and Protestant canons, Daniel 7–12 is the biblical text most concerned with the Hellenistic period—from the exploits of Alexander against Persia, to the division of his empire among his generals and other successors, to the rise of Antiochus IV and his actions against Yehud. Daniel 10–12 provides an especially important witness to events during the reigns of Antiochus III and Antiochus IV, being written by a living contemporary of those events.[1] The testimony of Daniel is greatly supplemented by 1–2 Maccabees, two historical books found among the deuterocanonical books of the Roman Catholic and Orthodox Bibles. Once its obvious partisan interests are taken into account, 1 Maccabees becomes an essential source for the Maccabean Revolt and establishment of the Hasmonean dynasty (167–141). Second Mac-

---

1. John J. Collins, *Daniel* (Hermeneia; Minneapolis: Fortress, 1993), 21–38; John Goldingay, *Daniel* (WBC 30; Waco: Word, 1989), 320–29; Louis F. Hartman and Alexander A. Di Lella, *The Book of Daniel: A New Translation with Introduction and Commentary* (AB 23; Garden City, NY: Doubleday, 1977), 9–18. A traditional date for Daniel is defended in Stephen R. Miller, *Daniel* (NAC 18; Nashville: Broadman & Holman, 1994), 22–43 (but see my critique: David A. deSilva, review of Stephen R. Miller, *Daniel*, *ATJ* 28 [1996]: 140–43). Miller nevertheless agrees that the text is concerned with events in the Hellenistic period.

cabees, an abridgement of a five-volume history of the Maccabean Revolt by Jason of Cyrene, himself perhaps a contemporary of the events, is the most important source for understanding the inner-Jewish partisan strife and the hellenizing crisis that led up to the revolt, as well as a supplementary source for Judas's campaigns before his death (175–161). Second Maccabees may have been written prior to 124 BCE, with 1 Maccabees perhaps being written somewhat later; neither postdates 63 BCE.[2]

Greek and Latin historians ultimately provide the larger historical framework within which the events treated in the canonical and deuterocanonical sources fit. Of these, the most important are Polybius's *Histories*, the eleventh book of Appian's *Roman History* (the *Syriake*, or *Syrian Wars*), Livy's *History*, and the *Bibliotheca historica* of Diodorus Siculus. These historians are excellent sources for the actions of the Seleucids and Ptolemies against each other and in regard to the West, but they show almost no interest in the affairs of Judea proper (e.g., there is virtually no mention of the Maccabean Revolt or the Hasmonean dynasty as a whole). For the latter, we rely almost wholly on 1–2 Maccabees and the works of Josephus (especially books 12–14 of his *Jewish Antiquities* and the opening sections of his *Jewish War*). Jewish texts of other genres occasionally provide windows into Jewish history, as, for example, the Qumran pesharim and the *Damascus Covenant*, which contain cryptic references to events in Yehud, or the *Psalms of Solomon*, which reflect on the later Hasmoneans, Pompey's invasion, and its aftermath.

From Alexander to Antiochus III

The Persian period in Yehud came to an end when, in 334–31 BCE, Alexander's armies swept eastward through Asia Minor and southward through Syria, the Palestinian coastlands, and Egypt (itself subsumed by the Persian Empire since Cambyses II's invasion in 525 BCE). The cities of Tyre and Gaza tried to withstand Alexander, but Egypt yielded peaceably to his domination. Josephus relates a tale of Alexander's visit to Jerusalem following his nine-month siege of Tyre and two-month siege of Gaza, en route to take Egypt (*Ant.* 11.325–345), though this story is generally rejected as legendary.[3] More

2. On the scholarly conversations regarding the dates of these books, see David A. deSilva, *Introducing the Apocrypha: Message, Context, and Significance* (Grand Rapids: Baker Academic, 2002), 247–48, 268–70; on the *Tendenz* of 1 Maccabees, see 255–62.

3. Victor Tcherikover, *Hellenistic Civilization and the Jews* (Philadelphia: Jewish Publication Society, 1959), 41, 49; Solomon Zeitlin, *The Rise and Fall of the Judaean State: A Political, Social, and Religious History of the Second Commonwealth* (Philadelphia: Jewish Publication Society, 1962), 41; John H. Hayes and Sara R. Mandell, *The Jewish People in Classical Antiquity: From*

probably, representatives from Jerusalem met Alexander in the coastal region to acknowledge his sovereignty. The legend suggests, at least, a memory of Yehud's peaceful acceptance of Greco-Macedonian rule.

Alexander's untimely death in 323 BCE left the empire with no viable heirs, leading to decades of wars among Alexander's generals (the Diadochoi, or "Successors"), during which time Alexander's half-brother and his young son by Roxane were murdered.[4] These wars eventually led to a four-way division of his empire (Dan. 8:8, 21–22; 11:3–4). General Ptolemy immediately seized Egypt, becoming Ptolemy I Soter (322–285), the first "king of the south" (Dan. 11:5; the "south" being identified explicitly as Egypt in 11:8). He was remembered to have captured Jerusalem, which was part of the territory first claimed by the rival general Antigonus, on a Sabbath (Josephus, *Ag. Ap.* 1.209–212; *Ant.* 12.4–6) and to have dealt harshly with the inhabitants (*Let. Arist.* 12–13).

Seleucus (later Seleucus I Nicator, the first "king of the north" [312–280 BCE]), another leader in Alexander's army and for a time a general under Ptolemy, secured Babylon and Syria by 312 with Ptolemy's assistance (Dan. 11:5). It was only after the Battle of Ipsus (301) and the defeat of Antigonus, however, that his claim was recognized by the other successors to Alexander.[5] Although the treaty following the Battle of Ipsus actually awarded Palestine to Seleucus I as well (Ptolemy had not participated in the battle), Ptolemy did not relinquish his hold upon it, and his old comrade-in-arms did not force his claim—appropriately so, since he owed his position, in part at least, to Ptolemy.[6] This would be a point of contention, however, for the next century and a half. Daniel's summarizing history of the descendants of Ptolemy and Seleucus as an alternation between uneasy truces and attempts to conquer each other's territory for themselves is quite accurate (Dan. 2:41–43).

Around 250 BCE Antiochus II Theos (261–246) and Ptolemy II Philadelphus (285–246) attempted to form an alliance through marriage, with Ptolemy's daughter Berenice being married to Antiochus II after the latter's divorce from Laodice. Antiochus II left Berenice, however, to return to Laodice once again. After Antiochus II's suspicious death, Laodice had Berenice and her young son executed so as to secure the succession for her own offspring (Dan. 11:6). Berenice's brother, Ptolemy III Euergetes (246–221), ascended to the throne of

---

Alexander to Bar Kochba (Louisville: Westminster John Knox, 1998), 24; Lester L. Grabbe, *The Persian and Greek Periods* (vol. 1 of *Judaism from Cyrus to Hadrian*; Minneapolis: Fortress, 1992), 174.

4. Diodorus Siculus (*Bib. hist.* 18.1–21.5) recounts these wars in detail down through the Battle of Ipsus (323–303 BCE).

5. The other two principal successors were Cassander, who secured Greece and Macedonia; and Lysimachus, who took Thrace and Asia Minor.

6. Tcherikover, *Hellenistic Civilization*, 53; Grabbe, *Persian and Greek Periods*, 204.

Egypt in 246 BCE. He sought to give support to his sister and nephew and, after their murder, to avenge their deaths, launching a campaign against Seleucus II Callinicus (246–226) that drove the latter out of Syria and the western parts of Babylonia. Ptolemy III returned to Egypt in triumph, even having recovered some of the Egyptian idols that had been carried off long before during the Persian invasion of Egypt in 525 BCE (Dan. 11:7–8), an achievement celebrated in a priestly inscription known as the Canopus Decree. Ptolemy III did not maintain a hold on Seleucid territory, perhaps being more interested to punish than to colonize, such that Seleucus II later recovered his Syro-Mesopotamian territory and even attempted to push into Palestine. Ptolemy III would not permit the latter, however, turning him back in 242 BCE (Dan. 11:9).

Since the end of Persian domination of Judea, under which both a Persian-appointed governor and the Judean high priest shared administrative responsibilities, the high priest became the chief administrator over the Greek province of Judea, aided by a *gerousia*, a senate of ruling elders.[7] This put a hitherto unparalleled spectrum of responsibilities and authority in the hands of the high priest, including ultimate responsibility for tax farming on behalf of the Ptolemaic overlords. Under Ptolemy III Euergetes, the high priest Onias II, father of the high priest Simon praised by Ben Sira (Sir. 50:1–21), defaulted on paying these taxes. Josephus attributes this to Onias's alleged miserliness, but it may also be a sign of his pro-Seleucid leanings and his anticipation that Judea would not long remain a Ptolemaic possession.[8] Whatever his motive, his default gave an enterprising aristocratic (but nonpriestly) Jew, Joseph ben Tobiah, the opportunity to secure the responsibilities of tax farming, as well as the position of official representative for Judea at Ptolemy's court (the *prostasia*), for himself.[9] His family, known as the Tobiads, would prove formidable rivals for power to the high-priestly Oniads. The Tobiad family had few scruples about being all things to all people. In a letter from Tobiah to Apollonius, a gentile associate, he writes, "Thanks be to the gods," and includes details about both circumcised and uncircumcised boys sent as slaves to the same (in violation of Torah on the counts of giving a Jew as a slave to a gentile and leaving slaves uncircumcised).[10] Nonetheless, Josephus would remember Joseph ben Tobiah as having "brought the Jews out of a state of poverty and lowliness, to one that was more splendid" (*Ant.* 12.224).

7. Hayes and Mandell, *Jewish People*, 32; Grabbe, *Persian and Greek Periods*, 191; Tcherikover, *Hellenistic Civilization*, 59.
8. Grabbe, *Persian and Greek Periods*, 196–97.
9. See Josephus, *Ant.* 12.154–241; Grabbe, *Persian and Greek Periods*, 192–98.
10. See further Tcherikover, *Hellenistic Civilization*, 64–65, 71, 126–42; Hayes and Mandell, *Jewish People*, 35–37; Grabbe, *Persian and Greek Periods*, 196–98; Zeitlin, *Rise and Fall*, 63.

Seleucus II had two sons, who began their reign jointly: Seleucus III Soter (226–223) and Antiochus III, later called "the Great" (226–187). The latter pursued a policy of military expansion. Antiochus III attempted to take Palestine from Ptolemaic control in 219–217 BCE. He succeeded in recovering some of the coastal territories of Phoenicia but was soundly defeated by Ptolemy IV Philopator (221–203) at the Battle of Raphia in 217 (Dan. 11:10–11; Polybius, *Hist.* 5.31–87). According to Polybius (*Hist.* 14.12.1), it was only Ptolemy IV's lazy character that prevented Egypt from exploiting this opportunity to gain a substantial share of Seleucid territory.

Antiochus III focused his attentions on expanding into Asia Minor and into territories east of Babylon, with stunning (though ultimately short-lived) success. His armies and resources replenished, he moved again into Palestine. Egypt now had a child on the throne, Ptolemy V Epiphanes (203–181), and his generals lacked the resources and leadership to defend against Antiochus III. The Seleucids finally seized control of Palestine after the Battle of Panion and the siege of Sidon, the "fortified city" where Ptolemy's general Scopas and his remaining troops sought refuge, in 198 BCE (Dan. 11:13–16; Polybius, *Hist.* 16.18–19).[11] Antiochus III visited Jerusalem, where he was greeted magnificently. Simon the Just, the high priest, had ordered military support to be given to Antiochus for his efforts in Palestine against Scopas and against the Ptolemaic garrison in Jerusalem, which deeply ingratiated the Judeans to their new overlord (Josephus, *Ant.* 12.133–34; Dan. 11:14). Josephus reports that in return for their support, Antiochus III granted the Judeans important rights and concessions (*Ant.* 12.138–53). Allowing for some embellishment, this report is generally regarded as accurate.[12] These rights included the permission for Judeans to govern themselves by their ancestral law, provision for temple sacrifices out of the royal treasury, and allowances for relief from taxes and tribute for three years while the land recovered (on the damage done to Judea in the course of the wars between Antiochus III and the Ptolemies, see Polybius, *Hist.* 16.39). It appears that Simon the Just enjoyed oversight of Jerusalem and its environs in both civil and religious matters, as he is remembered for repairing the temple, fortifying the temple and the city walls, and increasing the city's water supply (Sir. 50:1–4).[13]

---

11. Félix-Marie Abel, *De la conquête d'Alexandre jusqu'a la guerre juive* (vol. 1 of *Histoire de la Palestine depuis la conquête d'Alexandre jusqu'à l'invasion Arabe* (ÉBib; Paris: Gabalda, 1952), 72–87.

12. Abel, *De la conquête d'Alexandre*, 88–93; Tcherikover, *Hellenistic Civilization*, 82–88; Grabbe, *Persian and Greek Periods*, 246.

13. Menahem Stern, "The Period of the Second Temple," in *A History of the Jewish People* (ed. H. H. Ben-Sasson; Cambridge, MA: Harvard University Press, 1976), 185–303, esp. 191–93.

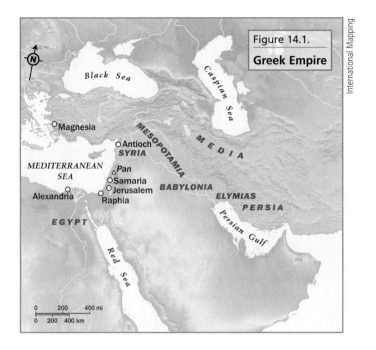

Figure 14.1.

Greek Empire

Antiochus III sought an alliance with Ptolemy V in 193 BCE by marrying the latter to his daughter Cleopatra, the first queen of Egypt by that name (Livy, *Hist*. 35.13.4). Antiochus may have hoped to use Cleopatra as an "inside agent" to secure the throne of Egypt for his own line, but Cleopatra proved a loyal wife to Ptolemy and queen to her new homeland (Dan. 11:17). Antiochus turned his attention to the coastlands of Asia Minor, with designs on Greece itself, but his efforts were halted by the power of Rome, which regarded him as a potential threat to their own interests in the East (Polybius, *Hist*. 16.46.14–16.47.3; 16.49–52; Appian, *Hist. rom*. 11.1.1–11.6.36). After Antiochus was driven back from Greece, Ptolemy V and Cleopatra I sent envoys to Rome, urging the Romans to occupy Asia Minor as well and drive him back even farther (Livy, *Hist*. 37.3.8–11).

The Roman navy defeated Antiochus's fleet (Livy, *Hist*. 36.42.1–36.45.9), and a few years later their armies defeated his at Magnesia in 190 BCE (Livy, *Hist*. 37.38.1–37.44.7). Rome thus placed an absolute limit on his westward expansion, crafted a treaty that severely limited his initiatives, and imposed a heavy financial penalty on him for "war reparations"—the heaviest ever to be imposed in the ancient world.[14] Polybius sought to write the history of "how

14. For the precise circumstances and terms, see Polybius, *Hist*. 21.13–17, 42, 45; Diodorus Siculus, *Bib. hist*. 29.10.1–11.1; 29.13.1; Livy, *Hist*. 38.38.1–18; Appian, *Hist. rom*. 11.7.37–39.

the Romans managed everything to ensure the subjection of the entire known world to their rule" (*Hist.* 5.3.3), and this certainly proved true in regard to their interventions in the Seleucid and Ptolemaic Empires during the reigns of Antiochus III and Antiochus IV.

The financial burden imposed on Antiochus III by Rome would play a large part in Seleucid policy in Judea, among other places, and should not be forgotten as one factor contributing to the disasters that would ensue in Jerusalem. Antiochus returned to his own territory and then died while attempting to plunder the funds deposited in a temple of Bel in Elymais in 187 BCE (Dan. 11:18–19; Diodorus Siculus, *Bib. hist.* 28.3.1; 29.15.1), impelled both by his debt to Rome and his expenses in waging an unsuccessful war in western Asia and Greece.

It would be appropriate to give some consideration to the situation of the Samaritans during this period. The residents of Samaria and its environs regarded themselves as the descendants of the northern tribes of Israel, who faithfully worshiped at Mount Gerizim. Judeans denied them this genealogical continuity, regarding the Samaritans rather as a mixed breed of religious syncretists (e.g., 2 Kings 17:24–31).[15] The Jerusalemites' rejection of the Samaritans' offer to help rebuild the Jerusalem temple in the Persian period (Ezra 4:1–5) was a decisive rejection of any kinship. This hostility continued through the Hellenistic period, reflected for example in Ben Sira's contempt for "the foolish people that live in Shechem" (Sir. 50:25–26). The nadir of Judean-Samaritan relations, however, would come in the Hasmonean period with the destruction of Samaria, Shechem, and the Samaritan temple by John Hyrcanus I (135–104) (see Josephus, *Ant.* 13.254–256; 13.275–283).

Earlier, Sanballat III, ruler of Samaria in 333 BCE, had established good diplomatic relations with Alexander on the latter's entrance into Palestine, securing permission to build a temple at Mount Gerizim (Josephus, *Ant.* 11.302–325), the foundations for which have since been discovered by archaeologists.[16] Following Sanballat's death shortly thereafter, the Samarians rebelled against Alexander, killing his deputy Andromachus. The reprisal, whether by Alexander or his general Perdiccas acting on his behalf, was terrible and decisive: Samaria was utterly destroyed. The survivors of Samaria resettled in and around Shechem and rebuilt their temple on Mount Gerizim by the

---

    15. James D. Purvis, "The Samaritans," in *The Hellenistic Period* (vol. 2 of *The Cambridge History of Judaism*; ed. W. D. Davies and Louis Finkelstein; Cambridge: Cambridge University Press, 1989), 591–613, esp. 591–92.
    16. Ibid., 597; Marie-Christine Halpern-Zylberstein, "The Archaeology of Hellenistic Palestine," in Davies and Finkelstein, *Hellenistic Period*, 1–34, esp. 24–26.

Wadi ed-Daliyeh

The excavations of the caves at Wadi ed-Daliyeh, about eight miles north of Jericho, produced a cache of papyrus documents written in Aramaic between 375 and 335 BCE.[a] These documents show that multiple rulers of Samaria bore the name "Sanballat," suggesting that Josephus's story of the building of the Samaritan temple was not misplaced by him from the Persian period to the Greek period.[b] These caves also yielded the skeletons of about two hundred Samaritan men, women, and children who sought refuge on this site from the sacking of Samaria by Alexander's army, whom Alexander's soldiers tracked down and slaughtered here.[c]

a. John H. Hayes and Sara R. Mandell, *The Jewish People in Classical Antiquity: From Alexander to Bar Kochba* (Louisville: Westminster John Knox, 1998), 25. See a translation of one papyrus on p. 424.
b. Against Victor Tcherikover, *Hellenistic Civilization and the Jews* (Philadelphia: Jewish Publication Society, 1959), 44.
c. Paul W. Lapp and Nancy L. Lapp, eds., *Discoveries in the Wâdi ed-Dâliyeh* (AASOR 41; Cambridge, MA: American Schools of Oriental Research, 1974).

second century BCE.[17] Samaria itself was rebuilt in Hellenistic fashion, to be inhabited by a military colony of Macedonians.[18]

The Hellenizing Reform and Its Aftermath

Antiochus III was succeeded by his older son, Seleucus IV Philopator (187–175). As a condition of the terms of the treaty with the Romans, Antiochus III had sent his younger son (who would become Antiochus IV Epiphanes) to Rome as a hostage, where he was treated well (Livy, *Hist.* 41; 42.6.8–9). Seleucus IV could do little as king beyond attempt to raise money to replenish the Seleucid coffers after his father's ruinous campaign in Asia Minor and Greece and to continue to pay the annualized fines imposed on his father by their new "allies" to the west. Daniel and the author of 2 Maccabees remember him primarily as concerned with finances, sending "an exactor of tribute" to Jerusalem (Dan. 11:20; 2 Macc. 3:4–40). The internal intrigues within the Judean leadership become quite visible in this situation. First, there are intrigues among the sons of Joseph ben Tobiah. The older sons were pro-Seleucid; the youngest brother, Hyrcanus, was pro-Ptolemaic and thoroughly alienated from his brothers. The

17. Andrea M. Berlin, "Between Large Forces: Palestine in the Hellenistic Period," *BA* 60 (1997): 2–51, esp. 10.
18. Tcherikover, *Hellenistic Civilization*, 47–48; Purvis, "Samaritans," 600–601.

fact that the high priest Onias III, son of Simon the Just, sheltered Hyrcanus's money in the temple treasury might suggest Onias's alienation from the older brothers as well.[19] Second, a certain Simon, a temple official,[20] sought to discredit Onias III by informing Seleucus IV about these funds. Seleucus sent a deputy, Heliodorus, to confiscate this money; thus Seleucus would both enjoy a windfall toward paying his debts and deprive a potential enemy (Hyrcanus) of resources. When Heliodorus arrived in Jerusalem, the whole city turned out in protest, praying to God to prevent the sacrilege, and their prayers were answered. Heliodorus returned to Seleucus empty-handed.

Continued trouble from Simon led Onias to appeal to Seleucus IV for support to defuse the rivalry (2 Macc. 4:1–6), but after his return to Antioch, Heliodorus participated in a conspiracy to murder Seleucus, probably in an attempt to secure power for Seleucus's younger son (Appian, *Hist. rom.* 11.8.45). Antiochus IV, who had been released by the Romans in exchange for Seleucus's older son, Demetrius (later Demetrius I Soter [162–150 BCE]), was a magistrate in Athens at this time, well within striking distance of his father's domain. With the support of King Attalus of Pergamum and allies in the Seleucid court, he managed to gain power for himself, thus supplanting two rightful heirs (Seleucus IV's two sons) and, it may have been suspected, Seleucus IV himself (whence the three plucked-up horns of Dan. 7:8, 20).

With the accession of a new king and Onias III under some suspicion, the more progressive elements among the Jerusalem elite made their move against the conservative high priest and toward a new Jerusalem. Jeshua, who took the name "Jason," was Onias's more progressive younger brother. Jason appealed to Antiochus IV to be made high priest in his brother's place, securing this with a massive bribe. Jason promised an additional 150 talents if the king would give him permission to re-create Jerusalem as a Greek city (a *polis*) with a new constitution. Antiochus IV, always in need of money to pay Rome's tribute and to finance his planned campaigns of expansion, accepted Jason's offer. Onias III, the "prince of the covenant," was removed by Antiochus IV (Dan. 11:22), and would eventually succumb to foul play (2 Macc. 4:32–34).

Jason enrolled those Jewish elites who were sympathetic to his agenda as citizens of the new Jerusalem and stocked the senate (*gerousia*) from this pool.

---

19. Tcherikover, *Hellenistic Civilization*, 156–57.

20. Simon probably enjoyed the support of the older sons of Joseph ben Tobiah, as would his brother Menelaus in the intrigues to follow. They were not, contrary to Zeitlin (*Rise and Fall*, 73, 78), sons of Joseph themselves. The Greek text of 2 Macc. 3:4 calls Simon a member of the tribe of Benjamin, but the Old Latin and Armenian correct this by connecting him to the priestly clan of Bilgah, named in 1 Chron. 24:14. The latter is probably more correct, given the easy accession of Menelaus to the high priesthood (Hayes and Mandell, *Jewish People*, 48).

He built a gymnasium for the training of Jerusalem's elite youths in Greek language, literature, and culture (including, prominently, athletics). The Torah was formally displaced as the basis for civil and political law, though not as the basis for public religious and private devotional practice (see 1 Macc. 1:10–15; 2 Macc. 3–4; Josephus, *Ant.* 12.237–241; *J.W.* 1.31–33).

This policy of voluntary hellenization enjoyed widespread support among the upper classes. All sources agree that a group of "renegade" Jews sought after the hellenization of Judea (Dan. 11:30; 1 Macc. 1:11), believing that this would put them on an equal footing with the people around them under Greek rule.[21] The sum of money that Jason promised also suggests widespread support among those who would most profit from the "reforms" that would position them for unimpeded access to both economic and political advancement in the larger arena of the Hellenistic kingdoms. The Tobiads may well have backed Jason against Onias, the former being more congenial to their own desires for Jerusalem's reform. Antiochus IV, moreover, would welcome such enthusiasm for Hellenistic ways. The de-emphasizing of native culture, customs, and hopes in favor of Hellenistic culture and ambitions would make Judea a more pacified possession. Antiochus had designs on conquering Egypt, and a secure Judea was an aid to his imperial aspirations. There appears to have been no overt resistance to these measures, perhaps because they left the matter of religious and cultic observances untouched. When Antiochus IV made his first visit to Jerusalem in 172 BCE, there were no demonstrations against him (2 Macc. 4:21–22).

Matters became more complicated later in 172 BCE when a certain Menelaus (a brother of the Simon who opposed Onias III) made a bid to Antiochus IV for the high priesthood, raising Jason's annual tribute by three hundred talents. This move may reflect a shift in the Tobiads's allegiance from Jason to a yet more pliable puppet (Josephus, *Ant.* 12.239).[22] Again, always in need of cash, Antiochus removed Jason and appointed Menelaus as high priest.

---

21. See Otto Mørkholm, "Antiochus IV," in Davies and Finkelstein, *Hellenistic Period*, 278–91, esp. 281. The hellenization of Palestine had advanced and would continue to advance in ways that were not seen as "critical" or threatening to the survival of Judaism, including the introduction of Greek language alongside Aramaic and Hebrew; a growing awareness of and dialogue with Greek literature, philosophy, and the traditions and stories that constitute "cultural literacy"; and increasing use of Greek forms of argumentation and rhetoric. In all these areas, "hellenizing" would not be seen as antithetical in and of itself to remaining a faithful Jew. See Martin Hengel, *Judaism and Hellenism: Studies in Their Encounter in Palestine during the Early Hellenistic Period* (trans. John Bowden; 2 vols.; Philadelphia: Fortress, 1974); John M. G. Barclay, *Jews in the Mediterranean Diaspora from Alexander to Trajan (323 BCE–117 CE)* (Edinburgh: T&T Clark, 1996), 88–91.

22. Mørkholm, "Antiochus IV," 281.

Seleucid interference in the appointment of the high priest, along with the overt buying and selling of the most sacred office, became increasingly problematic for the Judeans. Jason had been, at least, a Zadokite and therefore an acceptable incumbent. Menelaus, however, had no such claim to the high priesthood (2 Macc. 4:25). This change of priesthood appears also to have split the upper class and military personnel; Jason himself fled Jerusalem but retained a large number of supporters.

Menelaus was unable to pay Antiochus the promised sums and was summoned to Antioch to answer for it. A revolt in Tarsus, however, bought Menelaus a reprieve. He appropriated funds from the temple treasuries to bribe Syrian officials and to increase his own liquid resources, a move that deeply alienated the local population (2 Macc. 4:27–32). When Antiochus was at last free to hear charges against Menelaus, the latter had the means to make his payment to the king. Continued pillaging of the temple got Lysimachus, Menelaus's other brother and deputy, killed in a riot (4:39–42). Members of the *gerousia* finally brought formal complaints before Antiochus against Menelaus, who was again called to account, but the latter used bribes to manipulate the inquest in his favor, with the result that he even got his accusers executed (4:43–47). It is noteworthy that there was such opposition to Menelaus even among the hellenizing elite.[23]

The situation in Judea worsened against the backdrop of Antiochus IV's campaigns against Egypt. In 169 BCE Ptolemy VI Philometor (181–146) instigated a war with Antiochus IV by invading Palestine, but he was soundly defeated and captured (Polybius, *Hist.* 27.19; 28.1.4–6). Meanwhile, Ptolemy VI's younger brother, Ptolemy VIII Euergetes II, was made king in his place. Antiochus attempted an alliance with Ptolemy VI (his nephew, incidentally), promising to restore the latter to the throne as his vassal and thus using him as a pretext for war (see Dan. 11:27; Livy, *Hist.* 44.19.8; 45.11.1–6; Diodorus Siculus, *Bib. hist.* 31.1.1). Ptolemy VI appears to have been aware of Antiochus's insincerity, suspecting that his overall plan was to so weaken Egypt through civil war as to leave it all the more vulnerable to himself. Thus Ptolemy VI worked behind the scenes, with the help of his mother, Cleopatra, to be reconciled to his younger brother, whence Daniel's remembrance of the "double-cross" at the table.[24]

Major Figures in the Ptolemaic Empire

Ptolemy I Soter (322–285 BCE)

Ptolemy II Philadelphus (285–246 BCE)

23. Tcherikover, *Hellenistic Civilization*, 171.
24. Hartman and Di Lella, *Daniel*, 297.

Ptolemy III Euergetes (246–221 BCE)

Ptolemy IV Philopator (221–203 BCE)

Ptolemy V Epiphanes (203–181 BCE) (married Cleopatra I)

Ptolemy VI Philometor (181–146 BCE)

Ptolemy VII Neos, son of Philometor (briefly in 145 BCE)

Ptolemy VIII Euergetes II, brother of Philometor (jointly, 170–146; singly, 146–116 BCE)

Daniel 11:28 suggests that Antiochus IV took some action "against the holy covenant" between his two wars with Egypt. It is admittedly difficult to correlate Antiochus's actions in Jerusalem with his two campaigns.[25] It is likely that the king's actions at this point involved raiding the temple treasury and its supply of sacred vessels of gold and silver for the value of their metal content to replenish his war coffer, as Menelaus was ever in arrears in regard to his tribute, an action that no doubt increased anti-Seleucid sentiments in Jerusalem.[26]

The following year, Antiochus IV initiated an invasion of Egypt (Polybius, *Hist.* 28.18–23). He would have succeeded, except for the intervention of the Romans, under whose protection Egypt had placed itself at the instigation of Cleopatra I, Antiochus IV's sister. Ptolemy VI appealed to Rome for help (Livy, *Hist.* 44.19.6–14), with the result that "ships from Kittim" (Dan. 11:30) arrived in Alexandria carrying a Roman legate who ordered Antiochus to cease and desist from his efforts to take possession of Egypt or else risk war with Rome (Appian, *Hist. rom.* 11.66; Polybius, *Hist.* 29.27.1–7; Livy, *Hist.* 45.12.1–8; 45.13.1–7; Diodorus Siculus, *Bib. hist.* 31.2.1–2). Antiochus IV set out for his own territory, all the more bitterly defeated by Roman fiat after he had successfully conquered by right of arms.

During Antiochus's second campaign against Egypt, a rumor of his death roused Jason to seize the opportunity to regain control of the high priesthood. Raising a sizeable force (supported by Egypt? by Hyrcanus's surviving family?), he attacked Menelaus in Jerusalem, besieging him in the citadel. Antiochus received word of this as he returned from Egypt and regarded Jason's attack on Menelaus—still his appointee, whatever his competence—as an attack on his own rule, perhaps even as an attempt by a pro-Ptolemaic faction to undermine his hold on Judea. He responded brutally by slaughtering thousands (Dan. 11:30–31). It appears from our sources, however, that Jason had

25. Hayes and Mandell, *Jewish People*, 58. Sources include Dan. 11:29–31; 1 Macc. 1:20–23; 2 Macc. 5:1–22; Josephus, *Ant.* 12.239–250; *J.W.* 1.31–33.

26. Mørkholm, "Antiochus IV," 283.

actually withdrawn from Jerusalem before Antiochus's arrival, leading to the plausible theory that the tumult in Jerusalem gave Jewish resistance its first opportunity to crystallize, both driving out Jason and continuing to besiege Menelaus.[27] This alone would account for Antiochus's actions on his arrival (2 Macc. 5:5–7, 11–14).[28] Menelaus led Antiochus into the temple so as to pay the latter his due tribute from the treasury, an act of desecration that deeply galled the populace.

After Antiochus restored Menelaus, armed resistance must again have flared up, with the result that, in early 167, it was necessary for troops under the command of Apollonius to enter Jerusalem by force and subterfuge (1 Macc. 1:29–32; 2 Macc. 5:23b–26).[29] Apollonius established the Akra, a military garrison that would also serve as a fortress for the hellenized population of "Antioch-at-Jerusalem" (1 Macc. 1:33–36). This fortress remained a Seleucid stronghold until 142 BCE. Many residents of Jerusalem fled into the countryside; many more were dispossessed of houses and property in order to furnish the settled soldiers. The Jerusalem temple now had to make room for all citizens of Antioch-at-Jerusalem—Greek, Syrian, and Jewish—and so the sacred space was redecorated and furnished accordingly and its rites altered to accommodate the syncretistic practices of the inhabitants of the Akra.[30] This change in cult practice would be remembered in the sources as the "abomination of desolation" or "desolating sacrilege" (Dan. 11:31; 12:11; 1 Macc. 1:54).

The precise nature of the cult established there remains a mystery. Was the temple now dedicated to Zeus Olympios (2 Macc. 6:2),[31] or to a Syrian god (Baal Shamen), or to both, jointly identified with the God of Israel? Did the "desolating sacrilege" (Dan. 11:31; 1 Macc. 1:54) involve the introduction of a cult image, as one would expect for non-Jewish worship? If so, it is difficult to explain the silence in the sources about an idol being introduced. For example, 2 Maccabees 6:1–7 speaks only of rededicating the temple to Zeus, the defiling behavior in the temple (cult prostitutes, covering the altar with "abominable offerings forbidden by the law"), and the compulsory participation in the cults of the king and of Dionysus. It is also difficult to discern what religious tradi-

27. The authors of 1 and 2 Maccabees could understandably have omitted or underplayed references to armed resistance prior to the actions of Judas Maccabaeus and his family, the heroes of both histories.

28. Tcherikover, *Hellenistic Civilization*, 186–88. The most important sources for Antiochus's actions against Jerusalem are 1 Macc. 1:16–63; 2 Macc. 5–7; Josephus, *Ant.* 12.242–264; *J.W.* 1.34–35. Diodorus Siculus (*Bib. hist.* 34/35.1.3–5) makes brief mention of Antiochus's actions but appears to lack a firm grasp of their details.

29. Tcherikover, *Hellenistic Civilization*, 188.

30. Ibid., 194–96.

31. Mørkholm, "Antiochus IV," 286.

tion is reflected in the rites described, particularly involving the sacrifice of pigs.[32] It has been suggested that this was a cult of Menelaus's own invention, since it appears not to align with known Greek or Syrian practice.[33] What is clear is that the temple and its new, "inclusive" cult excluded all faithful Jews, including, no doubt, many who were avid promoters of Hellenism.

Perhaps as part of Apollonius's punitive measures, perhaps in response to further violent resistance to the innovations in the temple,[34] the practice of Judaism was proscribed. If "zeal for the Torah" stood at the center of the Judeans' resistance to Antiochus's measures to procure the peace of Jerusalem, then the Torah itself, and the way of life that exalted it, needed to be eliminated.[35] The symbols of Jewish exclusivism were particularly targeted: circumcision of infants brought death to the family; the sign of acquiescence to, and acceptance of, the religious pluralism of the new Antioch-at-Jerusalem was eating a morsel of pork; possession of a copy of the Torah was grounds for execution (1 Macc. 1:44–50, 57–63; 2 Macc. 6:1, 8–11; 6:18–7:42). As long as people outside the regime had access to the Torah, the legitimacy of the new cult promoted under Menelaus (and symbolizing the peaceful coexistence of Jew and gentile in Judea) would be threatened. So began the first systematic attempt to enforce the abandonment of the exclusivist form—the traditional form—of Judaism, and this attempt claimed many victims. At this point, the process of hellenization had overstepped the limits of the people's tolerance, and a revolution against Menelaus's priesthood and Syrian rule ensued.

Important questions remain concerning Antiochus's motivations for his actions in Judea and the degree to which pro-hellenizing Jews cooperated in these actions. The fact that some Jews actively and enthusiastically sought after the formal hellenization of Jerusalem cannot be denied (Dan. 11:30; 1 Macc. 1:11–15; 2 Macc. 4:7–15), such that Antiochus IV cannot be painted simply as a tyrant seeking to unify his realm by unilaterally imposing Greek culture and suppressing native cultures and religion (contra 1 Macc. 1:41–43).[36]

32. Ibid.

33. Klaus Bringmann, *Hellenistische Reform und Religionsverfolgung in Judäa: Eine Untersuchung zur jüdisch-hellenistischen Geschichte (175–163 v. Chr.)* (AAWG 3/132; Göttingen: Vandenhoeck & Ruprecht, 1983), 109–10; see further Elias J. Bickerman, *The God of the Maccabees: Studies on the Meaning and Origin of the Maccabean Revolt* (trans. Horst R. Moehring; SJLA 32; Leiden: Brill, 1979), 61–75; Grabbe, *Persian and Greek Periods*, 258–59.

34. Tcherikover (*Hellenistic Civilization*, 195, 198) looks to the Hasidim as a resistance movement active in Jerusalem prior to the outbreak of the persecution: though they might not defend themselves on the Sabbath, there were six other days on which they could offer "sturdy resistance."

35. Ibid., 198.

36. The Roman historian Tacitus (early second century CE) refers briefly to this period: "King Antiochus made an effort to get rid of their primitive cult and hellenize them, but his

Antiochus IV was no more avid a hellenizer than were his predecessors, and there is no evidence that other local cults and cultures were suppressed under his rule.[37]

Nor was Antiochus IV a particularly zealous apostle of Zeus Olympios (contra Dan. 11:37–38).[38] Zeus had been claimed as the patron deity of Antiochus's predecessors (the switch from Apollo having happened considerably earlier than Antiochus, to judge from coins).[39] Moreover, the suppression of native cults in favor of worship of Zeus is not elsewhere attested in Antiochus IV's reign.[40] The suppression of Torah observance was local to Judea. Samaria was unmolested and, apart from some agitation against Jews in the cities of Philistia, Jews in the Diaspora were unaffected.[41] Antiochus's actions in Judea "must be regarded as [a] purely political measure."[42] They were a response to resistance, even open revolt, in Judea.

A closely related question concerns the role of hellenizing Jewish leaders like Menelaus in the instigation of religious repression and forced syncretism. Did Antiochus IV settle on the suppression of Judaism in Judea himself? Was the program of overturning the Jewish religion a measure invented by Menelaus or others among the extreme hellenizers, supported by Antiochus IV as a plausible plan to rout resistance? While some scholars speak of the repression of Judaism as Antiochus's idea and initiative, with which Menelaus and his supporters went along only reluctantly,[43] it seems more likely that Antiochus

---

would-be reform of this degraded nation was foiled by the outbreak of war with Parthia, for this was the moment of Arsaces's insurrection" (*Hist.* 5.8). Although Tacitus is mistaken about the exact problem in the east, he is correct that Antiochus's energies and forces were needed in the eastern part of his empire and would shortly dispose him and his son to make concessions in Judea. Tacitus seems to be completely unaware, however, that many elite Jews shared his own position on the benefits of hellenization for the nation.

37. Grabbe, *Persian and Greek Periods*, 248–49; E. J. Bickermann, *The Jews in the Greek Age* (Cambridge, MA: Harvard University Press, 1988), 61–68.

38. Abel, *De la conquête d'Alexandre*, 124–25.

39. Hartman and Di Lella, *Daniel*, 302.

40. Goldingay, *Daniel*, 302.

41. The Samaritans averted difficulties with Antiochus by disavowing their connection with Jerusalem and by accepting the identification of the God of Mount Gerizim and Zeus (Josephus, *Ant.* 12.257–264; see also 2 Macc. 6:2, which presumes that the Shechemites had adopted this name for their temple sometime previously). The Samaritans may also have been split between a dominant pro-hellenizing faction and a more conservative group, as was Jerusalem (Zeitlin, *Rise and Fall*, 93). On Jews in the Diaspora during the Hellenistic and Roman periods, see David A. deSilva, "Jews in the Diaspora," in *The World of the New Testament: Cultural, Social, and Historical Contexts* (ed. Joel B. Green and Lee M. McDonald; Grand Rapids: Baker Academic, 2013), 272–90, and the literature cited therein.

42. Otto Mørkholm, *Antiochus IV of Syria* (CMD 8; Copenhagen: Gyldendal, 1966), 186; so also Grabbe, *Persian and Greek Periods*, 256.

43. So, e.g., Zeitlin, *Rise and Fall*, 90; Stern, "Period of the Second Temple," 204–5.

Rise of Apocalyptic Literature

Although there are important precursors to apocalyptic literature in the prophetic period, the genre and the worldview that nourished it actually took shape during the Hellenistic era. Apocalypses generally communicate a revelation of realities beyond normally experienced space and time. The reader thereby gains knowledge of a much larger "map" of heavenly and infernal spaces and of past and future history, all of which functions to provide an interpretive context for the realities and challenges encountered in lived time and space.[a] This revelation comes through supernatural means, whether in visions, in conversations with angelic (or higher) intermediaries, or in other ecstatic experiences. As such, it claims priority over other forms of public knowledge and discourse communicated through mundane means, including public discourse about the rule of kings and emperors and their place in the cosmos. This makes apocalypse an ideal genre for expressing resistance to, and critique of, current political and social arrangements.[b]

The earliest specimens of apocalypse appear in Palestine during the Ptolemaic period, in texts that come to be included in *1 Enoch*. The revelation of the movements of the astral bodies (the Astronomical Book [*1 En.* 72–82]) becomes an authoritative warrant for a solar calendar and a particular method of intercalating the required additional days. The wars of the Diadochi may provide the impetus for Jewish reflection on the demigods who wreak havoc in the land, developing the legend of the fallen angels and their giant offspring (Gen. 6:1–4) as found in the Book of the Watchers (*1 En.* 6–16).[c] A number of prophetic forecasts of history (mostly written after the fact) support resistance to the measures of Antiochus IV and promote hope in the wars of Judas (the Apocalypse of Weeks and the Animal Apocalypse [*1 En.* 93.1–10 + 91.11–17; 85–90]).

Daniel 7–12, the earliest canonical witness to the genre, arose in response to the actions of Antiochus IV against Judea, again as a means to promote resistance to the program for Judea of the imperial overlords and their Judean partners by drawing a larger map in which God and God's faithful ones ultimately emerge victorious. The genre would continue to be an important venue for reaffirming the viability of the subaltern culture's view of the cosmos and for the commitments and way of life nurtured by that view, becoming particularly prevalent in the wake of Rome's destruction of the second temple (Revelation; *4 Ezra*; *2 Baruch*; *Apocalypse of Abraham*).

a. David A. deSilva, *Seeing Things John's Way: The Rhetoric of the Book of Revelation* (Louisville: Westminster John Knox, 2009), 11–14.

b. David A. deSilva, *Seeing Things John's Way*; Anathea Portier-Young, *Apocalypse against Empire: Theologies of Resistance in Early Judaism* (Grand Rapids: Eerdmans, 2010).

c. George W. E. Nickelsburg, *Jewish Literature between the Bible and the Mishnah: A Historical and Literary Introduction* (Minneapolis: Fortress, 1981), 51–52.

would have relied on their insider advice concerning the power of Torah as a rallying cry for resistance and how best to respond.[44] Some ancient sources are also willing to assign a good portion of the blame to Menelaus (2 Macc. 13:4; Josephus, *Ant.* 12.384).

Antiochus IV soon met his demise, but not as the author of Daniel 10–12 predicted (Dan. 11:40–45). He died not in battle between Jerusalem and the seacoast, but ignominiously following an attempt to raid the treasury of another temple: the sanctuary of Artemis at Elymaïs (Polybius, *Hist.* 31.9; Diodorus Siculus, *Bib. hist.* 31.18a.1).

Relevant Rulers of the Seleucid Empire

Seleucus I Nicator (312–280 BCE)

Antiochus I Soter (coregent, 291–280; king, 280–261 BCE)

Antiochus II Theos (261–246 BCE)

Seleucus II Callinicus (246–226 BCE)

Seleucus III Soter (226–223 BCE)

Antiochus III "the Great" (coregent, 226–223; king, 223–187 BCE)

Seleucus IV Philopator (187–175 BCE)

Antiochus IV Epiphanes (175–163 BCE)

Antiochus V Eupator (163–162 BCE)

Demetrius I Soter (162–150 BCE) versus Alexander Balas I (152–145 BCE)

Demetrius II Nicator (145–138 BCE) versus Antiochus VI Dionysos (145–140 BCE)

Diodotos Tryphon (140–138 BCE)

Antiochus VII Sidetes (139–129 BCE)

The Maccabean Revolution

The author of Daniel wrote before the greater victories of Mattathias and his sons, though perhaps he was a witness to some early, small-scale strikes against renegades and Syrians (Dan. 11:34). The principal sources for this history are 1 Maccabees 2–9 and 2 Maccabees 8–15. Josephus also relates events of the revolution, but he depends principally on 1 Maccabees.[45]

---

44. Bickerman, *God of the Maccabees*, 76–90; Mørkholm, "Antiochus IV," 284–85; Grabbe, *Persian and Greek Periods*, 284.

45. On the military history of the revolt, see further Bezalel Bar-Kochva, *Judas Maccabeus: The Jewish Struggle against the Seleucids* (Cambridge: Cambridge University Press, 1989); Tcherikover, *Hellenistic Civilization*, 204–34.

There are a number of conflicting data in the two principal sources. According to both, the Seleucid general Lysias initiates two campaigns involving an attack on the fortress of Beth Zur (1 Macc. 4:26–35; 6:26–31, 48–50; 2 Macc. 11:5–15; 13:18–26). According to 1 Maccabees, however, the first of these preceded the rededication of the temple (and provides the occasion for it, as Lysias withdraws in defeat to gather more troops), whereas both are placed after the rededication in 2 Maccabees. Similarly, the timing of Antiochus IV's death differs: in 2 Maccabees it precedes the rededication (2 Macc. 9:1–29); in 1 Maccabees it postdates both the rededication and Judas's campaigns against neighboring cities to defend their Jewish residents (1 Macc. 6:1–17). The timing of the latter campaigns also varies between the two sources. These are generally resolved in favor of the chronology in 1 Maccabees. Maccabean-era dates also present a general problem due to the use of two calendars within the Seleucid Empire, one beginning the year in April and a second starting it in October. This is further complicated by the likelihood that the author of 1 Maccabees used different sources that themselves followed different calendars,[46] and by the difficulties involved in reconciling dates in 1 Maccabees and 2 Maccabees.[47]

Another issue centers on the historical value and authenticity of the diplomatic correspondence and other documents preserved in 1 Maccabees, and therefore on the reliability of these documents as contemporary witnesses to events narrated in these books.[48] The most important of these documents include

1. internal Jewish documents
   a. a letter from Jews in Gilead to Judas (5:10–13)
   b. a decree concerning the appointment of Simon and his descendants to the high priesthood (14:27–45)
2. correspondence between the Jews and Rome
   a. a letter from the Roman senate to the Jewish people (8:23–32)
   b. a circular letter from the Romans concerning the Jews (15:16–21)
3. correspondence between the Jews and Sparta
   a. a letter from Jonathan to the Spartans (12:6–18)

46. Harold W. Attridge, "Jewish Historiography," in *Early Judaism and Its Modern Interpreters*, ed. Robert A. Kraft and George W. E. Nickelsburg (Philadelphia: Fortress, 1986), 319; see further, John R. Bartlett, *1 Maccabees* (GAP; Sheffield: Sheffield Academic Press, 1998), 36–53.

47. See Lester L. Grabbe, "Maccabean Chronology: 167–164 or 168–165 BCE?," *JBL* 110 (1991): 59–74; Bringmann, *Hellenistische Reform*, 15–40; Bartlett, *1 Maccabees*, 36–53.

48. See W. O. E. Oesterley, "1 Maccabees," in *Apocrypha* (vol. 1 of *The Apocrypha and Pseudepigrapha of the Old Testament*; ed. R. H. Charles; Oxford: Oxford University Press, 1913), 59–124, esp. 61–65; Sidney Tedesche and Solomon Zeitlin, *The First Book of Maccabees: An English Translation* (New York: Harper, 1950), 38–48; Grabbe, *Persian and Greek Periods*, 223–24, 260–63; Bartlett, *1 Maccabees*, 81–83, 87–99.

    b. a letter from Arius, king of Sparta, to Onias, high priest (12:20–23)

    c. a letter from Sparta to Simon (14:20–23)

4. letters between Jewish leaders and Seleucid monarchs

    a. from Demetrius I to Jonathan (10:3–6)

    b. Alexander Balas to Jonathan (10:18–20)

    c. Demetrius I to Jonathan (10:25–45)

    d. Demetrius II to Jonathan (11:29–37)

    e. Demetrius II to Simon (13:3–40)

    f. Antiochus VII to Simon (15:1–9)[49]

Verdicts concerning the authenticity of these documents range widely, from seeing them as verbatim reproductions of authentic records, to imaginative expansions or rewritten versions of such texts, to summaries of original texts, to fictitious compositions by the author. Factors considered in the discussion include the likelihood that such a document would have been written, preserved, and available for the author's inspection, whether or not the style of the letter conforms to chancery styles appropriate for each type, and whether or not a document shows signs of being altered in favor of advancing the image or interests that the author wishes to project or promote. The likelihood that the Hasmonean leaders kept archives of their dealings with foreign powers and internal resolutions makes it probable that many of these documents contain reliable information, even those that show signs of being summaries or rewritten versions of a document,[50] except for the correspondence with Sparta (though the literary fiction does not rule out the possibility of real diplomatic relations with Sparta in pre-Maccabean and Hasmonean Judea.)[51] Similar questions are raised in regard to the documents represented in 2 Maccabees 11.[52]

Mattathias was a priest in the line of Joarib (1 Chron. 24:7; Neh. 11:10); with his five sons—John, Simon, Judas, Eleazar, and Jonathan—he left Jerusalem for the village of Modein during the radical reforms and rallied a guerrilla army (1 Macc. 2:1–28). Their initial targets were other Jews who

49. W. O. E. Oesterley, *An Introduction to the Books of the Apocrypha* (London: SPCK, 1935), 303.

50. Oesterley ("1 Maccabees," 61–65) offers the following verdicts (keyed to the outline in the preceding paragraph): 1a, 2a, and 4b are summary reports of genuine documents; 1b, 3b, 3c, and 4e are genuine; 2b and 4d are basically genuine; 3a is a forgery, reflecting, however, a genuine diplomatic relationship with Sparta; 4c and 4f are exaggerated rewrites of a genuine letter; 4a is not discussed. Bartlett (*1 Maccabees*, 83–97) provides a similarly detailed examination of each on its own merits and is essentially in agreement with Oesterley, except that Bartlett rejects 3b and 3c as forgeries.

51. Bartlett, *1 Maccabees*, 95–97.

52. See Tcherikover, *Hellenistic Civilization*, 213–18.

had abandoned observance of the exclusivist commands of Torah. Boys left uncircumcised were forcibly circumcised; Jews who had accommodated too far feared for their lives (1 Macc. 2:44–48; 3:5–8).[53]

The movement gained momentum under Judas's leadership. The local Seleucid officials did not take the threat sufficiently seriously at the outset, allowing Judas and his band to enjoy some early victories that fueled the fire of resistance and demoralized the Syrian occupying forces, more or less setting the tone for the campaigns that followed. During 165 and 164 BCE the Seleucid administration sent out increasingly larger forces, but Judas's army grew as well on account of his initial victories. A series of Seleucid defeats in major battles led to a temporary cease-fire (1 Macc. 3:10–4:35; 2 Macc. 8:5–36, with significant differences). Judas seized on this opportunity to besiege, capture, and cleanse the temple (1 Macc. 4:36–61; 2 Macc. 10:1–8). The pagan paraphernalia were removed, and the temple was rededicated to the Torah-regulated service of God. Judas may also have taken this opportunity to strike back at gentile cities in surrounding territories that had ostensibly harassed their Jewish residents (1 Macc. 5–6; 2 Macc. 12:1–9) as well as to engage in smaller skirmishes against Seleucid forces left in the region (2 Macc. 12:10–45).

The reprieve was short-lived: Lysias's armies returned in force (1 Macc. 6:18–63; 2 Macc. 11:1–15; 13:1–26), in part no doubt responding to the continued unrest in Judea. Intrigues within the Seleucid government began here to work in Judea's favor. First, Lysias received word about the return of another of Antiochus IV's generals, Philip, with designs on taking control of the empire from Lysias and his ward, Antiochus V Eupator. Lysias pushed the latter to confirm the Jews' religious liberty and ratify the reestablishment of the traditional cult (1 Macc. 6:55–63; 2 Macc. 11:22–26).[54] Menelaus himself was finally executed as "the source of all the trouble" (2 Macc. 13:4).[55] At this point, many Jews were willing to lay down their arms. Judas and his brothers, together with their army, however, refused to abandon the field. What began as a war for the restoration of Torah had become a war for political independence.

A more serious battle for succession arose between Antiochus IV's nephew, Demetrius I Soter (161–150), and Antiochus V (see Polybius, *Hist.* 31.2.1–6; 31.11–15), resulting in the deaths of Antiochus V and his guardian, Lysias

53. The claim in Daniel that "many shall join them insincerely" (Dan. 11:34) may refer to Mattathias and Judas's early policy of concentrating their fury against disloyal Jews, such that, in some areas, it might have become safer to join the Maccabees than to remain under the protection of the high priest appointed by Antiochus (Hartman and Di Lella, *Daniel*, 300). The book of 2 Maccabees is silent concerning these assaults on fellow Jews.

54. Tcherikover, *Hellenistic Civilization*, 225–26.

55. Mørkholm, "Antiochus IV," 288–90.

(1 Macc. 7:1–4; 2 Macc. 14:1–2). Demetrius continued to press the war in Judea. After defeating the first force under Nicanor (1 Macc. 7:26–50; 2 Macc. 14:11–15:37), Judas finally died in battle against an army led by Bacchides, a serious reversal for the conservative party in Judea (1 Macc. 9:5–27).

Leadership of the revolution fell to Judas's younger brother, Jonathan. He led the Judean army twice to victory over Bacchides, leading to terms of peace (1 Macc. 9:43–73). Further intrigues among claimants for the Seleucid throne greatly weakened Seleucid power to coerce and greatly strengthened Jonathan's position to negotiate. Both Demetrius I and his rival, Alexander Balas I (152–145), tried to enlist Judea's military support, each trying to best the other's offers to Jonathan as the de facto leader of Judea. In this process, Jonathan was appointed to the high-priestly office in 153 BCE by Alexander Balas (1 Macc. 10:15–21), with whom he ultimately sided, and was confirmed as such by Balas's successors in the ongoing strife within the Seleucid dynasty (10:48–12:38).

When Jonathan fell to treachery (1 Macc. 12:39–53; 13:12–30), his last surviving (though elder) brother Simon was chosen to lead the people (13:1–9), continuing also in his brother's stead as high priest. Simon allied himself with Demetrius II (against whom Jonathan had avidly fought [11:45–74; 12:24–38]), by whose order in 142 BCE the Seleucid troops stationed in the Akra in Jerusalem were finally withdrawn and, thus, the "yoke of the Gentiles" decisively removed. Judea and its environs became an independent state under the last surviving brother of Judas after four hundred years of foreign domination (1 Macc. 13:41–52).

The Archaeology of Hellenistic Palestine

Excavations of monuments from the Hellenistic and Hasmonean period have not been as plentiful as, for example, monuments from the Herodian period. Nevertheless, a number of discoveries provide corroborative or complementary data for the study of this period.

Digs in Samaria have unearthed evidence of sturdily built round towers against the old wall, dating from about 323–321 BCE, when Perdiccas rebuilt the city, as well as the remains of a Hellenistic-period settlement and a later Seleucid-era fortress.[56] The discovery of over two thousand handles of Greek wine jugs testify to Greco-Syrian presence there. A major settlement from the

---

56. William F. Albright, *The Archaeology of Palestine* (rev. ed.; Baltimore: Penguin, 1954), 150; Halpern-Zylberstein, "Archaeology of Hellenistic Palestine," 3–5; Berlin, "Between Large Forces," 10.

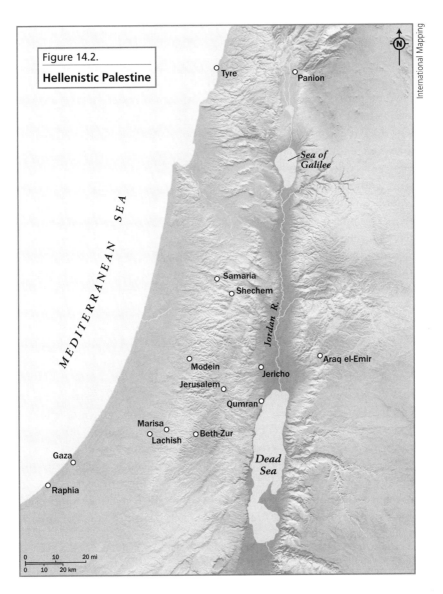

Figure 14.2.

Hellenistic Palestine

International Mapping

third-century BCE was Marisa (Mareshah) in Idumea, a city that benefited from the rise of Gaza's importance as the center of customs for export to Egypt's markets. Excavations revealed a city laid out in the grid pattern more typical of Greek urban planning, formidable fortifications, and extensive facilities for producing olive oil and raising doves.[57]

57. Berlin, "Between Large Forces," 6–8.

One site that has enjoyed extensive excavation is Beth Zur, about four miles north of Hebron. Beth Zur figures prominently in the history of this period (1 Macc. 4:29, 61; 6:7, 26, 31, 49–50; 9:52; 10:14; 11:65; 14:7, 33; 2 Macc. 11:5; 13:19, 22). Digs have revealed fortifications from the Persian or early Ptolemaic period, a second phase of fortification under Judas Maccabeus between 165 and 163 BCE, and a third phase of fortification under Bacchides in 161 BCE (see 1 Macc. 9:52).[58] Coins of Antiochus IV and Antiochus V Eupator were found in particular abundance (126 out of about 300), as well as scores of wine-jar handles stamped with the seal of a Rhodian potter, suggesting a large amount of imported Greek wine for the gentile garrison there (the supposition being that imported soldiers would have a taste for imported wine).[59] Excavations at Gezer have revealed the ruins of fortifications undertaken under Bacchides and a fortress of Simon.[60] Coins from the period after Alexander Janneus are not found at Beth Zur, Gezer, or Marisa, in keeping with the historical record. Janneus had significantly pushed the boundaries of his territory beyond these southern and western frontier forts, rendering their ongoing occupation unnecessary.[61]

Archaeologists have yet to discover the Seleucid Akra. Preferred locations include a site in the Lower City, the Ophel rise on the southeastern hill of Jerusalem, as Josephus relates;[62] a site directly adjacent to the northwestern or southeastern corner of the Temple Mount;[63] and a site in the Upper City, across the Tyropoeon Valley.[64] So far, no Hellenistic-era constructions have been found in the last area, nor Hellenistic-era pottery or coins. However, Hellenistic-era pottery and coins have been found in the Lower City southwest of the temple, giving some credence to Josephus's alternative.[65]

Tombs from the period show the influence of Hellenistic styles. For example, the mausoleum of the Tobiad family at 'Araq el-Emir in central Transjordan, adjacent to a more primitive third-century-BCE rock-cut tomb bearing Tobiah's name, has an elaborate façade carved into the face of the rock,

58. Albright, *Archaeology of Palestine*, 150–52; Halpern-Zylberstein, "Archaeology of Hellenistic Palestine," 8–9; Berlin, "Between Large Forces," 21–22.

59. Halpern-Zylberstein, "Archaeology of Hellenistic Palestine," 32.

60. Albright, *Archaeology of Palestine*, 152; Halpern-Zylberstein, "Archaeology of Hellenistic Palestine," 10; Berlin, "Between Large Forces," 29.

61. Albright, *Archaeology of Palestine*, 153; Halpern-Zylberstein, "Archaeology of Hellenistic Palestine," 8.

62. Bar-Kochva, *Judas Maccabeus*, 445–65.

63. Berlin, "Between Large Forces," 18.

64. Halpern-Zylberstein, "Archaeology of Hellenistic Palestine," 12n4.

65. Yoram Tsafrir, "The Location of the Seleucid Akra in Jerusalem," in *Jerusalem Revealed: Archaeology in the Holy City, 1968–1974* (ed. Yigael Yadin; trans. Rafi Grafman; Jerusalem: Israel Exploration Society, 1975), 85–86.

which includes carved columns with Corinthian capitals. This dates from about 175 BCE, around the time of the demise of Hyrcanus, son of Joseph ben Tobiah.[66] Similarly, the tomb of the Bene Hezir, carved out of the side of a mountain, combines a Greek-styled temple façade with Ionic columns supporting a pyramidal roof.[67] Tombs in Marisa show a penchant for Greek and Egyptian decoration, including painted columns and faux friezes to give the impression of architectural ornament, as well as frescoes depicting animals, amphorae, wreaths, and musicians.[68]

Partisan Judaism in the Hellenistic Period

According to Josephus, the Pharisees, Sadducees, and Essenes already existed as distinct parties within Judaism during the time of Jonathan's high priesthood (*Ant.* 13.171–173). The events of 175–150 BCE certainly provided sufficient opportunities for the formation of some, if not all, of these parties, though our sources give no sure reports concerning how any one of these parties originated.[69]

During the hellenizing crisis and the ensuing persecution of pious Jews, the Hasidim (or Hasidaioi, or Hasideans [1 Macc. 2:42; 7:13; 2 Macc. 14:6]) emerged as an identifiable group characterized by their deep piety and by their willingness to fight zealously to preserve that piety.[70] Many scholars have sought the origins of the Pharisees, the Essenes, or both parties in this resistance group. Solomon Zeitlin draws on Josippon (third century CE) to support identifying the Hasidim as the root of the Essene movement, since where Josephus reads "Essenes," Josippon often reads "Hasidim" as the third party alongside Pharisees and Sadducees.[71] He finds further support in Philo's etymology of "Essene" as a derivation of the Hebrew word for "piety" (*ḥesed*)

---

66. Albright, *Archaeology of Palestine*, 149–50. Alternatively, this more elaborate building may represent the entranceway into Hyrcanus's fortress, as described in Josephus, *Ant.* 12.230–233 (see Berlin, "Between Large Forces," 11–12). The fact that this hall, carved into the mountain, was used as a church in the Byzantine period has obscured its original use.

67. Albright, *Archaeology of Palestine*, 157. Halpern-Zylberstein ("Archaeology of Hellenistic Palestine," 23n2), however, places this tomb in the Herodian period. Her essay also provides a more detailed treatment of the archaeology of the period.

68. Berlin, "Between Large Forces," 15; David M. Jacobson, *The Hellenistic Paintings of Marisa* (PEFM 7; London: Maney, 2007).

69. For a survey of references to these various parties in Josephus, Philo, the New Testament, and other sources, see Shaye J. D. Cohen, *From the Maccabees to the Mishnah* (Philadelphia: Westminster, 1987), 144–59.

70. The author of Daniel speaks of "the wise" (Dan. 11:33) at about the same time in a manner that might likewise suggest an identifiable group within Judaism.

71. Zeitlin, *Rise and Fall*, 188–89.

and "pious ones" (*ḥasidîm*).[72] John Kampen argues for a connection between the Hasidim and the later Pharisees, observing that both appear to emerge from scribal circles, and that the Hasidim are portrayed in ways reminiscent of Pharisees (e.g., the Pharisees' lack of support for Hasmonean policies in the periods of John Hyrcanus I and Alexander Janneus), suggesting that the author of 1 Maccabees, at least, saw a connection.[73] Others, however, regard the Hasidim merely as a "loose association of pietists," and not the forerunner of either party.[74]

Some scholars have argued that both Pharisees and Sadducees existed well before the Hasmonean period. Rabbinic traditions speak of "pairs" of leaders of the "Great Synagogue," a judicial body that existed prior to the more hellenized *gerousia* under Jason. Identifying most of these names with known Pharisees, Louis Finkelstein believes that the Pharisees actively contributed to developing legal rulings in the late Persian and Ptolemaic periods, though they lost their influence during the hellenizing crisis.[75] Lawrence Schiffman sees evidence in a document known as *Some Precepts of the Torah* (4QHalakhic Letter)—found in multiple copies among the Dead Sea Scrolls (4QMMT = 4Q394–399)—that the people entrusted with administering the temple in the early Hasmonean period followed rulings regarding ritual purity and handling sacrifices that would later be explicitly identified as Pharisaic halakah, as opposed to the author of *4QHalakhic Letter*, who argued for the correctness of rulings that would later be attributed to the Sadducees.[76] This could suggest the influence of Pharisees (or the Pharisees' forerunners) in the temple cult and interpretation of the Torah prior to John Hyrcanus and Alexander Jan-

---

72. Géza Vermès also identifies the "Teacher of Righteousness" as, at first, "the priestly head of the Hasidim" (*The Dead Sea Scrolls in English* [4th ed.; London: Penguin, 1995], 36).

73. John Kampen, *The Hasideans and the Origins of Pharisaism: A Study in 1 and 2 Maccabees* (SBLSCSS 24; Atlanta: Scholars Press, 1988), 212–19. Kampen provides a lengthy list of adherents to such views (38n145).

74. Lawrence H. Schiffman, *Reclaiming the Dead Sea Scrolls: The History of Judaism, the Background of Christianity, the Lost Library of Qumran* (ABRL; New York: Doubleday, 1995), 76; Anthony J. Saldarini, *Pharisees, Scribes and Sadducees in Palestinian Society: A Sociological Approach* (Wilmington, DE: Michael Glazier, 1988), 253; Philip R. Davies, "Hasidim in the Maccabean Period," *JJS* 28 (1977): 127–40.

75. Louis Finkelstein, "The Pharisaic Leadership of the Great Synagogue (ca. 400–170 BCE)," in Davies and Finkelstein, *Hellenistic Period*, 245–77.

76. Schiffman, *Reclaiming the Dead Sea Scrolls*, 78. For example, 4Q396 II, 6–9 asserts that an unbroken liquid stream communicates impurity in either direction (from the source vessel to the receptacle, or from the receptacle back to the source vessel), a position in line with the view later attributed to Sadducees (*m. Yad.* 4.7, versus *m. Ṭahor.* 8.9, which gives the rabbinic ruling, reportedly in line with Pharisaic halakah). Similarly, 4Q394 3–7, I, 16–19 states that the priest involved in the ceremony of the red heifer does not become clean again until the sun has set (i.e., not before sunset, which would come to be known as the Pharisaic position).

neus's intentional alignment with the Sadducees' halakah (thus against the Pharisees' positions).

The Greek word *pharisaioi* (Pharisees) is derived from the Hebrew *pĕrûšîm* (separate ones).[77] This group exhibited a care for maintaining ritual purity beyond that of the typical pious Jew. As a result, they felt it necessary to restrict their table fellowship (eating being an activity fraught with many potential opportunities for impurity) to Jews committed to maintaining similarly higher standards of ritual purity.[78] Thus they formed "associations" and spoke of their "associates" (*ḥăbērîm*).[79] They were not, however, introversionist in their approach to life in general (unlike the community at Qumran or the Essenes as a whole). At one point in the Dead Sea Scrolls, the Pharisees may be reflected in the sobriquet "seekers after smooth things [*ḥălāqôt*]," perhaps a pun on *ḥălākôt*, the specific rulings about following Torah in particular situations sought by Pharisees (4QNahum Pesher).[80] The identification is not certain,[81] but it would provide an interesting counterpoint to New Testament texts that accuse Pharisees of being too stringent!

There appear to have been a number of significant splits within the priestly class during this period, spawned by widespread discontent with the administration of the temple, first by the hellenizing high priests and then by the Hasmoneans. Scholars tend to speak of "Sadducees" as essentially an equivalent term for "Zadokites," priests who were of, or were committed to, a particular high-priestly family line that had been entrusted with administration of the temple and its sacrifices (Ezek. 44:15–16). Schiffman speaks of the pre-Hasmonean, hellenizing high priests as Sadducees, though he rightly notes, "Many Sadducean priests during this period continued to be pious, maintaining the ancient traditions of the Temple in Jerusalem."[82] Onias III and his son Onias IV would have been such priests. If "Sadducee" was already a meaningful term in 175 BCE, however, we should not assume that it meant what Josephus would describe on the basis of his experience of Sadducees (and Pharisees) in the first century CE.

Louis Finkelstein posits that a number of these pious Sadducees broke from the majority of their party over the direction in which the priestly elite was taking Jerusalem, siding instead with the Pharisees (who surely would

---

77. Saldarini, *Pharisees, Scribes and Sadducees*, 220–25.

78. Schiffman, *Reclaiming the Dead Sea Scrolls*, 76.

79. Although Pharisees formed associations and were called *ḥăbērîm*, not all *ḥăbērîm* were Pharisees (Zeitlin, *Rise and Fall*, 201).

80. See 4Q169 3 +4 I, 2, 7; 3–4 II, 2, 4; 3–4 III, 3, 6–7.

81. Saldarini, *Pharisees, Scribes and Sadducees*, 279.

82. Schiffman, *Reclaiming the Dead Sea Scrolls*, 71.

have been found among the resistance against Antiochus IV and his appointed high priests).[83] What bound these parties together at this time was greater than what separated them, and this forged a sufficiently strong foundation to allow two very different schools to accept each other, even while they debated vociferously. The ex-Sadducean Pharisees were stricter in their interpretation of the Torah, and their line came to be associated with the school of Shammai in the mid-first century BCE, while the historic Pharisaic line came to be associated with Hillel.

Another theory connects pious, disenfranchised Zadokites (or members of their party) with the emergence of the sectarian community at Qumran. According to Schiffman, the emergence of high priests from a non-Zadokite family (in particular, Jonathan the Hasmonean) provided the occasion for pious Sadducean opposition to the new regime.[84] These Sadducean priests formed the core of the separatist faction that would become the Qumran sect, opposing the Pharisaic influence on Jonathan's conduct of the temple.[85] So *4QHalakhic Letter*, then, would represent an attempt on the part of these Sadducees to convince Jonathan of the correctness of their *hălākôt* and thus reconcile the new regime to their party.[86] Even if the Qumran sect's origins were Sadducean, the sect would quickly move in a direction that resembled Essenism far more closely than Sadducean Judaism as Josephus describes it (e.g., in Qumran's belief in afterlife and in their lively angelology, both of which the Sadducees would reject).[87] The more moderate and "moderately hellenized" Sadducees remained in Jerusalem; these are the people who would be remembered as Sadducees.

A more typical view locates the origins of Essenism in other priestly circles, perhaps circles that also produced and preserved texts such as *1 Enoch*, *Jubilees*, and *Testaments of the Twelve Patriarchs*.[88] Essene communities, including

83. Finkelstein, "Pharisaic Leadership," 245, 254; see also Zeitlin, *Rise and Fall*, 176.

84. Schiffman, *Reclaiming the Dead Sea Scrolls*, 71.

85. Gabriele Boccaccini agrees that Essenism and, ultimately, the Qumran sect arose from priestly circles, but not Zadokite/Sadducean circles specifically (*Beyond the Essene Hypothesis: The Parting of the Ways between Qumran and Enochic Judaism* [Grand Rapids: Eerdmans, 1998], 185–86).

86. Schiffman, *Reclaiming the Dead Sea Scrolls*, 84.

87. Their denial of resurrection and angels does not make Sadducees less religious than Pharisees or Essenes. If anything, it makes them more religiously conservative, since the Hebrew Bible does not clearly attest to doctrines of life after death or resurrection from the dead, beliefs that took shape among Jews in the Hellenistic period (Saldarini, *Pharisees, Scribes and Sadducees*, 304).

88. The Essenes' interest, e.g., in the "names of angels" (Josephus, *J.W.* 2.142) is reflected in the lists of angels in *1 En.* 6–9; 69 (Boccaccini, *Essene Hypothesis*, 170). Sources on Essenes and their various manifestations include Philo, *Good Person 75–91*; *Hypoth.* 11; Josephus, *J.W.* 2.119–161; *Ant.* 13:171–172; 18:11, 18–22; Pliny the Elder, *Nat.* 5.70–73; and the Dead Sea Scrolls.

the Qumran sect,[89] regulated their communal life by the *Damascus Covenant* (CD) and the *Rule of the Community* (1QS). The two rules, though closely related, are clearly not identical, presuming two different kinds of community. The preservation of both rules together among the Dead Sea Scrolls, in relatively high numbers of manuscript fragments, suggests that the communities regulated by these different rules were bound to one another in a cooperative relationship rather than as rivals.[90] The Qumran sect is the more radical group, rejecting family life and the validity of the Jerusalem temple altogether (replacing it with their own bloodless offerings of righteousness and devotion to the covenant [1QS VIII, 8–12; IX, 4–6]), but it is not therefore a schismatic offshoot of Essenism, whose texts it still cherished.[91] The two branches might have been aiming, instead, for different levels of holiness and ritual purity, with the sect at Qumran serving as a kind of spiritual elite for the whole movement.

Khirbet Qumran is, of course, one of the most thoroughly excavated sites from the late Hellenistic and early Roman periods, which, given its connection to the celebrated Dead Sea Scrolls, is hardly surprising. Preliminary archaeological reports suggested that a small group occupied the abandoned Iron Age site, restoring its main building and cistern and digging several more cisterns. This may have occurred as early as the period of Jonathan or Simon, though some would date the beginnings of the settlement to the time of Alexander Janneus. Early in the reign of John Hyrcanus, more settlers joined the community, expanding the complex to include the defensive tower, several more communal buildings (probably including a scriptorium, dining hall, and pantry), a pottery kiln and workshop, and a much more extensive water system with additional ritual baths. The site is notable for the complete absence of decorative and luxury goods.[92]

The *Damascus Covenant* and the pesharim are particularly important for historical questions about the movement. The former paints a picture of a group forming 390 years after the destruction of the first temple (587–586 BCE)

89. John J. Collins, *Beyond the Qumran Community: The Sectarian Movement of the Dead Sea Scrolls* (Grand Rapids: Eerdmans, 2010), 122–56.

90. Vermès, *Dead Sea Scrolls*, 17; Collins, *Qumran Community*, 2–6, 48–50, 209.

91. Contrary to Boccaccini, *Essene Hypothesis*, 166, 178–85. Although they regarded sexual intercourse as inherently impure, Essenes nevertheless married and raised families, not neglecting their duty to perpetuate the human race (Josephus, *J.W.* 2.120–21, 160–61; CD-A VII, 7–9; cf. *T. Iss.* 2.1–3). They sought to live lives of simplicity, working at agriculture or fishing, sharing their possessions (Philo, *Good Person* 76, 79). Essenes continued to send offerings to the temple, despite their questions about the legitimacy of how the cult was being administered (Josephus, *Ant.* 18.19).

92. Berlin, "Between Large Forces," 34–35; see further Roland de Vaux, *Archaeology and the Dead Sea Scrolls* (London: Oxford University Press, 1973); Jodi Magness, *The Archaeology of Qumran and the Dead Sea Scrolls* (Grand Rapids: Eerdmans, 2003).

but lacking direction for twenty years until the "Teacher of Righteousness" (or simply "a righteous teacher") came (CD-A I, 4–11; CD-B XIX, 35; XX, 1, 28–32). After the Teacher of Righteousness died, the group expected another forty years to pass before "the end of all the men of war who deserted to the Liar." John Hayes and Sara Mandell suggest that these dates should be read as essentially accurate.[93] In 198 BCE something of sufficient significance happened to warrant a sectarian split: the Seleucids took over Palestine. Since the Seleucid Empire used a lunar calendar, this might have been the occasion on which temple officials began to follow the lunar calendar as well. The issue of whether to calculate Sabbaths and festivals following the lunar calendar or the solar calendar (and, among those following the latter, the question of when to intercalate the four additional days) was of great importance to the circles that produced the Enochic literature and the book of *Jubilees* and those who lived at Qumran (see *1 En.* 72–82; *Jubilees*, which is cited in CD-A XVI, 2–4; *4QCalendrical Document* [4Q320–330]; 1QS X, 1–6).

Few scholars, however, take these dates so precisely, preferring to understand the source of the 390 years in a sectarian exegesis of Ezekiel 4:5, where God commands Ezekiel to lie on his left side for "three hundred ninety days, the same number as the years of their punishment,"[94] possibly in conjunction with an exegesis of Daniel's seventy weeks of years (if the Teacher's active ministry runs forty years, the time from the destruction of the first temple to the eschatological intervention of God is 490 years). References in the pesharim place the Teacher of Righteousness and his nemesis, the "Wicked Priest," more surely in the Hasmonean period. These two figures appear to have been allies at one point, with the former feeling betrayed by the latter, perhaps in connection with the latter's assumption of the high priesthood, if the former thought that he had a more legitimate claim and the latter's support. The harsh criticism of the temple and its rites, the emphasis on observing the proper calendar, and the level of purity required among the Essenes (especially at Qumran)—all point to the priestly location and concern (indeed, obsession) of the Teacher of Righteousness. The fact that the community he led became a substitute for the cultic system of the temple might also point in this direction (similar to Onias IV's solution, though without the construction of an alternative temple for cultic sacrifice).

Jonathan, brother of Judas Maccabeus, is frequently regarded as a prime candidate for being the Wicked Priest.[95] He had a good reputation with the

---

93. Hayes and Mandell, *Jewish People*, 88–90.

94. See Collins, *Qumran Community*, 8.

95. See Hanan Eshel, *The Dead Sea Scrolls and the Hasmonean State* (Grand Rapids: Eerdmans; Jerusalem: Yad Ben-Zvi Press, 2008), 29–61.

pious, along with his brothers, at the outset of his activity (1QpHab VIII, 9–14). His assumption of the high priesthood, appointed by a Seleucid king, would have given occasion for a change in this reputation among some. He was killed by an agent of the Greco-Syrian kings (4Q171 IV, 5–11; 1 Macc. 13:23). Documents such as *4QHalakhic Letter*, however, suggest that disaffection with the way the temple cult was being performed and the way rules of purity were observed under Jonathan was of greater significance than questions of lineage.

The Hasmonean Dynasty and Its Decline

Roman historians give scant attention to the events in Judea prior to Pompey's intervention in 63 BCE. Tacitus makes only this brief reference to the Hasmonean dynasty:

> Since the Hellenistic rulers were weak, . . . the Jews established a dynasty of their own. These kings were expelled by the fickle mob, but regained control by force, setting up a reign of terror which embraced, among other typical acts of despotism, the banishment of fellow-citizens, the destruction of cities, and the murder of brothers, wives and parents. The kings encouraged the superstitious Jewish religion, for they assumed the office of High Priest in order to buttress their regime. (*Hist.* 5.8)[96]

Tacitus's characterization of Hasmonean rule is grossly one-sided. Nevertheless, he accurately reflects the fact that it was the strife within the Seleucid dynasty that allowed for the establishment of the Hasmonean dynasty. Tacitus is also correct that this family did much to alienate their subjects and arouse significant animus, such as appears in some Jewish literature from the period. John Hyrcanus I and Alexander Janneus did, in fact, destroy cities in neighboring territories as part of their territorial expansion (notably Samaria to the north), and Judah Aristobulus I (104–103) was guilty of murdering his mother and one of his brothers. Many "fellow-citizens" would have preferred banishment to the fate they suffered under some of these kings—for example, the eight hundred crucified under Janneus while their families were butchered. Tacitus's final comment, betraying his bitter anti-Jewish prejudices, actually inverts the Hasmoneans' policy: they assumed the office of "king" to buttress their regime, having begun with the office of "high priest" as a hereditary possession. For historical reconstruction, we rely primarily on Josephus,

---

96. Tacitus, *The Histories* (trans. Kenneth Wellesley; rev. ed.; London: Penguin, 1986), 276.

Antiquities, and occasional, if oblique, references in the Qumran pesharim, the *Damascus Covenant*, and *Psalms of Solomon*.[97]

John Hyrcanus I (135–104), the son of Simon ben Mattathias, defended against attempts by Antiochus VII Sidetes (139–129) to reassert Seleucid control over the region. The latter even besieged Jerusalem, to the point that Hyrcanus had to agree to pay a heavy tribute and pledge soldiers to support the king's campaigns. Internal struggles over the Seleucid throne ensued after Sidetes's death, however, with the result that Hyrcanus reneged on the terms and began expanding the territory of his realm. He captured Shechem in 128 BCE and destroyed Samaria and Shechem about twenty years later (Josephus, *Ant.* 13.254–256, 275–283), annexing territory as far north as Scythopolis. He invaded Idumea as far south as Beersheba, forcing its inhabitants to accept circumcision and adopt Judaism (Josephus, *Ant.* 13.257–258), and he captured several cities in the region beyond the Jordan. The archaeological evidence supports Josephus's accounts of both campaigns.[98] One of the more impressive structures from the later Hellenistic period is the palace constructed by Hyrcanus, later expanded by his descendants, in the oasis of Jericho. This complex included a massive main house, a heated bath, a ritual bath, and a large garden area with two swimming pools.[99] Hyrcanus had a falling-out with the Pharisees after one of them questioned his genealogical fitness to retain the high priesthood (though not the secular power); the remainder urged a more lenient punishment for the offender than the death sentence that Hyrcanus wished to impose, with the result that the Sadducees gained in influence toward the end of his rule (Josephus, *Ant.* 13.288–299).

Hyrcanus had intended for his wife to succeed to his civil authority, but his eldest son, Judah Aristobulus I (104–103), moved to gain both the high priesthood and civil rule. He killed his mother and imprisoned three of his brothers, one of whom, Antigonus, was also eventually executed (Josephus, *Ant.* 13.301–313). Aristobulus began to use the title "king" (Josephus, *Ant.* 13.301). Now the Hasmoneans had usurped not only the high priesthood (traditionally belonging to the Zadokite line), but also the kingship (belonging to David's line). During his short reign Aristobulus was able to expand into Upper Galilee and possibly annexed Iturea, though the archaeological record in that region does not show evidence of battle and destruction in this period.[100] It is possible that one of the documents found among the Dead Sea

97. On the Hasmonean state, see further Stern, "Period of the Second Temple," 217–38; Tcherikover, *Hellenistic Civilization*, 235–65.
98. Berlin, "Between Large Forces," 31–32.
99. Ibid., 34–35, 42.
100. Ibid., 37.

Scrolls speaks in retrospect against John Hyrcanus I, referring to the deaths of two of his sons (Antigonus and Aristobulus) as a fulfillment of the divine curse against the person who would rebuild Jericho, as Hyrcanus did.[101]

The widow of Aristobulus, Salome Alexandra, released the remaining two brothers and married one, Alexander Janneus (103–76), making him king and high priest (Josephus, *Ant.* 13.320). Coins minted by Janneus with inscriptions in Greek and Hebrew bear witness to his use of the title "king."[102] Janneus continued to expand the borders of the Hasmonean state, gaining control over all the coastal cities from Gaza to Dora as well as the region of the Decapolis (Josephus, *Ant.* 13.395–397). He aroused much internal opposition, crushing the same with excessive brutality. His rule was so intolerable for some Jews that in 88 BCE they appealed to one of the rivals for the Seleucid throne, Demetrius III, for intervention (4Q169 3 +4 I, 1–5). Demetrius defeated Janneus in battle at Shechem, but after the former's withdrawal, Janneus took bitter revenge against his opponents, crucifying eight hundred Jews and slaughtering their families before their eyes (Josephus, *Ant.* 13.380; 4Q169 3 +4 I, 6–7).[103]

Hasmonean High Priests and Rulers

Name	Title	Period
Jonathan, brother of Judas	high priest	161–142 BCE
Simon, brother of Judas	high priest	142–135 BCE
John Hyrcanus I, son of Simon	high priest	135–104 BCE
Judah Aristobulus I, son of John Hyrcanus I	king and high priest	104–103 BCE
Alexander Janneus, son of John Hyrcanus I	king and high priest	103–76 BCE
Salome Alexandra, widow of Alexander Janneus	queen	76–67 BCE
John Hyrcanus II, son of Alexander Janneus	high priest	76–67 and 63–40 BCE
Judah Aristobulus II, son of Alexander Janneus	king and high priest	67–63 BE

Following Janneus's death, and possibly on his advice, his widow, Salome Alexandra (76–67), reconciled the dynasty to the Pharisees, restoring them to some degree of power (which they apparently used both to introduce their interpretations of Torah as the official rulings and to seek revenge against their enemies [Josephus, *Ant.* 13.405–409; *J.W.* 1.111–114]). Salome managed

101. See 4Q175 and 4Q379, discussed in Eshel, *Dead Sea Scrolls*, 63–90.
102. Berlin, "Between Large Forces," 37.
103. Eshel, *Dead Sea Scrolls*, 117–31.

to maintain the boundaries established by her husband. John Hyrcanus II, the elder son of Salome Alexandra, had functioned as high priest since the death of Alexander Janneus and was to become king on his mother's death. Judah Aristobulus II (67–63), the younger son, had other plans (see Josephus, *Ant.* 14.1–79; *J.W.* 1.120–158).

Supported by his personal allies, Aristobulus seized the strongholds throughout Judea, used the money stored therein to raise an army of hired soldiers, and proclaimed himself king and high priest. Hyrcanus lacked the support necessary to prevail, and he came to terms with Aristobulus. Antipater, an Idumean whose son Herod would become a major player in Judea, persuaded Hyrcanus to break his truce, flee to King Aretas in Petra, and seek support for seizing back his birthright. Aretas provided fifty thousand soldiers, allowing Hyrcanus to drive Aristobulus and his army back into Jerusalem, where they were besieged.

At this point, Rome intervened in the affairs of its eastern allies. Pompey, the triumvir charged with eastern affairs, sent Scaurus, one of his generals, to lift the siege and investigate. The two brothers came to Syria to present their cases to Pompey, alongside a third party—an embassy of "leading men, more than two hundred in number," complaining about the tyranny and brutality of Hasmonean rule (Diodorus Siculus, *Bib. hist.* 40.2). Pompey instructed both brothers to maintain the peace until he could come to Judea personally to settle their affairs. Aristobulus, however, mobilized for war. Pompey marched his army against Jerusalem and Aristobulus. Even though Aristobulus abandoned hopes of resistance and left the city to meet Pompey, Aristobulus's supporters would not open Jerusalem's gates. Pompey prepared to lay siege to the city, but Hyrcanus's party got control of the gates and allowed Pompey to enter. Aristobulus's partisans took refuge in the temple area. After a three-month siege, Pompey gained access to the temple. He killed the partisans he found inside, including some priests who were carrying out the religious service and sacrifices. Pompey and his officers even went into the holy places, perhaps to ensure that no insurgents were hiding there, perhaps simply to see its treasures. Josephus affirms, however, that they did not confiscate any of the furnishings or wealth deposited in the temple, and that they even ordered the priests to perform the necessary purification rites and resume their services the next day.

Pompey made Hyrcanus high priest, but not king, committing political authority to a senate. Judea became a Roman province and was required to pay an annual tribute. The territories annexed by Hyrcanus I and his sons were made independent of Judea (though likewise answerable to Rome). Once again Judea fell under the yoke of the gentiles after a mere eighty years of independence.

The enduring legacy of the Maccabeans was a renewed zeal for the restoration and secure establishment of the kingdom of Israel. Even if Jews ceased to view the Hasmonean kings as worthy or faithful leaders, they would now continue to hope for a future king who would take the best achievements of the Hasmoneans and combine them with the perfect embodiment of traditional Jewish virtues. Thus messianism and the fostering of hopes for God's perfect restoration of Israel flourished during this period.

Selected Bibliography

Abegg, Martin, Jr., Peter Flint, and Eugene Ulrich. *The Dead Sea Scrolls Bible: The Oldest Known Bible*. San Francisco: HarperSanFrancisco, 1999.

Abraham, Kathleen. "An Inheritance Division among Judeans in Babylonia from the Early Persian Period." Pages 206–21 in *New Seals and Inscriptions, Hebrew, Idumean and Cuneiform*. Edited by Meir Lubetski. Hebrew Bible Monographs 8. Sheffield: Sheffield Phoenix Press, 2007.

———. "West Semitic and Judean Brides in Cuneiform Sources from the Sixth Century BCE: New Evidence from a Marriage Contract from Al-Yahudu." *Archiv für Orientforschung* 51 (2005–2006): 198–219.

Ackroyd, Peter R. "The Succession Narrative (So-Called)." *Interpretation* 35 (1981): 383–96.

Agut-Labordère, Damien. "Les frontières intérieures de la société militaire égyptienne: L'invasion de l'Égypte par Artaxerxès III à travers Diodore XVI.46.4–51.3." *Transeuphratène* 35 (2008): 17–27.

Aharoni, Miriam. "Arad." Pages 75–87 in vol. 1 of *The New Encyclopedia of Archaeological Excavations in the Holy Land*. Edited by Ephraim Stern. Jerusalem: Israel Exploration Society & Carta, 1993.

Aharoni, Yohanan. *Arad Inscriptions*. Translated by Judith Ben-Or. Edited by Anson F. Rainey. Judean Desert Studies. Jerusalem: Israel Exploration Society, 1981.

———. "Arad: Its Inscriptions and Temple." *Biblical Archaeologist* 31 (1968): 2–32.

———. *The Archaeology of the Land of Israel: From the Prehistoric Beginning to the End of the First Temple Period*. Translated by Anson F. Rainey. Philadelphia: Westminster, 1982.

———. *Excavations at Ramat Raḥel, Seasons 1961 and 1962*. Serie archeologica 6. Rome: Center for Semitic Studies, 1964.

———. "The Horned Altar of Beer-sheba." *Biblical Archaeologist* 37 (1974): 2–6.

———. "The Israelite Sanctuary at Arad." Pages 28–44 in *New Directions in Biblical Archaeology*. Edited by David Noel Freedman and Jonas C. Greenfield. Garden City, NY: Doubleday, 1971.

———. *The Land of the Bible: A Historical Geography*. Translated by Anson F. Rainey. 2nd ed. Philadelphia: Westminster, 1979.

Ahituv, Shmuel. *Echoes from the Past: Hebrew and Cognate Inscriptions from the Biblical Period*. Translated and edited by Anson F. Rainey. Jerusalem: Carta, 2008.

Ahlström, Gösta W. "Administration of the State in Canaan and Ancient Israel." Pages 587–603 in vol. 1 of *Civilizations of the Ancient Near East*. Edited by Jack M. Sasson. New York: Scribner, 1995.

———. *The History of Ancient Palestine from the Palaeolithic Period to Alexander's Conquest.* Edited by Diana Vikander Edelman. Journal for the Study of the Old Testament: Supplement Series 146. Sheffield: JSOT Press, 1993.

———. *Who Were the Israelites?* Winona Lake, IN: Eisenbrauns, 1986.

Akkermans, Peter M., and Glenn M. Schwartz. *The Archaeology of Syria: From Complex Hunter-Gatherers to Early Urban Societies (c. 16,000–300 BC).* Cambridge World Archaeology. Cambridge: Cambridge University Press, 2003.

Albertz, Rainer. "The Controversy about Judeans versus Israelite Identity and the Persian Government: A New Interpretation of the Bagoses Story (*Jewish Antiquities* XI.297–301)." Pages 483–504 in *Judah and the Judeans in the Achaemenid Period: Negotiating Identity in an International Context.* Edited by Oded Lipschits, Gary N. Knoppers, and Manfred Oeming. Winona Lake, IN: Eisenbrauns, 2011.

———. *From the Exile to the Maccabees.* Vol. 2 of *A History of Israelite Religion in the Old Testament Period.* Old Testament Library. Louisville: Westminster John Knox, 1994.

Albright, William F. *The Archaeology of Palestine.* Rev. ed. Baltimore: Penguin, 1954.

———. "The Chronology of the Divided Monarchy of Israel." *Bulletin of the American Schools of Oriental Research* 100 (1945): 16–22.

———. "The Israelite Conquest in the Light of Archaeology." *Bulletin of the American Schools of Oriental Research* 74 (1939): 11–23.

———. "Some Important Recent Discoveries: Alphabetic Origins and the Idrimi Statue." *Bulletin of the American Schools of Oriental Research* 118 (1950): 11–20.

———. "Syria, the Philistines, and Phoenicia." Pages 507–36 in *History of the Middle East and the Aegean Region, c. 1380–1000 B.C.* Vol. 2.2 of *The Cambridge Ancient History.* Edited by I. E. S. Edwards, N. G. L. Hammond,

and E. Sollberger. 3rd ed. Cambridge: Cambridge University Press, 1975.

Alexander, T. Desmond, and David W. Baker. *Dictionary of the Old Testament: Pentateuch.* Downers Grove, IL: InterVarsity, 2003.

Allen, James P. "A Report of Bedouin." Pages 16–17 in *Archival Documents from the Biblical World.* Vol. 3 of *The Context of Scripture.* Edited by William W. Hallo and K. Lawson Younger Jr. Leiden: Brill, 2003.

Alt, Albrecht. "The Settlement of the Israelite Tribes in Palestine." Pages 173–221 in *Essays on Old Testament History and Religion.* Translated by R. A. Wilson. New York: Doubleday, 1967. German original, 1925.

Alter, Robert. *The Art of Biblical Narrative.* New York: Basic Books, 1981.

———. *The David Story: A Translation with Commentary of 1 and 2 Samuel.* New York: Norton, 1999.

Althann, Robert. "Gedaliah (Person) 2–5." Pages 923–24 in vol. 2 of *The Anchor Bible Dictionary.* Edited by David Noel Freedman. New York: Doubleday, 1992.

Altman, Amnon. "How Many Treaty Traditions Existed in the Ancient Near East?" Pages 17–36 in *Pax Hethetica: Studies on the Hittites in Honour of Itamar Singer.* Edited by Yoram Cohen, Amir Gilan, and Jared L. Miller. Wiesbaden: Harrassowitz, 2010.

Andersen, Francis I. "Israelite Kinship Terminology and Social Structure." *The Bible Translator* 20 (1969): 29–39.

Andersen, Frances I., and David Noel Freedman. *Hosea: A New Translation with Introduction and Commentary.* Anchor Bible 24. Garden City, NY: Doubleday, 1980.

Angel, Hayim. "Hopping between Two Opinions: Understanding the Biblical Portrait of Ahab." *Jewish Bible Quarterly* 35 (2007): 3–10.

Anson, Edward. "Idumaean Ostraca and Early Hellenistic Chronology." *Journal of the American Oriental Society* 125 (2005): 263–66.

Antoun, Richard T. *The Arab Village: A Social Structural Study of a Transjordanian Peasant Community.* Bloomington: Indiana University Press, 1972.

Arnold, Bill T. *Genesis*. New Cambridge Bible Commentary. Cambridge: Cambridge University Press, 2009.

———. "Hezekiah." Pages 407–12 in *The Dictionary of the Old Testament: Historical Books*. Edited by Bill T. Arnold and H. G. M. Williamson. Downers Grove, IL: InterVarsity, 2005.

———. "History and Historiography, OT." Pages 833–37 in vol. 2 of *The New Interpreter's Dictionary of the Bible*. Edited by Katharine Doob Sakenfeld. Nashville: Abingdon, 2009.

———. "The Neo-Babylonian Chronicle Series." Pages 407–26 in *The Ancient Near East: Historical Sources in Translation*. Edited by Mark W. Chavalas. Malden, MA: Blackwell, 2006.

———. "Pentateuchal Criticism, History of." Pages 622–31 in *Dictionary of the Old Testament: Pentateuch*. Edited by T. Desmond Alexander and David W. Baker. Downers Grove, IL: InterVarsity, 2003.

———. *Who Were the Babylonians?* Society of Biblical Literature Archaeology and Biblical Studies 10. Atlanta: Society of Biblical Literature, 2004.

Arnold, Bill T., and John H. Choi. *A Guide to Biblical Hebrew Syntax*. Cambridge: Cambridge University Press, 2003.

Arnold, Bill T., and H. G. M. Williamson, eds. *Dictionary of the Old Testament: Historical Books*. Downers Grove, IL: InterVarsity, 2005.

Aro, Jussi. "Remarks on the Language of the Alalakh Texts." *Archiv für Orientforschung* 17 (1954–1956): 361–65.

Ash, Paul S. *David, Solomon and Egypt: A Reassessment*. Journal for the Study of the Old Testament: Supplement Series 297. Sheffield: Sheffield Academic Press, 1999.

Astour, Michael C. "841 B.C.: Assyria's First Invasion of Israel." *Journal of the American Oriental Society* 91 (1971): 383–89.

Auld, A. Graeme. "Gideon: Hacking at the Heart of the Old Testament." *Vetus Testamentum* 39 (1989): 257–67.

Averbeck, Richard E. "The Sumerian Historiographic Tradition and Its Implications for Genesis 1–11." Pages 79–102 in *Faith, Tradition, and History: Old Testament Historiography in Its Near Eastern Context*. Edited by Alan R. Millard, James K. Hoffmeier, and David W. Baker. Winona Lake, IN: Eisenbrauns, 1994.

Avigad, Nahman. *Bullae and Seals from a Post-Exilic Judean Archive*. Qedem 4. Jerusalem: Institute of Archaeology, Hebrew University of Jerusalem, 1976.

———. *Discovering Jerusalem*. Nashville: Nelson, 1983.

———. "Excavations in the Jewish Quarter of the Old City, 1969–1971." Pages 41–51 in *Jerusalem Revealed: Archaeology in the Holy City, 1968–1974*. Edited by Yigael Yadin. Translated by R. Grafman. Jerusalem: Israel Exploration Society, 1975.

———. *Hebrew Bullae from the Time of Jeremiah: Remnants of a Burnt Archive*. Jerusalem: Israel Exploration Society, 1986.

———. "Samaria (City)." Pages 1300–1310 in vol. 4 of *The New Encyclopedia of Archaeological Excavations in the Holy Land*. Edited by Ephraim Stern. Jerusalem: Israel Exploration Society & Carta, 1993.

Avigad, Nahman, and Benjamin Sass. *Corpus of West Semitic Stamp Seals*. Jerusalem: Israel Exploration Society, 1996.

Babcock, Brian C. *Sacred Ritual: A Study of West Semitic Ritual Calendars in Leviticus 23 and the Akkadian Text Emar 446*. Bulletin for Biblical Research Supplements 9. Winona Lake, IN: Eisenbrauns, 2014.

Bachhuber, Christoph, and R. Gareth Roberts, eds. *Forces of Transformation: The End of the Bronze Age in the Mediterranean*. Themes from the Ancient Near East, BANEA Publication Series 1. Oxford: Oxbow, 2010.

Barclay, John M. G. *Jews in the Mediterranean Diaspora from Alexander to Trajan (323 BCE–117 CE)*. Edinburgh: T&T Clark, 1996.

Barkay, Gabriel. "A Bulla of Ishmael, the King's Son." *Bulletin of the American Schools of Oriental Research* 290–291 (1993): 109–14.

———. "Excavations at Ketef Hinnom in Jerusalem." Pages 85–106 in *Ancient Jerusalem Revealed*. Edited by Hillel Geva. Jerusalem: Israel Exploration Society, 1994.

———. "The Iron Age II–III." Pages 302–73 *The Archaeology of Ancient Israel*. Edited by Amnon Ben-Tor. New Haven: Yale University Press, 1992.

———. "The King of Babylonia or a Judean Official?" *Israel Exploration Journal* 45 (1995): 41–47.

———. "The Redefining of Archaeological Periods: Does the Date 588/586 BCE Indeed Mark the End of the Iron Age Cultures?" Pages 107–8 in *Biblical Archaeology Today*. Edited by Avraham Biran and Joseph Aviram. Jerusalem: Israel Exploration Society, 1993.

Bar-Kochva, Bezalel. *Judas Maccabeus: The Jewish Struggle against the Seleucids*. Cambridge: Cambridge University Press, 1989.

Barstad, Hans M. "After the 'Myth in the Empty Land': Major Challenges in the Study of Neo-Babylonian Judah." Pages 3–20 in *Judah and the Judeans in the Neo-Babylonian Period*. Edited by Oded Lipschits and Joseph Blenkinsopp. Winona Lake, IN: Eisenbrauns, 2003.

———. *History and the Hebrew Bible: Studies in Ancient Israelite and Ancient Near Eastern Historiography*. Forschungen zum Alten Testament 61. Tübingen: Mohr Siebeck, 2008.

———. *The Myth of the Empty Land: A Study in the History and Archaeology of Judah during the "Exilic" Period*. Symbolae osloenses 28. Oslo: Scandinavian University Press, 1996.

Barth, Fredrik, ed. *Ethnic Groups and Boundaries: The Social Organization of Culture Difference*. Boston: Little, Brown, 1969.

Bartlett, John R. "Edom." Pages 287–95 in vol. 2 of *The Anchor Bible Dictionary*. Edited by David Noel Freedman. New York: Doubleday, 1992.

———. *1 Maccabees*. Guides to Apocrypha and Pseudepigrapha. Sheffield: Sheffield Academic Press, 1998.

Beach, Eleanor Ferris. "The Samaria Ivories, Marzeah, and Biblical Texts." *Biblical Archaeologist* 55 (1992): 130–39.

Beaulieu, Paul-Alain. *The Reign of Nabonidus, King of Babylon, 556–539 B.C.* Yale Near Eastern Researches 10. New Haven: Yale University Press, 1989.

———. "Yahwistic Names in Light of Late Babylonian Onomastics." Pages 245–66 in *Judah and the Judeans in the Achaemenid Period: Negotiating Identity in an International Context*. Edited by Oded Lipschits, Gary N. Knoppers, and Manfred Oeming. Winona Lake, IN: Eisenbrauns, 2011.

Beck, Pirhiya. "The Drawings from Horvat Teiman (Kuntillet 'Ajrud)." *Tel Aviv* 9 (1982): 3–68.

Beck, Pirhiya, and Moshe Kochavi. "Aphek (in Sharon)." Pages 62–72 in vol. 1 of *The New Encyclopedia of Archaeological Excavations in the Holy Land*. Edited by Ephraim Stern. Jerusalem: Israel Exploration Society & Carta, 1993.

Becking, Bob. "Drought, Hunger, and Redistribution: A Social Economic Reading of Nehemiah 5." Pages 137–49 in *The Historian and the Bible: Essays in Honour of Lester L. Grabbe*. Edited by Philip R. Davies and Diana Vikander Edelman. Library of Hebrew Bible/Old Testament Studies 530. London: T&T Clark, 2010.

———. *From David to Gedaliah: The Book of Kings as Story and History*. Orbis biblicus et orientalis 228. Fribourg: Academic Press; Göttingen: Vandenhoeck & Ruprecht, 2007.

———. "The Seal of Baalisha, King of the Ammonites: Some Remarks." *Biblische Notizen* 97 (1999): 14–17.

———. "'We All Returned as One!': Critical Notes on the Myth of the Mass Return." Pages 3–18 in *Judah and the Judeans in the Persian Period*. Edited by Oded Lipschits and Manfred Oeming. Winona Lake, IN: Eisenbrauns, 2006.

———. "Yehudite Identity in Elephantine." Pages 403–19 in *Judah and the Judeans in the Achaemenid Period: Negotiating Identity in an International Context*. Edited by Oded Lipschits, Gary N. Knoppers, and Manfred

Oeming. Winona Lake, IN: Eisenbrauns, 2011.

Beckman, Gary M. *Hittite Diplomatic Texts.* Edited by Harry A. Hoffner. 2nd ed. Society of Biblical Literature Writings from the Ancient World 7. Atlanta: Scholars Press, 1999.

Beit-Arieh, Itzhaq. "The Edomites in Cisjordan." Pages 33–40 in *You Shall Not Abhor an Edomite for He Is Your Brother: Edom and Seir in History and Tradition.* Edited by Diana Vikander Edelman. Society of Biblical Literature Archaeology and Biblical Studies 3. Atlanta: Scholars Press, 1995.

———, ed. *Tel 'Ira: A Stronghold in the Biblical Negev.* Tel Aviv University Institute of Archaeology Monographs 15. Tel Aviv: Emery and Claire Yass Publications in Archaeology of the Institute of Archaeology, Tel Aviv University, 1999.

———. "Tel-'Ira and Ḥorvat 'Uzzah: Negev Sites in the Late Israelite Period" [in Hebrew]. *Cathedra* 42 (1987): 34–38.

Ben-Tor, Amnon. "The Fall of Canaanite Hazor—The 'Who' and 'When' Questions." Pages 456–67 in *Mediterranean Peoples in Transition: Thirteenth to Early Tenth Centuries BCE.* Edited by Seymour Gitin, Amihai Mazar, and Ephraim Stern. Jerusalem: Israel Exploration Society, 1998.

———. "Hazor." Pages 1–5 in vol. 3 of *The Oxford Encyclopedia of Archaeology in the Near East.* Edited by Eric M. Meyers. Oxford: Oxford University Press, 1997.

———. "The Sad Fate of Statues and the Mutilated Statues of Hazor." Pages 3–16 in *Confronting the Past: Archaeological and Historical Essays on Ancient Israel in Honor of William G. Dever.* Edited by Seymour Gitin, J. Edward Wright, and J. P. Dessel. Winona Lake, IN: Eisenbrauns, 2006.

Ben Zvi, Ehud. "Prelude to a Reconstruction of the Historical Manassic Judah." *Biblische Notizen* 81 (1996): 31–44.

Ben Zvi, Ehud, and Christoph Levin, eds. *The Concept of Exile in Ancient Israel and Its Historical Contexts.* Beihefte zur Zeitschrift für die alttestamentliche Wissenschaft 404. Berlin: de Gruyter, 2010.

Berlin, Adele. "Characterization in Biblical Narrative: David's Wives." *Journal for the Study of the Old Testament* 23 (1982): 69–85.

Berlin, Andrea M. "Between Large Forces: Palestine in the Hellenistic Period." *Biblical Archaeologist* 60 (1997): 2–51.

Berman, Joshua. "CTH 133 and the Hittite Provenance of Deuteronomy 13." *Journal of Biblical Literature* 130 (2011): 25–44.

Beyer, Klaus. *The Aramaic Language: Its Distribution and Subdivisions.* Translated by John F. Healy. Göttingen: Vandenhoeck & Ruprecht, 1986.

Bickerman, Elias J. "The Babylonian Captivity." Pages 342–58 in *Introduction; The Persian Period.* Vol. 1 of *The Cambridge History of Judaism.* Edited by W. D. Davies and Louis Finkelstein. Cambridge: Cambridge University Press, 1984.

———. *The God of the Maccabees: Studies on the Meaning and Origin of the Maccabean Revolt.* Translated by Horst R. Moehring. Studies in Judaism in Late Antiquity 32. Leiden: Brill, 1979.

———. *The Jews in the Greek Age.* Cambridge, MA: Harvard University Press, 1988.

Bienkowski, Piotr, ed. *Busayra Excavations by Crystal-M. Bennett, 1971–1980.* Oxford: Oxford University Press, 2002.

Bienkowski, Piotr, and Leonie Sedman. "Busayra and Judah: Stylistic Parallels in the Material Culture." Pages 310–25 in *Studies in the Archaeology of the Iron Age in Israel and Jordan.* Edited by Amihai Mazar. Journal for the Study of the Old Testament: Supplement Series 331. Sheffield: Sheffield Academic Press, 2001.

Bietak, Manfred. "Comments on the Exodus." Pages 163–71 in *Egypt, Israel, Sinai: Archaeological and Historical Relationships in the Bible Period.* Edited by Anson F. Rainey. Tel Aviv: Tel Aviv University, 1987.

Bimson, J. J. "Archaeological Data and the Dating of the Patriarchs." Pages 53–89 in *Essays on the Patriarchal Narratives.* Edited by A. R. Millard and D. J. Wiseman. Leicester, UK: Inter-Varsity, 1980.

Biran, Avraham. "Dan (Place)." Pages 12–17 in vol. 2 of *The Anchor Bible Dictionary*. Edited by David Noel Freedman. New York: Doubleday, 1992.

———. "Dan, Tel." Pages 313–21 in vol. 1 of *Encyclopedia of Archaeological Excavations in the Holy Land*. Edited by Michael Avi-Yonah. Jerusalem: Israel Exploration Society; Massada Press, 1975.

———. "Tel Dan: Biblical Texts and Archaeological Data." Pages 1–17 in *Scripture and Other Artifacts: Essays on the Bible and Archaeology in Honor of Philip J. King*. Edited by Michael D. Coogan, Cheryl Exum, and Lawrence E. Stager. Louisville: Westminster John Knox, 1994.

Biran, Avraham, and Joseph Naveh. "An Aramaic Stele from Tel Dan." *Israel Exploration Journal* 43 (1993): 81–98.

———. "The Tel Dan Inscription: A New Fragment." *Israel Exploration Journal* 45 (1995): 1–18.

Birnbaum, Salomo A. "Sherds with Letters in Aramaic Script." Pages 25–33 in *The Objects from Samaria*. Edited by John W. Crowfoot, Grace M. Crowfoot, and Kathleen M. Kenyon. Samaria-Sebaste 3. London: Palestine Exploration Fund, 1957.

Bittel, Kurt. "Bildliche Darstellungen Ḫattušili III in Ägypten." Pages 39–48 in *Kaniššuwar: A Tribute to Hans G. Güterbock on His Seventy-Fifth Birthday, May 27, 1983*. Edited by Harry A. Hoffner Jr. and Gary M. Beckman. Assyriological Studies 23. Chicago: Oriental Institute of the University of Chicago, 1986.

Blakely, Jeffrey A. "Reconciling Two Maps: Archaeological Evidence for the Kingdoms of David and Solomon." *Bulletin of the American Schools of Oriental Research* 327 (2002): 49–54.

Blenkinsopp, Joseph. "Ahab of Israel and Jehoshaphat of Judah: The Syro-Palestinian Corridor in the Ninth Century." Pages 1309–19 in vol. 2 of *Civilizations of the Ancient Near East*. Edited by Jack M. Sasson. New York: Scribner, 1995.

———. *Ezra-Nehemiah*. Old Testament Library. Philadelphia: Westminster, 1988.

———. "Footnotes to the Rescript of Artaxerxes (Ezra 7:11–26)." Pages 150–58 in *The Historian and the Bible: Essays in Honour of Lester L. Grabbe*. Edited by Philip R. Davies and Diana Vikander Edelman. Library of Hebrew Bible/Old Testament Studies 530. London: T&T Clark, 2010.

———. *Judaism, the First Phase: The Place of Ezra and Nehemiah in the Origins of Judaism*. Grand Rapids: Eerdmans, 2009.

———. "The Mission of Udjahorresnet and Those of Ezra and Nehemiah." *Journal of Biblical Literature* 106 (1987): 409–21.

Bloch-Smith, Elizabeth. "Israelite Ethnicity in Iron I: Archaeology Preserves What Is Remembered and What Is Forgotten in Israel's History." *Journal of Biblical Literature* 122 (2003): 401–25.

Block, Daniel I. *The Book of Ezekiel*. 2 vols. New International Commentary on the Old Testament. Grand Rapids: Eerdmans, 1997–1998.

———, ed. *Israel: Ancient Kingdom or Late Invention?* Nashville: B&H Academic, 2008.

Blum, Erhard. "Esra, die Mosetora und die persische Politik." Pages 231–56 in *Religion und Religionskontakte im Zeitalter der Achämeniden*. Edited by Reinhard G. Kratz. Veröffentlichungen der Wissenschaftlichen Gesellschaft für Theologie 22. Gütersloh: Kaiser/Gütersloher Verlagshaus, 2002.

Boccaccini, Gabriele. *Beyond the Essene Hypothesis: The Parting of the Ways between Qumran and Enochic Judaism*. Grand Rapids: Eerdmans, 1998.

Bodi, Daniel. *The Demise of the Warlord: A New Look at the David Story*. Hebrew Bible Monographs 26. Sheffield: Sheffield Phoenix Press, 2010.

———. "Les différents genres de la correspondance divine." *Ktèma* 33 (2008): 245–58.

———. *Israël et Juda: À l'ombre des Babyloniens et des Perses*. Études d'archélogie et d'histoire ancienne. Paris: De Boccard, 2010.

———. *The Michal Affair: From Zimri-Lim to the Rabbis*. Hebrew Bible Monographs 3. Sheffield: Sheffield Phoenix Press, 2005.

Boling, Robert. *Judges: Introduction, Translation, and Commentary*. Anchor Bible 6A. Garden City, NY: Doubleday, 1975.

Borger, Riekele. *Babylonisch-Assyrische Lesestücke*. 3 vols. Rome: Pontifical Biblical Institute, 1963.

———. *Die Inschriften Asarhaddons, Königs von Assyrien*. Archiv für Orientforschung: Beiheft 9. Graz: Weidner, 1956.

Borowski, Oded. *Agriculture in Iron Age Israel*. Boston: American Schools of Oriental Research, 2002.

———. *Daily Life in Biblical Times*. Society of Biblical Literature Archaeology and Biblical Studies 5. Atlanta: Society of Biblical Literature, 2003.

———. "Hezekiah's Reform and the Revolt against Assyria." *Biblical Archaeologist* 58 (1995): 148–55.

———. "In the Path of Sennacherib." *Biblical Archaeology Review* 31, no. 3 (2005): 24–35.

Bottéro, Jean. "Les Habiru, les Nomades et les Sédentaires." Pages 89–107 in *Nomads and Sedentary Peoples: XXX International Congress of Human Sciences in Asia and North Africa*. Edited by Jorge Silva Castillo. México, D.F.: Colegio de México, 1981.

Breasted, James H. *Ancient Records of Egypt: Historical Documents from the Earliest Times to the Persian Conquest*. 5 vols. Chicago: University of Chicago Press, 1906–1907.

Briant, Pierre. *Histoire de l'Empire perse: De Cyrus à Alexandre*. Paris: Fayard, 1996.

Briend, J., and J. Sapin. "Archéologie." *Transeuphratène* 1 (1989): 147–54.

———. "Archéologie." *Transeuphratène* 10 (1995): 125–44.

———. "Archéologie." *Transeuphratène* 24 (2002): 113–35.

———. "Archéologie." *Transeuphratène* 32 (2006): 163–83.

Bright, John. *A History of Israel*. 4th ed. Louisville: Westminster John Knox, 2000.

Bringmann, Klaus. *Hellenistische Reform und Religionsverfolgung in Judäa: Eine Untersuchung zur jüdisch-hellenistischen Geschichte*

(175–163 v. Chr.). Abhandlungen der Akademie der Wissenschaften in Göttingen 3/132. Göttingen: Vandenhoeck & Ruprecht, 1983.

Brinkman, J. A. *Prelude to Empire: Babylonian Society and Politics, 747–626 B.C.* Occasional Papers of the Babylonian Fund 7. Philadelphia: The Babylonian Fund, University Museum, 1984.

Brody, Aaron J. "The Archaeology of the Extended Family: A Household Compound from Iron II Tell en-Naṣbeh." Pages 237–54 in *Household Archaeology in Ancient Israel and Beyond*. Edited by Assaf Yasur-Landau, Jennie R. Ebeling, and Laura B. Mazow. Culture and History of the Ancient Near East 50. Leiden: Brill, 2011.

Brooks, Simcha S. "From Gibeon to Gibeah: High Place of the Kingdom." Pages 40–59 in *Temple and Worship in Biblical Israel*. Edited by John Day. Library of Hebrew Bible/Old Testament Studies 422. London: T&T Clark, 2005.

Bruins, Hendrik J., and Johannes van der Plicht. "Tell Es-Sultan (Jericho): Radiocarbon Results of Short-Lived Cereal and Multiyear Charcoal Samples from the End of the Middle Bronze Age." *Radiocarbon* 37, no. 2 (1995): 213–20.

Bryce, Trevor. *The Kingdom of the Hittites*. Oxford: Oxford University Press, 2005.

———. *Letters of the Great Kings of the Ancient Near East: The Royal Correspondence of the Late Bronze Age*. London: Routledge, 2003.

Buccellati, Giorgio. "La 'carriera' di David a quelle di Idrimi re di Alalac." *Bibbia e Oriente* 4 (1962): 95–99.

Bunimovitz, Shlomo. "Area C." Pages 15–34 in *Shiloh: The Archaeology of a Biblical Site*. Edited by Israel Finkelstein, Shlomo Bunimovitz, and Zvi Lederman. Tel Aviv: Institute of Archaeology, Tel Aviv University, 1993.

Bunimovitz, Shlomo, and Avraham Faust. "Building Identity: The Four-Room House and the Israelite Mind." Pages 411–23 in *Symbiosis, Symbolism, and the Power of the Past: Canaan, Ancient Israel, and Their Neighbors from the Late Bronze Age through Roman Palaestina; Proceedings of* the Centennial Symposium, W. F. Albright Institute of Archaeological Research and American Schools of Oriental Research, Jerusalem, May 29/31, 2000. Edited by William G. Dever and Seymour Gitin. Winona Lake, IN: Eisenbrauns, 2003.

———. "Chronological Separation, Geographical Segregation, or Ethnic Demarcation? Ethnography and the Iron Age Low Chronology." Bulletin of the American Schools of Oriental Research 322 (2001): 1–10.

Bunimovitz, Shlomo, and Zvi Lederman. "The Archaeology of Border Communities: Renewed Excavations at Tel Beth-Shemesh, Part 1: The Iron Age." Near Eastern Archaeology 72 (2009): 128–31.

———. "The Iron Age Fortifications of Tel Beth-Shemesh: A 1990–2000 Perspective." Israel Exploration Journal 51 (2001): 121–48.

Byrne, Ryan. "Lie Back and Think of Judah: The Reproductive Politics of Pillar Figurines." Near Eastern Archaeology 6 (2004): 137–51.

———. "The Refuge of Scribalism in Iron I Palestine." Bulletin of the American Schools of Oriental Research 345 (2007): 2–23.

Cahill, Jane M. "Jerusalem at the Time of the United Monarchy: The Archaeological Evidence." Pages 13–80 in Jerusalem in Bible and Archaeology: The First Temple Period. Edited by Andrew G. Vaughn and Ann E. Killebrew. Society of Biblical Literature Symposium Series 18. Atlanta: Society of Biblical Literature, 2003.

———. "A Rejoinder to 'Was the Siloam Tunnel Built by Hezekiah?'" Biblical Archaeologist 60 (1997): 184–85.

Campbell, Antony. Unfolding the Deuteronomistic History: Origins, Upgrades, Present Text. Minneapolis: Fortress, 2000.

Campbell, Edward F. "A Land Divided: Judah and Israel from the Death of Solomon to the Fall of Samaria." Pages 206–41 in The Oxford History of the Biblical World. Edited by Michael D. Coogan. Oxford: Oxford University Press, 2001.

———. Text. Vol. 1 of Shechem III: The Stratigraphy and Architecture of Shechem/Tell Balâṭah. American Schools of Oriental Research Archaeological Reports 6. Boston: American Schools of Oriental Research, 2002.

Campbell, Edward F., and James F. Ross. "The Excavations of Shechem and the Biblical Tradition." Biblical Archaeologist 26 (1963): 2–27.

Cantrell, Deborah O'Daniel. The Horsemen of Israel: Horses and Chariotry in Monarchic Israel (Ninth–Eighth Centuries B.C.E.). History, Archaeology, and Culture of the Levant 1. Winona Lake, IN: Eisenbrauns, 2011.

———. "Stable Issues." Pages 630–42 in Megiddo IV: The 1998–2002 Seasons. Edited by Israel Finkelstein, David Ussishkin, and Baruch Halpern. 2 vols. Tel Aviv University Institute of Archaeology Monographs 24. Tel Aviv: Emery and Claire Yass Publications in Archaeology of the Institute of Archaeology, Tel Aviv University, 2006.

Cantrell, Deborah O'Daniel, and Israel Finkelstein. "A Kingdom for a Horse: The Megiddo Stables and Eighth Century Israel." Pages 643–65 in Megiddo IV: The 1998–2002 Seasons, 2 vols. Edited by Israel Finkelstein, David Ussishkin, and Baruch Halpern. Monograph Series 24. Tel Aviv: Institute of Archaeology, Tel Aviv University, 2006.

Cardascia, Guillaume, ed. and trans. Les archives des Muraŝû: Une famille d'hommes d'affaires babyloniens à l'époque perse (455–403 av. J.-C.). Paris: Imprimerie Nationale, 1951.

Carey, Greg. Ultimate Things: An Introduction to Jewish and Christian Apocalyptic Literature. St. Louis: Chalice, 2005.

Carlson, Rolf A. David, the Chosen King: A Traditio-Historical Approach to the Second Book of Samuel. Translated by Eric J. Sharpe and Stanley Rudman. Stockholm: Almqvist & Wiksell, 1964.

Carroll, Robert P. "The Myth of the Empty Land." Pages 79–93 in Ideological Criticism of Biblical Texts. Semeia 59. Edited by David Jobling and Tina Pippin. Atlanta: Scholars Press, 1992.

Carter, Charles E. *The Emergence of Yehud in the Persian Period: A Social and Demographic Study.* Journal for the Study of the Old Testament: Supplement Series 294. Sheffield: Sheffield Academic Press, 1999.

Cassin, Elena. "Le droit et le tordu I." Pages 50–71 in *Le semblable et le différent: Symbolisme du pouvoir dans le Proche-Orient ancien.* Paris: Découverte, 1987.

Cazelles, Henri. "Les localizations de l'exode et la critique litteraire." *Revue biblique* 62 (1955): 346–58.

———. "La mission d'Esdras." *Vetus Testamentum* 4 (1954): 113–40.

Çeçen, S., and K. Hecker. "*Ina Mātika Eblum*: Zu einem neuen Text zum Wegerecht in der Kültepe-Zeit." Pages 31–41 in *Vom Alten Orient zum Alten Testament: Festschrift für Wolfram Freiherrn von Soden zum 85. Geburtstag am 19. Juni 1993.* Edited by Manfred Dietrich and Oswald Loretz. Alter Orient und Altes Testament 240. Neukirchen-Vluyn: Neukirchener Verlag; Kevalaer: Butzon & Becker, 1995.

Chambon, Alain. *Tell el-Fârʿah I: L'âge du fer.* Éditions Recherche sur les civilisations: Mémoire 31. Paris: Éditions Recherche sur les civilisations, 1984.

Chaney, Marvin. "Ancient Palestinian Peasant Movements and the Formation of Premonarchic Israel." Pages 39–90 in *Palestine in Transition: The Emergence of Ancient Israel.* Edited by David Noel Freedman and David Frank Graf. Social World of Biblical Antiquity 2. Sheffield: Almond, 1983.

Charles, R. H., ed. *The Apocrypha and Pseudepigrapha of the Old Testament.* 2 vols. Oxford: Oxford University Press, 1913.

Charpin, Dominique. "Une campagne de Yahdun-Lîm en Haute-Mésopotamie." Pages 177–200 in *Florilegium marianum: Recueil d'études à la mémoire de Maurice Birot.* Edited by Dominique Charpin and Jean-Marie Durand. Nouvelles assyriologiques brèves et utilitaires 3. Paris: SEPOA, 1994.

———. *Hammu-rabi de Babylone.* Paris: Presses universitaires de France, 2003.

———. "Un souverain éphémère en Ida-Maraṣ: Išme-Addu d'Ašnakkum." *Mari: Annales de recherches interdisciplinaires* 7 (1993): 165–91.

———. *Writing, Law, and Kingship in Old Babylonian Mesopotamia.* Translated by Jane Marie Todd. Chicago: University of Chicago Press, 2010.

Charpin, Dominque, and Jean-Marie Durand. "La prise de pouvoir par Zimri-Lim." *Mari: Annales de recherches interdisciplinaires* 4 (1985): 293–343.

Chavalas, Mark W. "The Context of Early Israel Viewed through the Archaeology of Northern Mesopotamia and Syria." Pages 151–61 in *Critical Issues in Early Israelite History.* Edited by Richard S. Hess, Gerald A. Klingbeil, and Paul J. Ray Jr. Bulletin for Biblical Research Supplements 3. Winona Lake, IN: Eisenbrauns, 2008.

Chew, Sing C. *The Recurring Dark Ages: Ecological Stress, Climate Changes, and System Transformation.* Lanham, MD: Altamira, 2007.

Cinamon, Gilead. "The Tumuli South-West of Jerusalem and Their Significance to the Understanding of Jerusalem's Countryside in the Iron Age II." MA thesis, University of Tel Aviv, 2004.

Clédat, Jean. "Notes sur l'Isthme de Suez." *Bulletin de l'Institut français d'archéologie orientale* 16 (1919): 201–28.

———. "Notes sur l'Isthme de Suez [continued]." *Bulletin de l'Institut français d'archéologie orientale* 18 (1920): 203–15.

Cline, Eric. *1177 B.C.: The Year Civilization Collapsed.* Princeton: Princeton University Press, 2014.

Cody, Alfred. "Le titre égyptien et le nom propre du scribe de David." *Revue biblique* 72 (1965): 381–93.

Cogan, Mordechai. *Imperialism and Religion: Assyria, Judah, and Israel in the Eighth and Seventh Centuries B.C.E.* Society of Biblical Literature Monograph Series 19. Missoula, MT: Scholars Press, 1974.

———. "Into Exile: From the Assyrian Conquest of Israel to the Fall of Babylon." Pages

242–75 in *The Oxford History of the Biblical World*. Edited by Michael D. Coogan. Oxford: Oxford University Press, 1998.

———. *The Raging Torrent: Historical Inscriptions from Assyria and Babylonia Relating to Ancient Israel*. Jerusalem: Carta, 2008.

Cogan, Mordechai, and Hayim Tadmor. *II Kings: A New Translation with Introduction and Commentary*. Anchor Bible 11. Garden City, NY: Doubleday, 1988.

Cohen, Rudolph. "Kadesh-Barnea: The Israelite Fortress." Pages 843–47 in vol. 3 of *The New Encyclopedia of Archaeological Excavations in the Holy Land*. Edited by Ephraim Stern. Jerusalem: Israel Exploration Society & Carta, 1993.

Cohen, Shaye J. D. *From the Maccabees to the Mishnah*. Philadelphia: Westminster, 1987.

Cohn, Robert L. "The Literary Structure of Kings." Pages 107–22 in *The Books of Kings: Sources, Composition, Historiography, and Reception*. Edited by Baruch Halpern and André Lemaire. Supplements to Vetus Testamentum 129. Leiden: Brill, 2010.

Cole, Dan. "Archaeology and the Messiah Oracles of Isaiah 9 and 11." Pages 53–69 in *Scripture and Other Artifacts: Essays on the Bible and Archaeology in Honor of Philip J. King*. Edited by Michael D. Coogan, Cheryl Exum, and Lawrence E. Stager. Louisville: Westminster John Knox, 1994.

Cole, Steven W. "The Destruction of Orchards in Assyrian Warfare." Pages 29–40 in *Assyria 1995: Proceedings of the 10th Anniversary Symposium of the Neo-Assyrian Text Corpus Project Helsinki, September 7–11, 1995*. Edited by Simo Parpola and Robert M. Whiting. Helsinki: Neo-Assyrian Text Corpus Project, University of Helsinki, 1997.

Collins, Billie Jean. *The Hittites and Their World*. Society of Biblical Literature Archaeology and Biblical Studies 7. Atlanta: Society of Biblical Literature, 2007.

Collins, John J. *The Apocalyptic Imagination: An Introduction to the Jewish Matrix of Christianity*. 2nd ed. Grand Rapids: Eerdmans, 1998.

———. *Between Athens and Jerusalem: Jewish Identity in the Hellenistic Diaspora*. 2nd ed. Grand Rapids: Eerdmans, 2000.

———. *Beyond the Qumran Community: The Sectarian Movement of the Dead Sea Scrolls*. Grand Rapids: Eerdmans, 2010.

———. *Daniel*. Hermeneia. Minneapolis: Fortress, 1993.

Collins, Paul. *From Babylon to Egypt: The International Age, 1550–500 BC*. Cambridge, MA; London: Harvard University Press, 2008.

Conrad, Joachim. "Zum geschichtlichen Hintergrund der Darstellung von Davids Aufstieg." *Theologische Literaturzeitung* 97 (1972): 321–32.

Coogan, Michael D. *A Brief Introduction to the Old Testament: The Hebrew Bible in Its Context*. Oxford: Oxford University Press, 2009.

———. "Life in the Diaspora: Jews at Nippur in the Fifth Century BC." *Biblical Archaeologist* 37 (1974): 6–12.

———. "Patterns in Jewish Personal Names in the Diaspora." *Journal for the Study of Judaism in the Persian, Hellenistic, and Roman Periods* 4 (1973): 183–91.

———. *West Semitic Personal Names in the Murašû Documents*. Harvard Semitic Monographs 7. Missoula, MT: Scholars Press, 1976.

Cooley, Robert E., and Gary Davis Pratico. "Gathered to His People: An Archaeological Illustration from Tell Dothan's Western Cemetery." Pages 70–92 in *Scripture and Other Artifacts: Essays on the Bible and Archaeology in Honor of Philip J. King*. Edited by Michael D. Coogan, Cheryl Exum, and Lawrence E. Stager. Louisville: Westminster John Knox, 1994.

Cooper, Jerrold S. *Presargonic Inscriptions*. Vol. 1 of *Sumerian and Akkadian Royal Inscriptions*. Sumerian and Akkadian Royal Inscriptions 1. New Haven: American Oriental Society, 1986.

Coote, Robert B. *Ancient Israel: A New Horizon*. Minneapolis: Fortress, 1990.

Coote, Robert B., and Keith W. Whitelam. *The Emergence of Early Israel in Historical Perspective.* 2nd ed. Social World of Biblical Antiquity 5. Sheffield: Almond Press, 1987.

Couroyer, Bernard. "Un égyptianisme biblique 'depuis la fondation de l'Égypte' (Exode IX, 18)." *Revue biblique* 67 (1960): 42–48.

———. "Quelques égyptianismes dans l'Exode." *Revue biblique* 63 (1956): 209–19.

———. "La résidence ramesside du Delta et la Ramsès biblique." *Revue biblique* 53 (1946): 75–98.

Cowley, Arthur E., ed. and trans. *Aramaic Papyri of the Fifth Century B.C.* Oxford: Clarendon, 1923.

Crawford, Harriet E. W. *Sumer and the Sumerians.* 2nd ed. Cambridge: Cambridge University Press, 2004.

Cross, Frank Moore. *Canaanite Myth and Hebrew Epic: Essays in the History of the Religion of Israel.* Cambridge, MA: Harvard University Press, 1973.

———. *From Epic to Canon: History and Literature in Ancient Israel.* Baltimore: Johns Hopkins University Press, 1998.

———. "Traditional Narrative and the Reconstruction of Early Israelite Institutions." Pages 22–52 in *From Epic to Canon: History and Literature in Ancient Israel.* Baltimore: Johns Hopkins University Press, 1998.

Cross, Frank Moore, and David Noel Freedman. *Early Hebrew Orthography: A Study of the Epigraphic Evidence.* American Oriental Series 36. New Haven: American Oriental Society, 1952.

———. "Josiah's Revolt against Assyria." *Journal of Near Eastern Studies* 12 (1953): 56–58.

Crown, Alan D. "Toward a Reconstruction of the Climate of Palestine 8000 B.C.–0 B.C." *Journal of Near Eastern Studies* 31 (1972): 312–30.

Cryer, Frederick H. *Divination in Ancient Israel and Its Near Eastern Environment: A Socio-Historical Investigation.* Journal for the Study of the Old Testament: Supplement Series 142. Sheffield: JSOT Press, 1994.

Dagan, Yehuda. "The Shephelah during the Period of the Monarchy in Light of Archaeological Excavations and Surveys." MA thesis, Tel Aviv University, 1992.

Dagut, Menachem B. "2 Maccabees and the Death of Antiochus IV Epiphanes." *Journal of Biblical Literature* 72 (1953): 149–57.

Dalley, Stephanie, and Anne Goguel. "The Sela' Sculpture: A Neo-Babylonian Rock Relief in Southern Jordan." *Annual of the Department of Antiquities of Jordan* 41 (1997): 169–76.

Damrosch, David. *The Narrative Covenant: Transformations of Genre in the Growth of Biblical Literature.* San Francisco: Harper & Row, 1987.

Dar, Shimon. "Samaria (Archaeology of the Region)." Pages 926–31 in vol. 5 of *The Anchor Bible Dictionary.* Edited by David Noel Freedman. New York: Doubleday, 1992.

Davies, Graham I. "King Solomon's Stables: Still at Megiddo?" *Biblical Archaeology Review* 20, no. 1 (1994): 45–49.

Davies, Philip R. "Hasidim in the Maccabean Period." *Journal of Jewish Studies* 28 (1977): 127–40.

———. *In Search of "Ancient Israel."* Journal for the Study of the Old Testament: Supplement Series 148. Sheffield: Sheffield Academic Press, 1992.

Day, John, ed. *In Search of Pre-Exilic Israel: Proceedings of the Oxford Old Testament Seminar.* Journal for the Study of the Old Testament: Supplement Series 406. London: T&T Clark International, 2004.

De Odorico, Marco. *The Use of Numbers and Quantifications in the Assyrian Royal Inscriptions.* State Archives of Assyria Studies 3. Helsinki: Neo-Assyrian Text Corpus Project, University of Helsinki, 1995.

Depuydt, Leo. "Egypt, Egyptians." Pages 237–46 in *Dictionary of the Old Testament: Historical Books.* Edited by Bill T. Arnold and H. G. M. Williamson. Downers Grove, IL: InterVarsity, 2005.

deSilva, David A. *Introducing the Apocrypha: Message, Context, and Significance.* Grand Rapids: Baker Academic, 2002.

———. "Jews in the Diaspora." Pages 272–90 in *The World of the New Testament: Cultural, Social, and Historical Contexts*. Edited by Joel B. Green and Lee M. McDonald. Grand Rapids: Baker Academic, 2013.

———. *Seeing Things John's Way: The Rhetoric of the Book of Revelation*. Louisville: Westminster John Knox, 2009.

Deutsch, Robert. "An Ammonite Royal Seal." Pages 53–57 in *West Semitic Epigraphic News of the 1st Millennium*. Edited by Robert Deutsch and Michael Heltzer. Tel Aviv: Archaeological Center Publications, 1999.

———. *Biblical Period Hebrew Bullae: The Josef Chaim Kaufman Collection*. Tel Aviv: Archaeological Center Publications, 2003.

———. "Seal of Baalis Surfaces." *Biblical Archaeology Review* 25, no. 2 (1999): 46–49, 66.

de Vaux, Roland. *Ancient Israel: Its Life and Institutions*. Translated by John McHugh. London: Darton, Longman & Todd, 1961.

———. *Archaeology and the Dead Sea Scrolls*. London: Oxford University Press, 1973.

———. *The Early History of Israel*. Translated by David Smith. Philadelphia: Westminster, 1978.

———. "Titres et fonctionnaires égyptiens à la cour de David et de Salomon." *Revue biblique* 48 (1939): 394–405.

Dever, William G. "Archaeology and the Emergence of Early Israel." Pages 20–50 in *Archaeology and Biblical Interpretation*. Edited by John R. Bartlett. New York: Routledge, 1997.

———. "Archaeology, Syro-Palestinian and Biblical." Pages 354–67 in vol. 1 of *The Anchor Bible Dictionary*. Edited by David Noel Freedman. New York: Doubleday, 1992.

———. "A Case-Study in Biblical Archaeology: The Earthquake of ca. 760 BCE." *Eretz-Israel* 23 (1992): 27–35*.

———. *Did God Have a Wife? Archaeology and Folk Religion in Ancient Israel*. Grand Rapids: Eerdmans, 2005.

———. "Qedah, Tell El-." Pages 578–81 in vol. 5 of *The Anchor Bible Dictionary*. Edited by David Noel Freedman. New York: Doubleday, 1992.

———. *What Did the Biblical Writers Know, and When Did They Know It? What Archaeology Can Tell Us about the Reality of Ancient Israel*. Grand Rapids: Eerdmans, 2001.

———. *Who Were the Early Israelites, and Where Did They Come From?* Grand Rapids: Eerdmans, 2003.

De Vries, Simon J. *1 and 2 Chronicles*. Forms of the Old Testament Literature 11. Grand Rapids: Eerdmans, 1989.

———. *1 Kings*. Word Biblical Commentary 12. Dallas: Word, 1985.

de Wette, Wilhelm M. L. *Beiträge zur Einleitung in das Alte Testament*. 1806–1807. Repr., Hildesheim: G. Olms, 1971.

Dhorme, Edouard. "Les Habirou et les Hébreux." *Revue historique* 78 (1954): 256–64.

Dickinson, Oliver. *The Aegean from Bronze Age to Iron Age: Continuity and Change between the Twelfth and Eighth Centuries BC*. London: Routledge, 2007.

Dietrich, Walter. "*dāwīd, dôd* und *bytdwd.*" *Theologische Zeitschrift* 53 (1997): 17–32.

———. *Prophetie und Geschichte: Eine redaktionsgeschichtliche Untersuchung zum deuteronomistischen Geschichtswerk*. Forschungen zur Religion und Literatur des Alten und Neuen Testaments 108. Göttingen: Vandenhoeck & Ruprecht, 1972.

Dion, Paul-Eugène. "La religion des papyrus d'Éléphantine: Un reflet du Juda d'avant l'exil." Pages 243–54 in *Kein Land für sich allein: Studien zum Kulturkontakt in Kanaan, Israel/Palästina und Ebirnâri für Manfred Weippert zum 65. Geburtstag*. Edited by Ulrich Hübner and Ernst A. Knauf. Orbis biblicus et orientalis 186. Freiburg: Universitätsverlag; Göttingen: Vandenhoeck & Ruprecht, 2002.

Donbaz, Veysel. "Some Late Babylonian Texts Gleaned from the Assur Collection." Pages 163–79 in *Historiography in the Cuneiform World*. Vol. 1 of *Proceedings of the XLVe Recontre Assyriologique Internationale*. Edited by Tzvi Abusch et al. Bethesda, MD: CDL Press, 2001.

Donbaz, Veysel, and Matthew W. Stolper. *Istanbul Murašû Texts*. Uitgaven van het Nederlands Historisch-Archaeologisch Instituut te Istanbul 79. Istanbul: Nederlands Historisch-Archeologisch Instituut, 1997.

Donner, Herbert. *Von den Anfangen bis zur Staatenbildungszeit*. Vol. 1 of *Geschichte Volkes Israel und seiner Nachbarn in Grundzügen*. Grundrisse zum Alten Testament 4.1. Göttingen: Vandenhoeck & Ruprecht, 1995.

Doran, Robert. *Temple Propaganda: The Purpose and Character of 2 Maccabees*. Catholic Biblical Quarterly Monograph Series 12. Washington, DC: Catholic Biblical Association, 1981.

Dorsey, David A. *The Roads and Highways of Ancient Israel*. Library of Biblical and Near Eastern Archaeology. Baltimore: Johns Hopkins University Press, 1991.

Dossin, Georges. "Amurru, dieu cananéen." Pages 95–98 in *Symbolae biblicae et mesopotamicae: Francisco Mario Theodoro De Liagre Böhl dedicatae*. Edited by M. A. Beek et al. Studia Francisci Scholten memoriae diacata 4. Leiden: Brill, 1973.

———. "Archives de Sûmum-Iamam, roi de Mari." *Revue d'assyriologie et d'archéologie orientale* 64 (1970): 17–44.

Dothan, Trude. "Initial Philistine Settlement: From Migration to Coexistence." Pages 148–61 in *Mediterranean Peoples in Transition: Thirteenth to Early Tenth Centuries BCE*. Edited by Seymour Gitin, Amihai Mazar, and Ephraim Stern. Jerusalem: Israel Exploration Society, 1998.

———. *The Philistines and Their Material Culture*. New Haven: Yale University Press, 1982.

Dothan, Trude, and Seymour Gitin. "Miqne, Tel." Pages 30–35 in vol. 4 of *The Oxford Encyclopedia of Archaeology in the Near East*. Edited by Eric M. Meyers. Oxford: Oxford University Press, 1997.

Drews, Robert. *The End of the Bronze Age: Changes in Warfare and the Catastrophe ca. 1200 B.C.* Princeton: Princeton University Press, 1993.

Driver, G. R., and John C. Miles. *The Babylonian Laws*. Corrected ed. with additions. 2 vols. Aalen: Scientia Verlag, 1975.

Driver, S. R. *A Critical and Exegetical Commentary on Deuteronomy*. 3rd ed. International Critical Commentary. 1901. Repr., Edinburgh: T&T Clark, 1986.

Duke, Rodney K. "Chronicles, Book of." Pages 171–72 in *Dictionary of the Old Testament: Historical Books*. Edited by Bill T. Arnold and H. G. M. Williamson. Downers Grove, IL: InterVarsity, 2005.

Durand, Jean-Marie. "Les anciens de Talḥayum." *Revue d'assyriologie et d'archéologie orientale* 82 (1988): 97–113.

———. *Archives épistolaires de Mari I*. ARM 26. Paris: Éditions Recherche sur les Civilisations, 1988.

———. "Assyriologie: L'Étude de la société et du peuplement du Proche-Orient au XVIIIe siècle av. notre ère." *Annuaire du Collège de France* 104 (2003–2004): 817–59.

———. "Assyriologie: Le Problème des ḥabiru." *Annuaire du Collège de France* 105 (2004–2005): 563–84.

———. "Les dames du palais de Mari à l'époque du royaume de Haute-Mésopotamie." *Mari: Annales de recherches interdisciplinaires* 4 (1985): 385–436.

———. *Les documents épistolaires du palais de Mari*. 3 vols. Littératures anciennes du Proche-Orient 16–18. Paris: Cerf, 1997–2000.

———. "Mari (Texts)." Pages 529–36 in vol. 4 of *The Anchor Bible Dictionary*. Edited by David Noel Freedman. New York: Doubleday, 1992.

———. "Réalités amorrites et traditions bibliques." *Revue d'assyriologie et d'archéologie orientale* 92 (1998): 3–39.

———. "La religion amorrite en Syrie à l'époque des Archives de Mari." Pages 161–722 in *Mythologie et religion des Sémites occidentaux*. Edited by Gregorio del Olmo Lete. Orientalia lovaniensia analecta 162. Louven: Peeters, 2008.

Dušek, Jan. "Archaeology and Texts in the Persian Period: Focus on Sanballat." Pages 117–32 in *Congress Volume: Helsinki 2010*.

Edited by Martti Nissinen. Supplements to Vetus Testamentum 148. Leiden: Brill, 2012.

———. *Les manuscrits araméens du Wadi Daliyeh et la Samarie vers 450–332 av. J.-C.* Culture and History of the Ancient Near East 30. Leiden: Brill, 2007.

Edel, Elmar. *Die ägyptisch-hethitische Korrespondenz aus Boghazköi in babylonischer und hethitischer Sprache.* 2 vols. Abhandlungen der Rheinisch-Westfälischen Akademie der Wissenschaften 77. Opladen: Westdeutscher Verlag, 1994.

———. "Amasis und Nebukadrezar II." *Göttinger Miszellen* 29 (1978): 13–20.

Edelman, Diana Vikander. "Apples and Oranges: Textual and Archaeological Evidence for Reconstructing the History of Yehud in the Persian Period." Pages 133–44 in *Congress Volume: Helsinki 2010.* Edited by Martti Nissinen. Supplements to Vetus Testamentum 148. Leiden: Brill, 2012.

———. "From Prophets to Prophetic Books: The Fixing of the Divine Word." Pages 29–54 in *The Production of Prophecy: Constructing Prophecy and Prophets in Yehud.* Edited by Ehud Ben Zvi and Diana Vikander Edelman. London: Equinox, 2009.

———. *King Saul in the Historiography of Judah.* Journal for the Study of the Old Testament: Supplement Series 121. Sheffield: JSOT Press, 1991.

———. *The Origins of the "Second" Temple: Persian Imperial Policy and the Rebuilding of Jerusalem.* Bible World. London: Equinox, 2005.

———. "Saul ben Kish in History and Tradition." Pages 142–59 in *The Origins of the Ancient Israelite States.* Edited by Volkmar Fritz and Philip R. Davies. Journal for the Study of the Old Testament: Supplement Series 228. Sheffield: Sheffield Academic Press, 1996.

Eggler, Jürg, and Othmar Keel. *Corpus der Siegel-Amulette aus Jordanien: Vom Neolithikum bis zur Perserzeit.* Orbis biblicus et orientalis 25. Fribourg: Academic Press; Göttingen: Vandenhoeck & Ruprecht, 2006.

Ehrlich, Ernst L. "Der Aufenthalt des Königs Manasse in Babylon." *Theologische Zeitschrift* 21 (1965): 281–86.

Eichler, Barry L. "Nuzi and the Bible: A Retrospective." Pages 107–19 in *Dumu-E₂–Dub-Ba-A: Studies in Honor of Åke W. Sjöberg.* Edited by Hermann Behrens, Darlene Loding, and Martha T. Roth. Occasional Publications of the Samuel Noah Kramer Fund 11. Philadelphia: Samuel Noah Kramer Fund, University Museum, 1989.

Eidem, Jesper. "An Old Assyrian Treaty from Tell Leilan." Pages 185–206 in *Marchands, diplomates et empereurs: Études sur la civilisation mésopotamienne offertes à Paul Garelli.* Edited by Dominque Charpin and Francis Joannès. Paris: Éditions Recherche sur les civilisations, 1991.

———. *The Royal Archives from Tell Leilan: Old Babylonian Letters and Treaties from the Lower Town Palace East.* Uitgaven van het Nederlands Instituut voor het Nabije Oosten te Leiden 107. Leiden: Nederlands Instituut voor het Nabije Oosten, 2011.

Eissfeldt, Otto. "El and Yahweh." *Journal of Semitic Studies* 1 (1956): 25–37.

Elayi J., and A. Lemaire. "Numismatique." *Transeuphratène* 1 (1989): 155–64.

———. "Numismatique." *Transeuphratène* 4 (1991): 119–32.

———. "Numismatique." *Transeuphratène* 10 (1995): 151–87.

———. "Numismatique." *Transeuphratène* 17 (1999): 117–53.

———. "Numismatique." *Transeuphratène* 25 (2003): 63–105.

———. "Numismatique." *Transeuphratène* 33 (2007): 23–82.

Eph'al, Israel. *The City Besieged: Siege and Its Manifestations in the Ancient Near East.* Culture and History of the Ancient Near East 36. Leiden: Brill, 2009.

———. "Nebuchadnezzar the Warrior: Remarks on His Military Achievements." *Israel Exploration Journal* 53 (2003): 178–91.

———. "On the Political and Social Organization of the Jews in Babylonian Exile." Pages 106–12 in *XXI. Deutscher*

Orientalistentag: Vom 24. bis 29. März 1980 in Berlin. Edited by Fritz Steppat. Zeitschrift des deutschen morgenländischen Gesellschaft: Supplementbände 5. Wiesbaden: Franz Steiner, 1983.

————. "The Samarian(s) in the Assyrian Sources." Pages 36–45 in *Ah, Assyria . . . : Studies in Assyrian and Ancient Near Eastern Historiography Presented to Hayim Tadmor.* Edited by Mordechai Cogan and Israel Eph'al. Scripta hierosolymitana 33. Jerusalem: Magnes, 1991.

Eran, A. "Weights from Excavations 1981–1984 at Shiloh." *Zeitschrift des deutschen Palästina-Vereins* 110 (1994): 151–57.

Eshel, Hanan. *The Dead Sea Scrolls and the Hasmonean State.* Grand Rapids: Eerdmans; Jerusalem: Yad Ben-Zvi Press, 2008.

————. "The Governors of Samaria in the Fifth and Fourth Centuries BCE." Pages 223–34 in *Judah and the Judeans in the Fourth Century B.C.E.* Edited by Oded Lipschits, Gary N. Knoppers, and Rainer Albertz. Winona Lake, IN: Eisenbrauns, 2006.

————. "Hellenism in the Land of Israel from the Fifth to the Second Centuries BCE in Light of Semitic Epigraphy." Pages 116–24 in *A Time of Change: Judah and Its Neighbours in the Persian and Early Hellenistic Periods.* Edited by Yigal Levin. Library of Second Temple Studies 65. London: T&T Clark, 2007.

Eshel, Hanan, and Boaz Zissu. "Jericho: Archaeological Introduction." Pages 3–20 in *Miscellaneous Texts from the Judaean Desert*, by James Charlesworth et al. Discoveries in the Judaean Desert 38. Oxford: Clarendon, 2000.

Fagan, Brian. *The Long Summer: How Climate Changed Civilization.* New York: Basic Books, 2004.

Fales, Frederick Mario. "Preparing for War in Assyria." Pages 35–59 in *Économie antique: La guerre dans les économies antiques.* Entretiens d'archéologie et d'histoire 5. Edited by Jean Andreau, Pierre Briant, and Raymond Descant. Saint-Bertrand-de-Comminges: Musée d'archéologie départmentale, 2000.

Fantalkin, Alexander. "Meẓad Ḥashavyahu: Its Material Culture and Historical Background." *Tel Aviv* 28 (2001): 3–165.

Faust, Avraham. *The Archaeology of Israelite Society in Iron Age II.* Translated by Ruth Ludlum. Winona Lake, IN: Eisenbrauns, 2012.

————. "Household Economies in the Kingdoms of Israel and Judah." Pages 255–73 in *Household Archaeology in Ancient Israel and Beyond.* Edited by Assaf Yasur-Landau, Jennie R. Ebeling, and Laura B. Mazow. Culture and History of the Ancient Near East 50. Leiden: Brill, 2011.

————. "How Did Israel Become a People? The Genesis of Israelite Identity." *Biblical Archaeology Review* 35, no. 6 (2009): 62–69, 92–94.

————. "The Interests of the Assyrian Empire in the West: Olive Oil Production as a Test-Case." *Journal of the Economic and Social History of the Orient* 54 (2011): 62–85.

————. *Israel's Ethnogenesis: Settlement, Interaction, Expansion and Resistance.* Approaches to Anthropological Archaeology. London: Equinox, 2006.

————. "Judah in the Sixth Century B.C.E.: A Rural Perspective." *Palestine Exploration Quarterly* 135 (2003): 37–53.

————. "Settlement and Demography in Seventh-Century Judah and the Extent and Intensity of Sennacherib's Campaign." *Palestine Exploration Quarterly* 140 (2008): 168–94.

Faust, Avraham, and Ehud Weiss. "Between Assyria and the Mediterranean World: The Prosperity of Judah and Philistia in the Seventh Century BCE in Context." Pages 189–204 in *Interweaving Worlds: Systemic Interactions in Eurasia, 7th to 1st Millennia BC.* Edited by Toby C. Wilkinson, Susan Sherratt, and John Bennett. Oakville, CT: Oxbow, 2011.

————. "Judah, Philistia, and the Mediterranean World: Reconstructing the Economic System of the Seventh Century B.C.E." *Bulletin of the American Schools of Oriental Research* 338 (2005): 71–92.

Feldman, Louis H. "How Much Hellenism in Jewish Palestine?" *Hebrew Union College Annual* 57 (1986): 83–111.

———. *Jew and Gentile in the Ancient World: Attitudes and Interactions from Alexander to Justinian.* Princeton: Princeton University Press, 1993.

Fink, Amir. *Late Bronze Age Tell Atchana (Alalakh): Stratigraphy, Chronology, History.* Oxford: Archaeopress, 2010.

———. "Where Was the Statue of Idrimi Actually Found? The Later Temple of Tell Atchana (Alalakh) Revisited." *Ugarit-Forschungen* 39 (2007): 161–245.

Finkelstein, Israel. "The Archaeology of the Days of Manasseh." Pages 169–87 in *Scripture and Other Artifacts: Essays on the Bible and Archaeology in Honor of Philip J. King.* Edited by Michael D. Coogan, Cheryl Exum, and Lawrence E. Stager. Louisville: Westminster John Knox, 1994.

———. *The Archaeology of the Israelite Settlement.* Translated by D. Saltz. Jerusalem: Israel Exploration Society, 1988.

———. "The Archaeology of the United Monarchy: An Alternative View." *Levant* 28 (1996): 177–87.

———. "The Emergence of Israel in Canaan: Consensus, Mainstream and Dispute." *Scandinavian Journal of the Old Testament* 5, no. 2 (1991): 47–59.

———. "A Great United Monarchy? Archaeological and Historical Perspectives." Pages 3–28 in *One God—One Cult—One Nation: Archaeological and Biblical Perspectives.* Edited by Reinhard G. Kratz and Hermann Spieckermann. Beihefte zur Zeitschrift für die alttestamentliche Wissenschaft 405. Berlin: de Gruyter, 2010.

———. *'Izbet Ṣarṭah: An Early Iron Age Site near Rosh Ha'ayin.* British Archaeological Reports International Series 299. Oxford: British Archaeological Reports, 1986.

———. "Khirbat en-Nahas, Edom and Biblical History." *Tel Aviv* 32 (2005): 119–25.

———. "The Last Labayu: King Saul and the Expansion of the First North Israelite Territorial Entity." Pages 171–87 in *Essays on*

Ancient Israel in Its Near Eastern Context: A Tribute to Nadav Na'aman. Edited by Yairah Amit et al. Winona Lake, IN: Eisenbrauns, 2006.

———. "Pots and People Revisited: Ethnic Boundaries in the Iron Age I." Pages 227–30 in *The Archaeology of Israel: Constructing the Past, Interpreting the Present.* Edited by Neil Asher Silberman and David Small. Journal for the Study of the Old Testament: Supplement Series 237. Sheffield: Sheffield Academic Press, 1997.

———. "The Rise of Jerusalem and Judah: The Missing Link." *Levant* 33 (2001): 105–15.

———. "Seilun, Khirbet." Pages 1069–71 in vol. 5 of *The Anchor Bible Dictionary.* Edited by David Noel Freedman. New York: Doubleday, 1992.

———. "State Formation in Israel and Judah: A Contrast in Context, a Contrast in Trajectory." *Near Eastern Archaeology* 62 (1998): 35–52.

———. "Tell el-Ful Revisited: The Assyrian and Hellenistic Periods (with a New Identification)." *Palestine Exploration Quarterly* 143 (2011): 106–18.

———. "Two Notes on Northern Samaria." *Palestine Exploration Quarterly* 130 (1998): 94–98.

Finkelstein, Israel, Zvi Lederman, and Shlomo Bunimovitz. *Highlands of Many Cultures: The Southern Samaria Survey; The Sites.* 2 vols. Tel Aviv University Institute of Archaeology Monographs 14. Tel Aviv: Institute of Archaeology, Tel Aviv University, 1997.

Finkelstein, Israel, and Amihai Mazar. *The Quest for the Historical Israel: Debating Archaeology and the History of Early Israel.* Edited by Brian B. Schmidt. Society of Biblical Literature Archaeology and Biblical Studies 17. Atlanta: Society of Biblical Literature, 2007.

Finkelstein, Israel, and Nadav Na'aman. "The Judahite Shephelah in the Late 8th and Early 7th Centuries BCE." *Tel Aviv* 31 (2004): 60–79.

Finkelstein, Israel, and Neil Asher Silberman. *The Bible Unearthed: Archaeology's New Vision of Ancient Israel and the Origin of Its Sacred Texts*. New York: Free Press, 2001.

———. *David and Solomon: In Search of the Bible's Sacred Kings and the Roots of the Western Tradition*. New York: Free Press, 2006.

———. "Temple and Dynasty: Hezekiah, the Remaking of Judah and the Rise of the Pan-Israelite Ideology." *Journal for the Study of the Old Testament* 30 (2006): 259–85.

Finkelstein, Israel, and David Ussishkin. "Back to Megiddo: A New Expedition Will Explore the Jewel in the Crown of Canaan/Israel." *Biblical Archaeology Review* 20, no. 1 (1994): 26–43.

Finkelstein, Louis. "The Pharisaic Leadership of the Great Synagogue (ca. 400–170 BCE)." Pages 245–77 in *The Hellenistic Period*. Vol. 2 of *The Cambridge History of Judaism*. Edited by W. D. Davies and Louis Finkelstein. Cambridge: Cambridge University Press, 1989.

Fitzmyer, Joseph A. *The Aramaic Inscriptions of Sefire*. Rev. ed. Biblica et orientalia 19A. Rome: Pontifical Biblical Institute, 1967.

———. "The Inscriptions of Bar-Ga'yah and Mati'el from Sefire." Pages 213–17 in *Monumental Inscriptions from the Biblical World*. Vol. 2 of *The Context of Scripture*. Edited by William W. Hallo and K. Lawson Younger Jr. Leiden: Brill, 2003.

Flanagan, James. *David's Social Drama: A Hologram of Israel's Early Iron Age*. Journal for the Study of the Old Testament: Supplement Series 73. Sheffield: Almond, 1988.

Fleming, Daniel E. *Democracy's Ancient Ancestors: Mari and Early Collective Governance*. Cambridge: Cambridge University Press, 2004.

———. "From Joseph to David: Mari and Israelite Pastoral Traditions." Pages 78–96 in *Israel: Ancient Kingdom or Late Invention?* Edited by Daniel I. Block. Nashville: B&H Academic, 2008.

———. "Genesis in History and Tradition: The Syrian Background of Israel's Ancestors, Reprise." Pages 193–232 in *The Future of Biblical Archaeology: Reassessing Methodologies and Assumptions; The Proceedings of a Symposium, August 12–14, 2001 at Trinity International University*. Edited by James K. Hoffmeier and Alan R. Millard. Grand Rapids: Eerdmans, 2004.

———. "If El Is a Bull, Who Is a Calf? Reflections on Religion in Second-Millennium Syria-Palestine." Pages 23*–27* in *Frank Moore Cross Volume*. Edited by Baruch A. Levine et al. Eretz-Israel 26. Jerusalem: Israel Exploration Society, 1999.

———. *The Installation of Baal's High Priestess at Emar: A Window on Ancient Syrian Religion*. Harvard Semitic Studies 42. Atlanta: Scholars Press, 1992.

———. *The Legacy of Israel in Judah's Bible: History, Politics, and the Reinscribing of Tradition*. Cambridge: Cambridge University Press, 2012.

———. "Mari and the Possibilities of Biblical Memory." *Revue d'assyriologie et d'archéologie orientale* 92 (1998): 41–78.

———. "*Nābû* and *Munabbiātu*: Two New Syrian Religious Personnel." *Journal of the American Oriental Society* 113 (1993): 175–83.

———. "Prophets and Temple Personnel in the Mari Archives." Pages 44–64 in *The Priests in the Prophets: The Portrayal of Priests, Prophets and Other Religious Specialists in the Latter Prophets*. Edited by Lester L. Grabbe and Alice Ogden Bellis. Journal for the Study of the Old Testament: Supplement Series 408. London: T&T Clark, 2004.

———. *Time at Emar: The Cultic Calendar and the Rituals from the Diviner's Archive*. Mesopotamian Civilizations 11. Winona Lake, IN: Eisenbrauns, 2000.

Fox, Nili Sacher. *In the Service of the King: Officialdom in Ancient Israel and Judah*. Monographs of the Hebrew Union College 23. Cincinnati: Hebrew Union College Press, 2000.

Frahm, Eckart. *Einleitung in die Sanherib-Inschriften*. Archiv für Orientforschung: Beiheft 26. Vienna: Institut für Orientalistik der Universität Wien, 1997.

Frankel, Rafael. *Settlement Dynamics and Regional Diversity in Ancient Upper Galilee: Archaeological Survey of Upper Galilee.* Israel Antiquities Authority Reports 14. Jerusalem: Israel Antiquities Authority, 2001.

Frankfort, Henri. *Kingship and the Gods: A Study of Ancient Near Eastern Religion as the Integration of Society and Nature.* Oriental Institute Essays. Chicago: University of Chicago Press, 1978.

Freedman, David Noel, and Andrew Welch. "Amos's Earthquake and Israelite Prophecy." Pages 188–98 in *Scripture and Other Artifacts: Essays on the Bible and Archaeology in Honor of Philip J. King.* Edited by Michael D. Coogan, Cheryl Exum, and Lawrence E. Stager. Louisville: Westminster John Knox, 1994.

Frick, Frank S. *The Formation of the State in Ancient Israel: A Survey of Models and Theories.* Social World of Biblical Antiquity 4. Sheffield: Almond, 1985.

Fried, Lisbeth S. "The Land Lay Desolate: Conquest and Restoration in the Ancient Near East." Pages 21–54 in *Judah and the Judeans in the Neo-Babylonian Period.* Edited by Oded Lipschits and Joseph Blenkinsopp. Winona Lake, IN: Eisenbrauns, 2003.

———. *The Priest and the Great King: Temple-Palace Relations in the Persian Empire.* Biblical and Judaic Studies 10. Winona Lake, IN: Eisenbrauns, 2004.

———. "A Silver Coin of Yoḥanan Hakkohen." *Transeuphratène* 26 (2003): 65–85.

Fritz, Volkmar. *The Emergence of Israel in the 12th and 11th Centuries BCE.* Translated by James W. Barker. Society of Biblical Literature Biblical Encyclopedia Series 2. Leiden: Brill, 2011.

Gadot, Yuval. "Continuity and Change in the Late Bronze to Iron Age Transition in Israel's Coastal Plain: A Long-Term Perspective." Pages 55–73 in *Bene Israel: Studies in the Archaeology of Israel and the Levant during the Bronze and Iron Ages in Honour of Israel Finkelstein.* Edited by Alexander Fantalkin and Assaf Yasur-Landau. Culture and History of the Ancient Near East 31. Leiden: Brill, 2008.

———. "Houses and Households in Settlements along the Yarkon River, Israel, during the Iron Age I: Society, Economy, and Identity." Pages 155–81 in *Household Archaeology in Ancient Israel and Beyond.* Edited by Assaf Yasur-Landau, Jennie R. Ebeling, and Laura B. Mazow. Culture and History of the Ancient Near East 50. Leiden: Brill, 2011.

Gal, Zvi. *Lower Galilee during the Iron Age.* Translated by Marcia Reines Josephy. American Schools of Oriental Research Dissertation Series 9. Winona Lake, IN: Eisenbrauns, 1992.

Galil, Gershon. "The Hebrew Inscription from Khirbet Qeiyafa/Neta'im." *Ugarit-Forschungen* 41 (2009): 193–242.

Garbini, Giovanni. *History and Ideology in Ancient Israel.* Translated by John Bowden. New York: Crossroad, 1988.

Gardiner, Alan H. "The Geography of the Exodus." Pages 203–15 in *Recueil d'études égyptologiques dédiées à la mémoire de Jean-François Champollion à l'occasion du centenaire de la lettre à M. Dacier relative à l'alphabet des hieroglyphes phonétiques, lue à la l'Académie des Inscriptions et Belles-Lettres le 27 septembre 1822.* Bibliothèque de l'École des hautes études 4/234. Paris: E. Champion, 1922.

———. "The Geography of the Exodus: An Answer to Professor Naville and Others." *Journal of Egyptian Archaeology* 10 (1924): 87–96.

Garfinkel, Yosef, and Saar Ganor, eds. *Excavation Report 2007–2008.* Vol. 1 of *Khirbet Qeiyafa.* Jerusalem: Israel Exploration Society, 2009.

Garr, W. Randall. *Dialect Geography of Syria-Palestine, 1000–586 B.C.E.* Philadelphia: University of Pennsylvania Press, 1985.

Gass, Erasmus. "Der Passa-Papyrus (Cowl 21[1])—Mythos oder Realität?" *Biblische Notizen* 99 (1999): 55–68.

———. "Topographical Considerations and Redaction Criticism in 2 Kings 3." *Journal of Biblical Literature* 128 (2009): 65–84.

George, Andrew R. *The Epic of Gilgamesh: The Babylonian Epic Poem and Other Texts in Akkadian and Sumerian; Translated and with an Introduction.* New York: Barnes & Noble, 1999.

Geva, Hillel. *Jewish Quarter Excavations in the Old City of Jerusalem: Conducted by Nahman Avigad, 1969–1982.* 4 vols. Jerusalem: Institute of Archaeology, Hebrew University of Jerusalem, 2008.

Giacumakis, George. *The Akkadian of Alalakh.* Janua Linguarum: Series Practica 59. The Hague: Mouton, 1970.

Gill, Dan. "The Geology of the City of David and Its Ancient Subterranean Waterworks." Pages 1–28 in *Various Reports.* Vol. 4 of *Excavations at the City of David*, by Yigal Shiloh. Edited by Donald T. Ariel et al. Qedem 35. Jerusalem: Institute of Archaeology, Hebrew University of Jerusalem, 1996.

———. "How They Met: Geology Solves Long-Standing Mystery of Hezekiah's Tunnelers." *Biblical Archaeology Review* 20, no. 4 (1994): 20–33, 64.

Gitin, Seymour. "Philistia in Transition: The Tenth Century BCE and Beyond." Pages 162–83 in *Mediterranean Peoples in Transition: Thirteenth to Early Tenth Centuries BCE.* Edited by Seymour Gitin, Amihai Mazar, and Ephraim Stern. Jerusalem: Israel Exploration Society, 1998.

———. "Tel Miqne-Ekron in the 7th Century BC: City Plan Development and the Oil Industry." Pages 167–96, 219–43 in *Olive Oil in Antiquity: Israel and Neighbouring Countries from the Neolithic to the Early Arab Period.* Edited by David Eitam and Michael Heltzer. Studies in the History of the Ancient Near East 7. Padova: Sargon, 1996.

Gitin, Seymour, Amihai Mazar, and Ephraim Stern, eds. *Mediterranean Peoples in Transition: Thirteenth to Early Tenth Centuries BCE; In Honor of Professor Trude Dothan.* Jerusalem: Israel Exploration Society, 1998.

Gitler, Haim, and Catharine Lorber. "A New Chronology for the Ptolemaic Coins of Judah." *American Journal of Numismatics* 18 (2006): 1–41.

Glass, J., et al. "Petrographic Analysis of Middle Bronze Age III, Late Bronze Age and Iron Age I Ceramic Assemblages." Pages 171–77 in *Shiloh: The Archaeology of a Biblical Site.* Edited by Israel Finkelstein, Shlomo Bunimovitz, and Zvi Lederman. Tel Aviv: Institute of Archaeology, Tel Aviv University, 1993.

Glassner, Jean-Jacques. *Mesopotamian Chronicles.* Edited by Benjamin R. Foster. Society of Biblical Literature Writings from the Ancient World 19. Atlanta: Society of Biblical Literature, 2004.

Glazier-McDonald, Beth. "Edom in the Prophetical Corpus." Pages 23–32 in *You Shall Not Abhor an Edomite for He Is Your Brother: Edom and Seir in History and Tradition.* Edited by Diana Vikander Edelman. Society of Biblical Literature Archaeology and Biblical Studies 3. Atlanta: Scholars Press, 1995.

Goetze, Albrecht. "The Struggle for the Domination of Syria." Pages 1–20 in *History of the Middle East and the Aegean Region, c. 1380–1000 B.C.* Vol. 2.2 of *The Cambridge Ancient History.* Edited by I. E. S. Edwards, N. G. L. Hammond, and E. Sollberger. 3rd ed. Cambridge: Cambridge University Press, 1975.

Gogel, Sandra Landis. *A Grammar of Epigraphic Hebrew.* Society of Biblical Literature Resources for Biblical Study 23. Atlanta: Society of Biblical Literature, 1998.

Goldingay, John. *Daniel.* Word Biblical Commentary 30. Waco: Word, 1989.

———. "The Patriarchs in Scripture and History." Pages 1–34 in *Essays on the Patriarchal Narratives.* Edited by A. R. Millard and D. J. Wiseman. Leicester, UK: Inter-Varsity, 1980.

Goldstein, Jonathan. *1 Maccabees: A New Translation with Introduction and Commentary.* Anchor Bible 41. New York: Doubleday, 1976.

Goren, Yuval, Israel Finkelstein, and Nadav Na'aman. "The Expansion of the Kingdom of Amurru according to the Petrographic Investigation of the Amarna Tablets." *Bulletin of the American Schools of Oriental Research* 329 (2003): 2–11.

Gorny, Ronald L. "Environment, Archaeology, and History in Hittite Anatolia." *Biblical Archaeologist* 52 (1989): 78–96.

Gosse, Bernard. "La disparition de la dynastie davidique." *Transeuphratène* 39 (2010): 97–112.

Gottwald, Norman K. *The Tribes of Yahweh: A Sociology of the Religion of Liberated Israel, 1250–1050 B.C.E.* Maryknoll, NY: Orbis Books, 1979.

Grabbe, Lester L. *Ancient Israel: What Do We Know and How Do We Know It?* London: T&T Clark, 2007.

———. "Ancient Near Eastern Prophecy from an Anthropological Perspective." Pages 13–32 in *Prophecy in Its Ancient Near Eastern Context: Mesopotamian, Biblical, and Arabian Perspectives*. Edited by Martti Nissinen. Society of Biblical Literature Symposium Series 13. Atlanta: Society of Biblical Literature, 2000.

———, ed. *The Archaeology.* Vol. 1 of *Israel in Transition: From Late Bronze II to Iron IIA (c. 1250–850 BCE).* Library of Hebrew Bible/Old Testament Studies 491. London: T&T Clark, 2008.

———. "Are Historians of Ancient Palestine Fellow Creatures—or Different Animals?" Pages 19–36 in *Can a "History of Israel" Be Written?* Edited by Lester L. Grabbe. Journal for the Study of the Old Testament: Supplement Series 245. Sheffield: Sheffield Academic Press, 1997.

———, ed. *Good Kings and Bad Kings: The Kingdom of Judah in the Seventh Century BCE.* Library of Hebrew Bible/Old Testament Studies 393. London: T&T Clark, 2005.

———. "The Kingdom of Judah from Sennacherib's Invasion to the Fall of Jerusalem: If We Only Had the Bible . . ." Pages 78–122 in *Good Kings and Bad Kings: The Kingdom of Judah in the Seventh Century BCE.* Edited by Lester L. Grabbe. Library of Hebrew Bible/Old Testament Studies 393. London: T&T Clark, 2005.

———. "Maccabean Chronology: 167–164 or 168–165 BCE?" *Journal of Biblical Literature* 110 (1991): 59–74.

———. *The Persian and Greek Periods.* Vol. 1 of *Judaism from Cyrus to Hadrian.* Minneapolis: Fortress, 1992.

———. "The 'Persian Documents' in the Book of Ezra: Are They Authentic?" Pages 531–70 in *Judah and the Judeans in the Persian Period.* Edited by Oded Lipschits and Manfred Oeming. Winona Lake, IN: Eisenbrauns, 2006.

———. "What Was Ezra's Mission?" Pages 286–99 in *Second Temple Studies 2: Temple and Community in the Persian Period.* Edited by Tamara C. Eskenazi and Kent H. Richards. Journal for the Study of the Old Testament: Supplement Series 175. Sheffield: Sheffield Academic Press, 1994.

———. *Yehud: A History of the Persian Province of Judah.* Vol. 1 of *A History of the Jews and Judaism in the Second Temple Period.* Library of Second Temple Studies 47. London: T&T Clark, 2004.

Graham, John N. "'Vinedressers and Plowmen': 2 Kings 25:12 and Jeremiah 52:16." *Biblical Archaeologist* 47 (1984): 55–58.

Grayson, A. Kirk. *Assyrian and Babylonian Chronicles.* Texts from Cuneiform Sources 5. Locust Valley, NY: Augustin, 1975. Repr., Winona Lake, IN: Eisenbrauns, 2000.

———. "Shalmaneser III and the Levantine States: The Damascus Coalition." *Journal of Hebrew Scriptures* 5, art. 4 (2004). Online: http://www.jhsonline.org/Articles/article_34 .pdf.

Grayson, Kirk, and Jamie Novotny. *The Royal Inscriptions of Sennacherib, King of Assyria (704–681 BC), Part 1.* Royal Inscriptions of the Neo-Assyrian Period 3/1/. Winona Lake, IN: Eisenbrauns, 2012.

Green, Barbara. *How Are the Mighty Fallen? A Dialogical Study of King Saul in 1 Samuel.* Journal for the Study of the Old Testament: Supplement Series 365. Sheffield: Sheffield Academic Press, 2003.

Green, Peter. *Alexander to Actium: The Hellenistic Age.* London: Thames & Hudson, 1990.

Greene, John T. *The Role of the Messenger and Message in the Ancient Near East.* Brown Judaic Studies 169. Atlanta: Scholars Press, 1989.

Greengus, Samuel. *Laws in the Bible and in Early Rabbinic Collections: The Legal Legacy of the Ancient Near East*. Eugene, OR: Cascade Books, 2011.

———. "Legal and Social Institutions of Ancient Mesopotamia." Pages 469–84 in vol. 1 of *Civilizations of the Ancient Near East*. Edited by Jack M. Sasson. New York: Scribner, 1995.

———. "The Old Babylonian Marriage Contract." *Journal of the American Oriental Society* 89 (1969): 505–32.

———. *Old Babylonian Tablets from Ishchali and Vicinity*. Uitgaven van het Nederlands Historisch-Archeologisch Instituut te Istanbul 44. Istanbul: Nederlands Historisch-Archaeologisch Instituut, 1979.

———. "Redefining 'Inchoate Marriage' in Old Babylonian Contexts." Pages 123–39 in *Riches Hidden in Secret Places: Ancient Near Eastern Studies in Memory of Thorkild Jacobsen*. Edited by Tzvi Abusch. Winona Lake, IN: Eisenbrauns, 2002.

Greenstein, Edward L. "Autobiographies in Ancient Western Asia." Pages 2421–32 in vol. 4 of *Civilizations of the Ancient Near East*. Edited by Jack M. Sasson. New York: Scribner, 1995.

Greenstein, Edward L., and David Marcus. "The Akkadian Inscription of Idrimi." *Journal of the Ancient Near Eastern Society of Columbia University* 8 (1976): 59–96.

Greenwood, Kyle. "Campaigns of Tiglath-pileser I against the Arameans and Babylonia." Pages 156–57 in *The Ancient Near East: Historical Sources in Translation*. Edited by Mark W. Chavalas. Malden, MA: Blackwell, 2006.

———. "Labor Pains: The Relationship Between David's Census and Corvée Labor." *Bulletin for Biblical Research* 20 (2010): 467–78.

Greer, Jonathan S. "A Marzeaḥ and a Mizraq: A Prophet's Mêlée with Religious Diversity in Amos 6:4–7." *Journal for the Study of the Old Testament* 32 (2007): 243–62.

Gregor, Paul Z. "A Tripartite Pillared Building in Transjordan." *Annual of the Department of Antiquities of Jordan* 53 (2009): 9–19.

Grelot, Pierre. "La dernière étape de la rédaction sacerdotale." *Vetus Testamentum* 6 (1956): 174–89.

———. *Documents araméens d'Égypte*. Littératures anciennes du Proche-Orient 5. Paris: Cerf, 1972.

———. "Le papyrus pascal d'Éléphantine et le problème du Pentateuque." *Vetus Testamentum* 5 (1955): 250–65.

Grena, George M. *LMLK—a Mystery Belonging to the King*. Redondo Beach, CA: 4000 Years of Writing History, 2004.

Groll, Sarah. "The Historical Background to the Exodus: Papyrus Anastasi VIII." Pages 109–14 in *Études égyptologiques et bibliques: À la mémoire du Père B. Couroyer*. Edited by Marcel Sigrist. Cahiers de la Revue biblique 36. Paris: Gabalda, 1997.

Grønbaek, Jakob H. *Die Geschichte vom Aufstieg Davids (1 Sam. 15–2 Sam. 5): Tradition und Komposition*. Translated by Hanns Leister. Acta theologica danica 10. Copenhagen: Prostant apud Munksgaard, 1971.

Gropp, Douglas M. *The Samaria Papyri from Wadi Daliyeh*. Vol. 2 of *Wadi Daliyeh*. Discoveries in the Judaean Desert 28. Oxford: Clarendon, 2001.

Groves, J. Alan. *Judges*. Two Horizons Old Testament Commentary. Grand Rapids: Eerdmans, forthcoming.

Guichard, Michaël. "Un David raté ou une histoire de habiru à l'époque Amorite: Vie et mort de Samsī-Erah, chef de guerre et homme du people." Pages 29–93 in *Le jeune héros: Recherches sur la formation et la diffusion d'un thème littéraire au Proche-Orient ancien; Actes du colloque organisé par les chaires d'Assyriologie et des Milieux bibliques du Collège de France, Paris, les 6 et 7 avril 2009*. Edited by Jean-Marie Durand, Thomas Römer, and Michael Langlois. Orbis biblicus et orientalis 250. Fribourg: Academic Press; Göttingen: Vandenhoeck & Ruprecht, 2011.

———. "Un taité alliance entre Larsa, Uruk et Ešnunna contra Sabium de Babylone." *Semitica* 56 (2014): 9–24.

Günbatti, Cahit. "Two Treaty Texts Found at Kültepe." Pages 249–68 in *Assyria and*

Beyond: Studies Presented to Mogens Trolle Larsen. Edited by J. G. Dercksen. Uitgaven van het Nederlands Instituut voor het Nabije Oosten te Leiden 100. Leiden: Nederlands Instituut voor et Nabije Oosten, 2004.

Gunn, David M. *The Story of King David: Genre and Interpretation.* Journal for the Study of the Old Testament: Supplement Series 6. Sheffield: JSOT Press, 1989.

Guy, P. L. O. *New Light from Armageddon: Second Provisional Report (1927–29) on the Excavations at Megiddo in Palestine.* Oriental Institute Communications 9. Chicago: University of Chicago Press, 1931.

Habicht, Christian. "Royal Documents in II Maccabees." *Harvard Studies in Classical Philology* 80 (1976): 1–18.

———. *2 Makkabäerbuch.* Jüdische Schriften aus hellenistisch-römischer Zeit 1.3. Gütersloh: Mohn, 1976.

Hackett, Jo Ann, Frank M. Cross, P. Kyle McCarter, and Ada Yardeni. "Defusing Pseudo-Scholarship: The Siloam Inscription Ain't Hasmonean." *Biblical Archaeology Review* 23, no. 2 (1997): 41–50, 68.

Hadley, Judith. "Some Drawings and Inscription on Two Pithoi from Kuntillet ʿAjrud." *Vetus Testamentum* 37 (1987): 180–209.

Hallo, William W. "Antediluvian Cities." *Journal of Cuneiform Studies* 23 (1970): 57–67.

———. "From Qarqar to Carchemish: Assyria and Israel in the Light of New Discoveries." *Biblical Archaeologist* 23 (1960): 34–61.

Hallo, William W., and K. Lawson Younger Jr., eds. *Archival Documents from the Biblical World.* Vol. 3 of *The Context of Scripture.* Leiden: Brill, 2003.

Halpern, Baruch. *David's Secret Demons: Messiah, Murderer, Traitor, King.* The Bible in Its World. Grand Rapids: Eerdmans, 2001.

———. *The First Historians: The Hebrew Bible and History.* San Francisco: Harper & Row, 1988.

———. "The State of Israelite History." Pages 540–65 in *Reconsidering Israel and Judah: Recent Studies on the Deuteronomistic History.* Edited by Gary N. Knoppers and J. Gordon McConville. Sources for Biblical and Theological Study 8. Winona Lake, IN: Eisenbrauns, 2000.

Halpern, Baruch, and William G. Dever. "Two Views of a History of Ancient Israel." Review of Lester L. Grabbe, *Ancient Israel: What Do We Know and How Do We Know It? Bulletin of the American Schools of Oriental Research* 357 (2010): 77–83.

Halpern-Zylberstein, Marie-Christine. "The Archaeology of Hellenistic Palestine." Pages 1–34 in *The Hellenistic Period.* Vol. 2 of *The Cambridge History of Judaism.* Edited by W. D. Davies and Louis Finkelstein. Cambridge: Cambridge University Press, 1989.

Harrington, Daniel J. *The Maccabean Revolt: Anatomy of a Biblical Revolution.* Old Testament Studies 1. Wilmington, DE: Michael Glazier, 1988.

Harris, Rivkah. "Inanna-Ishtar as Paradox and a Coincidence of Opposites." *History of Religions* 30 (1991): 261–78.

Harrison, Timothy P. "The Late Bronze/Early Iron Age Transition in the Northern Orontes Valley." Pages 83–102 in *Societies in Transition: Evolutionary Processes in the Northern Levant between Late Bronze Age II and Early Iron Age; Papers Presented on the Occasion of the 20th Anniversary of the New Excavations in Tell Afis, Bologna, 15th November 2007.* Edited by Fabrizio Venturi. Studi e testi orientali 9. Bologna: CLUEB, 2010.

———. "Lifting the Veil on a 'Dark Age': Taʿyinat and the North Orontes Valley during the Early Iron Age." Pages 171–84 in *Exploring the Longue Durée: Essays in Honor of Lawrence E. Stager.* Edited by J. David Schloen. Winona Lake, IN: Eisenbrauns, 2009.

———. "Neo-Hittites in the North Orontes Valley: Recent Investigations at Tell Tayinat." *Journal of the Canadian Society for Mesopotamian Studies* 2 (2008): 59–68.

———. "Tayinat Archaeological Project Annual Reports." Online: http://www.utoronto.ca/tap/.

———. "Temples, Tablets and the Neo-Assyrian Provincial Capital of Kinalia." *Journal of the Canadian Society for Mesopotamian Studies* 6 (2011): 29–37.

Harrison, Timothy P., and James F. Osborne. "Building XVI and the Neo-Assyrian Sacred Precinct at Tell Tayinat." *Journal of Cuneiform Studies* 64 (2012): 125–43.

Hartman, Louis F., and Alexander A. Di Lella. *The Book of Daniel: A New Translation with Introduction and Commentary*. Anchor Bible 23. Garden City, NY: Doubleday, 1977.

Hasel, Michael G. *Domination and Resistance: Egyptian Military Activity in the Southern Levant, ca. 1300–1185 B.C.* Probleme der Ägyptologie 11. Leiden: Brill, 1998.

———. "Merneptah's Reference to Israel: Critical Issues for the Origin of Israel." Pages 47–59 in *Critical Issues in Early Israelite History*. Edited by Richard S. Hess, Gerald A. Klingbeil, and Paul J. Ray. Bulletin for Biblical Research Supplements 3. Winona Lake, IN: Eisenbrauns, 2008.

Hawkins, John David. "Azatiwata." Pages 124–26 in *Monumental Inscriptions from the Biblical World*. Vol. 2 of *The Context of Scripture*. Edited by William W. Hallo and K. Lawson Younger Jr. Leiden: Brill, 2003.

———. "Cilicia, the Amuq, and Aleppo: New Light in a Dark Age." *Near Eastern Archaeology* 72 (2009): 164–73.

———. *Inscriptions of the Iron Age*. Vol. 1 of *Corpus of Hieroglyphic Luwian Inscriptions*. Untersuchungen zur indogermanischen Sprach- und Kulturwissenschaft 8. Berlin: de Gruyter, 2000.

———. "Karkamish and Karatepe: Neo-Hittite City-States in North Syria." Pages 1295–1307 in vol. 2 of *Civilizations of the Ancient Near East*. Edited by Jack M. Sasson. New York: Scribner, 1995.

Hawkins, Ralph K. *How Israel Became a People*. Nashville: Abingdon, 2013.

———. *The Iron Age I Structure on Mt. Ebal: Excavation and Interpretation*. Bulletin for Biblical Research Supplements 6. Winona Lake, IN: Eisenbrauns, 2012.

Hayes, John H., and Paul K. Hooker. *A New Chronology for the Kings of Israel and Judah and Its Implications for Biblical History and Literature*. Atlanta: John Knox, 1988.

Hayes, John H., and Sara R. Mandell. *The Jewish People in Classical Antiquity: From Alexander to Bar Kochba*. Louisville: Westminster John Knox, 1998.

Hecker, Karl. "Staatsverträge." Pages 88–91 in *Staatsverträge, Herrscherinschriften und andere Documente zur politischen Geschichte*. Vol. 2 of *Texte aus der Umwelt des Alten Testaments*. Edited by Michael Lichtenstein. Gütersloh: Mohn, 2005.

Heimpel, Wolfgang. *Letters to the King of Mari: A New Translation, with Historical Introduction, Notes, and Commentary*. Mesopotamian Civilizations 12. Winona Lake, IN: Eisenbrauns, 2003.

Heintz, Jean-Georges. "'Dans la plénitude du coeur': A propos d'une formule d'alliance à Mari en Assyrie et dans la Bible." Pages 31–34 in *Ce Dieu qui vient: Études sur L'Ancien et le Nouveau Testament offertes au professeur Bernard Renaud à l'occasion de son soixante-cinquième anniversaire*. Edited by Raymond Kuntzmann. Lectio divina 159. Paris: Cerf, 1995.

———. "Nouveaux traités d'époque babylonienne ancienne et formules d'alliance dans la Bible hébraïque: Remarques préliminaires." Pages 69–94 in *Les relations internationales: Actes du colloque de Strasbourg, 15–17 juin 1993*. Edited by Edmond Frézouls and Alex Jacquemin. Travaux du Centre de recherche sur le Proche-Orient et la Grèce antiques 13. Strasbourg: Université des sciences humaines de Strasbourg, 1995.

Helck, Wolfgang. "*Ṯkw* und die Ramses-Stadt." *Vetus Testamentum* 15 (1965): 35–48.

Hendel, Ronald S. "The Date of the Siloam Inscription: A Rejoinder to Rogerson and Davies." *Biblical Archaeologist* 59 (1996): 233–37.

———. *Remembering Abraham: Culture, Memory, and History in the Hebrew Bible*. New York: Oxford University Press, 2005.

Hengel, Martin. *Judaism and Hellenism: Studies in Their Encounter in Palestine during the Early Hellenistic Period*. Translated by John Bowden. 2 vols. Philadelphia: Fortress, 1974.

Herr, Larry G. "The Iron Age II Period: Emerging Nations." *Biblical Archaeologist* 60 (1997): 115–83.

———. "Tripartite Pillared Buildings and the Market Place in Iron Age Palestine." *Bulletin* of the American Schools of Oriental Research 272 (1988): 47–67.

———. "Wine Production in the Hills of Southern Ammon and the Founding of Tall al-ʿUmayri in the Sixth Century B.C." Annual of the Department of Antiquities of Jordan 39 (1995): 121–25.

Herr, Larry G., and Mohammad Najjar. "The Iron Age." Pages 311–34 in Jordan: An Archaeological Reader. Edited by Russell B. Adams. London: Equinox, 2008.

Herzog, Zeʾev. "Settlement and Fortification Planning in the Iron Age." Pages 231–74 in The Architecture of Ancient Israel: From the Prehistoric to the Persian Periods; In Memory of Immanuel (Munya) Dunayevsky. Edited by Aharon Kempinski and Ronny Reich. Jerusalem: Israel Exploration Society, 1992.

Herzog, Zeʾev, Miriam Aharoni, and Anson F. Rainey. "Arad—an Ancient Israelite Fortress with a Temple to Yahweh." Biblical Archaeological Review 13, no. 2 (1987): 16–35.

Herzog, Zeʾev, Miriam Aharoni, Anson F. Rainey, and Shmuel Moshkovitz. "The Israelite Fortress at Arad." Bulletin of the American Schools of Oriental Research 254 (1984): 1–34.

Herzog, Zeʾev, and Lily Singer-Avitz. "Redefining the Centre: The Emergence of State in Judah." Tel Aviv 31 (2004): 209–44.

Hess, Richard S. "Alalakh: 1. Treaties." Pages 329–32 in Monumental Inscriptions from the Biblical World. Vol. 2 of The Context of Scripture. Edited by William W. Hallo and K. Lawson Younger Jr. Leiden: Brill, 2003.

———. "Alalakh Studies and the Bible: Obstacle or Contribution?" Pages 199–215 in Scripture and Other Artifacts: Essays on the Bible and Archaeology in Honor of Philip J. King. Edited by Michael D. Coogan, Cheryl Exum, and Lawrence E. Stager. Louisville: Westminster John Knox, 1994.

———. "Arrowheads from Iron Age I: Personal Names and Authenticity." Pages 113–29 in Ugarit at Seventy-Five: Proceedings of the Symposium "Ugarit at Seventy-Five," Held at Trinity International University, Deerfield, Illinois, February 18–20, 2005, under the Auspices of the Middle Western Branch of the American Oriental Society and the Mid-West Region of the Society of the Biblical Literature. Edited by K. Lawson Younger Jr. Winona Lake, IN: Eisenbrauns, 2007.

———. "Ashera or Asherata?" Orientalia 65 (1996): 209–19.

———. "The Bible and Alalakh." Pages 209–21 in Mesopotamia and the Bible: Comparative Explorations. Edited by Mark W. Chavalas and K. Lawson Younger Jr. Journal for the Study of the Old Testament: Supplement Series 341. Grand Rapids: Baker Academic, 2002.

———. "Canaan and Canaanite in Alalakh." Ugarit-Forschungen 31 (1999): 225–36.

———. "Early Israel in Canaan: A Survey of Recent Evidence and Interpretations." Palestine Exploration Quarterly 126 (1993): 125–42. Repr., pages 492–518 in Israel's Past in Present Research: Essays on Ancient Israelite Historiography. Edited by V. Philips Long. Sources for Biblical and Theological Study 7. Winona Lake, IN: Eisenbrauns, 1999.

———. "Eden—a Well-Watered Place." Bible Review 7, no. 6 (1991): 29–33.

———. "The Form and Structure of the Solomonic District List in 1 Kings 4:7–19." Pages 279–92 in Crossing Boundaries and Linking Horizons: Studies in Honor of Michael C. Astour on His 80th Birthday. Edited by Gordon D. Young, Mark W. Chavalas, and Richard E. Averbeck. Bethesda, MD: CDL Press, 1997.

———. "The Genealogies of Genesis 1–11 and Comparative Literature." Biblica 70 (1989): 241–54.

———. "Hezekiah and Sennacherib in 2 Kings 18–20." Pages 23–41 in Zion, City of Our God. Edited by Richard S. Hess and Gordon J. Wenham. Grand Rapids: Eerdmans, 2004.

———. "Israelite Identity and Personal Names from the Book of Judges." Hebrew Studies 44 (2003): 25–39.

———. Israelite Religions: An Archaeological and Biblical Survey. Grand Rapids: Baker Academic, 2007.

————. "The Jericho and Ai of the Book of Joshua." Pages 33–46 in *Critical Issues in Early Israelite History*. Edited by Richard S. Hess, Gerald A. Klingbeil, and Paul J. Ray Jr. Bulletin for Biblical Research Supplements 3. Winona Lake, IN: Eisenbrauns, 2008.

————. *Joshua: An Introduction and Commentary*. Tyndale Old Testament Commentaries 6. Downers Grove, IL: InterVarsity, 1996.

————. "Multi-Month Ritual Calendars in the West Semitic World: Emar 446 and Leviticus 23." Pages 233–53 in *The Future of Biblical Archaeology: Reassessing Methodologies and Assumptions; The Proceedings of a Symposium, August 12–14, 2001, at Trinity International University*. Edited by James K. Hoffmeier and Alan R. Millard. Grand Rapids: Eerdmans, 2004.

————. "Questions of Reading and Writing in Ancient Israel." *Bulletin for Biblical Research* 19 (2009): 1–9.

————. "Recent Studies in Old Testament History: A Review Article." *Themelios* 19, no. 2 (1994): 9–15.

————. Review of Wolfgang Heimpel, *Letters to the King of Mari*. *Denver Journal* 8 (2005). Online: http://www.denverseminary.edu/article/letters-to-the-king-of-mari.

————. "Seven Years of Barrenness before a Second Wife." Pages 252–53 in *Archival Documents from the Biblical World*. Vol. 3 of *The Context of Scripture*. Edited by William W. Hallo and K. Lawson Younger Jr. Leiden: Brill, 2003.

————. *Studies in the Personal Names of Genesis 1–11*. Winona Lake, IN: Eisenbrauns, 2009.

————. "Taxes, Taxation." Pages 950–54 in *Dictionary of the Old Testament: Historical Books*. Edited by Bill T. Arnold and H. G. M. Williamson. Downers Grove, IL: InterVarsity, 2005.

————. "Yahweh and His Asherah? Religious Pluralism in the Old Testament World." Pages 5–33 in *One God, One Lord: Christianity in a World of Religious Pluralism*. Edited by Andrew D. Clarke and Bruce W. Winter. 2nd ed. Exeter, UK: Paternoster; Grand Rapids: Baker Books, 1992.

Hess, Richard S., Gerald A. Klingbeil, and Paul J. Ray Jr., eds. *Critical Issues in Early Israelite History*. Bulletin for Biblical Research Supplements 3. Winona Lake, IN: Eisenbrauns, 2008.

Hess, Richard S., and David Toshio Tsumura, eds. *I Studied Inscriptions from before the Flood: Ancient Near Eastern, Literary, and Linguistic Approaches to Genesis 1–11*. Sources for Biblical and Theological Study 4. Winona Lake, IN: Eisenbrauns, 1994.

Hillers, Delbert R. *Treaty-Curses and the Old Testament Prophets*. Biblica et orientalia 16. Rome: Pontifical Biblical Institute, 1964.

Hirsch, Eileen N. "Ramses III und sein Verhältnis zur Levante." Pages 223–27 in *Das Königtum der Ramessidenzeit: Voraussetzungen, Verwirklichung, Vermächtnis; Akten des 3. Symposions zur ägyptischen Königsideologie in Bonn 7.–9.6.2001*. Edited by Rolf Gundlach and Ursula Rössler-Köhler. Ägypten und Altes Testament 36.3. Wiesbaden: Harrassowitz, 2001.

Hobbs, T. Raymond. *2 Kings*. Word Biblical Commentary 13. Dallas: Word, 1985.

Hoffmeier, James K. *Ancient Israel in Sinai: The Evidence for the Authenticity of the Wilderness Tradition*. New York: Oxford University Press, 2005.

————. *Israel in Egypt: The Evidence for the Authenticity of the Exodus Tradition*. New York: Oxford University Press, 1997.

Hoffmeier, James K., and Dennis R. Magary, eds. *Do Historical Matters Matter to Faith? A Critical Appraisal of Modern and Postmodern Approaches to Scripture*. Wheaton: Crossway, 2012.

Hoffmeier, James K., and Alan R. Millard, eds. *The Future of Biblical Archaeology: Reassessing Methodologies and Assumptions; The Proceedings of a Symposium, August 12–14, 2001, at Trinity International University*. Grand Rapids: Eerdmans, 2004.

Hoffmeier, James K. and Stephen Moshier. "A Highway Out of Egypt: The Main Road from Egypt to Canaan." Pages 485–510 in *Desert Road Archaeology in Ancient Egypt and Beyond*. Edited by Heiko Riemer and

Frank Förster. Africa Praehistorica 26. Köln: Heinrich Barth Institut, 2013.

Hoglund, Kenneth G. "Edomites." Pages 335–47 in *Peoples of the Old Testament World*. Edited by Alfred J. Hoerth, Gerald L. Mattingly, and Edwin M. Yamauchi. Grand Rapids: Baker Books, 1994.

Holladay, John S. "Hezekiah's Tribute, Long-Distance Trade, and the Wealth of Nations ca. 1000–600 BC: A New Perspective." Pages 311–31 in *Confronting the Past: Archaeological and Historical Essays on Ancient Israel in Honor of William G. Dever*. Edited by Seymour Gitin, J. Edward Wright, and J. P. Dessel. Winona Lake, IN: Eisenbrauns, 2006.

———. "The Kingdoms of Israel and Judah: Political and Economic Centralization in the Iron IIA-B (ca. 1000–750 BC)." Pages 368–415 in *The Archaeology of Society in the Holy Land*. Edited by Thomas E. Levy. New York: Facts on File, 1995.

———. "Red Slip, Burnish, and the Solomonic Gateway at Gezer." *Bulletin of the American Schools of Oriental Research* 277–78 (1990): 23–70.

Homan, Michael M. *To Your Tents, O Israel! The Terminology, Function, Form, and Symbolism of Tents in the Hebrew Bible and the Ancient Near East*. Culture and History of the Ancient Near East 12. Leiden: Brill, 2002.

Horn, Siegfried. "The Divided Monarchy: The Kingdoms of Judah and Israel." Pages 129–99 in *Ancient Israel: From Abraham to the Roman Destruction of the Temple*. Edited by Hershel Shanks. Rev. ed. Washington, DC: Biblical Archaeology Society, 1999.

Horowitz, Wayne, and Takayoshi Oshima. *Cuneiform in Canaan: Cuneiform Sources from the Land of Israel in Ancient Times*. Jerusalem: Israel Exploration and Hebrew University of Jerusalem, 2006.

Houtman, Cornelius. *Exodus*. Translated by Johan Rebel and Sierd Woudstra. 4 vols. Historical Commentary on the Old Testament. Leuven: Peeters; Kampen: Kok, 1993–2002.

Huehnergard, John. "Languages (Introduction)." Pages 155–70 in vol. 4 of *The Anchor Bible Dictionary*. Edited by David Noel Freedman. New York: Doubleday, 1992.

———. "On the Etymology and Meaning of Hebrew *nābî'*." *Eretz-Israel* 26 (1999): 88–93.

Huffmon, Herbert B. "The Expansion of Prophecy in the Mari Archives: New Texts, New Readings, New Information." Pages 7–22 in *Prophecy and Prophets: The Diversity of Contemporary Issues in Scholarship*. Society of Biblical Literature Semeia Studies. Edited by Yehoshua Gitay. Atlanta: Scholars Press, 1997.

Ilan, David. "Dan." Pages 107–12 in vol. 2 of *The Oxford Encyclopedia of Archaeology in the Near East*. Edited by Eric M. Meyers. Oxford: Oxford University Press, 1997.

Isserlin, B. S. J. *The Israelites*. Minneapolis: Augsburg Fortress, 2001.

Izre'el, Shlomo. "The Amarna Letters from Canaan." Pages 2411–19 in vol. 2 of *Civilizations of the Ancient Near East*. Edited by Jack M. Sasson. New York: Scribner, 1995.

Jackson, Bernard S. "Law in the Ninth Century: Jehoshaphat's 'Judicial Reform.'" Pages 369–97 in *Understanding the History of Ancient Israel*. Edited by H. G. M. Williamson. Proceedings of the British Academy 143. Oxford: Oxford University Press, 2007.

Jacobsen, Thorkild. "The Eridu Genesis." *Journal of Biblical Literature* 100 (1981): 513–29.

Jacobson, David M. *The Hellenistic Paintings of Marisa*. Palestinian Exploration Fund Monographs 7. Leeds, UK: Maney, 2007.

James, Peter J. "Dating Late Iron Age Ekron (Tel Miqne)." *Palestine Exploration Quarterly* 138 (2006): 85–97.

Jamieson-Drake, David W. *Scribes and Schools in Monarchic Judah: A Socio-Archaeological Approach*. Journal for the Study of the Old Testament: Supplement Series 109. Sheffield: Almond, 1991.

Janssen, Jozef M. A. "On the Ideal Lifetime of the Egyptians." *Oudheidkundige Mededelingen uit het Rijksmuseum van Oudheden te Leiden* 31 (1950): 33–41.

Japhet, Sara. *I & II Chronicles: A Commentary*. Old Testament Library. Louisville: Westminster John Knox, 1993.

———— "Periodization and Ideology II: Chronology and Ideology in Ezra-Nehemiah." Pages 491–508 in *Judah and the Judeans in the Persian Period*. Edited by Oded Lipschits and Manfred Oeming. Winona Lake, IN: Eisenbrauns, 2006.

Jastrow, Otto. "Old Aramaic and Neo-Aramaic: Some Reflections on Language History." Pages 1–10 in *Aramaic in Its Historical and Linguistic Setting*. Edited by Holger Gzella and Margaretha L. Folmer. Akademie der Wissenschaften und der Literatur Mainz Veröffentlichungen der Orientalischen Kommission 50. Wiesbaden: Harrassowitz, 2008.

Jean, Charles-François. *Lettres*. Archives royales de Mari 2. Paris: Librairie orientaliste P. Geuthner, 1941.

————. *Lettres diverses*. Archives royales de Mari 2. Paris: Imprimerie Nationale, 1950.

Jeffers, Ann. *Magic and Divination in Ancient Palestine and Syria*. Studies in the History and Culture of the Ancient Near East 8. Leiden: Brill, 1996.

Joannès, Francis, and André Lemaire. "Contrats babyloniens d'époque achéménide du Bît-Abî Râm avec une épigraphe araméenne." *Revue d'Assyriologie* 90 (1996): 41–60.

————. "Trois tablettes cunéiformes à l'onomastique ouest-sémitique." *Transeuphratène* 17 (1999): 17–34.

Joffe, Alexander H. "The Rise of Secondary States in the Iron Age Levant." *Journal of the Economic and Social History of the Orient* 45 (2002): 425–67.

Joisten-Pruschke, Anke. *Das religiöse Leben der Juden von Elephantine in der Achämenidenzeit*. Göttinger Orientforschungen 3. Iranica, N.F. 2. Wiesbaden: Harrassowitz, 2008.

Kahn, Dan'el. "Judean Auxiliaries in Egypt's Wars against Kush." *Journal of the American Oriental Society* 127 (2007): 507–16.

Kaiser, Otto. "Beobachtungen zur sogenannten Thronnachfolgeerzählung." *Ephemerides theologicae lovanienses* 64 (1988): 5–20.

————. "David und Jonathan." *Ephemerides theologicae lovanienses* 66 (1990): 281–96.

Kallai, Zecharia. "Biblical Narrative and History: A Programmatic Review." *Wiener Zeitschrift für die Kunde des Morgenlandes* 96 (2006): 133–57.

Kamlah, Jens. "Zwei nordpalästinische 'Heiligtümer' der persischen Zeit und ihre epigraphischen Funde." *Zeitschrift des deutschen Palästina-Vereins* 115 (1999): 163–90.

Kampen, John. *The Hasideans and the Origin of Pharisaism: A Study in 1 and 2 Maccabees*. Society of Biblical Literature Septuagint and Cognate Studies Series 24. Atlanta: Scholars Press, 1988.

Kaniewski, D., E. Paulissen, E. Van Campo, H. Weiss, T. Otto, J. Bretschneider, and K. Van Lerberghe. "Late Second-Early First Millennium BC Abrupt Climate Changes in Coastal Syria and Their Possible Significance for the History of the Eastern Mediterranean." *Quaternary Research* 74 (2010): 207–15.

Kaufman, Stephen A. "Languages (Aramaic)." Pages 176–78 in vol. 4 of *The Anchor Bible Dictionary*. Edited by David Noel Freedman. New York: Doubleday, 1992.

Keel, Othmar. *The Symbolism of the Biblical World: Ancient Near Eastern Iconography and the Book of Psalms*. Translated by Timothy J. Hallett. New York: Seabury, 1978.

Keel, Othmar, and Christoph Uehlinger. *Gods, Goddesses and Images of God in Ancient Israel*. Translated by Thomas H. Trapp. Minneapolis: Fortress, 1998.

Keil, C. F., and F. Delitzsch. *Minor Prophets*. Vol. 10 of *Commentary on the Old Testament*. Translated by James Martin. Peabody, MA: Hendrickson, 1989.

Kelle, Brad E. *Ancient Israel at War, 853–586 BC*. Essential Histories 67. Oxford: Osprey, 2007.

————. "What's in a Name? Neo-Assyrian Designations for the Northern Kingdom and Their Implications for Israelite History and Biblical Interpretation." *Journal of Biblical Literature* 121 (2002): 639–66.

Kelle, Brad E., and Brent A. Strawn. "History of Israel 5: Assyrian Period." Pages 462–78 in *Dictionary of the Old Testament:*

Historical Books. Edited by Bill T. Arnold and H. G. M. Williamson. Downers Grove, IL: InterVarsity, 2005.

Kenyon, Kathleen. *Archaeology in the Holy Land.* 3rd ed. New York: Praeger, 1970.

———. *Digging Up Jerusalem.* London: Benn, 1974.

———. *Royal Cities of the Old Testament.* London: Barrie & Jenkins, 1971.

Kessler, Rainer. "Die Sklavin als Ehefrau: Zur Stellung der *ʾāmāh*." *Vetus Testamentum* 52 (2002): 501–12.

Keys, Gillian. *The Wages of Sin: A Reappraisal of the "Succession Narrative."* Journal for the Study of the Old Testament: Supplement Series 221. Sheffield: Sheffield Academic Press, 1996.

Khoury, Philip S., and Joseph Kostiner, eds. *Tribes and State Formation in the Middle East.* Berkeley: University of California Press, 1990.

Killebrew, Ann E. *Biblical Peoples and Ethnicity: An Archaeological Study of Egyptians, Canaanites, Philistines, and Early Israel, 1300–1100 B.C.E.* Society of Biblical Literature Archaeology and Biblical Studies 9. Atlanta: Society of Biblical Literature, 2005.

King, Philip J. *Amos, Hosea, Micah: An Archaeological Commentary.* Philadelphia: Westminster, 1988.

———. "Why Lachish Matters." *Biblical Archaeology Review* 31, no. 4 (2005): 36–47.

King, Philip J., and Lawrence E. Stager. *Life in Biblical Israel.* Library of Ancient Israel. Louisville: Westminster John Knox, 2001.

Kitchen, Kenneth A. *Ancient Orient and Old Testament.* Downers Grove, IL: InterVarsity, 1966.

———. *The Bible in Its World: Archaeology and the Bible Today.* Exeter, UK: Paternoster, 1977.

———. "Chronology." Pages 181–88 in *Dictionary of the Old Testament: Historical Books.* Edited by Bill T. Arnold and H. G. M. Williamson. Downers Grove, IL: InterVarsity, 2005.

———. "Egypt, History of (Chronology)." Pages 321–31 in vol. 2 of *The Anchor Bible Dictionary.* Edited by David Noel Freedman. New York: Doubleday, 1992.

———. "Egypt, Ugarit, Qatna, and Covenant." *Ugarit-Forschungen* 11 (1979): 453–64.

———. "An Egyptian Inscribed Fragment from Late Bronze Hazor." *Israel Exploration Journal* 53 (2003): 20–28.

———. "Egyptian Interventions in the Levant in Iron Age II." Pages 113–32 in *Symbiosis, Symbolism, and the Power of the Past: Canaan, Ancient Israel, and Their Neighbors from the Late Bronze Age through Roman Palaestina; Proceedings of the Centennial Symposium, W. F. Albright Institute of Archaeological Research and American Schools of Oriental Research, Jerusalem, May 29/31, 2000.* Edited by William G. Dever and Seymour Gitin. Winona Lake, IN: Eisenbrauns, 2003.

———. "Egyptians and Hebrews, from Raʿamses to Jericho." Pages 65–131 in *The Origin of Early Israel—Current Debate: Biblical, Historical, and Archaeological Perspectives; Irene Levi-Sala Seminar, 1997.* Edited by Shmuel Ahituv and Eliezer D. Oren. Beer-Sheva: Ben-Gurion University of the Negev Press, 1998.

———. "The Fall and Rise of Covenant, Law, and Treaty." *Tyndale Bulletin* 40 (1989): 118–35.

———. *On the Reliability of the Old Testament.* Grand Rapids: Eerdmans, 2003.

———. *Pharaoh Triumphant: The Life and Times of Ramesses II, King of Egypt.* Warminster, UK: Aris & Phillips, 1982.

———. "A Possible Mention of David in the Late Tenth Century BCE, and Deity *Dod as Dead as the Dodo?" *Journal for the Study of the Old Testament* 76 (1997): 29–44.

———. Review of Kevin A. Wilson, *The Campaign of Pharaoh Shoshenq I into Palestine.* *Journal of Jewish Studies* 54 (2009): 274–76.

———. "Some New Light on the Asiatic Wars of Ramesses II." *Journal of Egyptian Archaeology* 50 (1964): 47–70.

———. "The Tabernacle—a Bronze Age Artifact." *Eretz-Israel* 24 (1993): 119–29.

———. *The Third Intermediate Period in Egypt, 1100–650 B.C.* 2nd ed. Warminster, UK: Aris & Phillips, 1986.

———. "The Victories of Merneptah, and the Nature of Their Record." *Journal for the Study of the Old Testament* 28 (2004): 259–72.

Kitchen, Kenneth A., and Paul J. N. Lawrence, eds. *Treaty, Law and Covenant in the Ancient Near East.* 3 vols. Wiesbaden: Harrassowitz, 2012.

Kitz, Anne Marie. "Prophecy as Divination." *Catholic Biblical Quarterly* 65 (2003): 22–41.

Klein, Ralph W. *2 Chronicles: A Commentary.* Edited by Paul D. Hanson. Hermeneia. Minneapolis: Fortress, 2012.

Klengel, Horst. *Mittel- und Südsyrien.* Vol. 2 of *Geschichte Syriens im 2. Jahrtausen v. u. Z.* Berlin: Akademie Verlag, 1969.

———. *Syria, 3000–300 B.C.: A Handbook of Political History.* Berlin: Akademie Verlag, 1992.

Kletter, Raz. "Chronology and United Monarchy: A Methodological Review." *Zeitschrift des deutschen Palästina-Vereins* 120 (2004): 13–54.

———. *The Judean Pillar-Figurines and the Archaeology of Asherah.* British Archaeological Reports International Series 636. Oxford: Tempus Reparatum, 1996.

Knauf, Ernst A. "Elephantine und das vorbiblische Judentum." Pages 179–88 in *Religion und Religionskontakte im Zeitalter der Achämeniden.* Edited by Reinhard G. Kratz. Veröffentlichungen der Wissenschaftlichen Gesellschaft für Theologie 22. Gütersloh: Kaiser/Gütersloher Verlagshaus, 2002.

———. "From Archeology to History, Bronze and Iron Ages with Special Regard to the Year 1200 B.C.E. and the Tenth Century." Pages 72–85 in *The Archaeology.* Vol. 1 of *Israel in Transition: From Late Bronze II to Iron IIA (c. 1250–850 BCE).* Edited by Lester Grabbe. Library of Hebrew Bible/ Old Testament Studies 491. London: T&T Clark, 2008.

———. "The Glorious Days of Manasseh." Pages 164–88 in *Good Kings and Bad Kings: The Kingdom of Judah in the Seventh Century BCE.* Edited by Lester L. Grabbe. Library of Hebrew Bible/Old Testament Studies 393. London: T&T Clark, 2005.

Knoppers, Gary N. "Aaron's Calf and Jeroboam's Calves." Pages 92–104 in *Fortunate the Eyes That See: Essays in Honor of David Noel Freedman in Celebration of His Seventieth Birthday.* Edited by Astrid B. Beck et al. Grand Rapids: Eerdmans, 1995.

———. "The Davidic Genealogy: Some Textual Considerations from the Ancient Mediterranean World." *Transeuphratène* 22 (2001): 35–50.

———. "Jehoshaphat's Judiciary and 'The Scroll of YHWH's Torah.'" *Journal of Biblical Literature* 113 (1994): 59–80.

———. "Reform and Regression: The Chronicler's Presentation of Jehoshaphat." *Biblica* 72 (1991): 500–524.

———. "Rehoboam in Chronicles: Villain or Victim?" *Journal of Biblical Literature* 109 (1990): 423–40.

———. *The Reign of Solomon and the Rise of Jeroboam.* Vol. 1 of *Two Nations under God: The Deuteronomistic History of Solomon and the Dual Monarchies.* Harvard Semitic Monographs 52. Atlanta: Scholars Press, 1993.

———. "The Vanishing Solomon: The Disappearance of the United Monarchy from Recent Histories of Ancient Israel." *Journal of Biblical Literature* 116 (1997): 19–44.

Koch, Heidemarie. "Elams Vertrag mit dem akkadischen König Narām-Sîn (2260–2223 v. Chr.)." Pages 283–86 in *Staatsverträge, Herrscherinschriften und andere Documente zur politischen Geschichte.* Vol. 2 of *Texte aus der Umwelt des Alten Testaments.* Edited by Michael Lichtenstein. Gütersloh: Mohn, 2005.

Kochavi, Moshe, Pirhiyah Beck, and Esther Yadin, eds. *Aphek-Antipatris I: Excavation of Areas A and B; The 1972–1976 Seasons.* Tel Aviv: Emery and Claire Yass Publications in Archaeology of the Institute of Archaeology, Tel Aviv University, 2000.

Kofoed, Jens Bruun. *Text and History: Historiography and the Study of the Biblical Text*. Winona Lake, IN: Eisenbrauns, 2005.

Kottsieper, Ingo. "Die Religionspolitik der Achämeniden und die Juden von Elephantine." Pages 150–78 in *Religion und Religionskontakte im Zeitalter der Achämeniden*. Edited by Reinhard G. Kratz. Veröffentlichungen der Wissenschaftlichen Gesellschaft für Theologie 22. Gütersloh: Kaiser/Gütersloher Verlagshaus, 2002.

———. "The Tel Dan Inscription (*KAI* 310) and the Political Relations between Aram-Damascus and Israel in the First Half of the First Millennium B.C.E." Pages 105–34 in *Ahab Agonistes: The Rise and Fall of the Omri Dynasty*. Edited by Lester L. Grabbe. Library of Hebrew Bible/Old Testament Studies 421. London: T&T Clark, 2007.

Kramer, Samuel N. "BM 29616: The Fashioning of the *gala*." *Acta Sumerologica* 3 (1981): 1–9.

Kratz, Reinhard G. "Judean Ambassadors and the Making of Jewish Identity: The Case of Hananiah, Ezra, and Nehemiah." Pages 421–44 in *Judah and the Judeans in the Achaemenid Period: Negotiating Identity in an International Context*. Edited by Oded Lipschits, Gary N. Knoppers, and Manfred Oeming. Winona Lake, IN: Eisenbrauns, 2011.

———, ed. *Religion und Religionskontakte im Zeitalter der Achämeniden*. Veröffentlichungen der Wissenschaftlichen Gesellschaft für Theologie 22. Gütersloh: Kaiser/Gütersloher Verlagshaus, 2002.

———. "The Second Temple of Jeb and of Jerusalem." Pages 247–64 in *Judah and the Judeans in the Persian Period*. Edited by Oded Lipschits and Manfred Oeming. Winona Lake, IN: Eisenbrauns, 2006.

———. "Zwischen Elephantine und Qumran: Das Alte Testament im Rahmen des antiken Judentums." Pages 129–46 in *Congress Volume: Ljubljana 2007*. Edited by André Lemaire. Supplements to Vetus Testamentum 133. Leiden: Brill, 2010.

Kuhnen, Hans-Peter. *Palästina in griechisch-römischer Zeit*. Handbuch der Archäologie 2. Munich: Beck, 1990.

Kupper, Jean R. *Correspondance de Baḫdi-Lim, préfet du palais de Mari*. Archives royales de Mari 6. Paris: Imprimerie Nationale, 1954.

Lafont, Bertrand. "International Relations in the Ancient Near East: The Birth of a Complete Diplomatic System." *Diplomacy and Statecraft* 12, no. 1 (2001): 39–60.

———. "Relations internationales, alliances et diplomatie au temps des rois de Mari." Pages 213–328 in vol. 2 of *Mari, Ébla et les Hourrites: Dix ans de travaux; Actes du colloque international (Paris, Mai 1993)*. Edited by Jean-Marie Durand and Dominique Charpin. Amurru 2. Paris: Éditions Recherche sur les civilisations, 2001.

Lafont, Sophie. "Nouvelles données sur la royauté mésopotamienne." *Revue historique de droit français et étranger* 73 (1975): 473–500.

———. "Le roi, le juge et l'étranger à Mari et dans la Bible." *Revue d'assyriologie et d'archéologie orientale* 92 (1998): 161–81.

Lambert, Wilfred G. "A Document from a Community of Exiles in Babylonia." Pages 201–5 in *New Seals and Inscriptions, Hebrew, Idumean and Cuneiform*. Edited by Meir Lubetski. Hebrew Bible Monographs 8. Sheffield: Sheffield Phoenix Press, 2007.

———. "Mesopotamian Sources and Pre-Exilic Israel." Pages 352–65 in *In Search of Pre-Exilic Israel: Proceedings of the Oxford Old Testament Seminar*. Edited by John Day. Journal for the Study of the Old Testament: Supplement Series 406. London: T&T Clark International, 2004.

———. Review of Hans Ulrich Steymans, *Deuteronomium 28 und die adê zur Thronfolgeregelung Asarhaddons: Segen und Fluch im Alten Orient und in Israel*. *Archiv für Orientforschung* 44–45 (1997–1998): 396–99.

Landsberger, Benno. "Assyrische Königsliste und 'Dunkeles Zeitalter.'" *Journal of Cuneiform Studies* 8 (1954): 47–73.

Laperrousaz, Ernest-Marie, and André Lemaire, eds. *La Palestine à l'époque perse*.

Études annexes de la Bible de Jérusalem. Paris: Cerf, 1994.

Lapp, Nancy L. "Ful, Tell el-." Page 346–47 in vol. 2 of *The Oxford Encyclopedia of Archaeology in the Near East*. Edited by Eric M. Meyers. New York: Oxford University Press, 1997.

———. *Shechem IV: The Persian-Hellenistic Potttery of Shechem/Tell Balâṭah*. Edited by Edward F. Campbell. American Schools of Oriental Research Archaeological Reports 11. Boston: American Schools of Oriental Research, 2008.

———. *The Third Campaign at Tel el-Fûl: The Excavations of 1964*. Annual of the American Schools of Oriental Research 45. Cambridge, MA: American Schools of Oriental Research, 1981.

Lapp, Paul W., and Nancy L. Lapp, eds. *Discoveries in the Wâdi ed-Dâliyeh*. Annual of the American Schools of Oriental Research 41. Cambridge, MA: American Schools of Oriental Research, 1974.

Laroche, Emmanuel. *Catalogue of Hittite Texts*. Online: http://www.hethport.uniwuerzburg.de/CTH/.

Lauringer, Jacob. "Esarhaddon's Succession Treaty at Tell Tayinat: Text and Commentary." *Journal of Cuneiform Studies* 64 (2012): 87–123.

———. "Some Preliminary Thoughts on the Tablet Collection in Building XVI from Tell Tayinat." *Journal of the Canadian Society for Mesopotamian Studies* 6 (2011): 5–14.

Lederman, Zvi. "An Early Iron Age Village at Khirbet Raddana: The Excavations of Joseph Callaway." PhD diss., Harvard University, 1999.

Lehmann, Gunnar. "The United Monarchy in the Countryside: Jerusalem, Judah and the Shephelah during the Tenth Century B.C.E." Pages 117–64 in *Jerusalem in Bible and Archaeology: The First Temple Period*. Edited by Andrew G. Vaughn and Ann E. Killebrew. Society of Biblical Literature Symposium Series 18. Atlanta: Society of Biblical Literature, 2003.

Lehmann, Gunnar, and Ann E. Killebrew. "Palace 6000 at Megiddo in Context: Iron Age Central Hall Tetra-Partite Residencies and the *Bit-Hilani* Building Tradition in the Levant." *Bulletin of the American Schools of Oriental Research* 359 (2010): 13–33.

Leichty, Earle. *The Royal Inscriptions of Esarhaddon, King of Assyria (680–669 BC)*. Royal Inscriptions of the Neo-Assyrian Period 4. Winona Lake, IN: Eisenbrauns, 2011.

Leith, Mary J. W. *The Wadi Daliyeh Seal Impressions*. Vol. 1 of *Wadi Daliyeh*. Discoveries in the Judaean Desert 24. Oxford: Clarendon, 1997.

Lemaire, André. "Das Achämenidische Juda und seine Nachbarn im Lichte der Epigraphie." Pages 210–30 in *Religion und Religionskontakte im Zeitalter der Achämeniden*. Edited by Reinhard G. Kratz. Veröffentlichungen der Wissenschaftlichen Gesellschaft für Theologie 22. Gütersloh: Kaiser/Gütersloher Verlagshaus, 2002.

———. "Administration in Fourth-Century B.C.E.: Judah in Light of Epigraphy and Numismatics." Pages 53–74 in *Judah and the Judeans in the Fourth Century B.C.E.* Edited by Oded Lipschits, Gary N. Knoppers, and Rainer Albertz. Winona Lake, IN: Eisenbrauns, 2007.

———. *Collections Moussaïeff, Jeselsohn, Welch et divers*. Vol. 2 of *Nouvelles inscriptions araméennes d'Idumées*. Supplements to Transeuphratène 9. Paris: Gabalda, 2002.

———. "Épigraphie." *Transeuphratène* 4 (1991): 113–18.

———. "Épigraphie." *Transeuphratène* 10 (1995): 145–50.

———. "Épigraphie." *Transeuphratène* 17 (1999): 111–16.

———. "Épigraphie." *Transeuphratène* 24 (2002): 137–41.

———. "Épigraphie." *Transeuphratène* 32 (2006): 185–94.

———. "La fin de la première période perse en Égypte et la chronologie judéenne vers 400 av. J.-C." *Transeuphratène* 9 (1995): 51–62.

———. "La haute Mésopotamie et l'origine des Benê Jacob." *Vetus Testamentum* 34 (1984): 95–101.

———. "Hebrew and West Semitic Inscriptions and Pre-Exilic Israel." Pages 366–85 in *In Search of Pre-exilic Israel: Proceedings of the Oxford Old Testament Seminar*. Edited by John Day. Journal for the Study of the Old Testament: Supplement Series 406. London: T&T Clark, 2004.

———. "'House of David' Restored in Moabite Inscription." *Biblical Archaeology Review* 20, no. 3 (1994): 30–37.

———. "Les inscriptions palestiniennes d'époque perse: Un bilan provisoire." *Transeuphratène* 1 (1989): 87–106.

———. "Judean Identity in Elephantine: Everyday Life according to the Ostraca." Pages 365–73 in *Judah and the Judeans in the Achaemenid Period: Negotiating Identity in an International Context*. Edited by Oded Lipschits, Gary N. Knoppers, and Manfred Oeming. Winona Lake, IN: Eisenbrauns, 2011.

———. "Nabonidus in Arabia and Judah in the Neo-Babylonian period." Pages 285–98 in *Judah and the Judeans in the Neo-Babylonian Period*. Edited by Oded Lipschits and Joseph Blenkinsopp. Winona Lake, IN: Eisenbrauns, 2003.

———. "Notes d'épigraphie nord-ouest sémitique." *Semitica* 35 (1985): 13–17.

———. "Nouveau temple de Yahô (IVe s. av. J.-C.)." Pages 265–73 in *"Basel und Bibel": Collected Communications to the XVIIth Congress of the International Organization for the Study of the Old Testament, Basel 2001*. Edited by Matthias Augustin and Hermann Michael Niemann. Beiträge zur Erforschung des Alten Testaments und des Antiken Judentums 51. Frankfurt: Peter Lang, 2004.

———. "Populations et territoires de la Palestine à l'époque perse." *Transeuphratène* 3 (1990): 31–74.

———. "Recherches d'épigraphie araméenne en Asie Mineure et en Égypte et le problème de l'acculturation." Pages 199–206 in *Asia Minor and Egypt: Old Cultures in a New Empire*. Edited by Heleen Sancisi-Weerdenburg

and Amélie Kuhrt. Achaemenid History 6. Leiden: Nederlands Instituut voor het Nabije Oosten, 1991.

———. Review of Hélène Lozachmeur, *La collection Clermont-Ganneau: Ostraca, épigraphes sur jarre, étiquettes de bois*. *Transeuphratène* 34 (2007): 177–83.

———. Review of Nahman Avigad, *Bullae and Seals from a Post-Exilic Judean Archive*. *Syria* 54 (1977): 129–31.

———. "Salomon et la fille de Pharaon: Un problème d'interprétation historique." Pages 699–710 in *"I Will Speak the Riddles of Ancient Times": Archaeological and Historical Studies in Honor of Amihai Mazar on the Occasion of His Sixtieth Birthday*. Edited by Aren M. Maeir and Pierre de Miroschedji. Winona Lake, IN: Eisenbrauns, 2006.

———. "La stèle araméenne d'Assouan (RES 438, 1806): Nouvel examen." Pages 289–304 in *Intertestamental Essays in Honour of Józef Tadeusz Milik*. Edited by Zdzisław J. Kapera. Qumranica Mogilanensia 6. Kraków: Enigma, 1992.

———. "Taxes et impôts dans le sud de la Palestine (IVe s. av. J.-C.)." *Transeuphratène* 28 (2004): 133–42.

———. "Traditions amorrites et Bible: Le prophétisme." *Revue d'assyriologie et d'archéologie orientale* 93 (1999): 49–56.

———. "West Semitic Inscriptions and Ninth-Century BCE Ancient Israel." Pages 207–303 in *Understanding the History of Ancient Israel*. Edited by H. G. M. Williamson. Proceedings of the British Academy 143. Oxford: Oxford University Press, 2007.

———. "Zorobabel et la Judée à la lumière de l'épigraphie (fin du VIe s. av. J.-C.)." *Revue biblique* 103 (1996): 48–57.

Lemche, Niels Peter. *Ancient Israel: A New History of Israelite Society*. Biblical Seminar 5. Sheffield: JSOT Press, 1988.

———. "David's Rise." *Journal for the Study of the Old Testament* 10 (1978): 2–25.

———. *Early Israel: Anthropological and Historical Studies on the Israelite Society before the Monarchy*. Supplements to Vetus Testamentum 37. Leiden: Brill, 1985.

Lesko, Leonard H. "Egypt in the 12th Century." Pages 151–56 in *The Crisis Years: The 12th Century B.C.; From beyond the Danube to the Tigris*. Edited by William A. Ward and Martha Sharp Joukowsky. Dubuque, IA: Kendall/Hunt, 1989.

Levine, Baruch A. "The Deir 'Alla Plaster Inscriptions." Pages 140–45 in *Monumental Inscriptions from the Biblical World*. Vol. 2 of *The Context of Scripture*. Edited by William W. Hallo and K. Lawson Younger Jr. Leiden: Brill, 2003.

Levinson, Bernard M. *Deuteronomy and the Hermeneutics of Legal Innovation*. Oxford: Oxford University Press, 1997.

Levy, Thomas E., ed. *The Archaeology of Society in the Holy Land*. New York: Facts on File, 1995.

Levy, Thomas E., and Mohammad Najjar. "Edom and Copper: The Emergence of Ancient Israel's Rival." *Biblical Archaeology Review* 32, no. 4 (2006): 24–35, 70.

Levy, Thomas E., Mohammad Najjar, Johannes van der Plicht, Neil Smith, Hendrick J. Bruins, and Thomas Higham. "Lowland Edom and the High and Low Chronologies: Edomite State Formation, the Bible and Recent Archaeological Research in Southern Jordan." Pages 129–63 in *The Bible and Radiocarbon Dating: Archaeology, Text and Science*. Edited by Thomas E. Levy and Thomas Higham. London: Equinox, 2005.

———. "Reassessing the Chronology of Biblical Edom: New Excavations and 14C Dates from Khirbat en-Nahas (Jordan)." *Antiquity* 302 (2004): 865–79.

Lewis, Theodore. "The Identity and Function of El/Baal Berith." *Journal of Biblical Literature* 115 (1996): 401–3.

Licona, Michael R. *The Resurrection of Jesus: A New Historiographical Approach*. Downers Grove, IL: IVP Academic; Nottingham, UK: Apollos, 2010.

Liebowitz, Harry A. "Ivory." Pages 584–87 in vol. 3 of *The Anchor Bible Dictionary*. Edited by David Noel Freedman. New York: Doubleday, 1992.

Limburg, James. "The Root *ryb* and the Prophetic Lawsuit Speeches." *Journal of Biblical Literature* 88 (1969): 291–304.

Lindsay, John. "The Babylonian Kings and Edom." *Palestine Exploration Quarterly* 108 (1976): 23–39.

Lipiński, Edward. *The Aramaeans: Their Ancient History, Culture, Religion*. Orientalia lovaniensia analecta 100. Leuven: Peeters, 2000.

Lipschits, Oded. "Demographic Changes in Judah between the Seventh and the Fifth Centuries BCE." Pages 323–76 in *Judah and the Judean in the Neo-Babylonian Period*. Edited by Oded Lipschits and Joseph Blenkinsopp. Winona Lake, IN: Eisenbrauns, 2003.

———. *The Fall and Rise of Jerusalem: Judah under Babylonian Rule*. Winona Lake, IN: Eisenbrauns, 2005.

———. "The History of the Benjamin Region under Babylonian Rule." *Tel Aviv* 26 (1999): 155–89.

———. "Judah, Jerusalem and the Temple 586–539 B.C." *Transeuphratène* 22 (2001): 129–42.

———. "Nebuchadrezzar's Policy in 'Hattu-Land' and the Fate of the Kingdom of Judah." *Ugarit-Forschungen* 30 (1999): 467–87.

———. "Persian Period Finds from Jerusalem: Facts and Interpretations." *Journal of Hebrew Scriptures* 9 (2009): 1–30.

———. "Shedding New Light on the Dark Years of the 'Exilic Period': New Studies, Further Elucidation, and Some Questions Regarding the Archaeology of Judah as an 'Empty Land.'" Pages 81–82 in *Interpreting Exile: Displacement and Deportation in Biblical and Modern Contexts*. Edited by Brad Kelle, Frank R. Ames, and Jacob L. Wright. Society of Biblical Literature Ancient Israel and Its Literature 10. Atlanta: Society of Biblical Literature, 2011.

Lipschits, Oded, and Yuval Gadot. "Ramat Raḥel and the Emeq Rephaim Sites—Links and Interpretations." Pages 88–96 in vol. 2 of *New Studies in the Archaeology of*

Jerusalem and Its Region: Collected Papers. Edited by David Amit and Guy D. Stiebel. Jerusalem: Israel Antiquities Authority, 2008.

Lipschits, Oded, Yuval Gadot, Benjamin Arubas, and Manfred Oeming. "Palace and Village, Paradise and Oblivion: Unraveling the Riddles of Ramat Raḥel." *Near Eastern Archaeology* 74 (2011): 2–49.

Lipschits, Oded, Gary N. Knoppers, and Rainer Albertz, eds. *Judah and the Judeans in the Fourth Century B.C.E.* Winona Lake, IN: Eisenbrauns, 2007.

Lipschits, Oded, Gary N. Knoppers, and Manfred Oeming, eds. *Judah and the Judeans in the Achaemenid Period: Negotiating Identity in an International Context.* Winona Lake, IN: Eisenbrauns, 2011.

Lipschits, Oded, Omer Sergi, and Ido Koch. "Royal Judahite Jar Handles: Reconsidering the Chronology of the *lmlk* Stamp Impressions." *Tel Aviv* 37 (2010): 3–32.

Lipschits, Oded, and David Vanderhooft. "A New Typology of the Yehud Stamp Impressions." *Tel Aviv* 34 (2007): 12–37.

———. "Yehud Stamp Impressions in the Fourth Century BCE: A Time of Administrative Consolidation?" Pages 75–94 in *Judah and the Judeans in the Achaemenid Period: Negotiating Identity in an International Context.* Edited by Oded Lipschits, Gary N. Knoppers, and Manfred Oeming. Winona Lake, IN: Eisenbrauns, 2011.

Liverani, Mario. "The Collapse of the Near Eastern Regional System at the End of the Bronze Age: The Case of Syria." In *Centre and Periphery in the Ancient World.* Edited by Michael Rowlands, Mogens Larsen, and Kristian Kristiansen. New Directions in Archaeology. Cambridge: Cambridge University Press, 1987.

———. *Israel's History and the History of Israel.* Translated by Chiara Peri and Philip R. Davies. Bible World. London: Equinox, 2005.

———. *Myth and Politics in Ancient Near Eastern Historiography.* Edited by Zainab Bahrani and Marc Van de Mieroop. Ithaca, NY: Cornell University Press, 2004.

———. *Prestige and Interest: International Relations in the Near East ca. 1600–1100 B.C.* Studies in the History of the Ancient Near East 1. Padova: Sargon, 1990.

Long, V. Philips. *The Art of Biblical History.* Foundations of Contemporary Interpretation 5. Grand Rapids: Zondervan, 1994.

———. "How Reliable Are Biblical Reports? Repeating Lester Grabbe's Comparative Experiment." *Vetus Testamentum* 52 (2002): 367–84.

———, ed. *Israel's Past in Present Research: Essays on Ancient Israelite Historiography.* Sources for Biblical and Theological Study 7. Winona Lake, IN: Eisenbrauns, 1999.

Long, V. Philips, David W. Baker, and Gordon J. Wenham, eds. *Windows into Old Testament History: Evidence, Argument, and the Crisis of "Biblical Israel."* Grand Rapids: Eerdmans, 2002.

Longman, Tremper, III. "The Autobiography of Idrimi." Pages 479–80 in *Canonical Compositions from the Biblical World.* Vol. 1 of *The Context of Scripture.* Edited by William W. Hallo and K. Lawson Younger Jr. Leiden: Brill, 2003.

Loretz, Oswald. *Habiru-Hebräer: Eine soziolinguistische Studie über die Herkunft des Gentiliziums ʿibrî vom Appelativum ḫabiru.* Beihefte zur Zeitschrift für die alttestamentliche Wissenschaft 160. Berlin: de Gruyter, 1984.

———. "Der juridische Begriff niḫlatum/nḫlt/naḥālāh 'Erbbesitz' als amurritisch-kanaanäische Hintergrund von Psalm 58." *Ugarit-Forschungen* 34 (2002): 453–79.

Lozachmeur, Hélène. *La collection Clermont-Ganneau: Ostraca, épigraphes sur jarre, étiquettes de bois.* Mémoires présentés à l'Academie des Inscriptions et Belles-Lettres 35. Paris: De Boccard, 2006.

Lubetski, Meir. "Ezion-Geber." Pages 723–25 in vol. 2 of *The Anchor Bible Dictionary.* Edited by David Noel Freedman. New York: Doubleday, 1992.

Lucas, Alfred. *The Route of the Exodus of the Israelites from Egypt.* London: E. Arnold, 1938.

MacDonald, Burton. *East of the Jordan: Territories and Sites of the Hebrew Scriptures.* American Schools of Oriental Research Books 6. Boston: American Schools of Oriental Research, 2000.

Maeir, Aren M., Oren Ackermann, and Hendrik J. Bruins. "The Ecological Consequences of a Siege: A Marginal Note on Deuteronomy 20:19–20." Pages 239–43 in *Confronting the Past: Archaeological and Historical Essays on Ancient Israel in Honor of William G. Dever.* Edited by Seymour Gitin, J. Edward Wright, and J. P. Dessel. Winona Lake, IN: Eisenbrauns, 2006.

Maeir, Aren M., and Pierre de Miroschedji, eds. *"I Will Speak the Riddles of Ancient Times": Archaeological and Historical Studies in Honor of Amihai Mazar.* 2 vols. Winona Lake, IN: Eisenbrauns, 2006.

Maeir, Aren M., Stefan J. Wimmer, Alexander Zukerman, and Aaron Demsky. "A Late Iron Age I/Early Iron Age II Old Canaanite Inscription from Tell es-Ṣâfi/Gath, Israel." *Bulletin of the American Schools of Oriental Research* 351 (2008): 39–71.

Magen, Yitzhak. "The Dating of the First Phase of the Samaritan Temple on Mount Gerizim in Light of the Archaeological Evidence." Pages 157–211 in *Judah and the Judeans in the Fourth Century B.C.E.* Edited by Oded Lipschits, Gary N. Knoppers, and Rainer Albertz. Winona Lake, IN: Eisenbrauns, 2007.

———. *A Temple City.* Vol. 2 of *Mount Gerizim Excavations.* Judea and Samaria Publications 8. Jerusalem: Israel Antiquities Authority, 2008.

Magen, Yitzhak, and Michael Dadon. "Nebi Samwil" (in Hebrew). *Qadmoniot* 118 (1999): 62–77.

Magen, Yitzhak, Haggai Misgav, and Levanna Tsfania. *The Aramaic, Hebrew and Samaritan Inscriptions.* Vol. 1 of *Mount Gerizim Excavations.* Judea and Samaria Publications 2. Jerusalem: Israel Antiquities Authority, 2004.

Magness, Jodi. *The Archaeology of Qumran and the Dead Sea Scrolls.* Grand Rapids: Eerdmans, 2003.

Maidman, Maynard Paul. "Historiographic Reflections on Israel's Origins: The Rise and Fall of the Patriarchal Age." *Eretz-Israel* 27 (2003): 120*–28*.

———. *Nuzi Texts and Their Uses as Historical Evidence.* Edited by Ann K. Guinan. Society of Biblical Literature Writings from the Ancient World 18. Atlanta: Society of Biblical Literature, 2010.

Malamat, Abraham. "Aspects of the Foreign Policies of David and Solomon." *Journal of Near Eastern Studies* 22 (1963): 1–17.

———. "The First Peace Treaty between Israel and Egypt." *Biblical Archaeology Review* 5, no. 5 (1979): 58–61.

———. "The Historical Background of the Assassination of Amon, King of Judah." *Israel Exploration Journal* 3 (1953): 26–29.

———. "Mari and the Bible: Some Patterns of Tribal Organization and Institution." *Journal of the American Oriental Society* 82 (1962): 143–50.

———. *Mari and the Early Israelite Experience.* Oxford: Oxford University Press, 1989.

———. "The Proto-History of Israel: A Study in Method." Pages 303–13 in *The Word of the Lord Shall Go Forth: Essays in Honor of David Noel Freedman in Celebration of His Sixtieth Birthday.* Edited by Carol L. Meyers and Michael Patrick O'Connor. Winona Lake, IN: Eisenbrauns, 1983.

———. "*Ummātum* in Old Babylonian Texts and Its Ugaritic and Biblical Counterparts." *Journal of the American Oriental Society* 11 (1979): 527–36.

Manor, Dale W. "Kadesh-Barnea." Pages 1–3 in vol. 4 of *The Anchor Bible Dictionary.* Edited by David Noel Freedman. New York: Doubleday, 1992.

Manor, Dale W., and Gary A. Herion. "Arad." Pages 331–35 in vol. 1 of *The Anchor Bible Dictionary.* Edited by David Noel Freedman. New York: Doubleday, 1992.

Marello, Pierre. "Vie nomade." Pages 115–25 in *Florilegium marianum: Recueil d'études en l'honneur de Michel Fleury.* Edited by Jean-Marie Durand. Nouvelles assyriologiques brèves et utilitaires 4. Paris: SEPOA, 1992.

Margueron, Jean-Claude. "Mari." Pages 413–17 in vol. 3 of *The Oxford Encyclopedia of Archaeology in the Near East.* Edited by Eric M. Meyers. New York: Oxford University Press, 1997.

———. "Mari (Archaeology)." Pages 525–29 in vol. 4 of *The Anchor Bible Dictionary.* Edited by David Noel Freedman. New York: Doubleday, 1992.

Master, Dan. "State Formation Theory and the Kingdom of Ancient Israel." *Journal of Near Eastern Studies* 60 (2001): 117–31.

Mazar, Amihai. "Archaeology and the Biblical Narrative: The Case of the United Monarchy." Pages 29–58 in *One God—One Cult—One Nation: Archaeological and Biblical Perspectives.* Edited by Reinhard G. Kratz and Hermann Spieckermann. Beihefte zur Zeitschrift für die alttestamentliche Wissenschaft 405. Berlin: de Gruyter, 2010.

———. *Archaeology of the Land of the Bible: 10,000–586 B.C.E.* Anchor Bible Reference Library. New York: Doubleday, 1990.

———. "The Bull Site." *Bulletin of the American Schools of Oriental Research* 247 (1982): 27–42.

———. "The Debate over the Chronology of the Iron Age in the Southern Levant: Its History, the Current Situation, and a Suggested Resolution." Pages 13–28 in *The Bible and Radiocarbon Dating: Archaeology, Text and Science.* Edited by Thomas E. Levy and Thomas Higham. London: Equinox, 2005.

———. "The 11th Century in the Land of Israel." Pages 39–57 in *Cyprus in the 11th Century B.C.: Proceedings of the International Symposium Organized by the Archaeological Research Unit of the University of Cyprus and the Anastasios G. Leventis Foundation, Nicosia, 30–31 October 1993.* Edited by Vassos Karageorghis. Nicosia: A. G. Leventis Foundation, University of Cyprus, 1994.

———. "Iron Age Chronology: A Reply to I. Finkelstein." *Levant* 29 (1997): 157–67.

———. "Jerusalem in the 10th Century BCE: The Glass Half Full." Pages 255–72 in *Essays on Ancient Israel in Its Near Eastern Context: A Tribute to Nadav Na'aman.* Edited by Yairah Amit et al. Winona Lake, IN: Eisenbrauns, 2006.

———. "The Spade and the Text: The Interaction between Archaeology and the Israelite History Relating to the Tenth–Ninth Centuries BC." Pages 143–71 in *Understanding the History of Ancient Isarel.* Edited by H. G. M. Williamson. Oxford: Oxford University Press, 2007.

———. "Temples of the Middle and Late Bronze Ages and the Iron Age." Pages 161–87 in *The Architecture of Ancient Israel: From the Prehistoric to the Persian Periods; In Memory of Immanuel (Munya) Dunayevsky.* Edited by Aharon Kempinski and Ronny Reich. Jerusalem: Israel Exploration Society, 1992.

Mazar, Benjamin. "Shishak's Campaign to the Land of Israel." Pages 139–50 in *The Early Biblical Period: Historical Studies.* Edited by Shmuel Ahituv and Baruch A. Levine. Jerusalem: Israel Exploration Society, 1986.

Mazar, Eilat. *Discovering the Solomonic Wall in Jerusalem: A Remarkable Archaeological Adventure.* Jerusalem: Shoham Academic Research and Publication, 2011.

———. *The Palace of King David: Excavations at the Summit of the City of David; Preliminary Report of Seasons 2005–2007.* Translated by Ben Gordon. Jerusalem: Shoham Academic Research and Publication, 2009.

———. "The Royal Quarter of Biblical Jerusalem: The Ophel." Pages 64–72 in *Ancient Jerusalem Revealed.* Edited by Hillel Geva. Jerusalem: Israel Exploration Society, 1994.

———. "The Spade and the Text: The Interaction between Archaeology and the Israelite History Relating to the Tenth–Ninth Centuries BC." Pages 143–71 in *Understanding the History of Ancient Israel.* Edited by H. G. M. Williamson. Proceedings of the British Academy 143. Oxford: Oxford University Press, 2007.

McCann, J. Clinton. *Judges.* Interpretation: A Bible Commentary for Teaching and Preaching. Louisville: Westminster John Knox, 2002.

McCarter, P. Kyle, Jr. *Ancient Inscriptions: Voices from the Biblical World.* Washington, DC: Biblical Archaeological Society, 1996.

———. *1 Samuel: A New Translation with Introduction, Notes, and Commentary*. Anchor Bible 8. Garden City, NY: Doubleday, 1980.

McCarthy, Dennis J. "Ebla, *orkia temnein, ṭb, šlm*: Addenda to *Treaty and Covenant*." *Biblica* 60 (1979): 247–53.

———. *Treaty and Covenant: A Study in Form in the Ancient Oriental Documents and in the Old Testament*. 2nd ed. Analecta Biblica 21A. Rome: Biblical Institute Press, 1978.

McKay, J. W. *Religion in Judah under the Assyrians, 732–609 BC*. Studies in Biblical Theology 26. Naperville, IL: Allenson, 1973.

McKenzie, Steven L. *King David: A Biography*. Oxford: Oxford University Press, 2000.

———. *The Trouble with Kings: The Composition of the Book of Kings in the Deuteronomistic History*. Supplements to Vetus Testamentum 42. Leiden: Brill, 1991.

McKnight, Scot. "Rehoboam." Pages 838–40 in *Dictionary of the Old Testament: Historical Books*. Edited by Bill T. Arnold and H. G. M. Williamson. Downers Grove, IL: InterVarsity, 2006.

Mead, James K. "Elijah." Pages 249–54 in *Dictionary of the Old Testament: Historical Books*. Edited by Bill T. Arnold and H. G. M. Williamson. Downers Grove, IL: InterVarsity, 2005.

———. "Elisha." Pages 254–58 in *Dictionary of the Old Testament: Historical Books*. Edited by Bill T. Arnold and H. G. M. Williamson. Downers Grove, IL: InterVarsity, 2005.

Meier, Samuel A. *The Messenger in the Ancient Semitic World*. Harvard Semitic Monographs 45. Atlanta: Scholars Press, 1988.

Melchert, H. Craig. "Indo-European Languages of Anatolia." Pages 2151–59 in vol. 4 of *Civilizations of the Ancient Near East*. Edited by Jack M. Sasson. New York: Scribner, 1995.

———, ed. *The Luwians*. Handbuch der Orientalistik 68. Leiden: Brill, 2003.

Melville, Sarah C. "Apology and Egyptian Campaigns." Pages 363–65 in *The Ancient Near East: Historical Sources in Translation*. Edited by Mark W. Chavalas. Malden, MA: Blackwell, 2006.

———. "The Bavarian Inscription: The Destruction of Babylon." Page 349 in *The Ancient Near East: Historical Sources in Translation*. Edited by Mark W. Chavalas. Malden, MA: Blackwell, 2006.

———. "Oriental Institute Prism: Campaigns in Babylonia and Judah." Pages 345–49 in *The Ancient Near East: Historical Sources in Translation*. Edited by Mark W. Chavalas. Malden, MA: Blackwell, 2006.

———. "The Succession Treaty of Esarhaddon." Pages 355–56 in *The Ancient Near East: Historical Sources in Translation*. Edited by Mark W. Chavalas. Malden, MA: Blackwell, 2006.

Mendenhall, George. "The Hebrew Conquest of Palestine." *Biblical Archaeologist* 25 (1962): 66–87.

———. *The Tenth Generation: The Origins of the Biblical Tradition*. Baltimore: Johns Hopkins University Press, 1985.

Merrill, Eugene H. *Kingdom of Priests: A History of Old Testament Israel*. 2nd ed. Grand Rapids: Baker Academic, 2008.

Meshel, Zeʾev. "Horvat Teman." Pages 460–64 in vol. 4 of *The New Encyclopedia of Archaeological Excavations in the Holy Land*. Edited by Ephraim Stern. Jerusalem: Israel Exploration Society & Carta, 1993.

———. *Kuntillet ʿAjrud (Horvat Teman): An Iron Age II Religious Site on the Judah-Sinai Border*. Jerusalem: Israel Exploration Society, 2012.

Meshorer, Yaʾakov. *A Treasury of Jewish Coins from the Persian Period to Bar Kokhba*. Jerusalem: Yad ben-Zvi; Nyack, NY: Amphora, 2001.

Meshorer, Yaʾakov, and Shraga Qedar. *Samarian Coinage*. Numismatic Studies and Researches 9. Jerusalem: Israel Numismatic Society, 1999.

Mettinger, Tryggve N. D. *King and Messiah: The Civil and Sacral Legitimation of the Israelite Kings*. Coniectanea biblica: Old Testament Series 8. Lund: Gleerup, 1976.

Meyers, Carol. "The Family in Early Israel." Pages 1–47 in *Families in Ancient Israel*, by Leo G. Perdue, Joseph Blenkinsopp, John J. Collins, and Carol L. Meyers. Louisville: Westminster John Knox, 1997.

———. "Kinship and Kingship: The Early Monarchy." Pages 165–205 in *The Oxford History of the Biblical World*. Edited by Michael D. Coogan. Oxford: Oxford University Press, 1998.

Meyers, Eric M. "The Shelomith Seal and the Judean Restoration—Some Additional Considerations." *Eretz-Israel* 18 (1985): 33–38.

Milgrom, Jacob. "The Nature and Extent of Idolatry in Eighth–Seventh Century Judah." *Hebrew Union College Annual* 69 (1998): 1–13.

Millard, Alan R. "Abraham." Pages 35–41 in vol. 1 of *The Anchor Bible Dictionary*. Edited by David Noel Freedman. New York: Doubleday, 1992.

———. *The Eponyms of the Assyrian Empire 910–612 BC*. State Archives of Assyria Studies 2. Helsinki: Neo-Assyrian Text Corpus Project, University of Helsinki, 1994.

———. "Hadad-Yith'i." Pages 153–54 in *Monumental Inscriptions from the Biblical World*. Vol. 2 of *The Context of Scripture*. Edited by William W. Hallo and K. Lawson Younger Jr. Leiden: Brill, 2003.

———. "The Hazael Booty Inscriptions." Pages 162–63 in *Monumental Inscriptions from the Biblical World*. Vol. 2 of *The Context of Scripture*. Edited by William W. Hallo and K. Lawson Younger Jr. Leiden: Brill, 2003.

———. "The Inscription of Zakkur, King of Hamath." Page 155 in *Monumental Inscriptions from the Biblical World*. Vol. 2 of *The Context of Scripture*. Edited by William W. Hallo and K. Lawson Younger Jr. Leiden: Brill, 2003.

———. "King Solomon in His Ancient Context." Pages 30–53 in *The Age of Solomon: Scholarship at the Turn of the Millennium*. Edited by Lowell K. Handy. Studies in the History and Culture of the Ancient Near East 11. Leiden: Brill, 1997.

———. "Large Numbers in Assyrian Royal Inscriptions." Pages 213–22 in *Ah, Assyria . . . : Studies in Assyrian and Ancient Near Eastern Historiography Presented to Hayim Tadmor*. Edited by Mordechai Cogan and Israel Eph'al. Scripta hierosolymitana 33. Jerusalem: Magnes, 1991.

———. "The Tell Dan Stele." Pages 161–62 in *Monumental Inscriptions from the Biblical World*. Vol. 2 of *The Context of Scripture*. Edited by William W. Hallo and K. Lawson Younger Jr. Leiden: Brill, 2003.

Millard, Alan R., James K. Hoffmeier, and David W. Baker, eds. *Faith, Tradition, and History: Old Testament Historiography in Its Near Eastern Context*. Winona Lake, IN: Eisenbrauns, 1994.

Miller, J. Maxwell. "The Elisha Cycle and the Accounts of the Omride Wars." *Journal of Biblical Literature* 85 (1966): 441–53.

———. "Old Testament History and Archaeology." *Biblical Archaeologist* 50 (1987): 301–12.

———. "Solomon: International Potentate or Local King?" *Palestine Exploration Quarterly* 123 (1991): 28–31.

Miller, J. Maxwell, and John H. Hayes. *A History of Ancient Israel and Judah*. Philadelphia: Westminster, 1986. 2nd ed., Louisville: Westminster John Knox, 2006.

Miller, Patrick D., Jr. "Eridu, Dunnu, and Babel: A Study in Comparative Mythology." *Hebrew Annual Review* 9 (1985): 227–51.

———. "The World and Message of the Prophets." Pages 97–112 in *Old Testament Interpretation: Past, Present, and Future; Essays in Honor of Gene M. Tucker*. Edited by James Luther Mays, David L. Petersen, and Kent Harold Richards. Nashville: Abingdon, 1995.

Miller, Robert D., II. *Chieftains of the Highland Clans: A History of Israel in Twelfth and Eleventh Centuries B.C.* Grand Rapids: Eerdmans, 2005.

———. "Modeling the Farm in Early Iron Age Israel." Pages 289–310 in *Life and Culture in the Ancient Near East*. Edited by Richard E.

Averbeck, Mark W. Chavalas, and David B. Weisberg. Bethesda, MD: CDL Press, 2003.

———. "A 'New Cultural History' of Early Israel." Pages 167–98 in *The Texts*. Vol. 2 of *Israel in Transition: From Late Bronze II to Iron IIA (c. 1250–850 BCE)*. Edited by Lester L. Grabbe. Library of Hebrew Bible/Old Testament Studies 521. London: T&T Clark, 2010.

———. *Oral Tradition in Ancient Israel*. Biblical Performance Criticism 4. Eugene, OR: Cascade Books, 2011.

———. "Shamanism in Early Israel." *Wiener Zeitschrift für die Kunde des Morgenlandes* 101 (2011): 309–42.

Miller, Stephen R. *Daniel*. New American Commentary 18. Nashville: Broadman & Holman, 1994.

Misgav, Haggai, Yosef Garfinkel, and Saar Ganor. "The Ostracon." Pages 243–60 in *Excavation Report 2007–2008*. Vol. 1 of *Khirbet Qeiyafa*. Edited by Yosef Garfinkel and Saar Ganor. Jerusalem: Israel Exploration Society, 2009.

Mitchell, T. C. *The Bible in the British Museum: Interpreting the Evidence*. London: British Museum Publications, 1988.

Mittmann, Siegfried. "Tobia, Sanballat und die persische Provinz Juda." *Journal of Northwest Semitic Languages* 26 (2000): 1–50.

Monson, John M. "The Temple of Solomon: Heart of Jerusalem." Pages 1–22 in *Zion, City of Our God*. Edited by Richard S. Hess and Gordon J. Wenham. Grand Rapids: Eerdmans, 2004.

Montet, Pierre. *Egypt and the Bible*. Translated by Leslie R. Keylock. Philadelphia: Fortress, 1968.

Moore, Megan Bishop. *Philosophy and Practice in Writing a History of Ancient Israel*. Library of Hebrew Bible/Old Testament Studies 435. London: T&T Clark, 2006.

Moore, Megan Bishop, and Brad E. Kelle. *Biblical History and Israel's Past: The Changing Study of the Bible and History*. Grand Rapids: Eerdmans, 2011.

Moors, Annelies. "Gender Hierarchy in a Palestinian Village." Pages 195–209 in *The Rural Middle East: Peasant Lives and Modes of Production*. Edited by Kathy Glavanis and Pandeli Glavanis. Birzeit: Birzeit University, 1989.

Moran, William L., ed. and trans. *The Amarna Letters*. Baltimore: Johns Hopkins University Press, 1992.

———. "The Gilgamesh Epic: A Masterpiece from Ancient Mesopotamia." Pages 2327–36 in vol. 4 of *Civilizations of the Ancient Near East*. Edited by Jack M. Sasson. New York: Scribner, 1995.

———. "New Evidence from Mari on the History of Prophecy." *Biblica* 50 (1969): 15–56.

Mørkholm, Otto. "Antiochus IV." Pages 278–91 in *The Hellenistic Period*. Vol. 2 of *The Cambridge History of Judaism*. Edited by W. D. Davies and Louis Finkelstein. Cambridge: Cambridge University Press, 1989.

———. *Antiochus IV of Syria*. Classica et mediaevalia: Dissertationes 8. Copenhagen: Gyldendal, 1966.

Moye, Richard H. "In the Beginning: Myth and History in Genesis and Exodus." *Journal of Biblical Literature* 109 (1990): 577–98.

Münger, Stefan. "Egyptian Stamp-Seal Amulets and Their Implications for the Chronology of the Early Iron Age." *Tel Aviv* 30 (2003): 66–82.

Münger, Stefan, Jürgen Zangenberg, and Juha Pakkala, in collaboration with Guy Bar-Oz et al. "Kinneret—An Urban Center at the Crossroads: Excavations on Iron IB Tel Kinrot at the Lake of Galilee." *Near Eastern Archaeology* 74 (2011): 68–90.

Myers, Jacob M. *II Chronicles: Introduction, Translation, and Notes*. 2nd ed. Anchor Bible 13. Garden City, NY: Doubleday, 1973.

Mykytiuk, Lawrence J. "Corrections and Updates to 'Identifying Biblical Persons in Northwest Semitic Inscriptions of 1200–539 B.C.E.'" *Maarav* 16, no. 1 (2009): 49–132.

———. *Identifying Biblical Persons in Northwest Semitic Inscriptions of 1200–539 B.C.E.* Society of Biblical Literature Academia Biblica 12. Atlanta: Society of Biblical Literature, 2004.

Myśliwiec, Karol. *The Twilight of Ancient Egypt: First Millennium B.C.E.* Translated by David Lorton. Ithaca, NY: Cornell University Press, 2000.

Na'aman, Nadav. "Ahab's Chariot Force at Qarqar." Pages 1–12 in *Ancient Israel and Its Neighbors: Interaction and Counteraction.* Vol. 1 of *Collected Essays.* Winona Lake, IN: Eisenbrauns, 2005.

———. *Ancient Israel and Its Neighbors: Interaction and Counteraction.* Vol. 1 of *Collected Essays.* Winona Lake, IN: Eisenbrauns, 2005.

———. *Ancient Israel's History and Historiography: The First Temple Period.* Vol. 3 of *Collected Essays.* Winona Lake, IN: Eisenbrauns, 2005.

———. *Borders and Districts in Biblical Historiography.* Jerusalem Biblical Studies 4. Jerusalem: Simor, 1996.

———. *Canaan in the Second Millennium B.C.E.* Vol. 2 of *Collected Essays.* Winona Lake, IN: Eisenbrauns, 2005.

———. "The 'Conquest of Canaan' in the Book of Joshua and in History." Pages 218–81 in *From Nomadism to Monarchy: Archaeological and Historical Aspects of Early Israel.* Edited by Israel Finkelstein and Nadav Na'aman. Jerusalem: Israel Exploration Society, 1994.

———. "The Contribution of the Amarna Letters to the Debate on Jerusalem's Political Position in the Tenth Century BCE." *Bulletin of the American Schools of Oriental Research* 304 (1996): 17–27.

———. "Ekron under the Assyrian and Egyptian Empires." *Bulletin of the American Schools of Oriental Research* 332 (2003): 81–91.

———. "Jehu Son of Omri: Legitimizing a Loyal Vassal by His Lord." Pages 13–15 in *Ancient Israel and Its Neighbors: Interaction and Counteraction.* Vol. 1 of *Collected Essays.* Winona Lake, IN: Eisenbrauns, 2005.

———. "Josiah and the Kingdom of Judah." Pages 189–247 in *Good Kings and Bad Kings: The Kingdom of Judah in the Seventh Century BCE.* Edited by Lester L. Grabbe.

Library of Hebrew Bible/Old Testament Studies 393. London: T&T Clark, 2005.

———. "The Kingdom of Judah under Josiah." *Tel Aviv* 18 (1991): 3–71.

———. "The Northern Kingdom in the Late Tenth–Ninth Centuries BCE." Pages 399–418 in *Understanding the History of Ancient Israel.* Edited by H. G. M. Williamson. Proceedings of the British Academy 143. Oxford: Oxford University Press, 2007.

———. "The Pre-Deuteronomistic Story of King Saul and Its Historical Significance." *Catholic Biblical Quarterly* 54 (1992): 638–58.

———. "Royal Inscription versus Prophetic Story: Mesha's Rebellion according to Biblical and Moabite Historiography." Pages 1345–83 in *Ahab Agonistes: The Rise and Fall of the Omri Dynasty.* Edited by Lester L. Grabbe. Library of Hebrew Bible/Old Testament Studies 421. London: T&T Clark, 2007.

———. "Royal Vassals or Governors? On the Status of Sheshbazzar and Zerubbabel in the Persian Empire." *Henoch* 22 (2000): 35–44.

———. "Solomon's District List (1 Kings 4:7–19) and the Assyrian Province System in Palestine." *Ugarit-Forschungen* 33 (2001): 419–35.

———. "Sources and Composition in the History of David." Pages 170–86 in *The Origins of the Ancient Israelite States.* Edited by Volkmar Fritz and Philip R. Davies. Journal for the Study of the Old Testament: Supplement Series 228. Sheffield: Sheffield Academic Press, 1996.

———. "When and How Did Jerusalem Become a Great City? The Rise of Jerusalem as Judah's Premier City in the Eighth–Seventh Centuries BCE." *Bulletin of the American Schools of Oriental Research* 347 (2007): 21–56.

Naveh, Joseph. "Hebrew and Aramaic Inscriptions." Pages 1–14 in *Inscriptions.* Vol. 6 of *Excavations at the City of David*, by Yigal Shiloh. Edited by Donald T. Ariel et al. Qedem 41. Jerusalem: Institute of Archaeology, Hebrew University of Jerusalem, 2000.

———. "A Hebrew Letter from the Seventh Century BC." *Israel Exploration Journal* 10 (1960): 129–39.

————. "Some Considerations on the Ostracon from 'Izbet Ṣarṭah." *Israel Exploration Journal* 28 (1978): 31–35.

Naveh, Joseph, and Shaul Shaked. *Aramaic Documents from Ancient Bactria (Fourth Century BCE)*. From the Khalili Collections. London: The Khalili Family Trust, 2012.

Naville, Édouard. "The Geography of the Exodus." *Journal of Egyptian Archaeology* 10 (1924): 18–39.

————. *The Shrine of the Saft El-Henneh and the Land of Goshen*. Egypt Exploration Fund Memoir 4. London: Trübner, 1887.

Nelson, Eric. *The Hebrew Republic: Jewish Sources and the Transformation of European Political Thought*. Cambridge, MA: Harvard University Press, 2010.

Nelson, Richard D. *The Double Redaction of the Deuteronomistic History*. Journal for the Study of the Old Testament: Supplement Series 18. Sheffield: JSOT Press, 1981.

Neumann, Hans. "Der Vertrag zwischen Ebla und Abarsal." Pages 2–8 in *Staatsverträge, Herrscherinschriften und andere Documente zur politischen Geschichte*. Vol. 2 of *Texte aus der Umwelt des Alten Testaments*. Edited by Michael Lichtenstein. Gütersloh: Mohn, 2005.

Neumann, Jehuda, and Simo Parpola. "Climatic Change and the Eleventh–Tenth-Century Eclipse of Assyria and Babylonia." *Journal of Near Eastern Studies* 46 (1987): 161–82.

Nicholson, Sarah. *Three Faces of Saul: An Intertextual Approach to Biblical Tragedy*. Journal for the Study of the Old Testament: Supplement Series 339. Sheffield: Sheffield Academic Press, 2002.

Nickelsburg, George W. E. *Jewish Literature between the Bible and the Mishnah: A Historical and Literary Introduction*. Minneapolis: Fortress, 1981.

Niehr, Herbert, and Daniel Schwemer. "Altsyrische Texte." Pages 161–85 in *Staatsverträge, Herrscherinschriften und andere Documente zur politischen Geschichte*. Vol. 2 of *Texte aus der Umwelt des Alten Testaments*. Edited by Michael Lichtenstein. Gütersloh: Mohn, 2005.

Niemann, Hermann. "The Socio-Political Shadow Cast by the Biblical Solomon." Pages 252–99 in *The Age of Solomon: Scholarship at the Turn of the Millennium*. Edited by Lowell K. Handy. Studies in the History and Culture of the Ancient Near East 11. Leiden: Brill, 1997.

Nissinen, Martti. "Fear Not: A Study on an Ancient Near Eastern Phrase." Pages 122–61 in *The Changing Face of Form Criticism for the Twenty-First Century*. Edited by Marvin A. Sweeney and Ehud Ben Zvi. Grand Rapids: Eerdmans, 2003.

————. "What Is Prophecy? An Ancient Near Eastern Perspective." Pages 17–37 in *Inspired Speech: Prophecy in the Ancient Near East; Essays in Honor of Herbert B. Huffmon*. Edited by John Kaltner and Louis Stulman. Journal for the Study of the Old Testament: Supplement Series 378. London: T&T Clark, 2004.

Nissinen, Martti, Choon-Leong Seow, and Robert K. Ritner. *Prophets and Prophecy in the Ancient Near East*. Edited by Peter Machinist. Society of Biblical Literature Writings from the Ancient World 12. Atlanta: Society of Biblical Literature, 2003.

Noegel, Scott. "Zakkur Inscription." Pages 307–11 in *The Ancient Near East: Historical Sources in Translation*. Edited by Mark W. Chavalas. Malden, MA: Blackwell, 2006.

Nogalski, James. *Literary Precursors to the Book of the Twelve*. Beihefte zur Zeitschrift für die alttestamentliche Wissenschaft 217. Berlin: de Gruyter, 1993.

Noth, Martin. *The Deuteronomistic History*. Journal for the Study of the Old Testament: Supplement Series 15. Sheffield: University of Sheffield, Department of Biblical Studies, 1981.

Nur, Amos, and Eric H. Cline. "Poseidon's Horses: Plate Tectonics and Earthquake Storms in the Late Bronze Age Aegean and Eastern Mediterranean." *Journal of Archaeological Science* (2000): 27, 43–63.

Nutkowicz, Hélène. "Éléphantine, ultime tragédie." *Transeuphatène* 40 (2011): 185–98.

———. "Les mariages mixtes à Éléphantine à l'époque perse." *Transeuphratène* 36 (2008): 125–39.

Oded, Bustenay. "Judah and the Exile." Pages 435–88 in *Israelite and Judaean History*. Edited by John H. Hayes and J. Maxwell Miller. Old Testament Library. Philadelphia: Westminster, 1977.

———. *Mass Deportations and Deportees in the Neo-Assyrian Empire*. Wiesbaden: Reichert, 1979.

Oesterley, W. O. E. "1 Maccabees." Pages 59–124 in *Apocrypha*. Vol. 1 of *The Apocrypha and Pseudepigrapha of the Old Testament*. Edited by R. H. Charles. Oxford: Oxford University Press, 1913.

Ofer, Avi. "'All the Hill Country of Judah': From a Settlement Fringe to a Prosperous Monarchy." Pages 92–122 in *From Nomadism to Monarchy: Archaeological and Historical Aspects of Early Israel*. Edited by Israel Finkelstein and Nadav Na'aman. Jerusalem: Israel Exploration Society, 1994.

Ogden, Graham S. "The Northern Extent of Josiah's Reform." *Australian Biblical Review* 26 (1978): 26–34.

Oppenheim, A. Leo. Review of Sidney Smith, *The Statue of Idri-mi*. *Journal of Near Eastern Studies* 14 (1955): 199–200.

———. "The Story of Idrimi, King of Alalakh." Pages 557–58 in *Ancient Near Eastern Texts Relating to the Old Testament*. Edited by James B. Pritchard. 3rd ed. Princeton: Princeton University Press, 1969.

Oren, Eliezer D., ed. *The Sea Peoples and Their World: A Reassessment*. Philadelphia: The University Museum, University of Pennsylvania, 2000.

Ortiz, Steven M. "The Archaeology of David and Solomon: Navigating the New Methods and Madness." Pages 497–516 in *Do Historical Matters Matter to Faith? A Critical Appraisal of Modern and Postmodern Approaches to Scripture*. Edited by James K. Hoffmeier and Dennis R. Magary. Wheaton: Crossway, 2012.

———. "Deconstructing and Reconstructing the United Monarchy: House of David or Tent of David? (Current Trends in Iron Age Research)." Pages 121–47 in *The Future of Biblical Archaeology: Reassessing Methodologies and Assumptions; The Proceedings of a Symposium, August 12–14, 2001, at Trinity International University*. Edited by James K. Hoffmeier and Alan R. Millard. Grand Rapids: Eerdmans, 2004.

———. "Does the Low Chronology Work? A Case Study of Qasile X, Gezer X, and Lachish V." Pages 587–612 in *"I Will Speak the Riddles of Ancient Times": Archaeological and Historical Studies in Honor of Amihai Mazar on the Occasion of His Sixtieth Birthday*. Edited by Aren M. Maeir and Pierre de Miroschedji. Winona Lake, IN: Eisenbrauns, 2006.

———. "Solomon's Egyptian Father-in-Law: A Reassessment of Egyptian Activity Based on Recent Archaeological Discoveries." *Near East Archaeology Society Bulletin* 56 (2011): 25–32.

Ortiz, Steven M., and Samuel Wolff. "Guarding the Border to Jerusalem: The Iron Age City of Gezer." *Near Eastern Archaeology* 75 (2012): 4–19.

Oswalt, John N. "Abraham's Experience of Yahweh: An Argument for the Historicity of the Patriarchal Narrative." Pages 33–43 in *Perspectives on Our Father Abraham: Essays in Honor of Marvin R. Wilson*. Edited by Steven A. Hunt and Marvin R. Wilson. Grand Rapids: Eerdmans, 2010.

———. *The Bible among the Myths: Unique Revelation or Just Ancient Literature?* Grand Rapids: Zondervan, 2009.

———. *Isaiah: Chapters 1–39*. New International Commentary on the Old Testament. Grand Rapids: Eerdmans, 1986.

Otzen, Benedikt. "Israel under the Assyrians." Pages 251–61 in *Power and Propaganda: A Symposium on Ancient Empires*. Edited by Mogens Trolle Larsen. Mesopotamia 7. Copenhagen: Akademisk Forlag, 1979.

Overholt, Thomas W. *Channels of Prophecy: The Social Dynamics of Prophetic Activity*. Minneapolis: Fortress, 1989.

———. *Prophecy in Cross-Cultural Perspective: A Sourcebook for Biblical Researchers*.

Society of Biblical Literature Sources for Biblical Study 17. Atlanta: Scholars Press, 1986.

Parpola, Simo. *Assyrian Prophecies*. State Archives of Assyria 9. Helsinki: Neo-Assyrian Text Corpus Project, University of Helsinki, 1997.

Parpola, Simo, and Kazuko Watanabe, eds. *Neo-Assyrian Treaties and Loyalty Oaths*. State Archives of Assyria 2. Helsinki: Neo-Assyrian Text Corpus Project, University of Helsinki, 1988.

Parzen, Herbert. "The Prophets and the Omri Dynasty." *Harvard Theological Review* 33 (1940): 69–96.

Payne, Annick. *Iron Age Hieroglyphic Luwian Inscriptions*. Society of Biblical Literature Writings from the Ancient World 29. Atlanta: Society of Biblical Literature, 2012.

Pearce, Laurie E. "'Judean': A Special Status in Neo-Babylonian and Achemenid Babylonia?" Pages 267–77 in *Judah and the Judeans in the Achaemenid Period: Negotiating Identity in an International Context*. Edited by Oded Lipschits, Gary N. Knoppers, and Manfred Oeming. Winona Lake, IN: Eisenbrauns, 2011.

———. "New Evidence for Judeans in Babylonia." Pages 399–411 in *Judah and the Judeans in the Persian Period*. Edited by Oded Lipschits and Manfred Oeming. Winona Lake, IN: Eisenbrauns, 2006.

Pearce, Laurie E., and Cornelia Wunsch. *Into the Hands of Many Peoples: Judeans and West Semitic Exiles in Mesopotamia*. Cornell University Studies in Assyriology and Sumerology 18. Bethesda, MD: CDL Press, forthcoming.

Peet, T. Eric. *Egypt and the Old Testament*. Liverpool: University Press of Liverpool, 1922.

Petersen, David L. "Prophet, Prophecy." Pages 622–48 in vol. 4 of *The New Interpreter's Dictionary of the Bible*. Edited by Katherine Doob Sakenfeld. Nashville: Abingdon, 2009.

———. *The Prophetic Literature: An Introduction*. Louisville: Westminster John Knox, 2002.

Petrie, W. M. Flinders. *Egypt and Israel*. London: Society for Promoting Christian Knowledge, 1911.

———. *Hyksos and Israelite Cities*. London: School of Archaeology, University College, 1906.

———. *Nebesheh (Am) and Defenneh (Tahpanhes)*. Egypt Exploration Fund Memoir 5. London: Trübner, 1888.

———. *Researches in Sinai*. New York: E. P. Dutton, 1906.

Pitard, Wayne T. *Ancient Damascus: A Historical Study of the Syrian City-State from Earliest Times until Its Fall to the Assyrians in 732 B.C.E.* Winona Lake, IN: Eisenbrauns, 1987.

———. "The Identity of the Bir-Hadad of the Melqart Stela." *Bulletin of the American Schools of Oriental Research* 272 (1988): 3–21.

———. "The Melqart Stela." Pages 152–53 in *Monumental Inscriptions from the Biblical World*. Vol. 2 of *The Context of Scripture*. Edited by William W. Hallo and K. Lawson Younger Jr. Leiden: Brill, 2003.

Podany, Amanda H. *Brotherhood of Kings: How International Relations Shaped the Ancient Near East*. Oxford: Oxford University Press, 2010.

Polanyi, Michael. *Meaning*. Chicago: University of Chicago Press, 1975.

Polzin, Robert. "*HWQY'* and Covenant Institutions in Israel." *Harvard Theological Review* 62 (1969): 227–40.

Pongratz-Leisten, Beate. *Herrschaftswissen in Mesopotamien: Formen der Kommunikation zwischen Gott und König im 2. und 1. Jahrtausend v. Chr.* State Archives of Assyria Studies 10. Helsinki: Neo-Assyrian Text Corpus Project, University of Helsinki, 1999.

Porten, Bezalel. *Archives from Elephantine: The Life of an Ancient Jewish Military Colony*. Berkeley: University of California Press, 1968.

———. "Settlement of the Jews at Elephantine and the Arameans at Syene." Pages 451–70 in *Judah and the Judeans in the*

Neo-Babylonian Period. Edited by Oded Lipschits and Joseph Blenkinsopp. Winona Lake, IN: Eisenbrauns, 2003.

Porten, Bezalel, and Ada Yardeni. "The Chronology of the Idumean Ostraca in the Decade or So after the Death of Alexander the Great and Its Relevance for Historical Events." Pages 237–49 in *Treasures on Camels' Humps: Historical and Literary Studies from the Ancient Near East Presented to Israel Eph'al*. Edited by Mordechai Cogan and Dan'el Kahn. Jerusalem: Magnes, 2008.

———. *Textbook of Aramaic Documents from Ancient Egypt*. 4 vols. Jerusalem: Department of the History of the Jewish People, Hebrew University; Winona Lake, IN: Eisenbrauns, 1986–1999.

Porteous, Norman. *Daniel: A Commentary*. Old Testament Library. Philadelphia: Westminster, 1965.

Portier-Young, Anathea. *Apocalypse against Empire: Theologies of Resistance in Early Judaism*. Grand Rapids: Eerdmans, 2010.

Provan, Iain, V. Philips Long, and Tremper Longman III. *A Biblical History of Israel*. Louisville: Westminster John Knox, 2003.

Puech, Émile. "L'Ostracon de Khirbet Qeiyafa et les débuts de la royauté en Israël." *Revue biblique* 17 (2010): 162–84.

Purvis, James D. "The Samaritans." Pages 591–613 in *The Hellenistic Period*. Vol. 2 of *The Cambridge History of Judaism*. Edited by W. D. Davies and Louis Finkelstein. Cambridge: Cambridge University Press, 1989.

Radner, Karen. *Die neuassyrischen Privatrechtsurkunden als Quelle für Mensch und Umwelt*. State Archives of Assyria Studies 6. Helsinki: Neo-Assyrian Text Corpus Project, University of Helsinki, 1997.

Rainey, Anson F. "Hezekiah's Reform and the Altars at Beer-sheba and Arad." Pages 333–54 in *Scripture and Other Artifacts: Essays on the Bible and Archaeology in Honor of Philip J. King*. Edited by Michael D. Coogan, Cheryl Exum, and Lawrence E. Stager. Louisville: Westminster John Knox, 1994.

———. "Israel in Merenptah's Inscription and Reliefs." *Israel Exploration Journal* 51 (2001): 57–75.

———. "Manasseh, King of Judah, in the Whirlpool of the Seventh Century BCE." Pages 147–64 in Kinattūtū ša dārâti: *Raphael Kutscher Memorial Volume*. Edited by Anson F. Rainey. Tel Aviv University Institute of Archaeology Publications 1. Tel Aviv: Institute of Archaeology, Tel Aviv University, 1993.

———. "Rainey's Challenge." *Biblical Archaeology Review* 17, no. 6 (1991): 58–60, 93.

———. "Taharqa and Syntax." *Tel Aviv* 3 (1976): 38–41.

———. "Whence Came the Israelites and Their Language?" *Israel Exploration Journal* 57 (2007): 41–64.

Rainey, Anson F., and R. Steven Notley. *The Sacred Bridge: Carta's Atlas of the Biblical World*. Jerusalem: Carta, 2006.

Reade, Julian. "Assyrian Kinglists, the Royal Tombs of Ur, and Indus Origins." *Journal of Near Eastern Studies* 60 (2001): 1–29.

Redford, Donald B. *Egypt, Canaan, and Israel in Ancient Times*. Princeton: Princeton University Press, 1992.

———. "An Egyptological Perspective on the Exodus Narrative." Pages 137–61 in *Egypt, Israel, Sinai: Archaeological and Historical Relationships in the Biblical Period*. Edited by Anson F. Rainey. Tel Aviv: Tel Aviv University, 1987.

———. "Exodus I 11." *Vetus Testamentum* 13 (1963): 401–18.

———. "The Land of Ramesses." Pages 175–78 in *Causing His Name to Live: Studies in Egyptian Epigraphy and History in Memory of William J. Murnane*. Edited by Peter J. Brand and Louise Cooper. Culture and History of the Ancient Near East 37. Leiden: Brill, 2009.

———. "Observations on the Sojourn of the Bene-Israel." Pages 56–66 in *Exodus: The Egyptian Evidence*. Edited by Ernest S. Frerichs and Leonard H. Lesko. Winona Lake, IN: Eisenbrauns, 1997.

———. "Studies in Relations between Palestine and Egypt during the First Millennium B.C." *Journal of the American Oriental Society* 93 (1973): 3–17.

———. *A Study of the Biblical Story of Joseph (Genesis 37–50).* Supplements to Vetus Testamentum 20. Leiden: Brill, 1970.

Reich, Ronny. "The Ancient Burial Ground in the Mamilla Neighbourhood, Jerusalem." Pages 111–18 in *Ancient Jerusalem Revealed.* Edited by Hillel Geva. Jerusalem: Israel Exploration Society, 1994.

———. *Excavating the City of David: Where Jerusalem's History Began.* Jerusalem: Israel Exploration Society, 2011.

———. "Light at the End of the Tunnel: Warren's Shaft Theory of David's Conquest Shattered." *Biblical Archaeology Review* 20, no. 2 (1999): 22–33, 72.

Reich, Ronny, and Eli Shukron. "The Urban Development of Jerusalem in the Late Eighth Century B.C.E." Pages 209–18 in *Jerusalem in Bible and Archaeology: The First Temple Period.* Edited by Andrew G. Vaughn and Ann E. Killebrew. Society of Biblical Literature Symposium Series 18. Atlanta: Society of Biblical Literature, 2003.

Reiner, Erica. "Akkadian Treaties from Syria and Assyria." Pages 531–41 in *Ancient Near Eastern Texts Relating to the Old Testament.* Edited by James B. Pritchard. 3rd ed. Princeton: Princeton University Press, 1969.

Reisner, George A., Clarence S. Fisher, and David G. Lyon. *Plans and Plates.* Vol. 2 of *Harvard Excavations at Samaria, 1908–1910.* Harvard Semitic Series. Cambridge, MA: Harvard University Press, 1924.

Rendsburg, Gary A. "Israel without the Bible." Pages 3–23 in *The Hebrew Bible: New Insights and Scholarship.* Edited by Frederick E. Greenspahn. New York: New York University Press, 2008.

Renfrew, Colin. "Archaeology of Religion." Pages 47–54 in *The Ancient Mind.* Edited by Colin Renfrew and Ezra B. W. Zubrow. New Directions in Archaeology. Cambridge: Cambridge University Press, 1994.

Reuveny, Rafael. "Climate Change-Induced Migration and Violent Conflict." *Political Geography* 26 (2007): 656–73.

Richter, Sandra. "Deuteronomistic History." Pages 219–30 in *Dictionary of the Old Testament: Historical Books.* Edited by Bill T. Arnold and H. G. M. Williamson. Downers Grove, IL: InterVarsity, 2006.

———. *The Deuteronomistic History and the Name Theology: lĕšakkēn šĕmô šām in the Bible and the Ancient Near East.* Beihefte zur Zeitschrift für die alttestamentliche Wissenschaft 318. Berlin: de Gruyter, 2002.

———. "Environmental Law in Deuteronomy." *Bulletin for Biblical Research* 20 (2010): 355–76.

———. *The Epic of Eden: A Christian Entry into the Old Testament.* Downers Grove, IL: IVP Academic, 2008.

Ringgren, Helmer. "רִיב." Pages 473–79 in vol. 13 of *Theological Dictionary of the Old Testament.* Edited by G. Johannes Botterweck, Helmer Ringgren, and Heinz-Josef Fabry. Translated by David E. Green. Grand Rapids: Eerdmans, 2004.

Ritner, Robert K. "Report of Wenamon." Pages 219–20 in *Prophets and Prophecy in the Ancient Near East,* by Martti Nissinen, Choon-Leong Seow, and Robert K. Ritner. Edited by Peter Machinist. Atlanta: Society of Biblical Literature, 2003.

Roaf, Michael. *Cultural Atlas of Mesopotamia and the Ancient Near East.* New York: Facts on File, 1990.

Roberts, J. J. M. "The Mari Prophetic Texts in Transliteration and English Translation." Pages 157–253 in *The Bible and the Ancient Near East: Collected Essays.* Winona Lake, IN: Eisenbrauns, 2002.

———. "Prophets and Kings: A New Look at the Royal Persecution of Prophets against Its Near Eastern Background." Pages 341–54 in *A God So Near: Essays on Old Testament Theology in Honor of Patrick D. Miller.* Edited by Brent A. Strawn and Nancy R. Bowen. Winona Lake, IN: Eisenbrauns, 2003.

Rogerson, John, and Philip R. Davies. "Was the Siloam Tunnel Built by Hezekiah?" *Biblical Archaeologist* 59 (1996): 138–49.

Rohling, Eelco J., Angela Hayes, Paul A. Mayewski, and Michal Kucera. "Holocene Climate Variability in the Eastern Mediterranean and the End of the Bronze Age." Pages 2–5 in *Forces of Transformation: The End of the Bronze Age in the Mediterranean*. Edited by Christoph R. Bachhuber and R. Gareth Roberts. Themes from the Ancient Near East, BANEA Publication Series 1. Oxford: Oxbow, 2010.

Römer, Thomas. *The So-Called Deuteronomistic History: Sociological, Historical and Literary Introduction*. London: T&T Clark, 2006.

Rosenthal, Franz. "The Treaty between *KTK* and Arpad." Pages 659–61 in *Ancient Near Eastern Texts Relating to the Old Testament*. Edited by James B. Pritchard. 3rd ed. Princeton: Princeton University Press, 1969.

Rost, Leonhard. *Die Überlieferung von der Thronnachfolge Davids*. Beiträge zur Wissenschaft vom Alten und Neuen Testament 42. Stuttgart: Kohlhammer, 1926. ET, *The Succession to the Throne of David*. Translated by Michael D. Rutter and David M. Gunn. Historic Texts and Interpreters in Biblical Scholarship 1. Sheffield: Almond, 1982.

Roth, Martha T. *Law Collections from Mesopotamia and Asia Minor*. Edited by Piotr Michalowski. Society of Biblical Literature Writings from the Ancient World 6. Atlanta: Scholars Press, 1997.

Rothenberg, Benno. *The Egyptian Mining Temple at Timna*. London: University College London, 1988.

Roux, Georges. *Ancient Iraq*. 3rd ed. London: Penguin Books, 1992.

Rowley, H. H. "The Chronological Order of Ezra and Nehemiah." Pages 135–68 in *The Servant of the Lord, and Other Essays on the Old Testament*. 2nd ed. Oxford: Blackwell, 1965.

Safrai, Shemuel, and Menahem Stern, eds. *The Jewish People in the First Century: Historical Geography, Political History, Social, Cultural and Religious Life and Institutions*. 2 vols. Compendia rerum iudaicarum ad Novum Testamentum 1. Assen: Van Gorcum; Philadelphia: Fortress, 1974–1976.

Sagrillo, Troy Leiland. "Šīšaq's Army: 2 Chronicles 12:2-3 from an Egyptological Perspective." Pages 425–50 in *The Ancient Near East in the 12th–10th Centuries BCE: Culture and History; Proceedings of the International Conference Held at the University of Haifa, 2–5 May, 2010*. Edited by Gershon Galil et al. Alter Orient und Altes Testament 392. Münster: Ugarit-Verlag, 2012.

Saldarini, Anthony J. *Pharisees, Scribes and Sadducees in Palestinian Society: A Sociological Approach*. Wilmington, DE: Michael Glazier, 1988.

Salmon, Pierre. "Les relations entre la Perse et l'Égypte du VIe au IVe s. av. J.-C." Pages 147–68 in *The Land of Israel: Cross-Roads of Civilizations*. Edited by Edward Lipiński. Orientalia lovaniensia analecta 19. Leuven: Peeters, 1985.

Sapin, J. "Archéologie." *Transeuphratène* 4 (1991): 103–11.

Sapin, J., and J. Briend. "Archéologie." *Transeuphratène* 17 (1999): 89–110.

Sartre, Maurice. *D'Alexandre à Zénobie: Histoire du Levant antique IVᵉ siècle avant J.-C.–IIIᵉ siècle après J.-C.* Paris: Fayard, 2001.

Sasson, Jack M. "About 'Mari and the Bible.'" *Revue d'assyriologie et d'archéologie orientale* 92 (1998): 97–123.

———. "The King and I: A Mari King in Changing Perceptions." *Journal of the American Oriental Society* 118 (1998): 453–70.

———. "Mari and the Holy Grail." Pages 186–98 in *Orientalism, Assyriology and the Bible*. Edited by Steven W. Holloway. Hebrew Bible Monographs 10. Sheffield: Sheffield Phoenix Press, 2007.

———. Review of George E. Mendenhall, *The Tenth Generation: The Origins of the Biblical Tradition*. *Journal of Biblical Literature* 93 (1974): 294–96.

Sauer, James A. "The River Runs Dry: Creation Story Preserves Historical Memory." *Biblical*

Archaeology Review 22, no. 4 (1996): 52–57, 64.

Schaper, Joachim. "Torah and Identity in the Persian Period." Pages 27–38 in *Judah and the Judeans in the Achaemenid Period: Negotiating Identity in an International Context*. Edited by Oded Lipschits, Gary N. Knoppers, and Manfred Oeming. Winona Lake, IN: Eisenbrauns, 2011.

Scheffler, Eben. "Saving Saul from the Deuteronomist." Pages 263–71 in *Past, Present, Future: The Deuteronomistic History and the Prophets*. Edited by Johannes C. de Moor and Harry F. van Rooy. Oudtestamentische studiën 44. Leiden: Brill, 2000.

Schiffman, Lawrence H. *Reclaiming the Dead Sea Scrolls: The History of Judaism, the Background of Christianity, the Lost Library of Qumran*. Anchor Bible Reference Library. New York: Doubleday, 1995.

Schipper, Bernd U. "Egypt and the Kingdom of Judah under Josiah and Jehoiakim." *Tel Aviv* 37 (2010): 200–229.

Schloen, J. David. *The House of the Father as Fact and Symbol: Patrimonialism in Ugarit and the Ancient Near East*. Studies in the Archaeology and History of the Levant 2. Winona Lake, IN: Eisenbrauns, 2001.

Schmidt, Brian B. "Moabite Stone." Pages 311–16 in *The Ancient Near East: Historical Sources in Translation*. Edited by Mark W. Chavalas. Malden, MA: Blackwell, 2006.

———. "Tel Dan Stele Inscription." Pages 305–6 in *The Ancient Near East: Historical Sources in Translation*. Edited by Mark W. Chavalas. Malden, MA: Blackwell, 2006.

Schneider, Tammi. "Rethinking Jehu." *Biblica* 77 (1996): 100–107.

Schniedewind, William M. "Excavating the Text of 1 Kings 9: In Search of the Gates of Solomon." Pages 241–49 in *Historical Biblical Archaeology and the Future: The New Pragmatism*. Edited by Thomas E. Levy. London: Equinox, 2010.

———. *Society and the Promise to David: The Reception History of 2 Samuel 7:1–17*. Oxford: Oxford University Press, 1999.

———. "The Source Citations of Manasseh: King Manasseh in History and Homily." *Vetus Testamentum* 41 (1991): 450–61.

———. "Tel Dan Stela: New Light on Aramaic and Jehu's Revolt." *Bulletin of the American Schools of Oriental Research* 302 (1996): 75–90.

Schunck, Klaus-Dietrich. *Die Quellen des I und II Makkabäerbuches*. Halle: Niemeyer, 1954.

Schwally, Friedrich. "Zur Quellenkritik der historischen Bücher." *Zeitschrift für die alttestamentliche Wissenschaft* 12 (1892): 153–61.

Schwartz, Daniel R. "On Some Papyri and Josephus' Sources and Chronology for the Persian Period." *Journal for the Study of Judaism in the Persian, Hellenistic, and Roman Periods* 21 (1990): 175–99.

Schwiderski, Dirk, ed. *Texte und Bibliographie*. Vol. 2 of *Die alt- und reicharamäischen Inschriften* [= *The Old and Imperial Aramaic Inscriptions*]. Fontes et subsidia ad Bibliam pertinentes 4. Berlin: de Gruyter, 2004.

Seger, J. D. "Shechem." Page 19–23 in vol. 5 of *The Oxford Encyclopedia of Archaeology in the Near East*. Edited by Eric M. Meyers. New York: Oxford University Press, 1997.

Sekunda, Nicholas. "The Might of the Persian Empire." Pages 67–86 in *The Ancient World at War: A Global History*. Edited by Philip de Souza. London: Thames & Hudson, 2008.

Selman, Martin J. "Chronicler's History." Pages 157–61 in *Dictionary of the Old Testament: Historical Books*. Edited by Bill T. Arnold and H. G. M. Williamson. Downers Grove, IL: InterVarsity, 2006.

Shaked, Shaul. "De Khulmi à Nikhšapaya: Les données des nouveaux documents araméens de Bactres sur la toponymie de la région (IVe siècle av. n. è.)." *Comptes rendus des séances de l'Academie des inscriptions et belles-lettres* 147, no. 4 (2003): 1517–35.

———. *Le satrape de Bactriane et son gouverneur: Documents araméens du IVe s. avant notre ère provenant de Bactriane*. Persika 4. Paris: De Boccard, 2004.

Shanks, Hershel, ed. *Ancient Israel: A Short History from Abraham to the Roman*

Destruction of the Temple. Englewood Cliffs, NJ: Prentice-Hall; Washington, DC: Biblical Archaeology Society, 1988.

———, ed. *Ancient Israel: From Abraham to the Roman Destruction of the Temple.* 3rd ed. Englewood Cliffs, NJ: Prentice-Hall, 2010.

Sharon, Ilan, and Anabel Zarzecki-Peleg. "Podium Structures with Lateral Access: Authority Ploys in Royal Architecture in the Iron Age Levant." Pages 145–67 in *Confronting the Past: Archaeological and Historical Essays on Ancient Israel in Honor of William G. Dever.* Edited by Seymour Gitin, J. Edward Wright, and J. P. Dessel. Winona Lake, IN: Eisenbrauns, 2006.

Shaver, Judson R. "Ezra and Nehemiah: On the Theological Significance of Making Them Contemporaries." Pages 76–86 in *Priests, Prophets, and Scribes: Essays on the Formation and Heritage of Second Temple Judaism in Honour of Joseph Blenkinsopp.* Edited by Eugene Ulrich et al. Journal for the Study of the Old Testament: Supplement Series 149. Sheffield: JSOT Press, 1992.

Shea, William H. "Famine." Pages 769–73 in vol. 2 of *The Anchor Bible Dictionary.* Edited by David Noel Freedman. New York: Doubleday, 1992.

———. "Sennacherib's Second Palestinian Campaign." *Journal of Biblical Literature* 104 (1985): 401–18.

Shiloh, Yigal. "Jerusalem." Pages 698–804 in vol. 2 of *The New Encyclopedia of Archaeological Excavations in the Holy Land.* Edited by Ephraim Stern. Jerusalem: Israel Exploration Society & Carta, 1993.

———. "Judah and Jerusalem in the Eighth–Sixth Centuries B.C.E." Pages 97–106 in *Recent Excavations in Israel: Studies in the Iron Age Archaeology.* Edited by Seymore Gitin and William G. Dever. Annual of the American Schools of Oriental Research 49. Winona Lake, IN: Eisenbrauns, 1989.

———. *1978–1982, Interim Report of the First Five Seasons.* Vol. 1 of *Excavations at the City of David.* Qedem 19. Jerusalem: Institute of Archaeology, Hebrew University of Jerusalem, 1984.

———. *The Proto-Aeolic Capital and Israelite Ashlar Masonry.* Qedem 11. Jerusalem: Israel Exploration Society, 1979.

Sigrist, Marcel, ed. *Études égyptologiques et bibliques: À la mémoire du Père B. Couroyer.* Cahiers de la Revue biblique 36. Paris: Gabalda, 1997.

Singer, Itamar. "The Beginning of Philistine Settlement in Canaan and the Northern Boundary of Philistia." *Tel Aviv* 12 (1985): 109–22.

———. "A Concise History of Amurru." Pages 197–42 in *The Calm before the Storm: Selected Writings of Itamar Singer on the End of the Late Bronze Age in Anatolia and the Levant.* Society of Biblical Literature Writings from the Ancient World: Supplement 1. Atlanta: Society of Biblical Literature, 2011.

———. "Egyptians, Canaanites, and Philistines in the Period of the Emergence of Israel." Pages 282–338 in *From Nomadism to Monarchy: Archaeological and Historical Aspects of Early Israel.* Edited by Israel Finkelstein and Nadav Na'aman. Jerusalem: Israel Exploration Society, 1994.

———. "The Treaties between Hatti and Amurru." Pages 93–100 in *Monumental Inscriptions from the Biblical World.* Vol. 2 of *The Context of Scripture.* Edited by William W. Hallo and K. Lawson Younger Jr. Leiden: Brill, 2003.

Singer-Avitz, Lily. "'Busayra Painted Ware' at Tel Beersheba." *Tel Aviv* 31 (2004): 80–89.

Smallwood, E. Mary. *The Jews under Roman Rule: From Pompey to Diocletian; A Study in Political Relations.* 2nd ed. Studies in Judaism in Late Antiquity 20. Leiden: Brill, 1981.

Smelik, Klaas A. D. "The Inscription of Mesha." Pages 137–38 in *Monumental Inscriptions from the Biblical World.* Vol. 2 of *The Context of Scripture.* Edited by William W. Hallo and K. Lawson Younger Jr. Leiden: Brill, 2003.

Smith, Sidney. *The Statue of Idri-mi.* Occasional Publications of the British Institute of Archaeology in Ankara 1. London: British Institute of Archaeology in Ankara, 1949.

Smith-Christopher, Daniel L. "The Book of Daniel." Pages 19–152 in vol. 7 of *The New Interpeter's Bible*. Edited by Leander E. Keck. Nashville: Abingdon, 1996.

Snell, Daniel C. "Taxes and Taxation." Pages 338–40 in vol. 6 of *The Anchor Bible Dictionary*. Edited by David Noel Freedman. New York: Doubleday, 1992.

Soggin, J. Alberto. *A History of Israel: From the Beginnings to the Bar Kochba Revolt, AD 135*. Translated by John Bowden. London: SCM, 1984.

———. *An Introduction to the History of Israel and Judah*. Translated by John Bowden. 2nd ed. Valley Forge, PA: Trinity Press International, 1993.

———. *Introduction to the Old Testament: From Its Origins to the Closing of the Alexandrian Canon*. Translated by John Bowden. Philadelphia: Westminster, 1976.

———. "Israel and the Nomads of Ancient Palestine." Pages 9–26 in *Community Identity in Judean Historiography: Biblical and Comparative Perspectives*. Edited by Gary N. Knoppers and Kenneth A. Ristau. Winona Lake, IN: Eisenbrauns, 2009.

Spalinger, Anthony J. "Egypt, History of (3d Intermediate-Saite Period [Dyn. 21–26])." Pages 353–64 in vol. 2 of *The Anchor Bible Dictionary*. Edited by David Noel Freedman. New York: Doubleday, 1992.

———. "The Foreign Policy of Egypt Preceding the Assyrian Conquest." *Chronique d'Egypt* 53 (1978): 22–47.

Sparks, Kenton L. *Ancient Texts for the Study of the Hebrew Bible: A Guide to the Background Literature*. Peabody, MA: Hendrickson, 2005.

Speiser, Ephraim A. "'People' and 'Nation' of Israel." *Journal of Biblical Literature* 79 (1960): 157–63.

Spieckermann, Hermann. *Juda unter Assur in der Sargonidenzeit*. Forschungen zur Religion und Literatur des Alten und Neuen Testaments 129. Göttingen: Vandenhoeck & Ruprecht, 1982.

Stager, Lawrence E. "The Archaeology of the Family in Ancient Israel." *Bulletin of the American Schools of Oriental Research* 260 (1985): 1–35.

———. "Biblical Philistines: A Hellenistic Literary Creation?" Pages 285–374 in vol. 2 of *"I Will Speak the Riddles of Ancient Times": Archaeological and Historical Studies in Honor of Amihai Mazar*. Edited by Aren Maeir et al. Winona Lake, IN: Eisenbrauns, 2006.

———. "The Finest Olive Oil in Samaria." *Journal of Semitic Studies* 28 (1983): 241–45.

———. "Inscribed Potsherd from the Eleventh Century BC." *Bulletin of the American Schools of Oriental Research* 194 (1969): 45–52.

———. "The Patrimonial Kingdom of Solomon." Pages 63–74 in *Symbiosis, Symbolism, and the Power of the Past: Canaan, Ancient Israel, and Their Neighbors from the Late Bronze Age through Roman Palaestina; Proceedings of the Centennial Symposium, W. F. Albright Institute of Archaeological Research and American Schools of Oriental Research, Jerusalem, May 29/31, 2000*. Edited by William G. Dever and Seymour Gitin. Winona Lake, IN: Eisenbrauns, 2003.

———. "Shemer's Estate." *Bulletin of American Society of Oriental Research* 277–78 (1990): 93–107.

Stamm, Johann J. *Beiträge zur hebräischen und altorientalischen Namenskunde*. Edited by Ernst Jenni and Martin A. Klopfenstein. Orbis biblicus et orientalis 30. Freiburg: Universitätsverlag, 1980.

Steiner, Margreet L. *The Settlement in the Bronze and Iron Ages*. Vol. 3 of *Excavations by Kathleen M. Kenyon in Jerusalem, 1961–1967*. Copenhagen International Series 9. London: Sheffield Academic Press, 2001.

Stern, Ephraim. *Archaeology of the Land of the Bible: The Assyrian, Babylonian, and Persian Periods, 732–332 B.C.E.* Anchor Bible Reference Library. New York: Doubleday, 2001.

———. "The Babylonian Gap: The Archaeological Reality." *Journal for the Study of the Old Testament* 28 (2004): 273–77.

———. *Material Culture of the Land of the Bible in the Persian Period, 538–332 B.C.* Warminster, UK: Aris & Phillips; Jerusalem: Israel Exploration Society, 1982.

Stern, Menahem [Menaḥem]. "The Period of the Second Temple." Pages 185–303 in *A History of the Jewish People.* Edited by H. H. Ben-Sasson. Cambridge, MA: Harvard University Press, 1976.

Sternberg, Meir. *The Poetics of Biblical Narrative: Ideological Literature and the Drama of Reading.* Bloomington: Indiana University Press, 1985.

Stiebing, William H. *Out of the Desert? Archaeology and the Exodus/Conquest Narratives.* Buffalo, NY: Prometheus Books, 1989.

Stolper, Matthew W. *Entrepreneurs and Empire: The Murašû Archive, the Murašû Firm, and Persian Rule in Babylonia.* Uitgaven van het Nederlands Historisch-Archaeologisch Instituut te Istanbul 54. Leiden: Brill, 1985.

———. "Fifth Century Nippur: Texts of the Murašûs and from Their Surroundings." *Journal of Cuneiform Studies* 53 (2001): 83–132.

———. "A Note on Yahwistic Personal Names in the Murašû Texts." *Bulletin of the American Schools of Oriental Research* 222 (1976): 25–28.

Stone, Lawson G. "The Book of Judges." In *Joshua, Judges, Ruth.* Edited by Philip W. Comfort. Cornerstone Biblical Commentary 3. Carol Stream, IL: Tyndale, 2012.

———. "Ethical and Apologetic Tendencies in the Redaction of Joshua." *Catholic Biblical Quarterly* 53 (1991): 25–36.

Strawn, Brent A. "Shalmaneser III." Pages 289–93 in *The Ancient Near East: Historical Sources in Translation.* Edited by Mark W. Chavalas. Malden, MA: Blackwell, 2006.

Streck, Maximilian. *Assurbanipal und die letzten assyrischen Könige bis zum Untergang Niniveh's.* 3 vols. Vorderasiastische Bibliothek 7. Leipzig: Hinrichs, 1916.

Streck, Michael. *Das amurritische Onomastikon der altbabylonischen Zeit.* Alter Orient und Altes Testament 271. Münster: Ugarit-Verlag, 2000.

Sweeney, Marvin A. *King Josiah of Judah: The Lost Messiah of Israel.* Oxford: Oxford University Press, 2001.

Szuchman, Jeffrey, ed. *Nomads, Tribes, and the State in the Ancient Near East: Cross-Disciplinary Perspectives.* Oriental Institute Seminars 5. Chicago: Oriental Institute of the University of Chicago, 2009.

Tadmor, Hayim. *The Inscriptions of Tiglath-Pileser III, King of Assyria: Critical Edition, with Introductions, Translations, and Commentary.* Jerusalem: Israel Academy of Sciences and Humanities, 1994.

———. "The Meunites in the Book of Chronicles in the Light of an Assyrian Document." Pages 793–804 in *"With My Many Chariots I Have Gone Up the Heights of the Mountains": Historical and Literary Studies on Ancient Mesopotamia and Israel.* Edited by Mordechai Cogan. Jerusalem: Israel Exploration Society, 2011.

———. "Que and Musri." *Israel Exploration Journal* 11 (1961): 143–50.

Tadmor, Hayim, and Shigeo Yamada. *The Royal Inscriptions of Tiglath-pileser III (744–727 BC) and Shalmaneser V (726–722 BC), Kings of Assyria.* Royal Inscriptions of the Neo-Assyrian Period 1. Winona Lake, IN: Eisenbrauns, 2011.

Tainter, Joseph. *The Collapse of Complex Societies.* New Studies in Archaeology. Cambridge: Cambridge University Press, 1988.

Tal, Oren. "Achaemenid to Greek Rule: The Contribution of Achaemenid-Ptolemaic Temples of Palestine." *Transeuphratène* 36 (2008): 165–83.

———. *The Archaeology of Hellenistic Palestine: Between Tradition and Renewal* (in Hebrew). Jerusalem: Bialik Institute, 2006.

———. "Negotiating Identity in an International Context under Achaemenid Rule: The Indigenous Coinages of Persian-Period Palestine as an Allegory." Pages 445–59 in *Judah and the Judeans in the Achaemenid Period: Negotiating Identity in an International Context.* Edited by Oded Lipschits, Gary N. Knoppers, and Manfred Oeming. Winona Lake, IN: Eisenbrauns, 2011.

Talmon, Shemaryahu, and Weston W. Fields. "The Collocation *mštyn bqyr w ʿṣwr w ʿzwb* and Its Meaning." *Zeitschrift für die alttestamentliche Wissenschaft* 101 (1989): 85–112.

Tanner, J. Paul. "The Gideon Narrative as the Focal Point of Judges." *Bibliotheca Sacra* 149 (1992): 149–61.

Tappy, Ron E. *The Archaeology of Israelite Samaria.* Harvard Semitic Studies 44. Atlanta: Scholars Press, 1992.

———. "Samaria." Pages 463–67 in vol. 4 of *The Oxford Encyclopedia of Archaeology in the Near East.* Edited by Eric M. Meyers. Oxford: Oxford University Press, 1997.

———. "Samaria." Pages 854–62 in *Dictionary of the Old Testament: Historical Books.* Edited by Bill T. Arnold and H. G. M. Williamson. Downers Grove, IL: InterVarsity, 2005.

Tappy, Ron E., and P. Kyle McCarter, eds. *Literate Culture and Tenth-Century Canaan: The Tel Zayit Abecedary in Context.* Winona Lake, IN: Eisenbrauns, 2008.

Tatum, Lynn. "Jerusalem in Conflict: The Evidence for the Seventh-Century BCE Religious Struggle over Jerusalem." Pages 291–306 in *Jerusalem in Bible and Archaeology: The First Temple Period.* Edited by Andrew G. Vaughn and Ann E. Killebrew. Society of Biblical Literature Symposium Series 18. Atlanta: Society of Biblical Literature, 2003.

Tcherikover, Victor. *Hellenistic Civilization and the Jews.* Philadelphia: Jewish Publication Society, 1959.

Thiele, Edwin R. *The Mysterious Numbers of the Hebrew Kings: A Reconstruction of the Chronology of the Kingdoms of Israel and Judah.* 3rd ed. Grand Rapids: Eerdmans, 1983.

Thompson, Thomas L. *Early History of the Israelite People: From the Written and Archaeological Sources.* Studies in the History of the Ancient Near East 4. Leiden: Brill, 1992.

———. *The Historicity of the Patriarchal Narratives: The Quest for the Historical Abraham.* Beihefte zur Zeitschrift für die alttestamentliche Wissenschaft 133. Berlin: de Gruyter, 1974.

Tigay, Jeffrey H. *Deuteronomy.* Jewish Publication Society Torah Commentary. Philadelphia: Jewish Publication Society, 1996.

Tollefson, Kenneth D., and H. G. M. Williamson. "Nehemiah as Cultural Revitalization: An Anthropological Perspective." *Journal for the Study of the Old Testament* 56 (1992): 41–68.

Toombs, Lawrence E. "Shechem (Place)." Pages 1174–86 in vol. 5 of *The Anchor Bible Dictionary.* Edited by David Noel Freedman. New York: Doubleday, 1992.

Torrey, Charles C. *The Chronicler's History of Israel: Chronicles-Ezra-Nehemiah Restored to Its Original Form.* New Haven: Yale University Press, 1954.

———. *The Composition and Historical Value of Ezra-Nehemiah.* Beihefte zur Zeitschrift für die alttestamentliche Wissenschaft 2. Giessen: J. Ricker, 1896.

Tov, Emanuel. *Textual Criticism of the Hebrew Bible.* 3rd rev. and exp. ed. Minneapolis: Fortress, 2012.

Trible, Phyllis. "Depatriarchalizing in Biblical Interpretation." *Journal of the American Academy of Religion* 41 (1973): 30–48.

Tsafrir, Yoram. "The Location of the Seleucid Akra in Jerusalem." Pages 85–86 in *Jerusalem Revealed: Archaeology in the Holy City, 1968–1974.* Edited by Yigael Yadin. Translated by Rafi Grafman. Jerusalem: Israel Exploration Society, 1975.

Tsevat, Matitiahu. "Alalakhiana." *Hebrew Union College Annual* 29 (1958): 109–35.

———. "Die Namengeburg Samuels und die Substitionstheorie." *Zeitschrift für die alttestamentliche Wissenschaft* 99 (1987): 250–54.

Tsumura, David Toshio. "Genesis and Ancient Near Eastern Stories of Creation and Flood: An Introduction." Pages 27–57 in *I Studied Inscriptions from before the Flood: Ancient Near Eastern, Literary, and Linguistic Approaches to Genesis 1–11.* Edited by Richard S. Hess and David Toshio Tsumura.

Sources for Biblical and Theological Study 4. Winona Lake, IN: Eisenbrauns, 1994.

Tubb, Jonathan N., ed. *Palestine in the Bronze and Iron Ages: Papers in Honour of Olga Tufnell*. University of London Institute of Archaeology Occasional Publications 11. London: University of London Institute of Archaeology, 1985.

Turkowski, Lucian. "Peasant Agriculture in the Judaean Hills." *Palestine Exploration Quarterly* 101 (1969): 21–33, 101–13.

Tushingham, A. Douglas. "New Evidence Bearing on the Two-Winged *LMLK* Stamp Impressions." *Bulletin of the American Schools of Oriental Research* 287 (1992): 61–65.

Uehlinger, Christoph. "Neither Eyewitnesses, nor Windows to the Past, but Valuable Testimony in Its Own Right: Remarks on Iconography, Source Criticism and Ancient Data Processing." Pages 173–228 in *Understanding the History of Ancient Israel*. Edited by H. G. M. Williamson. Proceedings of the British Academy 143. Oxford: Oxford University Press, 2007.

Unger, Merill F. *Archaeology and the New Testament*. Grand Rapids: Zondervan, 1962.

Ussishkin, David. "Archaeology of the Biblical Period: On Some Questions of Methodology and Chronology of the Iron Age." Pages 131–41 in *Understanding the History of Ancient Israel*. Edited by H. G. M. Willliamson. Proceedings of the British Academy 143. Oxford: Oxford University Press, 2007.

———. "The Borders and De Facto Size of Jerusalem in the Persian Period." Pages 147–66 in *Judah and the Judeans in the Persian Period*. Edited by Oded Lipschits and Manfred Oeming. Winona Lake, IN: Eisenbrauns, 2006.

———. "Building IV at Hamath and the Temples of Solomon and Tell Tayanat." *Israel Exploration Journal* 16 (1966): 104–10.

———. *The Conquest of Lachish by Sennacherib*. Tel Aviv University Institute of Archaeology Publications 6. Tel Aviv: Institute of Archaeology, Tel Aviv University, 1982.

———. "The Date of the Judaean Shrine at Arad." *Israel Exploration Journal* 38 (1988): 142–57.

———. "King Solomon's Palace and Building 1723 in Megiddo." *Israel Exploration Journal* 16 (1966): 174–86.

———. "Lachish." Pages 114–26 in vol. 4 of *The Anchor Bible Dictionary*. Edited by David Noel Freedman. New York: Doubleday, 1992.

———. "*Lmlk* Seal Impressions Once Again: A Second Rejoinder to Oded Lipschits." *Antiguo Oriente* 10 (2012): 13–24.

———. "Megiddo." Pages 666–79 in vol. 4 of *The Anchor Bible Dictionary*. Edited by David Noel Freedman. New York: Doubleday, 1992.

———. "Megiddo." Pages 460–69 in vol. 3 of *The Oxford Encyclopedia of Archaeology in the Near East*. Edited by Eric M. Meyers. Oxford: Oxford University Press, 1997.

———. *The Renewed Archaeological Excavations at Lachish (1973–1994)*. 5 vols. Tel Aviv University Institute of Archaeology Monographs 22. Tel Aviv: Emery and Claire Yass Publications in Archaeology of the Institute of Archaeology, Tel Aviv University, 2004.

———. "Solomon's Jerusalem: The Text and the Facts on the Ground." Pages 103–11 in *Jerusalem in Bible and Archaeology: The First Temple Period*. Edited by Andrew G. Vaughn and Ann E. Killebrew. Society of Biblical Literature Symposium Series 18. Atlanta: Society of Biblical Literature, 2003.

Uziel, Joe, and Itzhaq Shai. "Iron Age Jerusalem: Temple-Palace, Capital City." *Journal of the American Oriental Society* 127 (2007): 161–70.

Valkama, Kirsi. "What Do Archaeological Remains Reveal of the Settlements in Judah during the Mid-Sixth Century BCE?" Pages 39–59 in *The Concept of Exile in Ancient Israel and Its Historical Contexts*. Edited by Ehud Ben Zvi and Christoph Levin. Beihefte zur Zeitschrift für die alttestamentliche Wissenschaft 404. Berlin: de Gruyter, 2010.

van Bekkum, Koert. *From Conquest to Coexistence: Ideology and Antiquarian Intent in* the *Historiography of Israel's Settlement in Canaan. Culture and History of the Ancient Near East* 45. Leiden: Brill, 2011.

Van de Mieroop, Marc. *The Eastern Mediterranean in the Age of Ramesses II.* Oxford: Blackwell, 2007.

———. *A History of the Ancient Near East, ca. 3000–323 BC.* Malden, MA: Blackwell, 2004. 2nd ed., Malden, MA: Blackwell, 2007.

Vanderhooft, David. "*'el-mĕdînâ ûmĕdînâ kiktābāh*: Scribes and Scripts in Yehud and in Achaemenid Transeuphratene." Pages 529–44 in *Judah and the Judeans in the Achaemenid Period: Negotiating Identity in an International Context.* Edited by Oded Lipschits, Gary N. Knoppers, and Manfred Oeming. Winona Lake, IN: Eisenbrauns, 2011.

———. *The Neo-Babylonian Empire and Babylon in the Latter Prophets.* Harvard Semitic Monographs 59. Atlanta: Scholars Press, 1999.

Vanderhooft, David, and Wayne Horowitz. "The Cuneiform Inscription from Tell en-Naṣbeh: The Demise of an Unknown King." *Tel Aviv* 29 (2002): 318–27.

VanderKam, James C. *From Joshua to Caiaphas: High Priests after the Exile.* Minneapolis: Fortress; Assen: Van Gorcum: 2004.

van der Toorn, Karel. "Mesopotamian Prophecy between Immanence and Transcendence: A Comparison of Old Babylonian and Neo-Assyrian Prophecy." Pages 71–87 in *Prophecy in Its Ancient Near Eastern Context: Mesopotamian, Biblical, and Arabian Perspectives.* Edited by Martti Nissinen. Society of Biblical Literature Symposium Series 13. Atlanta: Society of Biblical Literature, 2000.

———. "Saul and the Rise of the Israelite State Religion." *Vetus Testamentum* 43 (1993): 519–42.

van der Veen, Peter G. "Arabian Seals and Bullae along the Trade Routes of Judah and Edom." *Journal of Epigraphy and Rock Drawings* 3 (2009): 25–39.

———. "Beschriftete Siegel als Beweis für das biblische Israel? Gedalja und seine Mörder par exemple (eine Antwort an Bob Becking)." Pages 253–55 in *Wort und Stein: Studien zur Theologie und Archäologie; Festschrift für Udo Worschech.* Edited by Friedbert Ninow. Beiträge zur Erforschung der antiken Moabitis (Ard el-Kerak) 4. Frankfurt: Peter Lang, 2003.

———. "The Final Phase of Iron Age IIC and the Babylonian Conquest: A Reassessment with Special Emphasis on Names and Bureaucratic Titles on Provenanced Seals and Bullae from Israel and Judah." PhD diss., University of Bristol, 2005.

———. "Gedaliah ben Ahiqam in the Light of Epigraphic Evidence (A Response to Bob Becking)." Pages 55–70 in *New Seals and Inscriptions, Hebrew, Idumean and Cuneiform.* Edited by Meir Lubetski. Hebrew Bible Monographs 8. Sheffield: Sheffield Phoenix Press, 2007.

———. "Gedaliah's Seal Material Revisited: Some Preliminary Notes on New Evidence from the City of David." Pages 21–33 in *New Inscriptions and Seals Relating to the Biblical World.* Edited by Meir Lubetski and Edith Lubetski. Society of Biblical Literature Archaeology and Biblical Studies 19. Atlanta: Scholars Press, 2012.

———. "An Inscribed Jar Handle from Ras el-'Amud: A New Reading and an Absolute Date." *Kleine Untersuchungen zur Sprache des Alten Testaments und seiner Umwelt* 11 (2010): 109–21.

———. "The Seal Material." Pages 79–84 in *Umm al-Biyara: Excavations by Crystal-M. Bennett in Petra, 1960–1965.* Edited by Piotr Bienkowski. Levant Supplementary Series 10. Oxford: Oxbow, 2011.

van der Veen, Peter G., and François Bron. "Arabian and Arabizing Epigraphic Finds from the Iron Age Southern Levant." In *Unearthing the Wilderness: Studies on the History and Archaeology of the Negev and Edom in the Iron Age.* Edited by Juan Manuel Tebes. Ancient Near Eastern Studies Supplement Series 45. Leuven: Peeters, forthcoming.

Van Hoonacker, Albin. *Néhémie en l'an 20 d'Artaxerxès I: Esdras en l'an 7 d'Artaxerxès II; Réponse à un mémoire de A. Kuenen.* Leipzig: H. Engelcke, 1892.

———. "Néhémie et Esdras." *Le Muséon* 9 (1890): 151–84, 317–51, 389–401.

———. "La question Néhémie et Esdras." *Revue biblique* 4 (1895): 186–92.

Van Seters, John. *Abraham in History and Tradition.* New Haven: Yale University Press, 1975.

———. *In Search of History: Historiography in the Ancient World and the Origins of Biblical History.* New Haven: Yale University Press, 1983.

Van Volsem, Cindy L. "The Babylonian Period in the Region of Benjamin (586–538 BCE)." MA thesis, Institute of Holy Land Studies, 1987.

Vaughn, Andrew G. *Theology, History, and Archaeology in the Chronicler's Account of Hezekiah.* Society of Biblical Literature Archaeology and Biblical Studies 4. Atlanta: Scholars Press, 1999.

Veijola, Timo. "Salomo—der erstgeborene Bathshebas." Pages 230–50 in *Studies in the Historical Books of the Old Testament.* Edited by J. A. Emerton. Supplements to Vetus Testamentum 30. Leiden: Brill, 1979.

Verhoef, Pieter A. "Prophecy." Pages 1067–78 in vol. 4 of *New International Dictionary of Old Testament Theology and Exegesis.* Edited by Willem A. VanGemeren. Grand Rapids: Zondervan, 1997.

Vermès, Géza. *The Dead Sea Scrolls in English.* 4th ed. London: Penguin, 1995.

Vermeylen, Jacques. *La loi du plus fort: Histoire de la rédaction des récits davidiques de 1 Samuel 8 à 1 Rois 2.* Bibliotheca ephemeridum theologicarum lovaniensium 154. Leuven: Peeters, 2000.

———. "La maison de Saül et la maison de David: Un écrit de propagande théologico-politique de 1S 11 à 2S 7." Pages 34–74 in *Figures de David à travers la Bible: XVIIe congrès de l'ACFEB, Lille, 1er–5 septembre 1997.* Edited by Louis Desrousseaux and Jacques Vermeylen. Lectio divina 177. Paris: Cerf, 1999.

Vernus, Pascal. "Inscriptions de la troisième période intermédiaire (I)." *Bulletin de l'Institut français d'archéologie orientale* 75 (1975): 1–66.

von Dassow, Eva. *State and Society in the Late Bronze Age: Alalaḫ under the Mittani Empire.* Edited by David I. Owen and Gernot Wilhelm. Studies on the Civilization and Culture of Nuzi and the Hurrians 17. Bethesda, MD: CDL Press, 2008.

von Rad, Gerhard. "The Beginning of Historical Writing in Ancient Israel." Pages 166–204 in *The Problem of the Hexateuch, and Other Essays.* Translated by E. W. Trueman Dicken. London: Oliver & Boyd, 1966.

———. *Old Testament Theology.* Translated by D. M. G. Stalker. 2 vols. New York: Harper & Row, 1962–1965.

Wacholder, Ben Zion. "The Letter from Judah Maccabee to Aristobulos: Is 2 Maccabees 1:10b–2:18 Authentic?" *Hebrew Union College Annual* 49 (1978): 89–133.

Wainwright, G. A. "Some Early Philistine History." *Vetus Testamentum* 9 (1959): 73–84.

Wallis, Gerhard. "Eine Parallele zu Richter 19,29ff und 1 Samuel 11,5ff aus dem Briefarchiv von Mari." *Zeitschrift für die alttestamentliche Wissenschaft* 64 (1952): 57–61.

Walløe, L. "Was the Disruption of the Mycenaean World Caused by Repeated Epidemics of Bubonic Plague?" *Opuscula Atheniensia* 24 (1999): 121–26.

Walton, John H. *Ancient Israelite Literature in Its Cultural Context: A Survey of Parallels between Biblical and Ancient Near Eastern Texts.* Library of Biblical Interpretation. Grand Rapids: Zondervan, 1989.

———. "Genealogies." Pages 309–16 in *Dictionary of the Old Testament: Historical Books.* Edited by Bill T. Arnold and H. G. M. Williamson. Downers Grove, IL: InterVarsity, 2005.

Ward, William A., and Martha Sharp Joukowsky, eds. *The Crisis Years: The 12th Century B.C.; From beyond the Danube to the Tigris.* Dubuque, IA: Kendall/Hunt, 1989.

Watson, Wilfred G. E., and Nicolas Wyatt, eds. *Handbook of Ugaritic Studies.* Handbuch der Orientalistik 1/39. Leiden: Brill, 1999.

Way, Kenneth C. *Donkeys in the Biblical World: Ceremony and Symbol.* History, Archaeology, and Culture of the Levant 2. Edited by Jeffrey A. Blakely and K. Lawson Younger Jr. Winona Lake, IN: Eisenbrauns, 2011.

———. "Jehoshaphat." Pages 531–34 in *Dictionary of the Old Testament: Historical Books.* Edited by Bill T. Arnold and H. G. M. Williamson. Downers Grove, IL: InterVarsity, 2006.

Weidner, Ernst F. "Jojachin, König von Juda, in babylonischen Keilschrifttexten." Pages 923–35 in vol. 2 of *Mélanges syriens offerts à Monsieur René Dussaud.* Paris: Geuthner, 1939.

Weinfeld, Moshe. *Deuteronomy and the Deuteronomic School.* Oxford: Clarendon, 1972.

Weinstein, James. "The Collapse of the Egyptian Empire in the Southern Levant." Pages 142–50 in *The Crisis Years: The 12th Century B.C.; From beyond the Danube to the Tigris.* Edited by William A. Ward and Martha Sharp Joukowsky. Dubuque, IA: Kendall/Hunt, 1989.

Weippert, Manfred. *Die Landnahme der israelitischen Stämme in der neuren wissenschaftlichen Diskussion: Ein kritischer Bericht.* Forschungen zur Religion und Literatur des Alten und Neuen Testaments 92. Göttingen: Vandenhoeck & Ruprecht, 1967. ET, *The Settlement of the Israelite Tribes in Palestine: A Critical Survey of Recent Debate.* Translated by James D. Martin. Studies in Biblical Theology 21. London: SCM, 1971.

Weiss, Barry. "The Decline of Late Bronze Age Civilization as a Possible Response to Climatic Change." *Climatic Change* 4 (1982): 172–98.

Weiss, Harvey, and Raymond S. Bradley. "What Drives Societal Collapse?" *Science* 291 (2001): 609–10.

Wellhausen, Julius. *The Pharisees and the Sadducees: An Examination of Internal Jewish History.* Translated by Mark E. Biddle. Mercer Library of Biblical Studies. Macon, GA: Mercer University Press, 2001.

Welten, Peter. *Geschichte und Geschichtsdarstellung in den Chronikbüchern.* Wissenschaftliche Monographien zum Alten und Neuen Testament 42. Neukirchen-Vluyn: Neukirchener Verlag, 1973.

Wenham, Gordon J. *Genesis 1–15.* Word Biblical Commentary 1. Waco: Word, 1987.

———. "Pondering the Pentateuch: The Search for a New Paradigm." Pages 116–44 in *The Face of Old Testament Studies: A Survey of Contemporary Approaches.* Edited by David W. Baker and Bill T. Arnold. Grand Rapids: Baker Books, 1999.

Wenham, John W. "Large Numbers in the Old Testament." *Tyndale Bulletin* 18 (1967): 19–53.

Westermann, Claus. *Basic Forms of Prophetic Speech.* Translated by Hugh Clayton White. Philadelphia: Westminster, 1967.

———. *Genesis 37–50: A Commentary.* Translated by John J. Scullion. Minneapolis: Augsburg, 1986.

White, Marsha. "Naboth's Vineyard and Jehu's Coup: The Legitimation of a Dynastic Extermination." *Vetus Testamentum* 44 (1994): 66–76.

Whitley, James. "Objects with Attitude: Biographical Facts and Fallacies in the Study of Late Bronze Age and Early Iron Age Warrior Graves." *Cambridge Archaeological Journal* 12 (2002): 217–32.

Whybray, R. N. *The Succession Narrative: A Study of II Sam. 9–20 and I Kings 1 and 2.* Studies in Biblical Theology 9. London: SCM, 1968.

Widengren, George. "The Persian Period." Pages 489–538 in *Israelite and Judaean History.* Edited by John H. Hayes and J. Maxwell Miller. Old Testament Library. Philadelphia: Westminster, 1977.

Wightman, Gregory J. "The Myth of Solomon." *Bulletin of the American Schools of Oriental Research* 277–78 (1990): 5–22.

Wilhelm, Gernot, et al. "Texte der Hethiter." Pages 95–159 in *Staatsverträge, Herrscherinschriften und andere Documente zur politischen Geschichte.* Vol. 2 of *Texte aus der Umwelt des Alten Testaments.* Edited by Michael Lichtenstein. Gütersloh: Mohn, 2005.

Willi, Thomas. "'Wie geschrieben steht'—Schriftbezug und Schrift: Überlegungen zur

frühjüdischen Literaturwerdung im perser-
zeitlichen Kontext." Pages 257–77 in *Reli-*
gion und Religionskontakte im Zeitalter der
Achämeniden. Edited by Reinhard G. Kratz.
Veröffentlichungen der Wissenschaftlichen
Gesellschaft für Theologie 22. Gütersloh:
Kaiser/Gütersloher Verlagshaus, 2002.

Williams, Ronald J. *Hebrew Syntax: An Out-*
line. 2nd ed. Toronto: University of Toronto
Press, 1976.

———. "'A People Come Out of Egypt': An
Egyptologist Looks at the Old Testament."
Pages 231–52 in *Congress Volume: Edin-*
burgh 1974. Edited by Luis Alonso Schökel.
Supplements to Vetus Testamentum 28.
Leiden: Brill, 1975.

Williams, Vivien. "The Works of R. J. Wil-
liams." Pages 126–28 in *Egyptological Mis-*
cellanies: A Tribute to Professor Ronald J.
Williams. Edited by J. K. Hoffmeier and
E. S. Meltzer. Ancient World 6. Chicago:
Ares, 1983.

Williamson, H. G. M. *Ezra, Nehemiah.* Word
Biblical Commentary 16. Waco: Word, 1985.

———. "The Origins of Israel: Can We Safely
Ignore the Bible?" Pages 141–51 in *The Ori-*
gin of Early Israel—Current Debate: Bibli-
cal, Historical, and Archaeological Perspec-
tives; Irene Levi-Sala Seminar, 1997. Edited
by Shmuel Ahituv and Eliezer D. Oren. Beer-
Sheva: Ben-Gurion University of the Negev
Press, 1998.

Wilson, John A. "The Report of a Frontier Of-
ficial." Pages 235–36 in *The Ancient Near*
East: An Anthology of Texts and Pictures.
Edited by James B. Pritchard. Princeton:
Princeton University Press, 2011.

Wilson, Kevin A. *The Campaign of Pharaoh*
Shoshenq I into Palestine. Forschungen zum
Alten Testament 2/9. Tübingen: Mohr Sie-
beck, 2005.

Wilson, Robert R. "Current Issues in the Study
of Old Testament Prophecy." Pages 38–48
in *Inspired Speech: Prophecy in the Ancient*
Near East; Essays in Honor of Herbert B.
Huffmon. Journal for the Study of the Old
Testament: Supplement Series 378. Edited by
John Kaltner and Louis Stulman. London:
T&T Clark, 2004.

———. *Prophecy and Society in Ancient Israel.*
Philadelphia: Fortress, 1980.

Wiseman, Donald J. *1 and 2 Kings: An Intro-*
duction and Commentary. Tyndale Old Testament Commentaries 9. Downers Grove, IL:
InterVarsity, 1993.

Wood, Bryant G. "The Search for Joshua's Ai."
Pages 205–40 in *Critical Issues in Early Is-*
raelite History. Edited by Richard S. Hess,
Gerald A. Klingbeil, and Paul J. Ray Jr. Bul-
letin for Biblical Research Supplements 3.
Winona Lake, IN: Eisenbrauns, 2008.

Wright, G. Ernest. "The Lawsuit of God: A
Form-Critical Study of Deuteronomy 32."
Pages 26–67 in *Israel's Prophetic Heritage:*
Essays in Honor of James Muilenburg. Ed-
ited by Bernhard W. Anderson and Walter
Harrelson. New York: Harper, 1962.

Wright, John W. "Remapping Yehud: The Borders of Yehud and the Genealogies of Chronicles." Pages 67–89 in *Judah and the Judeans*
in the Persian Period. Edited by Oded Lipschits and Manfred Oeming. Winona Lake,
IN: Eisenbrauns, 2006.

Wright, Paul H. "Ezion-geber." Pages 274–77
in *Dictionary of the Old Testament: His-*
torical Books. Edited by Bill T. Arnold and
H. G. M. Williamson. Downers Grove, IL:
InterVarsity, 2005.

Wunsch, Cornelia. "Glimpses on the Lives of
Deportees in Rural Babylonia." Pages 247–60
in *Arameans, Chaldeans, and Arabs in Baby-*
lonia and Palestine in the First Millennium
B.C. Edited by Angelika Berlejung and Michael P. Streck. Leipziger Altorientalistische
Studien 3. Wiesbaden: Harrassowitz, 2013.

———. *Judeans by the Waters of Babylon:*
New Historical Evidence in Sources from
Rural Babylonia; Texts from the Schøyen
Collection. Babylonische Archive 3. Dres-
den: ISLET-Verlag, forthcoming.

Würthwein, Ernst. *Die Erzählung von der*
Thronfolge Davids: Theologische oder poli-
tische Geschichtsschreibung? Theologische
Studien 115. Zurich: Theologischer Verlag,
1974.

Yadin, Yigael. *The Art of Warfare in Biblical*
Lands in the Light of Archaeological Study.

Translated by M. Pearlman. 2 vols. New York: McGraw-Hill, 1963.

———. "Beer-sheba: The High Place Destroyed by King Josiah." *Bulletin of the American Schools of Oriental Research* 222 (1976): 5–17.

———. "Hazor." Pages 474–95 in vol. 2 of *Encyclopedia of Archaeological Excavations in the Holy Land*. Edited by Michael Avi-Yonah. Jerusalem: Israel Exploration Society; Massada Press, 1976.

———. "New Light on Solomon's Megiddo." *Biblical Archaeologist* 23 (1960): 62–68.

———. "Solomon's City Wall and Gate at Gezer." *Israel Exploration Journal* 8 (1958): 80–86.

Yamada, Shigeo. *The Construction of the Assyrian Empire: A Historical Study of the Inscriptions of Shalmaneser III (859–824 BC) Relating to His Campaigns to the West*. Culture and History of the Ancient Near East 3. Leiden: Brill, 2003.

Yamauchi, Edwin M. "Abraham and Archaeology: Anachronisms or Adaptations?" Pages 15–32 in *Perspectives on Our Father Abraham: Essays in Honor of Marvin R. Wilson*. Edited by Steven A. Hunt. Grand Rapids: Eerdmans, 2010.

———. "Historic Homer." *Biblical Archaeology Review* 33, no. 2 (2007): 28–37, 76.

———. *Persia and the Bible*. Grand Rapids: Baker Books, 1996.

Yasur-Landau, Assaf. *The Philistines and Aegean Migration at the End of the Late Bronze Age*. Cambridge: Cambridge University Press, 2010.

Yasur-Landau, Assaf, Jennie R. Ebeling, and Laura B. Mazow, eds. *Household Archaeology in Ancient Israel and Beyond*. Culture and History of the Ancient Near East 50. Leiden: Brill, 2011.

Yon, Marguerite, and Daniel Arnaud. *Études Ougaritiques I: Travaux 1985–1995*. Ras Shamra-Ougarit 14. Paris: Éditions Recherche sur les civilisations, 2001.

Younger, K. Lawson, Jr. *Ancient Conquest Accounts: A Study in Ancient Near Eastern and Biblical History Writing*. Journal for the Study of the Old Testament: Supplement Series 98. Sheffield: JSOT Press, 1990.

———. "Annals: Aššur Clay Tablets." Pages 264–66 in *Monumental Inscriptions from the Biblical World*. Vol. 2 of *The Context of Scripture*. Edited by William W. Hallo and K. Lawson Younger Jr. Leiden: Brill, 2003.

———. "Annals: Calah Bulls." Pages 266–67 in *Monumental Inscriptions from the Biblical World*. Vol. 2 of *The Context of Scripture*. Edited by William W. Hallo and K. Lawson Younger Jr. Leiden: Brill, 2003.

———. "Annals: Marble Slab." Pages 267–68 in *Monumental Inscriptions from the Biblical World*. Vol. 2 of *The Context of Scripture*. Edited by William W. Hallo and K. Lawson Younger Jr. Leiden: Brill, 2003.

———. "Aššur Basalt Statue." Page 270 in *Monumental Inscriptions from the Biblical World*. Vol. 2 of *The Context of Scripture*. Edited by William W. Hallo and K. Lawson Younger Jr. Leiden: Brill, 2003.

———. "The Azatiwada Inscription." Pages 148–50 in *Monumental Inscriptions from the Biblical World*. Vol. 2 of *The Context of Scripture*. Edited by William W. Hallo and K. Lawson Younger Jr. Leiden: Brill, 2003.

———. "Black Obelisk." Pages 269–70 in *Monumental Inscriptions from the Biblical World*. Vol. 2 of *The Context of Scripture*. Edited by William W. Hallo and K. Lawson Younger Jr. Leiden: Brill, 2003.

———. "Black Stone Cylinder." Page 271 in *Monumental Inscriptions from the Biblical World*. Vol. 2 of *The Context of Scripture*. Edited by William W. Hallo and K. Lawson Younger Jr. Leiden: Brill, 2003.

———. "Calah Orthostat Slab." Pages 276–77 in *Monumental Inscriptions from the Biblical World*. Vol. 2 of *The Context of Scripture*. Edited by William W. Hallo and K. Lawson Younger Jr. Leiden: Brill, 2003.

———. "The Die (Pūru) of Yahli." Pages 271–72 in *Monumental Inscriptions from the Biblical World*. Vol. 2 of *The Context of Scripture*. Edited by William W. Hallo and K. Lawson Younger Jr. Leiden: Brill, 2003.

————. "The Fall of Samaria in Light of Recent Research." *Catholic Biblical Quarterly* 61 (1999): 461–82.

————. "The Hadad Inscription." Pages 156–58 in *Monumental Inscriptions from the Biblical World*. Vol. 2 of *The Context of Scripture*. Edited by William W. Hallo and K. Lawson Younger Jr. Leiden: Brill, 2003.

————. "Israelites in Exile: Their Names Appear at All Levels of Assyrian Society." *Biblical Archaeological Review* 29, no. 6 (2003): 36–45, 65–66.

————. "Kurba'il Statue." Pages 268–69 in *Monumental Inscriptions from the Biblical World*. Vol. 2 of *The Context of Scripture*. Edited by William W. Hallo and K. Lawson Younger Jr. Leiden: Brill, 2003.

————. "Kurkh Monolith." Pages 261–64 in *Monumental Inscriptions from the Biblical World*. Vol. 2 of *The Context of Scripture*. Edited by William W. Hallo and K. Lawson Younger Jr. Leiden: Brill, 2003.

————. "The Late Bronze/Iron Age Transition and the Origins of the Arameans." Pages 131–74 in *Ugarit at Seventy-Five: Proceedings of the Symposium "Ugarit at Seventy-Five," Held at Trinity International University, Deerfield, Illinois, February 18–20, 2005, under the Auspices of the Middle Western Branch of the American Oriental Society and the Mid-West Region of the Society of the Biblical Literature*. Edited by K. Lawson Younger Jr. Winona Lake, IN: Eisenbrauns, 2007.

————. "Neo-Assyrian and Israelite History in the Ninth Century: The Role of Shalmaneser III." Pages 243–77 in *Understanding the History of Ancient Israel*. Edited by H. G. M. Williamson. Proceedings of the British Academy 143. Oxford: Oxford University Press, 2007.

————. "The Rhetorical Structuring of the Joshua Conquest Narratives." Pages 3–32 in *Critical Issues in Early Israelite History*. Edited by Richard S. Hess, Gerald A. Klingbeil, and Paul J. Ray Jr. Bulletin for Biblical Research Supplements 3. Winona Lake, IN: Eisenbrauns, 2008.

————. "Tell Al Rimah Stela." Pages 275–76 in *Monumental Inscriptions from the Biblical World*. Vol. 2 of *The Context of Scripture*. Edited by William W. Hallo and K. Lawson Younger Jr. Leiden: Brill, 2003.

————, ed. *Ugarit at Seventy-Five: Proceedings of the Symposium "Ugarit at Seventy-Five," Held at Trinity International University, Deerfield, Illinois, February 18–20, 2005, under the Auspices of the Middle Western Branch of the American Oriental Society and the Mid-West Region of the Society of the Biblical Literature*. Winona Lake, IN: Eisenbrauns, 2007.

Younker, Randall W. "The Emergence of the Ammonites." Pages 189–218 in *Ancient Ammon*. Edited by Burton Macdonald and Randall W. Younker. Studies in the History and Culture of the Ancient Near East 17. Leiden: Brill, 1999.

Yurco, Frank J. "Merneptah's Canaanite Campaign and Israel's Origins." Pages 27–55 in *Exodus: The Egyptian Evidence*. Edited by Ernest S. Frerichs and Leonard H. Lesko. Winona Lake, IN: Eisenbrauns, 1997.

————. "The Shabaka-Shebitku Coregency and the Supposed Second Campaign of Sennacherib against Judah: A Critical Assessment." *Journal of Biblical Literature* 110 (1991): 35–45.

Zadok, Ran. *The Earliest Diaspora: Israelites and Judeans in Pre-Hellenistic Mesopotamia*. Publications of the Diaspora Research Institute 151. Tel Aviv: Diaspora Research Institute, Tel Aviv University, 2002.

————. *The Jews in Babylonia during the Chaldean and Achaemenian Periods according to Babylonian Sources*. Studies in the History of the Jewish People and the Land of Israel Monograph Series 3. Haifa: University of Haifa, 1979.

————. "A Prosopography of Samaria and Edom/Idumea." *Ugarit-Forschungen* 30 (1998): 781–828.

Zayadine, Fawzi. "Le relief néo-babylonien à Selaʿ près de Tafeleh: Interprétation historique." *Syria* 76 (1999): 83–90.

Zehnder, Markus. "Building on Stone? Deuteronomy and Esarhaddon's Loyalty Oaths

(Part 1); Some Preliminary Observations." *Bulletin for Biblical Research* 19 (2009): 341–74.

———. "Building on Stone? Deuteronomy and Esarhaddon's Loyalty Oaths (Part 2); Some Additional Observations." *Bulletin for Biblical Research* 19 (2009): 511–36.

Zeitlin, Solomon. *The Rise and Fall of the Judaean State: A Political, Social, and Religious History of the Second Commonwealth*. Philadelphia: Jewish Publication Society, 1962.

Zertal, Adam. "An Early Iron Age Cultic Site on Mount Ebal: Excavation Seasons 1982–1987, Preliminary Report." *Tel Aviv* 13–14 (1986–1987): 105–65.

———. "Has Joshua's Altar Been Found on Mt. Ebal?" *Biblical Archaeology Review* 11, no. 1 (1985): 26–35, 38–41, 43.

———. "Israel Enters Canaan—Following the Pottery Trail." *Biblical Archaeology Review* 17, no. 5 (1991): 28–38, 42–47.

———. *The Manasseh Hill Country Survey*. 2 vols. Culture and History of the Ancient Near East 21.1–2. Leiden: Brill, 2004–2008.

———. "The Pahwah of Samaria (Northern Israel) during the Persian Period: Types of Settlement, Economy, History and New Discoveries." *Transeuphratène* 3 (1990): 9–30.

———. *Seker Har Menasheh* [*The Manasseh Hill Country Survey*] [in Hebrew]. 2 vols. Haifa: Haifa University Press, 1996.

———. "'To the Land of the Perizzites and the Giants': On the Israelite Settlement in the Hill Country of Manasseh." Pages 47–69 in *From Nomadism to Monarchy: Archaeological and Historical Aspects of Early Israel*. Edited by Israel Finkelstein and Nadav Na'aman. Jerusalem: Israel Exploration Society, 1994.

Zertal, Adam, and Dror Ben-Yosef. "Bedhat esh-Sha'ab: An Iron Age I Enclosure in the Jordan Valley." Pages 517–29 in *Exploring the Longue Durée: Essays in Honor of Lawrence E. Stager*. Edited by J. David Schloen. Winona Lake, IN: Eisenbrauns, 2009.

Zettler, Richard L. "On the Chronological Range of Neo-Babylonian and Achaemenid Seals." *Journal of Near Eastern Studies* 38 (1979): 257–70.

Zevit, Ziony. "The Davidic-Solomonic Empire from the Perspective of Archaeological Bibliology." Pages 201–24 in vol. 1 of *Birkat Shalom: Studies in the Bible, Ancient Near Eastern Literature, and Postbiblical Judaism Presented to Shalom M. Paul on the Occasion of His Seventieth Birthday*. Edited by Chaim Cohen et al. Winona Lake, IN: Eisenbrauns, 2008.

Zorn, Jeffrey R. "Tell en-Naṣbeh and the Problem of the Material Culture of the Sixth Century." Pages 413–47 in *Judah and the Judeans in the Neo-Babylonian Period*. Edited by Oded Lipschits and Joseph Blenkinsopp. Winona Lake, IN: Eisenbrauns, 2003.

———. "Wedge- and Circle-Impressed Pottery—an Arabian Connection." Pages 689–98 in *Studies in the Archaeology of Israel and Neighboring Lands in Memory of Douglas L. Esse*. Edited by Samuel R. Wolff. Studies in Ancient Oriental Civilization 59. Chicago: Oriental Institute of the University of Chicago, 2001.

Zuckerman, Sharon. "Anatomy of a Destruction: Crisis Architecture, Termination Rituals and the Fall of Canaanite Hazor." *Journal of Mediterranean Archaeology* 20 (2007): 3–32.

———. "The Last Days of a Canaanite Kingdom: A View from Hazor." Pages 101–7 in *Forces of Transformation: The End of the Bronze Age in the Mediterranean*. Edited by Christoph Bachhuber and R. Gareth Roberts. Themes from the Ancient Near East, BANEA Publication Series 1. Oxford: Oxbow, 2009.

———. "Ruin Cults at Iron Age I Hazor." Pages 387–94 in *The Fire Signals of Lachish: Studies in the Archaeology and History of Israel in the Late Bronze Age, Iron Age, and Persian Period in Honor of David Ussishkin*. Edited by Israel Finkelstein and Nadav Na'aman. Winona Lake, IN: Eisenbrauns, 2011.

Zwickel, Wolfgang. "Der Beitrag der Ḫabiru zur Entstehung des Königtums." *Ugarit-Forschungen* 28 (1996): 751–66.

Contributors

Bill T. Arnold
Paul S. Amos Professor of Old Testament Interpretation
Asbury Theological Seminary

Daniel Bodi
Professor of Hebrew Bible and Semitic Languages
University of Paris 8, Vincennes Saint-Denis

David A. deSilva
Trustees' Distinguished Professor of New Testament and Greek
Ashland Theological Seminary

Samuel Greengus
Morgenstern Emeritus Professor of Bible and Near Eastern Literature
Hebrew Union College/Cincinnati

Kyle Greenwood
Associate Professor of Old Testament
Colorado Christian University

Richard S. Hess
Earl S. Kalland Professor of Old Testament and Semitic Languages
Denver Seminary

James K. Hoffmeier
Professor of Old Testament and Ancient Near Eastern History and Archaeology
Trinity Evangelical Divinity School

Brad E. Kelle
Professor of Old Testament
Point Loma Nazarene University

André Lemaire
École Pratique des Hautes Études, Paris

James K. Mead
Professor of Religion
Northwestern College

Robert D. Miller II
Associate Professor of Old Testament
Catholic University of America
Research Associate, Department of Old Testament Studies,
University of Pretoria

Steven M. Ortiz
Professor of Archaeology and Biblical Backgrounds
Southwestern Baptist Theological Seminary

Sandra Richter
Professor of Old Testament
Wheaton College

Lawson G. Stone
Professor of Old Testament
Asbury Theological Seminary

Peter van der Veen
Post-Doc, Evangelisch-Theologische Fakultät
Johannes Gutenberg-Universität Mainz

Author Index

523

Scripture Index

Old Testament

Old Testament Apocrypha

New Testament

Subject Index